Where To Stay In The
MID-ATLANTIC STATES

Where To Stay In The
MID-ATLANTIC STATES

Phil Philcox

Hunter Publishing, Inc.
300 Raritan Center Parkway
Edison NJ 08818
(908) 225 1900
Fax (908) 417 0482

ISBN 1-55650-631-7

© 1994 Phil Philcox

All rights reserved. No part of this publication may be reproduced, stored in a retrieval system, or transmitted in any form, or by any means, electronic, mechanical, by photocopying, recording, or otherwise, without written permission of the publisher.

Cover Photograph:
Jefferson Memorial, Washington D.C.
Robert Scurlock/Superstock

Contents

INTRODUCTION	1
Chain Hotels	2
ACCOMMODATIONS DIRECTORY	21
Delaware	21
Maryland	31
New Jersey	77
New York	127
Pennsylvania	248
Virginia	323
Washington D.C.	410
West Virginia	419

Introduction

If you're traveling for business or pleasure, this is the ultimate guide to finding a place to bed down for the night in the Mid-Atlantic states. Need a convenient downtown hotel within walking distance of the Convention Center in some major city or the serenity of a country inn tucked into the mountains far away from the maddening crowds? Prefer a high-rise apartment or private home rental for an extended stay? How about a spacious bedroom in a restored farmhouse on a working farm, complete with three meals a day and the opportunity to sample the farm life? If your choices range from out-of-the-way bed and breakfasts with a no smoking policy to hotel suites in the center of the business district that allow pets, you'll find something to your liking – and budget – in this guide.

Included are the names and telephone numbers of regional rental sources that handle an assortment of accommodation options – from private homes to condos and apartments. These agencies are excellent sources of information on what's available in each area in different price ranges and most have toll-free numbers and fax numbers you can call to request literature, rate cards and reservations.

Also included is a list of chain hotels and motels, their locations and descriptions of special clubs and offerings. Some properties offer discounts and programs for vacationers with children, theater goers, seniors, frequent travelers and government employees.

As of press time, the rates were current, based on interviews with the property owners. Rates are constantly changing and vary considerably with location and season, so use the rates listed to determine the price range of the property and always check prior to making your reservations. Use the toll-free number when available. Most toll-free numbers listed are valid from all states but some properties have outside-their-state numbers or in-state numbers. If you reach an invalid number, check with the toll-free operator at 800-555-1212.

To keep future editions up to date, we request you submit any new listing, information and current rates to Where-To-Stay, 131B North Bay Drive, Lynn Haven FL 32444. Please include all telephone numbers (including fax and toll-free) along with number of rooms, facilities and rates.

Abbreviations Used In This Guide:

SGL – single room – rate for one person
DBL – double room – rate for two people sharing one room
LS/HS – low season/high season rates
EFF – efficiency – usually one room with kitchen or kitchenette

STS – suites
APT – apartment
1BR/2BR/3BR – 1-, 2- or 3-bedroom apartment condo, apartment, villa or townhouse, usually with full kitchen facilities, washer/dryer, etc.
NO-SMOKING ROOMS – rooms available for non-smokers.
AIRPORT COURTESY CAR – free transportation to and from local airports.
AIRPORT TRANSPORTATION – transportation is available to and from local airports for a fee.
TRANSPORTATION TO LOCAL ATTRACTIONS – free transportation is available to local attractions.
EUROPEAN PLAN – no meals included in the room rates
MODIFIED AMERICAN PLAN – some meals included in the room rates, usually breakfast and dinner
AMERICAN PLAN – all meals included in the room rates
ALL MAJOR CREDIT CARDS – usually accepts American Express, MasterCard, Visa, Discover and others.

$00-$000 – daily rate span
$000W-$000W – weekly rate span
$00/$000W – daily rate followed by weekly rate
AP – charge for an additional person in the room.

Chain Hotels

Locations and Special Deals

($) indicates there is a cost for membership

Adam's Mark Hotels
11330 Olive St Road
St. Louis MO 63141
314-567-9000, Fax 314-567-7676
Reservations: 800-444-ADAM

Locations: Philadelphia PA; Memphis TN.

The Gold Mark Club provides corporate room rates, automatic upgrades when available, complimentary coffee and newspaper, gift shop discounts, free weekend stays and other benefits.

Adam Mark Discount Coupons provide a 10% discount on an overnight stay for each previous night's stay. Each certificate is worth a 10% discount and discounts are accumulative. Redeem ten coupons for one free night's stay.

Chain Hotels 3

Best Western
Box 10203
Phoenix AZ 85064
602-957-4200
Reservations: 800-528-1234

Locations: Wilmington DE; Aberdeen MD, Baltimore MD, College Park MD, Cumberland MD, Edgewood MD, Fredrick MD, Hagerstown MD, La Plata MD, Laurel MD, Ocean City MD, Salisbury MD; Atlantic City NJ, Cherry Hill NJ, Bordentown NJ, East Brunswick NJ, Fairfield NJ, Fanwood NJ, Gloucester City NJ; Hackensack NY, Lakewood NJ, Maple Shade NJ, Morristown NJ, New Providence NJ, Piscataway NJ, Pleasantville NJ, Princeton NJ, Ramsey NJ, Sommerville NJ, Westfield NJ, Binghamton NY, Boonville NY, Buffalo NY, Canton NY, Clifton Park NY, Cobleskill NY, Elmira NY, Endicott NY, Endwell NY, Farmington NY, Forest Hills NY, Hempstead, NY, Highland Falls NY, Horseheads NY, Ithaca NY, Johnson City NY, Lake George NY, Lake Placid NY, Little Falls NY, Lockport NY, Long Island City NY, Massapequa Park NY, Moira NY, Monticello NY, New York, Niagara Falls NY, North Creek NY, Nyack NY, Olean NY, Oswego NY, Painted Post NY, Riverhead NY, Saratoga Springs NY, Schenectady NY, Tully NY, Utical NY, Weedsport NY; Beaver Falls PA, Bedford PA, Breezewood PA, Butler PA, Carlisle PA, Clearfield PA, Concordville PA, Danville PA, Dubois PA, Erie PA, Gibsonia PA, Harrisburg PA, Hazleton PA, Hershey PA, Huntingdon PA, Indiana PA, Intercourse PA, Irwin PA, Lancaster PA, Lewisburg PA, Matamoras PA, Mechanicsburg PA, New Stanton PA, Paradise PA, Pittsburgh PA, Quakertown PA, Scranton PA, Shippensburg PA, State College PA, Stroudsburg PA, Tannersville PA, Washington PA, Waynesboro PA, Wilkes-Barre PA; Bedford VA, Blacksburg BA, Charlottesville VA, Chilhowie VA, Danville VA, Doswell VA, Franklin VA, Fredericksburg VA, Leesburg VA, Lexington VA, Manassas VA, Martinsville VA, Mount Jackson VA, Newport News VA, Norfolk VA, Petersburg VA, Radford VA, Richmond VA, Roanoke VA, Sandston VA, South Boston VA, Staunton VA, Triangle VA, Virginia Beach VA, Williamsburg VA, Winchester VA, Sytheville VA; Breckley WV, Davis WV, Elkins WV, Huntington WV, Martinsburg WV, Nitro WV, Parkersburg WV, Princeton WV, Ripley WV, Summersville WV, Wheeling WV; Washington D.C.

The Gold Crown Club International Card earns points redeemable for room nights and other awards. Many locations offer a 10% discount to senior travelers on a space-available basis with advanced reservations. The Government-Military Travel Program provides discounts to federal employees and military personnel.

Budget Host Inns
2601 Jackboro Highway
Fort Worth TX 76114
817-626-7064
Reservations: 800-BUD-HOST

Locations: Dover DE; Baltimore MD, Laurel MD, Salisbury MD, Niagara Falls NY, Ripley NY, Bellefonte PA, Berwick PA, Brookville PA, Carlisle PA, Gettysburg PA, Harrisburg PA, Indiana PA, Shippensburg PA, State College PA, Bristol VA, Marion VA, Roanoke VA, Rocky Mount VA, Salem VA, Williamsburg VA, Woodstock VA, Lewisburg WV, Washington D.C.

Budgetel Inns
250 West Wisconsin Ave
Milwaukee WI 53203

4 Introduction

414-274-0370
Reservations: 800-428-3438

Locations: Harrisburg PA, Hershey PA, Winchester VA.

The Road Runners Club offers a free night's stay after 12 paid nights.

Chatwell Hotels
234 West 48th St
New York NY 10036
212-262-1400
Reservations: 800-826-4667

Locations: New York NY.

Clarion-Choice Hotels
10750 Columbia Pike
Silver Spring MD 20901
301-593-5600, Fax: 301-681-7478
Reservation Numbers: Sleep Inn 800-62-SLEEP, Friendship Inn 800-453-4511, Econo Lodge 800-55-ECONO, Rodeway Inn 800-229-2000, Comfort Inn 800-228-5150, Quality Inn 800-228-5151, Clarion Hotels 800-CLARION

Locations: Dover DE, New Castle DE, Newark DE, Seaford DE; Annapolis MD, Baltimore MD, Cambridge MD, Clington MD, College Park MD, Easton MD, Edgewood MD, Frederick MD, Frostburg MD, Gaithersburg MD, Germantown MD, Hancock MD, Jessup MD, Kent Island MD, Landover Hills MD, Laurel MD, North Linthicum MD, Ocean City MD, Perryville MD, Pikesville MD, Pocomoke City MD, Salisbury MD, Silver Spring MD, Solomons MD, Towson MD, Westminster MD; Abeson NJ, Atlantic City NJ, Bordertown NJ, Edison NJ, Jersey City NJ, Lyndhurst NJ, Mahwah NJ, Mt. Laurel NJ, Newark NJ, North Brunswick NJ, Pleasantville NJ, Runnemede NJ, Saddle Brook NJ, Comerset NJ, Spring Lake NJ, Thorofare NJ, Toms River NJ, Albany NY, Binghamton NY, Buffalo NY, Corning NY, Dunkirk NY, East Elmhurst NY, Fulton NY, Hawthorne NY, Jamestown NY, Jericho NY, Latham NY, Lockport NY, New Hartford NY, New York NY, Newark NY, Newburgh NY, Niagara Falls NY, Ogdensburg NY, Plattsburgh NY, Rochester NY, Rome NY, Syracuse NY, Watertown NY, Woodbury NY; Allentown PA, Bartonsville PA, Bedford PA, Bensalem PA, Bethlehem PA, Bloomsburg PA, Breezewood PA, Enola PA, Erie PA, Essington PA, Exton PA, Gettysburg PA, Hamlin PA, Harrisburg PA, Hershey PA, Johnstown PA, King of Prussia PA, Kittanning PA, Lamar PA, Lancaster PA, Lebanon PA, Levittown PA, Mansfield PA, Mechanicsburg PA, Montgomeryville PA, New Castle PA, New Columbia PA, New Holland PA, Oakdale PA, Philadelphia PA, Pottstown PA, Pottsville PA, Reading PA, Selinsgrove PA, West Hazleton PA, West Middlesex PA, Williamsport PA; Abingdon VA, Alexandria VA, Altavista VA, Arlington VA, Ashland VA, Blacksburg VA, Bluefield VA, Bristol VA, Carmel Church VA, Chantilly VA, Charlottesville VA, Chesapeake VA, Chester VA, Covington VA, Culpeper VA, Dahlgren VA, Dublin VA, Dumfries VA, Emportia VA, Fairfax VA, Falls Church VA, Farmville VA, Fredericksburg VA, Front Royal VA, Hampton VA, Harrisonburg VA, Herndon VA, Hillsville VA, Hopewell VA, Lexington VA, Lynchburg VA, Manassas VA, Max Meadows VA, New Market VA, Newport News VA, Norfolk VA, Onley VA, Petersburg VA, Raphine VA, Richmond VA, Roanoke VA, Rocky Mount VA, Salem VA, South Hill Va, Staunton VA, Stephens City VA, Suffolk VA, Troutville VA, Virginia Beach VA, Warrenton VA, Waynesboro VA, Williamsburg VA, Winchester VA, Woodbridge VA, Wytheville VA; Barboursville WV, Beckley WV, Clarksburg WV, Fayetteville WV, Harpers Ferry WV, Martinsburg WV, Mineral

Wells WV, Morganton WV, Parkersburg WV, Princeton WV, Summersville WV, Weston WV; Washington D.C.

Clarion and Choice Hotels consist of Sleep Inn, Comfort Inns, Friendship Inn, Econo Lodges, Rodeway Inns, Quality Inns and Clarion Hotels and Resorts. Prime Time and Prime Time Senior Saver for people over age 60 offers a 10% discount at all hotels year-round and a 30% discount at limited locations when you call 800-221-2222 and ask for the Prime Time Senior Saver rate.

Special discounts of 10%-20% are available at participating locations for members of AAA. The Small Organizations Savings (SOS) Program is available to companies with over 10 employees and offers a 10% discount off the first 15 rooms used by company employees. The Weekender Rate Program offers special room rates of $20, $30 or $35 per night with an advanced reservation. All local, state and federal government employees and military personnel receive special per diem rates and upgrades when available at participating hotels.

Clubhouse Inn
7101 College Blvd
Overland Park KS 66210
913-451-1300
Reservations: 800-CLUB-INN

Locations: Pittsburgh PA.

Days Inn
2751 Buford Highway
Atlanta GA 30324
404-329-7466, Fax: 404-325-7731
Reservations: 800-325-2525

Locations: Dover DE, Newark DE; Aberdeen MD, Baltimore MD, College Park MD, Easton MD, Edgewood MD, Frederick MD, Gaithersburgh MD, Grantsville MD, Hagerstown MD, Lanham MD, Laurel MD, Ocean City MD, Pocomoke City MD, Rockville MD, Salisbury MD, Silver Spring MD, Waldorf MD, Westminster MD; Atlantic City NJ, Bridgeton NJ, Columbia NJ, cookstown NJ, Cranford NJ, East Rutherford NJ, East Windsor NJ, Fort Lee NJ, Lakewood NJ, Newark NJ, Parsippany NJ, Princeton NJ, Somerville NJ, South Plainfield NJ, Vineland NJ, Wrightstown NJ; Albany NY, Auburn NY, Bath NY, Binghamton NY, Brookhaven NY, Buffalo NY, Canasota NY, Corning NY, Dansville NY, Dunkirk NY, Geneseo NY, Geneva NY, Gloversville NY, Hicksville NY, Kingsport NY, Lake George NY, Liberty NY, Middletown NY, Montgomery NY, Nanuet NY, Newburgh NY, New Paltz NY, New York NY, Niagara Falls NY, Oswego NY, Plattsburgh NY, Poughkeepsie NY, Rochester NY, Schenectady NY, Syracuse NY, Utica NY, Watertown NY, White Plains NY; Allentown PA, Altoona PA, Barkeyville PA, Bensalem PA, Brookville PA, Butler PA, Carlisle PA, Chambersburg PA, Clarion PA, Danville PA, Donegal PA, Easton PA, Erie PA, Exton PA, Gettysburg PA, Harrisburg PA, Hershey PA, Horsham PA, Johnstown PA, Lancaster PA, Landsdale PA, Levittown PA, Lewisburg PA, Lock Haven PA, Meadville PA, New Castle PA, New Kensington PA, New Stanton PA, Philadelphia PA, Pittsburgh PA, Poconos PA, Pottstown PA, Reading PA, Scranton PA, Somerset PA, State College PA, Uniontown PA, Warfordsburg PA, Washington PA, Wilkes-Barre PA, York PA; Alexandria

VA, Arlington VA, Bristol VA, Carmel Church VA, Charlottesville VA, Chesapeake VA, Chester VA, Christiansburg VA, Colonial Beach VA, Emporia VA, Fancy Gap VA, Farmville VA, Franklin VA, Fredericksburg VA, Hampton VA, Harrisonberg VA, Leesburg VA, Lexington VA, Lynchburg VA, New Market VA, Newport News BA, Norfolk VA, Petersburg VA, Richmond VA, Roanoke VA, Staunton VA, Tappahannock VA, Tysons Corner VA, Virginia Beach VA, WaynesboroVA, Williamsburg VA, Winchester VA, Woodbridge VA, Wytheville V; Beckley WV, Fairmont WV, Martinsburg WV, Morgantown WV, Parkersburg WV, Princeton WV, St Albans WV, Sutton WV, Teys Valley WV, Wheeling WV; Washington D.C.

The September Days Club ($) offers travelers over the age of 50 up to 40% discounts on rooms, 10% discounts on food and gifts, a quarterly club magazine, seasonal room discounts and special tours and trips. The Inn Credible Card is designed for business travelers and provides up to 30% savings on room rates, free stays for spouses and other benefits. The Days Gem Club is a travel club for military personnel and government employees that offers up to 30% savings on room rates. School Days Club for academic staff and educators offers a minimum of 10% savings on room rates, special group rates and additional benefits. The Sport Plus Club is designed for coaches and team managers who organize team travel and offers 10% discounts on room rates, special team rates and late check-outs.

Doubletree Hotels
410 North 44th St,
New York NY 10022
602-220-6666
Reservations: 800-828-7447

Locations: Gaithersburg MD, Princeton NJ, Bensalem PA, Harrisburg PA, Alexandria VA, Crystal City VA.

Family Plans allow up to two children under the age of 18 to stay free when they share the rooms with their parents. A special discounted rate is available to seniors. A Corporate Plus Program is available at all business center locations.

Business Class offers quick check-in and check-out, free breakfast in a private lounge, free newspaper and additional benefits. The Entree Gold floor provides concierge services, exclusive lounge for guests, complimentary breakfast and cocktail hour and use of a private boardroom.

Embassy Suites
222 Las Colinas Blvd
Irving TX 75039
214-556-1133, Fax: 214-556-8222
Reservations: 800-528-1100

Locations: Baltimore MD; Parsippany NJ, Piscataway NJ, Secaucus NJ; New York NY, Syracuse NY; Philadelphia PA, Pittsburgh PA; Alexandria VA, Crystal City VA, Richmond VA, Tysons Corners VA, Vienna VA; Washington D.C.

Chain Hotels 7

Guest Quarters Suite Hotels
30 Rowes Wharf
Boston MA 02110
617-330-1440, Fax: 716-737-8752
Reservations 800-424-2900

Locations: Bethesda MD, Linthicum MD; Mt. Laurel NJ; Philadelphia PA, Plymouth Meeting PA, Valley Forge PA; Alexandria VA; Washington D.C.; Atlanta GA, Austin TX, Houston TX, Baltimore MD, Boston MA, Charlotte NC, Chicago IL, Cincinnati OH, Columbus OH, Detroit MI, Indianapolis IN, Nashville TN, Philadelphia PA, Washington D.C.

Hampton Inns
6800 Poplar
Memphis TN 38138
901-758-3100, Fax: 901-756-9479
Reservations: 800-426-7866

Locations: Wilmington DE, Baltimore MD, Frederick MD, Landover MD, Salisbury MD, Atlantic City NJ, Cherry Hill NJ, Mt. Laurel NJ, Newark NJ, Secaucus NJ, Albany NY, Buffalo NY, Long Island NY, Rochester NY, Syracuse NY, Allentown PA, Chambersburg PA, Downingtown PA, Harrisburg PA, Lancaster PA, Philadelphia PA, Pittsburgh PA, Reading PA, State College PA, Wilkes-Barre PA, York PA, Alexandria VA, Charlottesville VA, Chesapeake VA, Christiansburg VA, Emporia VA, Fairfax City VA, Fredericksburg VA, Hampton VA, Harrisonburg VA, Norfolk VA, Richmond VA, Roanoke VA, Sterling VA, Virginia Beach VA, Warrenton VA, Williamsburg VA, Winchester VA, Beckley WV, Morgantown WV, Wheeling WV, Washington D.C.

The LifeStyle 50 Club provides discounts for guests over age 50 with no charge for a third person staying in the room.

Harley/Helmsley Hotels
Box 818020
Cleveland OH 44189
216-891-3600
Reservations: 800-321-2323

Locations: New York NY.

Hilton Hotels
9336 Civic Center Drive
Beverly Hills CA 90209
213-278-4321, Fax: 213-205-4599
Reservations: 800-HILTON

Locations: Newark DE, Wilmington DE, Baltimore MD, Columbia MD, Mount Laurel NJ, Newark NJ, Secaucus NJ, Short Hills NJ, Somerset NJ, Woodcliff Lake NJ, Buffalo NY, New York NY, Rochester NY, Rye Brook NY, Lancaster PA, Malvern PA, King of Prussia PA, Philadelphia PA, Pittsburgh PA, Norfolk VA, Sandston VA, Springfield VA, Virginia Beach VA, Washington D.C.

8 Introduction

Zip-Out/Quick Check-Out is available to travelers using major credit cards. An itemized statement of charges is provided the night before departure. Many Hilton locations have hotels-within-hotels. Tower and Executive accommodations offer room upgrades, use of a private lounge, access to business services, complimentary cocktails and continental breakfast plus use of telex, fax machines and photocopying equipment.

The HHonors Guest Reward Program is a free program that earns points toward free or discounted stays at participating properties and members-only privileges that include rapid check-inns, free daily newspaper, free stay with spouse and free use of health club facilities when available.

The Corporate Rate Program offers business travelers guaranteed rates annually, speed reservations, Tower and Executive accommodations and Quick Check-Out facilities.

Hilton's Senior HHonors offers special amenities to travelers over the age of 60. Included are room discounts up to 50%, a 20% dinner discount and money- back guarantee, a private toll-free reservation number and automatic enrollment in Hilton's Guest Reward Programs. BounceBack Weekend offers a complimentary daily continental breakfast, children free in parents' rooms and special rates for Thursday to Sunday with a Saturday stay. During the summer, these discounted rates apply Monday to Wednesday when a Saturday stay is included.

Hilton Leisure Breaks includes packages for honeymooners and special occasions with special rates. Hilton Meeting 2,000 is a network of business meeting facilities available at some locations and includes special meeting room, audiovisual systems, refreshments and assistance in providing meeting rooms and programs.

Holiday Inn
1100 Ashwood Pkwy
Atlanta GA 30338
404-551-3500
Reservations: 800-HOLIDAY

Locations: Dover DE, Newark DE, Wilmington DE, Aberdeen MD, Annapolis MD, Timonium MD, Pikesville MD, Towson MD, Baltimore MD, Columbia MD, Cumberland MD, Frederick MD, Grantsville MD, Hagerstown MD, Ocean City MD, Salisbury MD, Solomons MD, Atlantic City NJ, Bridgeport NJ, Bridgewater NJ, Carteret NJ, Clinton NJ, Edison NJ, Hasbrouck Heights NC, Jamesbury NJ, Kenilworth NJ, Livingston NJ, Newark NJ, Paramus NJ, Parsippany NJ, Plainfield NJ, Runnemede NJ, Saddle Brook NJ, Secaucus NJ, Somerset NJ, Springfield NJ, Tinton Falls NJ, Toms River NJ, Totowa NJ, Wayne NJ, Albany NY, Amherst NY, Amsterdam NY, Auburn NY, Binghampton NY, Buffalo NY, Corning NY, Corland NY, Elmira NY, Fishkill NY, Ithaca NY, Jamestown NY, Johnstown NY, Kingston NY, Lake George NY, Lake Placid NY, Liberty NY, Middletown NY, Mt. Kisco NY, Newburgh NY, New York NY, Niagara Falls NY, Ogdensburg NY, Oneonta NY, Orangeburg NY, Plainview NY, Plattsburgh NY, Port Jervis NY, Poughkeepsie NY, Riverhead NY, Rochester NY, Ronkonkoma NY, Rockville Centre NY, Saratoga Springs NY, Schenectady NY, Stony Brook NY, Suggern NY, Syracuse NY, Utica NY, Waterloo NY,

Chain Hotels 9

Watertown NY, White Plains NY, Westbury NY, Allentown PA, Altoona PA, Bartonsville PA, Beaver Falls PA, Belle Vernon PA, Bethlehem PA, Chambersburg PA, Clarion PA, Du Bois PA, Erie PA, Exton PA, Fort Washington PA, Gettysburg PA, Harrisburg PA, Hazelton PA, Indiana PA, Johnstown PA, Lancaster PA, Kulpsville PA, King of Prussia PA, Lewistown PA, Monroeville PA, Morgantown PA, New Hope PA, Oil City PA, Philadelphia PA, Pittsburgh PA, Pottstown PA, Reading PA, Scranton PA, Sharon PA, Somerset PA, State College PA, Uniontown PA, Warren PA, Wilkes-Barre PA, York PA, Abingdon VA, Ashland VA, Blacksburg VA, Bristol VA, Charlottesville VA, Chesapeake VA, Covington VA, Culpeper VA, Emporia VA, Fredericksburg VA, Hampton VA, Harrisonburg VA, Lexington VA, Lynchburg VA, Marion VA, Newport News VA, Norfolk VA, Norton VA, Petersburg VA, Portsmouth VA, Richmond VA, Roanoke VA, Salem VA, South Hill VA, Staunton VA, Suffolk A, Virginia Beach VA, Waynesboro VA, Williamsburg VA, Winchester VA, Wytheville PA, Beckley WV, Bluefield WV, Charleston WV, Clarksburg WV, Fairmont WV, Huntington WV, Morgantown WV, Oak Hill WV, Parkersburg WV, Washington D.C.

Holiday Inn Preferred Senior Traveler offers a 20% savings on the single-person rate and a 10% discount at participating restaurants. Members of the American Association of Retired Persons receive a 10% discount at participating hotels.

Best Break Bed and Breakfast packages are offered at participating hotels and include a guest room and a breakfast coupon good for $12.

Great Rates are offered with advance reservations and include discounts of at least 10%. Most Holiday Inns offer Government-Military rates based on the per diem rate offered to government employees and contractors. Many hotels participate in the Government-Military Amenities program which offers coupons redeemable for free local phone calls with a $5 limit, 10% dinner discounts and a free continental breakfast.

The Priority Club is designed for frequent travelers and provides points that can be exchanged for travel and merchandise awards.

Homewood Suites
3742 Lamar Ave
Memphis TN 38195
901-362-4663, Fax: 901-362-4663
Reservations: 800-225-5466

Locations: Liverpool NY.

Homewood Suites offers apartment-style suites, complimentary breakfast and an evening social hour.

Hospitality International Inns
1726 Montreal Circle
Tucker GA 30084
404-872-6358
Reservations: 800-251-1962

10 Introduction

Locations: Baltimore MD, Havre de Grace MD, Laurel MD, LaVale MD, Ocean MD, Odenton MD, Mount Laurel NJ, Paramus NJ, Belle Vernon PA, Chambersburg PA, Philadelphia PA, Bristol VA, Culpeper VA, Emporia VA, Fredericksburg PA, Front Royal PA, Galax VA, Harrisonburg VA, Lynchburg BA, Martisville VA, Norfolk VA, Pulaski VA, Richmond VA, Staunton VA, Verona VA, Woodbridge VA, Clarksburg WV, Washington D.C.

Hospitality International consists of Red Carpet Inns, Scottish Inns, Passport Inns and Downtowner Motor Inns

The Identicard Program provides room discounts at participating inns and resorts.

Howard Johnson
8339 Jefferson Rd
Parsippany NJ 07054
201-428-9700
Reservations: 800-654-2000

Locations: Newark DE, Aberdeen MD, Annapolis MD, Baltimore MD, Hagerstown MD, Ocean City MD, Rockville MD, Salisbury MD, Waldorf MD, Asbury Park NJ, Atlantic City NJ, Blackwood NJ, Clark NJ, Lakewood NJ, Lawrenceville NJ, Middletown NJ, Mount Holly NJ, Neptune NJ, Ocean City NJ, Paramus NJ, Parsippany NJ, Penns Grove NJ, Phillipsburg NJ, Piscataway NJ, Plainfield NJ, Princeton NJ, Ramsey NJ, Rockaway NJ, Saddle Brook NJ, Springfield NJ, Toms River NJ, Trenton NJ, Wayne NJ, Whippany NJ, Williamstown NJ, Albany NY, Binghamton NY, Buffalo NY, Commack NY, Ellicottville NY, Elmire NY, Glens Falls NY, Hauppauge NY, Horseheads NY, Huntington NY, Ithaca NY, Jericho NY, Kingston NY, Lake George NY, Lake Placid NY, Latham NY, Middletown NY, Monticello NY, New York NY, Newburgh NY, Niagara Falls NY, Norwich NY, Orlean NY, Plainsview NY, Plattsburgh NY, Rochester NY, Rock Hill NY, Saugeries NY, Syracuse NY, Utica NY, Westbury NY, Williamsville NY, Needs NC, Allentown PA, Altoona PA, Bradford PA, Brookville PA, Carlisle PA, Chambersburg PA, Chester PA, Danville PA, Ebensburg PA, Erie PA, Gettysburg PA, Harrisburg PA, Lancaster PA, Mercer PA, Monroeville PA, New Stanton PA, Oakdale PA, Oakland PA, Pittsburgh PA, Philadelphia PA, Pittston PA, Pocono Mountains PA, Tannersville PA, Trevose PA, Valley Forge PA, Warren PA, Wilkes Barre PA, York PA, Alexandria VA, Arlington VA, Ashland VA, Blacksburg VA, Bristol VA, Charlottesville VA, Christiansburg VA, Fredericksburg VA, Lexington VA, Lynchburg VA, Manassas VA, Norfolk VA, Petersburg VA, Richmond VA, Roanoke VA, Virginia Beach VA, Williasmburg VA, Wytheville VA.

The Howard Johnson Road Rally Program offers discounts to senior travelers over the age of 60 and members of AARP and other national senior's organizations. With advanced reservations a 30% discount is available at some locations. The Family Plan lets children under 12 stay free at all locations with some properties extending the age limit to 18.

Government Rate Programs offer special rates to federal employees, military personnel and government contractors. The Corporate Rate Program offers special rates to companies and business travelers. Howard Johnson Executive Section offers guests special rooms, complimentary wake-up coffee and newspapers, and snacks. Kids Go Hojo provides children with free FunPacks filled with toys, puzzles, coloring books and games.

Chain Hotels

Hyatt Hotels International
Madison Plaza, 200 West Madison
Chicago IL 60606
312-720-1234, Fax: 312-750-8579
Reservations: 800-228-9000

Locations: Baltimore MD, Bethesda MD, New Brunswick NJ, Princeton NJ, Buffalo NY, New York NY, Pittsburgh PA, Arlington VA, Fairfax VA, Herndon VA, Reston VA, Richmond VA, Washington D.C.

Hyatt Gold Passport provides earned credits for free stays, a private toll-free reservation number, express check-in, special members-only rooms, free newspaper daily, complimentary morning coffee and use of fitness centers where available. Hyatt Reserved Upgrade coupon booklets are available for confirmed room upgrades. Hyatt Gold Passport At Leisure is available at over 155 locations worldwide and includes invitations to private receptions, room amenities, priority room and dining reservations and a quarterly newsletter with member-only offers.

The Regency Club is a hotel within a hotel offering VIP accommodations. Located on the topmost floors of participating hotels, the rooms are reached by special elevators requiring a passkey. Also include is a free morning paper, complimentary breakfast, plus afternoon hors d'oeuvres, wine and cocktails.

Camp Hyatt is for children and their parents. Upon arrival at any Hyatt hotel or resort, children receive a free cap, frequent travel passport and a registration card. The program offers special childrens' menus in the dinning room, room discounts, kitchen tours and other pastimes.

Journey's End Hotels and Suites
199 Front St
Belleville Ontario
Canada K8N 5E2
613-966-8020
Reservations: 800-668-4200

Locations: Buffalo NY, New York NY.

Knights Inn, Knights Court, Knights Stop, Arborgate Inn
26650 Emery Pkwy
Cleveland OH 44128
216-464-5055
Reservations: 800-843-5644

Locations: Elkton MD, Frederick MD, Laurel MD; Syracuse NY; Breezewood PA, Bridgeville PA, Carlisle PA, Clarion PA, Erie PA, Greensburg PA, Harrisburg PA, Irwin PA, New Stanton PA, Philadelphia PA, Scranton PA, Somerset PA, Washington PA, Charlottesville VA, Covington VA, Harrisonburg VA, Newport News VA, Roanoke VA, Charleston WV, Clarksburg WV, Martinsburg WV.

12   Introduction

The Knight Lodging System Royalty Club offers special discounts, express check-in service and a periodic newsletter. Discounts are available to AAA and AARP members and to guests over 55 years of age. All properties offer a discount to frequent guests.

LaQuinta Inns
10010 San Pedro
San Antonio TX 78279
512-366-6000, Fax 512-366-6100
Reservations: 800-531-5900

Locations: Pittsburgh PA; Newport News VA, Richmond VA, Virginia Beach VA.

Special rates are available to business travelers, government and military employees, seniors over the age of 55 and families.

La Quinta Returns Club offers discounted room rates, credit for a free 1-night stay, guaranteed reservations and $50 check cashing privileges. La Quinta Senior Class ($) is for travelers over the age of 60 and offers a 20% discount on room rates, credit for free night stays and guaranteed reservations. La Quint Per Diem Preferred offers credits and discounts to military personnel, U.S. government workers and cost reimbursable contractors.

Loews Hotels
667 Madison Ave
New York NY 10021
212-545-2000, Fax 212-935-6796
Reservations: 800-235-6397

Locations: Dallas TX, Denver CO, Nashville TN, New York NY, Tucson AZ, Washington D.C.

Manhattan East Suite Hotels
505 East 75th St
New York NY 10021
212-772-2900, Fax 212-628-6243
Reservations: 800-ME-SUITE

Locations: New York NY

Marriott
Marriott Drive
Washington D.C. 20058
301-380-9000
Reservations: Marriott Hotels 800-228-9290, Courtyard by Marriott 800-321-2211, Fairfield Inn 800-228-2800, Residence Inn 800-331-3131

Marriott consists of Marriott Hotels and Resorts, Marriott Suites, Courtyard by Marriott, Residence Inns and Fairfield Inns.

Chain Hotels 13

Marriott Hotel Locations: *Wilmington DE, Portland ME, Annapolis MD, Baltimore MD, Bethesda MD, Gaithersburg MD, Greenbelt MD, Rockville MD, Atlantic City NJ, Newark NJ, Park Ridge NJ, Princeton NJ, Saddle Brook NJ, Somerset NJ, Whippany NJ, Albany NY, Buffalo NY, Hauppauge NY, New York NY, Rochester NY, Syracuse NY, Uniondale NY, Westchester NY, Harrisburg PA, Philadelphia PA, Pittsburgh PA, Alexandria VA, Arlington VA, Blacksburg VA, Falls Church VA, Herndon VA, Norfoldk VA, Richmond VA, Roanoke VA, Vieena VA, Charleston WV, Washington D.C.*

Courtyard by Marriott Locations: *Wilmington DE, Annapolis MD, Baltimore MD, Columbia MD, Greenbelt MD, Landover MD, Rockville MD, Silver Spring MD, Hanover NJ, Lincroft NJ, Mahwah NJ, Mt. Laurel NJ, Newark NJ, Tinton Falls NJ, Fishkill NY, Poughkeepsie NY, Rochester NY, Rye NY, Syracuse NY, Tarrytown NY, Philadelphia PA, Pittsburgh PA, Willow Grove PA, Newport RI, Chantilly VA, Charlottesville VA, Fairfax VA, Hampton VA, Herndon VA, Manassas VA, Richmond VA, Rosslyn VA, Virginia Beach VA, Williamsburg VA.*

Fairfield Inn Locations: *Wilmington DE, Frederick MD, Buffalo NY, Syracuse NY, Harrisburg PA, Pittsburgh PA, Hampton VA, Virginia Beach VA.*

Residence Inn Locations: *Newark DE, Annapolis MD, Bethesda MD, Cockeysville MD, Atlantic City NJ, Cherry Hill NJ, Monmouth NJ, Princeton NJ, Albany NY, Binghamton NY, Brookhaven NY, Buffalo NY, Fishkill NY, Plainville NY, Rochester NY, Syracuse NY, Harrisburg PA, Philadelphia PA, Pittsburgh PA, Herndon VA, Richmond VA, Tysons Corner VA.*

SuperSaver rates offer discounts on weekday and weekend stays at participating hotels. Discounts range from 10% and up. The TFB program (Two For Breakfast) offers discounts for weekend stays for two adults that includes complimentary breakfasts.

Advance Purchase Rates are discounts of up to 50% for advance, prepaid, non-refundable reservations seven, 14, 21 and 30 days in advance. Senior Citizen discounts for members of AARP and other senior groups are available at all participating hotels.

The Marriott Honored Guest Award offers special upgrades to members at participating hotels. After a 15 night stay during a 12 month period, members receive express checkout services, complimentary newspaper, check cashing privileges, free luggage tags and discounts.

Motel 6
14651 Dallas Pkwy
Dallas TX 75240
214-386-6161, Fax 214-991-2976
Reservations: 800-437-7486, 505-891-6161

Locations: *Wilmington DE, Baltimore MD, Camp Spring MD, Capitol Heights MD, Elkton MD, Laurel MD, East Brunswick NJ, Piscataway NJ, Albany NY, Binghamton NY, Buffalo NY, Elmire NY, Geneva NY, Jamestown NY, Rochester NY, Syracuse NY, Utica NY, Harrisburg PA, Pittsburgh PA, Fredericksburg VA, Harrisonburg VA, Norfolk VA, Richmond VA, Roanoke VA, Williamsburg VA, Wytheville VA, Charleston WV, Wheeling WV, Washington D.C.*

Nikko Hotels
1700 Broadway
New York NY 10019
Reservations: 800-645-5687

Locations: New York NY.

Fountains Club offers preferred reservation service, early check-in and late check-out service; a complimentary drink upon arrival, a free continental breakfast and special room discounts.

Novotel
Two Overhill Rd
Scarsdale NY 10583
Reservations: 800-221-4542

Locations: Lyndhurst NJ, New York NY.

Omni Hotels
500 Lafayette Rd
Hampton NJ 03842
603-926-8911
Reservations: 800-THE-OMNI

Locations: Baltimore MD, New York NY, Philadelphia PA, Virginia Beach VA, Washington D.C.

The Omni Club Program is available at selected hotels and offers concierge service, private lounge facilities, complimentary breakfast, evening cocktails and hors d'oeuvres and specially-appointed rooms.

The Omni Hotel Select Guest Program provides special services, priority room availability, accommodation upgrades, complimentary coffee and morning newspaper and a newsletter announcing additional programs.

The Omni Hotel Executive Service Plan is available to corporate members and includes a variety of special benefits. For planning and scheduling meetings, the Omni Hotel Gavel Service and Omni-Express Program provide assistance by experienced meeting planners. City'scapes is a special weekend package that offers discounts and special amenities.

Park Inn Resorts International
4425 West Airport Freeway
Irving TX 75062
Reservations: 800-437-PARK

Locations: Olean NY, Virginia Beach VA.

The Silver Citizens Club offers a 20% room discount and 10% food discount at participating hotels, free morning paper and coffee, special directory, all-night emergency pharmacy telephone number and personal check cashing.

Preferred Hotels
1901 South Meyers Rd
708-953-0404
Oakbrook Terrace IL 60181
Reservations: 800-323-7500

Locations: Baltimore MD, New York NY, Philadelphia PA, Washington D.C.

Radisson Hotels International
Carlson Pkwy
Minneapolis MN 55459
612-540-5526, Fax 612-449-3400
Reservations: 800-333-3333

Locations: Wilmington DE, Baltimore MD, Cape May NJ, Englewood NJ, Newark NJ, Paramus NJ, Hauppauge NY, Melville NY, New York NY, Niagara Falls NY, Poughkeepsie NY, Rochester NY, Utica NY, Allentown PA, Monroeville PA, Philadelphia PA, Alexandria VA, Hampton VA, Lynchburg VA, Richmond VA, Virginia Beach VA, Huntington WV, Washington D.C.

Radisson operates 270 hotels and affiliates worldwide. Plaza Hotels are usually located in the city center or suburban locations. Suite Hotels offer oversized rooms with a living room, mini-bar and kitchenette. Resort Hotels are usually near beaches, golf course and recreational facilities.

Ramada Inn
1850 Pkwy Place
Marietta GA 30067
404-423-7773, Fax 404-423-7741
Reservations: 800-2-RAMADA

Locations: Wilmington DE, Annapolis MD, Baltimore MD, Beltsville MD, Bethesda MD, Calverton MD, Camp Springs MD, Hagerstown MD, Hanover MD, Laurel MD, Oxon Hill MD, Rockville MD, Towson MD, Atlantic City NJ, Clark NJ, Clifton NJ, East Brunswick NJ, East Hanover NJ, East Windsor NJ, Fairfield NJ, Hammonton NJ, Hazlet NJ, Mahwah NJ, Montvale NJ, Mt. Laurel NJ, Newark NJ, Princeton NJ, Rochelle Park NJ, Secaucus NJ, Somerset NJ, Toms River NJ, Vineland NJ, Weehawken NJ, West Long Branch NJ, Albany NY, Armonk NY, Binghampton NY, Buffalo NY, East Elmhurst NY, Elmsford NY, Glens Falls NY, Ithaca NY, Kingston NY, Lake George NY, Lake Placid NY, Long Island NY, Menands NY, New Rochelle NY, New York NY, Newburgh NY, Niagara Falls NY, Poughkeepsie NY, Queensbury NY, Rochester NY, Saratoga Springs NY, Schenectady NY, Syracuse NY, Watertown NY, Woodbury NY, Allentown PA, Altoona PA, Breezewood PA, Clarks Summit PA, Coraopolis PA, Delaware Water Gap PA, Du Bois PA, Erie PA, Essington PA, Fort Washington PA, Gettysburg PA, Glen Mills PA, Harrisburg PA, Lake Harmony PA, Philadelphia PA, Pittsburgh PA, Poconos PA, Pottstown PA, Scranton PA, Somerset PA, Trevose PA, Washington PA, West Middlesex PA, Whitehall PA, Wilkes-Barre PA, York PA, Alexandria VA, Arlington VA, Ashland VA, Duffield VA, Falls Church VA, Fredericksburg VA, Herndon VA, Lexington VA, Luray VA, Lynchburg VA, Manassas VA, Newport News BA, Norfolk VA, Petersburg VA, Richmond VA, Tysons Corner VA, Virginia

16 Introduction

Beach VA, Williamsburg VA, Woodstock VA, Wytheville VA, Bluefield WV, Charleston WV, Huntington WV, Morgantown WV, Washington D.C.

Ramada Inn has 700 locations world-wide consisting of Ramada Inns, Ramada Hotels and Ramada Renaissance Hotels. The Hotels are designed to five-star international standards and include convention and banquet facilities, restaurants, 24-hour room service, entertainment and lounges. Most Renaissance Hotels offer a club floor with concierge services, upgraded room amenities and lounge.

Membership in the Ramada Business Card Program earns points for trips and merchandise based on dollars spent at Ramada properties. The card is available free. Membership includes favorable rates, automatic room upgrade when available, express check-in and check-out, free newspaper on business days, free same-room accommodations for your spouse when you travel together, extended check-out times, newsletter and points redeemable for hotel stays, air travel, car rentals and over 10,000 Service Merchandise catalog items.

Participating Ramada Inn properties offer SuperSaver Weekend discounts. These rates apply on Friday, Saturday and Sunday for 1-, 2- and 3-night stays. Extra person rates may apply for a third or fourth person in the room. Because some hotels limit availability on some dates, reservations are recommended.

When traveling with family or friends, the Ramada Four-for-One Program permits up to four people to share the same room and pay the single rate. At participating properties, the Best Years Seniors Program provides travelers over the age of 60 who are members of AARP, the Global Horizons Club, Catholic Golden Age, The Golden Buckeye Club, Humana Seniors Association, The Retired Enlisted Association, The Retired Officers Association or United Airlines Silver Wings Plus, with a 25% discount off regular room rates.

The Ramada Per Diem Value Program is available at more than 350 locations. Properties honor the maximum lodging per diem rates set by the U.S. General Services Administration. Federal employees, military personnel and employees of Cost Reimbursable Contractors traveling on official government business are eligible. In addition to the per diem limits for lodging, the single person room rate at participating locations includes full breakfast and all applicable taxes. All Ramada properties provide corporate customers with favorable rates. Companies need a minimum of 10 travelers with a combined total of 100 room nights per year.

Red Roof Inns
4355 Davidson Rd
Hilliard OH 43026
Reservations: 800-843-7663

Chain Hotels 17

Locations: Wilmington DE, Columbia MD, Gaithersburg MD, Hanover MD, Lanham MD, Laurel MD, Oxon Hill MD, Edison NJ, Mount Laurel NJ, Parsippany NJ, Princeton NJ, Albany NY, Binghamton NY, Buffalo NY, Rochester NY, Syracuse NY, Utical NY, Allentown PA, Danville PA, Erie PA, Harrisburgh PA, Philadelphia PA, Pittsburgh PA, Washington PA, Wilkes-Barre PA, York PA, Alexandria VA, Chesapeake VA, Hampton VA, Richmond VA, Virginia Beach VA, Charleston WV, Fairmont WV, Huntington WV, Parkersburg WV, Washington D.C.

Redi Card membership offers 8 p.m. holds on reservations, complimentary USA Today newspaper, member-only newsletter, first priority advance room requests, check cashing privileges up to $50 per stay, express check-in and check-out and complimentary late-stays upon request.

Ritz Carlton Hotels
3414 Peachtree Rd NE
Atlanta GA 30326
404-237-5500, Fax 404-365-9643
Reservations: 800-241-3333

Locations: New York NY, Philadelphia PA, Arlington VA, McLean VA, Washington D.C.

Sheraton Hotels, Inns and Resorts
60 State St
Boston MA 02109
617-367-3600, Fax 617-367-5676
Reservations: 800-325-3535

Locations: Dover DE, Wilmington DE, Aberdeen MD, Hagerstown MD, Ocean City MD, Salisbury MD, Towson MD, Atlantic City NJ, Cherry Hill NJ, East Brunswick NJ, East Rutherford NJ, Fairfield NJ, Hasbrouch Heights NJ, Mahwah NJ, Mt. Arlington NJ, Newark NJ, Parsippany NJ, Woodbridge NJ, Albany NY, Batavia NY, Buffalo NY, Canandaigua NY, Dunkirk NY, Ithaca NY, Naneu NY, Smithtown NY, Syracuse NY, Allentown PA, Fraxer PA, Harrisburg PA, Langhorne PA, Philadelphia PA, Pittsburgh PA, Reading PA, Scranton PA, Stroudsburg PA, Valley Forge PA, Williamsport PA, Alexandria VA, Arlington VA, Charlottesville VA, Crystal City VA, Fredericksburg VA, Hampton VA, Norfolk VA, Richmond VA, Roanoke VA, Staunton VA, Tysons Corner VA, Virginia Beach VA, Martinsburg WV, Washington D.C.

ITT Sheraton Club International ($) provides additional guest services at over 400 participating hotels worldwide. Benefits include: automatic room upgrade when available, guaranteed 4 p.m. late check-out, Double Club points and free nights in select hotels throughout the year, and Express pass check-in and check-out service with key ready upon arrival.

Hotel Sofitel International and Pullman Hotels
Two Overhill Rd
Scarsdale NY 10583
914-575-5055
Reservations: 800-221-4542

Locations: Washington D.C.

Stouffer Hotels
29800 Bainbridge Rd
Cleveland OH 44139
Reservations: 800-HOTELS-1

Locations: Baltimore MD, White Plains NY, Philadelphia PA, Washington D.C., Atlanta GA, Austin TX, Coston MA, Chicago IL, Cleveland OH, Columbus OH, Dallas TX, Denver CO, Houston TX, Los Angeles CA, Nashville TN, St Louis MO, San Francisco CA, Seattle WA.

Club Express offers automatic room upgrades, express check-in and check-out, credits for free stays, and American Express Gift Cheques and Savings Bonds.

Summerfield Suites
8100 East 22nd St North
Wichita KS 67226
316-681-5100, Fax 681-0905
Reservations: 800-833-4353

Locations: Princeton NJ, Somerset NJ, Malvern PA, Washington D.C.

All Summerfield Suites Hotels provide 2-bedroom suites with fully-equipped kitchens, hotel pools, whirlpools and exercise rooms. Living rooms have TV with VCRs and movie are available 24-hours a day. Complimentary breakfast and evening social hour are included in the suite rate and there is an on-site convenience store.

Super 8 Motels
1910 8th Ave NE
Aberdeen SD 57402
605-225-2272, Fax 605-225-1140
Reservations: 800-800-8000, 800-848-8888

Locations: New Castle DE, Aberdeen MD, Capitol Heights MD, College Park MD, Cumberland MD, Essex MD, Frederick MD, Hagerstown MD, Havre de Grace MD, La Plata MD, Lexingtin Park MD, Salisbury MD, Thurmont MD, Waldorf MD, Atlantic City NJ, Barrington NJ, Fairfield NJ, North Bergen NJ, Albany NY, Amherst NY, Amsterdam NY, Auburn NY, Bath NY, Binghamton NY, Catskill NY, Corland NY, Glens Falls NY, Goversville NY, Governor's Island NY, Hornell NY, Ithaca NY, Kingston NY, Lake George NY, Latham NY, Liverpool NY, Massena NY, Maybrook NY, Middletown NY, New Paltz NY, Newburgh NY, Niagara Falls NY, Norwich NY, Nyack NY, Oneida NY, Oneonta NY, Plattasburgh NY, Poughkeepsie NY, Pulaski NY, Rochester NY, Saugerties NY, Sidney NY, Ticonderoga NY, Troy NY, Warrensburg NY, Allentown PA, Altoona PA, Bedford PA, Brookville PA, Butler PA, Carlisle PA, Gettysbrug PA, Greensburg PA, Hershey PA, Harrisburg PA, Johnstown PA, Lancaster PA, Lewiston PA, Meadville PA, Miffinville PA, New Castle PA, New Stanton PA, Philadelphia PA, Somerset PA, Stroudsburg PA, Warren PA, Waynesburg PA, Williamsport PA, York PA: Abingdon VA, Appomattox VA, Cristol VA, Charlottesville VA, Chesapeak VA, Christiansburg VA, Culpeper VA, Danville VA, Dumfries VA, Farmville VA, Franklin VA, Fredericksburg VA, Front Royal VA, Hampton VA, Harrisonburg VA, Lexington VA, Newport News VA, Norfolk VA, Norton VA, Petersburg VA, Radford VA, Richmond VA, Roanoke VA, Salem VA, South Boston VA, South Hill

VA, Suffolk VA, Tappahannock VA, Waynesboro VA, Williamsburg VA, Winchester VA, Wytheville VA, Beckley WV, Dunbar WV, Elkins WV, Lewisburg WV, Logan WV, Martinsburg WV, Ripley WV, Summersville WV, Weston WV, Washinton D.C.

Suisse Chalet
One Chalet Drive
Wilton NH 03086
603-654-2000
Reservations: 800-5-CHALET

Locations: Baltimore MD, Albany NY, Washington D.C.

Travelers Inns
1800 East Imperial Highway
Brea CA 92621
Reservations: 800-633-8300

Locations: Albuquerque NM, Dallas TX, El Paso TX, Denver CO, Fresno CA, Oklahoma City OK, Phoenix AZ, Sacramento CA, San Antonio TX, Tulsa OK.

TraveLodge
1973 Friendship Drive
El Cajon CA 92020
619-448-1884, Fax 619-562-0901
Reservations: 800-255-3050

Locations: Newark DE, New Castle DE, Hagerstown MD, Atlantic City NJ, Lake George NY, New York NY, Niagara Falls NY, Schenectady NY, Utica NY, Mt. Chambersburg PA, Lancaster PA, Laurel PA, Pittsburgh PA, York PA, Arlington VA, Ashland VA, Emporia VA, Fredericksburg VA, Cheseapeake VA, Petersburg VA, Roanoke VA, Virginia Beach VA, Williamsburg VA, Winchester VA, Washington DC, Dunbar WV.

The Business Break Club Program offers a 10% discount off the lowest published room rate, express check-in and check-out, free local telephone call, morning coffee and a special 800-number for fast reservations. The Corporate Business Break Club provides a 10% room discount off the lowest published rate, free morning coffee, newsletters and car rental discounts.

The Classic Travel Club is available to travelers over the age of 50. It offers room discounts of 15%, a quarterly newsletter, check-cashing privileges, free morning coffee, car rental discounts and express check-in, check-out services.

Coaches, Athletic Directors and Educators are eligible for Team TraveLodge which offers a free stay for groups of 10 or more, a minimum 10% discount, upgrades for group leaders, late check-out, free morning coffee, newsletter and car rental discounts.

All federal, state and local government employees and members of the armed forces and their families traveling on official government business or pleasure receive special rates equal to or less than the prevailing per diem rates. Information on these rates is available from 800-GOVT-RES.

Under the Family Plan, there is no charge for children under the age of 17 when sharing a room with their parents. The Government Traveler- Value America Plan offers rates equal to or less than the prevailing per diem rates paid and is available to federal employees, military personnel and contractors on government business.

Westin Hotels and Resorts
The Westin Building
Seattle WA 98121
206-443-5096, Fax 206-443-5096
Reservations: 800-228-3000

Locations: New York NY; Pittsburgh PA; Washington D.C.

At Westin hotels or resorts there is no charge for children under the age of 18 when they share the room with parents or guardians. If more than one room is required to accommodate a family, the single guest room rate will apply to each room, regardless of the number of people occupying the room.

Wyndham Hotels and Resort
2001 Bryan St, Suite 2300
Dallas TX 75210
214-978-4500
Reservations: 800-822-4200

Locations: Philadelphia PA.

Accommodations Directory

Delaware

Rental and Reservation Services

Bed and Breakfast Delaware (3650 Silverside Rd, Wilmington 19810; 302-479-9500, 800-233-4689) reservations service for bed and breakfasts and accommodations in private homes.

Bethany Beach
Area Code 302

Rental and Reservation Services

Bethany Beach Realty (5th St, 19930; 539-1600, 800-445-4770) rental condos and apartments.

Coldwell Banker (Pennsylvania Ave and Garfield Pkwy, 19930; 539-3005, 800-800-4089) rental homes, cottages, townhouses and condos.

East Coast Resorts (Rte 26, 19930; 539-7000, 800-444-8055) rental homes, townhouses and condos.

Jack Hickman Real Estate (South Rte 1, 19930; 539-8000, 800-537-8003) rental homes and condos.

Long and Foster (Bethany Beach, 19930; 539-9767, 800-562-3224) rental homes and condos.

Tidewater Realty (Starboard Center, 19930; 539-7500).

❑ ❑ ❑

Blue Surf Motel (Boardwalk and Garfield Pkwy, 19930; 539-7531) rooms and efficiencies, water view. SGL/DBL$48-$56.

Harbor View Motel (Bethany Beach 19930; 539-0500) 60 rooms and efficiencies, restaurant, pool, a/c, TV, beach. SGL/DBL$65-$75.

Westward Pines Motel (10 Kent Ave, 19930; 539-7426) 10 rooms, a/c, TV, in-room coffee makers, fireplace, jacuzzi, year-round. SGL/DBL$38-$58.

Bridgeville
Area Code 302

Teddy Bear Bed and Breakfast (303 Market St, 19933; 337-3134) 3 rooms, free breakfast, 1920s home, no smoking. SGL/DBL$50-$75.

Claymont
Area Code 302

Hilton Hotel (I-95 and Naamans Rd, 19703; 792-2700, Fax 798-6182, 800-HILTONS) 193 rooms and suites, restaurant, lounge, entertainment, outdoor pool, exercise facilities, children stay free with parents, no-smoking rooms, complimentary newspapers, free parking, wheelchair access, pets allowed, a/c, TV, business services, 10,000 square feet of meeting and exhibition space, major credit cards. SGL/DBL$95-$125.

Dewey Beach
Area Code 302

Adam's Ocean Front Motel (Two Read St, 19971; 227-3030, 800-448-8080) 23 2-bedroom condos, free breakfast, pool, kitchenette, water view, no pets, TV, a/c. SGL/DBL$55-$125.

Atlantic Oceanside Motel (Dewey Beach 19971; 227-8811) 59 rooms and apartments, restaurant, pool, major credit cards. SGL/DBL$29-$95.

Bay Resort (Dewey Beach 19971; 227-6400, 800-922-9240) 68 rooms and efficiencies, free breakfast, children stay free with parents, pool, a/c, TV, laundry facilities, no pets, major credit cards. SGL/DBL$98-$129.

Bay View Inn (Dewey Beach 19971; 227-4343) 33 efficiencies, pool, wheelchair access, water view, no pets, a/c, TV. SGL/DBL$45-$95.

Best Western (Dewey Beach 19971; 226-1100, Fax 226-9785, 800-528-1234) 75 rooms, restaurant, free breakfast, lounge, pool, exercise facilities, children stay free with parents, a/c, TV, no-smoking rooms, wheelchair access, pets allowed, in-room refrigerators, senior citizen rates, meeting facilities, major credit cards. SGL/DBL$130.

Boardwalk Plaza (Dewey Beach 19971; 227-7169, 800-33-BEACH) 3 2-bedroom apartments, indoor and outdoor pool, restaurant, a/c, TV, water view. SGL/DBL$1,800W-$2,200W.

Dewey Beach Suites and Motel (1406 Hwy 1, 19971; 226-0233) 24 rooms and 2-bedroom suites, kitchenettes, TV, a/c, laundry facilities, no pets, major credit cards. SGL/DBL$28-$169.

Joseph's Cottages and Rooms (506 Rehoboth Ave, 19971; 227-2222) rooms and cottages, kitchenettes. SGL/DBL$55-$65.

Dover
Area Code 302

Best Western Inn (1700 East Lebanon Rd, 19901; 735-4700, Fax 735-4705, 800-528-1234) 64 rooms, restaurant, free breakfast, lounge, pool, exercise facilities, whirlpool tubs, children stay free with parents, a/c, TV, no-smoking rooms, wheelchair access, no pets, senior citizen rates, meeting facilities, major credit cards. SGL/DBL$45-$60.

Budget Host Capitol City Lodge (246 North DuPont Hwy, 19901; 678-0161, 800-BUD-HOST) 112 rooms, in-room refrigerators, no-smoking rooms, TV, VCRs, kitchenettes, a/c, wheelchair access, children stay free with patents, senior citizen rates, meeting facilities, major credit cards. SGL$30-$35, DBL$32-$37, AP$4.

Budget Inn (1426 North DuPont Hwy, 19901; 734-4433) 68 rooms, pool, laundry facilities, wheelchair access, no-smoking rooms, a/c, TV. SGL/DBL$45-$65.

Comfort Inn (222 South DuPont Hwy, 19901; 674-3300, 800-221-2222) 94 rooms, restaurant, pool, wheelchair access, no-smoking rooms, no pets, children under 18 stay free with parents, in-room refrigerators, senior citizen rates, a/c, TV, meeting facilities, major credit cards. SGL$41-$45, DBL$46-$53, AP$5.

Days Inn Downtown (272 North DuPont Hwy, 19901; 674-8002, Fax 674-2195, 800-325-2525) 81 rooms, restaurant, lounge, pool, children stay free with parents, room service, laundry service, kitchenettes, a/c, TV, free local calls, no pets, wheelchair access, no-smoking rooms, senior citizen rates, major credit cards. SGL$30-$45, DBL$35-$55, EFF$44-$79.

Econo Lodge (561 North DuPont Hwy, 19901; 678-8900, Fax 678-2245, 800-4-CHOICE) 133 rooms, free breakfast, pool, TV, children under 12 stay free with parents, laundry service, no pets, senior citizen rates, wheelchair access, a/c, TV, major credit cards. SGL/DBL$37-$45.

Holiday Inn (348 North DuPont Hwy, 19901; 734-5701, Fax 674-4788, 800-HOLIDAY) rooms and 2-room suites, restaurant, lounge, entertainment, outdoor pool, exercise facilities, children under 19 stay free with parents, wheelchair access, a/c, TV, no-smoking rooms, fax service, room service, pets allowed, laundry service, senior citizen rates, meeting facilities for 100, major credit cards. SGL/DBL$39-$60.

The Inn At Meeting House Square (305 South Governors Ave, 19901; 678-1242) 4 rooms, bed and breakfast, private baths, no pets, a/c, TV, 1840s inn. SGL$35-$50, DBL$45-$60.

Noble Guest House (33 South Bradford St, 19901; 674-4084) B&B, free breakfast, 1880s home, antique furnishings. SGL/DBL$55-$110.

Sheraton Inn (1570 North DuPont Hwy, 19901; 678-8500, Fax 678-8500 ext 226, 800-325-3535) 145 rooms and suites, restaurant, lounge, entertainment, outdoor pool, exercise facilities, no-smoking rooms, a/c, gift shop, TV, children stay free with parents, wheelchair access, 5,000 square feet of meeting and exhibition space, 9 meeting rooms, meeting facilities for 400, major credit cards. SGL/DBL$55-$60.

Fenwick Island
Area Code 302

Atlantic Budget Inn (Ocean Hwy, 19944; 539-7673) 48 rooms and efficiencies, pool, a/c, TV. SGL/DBL$65-$95.

Sea Charm Motel (Oceanfront and Lighthouse Rd, 19944; 539-9613) rooms and efficiencies, pool, kitchenettes, a/c, beach, laundry facilities, TV. SGL/DBL$38-$65.

Laurel
Area Code 302

Spring Garden Bed and Breakfast (Delaware Ave, 19956; 875-7015) 5 rooms and suites, antique furnishings, fireplaces. SGL/DBL$55-$110.

Lewes
Area Code 302

Rental and Reservation Services

Wilgus Associates (645-9215, 800-441-8118) rental homes and condos.

□ □ □

Anglers Motel (110 Anglers Rd, 19958; 645-2831) 25 rooms, water view, TV, a/c, kitchenettes, major credit cards. SGL/DBL$55-$80.

The New Devon Inn (Meeting and 2nd St, 19958; 645-6466) 23 rooms and suites, restaurant, free breakfast, open year-round, antique furnishings, meeting facilities for 100. SGL/DBL$100-$145.

Seaport Inn (306 Savannah Rd, 19958; 645-1000) 13 rooms. SGL/DBL$38-$43.

Vesuvio Motel (105 Savannah Rd, 19958; 645-2224) SGL/DBL$45-$55.

Millsboro
Area Code 302

Atlantic Budget Inn (210 West DuPont Hwy, 19966; 934-6711) 82 rooms, pool, a/c, laundry facilities, TV. SGL/DBL$48-$65.

Newark
Area Code 302

Comfort Inn (State Rd 896, 19713; 368-8725, Fax 368-6454, 800-221-2222) 102 rooms, restaurant, free breakfast, pool, wheelchair access, no-smoking rooms, pets allowed, in-room refrigerators, children under 18 stay free with parents, senior citizen rates, a/c, TV, meeting facilities, major credit cards. SGL$42-$50, DBL$44-$54.

Courtyard by Marriott (48 Geoffrey Dr., 19713; 456-3800, Fax 456-2824, 800-321-2211) 152 rooms and suites, restaurant, lounge, pool, exercise facilities, whirlpools, children stay free with parents, laundry service, meeting facilities, no pets, senior citizen rates, major credit cards. SGL/DBL$56-$84.

Days Inn (900 Churchman Rd, 19713; 368-2400, Fax 731-8620, 800-325-2525) 150 rooms, restaurant, complimentary breakfast, lounge, outdoor pool, children stay free with parents, room service, laundry service, a/c, TV, free local calls, no pets, wheelchair access, no-smoking rooms, senior citizen rates, major credit cards. SGL$37-$47, DBL$39-$49.

Fairfield Inn (65 Geoffrey Dr., 19713; 292-1500) 135 rooms, pool, TV, a/c, no pets, major credit cards. SGL/DBL$36-$56.

Hampton Inn (Three Concord Lane, 19713; 737-3900, Fax 737-2630, 800-HAMPTON) 122 rooms, restaurant, free breakfast, pool, exercise facilities, children under 18 stay free with parents, no-smoking rooms, wheelchair access, computer hookups, fax, TV, a/c, laundry facilities, free local calls, pets allowed, meeting facilities, major credit cards. SGL/DBL$55-$70.

Hilton Christiana Hotel (100 Continental Dr., 19713; 454-1500, Fax 454-0233, 800-HILTONS) 266 rooms and suites, restaurant, lounge, entertainment, outdoor pool, exercise facilities, whirlpools, children stay free with parents, no-smoking rooms, free parking, wheelchair access, transportation to local attractions, free newspaper, pets allowed, a/c, TV, business services, meeting facilities, major credit cards. SGL/DBL$85-$140.

Holiday Inn (1203 Christiana Rd, 19713; 737-2700, Fax 737-3214, 800-HOLIDAY) 144 rooms, restaurant, lounge, outdoor pool, exercise facilities, children under 19 stay free with parents, wheelchair access, a/c, TV, no-smoking rooms, laundry facilities, fax service, room service, no pets, laundry service, meeting facilities, senior citizen rates, major credit cards. SGL/DBL$55-$75.

Howard Johnson Lodge and Suites (1119 South College Ave, 19713; 368-8521, Fax 368-9868, 800-I-GO-HOJO) 142 rooms, restaurant, free breakfast, lounge, pool, in-room refrigerators and microwaves, laundry facilities, children stay free with parents, wheelchair access, no-smoking rooms, TV, a/c, pets allowed, free parking, meeting facilities, senior citizen rates, major credit cards. SGL$49-$99, DBL$59-$109.

McIntosh Motor Inn Of Newark (Rte 273 North, 19713; 453-9100) 104 rooms, restaurant, a/c, TV, no-smoking rooms, no pets, in-room refrigerators and microwaves, wheelchair access, major credit cards. SGL/DBL$30-$40.

Red Roof Inn (415 Stanton Christiana Rd, 19713; 292-2870, 800-843-7663) 119 rooms, restaurant, no-smoking rooms, fax service, wheelchair access, free newspaper, children stay free with parents, pets allowed, free local calls, in-room computer hookups, major credit cards. SGL/DBL$42-$51.

Residence Inn (240 Chapman Rd, 19702; 453-9200, Fax 453-8122, 800-331-3131) rooms and suites, free breakfast, pool, spa, in-room refrigerators, coffee makers and microwaves, laundry facilities, free parking, TV, a/c, VCRs, pets allowed, fireplaces, children stay free with parents, no-smoking rooms, wheelchair access, major credit cards. SGL/DBL$115-$135.

Sheraton Inn (260 Chapman Rd, 19702; 738-3400, 800-325-3535) 99 rooms and suites, restaurant, lounge, pool, exercise facilities, no-smoking rooms, a/c, TV, room service, children stay free with parents, wheelchair access, meeting facilities, major credit cards. SGL/DBL$49-$79.

TraveLodge (268 East Main St, 19711; 737-5050, Fax 737-4089, 800-255-3050) 47 rooms, restaurant, lounge, complimentary breakfast, pool, wheelchair access, free newspaper, laundry service, TV, a/c, free local calls, fax service, no-smoking rooms, free in-room coffee and tea service, in-room refrigerators and microwaves, no pets, major credit cards. SGL$42-$56, DBL$47-$61, AP$5.

New Castle
Area Code 302

The David Finney Inn (216 Delaware St, 19720; 322-6367, 800-334-6640) 20 rooms and suites, restaurant, complimentary breakfast, lounge, entertainment, private baths, antique furnishings, wheelchair access, major credit cards. SGL/DBL$70-$135.

Econo Lodge (Three Memorial Dr., 19720; 654-5400, Fax 654-5775, 800-4-CHOICE) 48 rooms, complimentary breakfast, pool, children under 12 stay free with parents, in-room refrigerators, pets allowed, senior citizen rates, wheelchair access, a/c, TV, major credit cards. SGL/DBL$38-$44.

Econo Lodge Airport (232 DuPont Hwy, 19720; 322-4500, 800-4-CHOICE) 67 rooms, complimentary breakfast, pool, children under 12 stay free with parents, pets allowed, senior citizen rates, wheelchair access, a/c, TV, major credit cards. SGL/DBL$34-$42.

New Castle 27

Howard Johnson Motor Lodge (2162 New Castle Ave, 19720; 656-7771, 800-I-GO-HOJO) 103 rooms, restaurant, lounge, pool, children stay free with parents, wheelchair access, no-smoking rooms, TV, a/c, pets allowed, free parking, meeting facilities, senior citizen rates, major credit cards. SGL/DBL$50-$80.

Jefferson House Bed and Breakfast (New Castle 19720; 323-0999) complimentary breakfast, 1790s home, children under 6 stay free with parents, antique furnishings, a/c, fireplace, no pets, private baths, major credit cards. SGL/DBL$65-$85.

Motel 6 (1200 West Ave, 19720; 571-1200) 159 rooms, outdoor pool, TV, a/c, free local calls, wheelchair access, Modified American Plan available. SGL/DBL$30-$45.

Quality Inn Skyways (147 North Dupont Hwy, 19720; 328-6666, 800-221-2222) 100 rooms, restaurant, lounge, free breakfast, outdoor pool, no pets, no smoking rooms, children under 18 stay free with parents, TV, a/c, senior citizen rates, meeting facilities, major credit cards. SGL/DBL$50-$58.

Ramada Inn (New Castle 19720; 658-8511, 800-2-RAMADA) 136 rooms, restaurant, lounge, pool, wheelchair access, no-smoking rooms, airport transportation, free parking, pets allowed, wheelchair access, a/c, TV, room service, laundry facilities, meeting facilities, senior citizen rates, major credit cards. SGL$67-$75, DBL$73-$85, AP$6.

Rodeway Inn (111 South DuPont Hwy, 19720; 328-6246, Fax 328-9493) 41 rooms, restaurant, in-room refrigerators, transportation to local attractions, no-smoking rooms, pets allowed, children stay free with parents, a/c, TV. SGL/DBL$39-$54.

The Ross House (129 East Second St, 19720; 322-7787) free breakfast, 1720s home, a/c, VCR, in-room refrigerators, TV. SGL/DBL$65-$75.

Super 8 Motel (215 South DuPont Hwy, 19720; 322-9480, 800-800-8000) 59 rooms and suites, complimentary breakfast, no pets, children under 12 stay free with parents, free local calls, a/c, TV, in-room refrigerators and microwaves, fax service, no-smoking rooms, senior citizen rates, wheelchair access, meeting facilities, major credit cards. SGL$38, DBL$43.

TraveLodge (1213 West Ave, 19720; 654-5544, Fax 652-0146, 800-255-3050) 109 rooms, restaurant, lounge, free breakfast, pool, wheelchair access, complimentary newspaper, laundry service, TV, a/c, free local calls, fax, no-smoking rooms, free in-room coffee and tea service, in-room refrigerators and microwaves, pets allowed, major credit cards. SGL/DBL$38-$42.

William Penn Guest House (206 Delaware St, 19720; 328-7736) 4 rooms, bed and breakfast, no smoking, no pets, 1680s home, private bath, major credit cards. SGL$75-$100, DBL$85-$135.

Odessa
Area Code 302

Cantwell House (107 High St, 19730; 378-4179) 4 rooms, bed and breakfast, 1840s home, antique furnishings. SGL/DBL$58-$78.

Rehoboth Beach
Area Code 302

Rental and Reservation Services

Anderson-Stokes Realtors (146 Rehoboth Ave, 19971; 227-2541, 800-GO-BEACH).

❏ ❏ ❏

Admiral Motel (Two Baltimore Ave, 19971; 227-2103, Fax 227-3620) 73 rooms, restaurant, pool, in-room refrigerators, a/c, TV, no pets, major credit cards. SGL/DBL$36-$113.

Atlantic Budget Inn (154 Rehoboth Ave, 19971; 227-9446, 800-245-2112 in the northeast) 97 rooms and efficiencies, pool, no-smoking rooms, children stay free with parents, in-room refrigerators. SGL/DBL$85-$100.

Atlantic Sands Hotel and Suites (Rehoboth Beach 19971; 227-2511, Fax 227-9576, 800-422-2511) 114 rooms and suites, water view, kitchenettes, pool, whirlpool tubs, a/c, wheelchair access, children stay free with parents, no-smoking rooms, in-room refrigerators, TV, open year-round, major credit cards. SGL/DBL$135-$250.

Atlantic View Motel (Two Clayton St, 19971; 227-3878) 35 rooms, pool, a/c, TV, no pets, water view, major credit cards. SGL/DBL$48-$102.

Bay Resort (Rehoboth Beach 19971; 227-6400, 800-292-9240) 68 rooms and efficiencies, free breakfast, pool, laundry facilities, in-room refrigerators, children stay free with parents, a/c, TV. SGL/DBL$100-$135.

Beach View Motel (Six Wilmington Ave, 19971; 227-2999, 800-288-5962) 38 rooms, restaurant, free breakfast, pool, no pets, laundry facilities, gift shop, in-room refrigerators, major credit cards. SGL/DBL$49-$107.

Bellbouy Motel (21 Van Dyke St, 19971; 227-6000) 16 rooms and apartments, a/c, TV, pets allowed, in-room refrigerators. SGL/DBL$38-$95.

Best Western Gold Leaf (1400 Hwy One, 19971; 226-1100, 800-528-1234) restaurant, free breakfast, lounge, pool, exercise facilities, in-room refrigerators, children stay free with parents, a/c, TV, no-smoking rooms, wheelchair access, no pets, senior citizen rates, meeting facilities, major credit cards. SGL/DBL$45-$129.

Boardwalk Plaza Hotel (Two Olive Ave, 19971; 227-7169, Fax 227-0651, 800-332-3224) 84 rooms and suites, restaurant, pool, exercise facilities, whirlpool tubs, in-room refrigerators, a/c, TV, water view, no pets, children stay free with parents, no-smoking rooms, wheelchair access, major credit cards. SGL/DBL$60-$275.

Brighton Suites (34 Wilmington Ave, 19971; 227-5780) 67 suites, pool, exercise facilities, in-room refrigerators, open year-round, free parking, private baths, no pets, TV, a/c, children stay free with parents, meeting facilities, major credit cards. SGL/DBL$59-$189.

Commodore Motel (50 Rehoboth Ave, 19971; 227-9446, 800-245-2112) 75 rooms and suites, pool, exercise facilities, pets allowed, open year-round, a/c, TV, meeting facilities for 125, major credit cards. SGL/DBL$75-$85.

Dinner Bell Motel (Two Christian St, 19971; 227-2561) 32 rooms and housekeeping cottages, restaurant, TV, a/c, children stay free with parents, open April to September. SGL/DBL$80-$100.

Econo Lodge (4361 Hwy One, 19971; 227-0500, Fax 227-2170, 800-446-6900) 79 rooms, complimentary breakfast, pool, children under 12 stay free with parents, in-room refrigerators, pets allowed, senior citizen rates, a/c, TV, major credit cards. SGL$75-$120.

Edgewater House Condominiums (Rehoboth Beach, 19971; 227-9120) efficiencies and 1- and 2-bedroom condos, kitchenettes, TV, a/c, pool, major credit cards. SGL/DBL$85-$165.

The Henlopen Condominium (Surf Ave and Boardwalk, 19971; 227-6409, Fax 227-8147) 93 condos, kitchenettes, TV, a/c, no-smoking rooms, beach, children stay free with parents, major credit cards. SGL/DBL$140-$200.

Oceanus Motel (Six 2nd St, 19972; 227-9436, 800-852-5011) 38 rooms, restaurant, free breakfast, pool, a/c, in-room refrigerators, TV. SGL/DBL$39-$119.

Sandcastle Motel (123 2nd St, 19971; 227-0400, 800-372-2112) 60 rooms, indoor pool, sauna, whirlpools, children stay free with parents, a/c, TV, meeting facilities. SGL/DBL$100-$120.

Sea Ranch Motel (2909 Hwy 1, 19971; 227-8609) 22 rooms and apartments, pool, in-room refrigerators, a/c, TV, major credit cards. SGL/DBL$24-$80.

Tembo Bed and Breakfast (100 Laurel St, 19971; 227-3360) complimentary breakfast, no smoking. SGL/DBL$55-$65.

Seaford
Area Code 302

Comfort Inn (Beaverdam Dr., 19973; 629-8385, 800-228-5150, 800-221-2222) 93 rooms and suites, restaurant, indoor pool, exercise facilities, sauna, water view, fax, whirlpools, wheelchair access, no-smoking rooms, pets allowed, whirlpools, children under 18 stay free with parents, senior citizen rates, a/c, TV, meeting facilities, major credit cards. SGL$49-$65.

Wilmington
Area Code 302

Best Western Inn (1807 Concord Pike, 19803; 656-9436, 800-528-1234) 101 rooms, restaurant, free breakfast, lounge, pool, exercise facilities, children stay free with parents, a/c, TV, no-smoking rooms, pets allowed, wheelchair access, laundry facilities, meeting facilities, senior citizen rates, major credit cards. SGL/DBL$50-$80.

Christina House (707 North King St, 19801; 656-9300, Fax 656-2459) 39 rooms, in-room refrigerators, airport transportation, pets allowed, TV, major credit cards. SGL/DBL$75-$125.

Days Inn (1102 West St, 19801; 429-7600, 800-325-2525) 126 rooms, restaurant, lounge, whirlpools, children stay free with parents, room service, laundry service, in-room refrigerators, a/c, TV, free local calls, no pets, fax, wheelchair access, no-smoking rooms, senior citizen rates, major credit cards. SGL/DBL$75-$120.

Holiday Inn (700 King St, 19801; 655-0400, Fax 655-5488, 800-HOLIDAY) 217 rooms, restaurant, lounge, indoor pool, exercise facilities, whirlpools, children under 19 stay free with parents, wheelchair access, a/c, TV, no-smoking rooms, fax, room service, pets allowed, laundry service, meeting facilities, senior citizen rates, major credit cards. SGL/DBL$70-$100.

Hotel Du Pont (Market and 11th Streets, 19899; 549-3100) 217 rooms, restaurant, exercise facilities, a/c, TV, no pets, major credit cards. SGL/DBL$175-$225.

Sheraton Inn (4727 Concord Pike, 19803; 478-6000, Fax 477-1492, 800-325-3535) 154 rooms and suites, restaurant, lounge, entertainment, indoor pool, exercise facilities, no-smoking rooms, a/c, TV, airport transportation, in-room refrigerators, children stay free with parents, wheelchair access, meeting facilities, major credit cards. SGL/DBL$60-$140.

Sheraton Suites Hotel (422 Delaware Ave, 19801; 654-8300, Fax 654-6036, 800-325-3535) 230 rooms and suites, restaurant, lounge, entertainment, indoor pool, exercise facilities, sauna, no-smoking rooms, children stay free with parents, a/c, TV, no pets, VCRs, wheelchair access, meeting facilities, major credit cards. SGL/DBL$90-$195.

Tally-Ho Motor Lodge (5209 Concord Pike, 19803; 478-0300) 100 rooms, a/c, TV, laundry facilities, pets OK, major credit cards. SGL/DBL$38-$45.

Maryland

Rental and Reservation Services

Amanda's Bed and Breakfast Reservation Service (1428 Park Ave, Baltimore 21217; 410-225-0001, Fax 410-728-8957, 800-899-7533).

B&B of Maryland (Box 2277, Annapolis 21404; 410-269-6232, 800-736-4667).

The Inns of The Blue Ridge (Box 33, New Market 21774).

Aberdeen
Area Code 410

Days Inn (783 West Bel Air Ave, 21001; 272-8500, Fax 272-5782, 800-325-2525) 49 rooms, restaurant, lounge, pool, children stay free with parents, room service, laundry service, a/c, TV, free local calls, pets allowed, wheelchair access, no-smoking rooms, senior citizen rates, major credit cards. SGL/DBL$38-$46.

Econo Lodge (820 Bel Air Ave, 21001; 272-5500, Fax 272-7648, 800-4-CHOICE) 61 rooms, free breakfast, pool, children under 12 stay free with parents, no pets, senior citizen rates, wheelchair access, a/c, TV, major credit cards. SGL/DBL$36-$45.

Friendship Inn (424 South Philadelphia Blvd, 21001; 272-3666, 800-424-4777) 37 rooms, exercise facilities, a/c, TV, no pets, no-smoking rooms, children stay free with parents, wheelchair access, major credit cards. SGL/DBL$38-$56.

Holiday Inn Chesapeake House (1007 Beards Hill Rd, 21001; 272-8100, Fax 272-1714, 800-HOLIDAY) 123 rooms and efficiencies, restaurant, lounge, indoor pool, exercise facilities, kitchenettes, children under 19 stay free with parents, wheelchair access, a/c, TV, no-smoking rooms, fax service, room service, pets allowed, laundry service, meeting facilities, senior citizen rates, major credit cards. SGL/DBL$75-$100.

Howard Johnson Lodge (793 West Bel Air Ave, 21001; 272-6000, Fax 272-2287, 800-I-GO-HOJO) 124 rooms, restaurant, lounge, pool, children stay free with parents, wheelchair access, fax service, no-smoking rooms,

TV, a/c, pets allowed, laundry facilities, free parking, senior citizen rates, meeting facilities, major credit cards. SGL/DBL$46-$58.

Red Roof Inn (988 Beards Hill Rd, 21001; 273-7800, Fax 273-7800, 800-843-7663) 109 rooms, restaurant, no-smoking rooms, fax service, wheelchair access, free newspaper, children stay free with parents, pets allowed, free local calls, major credit cards. SGL/DBL$38-$51.

Sheraton Aberdeen Hotel (980 Beards Hill Rd, 21001; 273-6300, Fax 575-7195, 800-325-3535) 131 rooms and suites, restaurant, lounge, pool, exercise facilities, tennis courts, whirlpools, no-smoking rooms, a/c, TV, pets allowed, children stay free with parents, wheelchair access, 4,450 square feet of meeting and exhibition space, meeting facilities for 400, major credit cards. SGL/DBL$59-$110.

Super 8 Motel (1008 Beards Hill Rd, 21001; 272-5420, 800-800-8000) 62 rooms, free breakfast, no pets, children under 12 stay free with parents, free local calls, a/c, in-room refrigerators and microwaves, TV, fax service, no-smoking rooms, senior citizen rates, wheelchair access, major credit cards. SGL/DBL$38-$43.

Annapolis
Area Code 410

Rental and Reservation Services

B&B of Maryland (Box 2277, 21404; 269-6232, 800-736-4667).

Harborview Boat and Breakfast (980 Awald Dr., 21403; 268-9330, 800-877-9330) accommodations aboard boats. SGL/DBL$75-$200.

Historic Inns Of Annapolis (16 Church Circle, 21401; 263-2641, 800-847-8882).

Roomfinders (66 Maryland Ave, 21401; 263-3262, 800-84VISIT).

The Traveler In Maryland (33 West St, 21401; 269-6232) for B&Bs.

ooo

The Ark and Dove Bed and Breakfast (149 Prince George St, 21401; 268-6277) complimentary breakfast, antique furnishings, no smoking, no pets, major credit cards. SGL/DBL$60-$80.

Casa Bahia (262 King George St, 21401; 268-3106) bed and breakfast, children stay free with parents, 1860s home. SGL/DBL$70-$90.

Annapolis 33

The Charles Inn (74 Charles St, 21401; 268-1451) 4 rooms, bed and breakfast, 1860s home, TV, jacuzzi, private baths, antique furnishings, water view, a/c, major credit cards. SGL/DBL$55-$100.

College House Suites (One College Ave, 21401; 263-6124) 2 suites, bed and breakfast, no smoking, antique furnishings, no children allowed, no pets, private baths. SGL/DBL$147.

Comfort Inn (Old Mill Bottom, 21401; 757-8500, Fax 757-4409, 800-221-2222) 60 rooms, restaurant, pool, wheelchair access, no-smoking rooms, no pets, children under 18 stay free with parents, laundry facilities, VCRs, senior citizen rates, a/c, whirlpool, TV, meeting facilities, major credit cards. SGL/DBL$50-$90.

Courtyard by Marriott (2559 Riva Rd, 21401; 266-1555, Fax 266-6387, 800-321-2211) 149 rooms and suites, restaurant, lounge, indoor pool, exercise facilities, whirlpool, children stay free with parents, no pets, laundry service, meeting facilities, senior citizen rates, major credit cards. SGL/DBL$46-$66.

Days Inn (591 Revell Hwy, 21401; 974-4440, 800-325-2525) restaurant, lounge, pool, children stay free with parents, room service, laundry service, a/c, TV, free local calls, no pets, wheelchair access, no-smoking rooms, senior citizen rates, major credit cards. SGL/DBL$45-$65.

Days Inn (1542 Whitehall Rd, 21401; 974-4440, 800-325-2525) 74 rooms, restaurant, free breakfast, lounge, pool, children stay free with parents, room service, laundry service, a/c, TV, free local calls, in-room refrigerators and microwaves, pets allowed, wheelchair access, no-smoking rooms, senior citizen rates, major credit cards. SGL/DBL$43-$58.

Econo Lodge (2451 Riva Rd, 21401; 224-4317, Fax 224-6010, 800-4-CHOICE) 68 rooms, free breakfast, pool, TV, VCRs, children under 12 stay free with parents, no pets, whirlpools, in-room refrigerators and microwaves, senior citizen rates, wheelchair access, a/c, TV, major credit cards. SGL/DBL$48-$130.

Flag House Inn (26 Randall St, 21401; 280-2721, 800-437-4825) 4 rooms, bed and breakfast, a/c, private baths, antique furnishings, 1850s inn. SGL/DBL$65-$80.

Gibson's Lodging (110 Prince George St, 21401; 268-5555) 21 rooms and suites, bed and breakfast, no smoking, no pets, private baths, antique furnishings, major credit cards. SGL/DBL$65-$135.

Governor Calvert House (58 State Circle, 21401; 263-2641, Fax 268-3813, 800-847-8882) 51 rooms, pool, wheelchair access, in-room refrigerators, antique furnishings, no pets, whirlpool, a/c, TV, airport courtesy car, major credit cards. SGL/DBL$100-$185.

Maryland

Holiday Inn Hotel and Conference Center (210 Holiday Court, 21401; 224-3150, 800-HOLIDAY) 220 rooms and efficiencies, restaurant, lounge, outdoor pool, exercise facilities, children under 19 stay free with parents, wheelchair access, a/c, TV, no-smoking rooms, fax service, room service, pets allowed, laundry service, meeting facilities for 700, senior citizen rates, major credit cards. SGL/DBL$59.

Howard Johnson Lodge (69 Old Mill Bottom Rd North, 21401; 757-1600, Fax 757-1949, 800-I-GO-HOJO) 70 rooms, restaurant, lounge, pool, jacuzzi, kitchenettes, children stay free with parents, wheelchair access, no-smoking rooms, TV, a/c, pets allowed, free parking, senior citizen rates, meeting facilities, major credit cards. SGL$29-$81, DBL$33-$98.

Loew's Annapolis Hotel (126 West St, 21401; 263-7777, Fax 263-0084, 800-223-0888) 217 rooms and suites, restaurant, pool, tennis courts, pets allowed, a/c, barber and beauty shop, gift shop, TV, children stay free with parents, in-room refrigerators, major credit cards. SGL/DBL$115-$175.

Marriott Waterfront Hotel (80 Compromise St, 21401; 268-7555, Fax 269-5864, 800-336-0072, 800-228-9290) 150 rooms, restaurant, lounge, entertainment, water view, wheelchair access, TV, a/c, no-smoking rooms, gift shop, no pets, children stay free with parents, business services, meeting facilities, major credit cards. SGL/DBL$145-$295.

The Maryland Inn (Main St, 21401; 263-2641, Fax 268-3813, 800-847-8882) 44 rooms and suites, restaurant, lounge, entertainment, pool, exercise facilities, tennis courts, in-room refrigerators, no pets, airport transportation, TV, a/c, no-smoking rooms, water view, 1700s inn, antique furnishings, children stay free with parents, major credit cards. SGL/DBL$100-$185.

Prince George Inn (232 Prince George St, 21401; 263-6418) 4 rooms, bed and breakfast, no smoking, antique furnishings, no children allowed, no pets. SGL/DBL$65-$80.

Ramada Hotel (173 Jennifer Rd, 21401; 266-3131, Fax 266-6247, 800-2-RAMADA) 197 rooms and suites, restaurant, lounge, entertainment, indoor pool, no-smoking rooms, airport transportation, free parking, pets allowed, wheelchair access, a/c, TV, room service, laundry facilities, 10 meeting rooms, meeting facilities for 900, senior citizen rates, major credit cards. SGL/DBL$79-$109.

Residence Inn (Admiral Cochrane Dr., 21401; 573-0300, Fax 573-0316, 800-331-3131) rooms and suites, free breakfast, pool, exercise facilities, in-room refrigerators, coffee makers and microwaves, pets allowed, laundry facilities, free parking, TV, a/c, VCRs, fireplaces, children stay free with parents, no-smoking rooms, airport transportation, wheelchair access, meeting facilities, major credit cards. SGL/DBL$109-$145.

The Robert Johnson House (23 State Circle, 21401; 263-2641, Fax 268-3813, 800-847-8882) 29 rooms and suites, pool, tennis courts, wheelchair access, in-room refrigerators, a/c, TV, airport transportation, no pets, antique furnishings, major credit cards. SGL/DBL$100-$185.

Shaw's Fancy Bed and Breakfast (161 Green St, 21401; 268-9750) rooms and suites, hot tub, private baths, no smoking, no pets, no children allowed. SGL/DBL$70-$110, AP$25.

State House Inn (16 Church Circle, 21401; 263-2641, Fax 268-3813, 800-847-8882) 9 rooms, 1820s inn, antique furnishings, children stay free with parents, in-room refrigerators, no pets, whirlpools, airport transportation, major credit cards. SGL/DBL$117-$175.

William Page Inn (Eight Martin St, 21401; 626-1506) 5 rooms, bed and breakfast, antique furnishings, no smoking, private baths, airport transportation, no pets, major credit cards. SGL/DBL$90-$150.

Baltimore
Area Code 301

Rental and Reservation Services

Amanda's B&B Reservation Service (1428 Park Ave, 21217; 225-0001).

Downtown Baltimore

Admiral Fell Inn (888 South Broadway, 21231; 522-7377, Fax 522-0707, 800-292-INNS, 800-528-1234) 38 rooms, 2 restaurants, jacuzzi, transportation to local attractions, wheelchair access, no-smoking rooms, a/c, TV, 2 meeting rooms, major credit cards. SGL/DBL$125.

Belvedere Hotel (One East Chase St, 21202; 332-1000, Fax 332-1422) 100 rooms, restaurant, lounge, entertainment, free breakfast, pool, sauna, exercise center, barber and beauty shop, wheelchair access, no-smoking rooms, a/c, TV, children stay free with parents, airport courtesy car, major credit cards. SGL/DBL$65-$95.

Brookshire Inner Harbor Suite Hotel (120 East Lombard St, 21202; 625-1300, Fax 625-0912, 800-647-0013) 90 suites, restaurant, lounge, entertainment, exercise center, wheelchair access, no-smoking rooms, a/c, TV, children stay free with parents, free newspaper, 4 meeting rooms, meeting facilities for 125. Near the Convention Center. STS$99-$450.

Clarion Hotel Inner Harbor (711 Eastern Ave, 783-5553, Fax 783-1787, 800-252-7466) 71 rooms and suites, restaurant, lounge, entertainment, exercise center, in-room refrigerators, airport transportation, wheelchair access, no-smoking rooms, a/c, TV, meeting facilities for 500, major credit cards. Near the Convention Center, 10 miles from the Baltimore-Washington Airport. SGL/DBL$139-$149.

Comfort Inn at Baltimore's Mt. Vernon (24 West Franklin St, 21210; 532-6900, 800-245-5256, 800-221-2222) 195 rooms and suites, restaurant, lounge, jacuzzi, spa, wheelchair access, no-smoking rooms, a/c, TV, limousine service, no pets, airport courtesy car, meeting facilities for 300, major credit cards. Near the Inner Harbor, 9 miles from the Baltimore-Washington Airport. SGL/DBL$69, STS$105.

Cross Keys Inn (5100 Falls Rd, 21210; 532-6900, Fax 532-2403, 800-532-5397) 148 rooms and suites, restaurants, outdoor pool, jacuzzi, sauna, exercise center, tennis courts, airport courtesy car, boutiques, wheelchair access, no-smoking rooms, a/c, TV, barber and beauty shop, transportation to local attractions, 10 meeting rooms, major credit cards. SGL/DBL$99, STS$140-$340.

Days Inn Inner Harbor (100 Hopkins Place, 21201; 576-1000, 800-325-2525) 251 rooms and suites, 2 restaurants, lounge, outdoor pool, airport transportation, children stay free with parents, free local calls, wheelchair access, no-smoking rooms, a/c, TV, 4 meeting rooms, meeting facilities for 110, major credit cards. Near Inner Harbor, 8 miles from the Baltimore-Washington Airport. SGL$50-$92, DBL$60-$102, STS$55-$125.

Doubletree Inn at the Colonnade (Four West University Pkwy, 21201; 235-5400, Fax 235-5572) 125 rooms and suites, restaurant, indoor pool, jacuzzi, 24-hour room service, transportation to local attractions, pets allowed, no-smoking rooms, a/c, TV, 4 meeting rooms, meeting facilities for 150, major credit cards. SGL/DBL$65-$85.

Harbor Court Hotel (550 Light St, 21202; 234-0550, Fax 659-5925, 800-824-0076) 203 rooms and suites, 2 restaurants, lounge, entertainment, pool, sauna, tennis courts, exercise center, in-room refrigerators, barber and beauty shop, airport transportation, no-smoking rooms, a/c, TV, wheelchair access, pets allowed, 11 meeting rooms, meeting facilities for 500, major credit cards. Near the Convention Center and National Aquarium. SGL$205-$235, DBL$220-$260, 1BR$550, 2BR$650-$2,000.

Holiday Inn Inner Harbor (301 West Lombard St; 685-3500, Fax 685-3500 ext 7178, 800-HOLIDAY) 374 rooms and suites, restaurant, lounge, indoor pool, exercise center, children stay free with parents, wheelchair access, no-smoking rooms, a/c, TV, fax service, room service, free newspaper, meeting facilities for 1,200, major credit cards. Near the Convention Center and Festival Hall, 8 miles from Baltimore-Washington Airport. SGL/DBL$109.

Hyatt Regency Inner Harbor (300 Light St, 21202; 528-1234, Fax 685-3362, 800-233-1234) 489 rooms and suites, 2 restaurants, lounge, entertainment, outdoor pool, jogging track, tennis courts, exercise center, gift shop, barber and beauty shop, children stay free with parents, wheelchair access, no-smoking rooms, a/c, TV, airport courtesy car, 20 meeting rooms, 29,200 square feet of meeting and exhibition space, major credit cards. Near the Convention Center, Inner Harbor, the Science Center, Aquarium and Harbor Place, 15 minutes from Baltimore-Washington Airport. SGL/DBL$180, STS$300-$850.

Inn at Henderson Wharf (1000 Fell St, 21231; 522-7777, Fax 522-7087, 800-522-2088) 38 rooms and suites, bed and breakfast, children stay free with parents, laundry service, free parking, no-smoking, no pets, wheelchair access, fax service, free newspaper, meeting facilities for 150, major credit cards. Near Harbor Place, 20 minutes from Baltimore-Washington Airport. SGL$85-$120, DBL$100-$135, STS$250.

Johns Hopkins Inn (400 North Broadway, 21231; 675-6800, 800-638-1889 in Maryland) 145 rooms, restaurant, lounge, pool, lighted tennis courts, airport courtesy car, children stay free with parents, meeting facilities, major credit cards. Near Johns Hopkins Hospital. SGL/DBL$85, STS$97.

Latham Hotel (612 Cathedral St, 21201; 727-7101, Fax 789-3312, 800-528-4261) 104 rooms and suites, 2 restaurants, complimentary breakfast, lounge, entertainment, pool, jacuzzi, sauna, lighted tennis courts, wheelchair access, no-smoking rooms, a/c, TV, children stay free with parents, airport courtesy car, 9 meeting rooms, major credit cards. SGL/DBL$89, STS$150-$750.

Marriott Inner Harbor (110 South Eutaw St, 21201; 962-0202, 800-228-9290) 525 rooms and suites, Concierge Level, restaurant, lounge, indoor pool, whirlpool, sauna, exercise center, gift shop, transportation to local attractions, wheelchair access, no-smoking rooms, a/c, TV, pets allowed, 20,000 square feet of meeting and exhibition space, 20 meeting rooms, major credit cards. Near the Convention Center. SGL/DBL$149.

Mulberry House (111 West Mulberry St, 21201; 576-0111) 4 rooms, complimentary breakfast, no smoking, no pets, no children, major credit cards. SGL/DBL$65+.

Omni Inner Harbor Hotel (101 West Fayette St, 21201; 752-1100, Fax 752-0832, 800-843-6664), 800-THE-OMNI) 702 rooms and suites, Omni Club Level, restaurant, lounge, entertainment, pool, exercise center, laundry service, concierge, wheelchair access, no-smoking rooms, a/c, TV, transportation to local attractions, 5 meeting rooms, 28,000 square feet of meeting and exhibition space, meeting facilities for 1,200, major credit cards. Near the Convention Center and Inner Harbor, 8 miles from the Baltimore-Washington Airport. SGL/DBL$99.

Quality Inn Inner Harbor (1701 Russell St, 21230; 727-3400, Fax 547-0586) 120 rooms, pool, children stay free with parents, no pets, no-smoking

38 Maryland

rooms, a/c, TV, fax service, meeting facilities, major credit cards. 8 miles from the Baltimore-Washington Airport. SGL/DBL$55-$65.

Radisson Park Lord Baltimore (20 West Baltimore St, 21201; 539-8400, 800-333-3333) 440 rooms and 1- and 2-bedroom suites, 3 restaurants, lounge, sauna, exercise center, airport transportation, no-smoking rooms, a/c, TV, wheelchair access, 18 meeting rooms, meeting facilities for 2,000, major credit cards. Near the Convention Center. SGL/DBL$119-$139, STS$199-$325.

Ramada Inn Harbor (8 North Howard St, 21201; 539-1188, Fax 539-6411, 800-2-RAMADA) 92 rooms and suites, restaurant, lounge, children stay free parents, no pets, fax service, meeting facilities, no-smoking rooms, a/c, TV, 1,000 square feet of meeting space, meeting facilities for 85, major credit cards. SGL/DBL$65-$85.

Sheraton Inner Harbor (300 South Charles St, 21201; 728-6550, Fax 962-8211, 800-325-3535) 339 rooms and suites, restaurant, lounge, entertainment, indoor pool, sauna, exercise center, gift shop, wheelchair access, no-smoking rooms, a/c, TV, in-room refrigerators, 24-hour room service, airport transportation, 12 meeting rooms, 15,000 square feet of meeting and exhibition space, meeting facilities for 900, major credit cards. Near the Convention Center and Inner Harbor, 13 miles from the Baltimore-Washington Airport. SGL/DBL$145.

Shirley Madison (205 West Madison St, 21201; 728-6550, 728-5829, 800-868-5064) 16 rooms and suites, complimentary breakfast, children stay free with parents, in-room refrigerators, free newspaper, free parking, no-smoking rooms, a/c, TV, no pets, airport transportation, fax service, meeting facilities for 25, major credit cards. 10 miles from the Baltimore-Washington Airport. SGL/DBL$85, STS$95-$105.

Society Hill Hotel (58 West Biddle St, 21201; 837-3630, Fax 837-4654) 15 rooms, restaurant, lounge, entertainment, free breakfast, transportation to local attractions, a/c, TV, major credit cards. SGL/DBL$45-$85.

Society Hill Government House (1125 North Calvert St, 21202; 752-7722, Fax 752-6278) 15 rooms, free breakfast, no pets, private bath, transportation to local attractions, major credit cards. SGL$100-$130.

Stouffer Harborplace Hotel (202 East Pratt St, 21202; 547-1200, Fax 783-9676, 800-468-3571) 622 rooms and suites, Executive Floor, restaurant, 2 lounges, entertainment, indoor pool, exercise center, jacuzzi, wheelchair access, no-smoking rooms, a/c, TV, free newspaper, 24-hour room service, in-room refrigerators, children stay free with parents, boutiques, 14,560 square feet of meeting and exhibition space, 18 meeting rooms, major credit cards. Near the Convention Center. SGL/DBL$200-$230.

Baltimore 39

Tremont Hotel (Eight East Pleasant St, 21202; 576-1200, Fax 685-4215) 59 rooms, restaurant, lounge, exercise center, children stay free with parents, pets allowed, laundry service, no-smoking rooms, a/c, TV, meeting facilities, Near the Convention Center, major credit cards. SGL/DBL$79-$115.

Tremont Plaza Hotel (222 St Paul Place, 21202; 727-2222, Fax 685-4216, 800-TRE-MONT) 228 1- and 2-bedroom suites, Executive Floor, 2 restaurants, lounge, outdoor pool, sauna, exercise center, complimentary newspaper, children stay free with parents, wheelchair access, no-smoking rooms, a/c, TV, fax service, room service, no pets, laundry service, 9 meeting rooms, meeting facilities for 650, major credit cards. Near the Inner Harbor and Convention Center, 15 miles from the Baltimore-Washington Airport. 1BR$115, 2BR$225.

Airport Area

Best Western Baltimore Washington Airport (Rte 176, 21227; 796-3300, Fax 379-0471, 800-528-1234) 134 rooms, restaurant, lounge, indoor pool, sauna, whirlpool, airport courtesy car, fax service, no pets, meeting facilities, major credit cards. SGL$69-$76, DBL$74-$79.

Comfort Inn At BWI (6921 Baltimore Annapolis Blvd, 789-9100, 800-228-5150) 189 rooms, complimentary breakfast, sauna, exercise center, wheelchair access, no-smoking rooms, a/c, TV, free newspaper, no pets, meeting facilities, major credit cards. Near the Baltimore-Washington Airport. SGL/DBL$76.

Sheraton International Hotel on BWI Airport (7032 Elm Rd, 21240; 859-3300, Fax 859-0565, 800-638-5858, 800-325-3535) 196 rooms and suites, restaurant, lounge, entertainment, outdoor pool, jogging track, exercise center, wheelchair access, 24-hour room service, no-smoking rooms, a/c, TV, 10 meeting rooms, 8,500 square feet of meeting space, major credit cards. At the airport near Harbor Place, Marley Station Mall, 12 miles from the Laurel Racecourse. SGL/DBL$122-$140, STS$140-$195.

Suburban Baltimore

Best Western Welcome Inn (Whitehead Rd, 21207; 944-7400, Fax 944-7905, 800-528-1234) 100 rooms, restaurant, lounge, complimentary breakfast, pool, jacuzzi, no pets, fax service, laundry service, in-room refrigerators, wheelchair access, no-smoking rooms, a/c, TV, children stay free with parents, major credit cards. SGL$44-$48, DBL$44-$52.

Comfort Inn (8828 Baltimore Washington Blvd, 20794; 880-3131, 800-228-5150) 64 rooms, free breakfast, sauna, exercise center, wheelchair access, no-smoking rooms, a/c, TV, complimentary newspaper, no pets, meeting facilities, major credit cards. Ten miles from the Baltimore-Washington Airport, 15 miles from the downtown area. SGL/DBL$58-$78.

40 Maryland

Days Inn West (6700 Security Blvd, 21207; 281-1800, Fax 281-9148, 800-325-2525) 170 rooms, restaurant, pool, airport transportation, meeting facilities, children stay free with parents, free local calls, wheelchair access, no pets, no-smoking rooms, a/c, TV, fax, major credit cards. 8 miles from the Inner Harbor, 10 miles from the BWI Airport. SGL/DBL$39-$70, AP$5.

Holiday Inn (1800 Belmont Ave, 21207; 265-1400, Fax 281-9569, 800-HOLIDAY) 136 rooms, restaurant, lounge, children stay free with parents, wheelchair access, no-smoking rooms, a/c, TV, fax, room service, pets allowed, meeting facilities for 200, major credit cards. Near the Security Mall, 12 miles from the BWI Airport, 15 miles from Inner Harbor. SGL/DBL$75.

Howard Johnson Hotel (5701 Baltimore National Pike, 21228; 747-8900, Fax 744-3522, 800-654-2000) 145 rooms, restaurant, pool, whirlpool, children stay free, no-smoking rooms, a/c, TV, wheelchair access, free newspaper, pets allowed, meeting facilities, major credit cards. 10 miles from BWI Airport, 7 miles from the downtown area. SGL/DBL$40+.

Pikesville Hilton Inn (1726 Reisterstown Rd, 21208; 653-1100, Fax 484-4138, 800-HILTONS) 171 rooms and suites, restaurant, complimentary breakfast, lounge, entertainment, outdoor pool, sauna, tennis, exercise center, wheelchair access, no-smoking rooms, a/c, TV, free parking, business services, meeting facilities for 800, major credit cards. Thirty minutes from the BWI Airport. SGL/DBL$98, STS$175-$300.

Ramada Hotel (1701 Belmont Ave, 21207; 265-1100, Fax 944-2326, 800-2-RAMADA) 205 rooms and suites, restaurant, lounge, indoor pool, exercise center, audio-visual equipment, airport transportation, wheelchair access, no-smoking rooms, a/c, TV, children stay free with parents, 12 meeting rooms, meeting facilities for 275, major credit cards. Near the Social Security Administration Building and the BWI Airport, 15 miles from the Inner Harbor. SGL/DBL$59, STS$125.

Other Locations

Best Western East (5625 O'Donnell St, 21224; 633-9500, Fax 633-4313, 800-221-2222) 173 rooms and suites, 2 restaurants, lounge, entertainment, indoor pool, exercise center, sauna, pets allowed, free parking, wheelchair access, no-smoking rooms, a/c, TV, 7 meeting rooms, major credit cards. 17 miles from BWI Airport, 4.5 miles from Harbor Place. SGL$69-$84, DBL$74-$94.

Betsy's Bed and Breakfast (1428 Park Ave, 21217; 383-1274) 3 rooms, complimentary breakfast, private baths, major credit cards. SGL$60, DBL$65-$75.

Christlen (8733 Pulaski Hwy, 21237; 687-1740) 28 rooms, restaurant, in-room refrigerators, wheelchair access, major credit cards. SGL/DBL$45-$65.

Holiday Inn Moravia (6510 Frankford Ave, 21206; 485-7900, Fax 485-7900 ext 117, 800-HOLIDAY) 139 rooms, restaurant, lounge, children stay free with parents, wheelchair access, no-smoking rooms, a/c, TV, fax service, room service, no pets, laundry service, airport courtesy car, beauty shop, meeting facilities for 300, major credit cards. 5 miles from Inner Harbor, 3 miles from Memorial Stadium, 6 miles from BWI Airport. SGL/DBL$69.

Mr. Mole Bed and Breakfast (1601 Bolton St, 21217; 728-1179) 3 2-room suites, free breakfast, no-smoking, a/c, TV, no pets, private baths, major credit cards. SGL/DBL$95-$150.

Mount Washington Conference Center (5801 Smith Ave, 21209; 578-7694, Fax 578-4213) 48 rooms and suites, indoor pool, exercise center, audio-visual equipment, 12 meeting rooms, major credit cards. SGL/DBL$45-$90.

The Paulus Guesthouse (2406 Kentucky Ave, 21213; 467-1688) 2 rooms, bed and breakfast, no-smoking, no pets, SGL/DBL$55-$65.

Shoney's Inn (1401 Bloomfield Ave, 21226; 646-1700, 800-222-2222) 179 rooms, restaurant, lounge, pool, free parking, major credit cards. SGL/DBL$52-$55.

Suisse Chalet (Four Philadelphia Ct., 21237; 574-8100, Fax 574-8204, 800-258-1980) 132 rooms, complimentary breakfast, outdoor pool, wheelchair access, in-room computer hookups, major credit cards. SGL/DBL$50-$60.

Beltsville
Area Code 301

Ramada Inn (4050 Powder Mill Rd, 20705; 572-7100, Fax 572-8078, 800-2-RAMADA) 168 rooms, restaurant, lounge, pool, wheelchair access, no-smoking rooms, airport transportation, free parking, pets allowed, a/c, gift shop, TV, room service, laundry facilities, meeting facilities, senior citizen rates, major credit cards. SGL/DBL$70-$85.

Berlin
Area Code 301

Atlantic Hotel Inn (Two North Main St, 21811; 641-3589) 16 rooms, bed and breakfast, restaurant, lounge, private baths, no pets, a/c, TV, antique furnishings, 1890s inn, meeting facilities for 30, major credit cards. LS SGL/DBL$55; HS SGL/DBL$55-$125.

Merry Sherwood Plantation (8909 Worcester Hwy, 21811; 641-2112) 8 rooms, free breakfast, private baths, children over 12 only, 1850s home, no smoking, airport transportation, TV, a/c, major credit cards. SGL/DBL$100-$150.

Bethesda
Area Code 301

American Inn of Bethesda (8130 Wisconsin Ave, 20814; 656-9300, 800-323-7081) 76 rooms, restaurant, private baths, pool. SGL/DBL$62-$75.

Hyatt Regency Bethesda (One Bethesda Metro Center, 20814; 657-1234, Fax 657-6478, 800-233-1234) 380 rooms and suites, restaurant, lounge, entertainment, outdoor pool, whirlpool, exercise facilities, sauna, 16,000 square feet of meeting and exhibition space, 19 meeting rooms, major credit cards. SGL/DBL$69-$159+.

Marriott Bethesda Hotel (5151 Pooks Hill Rd, 20814; 897-9400, Fax 897-0192, 800-228-9290) 407 rooms and suites, restaurant, lounge, entertainment, indoor and outdoor pools, exercise facilities, whirlpool, jogging track, transportation to local attractions, barber and beauty shop, wheelchair access, TV, a/c, no-smoking rooms, gift shop, children stay free with parents, business services, meeting facilities, major credit cards. SGL/DBL$75-$125.

Marriott Bethesda Suites Hotel (6711 Democracy Blvd, 20817; 897-5600, Fax 530-1427, 800-228-9290) 274 2-room suites, restaurant, complimentary breakfast, lounge, indoor and outdoor pool, exercise facilities, whirlpool, wheelchair access, TV, free parking, transportation to local attractions, fax service, a/c, no-smoking rooms, children stay free with parents, business services, meeting facilities, major credit cards. SGL/DBL$110-$235.

Residence Inn (7335 Wisconsin Ave, 20814; 718-0200, 800-331-3131) 187 rooms and suites, free breakfast, pool, exercise facilities, in-room refrigerators, coffee makers and microwaves, laundry facilities, free parking, TV, a/c, VCRs, pets allowed, fireplaces, children stay free with parents, no-smoking rooms, wheelchair access, meeting facilities for 200, major credit cards. SGL/DBL$149, STS$199.

Bowie
Area Code 301

Econo Lodge (4500 Crain Hwy, 20718; 464-2200, 800-4-CHOICE) 76 rooms, complimentary breakfast, pool, children under 12 stay free with parents, pets allowed, senior citizen rates, wheelchair access, a/c, TV, major credit cards. SGL/DBL45-$58.

Buckeystown
Area Code 301

The Inn At Buckeystown (3521 Buckeystown Pike, 21717; 874-5755, 800-272-1190) 9 rooms and cottages, restaurant, 1890s Victorian inn, no-smoking rooms, children stay free with parents, a/c, antique furnishings, no pets, TV, Modified American Plan available, major credit cards. SGL/DBL$92-$272.

Cambridge
Area Code 301

Commodore's Cottage (215 Glenburn Ave, 21613; 228-6928) 2 cottages, complimentary breakfast, no pets, TV, a/c, major credit cards. SGL/DBL$80-$90.

Econo Lodge East (Box 1107, 21613; 221-0800, 800-4-CHOICE) 101 rooms, free breakfast, pool, children under 12 stay free with parents, pets allowed, whirlpools, senior citizen rates, wheelchair access, a/c, TV, laundry facilities, major credit cards. SGL/DBL42-$60.

Quality Inn (Crusader Rd, 21613; 228-6900, 800-368-5689) 60 rooms and suites, restaurant, room service, exercise facilities, children stay free with parents, a/c, TV, laundry service, no-smoking rooms, meeting facilities, major credit cards. SGL$40-$46, DBL$46-$52.

Camp Springs
Area Code 301

Motel 6 (5701 Allentown Rd, 20746; 702-1061) 147 rooms, free local calls, children under 17 stay free with parents, a/c, TV, major credit cards. SGL/DBL$33-$40.

Capitol Heights
Area Code 301

Days Inn (55 Hampton Park Blvd, 20743; 336-8900, Fax 336-6419, 800-325-2525) 191 rooms, restaurant, lounge, outdoor pool, children stay free with parents, room service, laundry service, a/c, TV, free local calls, no pets, wheelchair access, no-smoking rooms, senior citizen rates, major credit cards. SGL/DBL$42-$68.

Motel 6 (75 Hampton Park Blvd, 20743; 499-0800) 122 rooms, pool, free local calls, children under 17 stay free with parents, a/c, TV, major credit cards. SGL/DBL$32-$38.

Super 8 Motel (150 Hampton Park Blvd, 20743; 350-8899, 800-800-8000) 86 rooms and suites, no pets, children under 12 stay free with parents, free local calls, a/c, TV, fax service, no-smoking rooms, senior citizen rates, wheelchair access, major credit cards. SGL/DBL$44-$49.

Cascade
Area Code 301

Bluebird On The Mountain (14700 Eyler Ave, 21719; 241-4161) 4 suites, bed and breakfast, jacuzzis, fireplace, private baths. SGL/DBL$85-$115.

Cantonsville
Area Code 410

Econo Lodge West (5801 Baltimore National Pike, 21228; 744-4000, 800-4-CHOICE) 217 rooms, restaurant, pool, children under 12 stay free with parents, transportation to local attractions, no pets, senior citizen rates, wheelchair access, a/c, TV, meeting facilities, major credit cards. SGL/DBL$40-$53.

Chestertown
Area Code 301

Brampton Inn (Rte 20, 21620; 778-1832) 4 rooms. SGL/DBL$85-$95.

Great Oak Manor (Chestertown 21620; 800-345-4665) complimentary breakfast, private baths, water view, beach. SGL/DBL$90-$175.

The Imperial Hotel (208 High St, 21620; 778-2300) 11 rooms and suites, restaurant, in-room refrigerators, antique furnishings, major credit cards. SGL/DBL$110.

The Inn At Michell House (Box 329, 21620; 778-6500) 6 rooms, restaurant, free breakfast, transportation to local attractions, fireplaces, a/c, TV, 1700s home, children stay free with parents, meeting facilities, major credit cards. SGL/DBL$75-$100.

The Inn At Rolph's Wharf (Rolphs' Wharf Rd, 21620; 800-345-4665) complimentary breakfast, 1830s inn, private baths, on 6 acres, water view, major credit cards. SGL/DBL$90-$125.

Radcliffe Cross (Rte 3, 21620; 778-5540) bed and breakfast, no smoking, no pets, antique furnishings, private baths. SGL/DBL$65-$70.

The White Swan Tavern (231 High St, 21620; 778-2300) 6 rooms, complimentary breakfast, no pets, private baths, game room, 1700s home, antique furnishings, a/c. SGL/DBL$75-$125.

Clinton
Area Code 301

Comfort Inn (7979 Malcolm Rd, 20735; 856-5200, 800-221-2222) 94 rooms, restaurant, wheelchair access, no-smoking rooms, no pets, children under 18 stay free with parents, senior citizen rates, a/c, TV, meeting facilities, major credit cards. SGL$50-$64, DBL$54-$70, AP$4.

Cockneysville
Area Code 301

Rental and Reservation Services

Maryland Reservation Center (825 West Padonia Rd, 21030; 561-1590, 800-654-9303).

☐ ☐ ☐

Residence Inn (20710 Beaver Dam Rd, 21030; 584-7370, Fax 584-7834, 800-331-3131) rooms and suites, complimentary breakfast, pool, spa, in-room refrigerators, coffee makers and microwaves, laundry facilities, free parking, TV, a/c, VCRs, pets allowed, free newspaper, fireplaces, children stay free with parents, no-smoking rooms, wheelchair access, meeting facilities for 30, major credit cards. SGL/DBL$65-$105.

College Park
Area Code 301

Best Western Inn (8601 Baltimore Blvd, 20740; 474-2800, Fax 474-0714, 800-528-1234) 150 rooms, restaurant, complimentary breakfast, lounge, pool, exercise facilities, sauna, whirlpools, children stay free with parents, a/c, TV, no-smoking rooms, wheelchair access, pets allowed, senior citizen rates, meeting facilities, major credit cards. SGL/DBL$65-$75.

Comfort Inn (9020 Baltimore Blvd, 20704; 441-8110, 800-221-2222) 160 rooms, restaurant, free breakfast, pool, sauna, wheelchair access, no-smoking rooms, no pets, children under 18 stay free with parents, airport transportation, senior citizen rates, a/c, TV, meeting facilities, major credit cards. SGL$39-$68, DBL$44-$72.

Days Inn (9137 Baltimore Blvd, 20740; 345-5000, Fax 345-4577, 800-325-2525) 68 rooms, restaurant, lounge, pool, children stay free with parents, room service, laundry service, car rental desk, a/c, TV, free local calls, no pets, wheelchair access, no-smoking rooms, senior citizen rates, major credit cards. SGL/DBL$44-$65.

Holiday Inn (10000 Baltimore Blvd, 20740; 345-6700, Fax 441-4923, 800-HOLIDAY) 222 rooms, restaurant, lounge, indoor pool, exercise facilities, whirlpools, children under 19 stay free with parents, wheelchair access, a/c, TV, no-smoking rooms, fax service, room service, no pets, laundry service, meeting facilities, senior citizen rates, major credit cards. SGL/DBL$65-$85.

Quality Inn (7200 Baltimore Blvd, 20740; 864-5820, 800-368-5689) 178 rooms and suites, restaurant, room service, exercise facilities, children stay free with parents, a/c, TV, laundry service, no-smoking rooms, meeting facilities, major credit cards. SGL$34-$63, DBL$39-$68.

Maryland

Super 8 Motel (9150 Baltimore Ave, 20740; 474-0894, Fax 474-0894 ext 104, 800-800-8000) 51 rooms and suites, complimentary breakfast, no pets, children under 12 stay free with parents, free local calls, a/c, TV, fax service, no-smoking rooms, senior citizen rates, wheelchair access, major credit cards. SGL/DBL44-$50.

Columbia
Area Code 207

Columbia Inn (10207 Wincopin Circle, 21044; 730-3900, Fax 730-1290, 800-638-2817) 289 rooms and suites, restaurant, lounge, entertainment, indoor pool, whirlpools, sauna, tennis courts, jogging track, laundry facilities, airport transportation, pets allowed, 14 meeting rooms, major credit cards. SGL/DBL$105-$120.

Columbia Hilton (5485 Twin Knolls Rd, 21045; 997-1060, 800-HILTONS) 152 rooms and 1- and 2-bedroom suites, restaurant, lounge, indoor pool, jacuzzi, sauna, a/c, TV, tennis courts, transportation to local attractions, free parking, no pets, room service, children stay free with parents, no-smoking rooms, wheelchair access, meeting facilities, major credit cards. SGL/DBL$89-$130.

Courtyard by Marriott (8910 Stanford Blvd, 21045; 290-0002, Fax 290-1663, 800-321-2211) 152 rooms and suites, restaurant, lounge, indoor pool, exercise facilities, whirlpools, children stay free with parents, laundry service, meeting facilities, in-room refrigerators, senior citizen rates, major credit cards. SGL/DBL$56-$66.

Crisfield
Area Code 410

Pines Motel (North Somerset Ave, 21817; 968-0900) 40 rooms and efficiencies, outdoor pool, a/c, no pets, TV, children stay free with parents, kitchenettes, no-smoking rooms. SGL/DBL$40-$70.

Somers Cove Motel (Jersey Island Rd, 21817; 968-1900) 42 rooms and efficiencies, outdoor pool, water view, a/c, in-room refrigerators, no pets, TV. SGL/DBL$30-$75.

Cumberland
Area Code 301

Continental Motor Inn (Box 393A, 21502; 729-2201, Fax 689-8835) 54 rooms, restaurant, pool, airport transportation, no pets, whirlpools, major credit cards. SGL/DBL$40-$55.

Diplomat Motel (Box 216, 21502; 729-2311) 15 rooms, a/c, TV, wheelchair access, pets allowed, major credit cards. SGL/DBL$29-$37.

Holiday Inn (100 South George St, 21502; 724-8800, Fax 724-4001, 800-HOLIDAY) 130 rooms, restaurant, lounge, entertainment, outdoor pool, exercise facilities, children under 19 stay free with parents, wheelchair access, a/c, TV, no-smoking rooms, fax service, room service, pets allowed, laundry service, meeting facilities for 400, senior citizen rates, major credit cards. SGL/DBL$58-$70.

The Inn At Walnut Bottom (120 Green St, 21502; 777-0003) 12 rooms and suites, complimentary breakfast, restaurant, 1800s home, antique furnishings, no smoking, meeting facilities, TV. SGL/DBL$60-$120.

Scottish Inn (1262 National Hwy, 21502; 729-2880) 25 rooms, a/c, TV, no pets, major credit cards. SGL/DBL$30-$40.

Super 8 Motel (1301 National Hwy, 21502; 729-6265, Fax 729-6265 ext 40, 800-800-8000) 63 rooms and suites, no pets, children under 12 stay free with parents, free local calls, a/c, TV, fax service, no-smoking rooms, senior citizen rates, wheelchair access, meeting facilities, major credit cards. SGL/DBL$36-$42.

Turkey Flight Manor (Hwy 68 East, 21502; 777-3553) 12 rooms, restaurant, lounge, pets allowed, wheelchair access, major credit cards. SGL/DBL$25-$40.

Dameron
Area Code 301

Rental and Reservation Services

Country Hosting (Star Rte, 20628; 862-2589) reservation service for local hotels and bed and breakfasts.

Deale
Area Code 301

Makai Pierside Bed and Breakfast (5960 Vacation Lane, 20751; 867-0998) complimentary breakfast, water view, no smoking, TV, in-room refrigerators and coffee makers, private baths. SGL/DBL$50-$65.

Delmar
Area Code 410

Atlantic Budget Inn (Rte 4, 21875) 90 rooms, restaurant, pool, a/c, TV, meeting facilities. SGL/DBL$38-$48.

Traveler Motel (Hwy 13, 19940; 742-8701) 13 rooms. SGL/DBL$40-$50.

Easton
Area Code 301

Comfort Inn (310 North Hwy 50, 21601; 820-8333, 800-221-2222) 84 rooms, restaurant, pool, wheelchair access, no-smoking rooms, no pets, children under 18 stay free with parents, senior citizen rates, a/c, TV, whirlpools, meeting facilities, major credit cards. SGL$56-$70, DBL$53-$75.

Days Inn (Easton 21601; 822-4600, Fax 820-9723, 800-325-2525) 80 rooms and suites, restaurant, lounge, outdoor pool, children stay free with parents, room service, laundry service, a/c, TV, free local calls, pets allowed, wheelchair access, no-smoking rooms, senior citizen rates, major credit cards. SGL/DBL$45-$65, STS$55-$65.

Econo Lodge (8175 Ocean Gateway, 21601; 820-5555, 800-4-CHOICE) 48 rooms, complimentary breakfast, pool, children under 12 stay free with parents, pets allowed, senior citizen rates, wheelchair access, a/c, in-room refrigerators and microwaves, TV, VCRs, major credit cards. SGL/DBL$37-$53.

Tidewater Inn (Dover and Harrison Streets, 21601; 822-1300) 199 rooms and suites, restaurant, lounge, pool, a/c, TV, no pets, no-smoking rooms, wheelchair access, meeting facilities, major credit cards. SGL/DBL$109-$150.

Edgewater
Area Code 410

Best Western Inn (1709 Edgewood Rd, 21040; 679-9700, 800-528-1234) 159 rooms, restaurant, complimentary breakfast, lounge, pool, exercise facilities, children stay free with parents, a/c, TV, no-smoking rooms, wheelchair access, no pets, senior citizen rates, meeting facilities, major credit cards. SGL/DBL$49-$52.

Comfort Inn (1700 Van Bibber Rd, 21040; 679-0770, 800-221-2222) 157 rooms and suites, restaurant, pool, wheelchair access, no-smoking rooms, no pets, children under 18 stay free with parents, senior citizen rates, a/c, TV, meeting facilities, major credit cards. SGL/DBL$48-$51.

Days Inn (2116 Emmorton Park Rd, 21040; 671-9990, Fax 671-7802, 800-325-2525) 75 rooms, restaurant, complimentary breakfast, lounge, pool, children stay free with parents, room service, laundry service, a/c, TV, free local calls, pets allowed, wheelchair access, no-smoking rooms, senior citizen rates, major credit cards. SGL/DBL$43-$50.

Motel Edgewood (2209 Pulaski Hwy, 21040; 676-4466, Fax 679-6110) 22 rooms and 2-bedroom efficiencies, a/c, TV, no pets, major credit cards. SGL/DBL$35-$40.

Elkton
Area Code 301

Knights Inn (262 Belle Hill Rd, 21921; 392-6680, 800-843-5644) 120 rooms and efficiencies, pool, wheelchair access, no-smoking rooms, TV, a/c, in-room refrigerators and microwaves, pets allowed, fax service, free parking, VCRs, senior citizen rates, major credit cards. SGL/DBL$33-$42.

Motel 6 (223 Belle Hill Rd, 21921; 392-5020) 127 rooms, pool, free local calls, children under 17 stay free with parents, a/c, TV, major credit cards. SGL/DBL$25-$31.

Sutton Motel (405 East Pulaski Hwy, 21921; 398-3830) 11 rooms, a/c, TV, no pets. SGL/DBL$29-$33.

Ellicott City
Area Code 301

Turf Valley Hotel and Country Club (2700 Turf Valley Rd, 21042; 465-1500, Fax 465-8280, 800-666-8873) 173 rooms and 1- and 2-bedroom suites, restaurant, lounge, entertainment, exercise facilities, lighted tennis courts, gift shop, no-smoking rooms, no pets, a/c, TV, wheelchair access, major credit cards. SGL/DBL$85-$125.

The Wayside Inn (4344 Columbia Rd, 21043; 461-4636) bed and breakfast, no smoking, no children allowed, no pets, private baths, major credit cards. SGL/DBL$75-$95.

Essex
Area Code 301

Super 8 Motel (98 Stemmers Run Rd, 21221; 780-0030, Fax 780-0030 ext 401, 800-800-8000) 49 rooms and suites, restaurant, complimentary breakfast, children stay free with parents, no pets, in-room refrigerators and microwaves, no-smoking rooms, wheelchair access, computer hookups, fax service, free local calls, meeting facilities, major credit cards. SGL/DBL$49, STS$57.

Ewell
Area Code 410

Scattered Pines Retreat (Ewell 21824; 425-2320) 3 rooms, bed and breakfast, complimentary breakfast. SGL/DBL$60-$120.

Smith Island Motel (Ewell 21824; 425-4441) 8 rooms, complimentary breakfast. SGL/DBL$56-$76.

Frederick
Area Code 301

Rental and Reservations Services

Inns Of The Blue Ridge (7945 Worman's Mill Rd, 21707; 694-044).

□ □ □

Comfort Inn (420 Prospect Blvd, 21701; 695-6200, 800-221-2222) 118 rooms, restaurant, complimentary breakfast, laundry facilities, pool, wheelchair access, no-smoking rooms, in-room refrigerators, pets allowed, children under 18 stay free with parents, senior citizen rates, a/c, TV, meeting facilities, major credit cards. SGL/DBL$49-$64.

Dan Dee Motel (7817 Baltimore National Pike, 21702; 473-8282)restaurant, TV, a/c. SGL/DBL$45-$65.

Days Inn (5646 Buckeystown Pike, 21701; 694-6600, Fax 831-4242, 800-325-2525) 119 rooms and suites, restaurant, lounge, outdoor pool, children stay free with parents, room service, laundry service, a/c, TV, free local calls, pets allowed, airport transportation, wheelchair access, no-smoking rooms, senior citizen rates, meeting facilities for 200, major credit cards. SGL/DBL$49-$57.

Hampton Inn (5311 Buckeystown Pike, 21701; 698-2500, 800-HAMPTON) 160 rooms, restaurant, complimentary breakfast, pool, exercise facilities, children under 18 stay free with parents, no-smoking rooms, wheelchair access, computer hookups, fax service, TV, a/c, free local calls, pets allowed, meeting facilities, major credit cards. SGL/DBL$49-$59.

Holiday Inn (999 West Patrick St, 21702; 662-5141, Fax 663-5290, 800-HOLIDAY) 156 rooms, restaurant, lounge, outdoor pool, exercise facilities, children under 19 stay free with parents, wheelchair access, a/c, TV, no-smoking rooms, fax service, room service, pets allowed, laundry service, meeting facilities for 200, senior citizen rates, major credit cards. SGL/DBL$75.

Holiday Inn (5400 Holiday Dr., 21701; 694-7500, Fax 694-0589, 800-HOLIDAY) 155 rooms, restaurant, lounge, indoor pool, exercise facilities, children under 19 stay free with parents, wheelchair access, a/c, TV, whirlpools, VCRs, no-smoking rooms, fax service, room service, pets allowed, laundry service, meeting facilities for 900, senior citizen rates, major credit cards. SGL/DBL$77-$95.

Knights Inn (6005 Urbana Pike, 21701; 698-0555, 800-843-5644)rooms and efficiencies, pool, wheelchair access, no-smoking rooms, TV, a/c, in-room refrigerators and microwaves, fax service, free parking, pets allowed, VCRs, senior citizen rates, major credit cards. SGL/DBL$37-$46.

Masser's Motel (Hwy 40, 21702; 663-3698) restaurant, TV. SGL/DBL$30.

Middle Plantation Inn (9549 Liberty Rd, 21701; 898-7128) bed and breakfast, no smoking, no children allowed, on 25 acres, private bath, a/c, TV, no pets, antique furnishings. SGL/DBL$75-$85.

Red Horse Motor Inn (990 West Patrick St, 21702; 662-0281, 800-245-6701) 72 rooms, restaurant, in-room refrigerators, pets allowed, no-smoking rooms, a/c, TV. SGL/DBL$38-$60.

Spring Bank Bed and Breakfast (7945 Worman's Mill Rd, 21701; 694-0440) complimentary breakfast, restaurant, 1880s home, antique furnishings, no smoking, no pets, no children allowed. SGL/DBL$65-$90.

Super 8 Motel (5579 Spectrum Dr., 21701; 695-2881, Fax 695-7939, 800-626-9849, 800-800-8000) 102 rooms and suites, restaurant, pets allowed, children under 12 stay free with parents, free local calls, a/c, laundry facilities, in-room refrigerators and microwaves, TV, fax service, no-smoking rooms, senior citizen rates, wheelchair access, meeting facilities, major credit cards. SGL/DBL$44-$49.

Friendship
Area Code 410

Herrington Harbour Inn (Rose Haven On The Bay, 20758; 741-5100)restaurant, pool, tennis courts. SGL/DBL$38-$43.

Friendsville
Area Code 301

Yough Valley Motel (Friendsville 21531; 746-5836) SGL/DBL$28-$48.

Frostburg
Area Code 301

Charlie's Motel (220 West Main St, 21532; 689-6557) 10 rooms, wheelchair access, pets allowed. SGL/DBL$22-$35.

Comfort Inn (State Rd 36 North, 21532; 689-2050, 800-221-2222) 100 rooms, restaurant, whirlpools, exercise facilities, sauna, wheelchair access, no-smoking rooms, pets allowed, children under 18 stay free with parents, senior citizen rates, a/c, TV, meeting facilities, major credit cards. SGL/DBL$45-$50.

Failinger's Hotel Gunter (11 West Main St, 21532; 689-6511) 17 rooms, dining rooms, lounge, wheelchair access, a/c, TV, senior citizen rates, meeting facilities for 200, major credit cards. SGL/DBL$44.

Funkstown
Area Code 301

Edmar Manor Bed and Breakfast (Six High St, 21734; 416-7270) 4 rooms, complimentary breakfast, 1790s home, antique furnishings, fireplace, major credit cards. SGL/DBL$50-$100.

Gaithersburg
Area Code 301

Comfort Inn (16216 Frederick Rd, 20877; 330-0023, 800-221-2222) 127 rooms, complimentary breakfast, pool, wheelchair access, no-smoking rooms, no pets, children under 18 stay free with parents, senior citizen rates, a/c, TV, meeting facilities, major credit cards. SGL$53-$59, DBL$59-$69, AP$10.

Courtyard by Marriott (805 Russell Ave, 20879; 670-0008, Fax 948-4538, 800-321-2211) 203 rooms and suites, restaurant, lounge, pool, exercise facilities, whirlpools, lighted tennis courts, in-room refrigerators, children stay free with parents, laundry service, meeting facilities, senior citizen rates, major credit cards. SGL/DBL$85-$250.

Gaithersburg Hospitality (18908 Chimney Place, 20879; 977-7377)bed and breakfast, antique furnishings, no smoking, no pets, private baths. SGL/DBL$45-$55.

Holiday Inn (Two Montgomery Village Ave, 20879; 948-8900, 800-HOLIDAY) 304 rooms and suites, restaurant, lounge, indoor pool, exercise facilities, whirlpools, children under 19 stay free with parents, wheelchair access, a/c, TV, no-smoking rooms, fax service, room service, pets allowed, transportation to local attractions, in-room refrigerators, laundry service, meeting facilities, senior citizen rates, major credit cards. SGL/DBL$90-$105, STS$300.

Marriott Hotel (620 Perry Pkwy, 20877; 977-8900, Fax 869-8597, 800-228-9290) 299 rooms and suites, restaurant, lounge, entertainment, indoor and outdoor pool, exercise facilities, whirlpools, sauna, jogging track, free parking, wheelchair access, pets allowed, TV, a/c, no-smoking rooms, airport transportation, game room, in-room refrigerators, gift shop, children stay free with parents, business services, meeting facilities, major credit cards. SGL/DBL$60-$125.

Marriott Washington Center Hotel (9751 Washingtonian Blvd, 20878; 309-0333, Fax 762-6448, 800-228-9290) 284 rooms and suites, restaurant, lounge, indoor pool, exercise facilities, sauna, jogging track, whirlpools, wheelchair access, TV, a/c, no-smoking rooms, free parking, gift shop, children stay free with parents, business services, meeting facilities, major credit cards. SGL/DBL$99-$109.

Germantown
Area Code 301

Comfort Inn (20260 Goldenrod Lane, 20874; 428-1300, 800-221-2222) 203 rooms, restaurant, complimentary breakfast, pool, wheelchair access, airport transportation, no-smoking rooms, no pets, children under 18 stay free with parents, senior citizen rates, a/c, TV, meeting facilities, major credit cards. SGL/DBL$39-$75, AP$6.

Glen Burnie
Area Code 410

Hampton Inn (6618 Governor Ritchie Hwy, 21061; 761-7666, Fax 761-0254, 800-HAMPTON) 115 rooms, restaurant, complimentary breakfast, pool, exercise facilities, children under 18 stay free with parents, no-smoking rooms, wheelchair access, computer hookups, fax service, TV, a/c, free local calls, pets allowed, meeting facilities, major credit cards. SGL$60, DBL$64.

Holiday Inn (6600 Ritchie Hwy, 21061; 761-8300, 800-HOLIDAY) 100 rooms, restaurant, lounge, outdoor pool, exercise facilities, children under 19 stay free with parents, wheelchair access, a/c, TV, no-smoking rooms, air fax service, room service, no pets, laundry service, meeting facilities for 50, senior citizen rates, major credit cards. SGL/DBL$75-$85.

Holiday Inn (6323 Ritchie Hwy, 21061; 636-4300, Fax 636-2630, 800-HOLIDAY) 128 rooms, restaurant, lounge, outdoor pool, children stay free with parents, wheelchair access, no-smoking rooms, a/c, TV, pets allowed, meeting facilities for 150, major credit cards. SGL/DBL$74-$95.

Grantsville
Area Code 302

Holiday Inn (Hwy. I-68, 21536; 895-5993, 800-833-6107, 800-HOLIDAY)restaurant, lounge, indoor pool, exercise facilities, sauna, jacuzzi, children under 19 stay free with parents, wheelchair access, a/c, TV, no-smoking rooms, fax service, room service, pets allowed, laundry service, meeting facilities for 200, senior citizen rates, major credit cards. SGL/DBL$39-$54.

Grasonville
Area Code 410

Chesapeake Motel (Rte One, 21638; 827-7272, 800-562-8196) 42 rooms, children stay free with parents, pets allowed, a/c, TV, no-smoking rooms, wheelchair access, major credit cards. SGL/DBL$30-$45.

Comfort Inn (Rte 2, 21638; 827-6767, Fax 827-8626, 800-221-2222) 86 rooms and suites, restaurant, pool, wheelchair access, no-smoking rooms, no pets, children under 18 stay free with parents, laundry facilities, in-room refrigerators, game room, senior citizen rates, a/c, TV, meeting facilities, major credit cards. SGL/DBL$75-$100, STS$125-$150.

Greenbelt
Area Code 301

Marriott Hotel (6400 Ivy Lane, 20770; 441-3700, Fax 474-9128, 800-228-9290) 283 rooms and suites, restaurant, lounge, entertainment, indoor and outdoor pools, jogging track, sauna, exercise facilities, whirlpools, wheelchair access, TV, a/c, no-smoking rooms, gift shop, children stay free with parents, pets allowed, free parking, business services, meeting facilities, major credit cards. SGL/DBL$80-$150.

Hagerstown
Area Code 301

Beaver Creek House (Rte 9, 21740; 797-4764) 5 rooms, bed and breakfast, no smoking, no children allowed, private baths, no pets, antique furnishings. SGL/DBL$65-$75.

Best Western Venice Inn (431 Dual Hwy, 21740; 733-0830, Fax 733-4978, 800-2-VENICE, 800-528-1234) 240 rooms and efficiencies, restaurant, complimentary breakfast, lounge, entertainment, pool, exercise facilities, whirlpools, children stay free with parents, a/c, TV, no-smoking rooms, airport transportation, wheelchair access, pets allowed, beauty shop, in-room refrigerators, senior citizen rates, meeting facilities, major credit cards. SGL/DBL$48-$64.

Best Western (18221 Mason Dixon Rd, 21742; 791-3560, Fax 791-3519, 800-528-1234) 57 rooms, restaurant, complimentary breakfast, lounge, pool, exercise facilities, children stay free with parents, a/c, TV, no-smoking rooms, wheelchair access, pets allowed, senior citizen rates, meeting facilities, major credit cards. SGL/DBL$30-$50.

Beaver Creek House (20432 Beaver Creek Rd, 21740; 797-4764)bed and breakfast, complimentary breakfast. SGL/DBL$50-$75.

The Dagmar Hotel (50 Summit Ave, 21740; 733-4363, Fax 733-5675) 74 rooms and suites, restaurant, lounge, exercise facilities, airport courtesy car, game room, children stay free with parents, a/c, TV, wheelchair access, no-smoking rooms, major credit cards. SGL/DBL$30-$50.

Econo Lodge (Rte 6, 21740; 791-3560, 800-446-6900, 800-4-CHOICE) 57 rooms, restaurant, complimentary breakfast, pool, children under 12 stay free with parents, pets allowed, senior citizen rates, wheelchair access, a/c, TV, major credit cards. SGL/DBL$35-$65.

Holiday Inn (900 Dual Hwy, 21740; 739-9050, Fax 739-8347, 800-HOLIDAY) 140 rooms, restaurant, lounge, outdoor pool, exercise facilities, children under 19 stay free with parents, wheelchair access, a/c, TV, VCRs, whirlpools, no-smoking rooms, fax service, room service, no pets, airport transportation, laundry service, meeting facilities for 150, senior citizen rates, major credit cards. SGL/DBL$50-$66.

Howard Johnson Plaza Hotel (107 Underpass Way, 21740; 797-2500, 800-732-0906, 800-I-GO-HOJO) 165 rooms and suites, restaurant, lounge, pool, whirlpools, exercise facilities, in-room refrigerators and coffee makers, children stay free with parents, wheelchair access, no-smoking rooms, TV, a/c, pets allowed, free parking, senior citizen rates, meeting facilities, major credit cards. SGL$49-$61, DBL$58-$66.

Lewrene Farm Bed and Breakfast (Downsville Pike, 21740; 582-1735) 6 rooms, complimentary breakfast, on 100 acres, fireplace, antique furnishings, private bath, no smoking. SGL/DBL$50-$70.

Ramada Inn Convention Center (901 Dual Hwy, 21740; 733-5100, Fax 733-9192, 800-2-RAMADA) 210 rooms, restaurant, lounge, indoor pool, sauna, wheelchair access, no-smoking rooms, airport transportation, free parking, pets allowed, a/c, TV, room service, laundry facilities, meeting facilities, senior citizen rates, major credit cards. SGL/DBL$59-$69.

Sheraton Inn Conference Center (1910 Dual Hwy, 21740; 790-3010, Fax 733-4559, 800-325-3535) 108 rooms and suites, restaurant, lounge, outdoor pool, exercise facilities, no-smoking rooms, a/c, TV, children stay free with parents, whirlpools, in-room refrigerators, pets allowed, wheelchair access, 9,225 square feet of meeting and exhibition space, 9 meeting rooms, meeting facilities for 600, major credit cards. SGL/DBL$56-$64.

Sunday's Bed and Breakfast (39 Broadway, 21740; 797-4331, 800-221-4824) 3 rooms, complimentary breakfast, Victorian home, antique furnishings. SGL/DBL$55-$95.

Super 8 Motel (1220 Dual Hwy, 21740; 739-5800, Fax 739-5800 ext 405, 800-800-8000) 62 rooms and suites, no pets, children under 12 stay free with parents, free local calls, a/c, TV, fax service, no-smoking rooms, senior citizen rates, wheelchair access, meeting facilities, major credit cards. SGL/DBL$36-$42.

Sword Fireplace Country Living (12238 Walnut Point Rd, 21740; 582-4702) rooms and 1- and 2-bedroom apartments, private baths, TV, in-room refrigerators and microwaves, a/c, VCR. SGL/DBL$65-$135.

Travelodge Inn (101 Massey Blvd, 21740; 582-4445, Fax 582-0942, 800-HAMPTON) 103 rooms and efficiencies, restaurant, complimentary breakfast, pool, exercise facilities, children under 18 stay free with parents, no-smoking rooms, wheelchair access, computer hookups, fax service, TV, VCRs, a/c, free local calls, pets allowed, meeting facilities, major credit cards. SGL/DBL$33-$40.

Wellesley Inn (1101 Dual Hwy, 21740; 733-2700) 84 rooms, restaurant, pets allowed, VCRs, wheelchair access, a/c, TV, major credit cards. SGL/DBL$37-$60.

Hancock
Area Code 301

Comfort Inn (118 Limestone Rd, 21750; 678-6101, 800-221-2222) 50 rooms, restaurant, exercise facilities, wheelchair access, no-smoking rooms, no pets, children under 18 stay free with parents, whirlpools, senior citizen rates, a/c, TV, meeting facilities, major credit cards. SGL/DBL$39-$43.

Hancock Motel (Hwy. 522 South, 21750; 678-6106) 22 rooms and 2-bedroom efficiencies, a/c, TV, no pets, major credit cards. SGL/DBL$34-$45.

Hanover
Area Code 410

Days Inn Airport (7481 Ridge Rd, 21076; 684-3388, Fax 684-3919, 800-325-2525) 159 rooms and suites, restaurant, outdoor pool, exercise facilities, airport courtesy car, in-room computer hookups, wheelchair access, children stay free with parents, no pets, TV, a/c, no-smoking rooms, fax service, meeting facilities, major credit cards. SGL$59-$65, DBL$65-$75, STS$85-$115, AP$10.

Ramada Inn Airport (7253 Pkwy Dr., 21076; 712-4300, Fax 712-0921, 800-2-RAMADA) 132 rooms, restaurant, lounge, pool, wheelchair access, TV, a/c, children stay free with parents, no-smoking rooms, airport transportation, meeting facilities for 200, major credit cards. SGL$45-$85, DBL$49-$90, AP$5.

Red Roof Inn (7306 Pkwy Dr., 21076; 712-4070, 712-4070 ext 444, 800-843-7663) 109 rooms, no-smoking rooms, fax service, wheelchair access, TV, a/c, complimentary newspaper, free local calls, in-room computer hookups, major credit cards. SGL/DBL$37-$45.

Havre De Grace
Area Code 410

Super 8 Motel (929 Pulaski Hwy, 21078; 939-1880, Fax 939-1880 ext 402, 800-800-8000) 63 rooms and suites, no pets, children under 12 stay free with parents, free local calls, a/c, TV, in-room refrigerators and microwaves, fax service, no-smoking rooms, senior citizen rates, wheelchair access, meeting facilities, major credit cards. SGL/DBL$37-$42.

Vandiver Inn (301 South Union Ave, 21078; 939-5200) 8 rooms, complimentary breakfast, restaurant, 1880s inn, antique furnishings, no pets, fireplaces, wheelchair access, no-smoking rooms, TV, a/c, major credit cards. SGL/DBL$65-$95.

Hunt Valley
Area Code 410

Embassy Suites (213 International Circle, 21030; 584-1400, Fax 584-7306, 800-362-2779) 224 2-room suites, restaurant, lounge, complimentary breakfast, indoor pool, jacuzzi, sauna, wheelchair access, laundry service, room service, no-smoking rooms, airport transportation, gift shop, business services, meeting facilities, major credit cards. SGL/DBL$99-$109.

Courtyard by Marriott (221 International Circle, 21030; 584-7070, Fax 584-8151, 800-321-2211) 146 rooms and suites, restaurant, lounge, indoor pool, exercise facilities, whirlpools, children stay free with parents, in-room refrigerators, laundry service, no pets, meeting facilities, senior citizen rates, major credit cards. SGL/DBL$59-$84.

Hampton Inn (11200 York Rd, 21031; 527-1500, Fax 771-0819, 800-HAMPTON) 126 rooms, restaurant, complimentary breakfast, pool, exercise facilities, children under 18 stay free with parents, no-smoking rooms, wheelchair access, computer hookups, fax service, TV, a/c, free local calls, pets allowed, meeting facilities, major credit cards. SGL/DBL$52-$61.

Marriott Valley Inn (245 Shawan Rd, 21031; 785-7000, Fax 785-0341, 800-228-9290) 392 rooms and suites, Concierge Level, restaurant, lounge, entertainment, indoor and outdoor pool, sauna, whirlpools, tennis courts, gift shop, beauty shop, free parking, no-smoking rooms, wheelchair access, pets allowed, TV, a/c, business services, meeting facilities, major credit cards. SGL/DBL$89-$128.

Residence Inn by Marriott (10710 Beaver Dam Rd, 21030; 584-7370, Fax 584-7843, 800-331-3131) 96 rooms and 2-bedroom suites, complimentary breakfast, pool, spa, in-room refrigerators, coffee makers and microwaves, laundry facilities, free parking, TV, a/c, VCRs, pets allowed, airport transportation, pets allowed, complimentary newspaper, fireplaces, children stay free with parents, no-smoking rooms, wheelchair access, meeting facilities, major credit cards. SGL/DBL$94-$124.

Jessup
Area Code 301

Comfort Inn (8828 Baltimore-Washington Blvd, 20794; 880-3131, 800-221-2222) 63 rooms, restaurant, complimentary breakfast, sauna, wheelchair access, no-smoking rooms, no pets, children under 18 stay free with parents, complimentary newspaper, senior citizen rates, a/c, TV, meeting facilities, major credit cards. SGL$30-$46, DBL$35-$49.

Holiday Inn (7900 Washington Blvd, 20794; 799-7500, Fax 799-1924, 800-HOLIDAY) 243 rooms, restaurant, lounge, entertainment, children stay free with parents, a/c, TV, wheelchair access, no-smoking rooms, no pets, major credit cards. SGL/DBL$80-$82.

Red Roof Inn (8094 Washington Blvd, 20794; 410-796-0380, Fax 410-796-0380 ext 344, 800-843-7663) 108 rooms, no-smoking rooms, fax service, wheelchair access, complimentary newspaper, free local calls, in-room computer hookups, pets allowed, a/c, TV, major credit cards. SGL/DBL$44-$52.

Suisse Chalet (7300 Crestmount Rd, 20794; 799-1500, 800-5-CHALET) 104 rooms, restaurant, complimentary breakfast, pool, no-smoking rooms, a/c, children stay free with parents, laundry facilities, airport transportation, no pets, TV, wheelchair access, senior citizen rates, major credit cards. SGL/DBL$51-$58.

Kent Island
Area Code 301

Comfort Inn (Kent Island 21638; 827-6767, 800-823-3361, 800-221-2222) 87 rooms, restaurant, indoor pool, exercise facilities, in-room refrigerators, microwaves and coffee-makers, kitchenettes, water view, wheelchair access, no-smoking rooms, pets allowed, VCRs, laundry facilities, whirlpools, children under 18 stay free with parents, senior citizen rates, a/c, TV, meeting facilities, major credit cards. SGL$54-$98.

Kent Manor (Kent Island 21666; 643-5757, Fax 643-8315) 24 rooms, restaurant, complimentary breakfast, pool, transportation to local attractions, 1820s home, antique furnishings, TV, a/c, major credit cards. SGL/DBL$80-$150.

Landover Hills
Area Code 301

Comfort Inn (6205 Annapolis Rd, 20784; 322-6000, 800-221-2222) 84 rooms, restaurant, exercise facilities, wheelchair access, no-smoking rooms, no pets, children under 18 stay free with parents, senior citizen rates, a/c, TV, meeting facilities, major credit cards. SGL$42-$57, DBL$44-$64.

Courtyard by Marriott (8300 Corporate Dr., 20785; 577-3373, Fax 577-1780, 800-321-2211) 150 rooms and suites, restaurant, lounge, pool, exercise facilities, whirlpools, children stay free with parents, laundry service, meeting facilities, senior citizen rates, major credit cards. SGL/DBL$85-$100.

Lanham
Area Code 301

Days Inn (9023 Annapolis Rd, 20706; 459-6600, Fax 459-6002, 800-325-2525) 114 rooms, restaurant, lounge, pool, children stay free with parents, room service, laundry service, a/c, TV, free local calls, no pets, wheelchair access, no-smoking rooms, senior citizen rates, major credit cards. SGL/DBL$48-$58.

La Plata
Area Code 301

Best Western Inn (400 South 301, 20646; 934-4900, Fax 934-5389, 800-528-1234) 74 rooms and suites, restaurant, complimentary breakfast, lounge, pool, exercise facilities, children stay free with parents, a/c, no-smoking rooms, in-room refrigerators, TV, wheelchair access, pets allowed, senior citizen rates, meeting facilities, major credit cards. SGL/DBL$48-$57.

Super 8 Motel (729 Hwy 301, 20646; 934-3465, Fax 934-3709, 800-800-8000) 45 rooms and suites, complimentary breakfast, no pets, children under 12 stay free with parents, free local calls, a/c, TV, fax service, no-smoking rooms, senior citizen rates, wheelchair access, meeting facilities, major credit cards. SGL/DBL$36-$40.

Laurel
Area Code 301

Best Western Inn (1501 Sweitzer Lane, 20707; 776-5300, Fax 604-3667, 800-528-1234) 205 rooms, restaurant, complimentary breakfast, lounge, pool, exercise facilities, children stay free with parents, a/c, TV, no-smoking rooms, wheelchair access, no pets, senior citizen rates, meeting facilities, major credit cards. SGL/DBL$65-$95.

Budget Host Valencia Motel (10131 Washington Blvd, 20723; 725-4200, 800-336-4366) 80 rooms and efficiencies, wheelchair access, children stay free with parents, no pets, a/c, TV, major credit cards. SGL/DBL$36-$50.

Comfort Suites Hotel (14402 Laurel Place, 20707; 206-2500, Fax 725-0056, 800-628-7760, 800-221-2222) 118 rooms and suites, restaurant, indoor pool, wheelchair access, no-smoking rooms, no pets, children under 18 stay free with parents, senior citizen rates, a/c, in-room refrigerators, TV, airport transportation, in-room microwaves, meeting facilities, major credit cards. SGL/DBL$49-$90.

Days Inn (13700 Baltimore Ave, 20707; 498-8900, Fax 498-5721, 800-325-2525) 110 rooms and suites, restaurant, complimentary breakfast, lounge, pool, children stay free with parents, room service, laundry service, a/c, TV, free local calls, no pets, wheelchair access, no-smoking rooms, senior citizen rates, major credit cards. SGL/DBL$49-$64.

Holiday Inn (3400 Fort Meade Rd, 20707; 498-0900, Fax 498-0900 ext 160, 800-HOLIDAY) 120 rooms, restaurant, lounge, outdoor pool, exercise facilities, children under 19 stay free with parents, wheelchair access, a/c, TV, no-smoking rooms, fax service, room service, no pets, laundry service, meeting facilities, senior citizen rates, major credit cards. SGL/DBL$55.

Knights Inn (Baltimore-Washington Expressway, 20724; 498-5553, 800-843-5644) 119 rooms and efficiencies, pool, wheelchair access, no-smoking rooms, TV, a/c, in-room refrigerators and microwaves, pets allowed, fax service, free parking, VCRs, senior citizen rates, major credit cards. SGL/DBL$39-$49.

Motel 6 (3510 Old Annapolis Rd, 20724; 497-1544) 126 rooms, pool, free local calls, children under 17 stay free with parents, a/c, TV, major credit cards. SGL/DBL$28-$34.

Ramada Inn (9920 Hwy 1, 20723; 498-7750, Fax 498-7582, 800-2-RAMADA) 78 rooms, restaurant, lounge, pool, wheelchair access, no-smoking rooms, airport transportation, free parking, pets allowed, in-room refrigerators and microwaves, a/c, TV, room service, laundry facilities, meeting facilities, senior citizen rates, major credit cards. SGL/DBL$33-$40.

Red Roof Inn (12525 Laurel Bowie Rd, 20708; 498-8811, Fax 498-1490, 800-843-7663) 120 rooms, no-smoking rooms, fax service, wheelchair access, complimentary newspaper, children stay free with parents, pets allowed, free local calls, in-room computer hookups, major credit cards. SGL/DBL$30-$38.

La Vale
Area Code 301

Best Western Braddock Motor Inn (1268 National Hwy, 21502; 729-3300, 800-296-6006, 800-528-1234) 198 rooms, restaurant, free breakfast, lounge, indoor pool, exercise facilities, children stay free with parents, game room, a/c, TV, no-smoking rooms, wheelchair access, pets allowed, senior citizen rates, meeting facilities, major credit cards. SGL/DBL$48-$72.

Continental Motor (Rte 40A, National Hwy, 21502; 729-2201) 54 rooms, restaurant, lounge, pool, a/c, TV, meeting facilities, major credit cards. SGL/DBL$40-$71.

Lexington Park
Area Code 301

Belvedere Motor Inn (60 Main St, 20653; 863-6666, 800-428-2871) 166 rooms and efficiencies, restaurant, complimentary breakfast, lounge, entertainment, pool, pets allowed, TV, a/c, no-smoking rooms, children stay free with parents. SGL/DBL$45-$50.

Patuxent Inn (Lexington Park 20619; 862-4100, Fax 862-4673) 120 rooms and efficiencies, restaurant, pool, lighted tennis courts, no-smoking rooms, children stay free with parents, TV, a/c, laundry facilities, transportation to local attractions, wheelchair access. SGL/DBL$50-$70.

Super 8 Motel (9290 3 Notch Rd, 20619; 862-9822, Fax 862-9822 ext 403, 800-800-8000) 62 rooms and suites, no pets, children under 12 stay free with parents, free local calls, a/c, TV, fax service, in-room refrigerators and microwaves, no-smoking rooms, senior citizen rates, wheelchair access, meeting facilities, major credit cards. SGL/DBL$39-$44.

Linthicum
Area Code 410

Guest Quarters Suite Hotel BWI Airport (1300 Concourse Dr., 21090; 850-0747, Fax 859-0816, 800-424-2900) 251 suites, Executive Level, restaurant, indoor pool, jacuzzi, TV, a/c, sauna, gift shop, airport courtesy car, free parking, 11 meeting rooms, meeting facilities for 250, major credit cards. SGL/DBL$89-$180.

Hampton Inn Washington Airport (829 Elkridge Landing Rd, 21090; 850-0600, Fax 850-0600 ext 607, 800-HAMPTON) 139 rooms, complimentary breakfast, children stay free with parents, airport transportation, pets allowed, a/c, TV, no-smoking rooms, wheelchair access, computer hookups, fax service, free local calls, meeting facilities, major credit cards. SGL$63, DBL$66-$69.

Holiday Inn (890 Elkridge Landing Rd, 21090; 859-8400, Fax 859-8400 ext 1196, 800-HOLIDAY) 254 rooms, restaurant, lounge, entertainment, pool, exercise facilities, children stay free with parents, wheelchair access, no-smoking rooms, fax service, laundry facilities, a/c, TV, room service, airport transportation, pets allowed, meeting facilities for 500, major credit cards. SGL/DBL$99.

Marriott Airport (1743 West Nursery Rd, 21090; 859-8300, Fax 859-3369, 800-445-5365, 800-228-9290) 310 rooms and suites, restaurant, lounge, entertainment, indoor pool, exercise facilities, a/c, TV, whirlpool, free parking, airport courtesy car, no-smoking rooms, wheelchair access, gift shop, 14 meeting rooms, major credit cards. SGL/DBL$135.

Motel 6 (5193 Raynor Ave, 21090; 636-9070, 136 rooms, pool, free local calls, children under 17 stay free with parents, a/c, TV, major credit cards. SGL/DBL$30-$46.

Red Roof Inn (827 Elkridge Landing Rd, 21090; 850-7600, Fax 850-7611, 800-843-7663) 129 rooms, no-smoking rooms, fax service, wheelchair access, complimentary newspaper, a/c, TV, free local calls, in-room computer hookups, major credit cards. SGL/DBL$38+.

Little Orleans
Area Code 301

Town Hill Hotel (Little Orleans 21766; 478-2794) 7 rooms, bed and breakfast, no smoking. SGL/DBL$49.

McHenry
Area Code 301

Wisp Resort Hotel and Conference Center (Marsh Hill Rd, 21541; 387-5581, Fax 387-4127, 800-462-9477) 168 rooms and suites, restaurant, indoor pool, game room, no pets, wheelchair access, no-smoking rooms, a/c, TV, major credit cards. SGL/DBL$65-$100.

New Market
Area Code 301

National Pike Inn (Nine West Main St, 21774; 865-5055) 4 rooms, bed and breakfast, no pets, no children allowed, private baths, a/c, antique furnishings, children over 12 welcome. SGL/DBL$55-$105.

Strawberry Inn (17 Main St, 21774; 865-3318) bed and breakfast, no pets, no children allowed, 1830s inn, private baths. SGL/DBL$80-$90.

North Beach
Area Code 401

Angels In The Attic - Westlawn Inn (Seventh and Chesapeake Ave, 20714; 855-2607) bed and breakfast, private baths, 1903 inn, beach, a/c. SGL/DBL$65.

North East
Area Code 301

The Mill House (102 Mill Lane, 21901; 287-3532) bed and breakfast, 1700s home, antique furnishings, no pets, on 3 acres, no smoking, major credit cards. SGL/DBL$50-$65.

Oakland
Area Code 301

Alpine Village (Rte 4, 21550; 387-5534) 29 rooms and efficiencies, restaurant, lounge, outdoor pool, a/c, TV, beach. SGL/DBL$50-$70.

Lake Breeze (Oakland 21550; 387-5564) 10 rooms, restaurant, pool, water view, beach, a/c, TV, Modified American Plan available. SGL/DBL$55-$65.

Lakeside Motor Court (Oakland 21550; 387-5566) 11 rooms and housekeeping cottage, restaurant, pool, water view, beach, Modified American Plan available, a/c, TV. SGL/DBL$55-$80.

Town Motel (210 North Third St, 21550; 387-5555) 17 rooms and efficiencies, kitchenettes. SGL/DBL$30-$65.

Ocean City
Area Code 410

Americana Hotel (10th St and Broadway, 21842; 289-6271, 800-321-9174) 94 efficiencies, indoor pool, kitchenettes, water view, in-room refrigerators and microwaves, year-round. LS SGL/DBL$25-$70; HS SGL/DBL$90-$105.

Annabell's Bed and Breakfast (10th St and Boardwalk, 21842; 289-8894) 6 rooms, complimentary breakfast, a/c, TV, open March through October. SGL/DBL$50-$70.

Barefoot Beachcomber Motel (7500 Coastal Hwy, 21842; 524-3712, 800-638-2104) 28 apartments, outdoor pool, water view, pets allowed, senior citizen rates, major credit cards. SGL/DBL$90.

The Barefoot Mailman (35th St and Oceanside, 21842; 289-5343, 800-395-3668) 28 rooms and efficiencies, outdoor pool, a/c, TV. LS SGL/DBL$39-$73; HS SGL/DBL$83-$94, EFF$45-$105.

Beachmark Motel (73rd St and Oceanside, 21842; 524-7300, 800-638-1600) 96 apartments, coffee shop, pool, in-room refrigerators and microwaves, open May to September. LS SGL/DBL$38-$68; HS SGL/DBL$84.

Best Western Flagship (28th St and Oceanfront; 21842; 289-3384, 800-638-2106, 800-528-1234) 93 rooms and 2-bedroom efficiencies, restaurant, lounge, indoor and outdoor pool, exercise facilities, jacuzzi, sauna, game room, tennis court, free parking, children stay free with parents, a/c, TV, no-smoking rooms, wheelchair access, no pets, senior citizen rates, meeting facilities, major credit cards. LS SGL/DBL$37; HS SGL/DBL$61, EFF$36-$144.

Breakers Hotel Oceanfront (Third St and Boardwalk, 21842; 289-9165) 45 rooms and apartments, restaurant, kitchenettes, open May through September, a/c, TV. SGL/DBL$65-$525W.

Brighton Suites Hotel (12500 Coastal Hwy, 21842; 257-7600, 800-227-5788) 57 suites, restaurant, indoor pool, kitchenettes, a/c, no pets, in-room refrigerators, TV, major credit cards. SGL/DBL$49-$169.

Coconut Malorie Hotel (201 60th St, 21842; 723-6100, Fax 524-9327, 800-767-6060) 85 suites, restaurant, lounge, pool, a/c, TV, no-smoking rooms, in-room refrigerators and coffee-makers, no pets, whirlpools, major credit cards. SGL/DBL$89-$219.

Comfort Inn (5th and Oceanfront, 21842; 524-3000, 800-221-2222) 84 rooms, restaurant, pool, wheelchair access, no-smoking rooms, no pets, children under 18 stay free with parents, kitchenettes, senior citizen rates, a/c, TV, meeting facilities, major credit cards. SGL/DBL$55-$135.

Maryland

Comfort Inn Gold Coast (11201 Coastal Hwy, 21842; 524-3000, 800-221-2222) 202 rooms, restaurant, indoor pool, whirlpools, wheelchair access, no-smoking rooms, no pets, children under 18 stay free with parents, open year-round, free parking, senior citizen rates, a/c, TV, meeting facilities, major credit cards. LS SGL/DBL$30-$115; HS SGL/DBL$110-$135.

Dunes Manor (28th St and Oceanfront, 21842; 289-1100, 800-523-2888) 160 rooms and suites, restaurant, lounge, pool, whirlpools, exercise facilities, in-room refrigerators, children stay free with parents, TV, a/c, no-smoking rooms, beach, major credit cards. SGL/DBL$55-$165.

Dunes Motel (2700 Baltimore Ave, 21842; 289-4414) 103 rooms and efficiencies, pool, a/c, TV, no pets, in-room refrigerators, major credit cards. SGL/DBL$50-$100.

Executive Motel (Baltimore Ave, 21842; 289-3101, 800-638-1600) 47 rooms, major credit cards. SGL/DBL$70-$80.

Gateway Motel (4800 Coastal Hwy, 21842; 524-6500, 800-382-2582) 59 efficiencies, restaurant, lounge, entertainment, pool, whirlpools, beach, children stay free with parents, a/c, TV, in-room coffee makers, laundry facilities. SGL/DBL$150-$200.

Georgia Belle Hotel (12004 Coastal Hwy, 21842; 250-4000, Fax 250-9014) 98 rooms and suites, restaurant, pool, in-room refrigerators and microwaves, a/c, TV. SGL/DBL$40-$175.

Golden Sands Club (10900 Coastal Hwy, 21842; 820-1446) 1-bedroom apartments, indoor pool, sauna, tennis court, exercise facilities, a/c, TV. 1BR$75-$95.

HoJo Inn (102 60th St, 21842; 524-5634, 800-776-5634, 800-I-GO-HOJO) 62 rooms, restaurant, lounge, outdoor pool, children stay free with parents, wheelchair access, no-smoking rooms, TV, a/c, pets allowed, free parking, senior citizen rates, meeting facilities, major credit cards. LS SGL$20-$60, DBL$25-$70; HS SGL$30-$60, DBL$35-$75.

Holiday Inn (6600 Coastal Hwy, 21842; 524-1600, 800-492-3147 in Maryland, 800-638-2106, 800-HOLIDAY)restaurant, lounge, indoor pool, exercise facilities, tennis court, in-room microwaves, children under 19 stay free with parents, game room, wheelchair access, a/c, TV, no-smoking rooms, fax service, room service, no pets, laundry service, meeting facilities, senior citizen rates, major credit cards. SGL/DBL$37-$200.

Howard Johnson Hotel (1109 Atlantic Ave, 21842; 289-7251, 800-926-1122, 800-I-GO-HOJO) 90 rooms, restaurant, lounge, pool, children stay free with parents, wheelchair access, no-smoking rooms, gift shop, boutiques, TV, a/c, pets allowed, free parking, senior citizen rates, meeting facilities, major credit cards. SGL/DBL$30-$169.

Lighthouse Club Hotel (56th St, 21842; 524-5400, 800-767-6060) 23 rooms, restaurant, complimentary breakfast, pool, whirlpools, in-room refrigerators, no pets, a/c, TV, no-smoking rooms, Modified American Plan available, major credit cards. SGL/DBL$200-$220.

Nassau Motel (6002 Coastal Hwy, 21842; 524-6451) 63 rooms, restaurant, pool, beach, major credit cards. SGL/DBL$85-$105.

Nock Apartments (608 North Baltimore Ave, 21842; 289-5141, 800-289-0194) 17 1-, 2- and 3-bedroom apartments, a/c, kitchenettes, TV. 1BR$93, 2BR$110, 3BR$170.

Phillips Beach Plaza (13th St and Oceanfront, 21842; 289-9121) 86 rooms and efficiencies, restaurant, lounge, entertainment, pool, a/c, TV, beach. SGL/DBL$100-$125.

Plum Plaza (Second St and Boardwalk, 21842; 289-6181, 800-492-3147) 181 rooms, restaurant, pool, whirlpools, in-room refrigerators, a/c, TV, major credit cards. SGL/DBL$70-$130.

Princess Royale Resort (91st St and Oceanfront, 21842; 524-7777, Fax 525-7787, 800-476-9253) 340 1-, 2- and 3-bedroom condos, restaurant, lounge, entertainment, pool, exercise facilities, whirlpools, lighted tennis courts, sauna, game room, beach, a/c, TV, no-smoking rooms, wheelchair access, major credit cards. SGL/DBL$65-$215.

Quality Inn Beachfront (Oceanfront at 33rd St, 21842; 289-1234, 800-368-5689) 75 rooms and suites, restaurant, room service, indoor and outdoor pool, whirlpools, exercise facilities, children stay free with parents, game room, a/c, TV, laundry service, no-smoking rooms, meeting facilities, major credit cards. SGL/DBL$39-$177.

Quality Inn Boardwalk (17th St and Boardwalk, 21824; 289-4401, 800-368-5689) 170 rooms and suites, restaurant, pool, room service, exercise facilities, children stay free with parents, game room, whirlpools, laundry facilities, gift shop, a/c, TV, laundry service, no-smoking rooms, meeting facilities, major credit cards. SGL/DBL$44-$185.

Quality Inn Oceanfront (5400 Beach Hwy, 21842; 524-7200, 800-368-5689) 130 rooms and suites, restaurant, pool, exercise facilities, sauna, game room, laundry facilities, whirlpools, fax service, room service, exercise facilities, children stay free with parents, a/c, TV, laundry service, no-smoking rooms, meeting facilities, major credit cards. SGL/DBL$34-$174.

Sahara Motel (19th St and Oceanfront; 21842; 289-8101; 800-638-1600) 161 rooms and efficiencies, outdoor pool, in-room refrigerators, a/c, TV, water view, major credit cards. SGL/DBL$28-$108.

Sea Hawk Motel (12410 Coastal Hwy, 21842; 250-3191, 800-942-9042) 103 rooms and efficiencies, TV, a/c, open April through September, major credit cards. LS SGL/DBL$39-$73; HS SGL/DBL$86-$120.

Shangri La Motel (8400 Coastal Hwy, 21842; 524-1373, 800-852-3791) 29 rooms and efficiencies, TV, a/c, open May through September, free parking. LS SGL/DBL$39-$73; HS SGL/DBL$80-$102.

Satellite Motel (24th St and Oceanfront, 21842; 289-6401) 72 rooms and efficiencies, restaurant, pool, beach, children stay free with parents, a/c, TV, transportation to local attractions, major credit cards. SGL/DBL$95-$105, EFF$100-$120.

Sheraton Ocean City Resort and Conference Center (10100 Ocean Hwy, 21842; 524-3535, Fax 524-3834, 800-325-3535) 250 rooms and suites, restaurant, lounge, entertainment, indoor pool, exercise facilities, tennis court, game room, no-smoking rooms, a/c, TV, children stay free with parents, gift shop, beauty shop, wheelchair access, 37,000 square feet of meeting and exhibition space, 14 meeting rooms, meeting facilities for 1,000, major credit cards. SGL/DBL$55-$190.

Spinnaker Motel (18th St and Broadway, 21842; 289-5444, 800-638-3244) 100 rooms, restaurant, lounge, outdoor pool, TV, a/c, major credit cards LS SGL/DBL$45; HS SGL/DBL$121.

Stardust Motel (32nd St and Oceanfront, 21842; 289-6444, 800-638-2106) 76 rooms, restaurant, pool, a/c, TV, VCRs, laundry facilities, beach, major credit cards. SGL/DBL$65-$144.

Sun N'Fun Motel (29th St and Baltimore Ave, 21842; 289-6060, 800-638-3244) 28 rooms, in-room refrigerators and microwaves, TV, a/c, major credit cards. LS SGL/DBL$42; HS SGL/DBL$89.

Sun Tan Motel (Second St and Baltimore Ave, 21842; 289-7407) 36 rooms, a/c, TV, open April through September. LS SGL$30, DBL$50; HS SGL$50, DBL$70.

Surf and Sand Motel (23rd St and Boardwalk, 21842; 289-7161) 97 rooms and efficiencies, restaurant, pool, beach, a/c, TV, children stay free with parents. SGL/DBL$90-$135.

Surf Villa Hotel and Apartments (705 Baltimore Ave, 21842; 289-9434) 31 rooms and efficiencies, kitchenettes, TV, a/c, free parking, open May through late September. SGL/DBL$30-$35.

Thunderbird Beach Motel (32nd St and Baltimore Ave, 21842; 289-8136, 800-638-3244) 63 rooms and efficiencies, outdoor pool, TV, a/c, in-room refrigerators and microwaves, major credit cards. LS SGL/DBL$44; HS SGL/DBL$93.

Tides Motel (71st St and Oceanside, 21842; 524-7100, 800-638-1600) 54 efficiencies, outdoor pool, a/c, TV, free parking, major credit cards. LS SGL/DBL$38-$58; HS SGL/DBL$78.

Olney
Area Code 301

The Thoroughbred Bed and Breakfast (16410 Batchellor's Forest Rd, 20832; 774-7649) complimentary breakfast, no smoking, private baths, pool, on 175 acres, major credit cards. SGL/DBL$70-$115.

Oxford
Area Code 301

1876 House Bed and Breakfast (110 North Morris St, 21654; 226-5496)complimentary breakfast, no pets, 1870s home, antique furnishings. SGL/DBL$80-$100.

Robert Morris Inn (Rte 333, 21654; 226-5111) 33 rooms and housekeeping cottages, restaurant, lounge, beach, antique furnishings, no pets, private baths, water view, children stay free with parents, no-smoking rooms, major credit cards. SGL/DBL$60-$200.

Oxon Hill
Area Code 301

Ramada Hotel (6400 Oxon Hill Rd, 20745; 630-4050, Fax 839-4221, 800-2-RAMADA) 194 rooms and suites, restaurant, lounge, entertainment, indoor pool, wheelchair access, no-smoking rooms, airport transportation, free parking, pets allowed, wheelchair access, gift shop, jacuzzi, a/c, TV, room service, laundry facilities, meeting facilities, senior citizen rates, major credit cards. SGL/DBL$59-$99, STS$110, AP$10.

Perryville
Area Code 410

Comfort Inn (Hwy. 222, 21903; 642-2866, 800-221-2222) 104 rooms and 1- and 2-bedroom efficiencies, restaurant, wheelchair access, no-smoking rooms, no pets, in-room refrigerators and microwaves, children under 18 stay free with parents, senior citizen rates, a/c, TV, meeting facilities, major credit cards. SGL$48, 1BR/2BR$50.

Pikesville
Area Code 301

Comfort Inn Northwest (10 Wooded Way, 21806; 484-7700, Fax 653-1516, 800-228-5150) 103 rooms, complimentary breakfast, sauna, exercise facilities, wheelchair access, no-smoking rooms, complimentary newspaper, no pets, meeting facilities. children stay free with parents. SGL$40-$95, DBL$47-$105.

Econo Lodge (407 Reisertown Rd, 21208; 484-1800, 800-4-CHOICE) 60 rooms, pool, children under 12 stay free with parents, no pets, senior citizen rates, wheelchair access, a/c, TV, major credit cards. SGL/DBL$40-$62.

Hilton Hotel (1725 Reisertown Rd, 21208; 653-1100, 800-HILTONS) 265 rooms and suites, restaurant, lounge, entertainment, outdoor pool, exercise facilities, tennis courts, children stay free with parents, no-smoking rooms, wheelchair access, airport transportation, pets allowed, a/c, TV, business services, meeting facilities, major credit cards. SGL/DBL$100-$110, STS$150-$350.

Holiday Inn (1721 Reisertown Rd, 21208; 486-5600, Fax 486-5600 ext 255, 800-HOLIDAY) 108 rooms, restaurant, lounge, outdoor pool, exercise facilities, children under 19 stay free with parents, wheelchair access, a/c, TV, no-smoking rooms, fax service, room service, pets allowed, laundry service, meeting facilities for 150, senior citizen rates, major credit cards. SGL/DBL$65-$95.

Pocomoke City
Area Code 301

Days Inn (1540 Ocean Hwy, 21851; 957-3000, Fax 957-3147, 800-325-2525) 87 rooms, restaurant, lounge, pool, children stay free with parents, room service, laundry service, a/c, TV, free local calls, pets allowed, wheelchair access, no-smoking rooms, senior citizen rates, major credit cards. SGL/DBL$35-$75.

Quality Inn (825 Ocean Hwy, 21851; 957-1300, 800-368-5689) 64 rooms and suites, restaurant, room service, hot tubs, in-room refrigerators, exercise facilities, children stay free with parents, a/c, TV, VCRs, pets allowed, whirlpools, laundry service, no-smoking rooms, meeting facilities, major credit cards. SGL/DBL$44-$75.

Prince Anne
Area Code 410

Econo Lodge (10936 Market Lane, 21853; 651-9400, 800-424-4777, 800-4-CHOICE)complimentary breakfast, pool, TV, children under 12 stay free with parents, pets allowed, senior citizen rates, wheelchair access, a/c, TV, major credit cards. SGL/DBL$38-$46.

Washington Motel (11784 Somerset Ave, 21853; 651-2525) 12 rooms, restaurant, coffee shop, private baths, 1700s inn, meeting facilities. SGL/DBL$46-$66.

Prince Frederick
Area Code 410

Hutchin's Heritage (2860 Adeline Rd, 20678; 535-1759)bed and breakfast, antique furnishings, private baths. SGL/DBL$55-$75.

Rock Hall
Area Code 410

Mariner's Motel (5681 Hawthorne Ave, 21661; 639-2291) 12 rooms, pool, a/c, TV, no pets, laundry facilities. SGL/DBL$44-$75.

Rockville
Area Code 301

Courtyard by Marriott (2500 Research Blvd, 20850; 670-6700, Fax 670-9023, 800-321-2211) 147 rooms and suites, restaurant, lounge, indoor pool, exercise facilities, whirlpools, children stay free with parents, room service, laundry service, meeting facilities, senior citizen rates, major credit cards. SGL/DBL$85-$110.

Days Inn (One Shady Grove Rd, 20850; 948-4300, 800-325-2525) 190 rooms, restaurant, lounge, pool, children stay free with parents, room service, laundry service, a/c, TV, free local calls, transportation to local attractions, pets allowed, wheelchair access, no-smoking rooms, senior citizen rates, major credit cards. SGL/DBL$39-$64.

Howard Johnson Hotel (1251 West Montgomery Ave, 20850; 424-4940, Fax 424-1046, 800-I-GO-HOJO) 165 rooms and suites, restaurant, lounge, outdoor pool, exercise facilities, children stay free with parents, wheelchair access, no-smoking rooms, fax service, gift shop, TV, a/c, pets allowed, free parking, senior citizen rates, meeting facilities, major credit cards. SGL/DBL$65-$74.

Ramada Inn (1775 Rockville Pike, 20852; 881-2300, Fax 881-9047, 800-2-RAMADA) 160 rooms, restaurant, lounge, entertainment, pool, wheelchair access, no-smoking rooms, airport transportation, free parking, pets allowed, a/c, TV, room service, laundry facilities, meeting facilities for 200, senior citizen rates, major credit cards. SGL$49-$69, DBL$54-$79.

Sheraton Hotel (Three Research Center, 20850; 840-0200, 800-325-3535) 170 rooms and suites, restaurant, lounge, pool, exercise facilities, whirlpools, no-smoking rooms, a/c, TV, children stay free with parents, wheelchair access, transportation to local attractions, pets allowed, meeting facilities, major credit cards. SGL/DBL$80-$125.

Woodfin Suites (1380 Piccard Dr., 20850; 590-9880, Fax 590-9614, 800-237-8811) 200 suites, restaurant, lounge, pool, whirlpools, transportation to local attractions, TV, a/c, in-room refrigerators, senior citizen rates, major credit cards. SGL/DBL$125-$150.

Salisbury
Area Code 301

Best Western Statesman (712 North Salisbury Blvd, 21801; 749-7155, 800-528-1234) 92 rooms, restaurant, complimentary breakfast, lounge, pool, exercise facilities, children stay free with parents, a/c, TV, no-smoking rooms, wheelchair access, pets allowed, senior citizen rates, meeting facilities, major credit cards. SGL/DBL$46-$61.

Budget Host Temple Hill (1510 South Salisbury Blvd, 21801; 742-3284, 800-BUD-HOST) 63 rooms, pool, in-room refrigerators, no-smoking rooms, TV, VCRs, a/c, wheelchair access, children stay free with parents, senior citizen rates, meeting facilities, major credit cards. SGL$28-$36, DBL$32-$48, AP$4.

Comfort Inn (Hwy. 13 North, 21901; 543-4666, 800-221-2222) 96 rooms, restaurant, sauna, whirlpools, in-room refrigerators, wheelchair access, no-smoking rooms, no pets, children under 18 stay free with parents, senior citizen rates, a/c, TV, meeting facilities for 20, major credit cards. SGL/DBL$37-$51.

Days Inn (Rte 13 North, 21801; 749-6200, Fax 749-7378, 800-325-2525) 98 rooms, restaurant, free breakfast, lounge, pool, children stay free with parents, room service, laundry service, a/c, TV, free local calls, pets allowed, in-room refrigerators and microwaves, wheelchair access, no-smoking rooms, senior citizen rates, major credit cards. SGL/DBL$46-$64.

Hampton Inn (1735 North Salisbury Blvd, 21801; 546-1300, Fax 546-0370, 800-HAMPTON) 102 rooms, restaurant, complimentary breakfast, pool, exercise facilities, children under 18 stay free with parents, no-smoking rooms, wheelchair access, computer hookups, airport transportation, fax service, TV, a/c, free local calls, pets allowed, meeting facilities, major credit cards. SGL$39-$47, DBL$47-$69.

HoJo Inn (Box 984, 21801; 742-5195, Fax 546-1497, 800-I-GO-HOJO) 56 rooms, restaurant, lounge, pool, children stay free with parents, wheelchair access, no-smoking rooms, TV, a/c, pets allowed, free parking, senior citizen rates, meeting facilities, major credit cards. SGL/DBL$34-$69.

Holiday Inn (Rte 11, 21801; 742-7194, 800-HOLIDAY) 123 rooms, restaurant, lounge, outdoor pool, exercise facilities, children under 19 stay free with parents, wheelchair access, a/c, TV, no-smoking rooms, fax service, room service, no pets, laundry service, meeting facilities, senior citizen rates, major credit cards. SGL/DBL$39-$88.

Holiday Inn (Rte 13 North, 21801; 742-7194, Fax 742-5195, 800-HOLIDAY) restaurant, lounge, entertainment, outdoor pool, sauna, exercise facilities, children under 19 stay free with parents, wheelchair access, a/c, TV, no-smoking rooms, fax service, room service, pets allowed, laundry service, meeting facilities for 100, senior citizen rates, major credit cards. SGL/DBL$45-$80.

Lord Salisbury Motel (Rte 11, 21801; 742-3251) 50 rooms and efficiencies, pool, a/c, TV. SGL/DBL$65-$75.

Sandman Motel (1500 North Salisbury Blvd, 21801; 749-6178) 34 rooms, a/c, TV. SGL/DBL$49-$55.

Sheraton Inn (300 South Salisbury Blvd, 21801; 546-4400, Fax 546-2528, 800-325-3535) 156 rooms and suites, restaurant, lounge, indoor pool, exercise facilities, no-smoking rooms, a/c, TV, children stay free with parents, wheelchair access, 4,000 square feet of meeting and exhibition space, 5 meeting rooms, meeting facilities for 300, major credit cards. SGL/DBL$65-$100.

Super 8 Motel (2615 North Salisbury Blvd, 21801; 749-5131, Fax 749-5131 ext 401, 800-800-8000) 48 rooms and suites, free breakfast, no pets, children under 12 stay free with parents, free local calls, a/c, TV, fax service, no-smoking rooms, in-room microwaves, senior citizen rates, wheelchair access, meeting facilities, major credit cards. SGL/DBL$34-$39.

Thrift Travel Inn (604 North Salisbury Blvd, 21801; 742-5135, 800-457-3341) 40 rooms, complimentary breakfast, a/c, TV, major credit cards. SGL/DBL$50-$60.

White Oak Inn Bed and Breakfast (804 Spring Hill Rd, 21801; 742-4887) complimentary breakfast, no smoking, no children allowed, private baths, no pets, water view. SGL/DBL$55-$70.

Sharpsburg
Area Code 301

Ground Squirrel Hollar (6736 Sharpsburg Pike, 21782; 432-8288) 3 rooms, bed and breakfast, on 5 acres, antique furnishings. SGL/DBL$50-$75.

Jacob Rohrbach Inn (138 West Main St, 21782; 432-5079)bed and breakfast, private baths. SGL/DBL$75-$100.

Silver Spring
Area Code 301

Courtyard by Marriott (1251 Prosperity Dr, 20904; 680-8500, Fax 680-9232, 800-321-2211) 146 rooms and suites, restaurant, lounge, pool, exercise facilities, whirlpools, children stay free with parents, laundry service, meeting facilities, senior citizen rates, major credit cards. SGL/DBL$85-$100, STS$100-$150.

Days Inn (Silver Spring 20910; 544-4400, Fax 587-2059, 800-325-2525) 143 rooms, restaurant, lounge, pool, children stay free with parents, room service, laundry service, a/c, TV, free local calls, transportation to local attractions, no pets, wheelchair access, no-smoking rooms, senior citizen rates, major credit cards. SGL$55, DBL$58-$63.

Econo Lodge (7990 Georgia Ave, 20910; 565-3444, 800-4-CHOICE) 130 rooms, restaurant, complimentary breakfast, pool, children under 12 stay free with parents, pets allowed, senior citizen rates, laundry facilities, wheelchair access, a/c, TV, major credit cards. SGL/DBL$50-$60.

Holiday Inn (8777 Georgia Ave, 20910; 589-0800, Fax 587-4791, 800-HOLIDAY) 227 rooms and suites, restaurant, lounge, outdoor pool, exercise facilities, children under 19 stay free with parents, wheelchair access, a/c, TV, no-smoking rooms, fax service, room service, no pets, gift shop, beauty shop, laundry service, meeting facilities for 500, senior citizen rates, major credit cards. SGL/DBL$80-$100, STS$125-$145.

Quality Hotel (8727 Colesville Rd, 20910; 589-5200, 800-368-5689) 254 rooms and suites, restaurant, room service, pool, sauna, exercise facilities, children stay free with parents, a/c, TV, laundry service, wheelchair access, no-smoking rooms, meeting facilities, major credit cards. SGL$49-$103, DBL$59-$104.

Snow Hill
Area Code 410

River House Inn (201 East Market St, 21863; 632-2722) 7 rooms, restaurant, a/c, TV, no pets, 1860s inn, Modified American Plan available. $50-$95.

Snow Hill Inn (104 East Market St, 21863; 632-2102) 3 rooms, restaurant, no pets, fireplace, a/c, antique furnishings. SGL/DBL$65-$70.

Solomons
Area Code 410

Rental and Reservations Services

Long & Foster (Solomons Island 20688; 326-6351, 800-732-1537).

□ □ □

Back Creek Inn and Bed and Breakfast (Solomons Island, 20688; 326-2022)rooms and suites, complimentary breakfast, 1880s home, antique furnishings, open February to December, water view. SGL/DBL$85-$105.

By-The-Bay Bed and Breakfast (Solomons Island, 20688; 326-3428) rooms and suites, complimentary breakfast, Victorian home, private baths, water view, a/c, open year-round. SGL/DBL$80.

Comfort Inn Beacon Marina (Lore Rd, 20688; 326-6303, Fax 326-6708, 800-221-2222) 60 rooms, restaurant, outdoor pool, jacuzzi, wheelchair access, no-smoking rooms, no pets, children under 18 stay free with parents, hot tubs, water view, senior citizen rates, a/c, TV, meeting facilities, major credit cards. SGL/DBL$48-$70.

Davis House Bed and Breakfast (Solomons Island, 20688; 326-4811) 7 rooms, complimentary breakfast, private baths, Victorian home, water view. SGL/DBL$65-$85.

The Grey Fox Inn (14560 Solomon Island Rd South, 20688; 326-6826)a/c, TV, major credit cards. SGL/DBL$45-$55.

Holiday Inn Conference Center and Marina (155 Holiday Dr., 20688; 326-6311, Fax 326-1069, 800-HOLIDAY) 326 rooms and efficiencies, restaurant, lounge, outdoor pool, exercise facilities, sauna, tennis courts, water view, children under 19 stay free with parents, wheelchair access, a/c, TV, no-smoking rooms, fax service, room service, no pets, laundry service, 20,000 square feet of meeting and exhibition space, meeting facilities for 600, senior citizen rates, major credit cards. SGL/DBL$68-$140.

Stevensville
Area Code 410

Kent Manor Inn (500 Kent Manor, 21666; 643-5757) 24 rooms, restaurant, pool, antique furnishings, a/c, TV, no pets, major credit cards. SGL/DBL$130-$150.

St. Michaels
Area Code 301

The Inn At Perry Cabin (308 Watkins Lane, 21663; 745-5178, 800-722-2949) 41 rooms and suites, restaurant, complimentary breakfast, indoor pool, exercise facilities, sauna, TV, children stay free with parents, no-smoking rooms, wheelchair access, a/c, major credit cards. SGL/DBL$200-$500.

Harbourtowne Resort (Rte 33, 21663; 745-9066) 81 rooms and cottages, restaurant, lounge, pool, tennis courts, laundry facilities, wheelchair access, no-smoking rooms, beach, a/c, TV, meeting facilities, major credit cards. SGL/DBL$125 $150.

The Parsonage (210 North Talbot St, 21663; 745-5519, 800-234-5519) 7 rooms, restaurant, complimentary breakfast, transportation to local attractions, children stay free with parents, a/c, no smoking, major credit cards. SGL/DBL$75-$85.

St. Michaels Harbor Inn (101 North Harbor Rd, 21663; 745-9001) 46 rooms, restaurant, pool, jacuzzi, water view, in-room refrigerators, a/c, TV, no pets, whirlpools, exercise facilities, meeting facilities, major credit cards. SGL/DBL$100-$325.

St. Michaels Motor Inn (1228 South Talbot St, 21663; 745-3333) 93 rooms, a/c, laundry facilities, TV, pets OK, major credit cards. SGL/DBL$50-$70.

Taneytown
Area Code 410

Antrim 1844 Country Inn (30 Trevanion Rd, 21787; 756-6812, 800-858-1844) 13 rooms, bed and breakfast. SGL/DBL$175-$250.

Glenburn Bed and Breakfast (3515 Runnymede Rd, 21787; 751-1187) complimentary breakfast. SGL/DBL$100-$125.

Thurmont
Area Code 301

Rambler Motel (Thurmont 21788; 271-2424) 30 rooms and 1- and 2-bedroom efficiencies, restaurant, a/c, TV, laundry facilities, major credit cards. SGL/DBL$42-$50.

Super 8 Motel (300 Tippin Dr., 21788; 271-7888, 800-800-8000) 46 rooms and suites, no pets, children under 12 stay free with parents, free local calls, a/c, TV, in-room refrigerators and microwaves, fax service, no-smoking rooms, senior citizen rates, wheelchair access, meeting facilities, major credit cards. SGL/DBL$37-$42.

Tilghman
Area Code 410

Black Walnut Point (Black Walnut Rd, 21671; 886-2452) 7 rooms, complimentary breakfast, pool, tennis courts, water view, 1800s inn, airport courtesy car, a/c, TV, no-smoking rooms. SGL/DBL$85-$125.

Timonium
Area Code 410

Days Hotel North and Conference Center (9615 Deereco Rd, 21093; 560-1000, Fax 561-3918, 800-325-2525) 146 rooms and suites, restaurant, complimentary breakfast, free local calls, in-room refrigerators and microwaves, VCRs, laundry service, no pets, children stay free with parents, airport courtesy car, meeting facilities for 500, major credit cards. SGL$35-$65, DBL$45-$70, STS$90-$110.

Holiday Inn (2004 Greenspring Dr., 21093; 252-7373, Fax 561-0182 ext 799, 800-HOLIDAY) 250 rooms, restaurant, lounge, indoor and outdoor pool, exercise facilities, pets allowed, children stay free with parents, wheelchair access, no-smoking rooms, pets allowed, meeting facilities for 750, major credit cards. SGL/DBL$72-$92.

Red Roof Inn (111 West Timonium Rd, 21093; 666-0380, 666-1509, 800-843-7663) 137 rooms, no-smoking rooms, fax service, wheelchair access, complimentary newspaper, free local calls, in-room computer hookups, major credit cards. SGL/DBL39-$42.

Towson
Area Code 410

Days Inn (8801 Loch Raven Blvd, 21204; 882-0900, Fax 882-4176, 800-325-2525, 800-666-0900) 180 rooms and suites, restaurant, lounge, in-room refrigerators and microwaves, children stay free with parents, no-smoking rooms, wheelchair access, pets allowed, laundry service, meeting facilities for 200, major credit cards. SGL$39-$48, DBL$46-$56, STS$79.

Holiday Inn Cromwell (1100 Cromwell Bridge Rd, 21204; 823-4410, Fax 823-4410 ext 261, 800-465-4329) 142 rooms, restaurant, lounge, pool, whirlpool, exercise facilities, laundry room, children stay free with parents, wheelchair access, no-smoking rooms, fax service, room service, meeting facilities for 400, major credit cards. SGL/DBL$79.

Holiday Inn (Loch Haven Blvd, 21204; 823-8750, Fax 823-8750 ext 753, 800-HOLIDAY) 123 rooms, restaurant, lounge, outdoor pool, exercise facilities, children under 19 stay free with parents, wheelchair access, a/c, TV, no-smoking rooms, fax service, room service, pets allowed, laundry service, senior citizen rates, meeting facilities for 120, major credit cards. SGL/DBL$65-$95.

Quality Inn Towson (1015 York Rd, 21204; 825-9190, 800-688-2522) 159 rooms and suites, restaurant, lounge, complimentary breakfast, indoor pool, sauna, exercise facilities, 15 meeting rooms, meeting facilities for 500, major credit cards. SGL$52-$79, DBL$55-$79.

Ramada Inn (8712 Loch Raven Blvd, 21286; 823-8750, Fax 823-8644, 800-2-RAMADA) 123 rooms, restaurant, lounge, outdoor pool, wheelchair access, no-smoking rooms, airport transportation, free parking, pets allowed, wheelchair access, a/c, TV, room service, laundry facilities, meeting facilities, senior citizen rates, major credit cards. SGL$49-$54, DBL$59-$64.

Sheraton Towson Conference Hotel (903 Dulaney Valley Rd, 21204; 321-7400, Fax 296-9534) 284 rooms and suites, restaurant, 2 lounges, entertainment, indoor pool, sauna, exercise facilities, wheelchair access, no-smoking rooms, gift shop, 13 meeting rooms, 17,000 square feet of meeting and exhibition space, meeting facilities for 1,000, major credit cards. SGL/DBL$111, STS$125-$135.

Tudor Hall
Area Code 301

Tudor Hall (Tudor Hall 21014; 838-0466) bed and breakfast, no pets, no children allowed, private baths. SGL/DBL$50.

Upper Marlboro
Area Code 301

Forest Hills Motel (2901 Crain Hwy, 20772; 627-2969) 13 rooms, in-room refrigerators, TV, a/c, children stay free with parents, major credit cards. SGL/DBL$38-$45.

Vienna
Area Code 301

The Tavern House (111 Water St, 21869; 376-3347)bed and breakfast, no pets, water view. SGL/DBL$60-$65.

Waldorf
Area Code 301

Days Inn (11370 Days Court, 20603; 932-9200, Fax 843-9816, 800-325-2525) 100 rooms and suites, restaurant, complimentary breakfast, lounge, pool, children stay free with parents, room service, laundry service, a/c, TV, in-room refrigerators and microwaves, free local calls, no pets, wheelchair access, no-smoking rooms, senior citizen rates, major credit cards. SGL/DBL$44-$49.

Econo Lodge (Four Business Park Dr., 20601; 645-0022, 800-4-CHOICE) 92 rooms, complimentary breakfast, pool, TV, children under 12 stay free with parents, in-room microwaves, pets allowed, senior citizen rates, wheelchair access, a/c, TV, major credit cards. SGL/DBL$42-$49.

HoJo Inn (Hwy. 301, 20603; 932-5090, 800-826-4504, 800-I-GO-HOJO) 110 rooms, restaurant, lounge, pool, children stay free with parents, wheelchair access, no-smoking rooms, kitchenettes, VCRs, room service, TV, a/c, pets allowed, free parking, meeting facilities, senior citizen rates, major credit cards. SGL/DBL$42-$46.

Super 8 Motel (5050 Hwy 301, 20603; 932-8957, Fax 932-8957 ext 403, 800-800-8000) 59 rooms and suites, pets allowed, children under 12 stay free with parents, free local calls, in-room refrigerators and microwaves, a/c, TV, fax service, no-smoking rooms, senior citizen rates, wheelchair access, meeting facilities, major credit cards. SGL/DBL$36-$41.

Westminster
Area Code 301

The Boston Inn (533 Baltimore Blvd, 21157; 848-9095, 800-634-0846) 115 rooms, pool, a/c, TV, wheelchair access. SGL/DBL$29-$38.

Comfort Inn (451 WMC Dr., 21158; 857-1900, 800-221-2222) 101 rooms, restaurant, free breakfast, pool, wheelchair access, whirlpools, fax, no-smoking rooms, no pets, children under 18 stay free with parents, senior citizen rates, a/c, TV, meeting facilities, major credit cards. SGL/DBL$39-$60.

Days Inn (25 South Cranberry Rd, 21157; 857-0500, Fax 857-1407, 800-325-2525) 96 rooms, restaurant, complimentary breakfast, lounge, pool, children stay free with parents, room service, laundry service, a/c, TV, free local calls, pets allowed, wheelchair access, no-smoking rooms, senior citizen rates, major credit cards. SGL/DBL$44-$60.

The Winchester Country Inn (430 Bishop St, 21157; 876-7373)bed and breakfast. SGL/DBL$45-$85.

Williamsport
Area Code 301

Days Inn (310 East Potomac St, 21795; 582-3500, Fax 223-8491, 800-325-2525) 122 rooms, restaurant, lounge, outdoor pool, children stay free with parents, room service, laundry service, a/c, TV, free local calls, pets allowed, wheelchair access, no-smoking rooms, senior citizen rates, major credit cards. SGL/DBL$49-$53.

New Jersey

Absecon
Area Code 609

Caprice Motor Lodge (206 East White Horse Pike, 08201; 652-3322) 22 rooms, a/c, TV, whirlpool, in-room refrigerators, major credit cards. SGL/DBL$35-$110.

Comfort Inn North (405 East Absecon Blvd, 08201; 646-5000, 800-221-2222) 200 rooms, pool, wheelchair access, no-smoking rooms, no pets, children under 18 stay free with parents, senior citizen rates, transportation to local attractions, a/c, TV, meeting facilities, major credit cards. SGL/DBL$49-$115.

Days Inn (224 East Whitehorse Pike, 08201; 652-2200, Fax 748-8005, 800-325-2525) 102 rooms and suites, restaurant, lounge, outdoor pool, children stay free with parents, room service, laundry service, a/c, TV, free local calls, no pets, wheelchair access, no-smoking rooms, senior citizen rates, major credit cards. SGL/DBL$45-$110, STS$65-$140.

Econo Lodge (328 White Horse Pike, 08201; 652-3300, 800-4-CHOICE) 62 rooms, complimentary breakfast, pool, TV, children under 12 stay free with parents, no pets, senior citizen rates, wheelchair access, a/c, TV, major credit cards. SGL/DBL$40-$100.

Friendship Inn (316 White Horse Pike, 08201; 652-0904, 800-424-4777) 27 rooms, exercise facilities, a/c, TV, no pets, no-smoking rooms, children stay free with parents, whirlpools, wheelchair access, no-smoking rooms, major credit cards. SGL/DBL$30-$95.

Hampton Inn (240 East White Horse Pike, 08201; 652-2500, Fax 652-2212, 800-HAMPTON) 129 rooms, restaurant, complimentary breakfast, pool, exercise facilities, children under 18 stay free with parents, no-smoking rooms, wheelchair access, whirlpool tub, in-room computer hookups, transportation to local attractions, fax service, TV, a/c, free local calls, no pets, meeting facilities, major credit cards. SGL/DBL$53-$100.

Howard Johnson (539 Absecon Blvd, 08201; 641-7272, 800-I-GO-HOJO) 208 rooms, restaurant, lounge, pool, children stay free with parents, wheelchair access, no-smoking rooms, TV, a/c, no pets, free parking, meeting facilities, senior citizen rates, meeting facilities, major credit cards. SGL/DBL$50-$175.

Marriott Seaview Resort (Rte 9, 08201; 652-1800, 800-228-9290) 298 rooms and suites, restaurant, lounge, entertainment, pool, exercise facilities, whirlpools, tennis courts, wheelchair access, TV, a/c, no-smoking rooms, gift shop, children stay free with parents, business services, meeting facilities, major credit cards. SGL/DBL$140-$200.

Super 8 Motel (229 East White Horse Pike, 08201; 652-2477, Fax 748-0666, 800-800-8000) 58 rooms and suites, no pets, children under 12 stay free with parents, free local calls, whirlpools, a/c, TV, in-room refrigerators and microwaves, fax, no-smoking rooms, senior citizen rates, wheelchair access, meeting facilities, major credit cards. SGL/DBL$30-$105.

Andover
Area Code 201

Holiday Motel (708 Hwy 206, 07821; 786-5260, Fax 786-7627) 19 rooms, a/c, TV, no pets, major credit cards. SGL/DBL$62.

Asbury Park
Area Code 201

Berkeley Carteret (1401 Ocean Ave, 07712; 776-6700, 800-524-1423) 254 rooms and suites, restaurant, lounge, pool, exercise facilities, beach, meeting facilities, major credit cards. SGL/DBL$95-$105.

Atlantic City
Area Code 609

Admiral's Quarters (655 Absecon Blvd, 08401; 344-2201) 74 rooms, pool, major credit cards. SGL/DBL$80.

Atlanta Palace (1507 Boardwalk, 08401; 334-1200, 800-527-8483) 300 rooms, restaurant, lounge, pool, jacuzzi, a/c, room service, TV, meeting facilities, major credit cards. SGL/DBL$105.

Bala Motor Inn (114 South Illinois Ave, 08401; 348-3031, Fax 347-6043) 108 rooms, a/c, TV, pool, Modified American Plan available, major credit cards. SGL/DBL$50-$125.

Bally's Grand Casino (Boston Ave and Pacific Ave, 08401; 347-7111, 800-257-8677) 518 rooms and suites, restaurant, lounge, entertainment, indoor pool, exercise facilities, sauna, jacuzzi, no pets, beauty salon, 24-hour room service, a/c, TV, meeting facilities, major credit cards. SGL/DBL$115-$200.

Bally's Park Place (Park Place and Boardwalk, 08401; 340-2000, 800-225-5977) 510 rooms, restaurant, restaurant, lounge, entertainment, pool, exercise facilities, sauna, jacuzzi, beauty salon, no pets, 24-hour room service, a/c, TV, meeting facilities, major credit cards. SGL/DBL$95-$215.

Best Western Inn (1416 Pacific Ave, 08401; 344-7117, Fax 344-5659, 800-528-1234) 75 rooms, restaurant, complimentary breakfast, lounge, pool, exercise facilities, children stay free with parents, a/c, TV, no-smoking rooms, TV, wheelchair access, whirlpools, no pets, senior citizen rates, meeting facilities, major credit cards. SGL/DBL$48-$125.

Caesars Hotel and Casino (2100 Pacific Ave, 08401; 348-4411, 800-257-8555) 300 rooms and suites, restaurant, lounge, entertainment, pool, exercise facilities, sauna, jacuzzi, beauty salon, a/c, TV, meeting facilities, major credit cards. SGL/DBL$105.

Claridge Casino Hotel (Indiana and Boardwalk, 08401; 340-3400, Fax 345-8909, 800-257-8585) 504 rooms and suites, restaurant, lounge, entertainment, indoor pool, exercise facilities, whirlpools, sauna, beauty shop, children stay free with parents, no pets, TV, water view, a/c, wheelchair access, meeting facilities, major credit cards. SGL/DBL$80-$165.

Days Inn (Morris Ave and Boardwalk, 08401; 344-6101, Fax 348-5335, 800-325-2525) 105 rooms, restaurant, lounge, pool, children stay free with parents, room service, laundry service, a/c, TV, free local calls, beach, no pets, wheelchair access, no-smoking rooms, senior citizen rates, major credit cards. SGL/DBL$50-$200.

Del Webb's Claridge (Indiana Ave and Boardwalk, 08401; 340-3400, 800-257-8585) 504 rooms and suites, restaurant, lounge, entertainment, pool, exercise facilities, sauna, jacuzzi, beauty salon, a/c, TV, meeting facilities, major credit cards. SGL/DBL$150.

Econo Lodge Beach Block (3001 Pacific Ave, 08401; 344-2925, 800-227-6638, 800-4-CHOICE) 65 rooms, children under 12 stay free with parents, no pets, senior citizen rates, wheelchair access, a/c, TV, major credit cards. SGL/DBL$40-$150.

Econo Lodge Boardwalk (117 South Kentucky Ave, 08401; 344-9093, Fax 340-8065, 800-4-CHOICE) 51 rooms, pool, children under 12 stay free with parents, no pets, senior citizen rates, whirlpools, spa, wheelchair access, a/c, TV, major credit cards. SGL/DBL$40-$175.

Enclave Suites (3851 Boardwalk, 08401; 347-0400, 800-362-5283) 150 rooms and suites, pool, jacuzzi, sauna, exercise facilities, a/c, TV, major credit cards. SGL/DBL$85.

Harrah's Marina (1725 Brigantine Blvd, 08401; 441-5000, 800-242-7724) 750 rooms and suites, restaurant, lounge, entertainment, pool, sauna, exercise facilities, tennis courts, room service, a/c, TV, beauty shop. SGL/DBL$100.

HoJo Downtown (1339 Pacific Ave, 08401; 344-4193, Fax 348-1263, 800-I-GO-HOJO) 72 rooms and 2-bedroom apartments, restaurant, lounge, pool, children stay free with parents, wheelchair access, no-smoking rooms, TV, a/c, no pets, free parking, meeting facilities, senior citizen rates, meeting facilities, major credit cards. SGL/DBL$75-$150.

Holiday Inn (Chelsea Ave and Boardwalk, 08401; 348-2200, Fax 345-5110, 800-HOLIDAY) 220 rooms, restaurant, lounge, outdoor pool, exercise facilities, children under 19 stay free with parents, wheelchair access, a/c, TV, no-smoking rooms, fax service, room service, no pets, laundry service, meeting facilities for 400, senior citizen rates, major credit cards. SGL/DBL$60-$160.

Lido Motel (1400 Absecon Blvd, 08401; 344-1975, 800-223-6360) 27 rooms, pool, a/c, TV, major credit cards. SGL/DBL$30-$70.

Madison House (123 South Illinois Ave, 08401; 345-1400, 800-458-9879) 209 rooms, meeting facilities. SGL/DBL$55.

Merv Griffin's Resort Casino Hotel (1133 Broadway, 08404; 344-6000, Fax 340-7684) 669 rooms and suites, restaurant, lounge, entertainment, pool, whirlpools, a/c, TV, no pets, major credit cards. SGL/DBL$110-$205.

Midtown Motor Inn (101 South Indiana Ave, 08401; 348-3031, 800-932-0534 in the eastern U.S.) 172 rooms, restaurant, lounge, heated indoor pool, a/c, TV, no pets, American plan and Modified American Plan available. SGL/DBL$50-$125.

Atlantic City 81

Quality Inn (South Carolina and Pacific Avenues, 08401; 345-7070, 800-368-5689) 203 rooms and suites, restaurant, room service, pool, whirlpools, sauna, exercise facilities, children stay free with parents, no pets, a/c, TV, laundry service, no-smoking rooms, meeting facilities, major credit cards. SGL/DBL$62-$125.

Radisson Flagship Hotel (60 North Main Ave, 08401; 343-7447, 800-228-9822, 800-777-1700) 440 rooms and suites, restaurant, lounge, entertainment, pool, jacuzzi, sauna, wheelchair access, free parking, no-smoking rooms, TV, a/c, children stay free with parents, pets allowed, major credit cards. SGL/DBL$85.

Ramada Renaissance Suites (1507 Boardwalk, 08410; 344-1200, Fax 347-6090, 800-228-9898, 800-2-RAMADA) 293 suites, restaurant, lounge, pool, jacuzzi, wheelchair access, no-smoking rooms, kitchenettes, airport transportation, free parking, pets allowed, wheelchair access, a/c, TV, room service, laundry facilities, meeting facilities, senior citizen rates, major credit cards. SGL/DBL$79-$299.

Resorts International (North Carolina and Boardwalk., 08404; 344-6000, 800-438-7424) 700 rooms and suites, restaurant, lounge, entertainment, pool, exercise facilities, sauna, jacuzzi, beauty salon, a/c, TV, meeting facilities, major credit cards. SGL/DBL$85.

Sands Hotel and Casino (Indiana Ave and Brighton Park, 08401; 441-4000, 800-257-8580) 500 rooms and suites, restaurant, lounge, entertainment, pool, exercise facilities, sauna, jacuzzi, beauty salon, no pets, a/c, TV, meeting facilities, major credit cards. SGL/DBL$99-$199.

The Showboat (801 Boardwalk, 08404; 340-2000, 800-621-0200) 516 rooms and suites, restaurant, lounge, entertainment, pool, exercise facilities, sauna, jacuzzi, beauty salon, a/c, TV, meeting facilities, major credit cards. SGL/DBL$125.

Sun N'Surf Motel (1600 Albany Ave, 08401; 344-2515) 25 rooms, a/c, TV, no pets, pool, major credit cards. SGL/DBL$30-$70.

Tropworld Casino (Brighton Ave and Boardwalk, 08404; 340-4000, 800-257-6227) 1000 rooms and suites, restaurant, lounge, entertainment, pool, exercise facilities, sauna, jacuzzi, beauty salon, a/c, TV, meeting facilities, major credit cards. SGL/DBL$90-$145.

Trump Plaza (Mississippi Ave and Boardwalk, 08401; 441-6000, Fax 441-7881, 800-441-0909) 583 rooms and suites, restaurant, lounge, entertainment, pool, jacuzzi, sauna, exercise facilities, beauty salon, tennis courts, a/c, no pets, TV, meeting facilities, room service, major credit cards. SGL/DBL$120-$205.

Trump's Castle Casino Resort (Brigantine Blvd, 08401; 441-2000, Fax 441-8541) 725 rooms and suites, restaurant, lounge, pool, lighted tennis courts, whirlpools, sauna, room service, a/c, TV, no pets, major credit cards. SGL/DBL$95-$195.

Trump Regency (2500 Boardwalk, 08401; 344-4000, 800-234-5678) 500 rooms and suites, restaurant, lounge, entertainment, pool, whirlpools, exercise facilities, children stay free with parents, a/c, TV, wheelchair access, no-smoking rooms, meeting facilities, water view, major credit cards. SGL/DBL$150-$450.

Avalon
Area Code 609

Beachcomber Resort Motel (7900 Dune Drive, 08202; 368-5121) 55 rooms, and 2-bedroom efficiencies, restaurant, pool, kitchenettes, a/c, laundry facilities, TV, no pets, major credit cards. SGL/DBL$60-$200.

Desert Sand Resort Complex (Avalon 08202; 368-5133, 800-458-6008) 89 rooms and suites, restaurant, lounge, indoor and outdoor pools, whirlpools, exercise facilities, room service, laundry facilities, meeting facilities, major credit cards. SGL/DBL$

Golden Inn (Oceanfront at 78th St, 08202; 368-5155, 800-426-4300) 160 rooms and efficiencies, restaurant, lounge, entertainment, pool, jacuzzi, children under 12 stay free with parents, a/c, TV, in-room refrigerators, children stay free with parents, meeting facilities, major credit cards. SGL/DBL$125-$160.

Avon-By-The-Sea
Area Code 908

The Avon Manor (109 Sylvania Ave, 07717; 988-6326) 7 rooms, bed and breakfast, no smoking, no pets. SGL/DBL$55-$100.

Barrington
Area Code 609

Super 8 Motel (308 White Horse Pike, 08007; 547-8000, Fax 573-9570, 800-800-8000) 47 rooms and suites, no pets, children under 12 stay free with parents, free local calls, a/c, TV, jacuzzis, fax service, no-smoking rooms, senior citizen rates, wheelchair access, meeting facilities, major credit cards. SGL/DBL$40-$45.

Bay Head
Area Code 201

Bay Head Gables (200 Main Ave, 08742; 892-9449) 11 rooms, complimentary breakfast, no children allowed, antique furnishings, a/c, no smoking, no pets, beach, major credit cards. SGL/DBL$95-$125.

Bay Head Inn (646 Main Ave, 08742; 892-4664) bed and breakfast, private baths, no smoking, no pets, antique furnishings. SGL/DBL$90-$135.

Greenville Hotel (345 Main Ave, 08742; 892-3100, Fax 892-0599) 33 rooms and suites, restaurant, complimentary breakfast, 1890s inn, antique furnishings, a/c, TV. SGL/DBL$75-$200.

Beach Haven
Area Code 609

Engleside Inn (30 Engleside Ave, 08008; 892-9844, 800-762-2214) 73 rooms and apartments, restaurant, lounge, a/c, TV, VCRs, pets allowed, water view, major credit cards. SGL/DBL$64-$242.

Bellmawr
Area Code 609

Bellmawr Motor Inn (312 Black Horse Pike, 08031; 931-6300) 28 rooms, restaurant, a/c, TV, no pets, major credit cards. SGL/DBL$36-$46.

Econo Lodge (301 South Black Horse Pike, 08031; 931-2800, 800-4-CHOICE) 46 rooms, children under 12 stay free with parents, no pets, senior citizen rates, wheelchair access, a/c, TV, meeting facilities, major credit cards. SGL/DBL$45-$65..

Belmar
Area Code 201

Belmar Motor Lodge (910 River Rd, 07719; 681-6600) 55 rooms, restaurant, pool, TV, a/c, no-smoking rooms, wheelchair access, laundry facilities, major credit cards. SGL/DBL$50-$88.

The Shillelagh Inn (102 7th Ave, 07719; 681-8950) bed and breakfast, private baths, no children allowed, no pets, no smoking, antique furnishings, water view. SGL/DBL$35-$80.

Bernardsville
Area Code 201

Old Mill Inn (North Maple Ave, 07924; 221-1100) 107 rooms and housekeeping cottages, restaurant, complimentary breakfast, pool, exercise facilities, pets allowed, a/c, children stay free with parents, TV, meeting facilities, major credit cards. SGL/DBL$65-$95, STS$150.

Blackwood
Area Code 609

HoJo Inn (832 North Black Horse Pike, 08012; 228-4040, Fax 227-7544, 800-I-GO-HOJO) 101 rooms, restaurant, lounge, pool, whirlpools, children stay free with parents, wheelchair access, no-smoking rooms, TV, a/c, pets allowed, fax service, free parking, meeting facilities, senior citizen rates, all major credit cards. SGL/DBL$45-$87.

Bordentown
Area Code 609

Best Western Inn (Dunnsmill Rd, 08505; 298-8000, Fax 291-9757, 800-528-1234) 102 rooms, restaurant, free breakfast, lounge, indoor pool, exercise facilities, children stay free with parents, whirlpools, a/c, TV, no-smoking rooms, TV, pets allowed, wheelchair access, pets allowed, senior citizen rates, meeting facilities, major credit cards. SGL/DBL$55-$70.

Days Inn (1073 Rte 206 North, 08505; 298-6100, Fax 298-7509, 800-325-2525) 131 rooms, restaurant, lounge, pool, children stay free with parents, room service, laundry service, a/c, TV, free local calls, no pets, wheelchair access, no-smoking rooms, senior citizen rates, meeting facilities for 250, major credit cards. SGL/DBL$49-$82.

Econo Lodge (Bordentown 08505; 298-5000, Fax 298-5009, 800-4-CHOICE) 60 rooms, restaurant, complimentary breakfast, pool, TV, children under 18 stay free with parents, pets allowed, whirlpool tub, senior citizen rates, wheelchair access, a/c, TV, major credit cards. SGL/DBL$42-$85.

Holiday Inn (Rte 206 North, 08505; 298-3200, Fax 298-8845, 800-HOLIDAY) 95 rooms, restaurant, lounge, outdoor pool, exercise facilities, children under 19 stay free with parents, wheelchair access, a/c, TV, no-smoking rooms, fax service, room service, no pets, in-room refrigerators and microwaves, laundry service, meeting facilities, senior citizen rates, major credit cards. SGL/DBL$55-$70.

Quality Inn (1083 Hwy 206, 08505; 298-3200, 800-368-5689) 100 rooms and suites, lounge, entertainment, pool, exercise facilities, children stay free with parents, a/c, TV, laundry service, no-smoking rooms, meeting facilities, major credit cards. SGL$50-$90, DBL$60-$100, AP$5.

Bridgeport
Area Code 609

Holiday Inn (Bridgeport 08014; 467-3322, Fax 467-3031, 800-HOLIDAY) 149 rooms and suites, restaurant, lounge, indoor pool, exercise facilities, children under 19 stay free with parents, wheelchair access, a/c, TV, no-smoking rooms, fax service, room service, airport transportation, no pets, laundry service, meeting facilities for 600, senior citizen rates, major credit cards. SGL/DBL$86-$120.

Bridgeton
Area Code 609

The Cohansey Hotel (11 East Broad St, 08032; 455-8600) 18 rooms, a/c, TV, in-room refrigerators and microwaves, Victorian inn, major credit cards. SGL/DBL$55-$80.

Days Inn (500 East Broad St, 08302; 455-1500, Fax 451-1556, 800-325-2525) 32 rooms, restaurant, lounge, pool, children stay free with parents, room service, laundry service, a/c, TV, free local calls, no pets, wheelchair access, no-smoking rooms, senior citizen rates, major credit cards. SGL/DBL$50-$55.

Bridgewater
Area Code 908

Best Western Inn (Rte 22W, 08807; 722-4000, Fax 722-4840, 800-722-4000, 800-528-1234) 111 rooms, restaurant, complimentary breakfast, lounge, pool, exercise facilities, children stay free with parents, a/c, TV, VCRs, no-smoking rooms, TV, wheelchair access, no pets, senior citizen rates, meeting facilities, major credit cards. SGL/DBL$48-$56.

Holiday Inn (Highway 22 East, 08807; 526-9500, Fax 526-2538, 800-HOLIDAY) 170 rooms, restaurant, lounge, outdoor pool, exercise facilities, children under 19 stay free with parents, wheelchair access, a/c, TV, no-smoking rooms, fax service, room service, no pets, laundry service, meeting facilities for 350, senior citizen rates, major credit cards. SGL/DBL$70-$95.

Brooklawn
Area Code 609

Days Inn (801 Rte 130, 08030; 456-6688, Fax 456-1413, 800-325-2525) 116 rooms, restaurant, complimentary breakfast, lounge, outdoor pool, children stay free with parents, room service, laundry service, a/c, in-room refrigerators and microwaves, TV, free local calls, no pets, wheelchair access, no-smoking rooms, senior citizen rates, major credit cards. SGL/DBL$49-$69.

Brunswick, East Brunswick & North Brunswick
Area Code 908

Motel 6 (244 Rte 18, 08816; 390-4545) 114 rooms, pool, free local calls, children under 17 stay free with parents, a/c, TV, major credit cards. SGL/DBL$36-$42.

Sheraton Inn East (195 Rte 18 South, 08816; 828-6900, Fax 937-4838, 800-325-3535) 137 rooms and suites, restaurant, lounge, outdoor pool, exercise facilities, no-smoking rooms, a/c, TV, children stay free with parents, wheelchair access, 10,000 square feet of meeting and exhibition space, 10 meeting rooms, meeting facilities for 180, major credit cards. SGL/DBL$85-$165.

Quality Inn Conference Center (Highway 1, 08902; 246-2800, 800-368-5689) 132 rooms and suites, restaurant, room service, exercise facilities, children stay free with parents, a/c, TV, laundry service, no-smoking rooms, meeting facilities, major credit cards. SGL/DBL$39-$52.

Ramada Renaissance Hotel (Three Tower Center Blvd, 08816; 828-2000, Fax 828-6958, 800-2-RAMADA) 405 rooms and suites, restaurant, lounge, indoor pool, wheelchair access, no-smoking rooms, airport transportation, free parking, pets allowed, wheelchair access, a/c, TV, room service, laundry facilities, meeting facilities, senior citizen rates, major credit cards. SGL$120-$160, DBL$140-$180.

Buena Vista
Area Code 609

Econo Lodge (146 Old Tuckahoe Rd, 08310; 697-9000, 800-4-CHOICE) 45 rooms, pool, children under 12 stay free with parents, no pets, senior citizen rates, free local calls, wheelchair access, a/c, TV, major credit cards. SGL/DBL$35-$80.

Cape May
Area Code 609

The Abbey (Columbia Ave and Gurney St, 08204; 884-4506) 14 rooms, bed and breakfast, 1869 inn, antique furnishings, no pets, in-room refrigerators, major credit cards. SGL/DBL$90-$190.

Angel Of The Sea (Five Trenton Ave, 08204; 884-3369, Fax 884-3331) 26 rooms, free breakfast, pool, no smoking, TV. SGL/DBL$125-$250.

Brass Bed Inn (719 Columbia Ave, 08204; 884-8075) 8 rooms, a/c, Victorian inn, major credit cards. SGL/DBL$65-$140.

Chalfonte Hotel (301 Howard St, 08204; 884-8409) 180 rooms, bed and breakfast, restaurant, lounge, entertainment, no pets, open May 1 to November 1, airport courtesy car, private baths, 1870s inn, major credit cards. SGL/DBL$60-$150.

Coachman's Motor Inn (205 Beach Drive, 08204; 884-8463) 65 rooms and efficiencies, restaurant, lounge, entertainment, pool, tennis court, a/c, TV, major credit cards. SGL/DBL$110-$150.

Columns By The Sea (1513 Beach Drive, 08204; 884-2228) bed and breakfast, no smoking, whirlpools, no children allowed, water view, no pets, antique furnishings, major credit cards. SGL/DBL$100-$175.

Cape May

Driftwood Motor Inn (15 Broadway, 08204; 884-8393) 17 rooms and 1- and 2-bedroom efficiencies, a/c, TV, no pets. SGL/DBL$45-$125.

Heritage Motor Inn (721 Beach Drive, 08204; 884-7342) 21 rooms and efficiencies, pool, a/c, TV, in-room refrigerators, water view, major credit cards. SGL/DBL$51-$115.

Heritage Southwinds (14 Patterson Ave, 08204; 884-4187) 17 rooms and efficiencies, a/c, TV, no pets, kitchenettes, major credit cards. SGL/DBL$46-$113.

The Humphrey Hughes House (29 Ocean St, 08204; 884-4428) bed and breakfast, no smoking, private baths, 1900s home, antique furnishings, no children allowed, major credit cards. SGL/DBL$80-$200.

The Inn Of Cape May (601 Beach Drive, 08204; 884-3500, Fax 884-0669, 800-257-0432) 78 rooms, restaurant, lounge, entertainment, pool, free breakfast, open May to late September, TV, antique furnishings, no-smoking rooms, Modified American Plan available. SGL/DBL$85-$250.

La Mer Motor Inn (Cape May 08204; 884-9000, Fax 884-5004) 67 rooms and 1- and 2-bedroom apartments, restaurant, pool, whirlpools, in-room refrigerators, airport transportation, laundry facilities, TV, VCRs, a/c. SGL/DBL$53-$138.

Mainstay Inn (635 Columbia Ave, 08240; 884-8690) 12 rooms, bed and breakfast, no smoking, April 1 to late November, 1870s inn, no children allowed, antique furnishings, no pets. SGL/DBL$95-$190.

Marquis de Lafayette Motel (501 Beach Drive, 08204; 884-0432) 73 rooms and efficiencies, restaurant, complimentary breakfast, pool, sauna, laundry facilities, a/c, TV, no-smoking rooms, wheelchair access, major credit cards. SGL/DBL$150-$250.

Montreal Inn (635 Columbia Ave, 08204; 884-7011) 70 rooms and efficiencies, restaurant, lounge, pool, exercise facilities, whirlpools, laundry facilities, a/c, TV, no pets. SGL/DBL$28-$130.

Mt. Vernon Motel (Beach Ave, 08204; 884-4665) 25 rooms and efficiencies, restaurant, pool, in-room refrigerators, a/c, TV. SGL/DBL$100-$120.

Periwinkle Inn (Cape May 08204; 884-9200) 50 rooms and efficiencies, restaurant, pool, a/c, TV, in-room refrigerators, no pets. SGL/DBL$65-$150.

Queen Victoria Inn (102 Ocean St, 08204; 884-8702) 23 rooms, complimentary breakfast, private baths, whirlpools, Victorian inn, antique furnishings, a/c, fireplaces, in-room refrigerators, no pets, major credit cards. SGL/DBL$60-$210.

Sea Crest Inn (101 Beach Ave, 08204; 884-4561) 55 rooms and 1- and 2-bedroom efficiencies, restaurant, a/c, TV, in-room refrigerators, no smoking, water view, no pets. SGL/DBL$45-$145.

Virginia Inn (25 Jackson St, 08204; 884-5700, Fax 884-1236, 800-732-4236) 24 rooms, restaurant, lounge, complimentary breakfast, 1870s inn, antique furnishings, TV, meeting facilities. SGL/DBL$130-$250.

White Dove Cottages (619 Hughes St, 08204; 884-0613) 6 1- and 2-bedroom cottages, bed and breakfast, no smoking, a/c, TV, no children allowed, private baths, antique-furnishings, no pets, 1860s home. SGL/DBL$75-$150.

Windward House (24 Jackson St, 08204; 884-3368) bed and breakfast, no pets, fireplace, private baths, no children allowed, a/c, major credit cards. SGL/DBL$80-$130.

The Wooden Rabbit (609 Hughes St, 08204; 884-7291) bed and breakfast, no smoking, private baths, no pets, a/c, TV. SGL/DBL$135-$160.

Woodleigh House (808 Washington St, 08204; 884-7123) bed and breakfast, no smoking, no pets, private baths, 1860s home, antique furnishings, major credit cards. SGL/DBL$85-$120.

Cardiff
Area Code 609

TraveLodge (1760 Tilton Rd, 08232, 641-3131, Fax 641-0555, 800-255-3050) 92 rooms, restaurant, lounge, complimentary breakfast, pool, wheelchair access, complimentary newspaper, laundry service, TV, a/c, free local calls, laundry facilities, fax service, no-smoking rooms, free in-room coffee and tea service, in-room refrigerators and microwaves, no pets. SGL/DBL$50-$80, AP$5.

Carlstadt
Area Code 201

Econo Lodge Meadowlands (395 Washington Ave, 07072; 935-4600, 800-4-CHOICE) 75 rooms, children under 12 stay free with parents, no pets, senior citizen rates, wheelchair access, a/c, TV, major credit cards. SGL/DBL$40-$60.

Carteret
Area Code 908

Holiday Inn (1000 Roosevelt Ave, 07008; 541-9500, Fax 541-9640, 800-HOLIDAY) restaurant, lounge, entertainment, outdoor pool, exercise facilities, children under 19 stay free with parents, wheelchair access, a/c, airport transportation, TV, no-smoking rooms, fax service, room service, pets allowed, laundry service, meeting facilities for 300, senior citizen rates, major credit cards. SGL/DBL$80-$110.

Chatham
Area Code 201

Grand Summit Hotel (570 Springfield Ave, 07901; 273-3000, Fax 273-4228, 800-346-0773) 145 rooms and suites, restaurant, lounge, entertainment, pool, exercise facilities, whirlpools, a/c, TV, airport transportation, gift shop. SGL/DBL$130-$150, STS$175-$750.

Cherry Hill
Area Code 609

Days Inn (Rte 28 East, 08002; 663-0100, Fax 663-6449, 800-325-2525) 50 rooms, restaurant, complimentary breakfast, lounge, pool, jacuzzi, kitchenettes, children stay free with parents, room service, laundry service, a/c, TV, free local calls, no pets, wheelchair access, no-smoking rooms, senior citizen rates, major credit cards. SGL/DBL$37-$60.

Econo Lodge New Jersey State Aquarium (Cuthbert Blvd, 08002; 665-3630, 800-4-CHOICE) 73 rooms, restaurant, lounge, pool, children under 12 stay free with parents, no pets, senior citizen rates, wheelchair access, a/c, TV, major credit cards. SGL/DBL$36-$75.

Holiday Inn (Sayer Ave, 08002; 663-5300, 800-HOLIDAY) 186 rooms, restaurant, lounge, outdoor pool, exercise facilities, children under 19 stay free with parents, wheelchair access, a/c, TV, no-smoking rooms, fax service, room service, pets allowed, laundry service, meeting facilities, senior citizen rates, major credit cards. SGL/DBL$68-$78.

Hyatt Cherry Hill (2349 West Marlton Pike, 08002; 609-662-1234, Fax 609-662-3676, 800-233-1234) 409 rooms and suites, restaurant, lounge, entertainment, outdoor pool, whirlpool, lighted tennis courts, exercise facilities, room service, TV, a/c, no-smoking rooms, wheelchair access, 11,000 square feet of meeting and exhibition space, meeting facilities for 1,500, major credit cards. SGL/DBL$75-$145.

Residence Inn (1821 Old Cuthbert Rd, 08034; 429-6111, Fax 429-0345, 800-331-3131) rooms and suites, complimentary breakfast, pool, spa, in-room refrigerators, coffee makers and microwaves, laundry facilities, free parking, TV, pets allowed, a/c, VCRs, pets allowed, fireplaces, children stay free with parents, no-smoking rooms, wheelchair access, meeting facilities, major credit cards. SGL/DBL$78-$160.

Sheraton Poste Inn (1450 Rte 70 East, 08034; 428-2300, Fax 354-7662, 800-257-8262, 800-325-3535) 213 rooms and suites, restaurant, lounge, entertainment, outdoor pool, tennis courts, exercise facilities, no-smoking rooms, a/c, TV, children stay free with parents, wheelchair access, 14,000 square feet of meeting and exhibition space, 12 meeting rooms, meeting facilities for 1,000, major credit cards. SGL/DBL$78-$110.

Chester
Area Code 908

The Publick House Inn (111 Main St, 07930; 879-6878) 10 rooms, restaurant, a/c, TV, no pets, major credit cards. SGL/DBL$60-$80.

Clark
Area Code 908

Howard Johnson Lodge (70 Central Ave, 07066; 381-6500, Fax 381-6076, 800-I-GO-HOJO) 115 rooms, restaurant, lounge, pool, children stay free with parents, wheelchair access, complimentary newspaper, no-smoking rooms, TV, a/c, no pets, free parking, meeting facilities, senior citizen rates, all major credit cards. LS SGL/DBL$49-$66; HS SGL/DBL$49-$70.

Ramada Hotel (36 Valley Rd, 07066; 574-0100, Fax 382-8742, 800-2-RAMADA) 191 rooms, restaurant, lounge, entertainment, pool, wheelchair access, no-smoking rooms, airport transportation, free parking, pets allowed, wheelchair access, a/c, in-room computer hookups, gift shop, car rental desk, game room, TV, room service, laundry facilities, meeting facilities for 550, senior citizen rates, major credit cards. SGL/DBL$49-$85.

Clifton
Area Code 201

Howard Johnson Lodge (680 Rte 3 West, 07014; 471-3800, Fax 471-3800 ext 500, 800-I-GO-HOJO) 117 rooms and suites, restaurant, lounge, pool, complimentary newspaper, free parking, children stay free with parents, wheelchair access, no-smoking rooms, TV, a/c, pets allowed, free parking, meeting facilities, senior citizen rates, meeting facilities, major credit cards. SGL$59-$85, DBL$59-$95.

Ramada Inn (265 East Rte 3, 07013; 778-6500, 800-2-RAMADA) 196 rooms, restaurant, lounge, pool, wheelchair access, no-smoking rooms, airport transportation, free parking, pets allowed, wheelchair access, a/c, TV, room service, laundry facilities, meeting facilities, senior citizen rates, major credit cards. SGL/DBL$60-$140.

Clinton
Area Code 908

Holiday Inn (Rte 173, 08809; 735-5111, 800-HOLIDAY) rooms and suites, restaurant, lounge, indoor pool, exercise facilities, children under 19 stay free with parents, wheelchair access, a/c, TV, no-smoking rooms, fax service, room service, no pets, laundry service, meeting facilities for 400, senior citizen rates, major credit cards. SGL/DBL$80-$110, STS$120-$150.

Colts Neck
Area Code 908

Colts Neck Inn (Colts Neck 07722; 409-1200, Fax 431-6640, 49 rooms and suites, restaurant, a/c, TV, no pets, whirlpools, major credit cards. SGL/DBL$65-$75.

Columbia
Area Code 908

Days Inn (State Rd 94, 07832; 496-8221, Fax 496-4809, 800-325-2525) 35 rooms, restaurant, lounge, pool, children stay free with parents, room service, laundry service, gift shop, a/c, TV, free local calls, no pets, wheelchair access, no-smoking rooms, senior citizen rates, major credit cards. SGL/DBL$35-$55.

Cookstown
Area Code 609

Days Inn (616 East Wrightstown-Cookstown Rd, 08511; 723-6500, Fax 723-7895, 800-325-2525) 102 rooms, restaurant, lounge, pool, jacuzzi, children stay free with parents, room service, laundry service, a/c, TV, free local calls, no pets, wheelchair access, no-smoking rooms, senior citizen rates, major credit cards. SGL/DBL$65-$90.

Cranford
Area Code 908

Days Inn (136 Garden State Pkwy, 07016; 272-4700, Fax 272-2065, 800-325-2525) 180 rooms, restaurant, lounge, pool, children stay free with parents, room service, laundry service, a/c, TV, free local calls, airport courtesy car, no pets, wheelchair access, no-smoking rooms, senior citizen rates, meeting facilities for 800, major credit cards. SGL/DBL$40-$90, STS$125.

Dayton
Area Code 908

Days Inn (2316 Rte 130, 08810; 329-3000, Fax 329-2548, 800-325-2525) 51 rooms, restaurant, lounge, pool, children stay free with parents, room service, laundry service, a/c, TV, free local calls, pets allowed, wheelchair access, no-smoking rooms, senior citizen rates, major credit cards. SGL/DBL$50-$65.

Denville
Area Code 201

Lakeside Bed and Breakfast (11 Sunset Trail, 07834; 625-5129) complimentary breakfast, water view, no smoking, TV, no pets. SGL/DBL$45-$50.

Eatontown
Area Code 908

Sheraton Eatontown Hotel and Conference Center (Industrial Way East, 07724; 542-6500, Fax 542-6607 800-325-3535) 208 rooms and suites, restaurant, lounge, entertainment, indoor and outdoor pool, jacuzzi, hot tubs, exercise facilities, no-smoking rooms, a/c, TV, children stay free with parents, wheelchair access, 21,000 square feet of meeting and exhibition space, meeting facilities for 1,500, major credit cards. SGL/DBL$100-$125.

Edison
Area Code 908

Clarion Hotel and Towers (2055 Lincoln Highway, 08817; 287-3500, 800-221-2222) 169 rooms, restaurant, free breakfast, lounge, pool, no pets, no-smoking rooms, children under 18 stay free with parents, senior citizen rates, complimentary newspaper, meeting facilities, a/c, TV, major credit cards. SGL$94-$104, DBL$105-$115.

Holiday Inn (Raritan Center Pkwy, 08837; 225-8300, Fax 225-0037, 800-HOLIDAY) 274 rooms, restaurant, lounge, outdoor pool, exercise facilities, children under 19 stay free with parents, wheelchair access, a/c, TV, no-smoking rooms, fax service, room service, no pets, laundry service, meeting facilities for 400, senior citizen rates, major credit cards. SGL/DBL$85-$95.

Ramada Inn Raritan Center (3050 Woodbridge Ave, 08837; 494-2000, Fax 417-1811, 800-2-RAMADA) 189 rooms, restaurant, lounge, indoor pool, wheelchair access, no-smoking rooms, airport transportation, free parking, pets allowed, transportation to local attractions, wheelchair access, a/c, TV, room service, laundry facilities, meeting facilities, senior citizen rates, major credit cards. SGL/DBL$75-$99.

Elizabeth
Area Code 908

Hampton Inn Airport (38 Spring St, 07207; 355-0500, Fax 355-4343, 800-HAMPTON) 152 rooms, restaurant, complimentary breakfast, pool, exercise facilities, children stay free with parents, no-smoking rooms, wheelchair access, computer hookups, fax service, free local calls, pets allowed, meeting facilities. SGL/DBL$50-$85.

Holiday Inn Newark Jetport (1000 Spring St, 07201; 355-1700, Fax 355-1700 ext 1170, 800-HOLIDAY) 392 rooms and suites, Concierge Floor, restaurant, lounge, indoor pool, exercise facilities, children under 12 stay free with parents, wheelchair access, no-smoking rooms, fax service, room service, gift shop, car rental desk, airport transportation, pets allowed, meeting facilities for 1,250, major credit cards. SGL/DBL$73-$115.

Sheraton Inn Newark Airport (901 Spring St, 07201; 527-1600, Fax 527-1327, 800-325-3535) 258 rooms and suites, restaurant, lounge, entertainment, indoor and outdoor pools, exercise facilities, gift shop, no-smoking rooms, wheelchair access, complimentary airport transportation, 6,225 square feet of meeting and exhibition space, 13 meeting rooms, meeting facilities for 500, major credit cards. SGL/DBL$65-$95.

Vista (1170 Spring St, 07201; 351-3900. Fax 351-9556) 376 rooms and suites, restaurant, lounge, indoor pool, airport transportation, in-room refrigerators, wheelchair access, no-smoking rooms, meeting facilities. SGL/DBL$100-$175, STS$290+.

Englewood
Area Code 201

Radisson Hotel (401 South Van Brunt St, 07631; 871-2020, Fax 871-7116, 800-777-1700) rooms and suites, restaurant, lounge, entertainment, indoor pool, wheelchair access, free parking, no-smoking rooms, TV, a/c, children under 18 stay free with parents, transportation to local attractions, pets allowed, meeting facilities, major credit cards. SGL/DBL$115-$150.

Fairfield
Area Code 201

Ramada Inn (Two Bridges Rd, 07004; 575-1742, Fax 575-9567, 800-2-RAMADA) 177 rooms, restaurant, lounge, entertainment, indoor pool, whirlpools, wheelchair access, no-smoking rooms, airport transportation, in-room refrigerators and microwaves, free parking, pets allowed, wheelchair access, a/c, TV, room service, laundry facilities, meeting facilities for 250, senior citizen rates, major credit cards. SGL/DBL$49-$99.

Sheraton Fairfield Hotel (690 Rte 46 East, 07004; 227-9200, Fax 227-4308, 800-325-3535) 205 rooms and suites, restaurant, lounge, indoor pool, sauna, exercise facilities, no-smoking rooms, a/c, TV, children stay free with parents, wheelchair access, 17,000 square feet of meeting and exhibition space, meeting facilities for 1,800, major credit cards. SGL/DBL$135-$150, STS$150-$300.

Flemington
Area Code 908

Cabbage Rose Inn (162 Main St, 08822; 788-0247) bed and breakfast, a/c, private baths, no smoking, no pets, antique furnishings, major credit cards. SGL/DBL$55-$95.

Jerica Will Bed and Breakfast (96 Broad St, 08822; 782-8234) complimentary breakfast, no smoking, no pets, fireplace, private baths, major credit cards. SGL/DBL$60-$100.

Fort Lee
Area Code 201

Days Inn (2339 Rte 4, 07024; 944-5000, Fax 944-0623, 800-325-2525) 175 rooms, restaurant, lounge, pool, children stay free with parents, room service, laundry service, a/c, TV, free local calls, no pets, wheelchair access, no-smoking rooms, senior citizen rates, major credit cards. SGL/DBL$66-$86.

Hammonton
Area Code 609

Ramada Inn (308 South White Horse Pike, 08037; 561-5700, Fax 561-2392, 800-2-RAMADA) 100 rooms, restaurant, lounge, pool, wheelchair access, no-smoking rooms, airport transportation, free parking, pets allowed, wheelchair access, laundry facilities, a/c, TV, room service, laundry facilities, meeting facilities, senior citizen rates, major credit cards. SGL$45-$60, DBL$49-$65.

East Hanover
Area Code 201

Marriott Hotel (1401 Rte 10 East, 07981; 538-8811, Fax 538-0291, 800-228-9290) 353 rooms and suites, restaurant, lounge, entertainment, indoor and outdoor pool, exercise facilities, whirlpools, jogging track, sauna, free parking, wheelchair access, TV, a/c, no-smoking rooms, gift shop, children stay free with parents, business services, meeting facilities, major credit cards. SGL/DBL$65-$105.

Ramada Inn (103 Rte 10 West, 07936; 386-5611, Fax 386-5724, 800-2-RAMADA) 255 rooms, restaurant, lounge, entertainment, wheelchair access, no-smoking rooms, airport transportation, free parking, pets allowed, wheelchair access, a/c, transportation to local attractions, TV, room service, laundry facilities, meeting facilities for 800, senior citizen rates, major credit cards. SGL$79-$115, DBL$100-$136.

Hasbrouck Heights
Area Code 201

Holiday Inn (283 Rte 17 South, 07604; 288-9600, Fax 288-4527, 800-HOLIDAY) restaurant, complimentary breakfast, lounge, outdoor pool, exercise facilities, children under 19 stay free with parents, wheelchair access, a/c, TV, no-smoking rooms, fax service, room service, no pets, laundry service, meeting facilities for 250, senior citizen rates, major credit cards. SGL/DBL$65-$95.

Sheraton Hasbrouck Heights Hotel (650 Terrace Ave, 07604; 288-6100, Fax 288-4717, 800-325-3535) 350 rooms and suites, restaurant, lounge, entertainment, outdoor pool, sauna, jacuzzi, exercise facilities, no-smoking rooms, a/c, TV, children stay free with parents, wheelchair access, 17,000 square feet of meeting and exhibition space, 16 meeting rooms, meeting facilities for 800, major credit cards. SGL/DBL$85-$135.

Hazlet
Area Code 908

Ramada Inn (2870 Hwy 35, 07730; 264-2400, Fax 739-9735, 800-2-RAMADA) 120 rooms, restaurant, lounge, entertainment, indoor pool, wheelchair access, no-smoking rooms, airport transportation, free parking, pets allowed, wheelchair access, a/c, TV, room service, laundry facilities, meeting facilities, senior citizen rates, major credit cards. SGL/DBL$45-$70.

Hope
Area Code 201

The Inn At Millrace Pond (Rte 519, 07844; 459-4884) 16 rooms and bungalows, a/c, TV, major credit cards. SGL/DBL$75-$85.

Iselin
Area Code 908

Days Inn (Rte 1 South, 08830; 634-4200, Fax 634-7840, 800-325-2525) 76 rooms and suites, restaurant, lounge, pool, children stay free with parents, room service, laundry service, a/c, TV, free local calls, no pets, wheelchair access, no-smoking rooms, senior citizen rates, major credit cards. SGL/DBL$45-$65, STS$60-$80.

Hilton Woodbridge Hotel (120 Wood Ave South, 08830; 494-6200, Fax 494-6200 ext 240, 800-HILTONS) 200 rooms and suites, restaurant, lounge, entertainment, indoor pool, exercise facilities, jacuzzi, children stay free with parents, no-smoking rooms, gift shop, VCRs, wheelchair access, pets allowed, a/c, TV, business services, meeting facilities, major credit cards. SGL/DBL$100-$115.

Sheraton Woodbridge Place Hotel (515 Rte 1 South, 08830; 634-3600, Fax 634-0258, 800-325-3535) 254 rooms and suites, restaurant, lounge, entertainment, indoor and outdoor pool, exercise facilities, jacuzzi, no-smoking rooms, a/c, TV, children stay free with parents, airport transportation, wheelchair access, 16,000 square feet of meeting and exhibition space, 15 meeting rooms, meeting facilities for 2,000, major credit cards. SGL/DBL$100-$125.

Jamesburg
Area Code 609

Holiday Inn (390 Forsgate Drive, 08831; 655-4775, 800-HOLIDAY) 150 rooms and suites, restaurant, lounge, outdoor pool, exercise facilities, children under 19 stay free with parents, wheelchair access, a/c, TV, no-smoking rooms, fax service, room service, no pets, laundry service, meeting facilities for 425, senior citizen rates, major credit cards. SGL/DBL$65-$115, STS$125.

Jersey City
Area Code 201

Quality Inn (180 12th St, 07302; 653-0300, 800-368-5689) 150 rooms and suites, restaurant, pool, room service, exercise facilities, spa, children stay free with parents, no pets, a/c, TV, laundry service, no-smoking rooms, meeting facilities, major credit cards. SGL$69-$77, DBL$74-$81.

Jobstown
Area Code 609

Belle Springs Farm (Jobstown 08041; 723-5364) bed and breakfast, no pets, fireplace, a/c. SGL/DBL$50-$85.

Kenilworth
Area Code 908

Holiday Inn (South 31st St, 07033; 241-4775, Fax 241-1413, 800-HOLIDAY) 120 rooms, restaurant, lounge, outdoor pool, whirlpools, exercise facilities, children under 19 stay free with parents, wheelchair access, a/c, TV, no-smoking rooms, fax service, room service, no pets, laundry service, meeting facilities for 250, senior citizen rates, major credit cards. SGL/DBL$80-$90.

Lakehurst
Area Code 908

Econo Lodge (2016 Hwy 37W, 08733; 657-7100, 800-4-CHOICE) 45 rooms, children under 12 stay free with parents, no pets, senior citizen rates, wheelchair access, a/c, TV, meeting facilities, major credit cards. SGL/DBL$44-$89.

Lakewood
Area Code 908

HoJo Inn (1000 Madison Ave, 08701; 364-2020, Fax 364-0257, 800-I-GO-HOJO) 50 rooms, restaurant, lounge, pool, children stay free with parents, wheelchair access, no-smoking rooms, TV, a/c, pets allowed, free parking, fax service, room service, meeting facilities, senior citizen rates, all major credit cards. SGL$45-$49, DBL$55-$59.

Lambertville
Area Code 609

The Inn at Lambertville Station (11 Bridge St, 08530; 397-4400, 800-524-1091) 45 rooms, restaurant, spa, jacuzzi, meeting facilities, a/c, TV, major credit cards. SGL/DBL$75-$100.

Lawrenceville
Area Code 609

Howard Johnson Lodge (2991 Brunswick Pike, 08648; 896-1100, Fax 895-1325, 800-I-GO-HOJO) 104 rooms, restaurant, lounge, pool, children stay free with parents, wheelchair access, no-smoking rooms, complimentary newspaper, TV, a/c, pets allowed, free parking, meeting facilities, senior citizen rates, all major credit cards. SGL$55-$85, DBL$65-$95.

Red Roof Inn (3203 Brunswick Place, 08648; 896-3388, 800-843-7663) 149 rooms, no-smoking rooms, fax service, wheelchair access, complimentary newspaper, children stay free with parents, pets allowed, free local calls, in-room computer hookups, major credit cards. SGL/DBL$45-$60.

Ledgewood
Area Code 201

Days Inn (Rte 46 West, 07852; 347-5100, Fax 347-6356, 800-325-2525) 98 rooms, restaurant, lounge, outdoor pool, exercise facilities, tennis courts, children stay free with parents, room service, laundry service, a/c, TV, free local calls, no pets, wheelchair access, no-smoking rooms, senior citizen rates, major credit cards. SGL/DBL$49-$89.

Livingston
Area Code 201

Holiday Inn (550 West Mt. Pleasant Ave, 07039; 994-3500, 800-HOLIDAY) 178 rooms and suites, restaurant, lounge, indoor pool, exercise facilities, children under 19 stay free with parents, wheelchair access, a/c, TV, no-smoking rooms, fax service, room service, no pets, laundry service, meeting facilities for 500, senior citizen rates, major credit cards. SGL/DBL$75-$105.

Long Branch
Area Code 908

Hilton Ocean Place Resort and Spa (One Ocean Blvd, 07740; 571-4000, Fax 571-3314, 800-HILTONS) 254 rooms and suites, restaurant, lounge, entertainment, indoor and outdoor pool, exercise facilities, whirlpools, lighted tennis courts, children stay free with parents, no-smoking rooms, free parking, wheelchair access, pets allowed, a/c, TV, business services, 33,000 square feet of meeting and exhibition space, major credit cards. SGL/DBL$140-$215, STS$350-$1,000.

Lyndhurst
Area Code 201

Quality Inn Sports Complex (10 Polito Ave, 07071; 933-9800, 800-368-5689) 150 rooms and suites, restaurant, complimentary breakfast, lounge, entertainment, pool, room service, exercise facilities, children stay free with parents, a/c, TV, laundry service, no-smoking rooms, meeting facilities, major credit cards. SGL/DBL$65-$80.

Mahwah
Area Code 201

Comfort Inn (160 State Rd 17 South, 07495; 512-0800, 800-221-2222) 77 rooms, restaurant, complimentary breakfast, hot tubs, wheelchair access, no-smoking rooms, no pets, children under 18 stay free with parents, senior citizen rates, a/c, TV, meeting facilities, major credit cards. SGL/DBL$55-$75.

Ramada Inn (180 Rte 17 South, 07430; 529-5880, Fax 529-4767, 800-2-RAMADA) 129 rooms and suites, restaurant, lounge, indoor pool, kitchenettes, exercise facilities, wheelchair access, no-smoking rooms, airport transportation, free parking, pets allowed, wheelchair access, a/c, TV, room service, laundry facilities, meeting facilities, senior citizen rates, major credit cards. SGL/DBL$80-$100.

Sheraton International Crossroads Hotel and Towers (One International Blvd, 07495; 529-1660, Fax 529-4709, 800-325-3535) 225 rooms and suites, restaurant, lounge, entertainment, pool, exercise facilities, hot tubs, sauna, no-smoking rooms, a/c, gift shop, TV, children stay free with parents, wheelchair access, 18,700 square feet of meeting and exhibition space, meeting facilities for 1,500, major credit cards. SGL/DBL$85-$135.

Manahawkin
Area Code 609

The Goose N'Berry Inn (190 North Main St, 08050; 597-6350) bed and breakfast, no pets, private bath, antique furnishings. SGL/DBL$43-$75.

Maple Shade
Area Code 609

Best Western Inn (Maple Shade 08052; 235-3550, 800-528-1234) 92 rooms, restaurant, complimentary breakfast, lounge, pool, exercise facilities, children stay free with parents, a/c, TV, no-smoking rooms, in-room refrigerators, TV, wheelchair access, pets allowed, senior citizen rates, meeting facilities, major credit cards. SGL/DBL$45-$55.

Landmark Inn (Maple Shade 08052; 235-6400, Fax 727-1027) 163 rooms, restaurant, lounge, entertainment, pool, exercise facilities, sauna, room service, in-room refrigerators, children under 18 stay free with parents, a/c, TV, no-smoking rooms. SGL/DBL$50-$60.

McAfee
Area Code 201

Days Inn (McAfee 07428; 827-4666, 800-325-2525) 37 rooms, restaurant, lounge, pool, children stay free with parents, room service, laundry service, a/c, TV, free local calls, no pets, wheelchair access, no-smoking rooms, senior citizen rates, major credit cards. SGL/DBL$40-$85.

Great Gorge's Mountain View (Rte 517, 07428; 827-6000) 617 rooms, restaurant, lounge, pool, jacuzzi, tennis courts, sauna, a/c, TV, room service, meeting facilities, major credit cards. SGL/DBL$125.

Middletown
Area Code 908

Howard Johnson Lodge (750 Hwy 35, 07748; 671-3400, Fax 671-3911, 800-I-GO-HOJO) 82 rooms, restaurant, lounge, pool, children stay free with parents, wheelchair access, no-smoking rooms, TV, a/c, in-room refrigerators and coffee makes, free newspaper, pets allowed, free parking, meeting facilities, senior citizen rates, all major credit cards. SGL$60-$70, DBL$64-$74.

Monmouth Junction
Area Code 908

Days Inn (4191 Rte One, 08852; 329-4555, Fax 329-1041, 800-325-2525) 73 rooms, restaurant, lounge, pool, children stay free with parents, room service, laundry service, a/c, TV, free local calls, in-room refrigerators and microwaves, no pets, wheelchair access, no-smoking rooms, senior citizen rates, major credit cards. SGL/DBL$40-$80.

Red Roof Inn (208 New Rd, 08852; 821-8800, 800-843-7663) no-smoking rooms, fax service, wheelchair access, complimentary newspaper, children stay free with parents, pets allowed, free local calls, in-room computer hookups, major credit cards. SGL/DBL$40-$53.

Montvale
Area Code 201

Ramada Inn (Chestnut Ridge Rd, 07645; 391-7700, Fax 391-6648, 800-2-RAMADA) 187 rooms and efficiencies, restaurant, lounge, entertainment, pool, exercise facilities, wheelchair access, no-smoking rooms, airport transportation, free parking, pets allowed, wheelchair access, a/c, TV, room service, laundry facilities, meeting facilities for 450, senior citizen rates, major credit cards. LS SGL/DBL$49-$59; HS SGL$75-$85, DBL$85-$95.

Morristown
Area Code 201

Governor Morris Inn (Two Whippany Rd, 07960; 539-7300) 200 rooms, pool, a/c, TV, meeting facilities, major credit cards. SGL/DBL$125.

Madison Hotel (One Convent Rd, 07960; 285-1800, 800-526-0729) 192 rooms, restaurant, pool, jacuzzi, sauna, a/c, TV, meeting facilities, major credit cards. SGL/DBL$125-$165.

Mount Holly
Area Code 609

Friendship Inn (State Rd 2, 08060; 267-7900, 800-424-4777) 47 rooms, restaurant, lounge, entertainment, pool, hot tub, exercise facilities, a/c, TV, no pets, no-smoking rooms, children stay free with parents, wheelchair access, no-smoking rooms, major credit cards. SGL/DBL$36-$44.

Howard Johnson Lodge (Rte 541, 08060; 267-6550, Fax 267-2575, 800-I-GO-HOJO) 138 rooms, restaurant, lounge, pool, children stay free with parents, wheelchair access, no-smoking rooms, TV, whirlpools, room service, a/c, no pets, free parking, meeting facilities, senior citizen rates, all major credit cards. SGL/DBL$49-$86, DBL$59-$86.

Mt. Arlington
Area Code 201

Sheraton Inn (15 Howard Blvd, 07856; 770-2000, 800-325-3535) 124 rooms and suites, restaurant, lounge, entertainment, indoor pool, exercise facilities, no-smoking rooms, a/c, TV, children stay free with parents, wheelchair access, 5,100 square feet of meeting and exhibition space, 7 meeting rooms, meeting facilities for 275, major credit cards. SGL/DBL$75-$115.

Mt. Laurel
Area Code 609

Budget Motor Lodge (Mount Laurel 08054; 235-7400, Fax 778-9729) 240 rooms, restaurant, lounge, entertainment, pool, children stay free with parent, laundry facilities, a/c, TV. SGL/DBL$38-$48.

Econo Lodge (611 Fellowship Rd, 08054; 722-1919, 800-4-CHOICE) 66 rooms, pool, children under 12 stay free with parents, no pets, senior citizen rates, wheelchair access, a/c, TV, major credit cards. SGL/DBL$36-$54.

Guest Quarters (515 Fellowship Rd North, 08054; 778-8999, 800-424-2900) 129 suites, restaurant, pool, exercise facilities, sauna, whirlpools, remote control TV, a/c, in-room refrigerators, coffee makers and microwaves, transportation to local attractions, laundry service, fax service, no-smoking rooms, wheelchair access, meeting facilities for 100, major credit cards. SGL/DBL$65-$90.

Hampton Inn (4000 Crawford Place, 08054; 778-5535, Fax 778-0377, 800-HAMPTON) 127 rooms, restaurant, complimentary breakfast, pool, exercise facilities, children under 18 stay free with parents, no-smoking rooms, wheelchair access, computer hookups, fax service, TV, a/c, free local calls, pets allowed, meeting facilities, major credit cards. SGL/DBL$65-$61.

Hilton Hotel (Mount Laurel 08054; 234-7300, Fax 866-9401, 800-HILTONS) 300 rooms and suites, restaurant, lounge, entertainment, outdoor pool, exercise facilities, children stay free with parents, no-smoking rooms, wheelchair access, pets allowed, a/c, TV, business services, meeting facilities, major credit cards. SGL/DBL$90-$130.

McIntosh Inn (Church Rd, 08054; 234-7194, 800-444-2775) 93 rooms, restaurant, no-smoking rooms, major credit cards. SGL/DBL$37-$45.

Ramada Inn (555 Fellowship Rd, 08054; 273-1900, Fax 235-5731, 800-2-RAMADA) 102 rooms, restaurant, lounge, pool, wheelchair access, no-smoking rooms, airport transportation, free parking, pets allowed, wheelchair access, a/c, TV, room service, laundry facilities, meeting facilities for 1,000, senior citizen rates, major credit cards. LS SGL$60, DBL$70; HS SGL$63, DBL$73.

TraveLodge (1111 Rte 73, 08054; 234-7000, Fax 235-3909, 800-255-3050) 250 rooms and suites, restaurant, lounge, complimentary breakfast, indoor pool, sauna, wheelchair access, complimentary newspaper, laundry service, TV, a/c, free local calls, in-room refrigerators, jogging track, fax service, no-smoking rooms, free in-room coffee and tea service, in-room refrigerators and microwaves, no pets, meeting facilities for 300, major credit cards. SGL$55-$79, DBL$60-$83, AP$5.

Neptune
Area Code 201

HoJo Inn (Rte 35, 07753; 776-9000, Fax 776-9014, 800-I-GO-HOJO) 60 rooms, restaurant, complimentary breakfast, lounge, pool, children stay free with parents, in-room refrigerators and coffee makers, wheelchair access, no-smoking rooms, TV, a/c, pets allowed, free parking, meeting facilities, senior citizen rates, all major credit cards. SGL/DBL$55-$65, DBL$65-$75.

Newark
Area Code 201

Comfort Inn International Airport (50 Port St, 07114; 344-1500, 800-221-2222) 170 rooms, restaurant, lounge, exercise center, wheelchair access, no-smoking rooms, a/c, TV, meeting facilities, major credit cards. 1 mile from the Newark International Airport, 17 miles from Manhattan, 4 miles from the downtown area. SGL$48, DBL$55-$68.

Courtyard by Marriott (600 US 1, 07114; 643-8599, Fax 648-0662, 800-321-2211) 146 rooms and suites, restaurant, lounge, indoor pool, exercise center, whirlpools, airport courtesy car, laundry service, meeting facilities, major credit cards. SGL/DBL$85-$125.

Days Inn (450 Rte 1 South, 07114; 242-0900, Fax 242-8480, 800-325-2525) 191 rooms and suites, restaurant, lounge, exercise center, in-room refrigerators and microwaves, laundry service, wheelchair access, airport courtesy car, no-smoking rooms, a/c, TV, fax service, no pets, in-room computer hookups, free parking, meeting facilities, major credit cards. 10 miles from Manhattan, 8 miles from the Midwinds Sports Center. SGL$50-$75, DBL$65-$85, STS$75-$120.

Hilton Gateway & Towers (Gateway Center, Raymond Blvd, 07102; 622-5000, Fax 824-2188, 800-HILTONS) 253 rooms and suites, restaurant, lounge, outdoor pool, exercise center, free parking, transportation to local attractions, wheelchair access, no-smoking rooms, a/c, TV, business services, meeting facilities for 450, major credit cards. 15 minutes from downtown Manhattan, 10 minutes from the Newark International Airport. SGL/DBL$99-$109.

Holiday Inn Airport (160 Holiday Plaza, 07114; 589-1000, Fax 589-2799, 800-HOLIDAY) 234 rooms and suites, restaurant, lounge, entertainment, indoor pool, whirlpools, exercise center, children under 12 stay free with parents, wheelchair access, no-smoking rooms, a/c, TV, fax service, room service, gift shop, car rental desk, airport transportation, pets allowed, 14 meeting rooms, meeting facilities for 1,400, major credit cards. 1.5 miles from the airport, 2 miles from the downtown area, 12 miles from Manhattan. SGL/DBL$65-$75.

Howard Johnson Airport (US 1 and Haynes Ave, 07114; 824-4000, 800-654-2000) 342 rooms, restaurant, lounge, pool, jacuzzi, children stay free with parents, no-smoking rooms, a/c, TV, wheelchair access, airport courtesy car, major credit cards. SGL/DBL$52-$61.

Marriott Newark Airport (Newark International Airport, 07114; 623-0006, Fax 504-6197, 800-882-1037, 800-228-9290) 600 rooms and suites, restaurant, lounge, entertainment, indoor and outdoor pool, sauna, exercise center, whirlpools, gift shop, 24-hour room service, wheelchair access, no-smoking rooms, a/c, TV, airport courtesy car, in-room refrigerators, meeting facilities, major credit cards. At the Newark International Airport, 30 minutes from downtown Manhattan. SGL$75-$95.

Newark Airport Vista (1170 Spring St, 07201; 351-3900, Fax 351-9556, 800-HILTONS) 376 rooms, restaurant, lounge, entertainment, pool, exercise center, 24-hour rooms, service, gift shop, airport transportation, wheelchair access, in-room refrigerators, no-smoking rooms, a/c, TV, business services, meeting facilities for 1,250. 1 mile from the airport. SGL/DBL$85+.

Quality Inn Park Place (50 Park Place, 07102; 622-1000, 800-228-5151, 800-221-2222) 169 rooms, restaurant, lounge, entertainment, exercise center, free parking, airport courtesy car, free parking, meeting facilities for 2,000, major credit cards. 3 miles from Newark International Airport, 15 minutes from Manhattan. SGL/DBL$35-$65.

Radisson Airport (128 Frontage Rd, 07114; 690-5500, Fax 465-7195, 800-228-9822) 500 rooms, restaurant, lounge, entertainment, indoor pool, exercise center, gift shop, wheelchair access, no-smoking rooms, a/c, TV, children stay free with parents, airport courtesy car, meeting facilities, major credit cards. SGL/DBL$110-$115.

Ramada Inn (Rte 1 South, 07114; 824-4000, Fax 824-2034, 800-2-RAMADA) 342 rooms and suites, restaurant, lounge, pool, exercise center, children under 18 stay free with parents, wheelchair access, no-smoking rooms, a/c, TV, airport transportation, 8 meeting rooms, meeting facilities for 250. 5 minutes from the Newark airport, 20 minutes from Manhattan, 15 minutes from the Meadowlands. SGL$70-$90, DBL$80-$100, STS$135+, AP$5.

New Brunswick
Area Code 908

Econo Lodge (Highway One, 08901; 828-8000, 800-4-CHOICE) 112 rooms, pool, children under 12 stay free with parents, laundry facilities, complimentary newspaper, no pets, senior citizen rates, wheelchair access, a/c, TV, major credit cards. SGL/DBL$45-$125.

Hyatt Regency New Brunswick (Two Albany St, 08901; 873-1234, Fax 873-1382, 800-233-1234) 286 rooms and suites, restaurant, lounge, entertainment, indoor pool, whirlpools, sauna, tennis courts, exercise facilities, room service, TV, a/c, no-smoking rooms, wheelchair access, 9,000 square feet of meeting and exhibition space, major credit cards. SGL/DBL$69-$159+.

North Bergen
Area Code 201

Days Inn (2750 Tonnelle Ave, 07047; 348-3600, Fax 330-8932, 800-325-2525) 250 rooms, restaurant, lounge, children stay free with parents, room service, laundry service, a/c, TV, free local calls, pets allowed, wheelchair access, no-smoking rooms, senior citizen rates, major credit cards. SGL/DBL$39-$59.

Super 8 Motel (2600 Tonnelle Ave, 07047; 866-0400, Fax 866-6007, 800-548-4206, 800-800-8000) 127 rooms and suites, outdoor pool, no pets, children under 12 stay free with parents, free local calls, a/c, TV, fax service, no-smoking rooms, senior citizen rates, wheelchair access, meeting facilities, major credit cards. SGL/DBL$55, DBL$60-$70.

Ocean City
Area Code 609

BarnaGate Bed and Breakfast (637 Wesley Ave, 08226; 391-9366) complimentary breakfast, private baths, no smoking, no pets. SGL/DBL$65-$75.

Bayberry Bed and Breakfast (604 Atlantic Ave, 08226; 398-4115) complimentary breakfast, no smoking, private baths, no pets, major credit cards. SGL/DBL$65-$90.

Carousel Hotel and Resort (118th St, 08226; 524-1000, 800-641-0011) 266 efficiencies, restaurant, lounge, entertainment, indoor pool, exercise facilities, jacuzzi, TV, tennis courts, a/c, Modified American Plan available, 15 meeting rooms, meeting facilities for 150, major credit cards. LS SGL/DBL$30-$40; HS SGL/DBL$100.

Castle In The Sand Hotel (37th St and Oceanfront, 08226; 289-6846, 800-552-SAND) 167 rooms and efficiencies, restaurant, pool, a/c, TV, meeting facilities for 200. LS SGL/DBL$65-$103; HS SGL/DBL$92-$159.

Coconut Malorie Hotel (59th St, 08226; 723-6100, 800-767-6060) 84 rooms and apartments, restaurant, in-room refrigerators and microwaves, room service, a/c, TV, major credit cards. SGL/DBL$89.

Comfort Inn Gold Coast (112th St and Coastal Highway, 08226; 524-3000, 800-221-2222) 202 rooms, restaurant, pool, jacuzzi, wheelchair access, no-smoking rooms, no pets, children under 18 stay free with parents, in-room refrigerators and microwaves, senior citizen rates, no pets, a/c, TV, meeting facilities, major credit cards. LS SGL/DBL$30-$180; HS SGL/DBL$80-$300.

Days Inn (Seventh and Boardwalk, 08226; 398-2200, Fax 391-2050, 800-325-2525) 80 rooms, restaurant, lounge, outdoor pool, children stay free with parents, room service, laundry service, a/c, TV, free local calls, no pets, wheelchair access, no-smoking rooms, senior citizen rates, major credit cards. SGL/DBL$57-$175.

Days Inn Bayside (4201 Coastal Highway, 08226; 289-6488, 800-456-DAYS, 800-325-2525) 162 rooms, restaurant, lounge, indoor pool, children stay free with parents, room service, laundry service, a/c, TV, free local calls, no pets, wheelchair access, no-smoking rooms, senior citizen rates, meeting facilities for 150, major credit cards. LS SGL/DBL$30; HS SGL/DBL$65.

Dunes Motel (27th St and the Beach, 08226; 289-4414) 103 rooms and efficiencies, restaurant, outdoor pool, in-room refrigerators, a/c, TV, open February 12 to October 31. LS SGL/DBL$25-$65; HS SGL/DBL$70-$98.

Econo Lodge (61st St and Bayside, 08226; 524-6100, 800-888-2229) 92 rooms, restaurant, outdoor pool, TV, children under 12 stay free with parents, pets allowed, senior citizen rates, a/c, in-room refrigerators and microwaves, TV, major credit cards. SGL/DBL$40-$74.

Econo Lodge Oceanside (145th St and Coastal Highway, 08226; 800-443-4557) 87 efficiencies, coffee shop, outdoor pool, water view, pool, TV, children under 12 stay free with parents, no pets, senior citizen rates, a/c, TV, major credit cards. LS SGL/DBL$46; HS SGL/DBL$116.

Empress Motel and Apartments (1910 Baltimore Ave, 08226; 289-6745) 33 rooms and 2- and 3-bedroom apartments, kitchenettes, children under 5 stay free with parents, a/c, TV, major credit cards. LS SGL/DBL$25-$76; HS SGL/DBL$80.

Enterprise Bed and Breakfast (1020 Central Ave, 08226; 398-1698) complimentary breakfast, no pets, private baths. SGL/DBL$70-$85.

Executive Motel (30th St and Baltimore Ave, 08226; 289-3101; 800-638-1600) 49 rooms, in-room refrigerators, a/c, TV, major credit cards. SGL/DBL$34-$64.

Fenwick Inn (13801 Coastal Highway, 08226; 250-1100, 800-638-1600) 201 rooms, restaurant, lounge, entertainment, indoor pool, hot tub, a/c, TV, pets allowed. LS SGL/DBL$39-$99; HS SGL/DBL$79-$159.

Flamingo Motel (3100 Baltimore Ave, 08226; 289-6464, 800-394-7465) 72 rooms and efficiencies, kitchenettes, outdoor pool, a/c, TV, open Mary to mid-October. LS SGL/DBL$45-$65; HS SGL/DBL$85-$110.

Flanders Hotel (11th St and Boardwalk, 08226; 399-1000, 800-345-0211) 219 rooms, restaurant, pool, sauna, exercise facilities, a/c, TV, beauty shop, meeting facilities, major credit cards. SGL/DBL$85-$125.

Fountain Court Motel (1900 Philadelphia Ave, 80226; 298-9131) 47 rooms, pool, a/c, TV. SGL/DBL$70.

Francis Scott Key Motel (Elm St and Rte 50, 08226; 289-7241) 130 rooms, restaurant, lounge, 2 pools, spa, transportation to local attraction, open June 15 to mid September. LS SGL/DBL$36; HS SGL/DBL$46.

French Quarter Motel (22nd St and Baltimore Ave, 08226; 289-9101) 50 rooms and efficiencies, restaurant, lounge, pool, kitchenettes, ;TV, a/c, major credit cards. SGL/DBL$45-$75, EFF$95-$650W.

New Jersey

Gateway Motel (49th St and Oceanfront, 08226; 524-6500, 800-382-2582) 60 condos, restaurant, lounge, entertainment, pool, jacuzzi, kitchenettes, beach, a/c, TV. LS SG/DBL$40-$80; HS SGL/DBL$130-$190.

Georgia Belle Hotel-Suites and Lodge (120th St, 08226; 250-4000, 800-542-4444) 105 rooms and suites, restaurant, outdoor pool, in-room refrigerators and microwaves, TV, a/c, wheelchair access. LS SGL/DBL$35; HS SGL/DBL$69.

Harrison Hall Hotel (15th St and Oceanfront, 08226; 289-6222, 800-638-2106, 800-492-3147 in Maryland) 96 rooms, restaurant, outdoor pool, jacuzzi, in-room refrigerators, open April through October, a/c, TV. LS SGL$25, DBL$35; HS SGL$47, DBL$54.

Holiday Inn Oceanfront (67th St and Oceanfront, 08226; 524-1600, 800-638-2106, 800-493-3147 in Maryland, 800-HOLIDAY) 216 efficiencies, kitchenettes, restaurant, lounge, outdoor pool, exercise facilities, children under 12 stay free with parents, game room, wheelchair access, a/c, TV, no-smoking rooms, fax, room service, no pets, laundry service, meeting facilities, senior citizen rates, major credit cards. SGL/DBL$37-$99.

Howard Johnson Lodge (12th and Ocean Avenues, 08226; 399-7800, 800-I-GO-HOJO) 74 rooms, restaurant, lounge, outdoor pool, children stay free with parents, wheelchair access, no-smoking rooms, TV, a/c, no pets, free parking, meeting facilities, senior citizen rates, all major credit cards. SGL/DBL$55-$150.

Inlet Lodge Hotel (804 South Broadway, 08226; 289-7552) 36 rooms, in-room refrigerators, TV, a/c. SGL/DBL$32-$60.

Inn Town Motel (211 North Baltimore Ave, 08226; 289-8607) 16 rooms, in-room refrigerators, a/c, TV, open May through October. SGL/DBL$65.

New Brighton Inn Bed and Breakfast (519 5th St, 08266; 399-2829) complimentary breakfast, no smoking, no pets, no children allowed, antique furnishings, major credit cards. SGL$45-$50, DBL$65-$70.

Northwood Inn (401 Wesley Ave, 08226; 399-6071) 9 rooms, bed and breakfast, no smoking, antique furnishings, 1890s home, private baths, no pets, open year-round. SGL/DBL$80-$150.

Port-A-Call Hotel (1510 Boardwalk, 08226; 399-8812) 99 rooms, restaurant, pool, sauna, a/c, TV, beauty shop, meeting facilities, major credit cards. SGL/DBL$75-$100.

Top O'The Waves (5447 Central Ave, 08226; 399-0477) bed and breakfast, no pets, private baths, beach, major credit cards. SGL/DBL$75-$175.

Ocean Grove
Area Code 201

Cordova Bed and Breakfast (26 Webb St, 07756; 774-3084) complimentary breakfast, 1890s home, antique furnishings, no pets, private baths. SGL/DBL$30-$60.

The Sampler Inn (28 Main Ave, 07756; 775-1905) bed and breakfast, no smoking, private baths, antique furnishings, no pets, major credit cards. SGL/DBL$28-$50.

Paramus
Area Code 201

Holiday Inn (50 Rte 17, 07652; 843-5400, 800-HOLIDAY) restaurant, lounge, outdoor pool, exercise facilities, children under 19 stay free with parents, wheelchair access, a/c, TV, no-smoking rooms, fax service, room service, no pets, laundry service, meeting facilities, senior citizen rates, major credit cards. SGL/DBL$70-$90.

Howard Johnson Lodge (393 Rte 17, 07653; 265-4200, Fax 265-0247, 800-I-GO-HOJO) 81 rooms, restaurant, lounge, pool, children stay free with parents, laundry facilities, complimentary newspaper, wheelchair access, no-smoking rooms, TV, a/c, pets allowed, free parking, meeting facilities, senior citizen rates, meeting facilities, major credit cards. SGL$48-$65, DBL$58-$73.

Radisson Hotel (601 From Rd, 07652; 262-6900, Fax 262-4955, 800-777-1700) rooms and suites, restaurant, lounge, entertainment, pool, wheelchair access, free parking, no-smoking rooms, TV, a/c, children stay free with parents, pets allowed, major credit cards. SGL/DBL$

Park Ridge
Area Code 201

Marriott Park Ridge Hotel (300 Brae Blvd, 07656; 307-0800, Fax 307-0859, 800-228-9290) 289 rooms and suites, restaurant, lounge, entertainment, indoor and outdoor pools, exercise facilities, whirlpools, jogging track, sauna, free parking, wheelchair access, TV, a/c, no-smoking rooms, gift shop, children stay free with parents, business services, meeting facilities, major credit cards. SGL/DBL$80-$165.

Parsippany
Area Code 201

Concord Place (Cherry Hill Rd, 07054; 263-0095, Fax 263-6133, 800-843-7522) 110 rooms, restaurant, lounge, entertainment, exercise facilities, a/c, TV, kitchenettes, room service, whirlpools, major credit cards. SGL/DBL$75-$95.

Days Inn (3159 Rte 46, 07054; 335-0200, Fax 263-3094, 800-325-2525) 121 rooms and suites, restaurant, pool, jacuzzi, in-room refrigerators and microwaves, wheelchair access, no-smoking rooms, pets allowed, fax service, laundry service, meeting facilities, major credit cards. SGL$45-$65, DBL$50-$70, STS$70-$110.

Embassy Suites (909 Parsippany Blvd, 07054; 334-1440, Fax 402-1188, 800-EMBASSY) 274 two-room suites, restaurant, lounge, complimentary breakfast, lounge, pool, whirlpool, exercise facilities, sauna, room service, laundry service, wheelchair access, complimentary newspaper, complimentary local calls, no-smoking rooms, gift shop, transportation to local attractions, business services, meeting facilities, major credit cards. SGL/DBL$45-$75.

HoJo Inn (625 Rte 46 East, 07054; 882-8600, Fax 882-3493, 800-I-GO-HOJO) 118 rooms, restaurant, lounge, swimming pool, children stay free with parents, wheelchair access, no-smoking rooms, fax, TV, a/c, no pets, free parking, meeting facilities, senior citizen rates, major credit cards. SGL/DBL$45-$60.

Holiday Inn (707 Rte 46 East, 07054; 263-2000, Fax 220-9020, 800-HOLIDAY) 193 rooms and suites, restaurant, lounge, indoor pool, exercise facilities, children under 12 stay free with parents, TV, a/c, wheelchair access, no-smoking rooms, fax service, room service, gift shop, car rental desk, airport transportation, pets allowed, meeting facilities, major credit cards. SGL/DBL$80-$120.

Howard Johnson Lodge (949 Rte 46, 07054; 335-5100, Fax 335-4525, 800-I-GO-HOJO) 72 rooms, restaurant, complimentary breakfast, lounge, pool, jacuzzi, room service, children stay free with parents, wheelchair access, no-smoking rooms, TV, a/c, pets allowed, free parking, meeting facilities, senior citizen rates, major credit cards. SGL/DBL$35-$65, DBL$40-$70.

Parsippany Hilton (One Hilton Court, 07054; 267-7373, Fax 984-6853, 800-HILTONS) 508 rooms and suites, 2 restaurants, 2 lounges, indoor and outdoor swimming pools, TV, a/c, jacuzzi, jogging track, exercise facilities, tennis courts, wheelchair access, no-smoking rooms, free parking, business services, transportation to local attractions, children stay free with parents, meeting facilities for 1,250, major credit cards. SGL/DBL$100-$139.

Red Roof Inn (855 Rte 46, 07054; 334-3737, Fax 334-1984, 800-843-7663) 68 rooms, no-smoking rooms, fax service, wheelchair access, complimentary newspaper, free local calls, in-room computer hookups, major credit cards. SGL/DBL$35-$45.

Sheraton Tara Hotel (199 Smith Rd, 07054; 515-2000, Fax 515-9798, 800-325-3535) 391 rooms and suites, restaurant, lounge, indoor and outdoor pool, sauna, exercise facilities, no-smoking rooms, a/c, TV, children stay free with parents, wheelchair access, 22,000 square feet of meeting and exhibition space, meeting facilities for 1,000, major credit cards. SGL/DBL$67-$117.

Penns Grove
Area Code 609

Holiday Inn (Penns Grove 08069; 299-4400, Fax 299-7532, 800-HOLIDAY) restaurant, lounge, outdoor pool, exercise facilities, children under 19 stay free with parents, wheelchair access, a/c, TV, no-smoking rooms, fax service, room service, no pets, laundry service, meeting facilities, senior citizen rates, major credit cards. SGL/DBL$75-$85.

Howard Johnson Lodge and Suites (10 Howard Johnson Lane, 08069; 299-3800, Fax 299-6982, 800-I-GO-HOJO) 142 rooms, restaurant, complimentary breakfast, lounge, pool, exercise facilities, laundry service, in-room refrigerators, children stay free with parents, wheelchair access, no-smoking rooms, TV, fax service, a/c, pets allowed, free parking, meeting facilities, senior citizen rates, all major credit cards. SGL$50-$94, DBL$55-$104.

Phillipsburg
Area Code 908

Howard Johnson Lodge (Highways 22 and I-78, 08865; 454-6461, 800-800-I-GEM, 800-I-GO-HOJO) 72 rooms, restaurant, lounge, pool, jacuzzi, children stay free with parents, wheelchair access, no-smoking rooms, TV, a/c, pets allowed, fax service, free parking, meeting facilities, senior citizen rates, all major credit cards. SGL$45-$55, DBL$65-$75.

Piscataway
Area Code 908

Embassy Suites (121 Centennial Ave, 08854; 980-0500, Fax 980-9473, 800-EMBASSY) 2-room suites, restaurant, lounge, complimentary breakfast, lounge, pool, whirlpool, exercise facilities, sauna, room service, laundry service, wheelchair access, complimentary newspaper, free local calls, no-smoking rooms, gift shop, transportation to local attractions, business services, meeting facilities, major credit cards. SGL/DBL$140-$150.

Motel 6 (1012 Stelton Rd, 08854; 981-9200) 136 rooms, pool, free local calls, children under 17 stay free with parents, a/c, TV, major credit cards. SGL/DBL$35-$41.

Plainfield, South Plainfield & North Plainfield
Area Code 908

Days Inn (2989 Hamilton Blvd, 07080; 753-8900, 800-325-2525) 143 rooms and suites, restaurant, lounge, pool, jacuzzi, children stay free with parents, room service, laundry service, a/c, TV, free local calls, no pets, wheelchair access, no-smoking rooms, senior citizen rates, major credit cards. SGL/DBL$54-$69, STS$84-$94.

Holiday Inn (4701 Stellon Rd South, 07080; 753-5500, Fax 753-5500 ext 620, 800-HOLIDAY) 173 rooms, restaurant, lounge, entertainment, outdoor pool, exercise facilities, children under 19 stay free with parents, in-room refrigerators and microwaves, wheelchair access, a/c, TV, no-smoking rooms, fax service, room service, no pets, laundry service, meeting facilities for 300, senior citizen rates, major credit cards. SGL/DBL$80-$94.

Howard Johnson Lodge (West End Ave, 07060; 853-6500, Fax 753-6791, 800-I-GO-HOJO) 70 rooms, restaurant, lounge, pool, free breakfast, complimentary newspaper, children stay free with parents, wheelchair access, no-smoking rooms, TV, a/c, pets allowed, free parking, meeting facilities, senior citizen rates, all major credit cards. SGL$52-$75, DBL$52-$79.

Howard Johnson Lodge (I-287 and Stellon Rd, 07080; 561-4488, Fax 561-4488 ext 261, 07060; 853-6500, 800-I-GO-HOJO) 100 rooms, restaurant, lounge, pool, complimentary breakfast, complimentary newspaper, children stay free with parents, wheelchair access, no-smoking rooms, complimentary newspaper, in-room refrigerators and microwaves, TV, a/c, pets allowed, free parking, meeting facilities, senior citizen rates, all major credit cards. SGL/DBL$39-$64.

Pleasantville
Area Code 609

Comfort Inn Victorian (1175 Black Horse Pike, 08232; 646-8880, 800-221-2222) 117 rooms, restaurant, pool, wheelchair access, no-smoking rooms, transportation to local attractions, no pets, children under 18 stay free with parents, senior citizen rates, a/c, TV, meeting facilities, major credit cards. LS SGL/DBL$45-$100; HS SGL/DBL$60-$125.

Days Inn Pleasantville (6708 Tilton Rd, 08232; 641-4500, 800-325-2525) 168 rooms and suites, restaurant, lounge, pool, children stay free with parents, room service, laundry service, a/c, TV, free local calls, no pets, in-room refrigerators and microwaves, wheelchair access, no-smoking rooms, senior citizen rates, major credit cards. SGL/DBL$45-$110, STS$70-$135.

Sheraton Admiral Royalty (1165 Black Horse Pike, 08232; 272-0200, 800-228-9290, 800-325-3535) 213 rooms and suites, restaurant, lounge, pool, exercise facilities, jacuzzi, airport transportation, no-smoking rooms, a/c,

TV, children stay free with parents, wheelchair access, meeting facilities, major credit cards. SGL/DBL$75-$115.

Point Pleasant Beach
Area Code 908

Point Beach Motel (Point Pleasant Beach 08742; 892-5100) 24 rooms, pool, children stay free with parents, a/c, TV, in-room refrigerators, major credit cards. SGL/DBL$95-$115.

Princeton
Area Code 609

Rental and Reservation Services

Peacock Inn Association (20 Bayard Lane, 08540; 924-1707).

◻ ◻ ◻

Best Western Palmer Inn (3499 Rte 1 South, 08540; 452-2500, 800-528-1234) restaurant, complimentary breakfast, lounge, outdoor pool, exercise facilities, children stay free with parents, a/c, TV, no-smoking rooms, TV, wheelchair access, pets allowed, senior citizen rates, meeting facilities, major credit cards. SGL/DBL$48-$68.

Hyatt Regency Princeton (102 Carnegie Center, 08540; 987-1234, Fax 987-2584, 800-233-1234) 348 rooms and suites, restaurant, lounge, entertainment, indoor pool, whirlpools, sauna, tennis courts, exercise facilities, room service, TV, a/c, no-smoking rooms, wheelchair access, 22,000 square feet of meeting and exhibition space, major credit cards. SGL/DBL$145-$185, STS$200-$350.

Marriott Forrestal Village Hotel (201 Village Blvd, 08540; 452-7900,Fax 452-1223, 800-228-9290) 196 rooms and suites, restaurant, lounge, entertainment, indoor and outdoor pools, exercise facilities, whirlpools, sauna, free parking, wheelchair access, TV, a/c, no-smoking rooms, gift shop, children stay free with parents, business services, meeting facilities, major credit cards. SGL/DBL$155-$175.

Peacock Inn (20 Bayard Lane, 08540; 924-1707) 16 rooms, complimentary breakfast, restaurant, a/c, TV, 1770s inn, antique furnishings. SGL/DBL$85-$125.

Ramada Hotel (Rte 1 and Ridge Rd, 08540; 452-2400, Fax 452-2494, 800-2-RAMADA) 244 rooms and suites, restaurant, lounge, entertainment, indoor pool, wheelchair access, no-smoking rooms, airport transportation, free parking, pets allowed, wheelchair access, a/c, TV, room service, in-room refrigerators, gift shop, laundry facilities, 10 meeting rooms, meeting facilities for 600, senior citizen rates, major credit cards. SGL/DBL$90-$110.

Residence Inn (4225 Rte 1, 08540; 329-9600, Fax 329-8422, 800-331-3131) rooms and suites, complimentary breakfast, outdoor pool, spa, in-room refrigerators, coffee makers and microwaves, laundry facilities, free parking, TV, a/c, VCRs, pets allowed, fireplaces, children stay free with parents, no-smoking rooms, wheelchair access, meeting facilities for 40, major credit cards. SGL/DBL$140.

Scanticon Princeton (105 College Rd East, 08540; 452-7800) 300 rooms, restaurant, lounge, entertainment, pool, sauna, lighted tennis courts, room service, a/c, gift shop, TV, meeting facilities, major credit cards. SGL/DBL$95-$160.

Ramsey
Area Code 201

Howard Johnson Lodge (1255 Rte 17 South, 07446; 327-4500, 800-I-GO-HOJO) 50 rooms, restaurant, complimentary breakfast, lounge, pool, children stay free with parents, wheelchair access, no-smoking rooms, TV, a/c, in-room refrigerators and microwaves, pets allowed, free parking, meeting facilities, senior citizen rates, all major credit cards. LS SGL$45-$70, DBL$55-$80; HS SGL$45-$80, DBL$55-$90.

Red Bank
Area Code 201

Courtyard by Marriott (225 Half Mile Rd, 07701; 530-5552, Fax 530-5756, 800-321-2211) 146 rooms and suites, restaurant, lounge, pool, exercise facilities, whirlpools, children stay free with parents, laundry service, meeting facilities, senior citizen rates, major credit cards. SGL/DBL$82-$102.

Oyster Point Hotel (14 Bodman Place, 07701; 530-8200, 800-345-3484) 58 rooms, restaurant, jacuzzi, exercise facilities, a/c, TV, in-room refrigerators, children stay free with parents, meeting facilities, major credit cards. SGL/DBL$95-$160.

Rochelle Park
Area Code 201

Ramada Hotel (375 West Passaic St, 07662; 845-3400, Fax 845-0412, 800-2-RAMADA) 175 rooms and suites, restaurant, lounge, entertainment, indoor pool, wheelchair access, no-smoking rooms, airport transportation, free parking, pets allowed, wheelchair access, a/c, TV, room service, laundry facilities, meeting facilities for 250, senior citizen rates, major credit cards. SGL/DBL$59-$117, DBL$70-$138, STS$150.

Rockaway
Area Code 201

Howard Johnson Lodge (I-80 and Hibernia Rd, 07866; 625-1200, Fax 625-1200 ext 350, 800-I-GO-HOJO) 64 rooms, restaurant, complimentary breakfast, lounge, pool, children stay free with parents, fax service, wheelchair access, no-smoking rooms, TV, a/c, pets allowed, free parking, meeting facilities, senior citizen rates, all major credit cards. LS SGL/DBL$55-$65, HS SGL/DBL$71-$82.

The Mountain Inn (Rockaway 07866; 627-8310, Fax 627-0556) 110 rooms and efficiencies, restaurant, lounge, complimentary breakfast, pool, a/c, TV, children stay free with parents, laundry facilities, major credit cards. SGL/DBL$45-$60.

Runnemede
Area Code 609

Comfort Inn (101 Ninth Ave, 08078; 939-6700, 800-221-2222) 40 rooms, restaurant, exercise facilities, wheelchair access, no-smoking rooms, no pets, children under 18 stay free with parents, senior citizen rates, a/c, TV, meeting facilities, major credit cards. SGL/DBL$50-$75, AP$5.

Holiday Inn (109 Ninth Ave, 08070; 939-4200, Fax 939-3761, 800-HOLIDAY) rooms and suites, restaurant, complimentary breakfast, lounge, outdoor pool, exercise facilities, children under 19 stay free with parents, wheelchair access, a/c, TV, no-smoking rooms, fax service, room service, no pets, laundry service, meeting facilities for 250, senior citizen rates, major credit cards. SGL/DBL$75-$95.

Rutherford & East Rutherford
Area Code 201

Days Inn (850 Rte 120, 07073; 800-325-2525) 140 rooms and suites, restaurant, lounge, exercise facilities, children stay free with parents, room service, laundry service, a/c, TV, free local calls, pets allowed, wheelchair access, no-smoking rooms, senior citizen rates, major credit cards. SGL/DBL$45-$79, STS$79-$89.

Sheraton Meadowlands (Two Meadowlands Plaza, 07073; 896-0500, Fax 896-9696, 800-325-3535) 430 rooms and suites, restaurant, lounge, indoor pool, exercise facilities, whirlpools, sauna, no-smoking rooms, a/c, TV, airport transportation, children stay free with parents, wheelchair access, 22,000 square feet of meeting and exhibition space, meeting facilities for 2,000, major credit cards. SGL/DBL$125-$150.

Saddle Brook
Area Code 201

Holiday Inn (50 Kenney Place, 07662; 843-0600, Fax 843-7172, 800-HOLIDAY) 144 rooms and suites, restaurant, lounge, entertainment, outdoor pool, exercise facilities, children under 19 stay free with parents, wheelchair access, a/c, TV, no-smoking rooms, fax service, in-room coffee makers, room service, pets allowed, laundry service, meeting facilities, senior citizen rates, major credit cards. SGL/DBL$100-$110, STS$150.

Howard Johnson Plaza-Hotel (129 Pehle Ave, 07662; 845-7800, Fax 845-7061, 800-I-GO-HOJO) 147 rooms, restaurant, lounge, indoor and outdoor pool, exercise facilities, spa, children stay free with parents, wheelchair access, airport courtesy car, no-smoking rooms, TV, a/c, pets allowed, free parking, meeting facilities, senior citizen rates, meeting facilities, major credit cards. SGL/DBL$49-$110.

Marriott Hotel (Garden State Pkwy and Hwy 80, 07662; 843-9500, Fax 843-7760, 800-228-9290) 281 rooms and suites, restaurant, lounge, entertainment, indoor and outdoor pools, exercise facilities, whirlpools, game room, sauna, wheelchair access, TV, a/c, no-smoking rooms, gift shop, free parking, children stay free with parents, business services, meeting facilities, major credit cards. SGL/DBL$145-$450.

Salem
Area Code 609

Brown's Historic House (41-43 Market St, 08079; 935-8595) 6 rooms, complimentary breakfast, 1730s home, no smoking, major credit cards. SGL/DBL$65.

Tide Mill Farm (100 Tide Mill Rd, 08079; 935-2798) 7 rooms, bed and breakfast, 1840s home, no pets, private baths, no children allowed, water view. SGL/DBL$55-$65.

Seaside Park
Area Code 908

Island Beach Motor Lodge (Seaside Park 08752; 793-5400) 59 rooms and efficiencies, pool, a/c, TV, in-room refrigerators, laundry facilities. SGL/DBL$80-$140.

Windjammer Motel (Central Ave, 08752; 830-2555) 63 rooms and efficiencies, restaurant, lounge, pool, kitchenettes, a/c, TV, major credit cards. SGL/DBL$90-$125.

Secaucus
Area Code 201

Days Inn (Harmon Meadow Blvd, 07094; 617-8888, 800-325-2525) 165 rooms and suites, restaurant, lounge, exercise facilities, children stay free with parents, room service, laundry service, a/c, TV, free local calls, gift shop, no pets, wheelchair access, no-smoking rooms, senior citizen rates, major credit cards. SGL/DBL$66-$122, STS$122-$135.

Embassy Suites (455 Plaza Drive, Secaucus 07094; 864-7300, Fax 864-5391, 800-EMBASSY) 261 2-room suites, restaurant, lounge, complimentary breakfast, lounge, pool, whirlpool, exercise facilities, sauna, room service, laundry service, wheelchair access, free newspaper, free local calls, no-smoking rooms, gift shop, transportation to local attractions, business services, meeting facilities, major credit cards. SGL/DBL$159-$179.

Hampton Inn (250 Harmon Meadows Blvd, 07094; 867-4400, Fax 865-7932, 800-HAMPTON) 151 rooms, restaurant, complimentary breakfast, pool, exercise facilities, children under 18 stay free with parents, no-smoking rooms, wheelchair access, computer hookups, fax service, TV, a/c, free local calls, pets allowed, meeting facilities, major credit cards. SGL/DBL$55-$81.

Hilton Meadowlands Hotel (Two Harmon Plaza, 07094; 348-6900, Fax 864-0963, 800-HILTONS) 295 rooms and suites, restaurant, lounge, entertainment, outdoor pool, exercise facilities, jogging track, laundry facilities, children stay free with parents, no-smoking rooms, wheelchair access, pets allowed, a/c, free parking, airport transportation, TV, business services, meeting facilities, major credit cards. SGL/DBL$125-$155.

Holiday Inn Harmon Meadow (300 Plaza Drive, 07094; 348-2000, Fax 348-6035, 800-HOLIDAY) 159 rooms and suites, restaurant, lounge, exercise facilities, boutiques, children under 19 stay free with parents, wheelchair access, a/c, TV, no-smoking rooms, fax service, room service, no pets, laundry service, meeting facilities for 200, senior citizen rates, major credit cards. SGL/DBL$125-$150.

Ramada Plaza Suite Hotel Six (350 Rte 3, 07094; 863-8700, Fax 863-6209, 800-544-9772) 151 2-room suites, restaurant, lounge, indoor pool, exercise facilities, laundry service, in-room refrigerators and coffee makers, wheelchair access, no-smoking rooms, airport transportation, free parking, pets allowed, wheelchair access, a/c, TV, room service, laundry facilities, meeting facilities, senior citizen rates, major credit cards. SGL$99-$149, DBL$109-$159, AP$15.

Short Hill
Area Code 201

Hilton At Short Hill (41 JFK Pkwy, 07078; 379-0100, 800-HILTONS) 300 rooms and suites, restaurant, lounge, entertainment, outdoor pool, exercise facilities, jacuzzi, sauna, beauty shop, airport courtesy car, children stay free with parents, no-smoking rooms, wheelchair access, pets allowed, a/c, TV, business services, meeting facilities, major credit cards. SGL/DBL$145-$165.

Somerset
Area Code 908

Hilton Hotel (200 Atrium Drive, 08873; 469-2600, Fax 560-8043, 800-HILTONS) 361 rooms and suites, restaurant, lounge, entertainment, indoor and outdoor pool, exercise facilities, tennis courts, whirlpools, sauna, children stay free with parents, no-smoking rooms, free parking, wheelchair access, pets allowed, a/c, TV, business services, meeting facilities, major credit cards. SGL/DBL$105-$175, STS$175-$250.

Holiday Inn (195 Davidson Ave, 08873; 356-1700, Fax 356-0939, 800-HOLIDAY) 280 rooms and suites, restaurant, lounge, entertainment, outdoor pool, exercise facilities, children under 19 stay free with parents, wheelchair access, a/c, TV, no-smoking rooms, fax service, room service, no pets, laundry service, meeting facilities for 500, senior citizen rates, major credit cards. SGL/DBL$75-$95.

Marriott Hotel (110 Davidson Ave, 08873; 560-0500, Fax 560-3669, 800-228-9290) 435 rooms and suites, restaurant, lounge, entertainment, indoor and outdoor pool, exercise facilities, whirlpools, sauna, game room, free parking, wheelchair access, TV, a/c, no-smoking rooms, gift shop, children stay free with parents, business services, meeting facilities, major credit cards. SGL/DBL$80-$130.

Quality Inn (1850 Easton Ave, 08873; 469-5050, 800-368-5689) 99 rooms and suites, restaurant, pool, room service, exercise facilities, children stay free with parents, a/c, TV, laundry service, no-smoking rooms, meeting facilities, major credit cards. SGL/DBL$53-$70.

Ramada Inn (Weston Canal St, 08873; 560-9880, Fax 356-7455, 800-2-RAMADA) 126 rooms, restaurant, lounge, indoor pool, wheelchair access, no-smoking rooms, airport transportation, free parking, pets allowed, wheelchair access, a/c, in-room refrigerators, microwaves and coffee makers, TV, room service, laundry facilities, meeting facilities, senior citizen rates, major credit cards. SGL$50-$105, DBL$60-$120.

Summerfield Suites Hotel (260 Davidson Ave, 08873; 356-8000, Fax 356-0782, 800-833-4353) 1- and 2-bedroom suites, complimentary breakfast, pool, whirlpools, exercise facilities, VCRs, TV, a/c, no-smoking rooms, major credit cards. SGL/DBL$119-$159.

Somers Point
Area Code 609

Econo Lodge (21 McArthur Blvd, 08244; 927-3220, 800-4-CHOICE) 50 rooms, pool, children under 12 stay free with parents, no pets, senior citizen rates, wheelchair access, a/c, TV, major credit cards. SGL/DBL$32-$90.

Residence Inn (900 Mays Landing Rd, 08244; 927-6400, 800-331-3131) rooms and suites, complimentary breakfast, pool, spa, golf course, in-room refrigerators, coffee makers and microwaves, laundry facilities, free parking, TV, a/c, VCRs, pets allowed, pets allowed, fireplaces, children stay free with parents, no-smoking rooms, wheelchair access, meeting facilities for 40, major credit cards. SGL/DBL$80.

Somerville
Area Code 908

Best Western Red Bull (1271 Hwy 22, 08876; 722-4000, 800-528-1234) 112 rooms, restaurant, complimentary breakfast, lounge, pool, exercise facilities, children stay free with parents, a/c, TV, no-smoking rooms, TV, wheelchair access, pets allowed, senior citizen rates, meeting facilities, major credit cards. SGL/DBL$60-$70.

Days Inn Hillsborough (118 Rte 206 South, 08876; 685-9000, Fax 685-0601, 800-325-2525) 102 rooms, restaurant, lounge, outdoor pool, children stay free with parents, room service, laundry service, a/c, TV, free local calls, no pets, wheelchair access, no-smoking rooms, senior citizen rates, major credit cards. SGL/DBL$60-$75.

Springfield
Area Code 201

Holiday Inn (304 Rte 22 West, 07081; 376-9400, Fax 376-9543, 800-HOLIDAY) rooms and suites, restaurant, lounge, entertainment, outdoor pool, exercise facilities, children under 19 stay free with parents, wheelchair access, a/c, TV, no-smoking rooms, fax service, room service, pets allowed, laundry service, meeting facilities for 200, senior citizen rates, major credit cards. SGL/DBL$65-$85.

Spring Lake & Spring Lake Heights
Area Code 908

The Breakers Hotel (1507 Ocean Ave, 07080; 449-7700) 70 rooms and suites, restaurant, pool, spa, exercise facilities, jacuzzi, whirlpools, transportation to local attractions, in-room refrigerators, beach, water view, a/c, TV, meeting facilities, major credit cards. SGL/DBL$130-$160, STS$175-$275.

The Chateau (500 Warren Ave, 07762; 974-2000) 35 rooms, complimentary breakfast, a/c, TV, in-room refrigerators, 1880s home, water view, major credit cards. SGL/DBL$84-$120.

Comfort Inn (1909 State Rd 35, 08=7762; 449-6146, 800-221-2222) 70 rooms, restaurant, complimentary breakfast, pool, exercise facilities, wheelchair access, no-smoking rooms, no pets, children under 18 stay free with parents, senior citizen rates, a/c, TV, meeting facilities, major credit cards. LS SGL$45-$70, DBL$50-$85; HS SGL/DBL$92-$115, AP$10.

Days Inn (2035 Hwy 35, 07719; 449-3676, Fax 449-1379, 800-325-2525) 48 rooms, restaurant, lounge, outdoor pool, children stay free with parents, room service, laundry service, a/c, TV, free local calls, no pets, wheelchair access, no-smoking rooms, senior citizen rates, major credit cards. LS SGL$35-$45, DBL$40-$55; HS SGL$50-$75, DBL$55-$79.

Hewitt Wellington Hotel (200 Monmouth Ave, 07719; 974-1212) 29 rooms and suites, restaurant, lounge, complimentary breakfast, pool, in-room refrigerators, a/c, TV, 1880s inn, meeting facilities, major credit cards. SGL/DBL$110-$170.

Mike Doolan's (Spring Lake Heights 07762; 449-3666, Fax 449-2601) 60 rooms, restaurant, free breakfast, lounge, entertainment, pool, exercise facilities, sauna, whirlpools, meeting facilities. SGL/DBL$80-4105.

Normandy Inn (21 Tuttle Ave, 07762; 449-7172, Fax 449-1070) 18 rooms, complimentary breakfast, 1880s home, antique furnishings, TV. SGL/DBL$90-$150.

Sea Crest By the Sea (19 Tuttle Ave, 07762; 449-9031) bed and breakfast, no smoking, private baths, antique furnishing, no pets, major credit cards. SGL/DBL$35-$150.

Shoreham Hotel (115 Monmouth Ave, 07762; 449-7100, 800-648-4175) 107 rooms and suites, restaurant, complimentary breakfast, lounge, pool, exercise facilities, whirlpools, laundry service, transportation to local attraction, room service, major credit cards. SGL/DBL$75-$200.

Stanhope
Area Code 201

The Whistling Swan Inn (110 Main St, 07874; 347-6369) 10 rooms and suites, complimentary breakfast, children stay free with parents, airport transportation, antique furnishing, no smoking, major credit cards. SGL/DBL$65-$96.

Stewartsville
Area Code 908

Stewart Inn (Stewartsville 08886; 479-6060, Fax 459-5889) 8 rooms, complimentary breakfast, pool, no smoking. SGL/DBL$85-$135.

Stockton
Area Code 609

Woolverton Inn (Six Woolverton Rd, 08559; 397-0802) 12 rooms, bed and breakfast, no pets, private baths, Victorian home, antique furnishings, on 10 acres, private baths, major credit cards. SGL/DBL$75-$125.

Stone Harbor
Area Code 609

Desert Sand Resort (79th St, 08202; 368-5133, 800-458-6008) 89 rooms and suites, pool, whirlpools, exercise facilities, laundry facilities, a/c, TV, meeting facilities, major credit cards. SGL/DBL$100-$150.

Teaneck
Area Code 201

Marriott Glenpointe Hotel (100 Frank West Burr Blvd, 07666; 836-0600, Fax 836-0638, 800-228-9290) 345 rooms and suites, restaurant, lounge, entertainment, pool, exercise facilities, spa, whirlpools, free parking, wheelchair access, TV, a/c, no-smoking rooms, gift shop, children stay free with parents, business services, 22,000 square feet of meeting and exhibition space, major credit cards. SGL/DBL$105-$125.

Tenafly
Area Code 201

Clinton Inn (145 Dean Drive, 07670; 871-3200, 800-275-4411) 112 rooms and suites, restaurant, a/c, TV, exercise facilities, room service, wheelchair access, no-smoking rooms, meeting facilities, major credit cards. SGL/DBL$100-$275.

Thorofare
Area Code 609

Quality Inn (101 Grove Rd, 08086; 848-4111, 800-368-5689) 100 rooms and suites, restaurant, pool, room service, exercise facilities, children stay free with parents, a/c, TV, laundry service, no-smoking rooms, meeting facilities, major credit cards. SGL/DBL$55-$75.

Tinton Falls
Area Code 908

The Appleton Inn (600 Hope Rd, 07724; 389-2100, 800-542-7753) 122 rooms, pool, a/c, TV, meeting facilities, major credit cards. SGL/DBL$90-$105.

Days Inn (11 Centre Plaza, 07724; 389-4646, Fax 389-4509, 800-325-2525) 120 rooms, restaurant, lounge, pool, children stay free with parents, room service, laundry service, a/c, TV, free local calls, pets allowed, wheelchair access, no-smoking rooms, senior citizen rates, major credit cards. SGL/DBL$52-$62.

Holiday Inn (700 Hope Rd, 07724; 544-9300, Fax 544-0570, 800-HOLIDAY) 171 rooms, restaurant, lounge, outdoor pool, exercise facilities, children under 19 stay free with parents, wheelchair access, gift shop, a/c, TV, no-smoking rooms, fax service, room service, no pets, laundry service, meeting facilities for 400, senior citizen rates, major credit cards. SGL/DBL$75-$95.

Residence Inn (90 Park Rd, 07724; 389-8100, Fax 389-1573, 800-331-3131) rooms and suites, complimentary breakfast, pool, spa, in-room refrigerators, coffee makers and microwaves, laundry facilities, free parking, TV, a/c, VCRs, pets allowed, fireplaces, children stay free with parents, no-smoking rooms, wheelchair access, meeting facilities for 40, major credit cards. SGL/DBL$65-$125.

Toms River
Area Code 908

Holiday Inn (290 Hwy 37 East, 08753; 244-4000, Fax 244-4000 ext 520, 800-HOLIDAY) 124 rooms, restaurant, lounge, entertainment, indoor pool, exercise facilities, sauna, whirlpools, children under 19 stay free with parents, wheelchair access, a/c, TV, no-smoking rooms, fax service, in-room refrigerators and microwaves, room service, no pets, laundry service, meeting facilities for 400, senior citizen rates, major credit cards. SGL/DBL$75-$105.

Howard Johnson (955 Hooper Ave, 08753; 244-1000, Fax 505-3194, 800-I-GO-HOJO) 96 rooms, restaurant, lounge, entertainment, indoor pool, children stay free with parents, wheelchair access, no-smoking rooms, TV, a/c, pets allowed, free parking, meeting facilities, senior citizen rates, all major credit cards. SGL$60-$65, DBL$65-$75.

Quality Inn (915 State Rd 37 West, 08755; 341-2400, 800-368-5689) 100 rooms and suites, restaurant, pool, sauna, room service, exercise facilities, children stay free with parents, a/c, TV, laundry service, no-smoking rooms, meeting facilities, major credit cards. LS SGL/DBL$60-$129; HS SGL/DBL$88-$159.

Ramada Inn (2373 Rte Nine, 08755; 905-2626, Fax 905-8735, 800-2-RAMADA) 102 rooms, restaurant, lounge, entertainment, pool, exercise facilities, wheelchair access, no-smoking rooms, airport transportation, free parking, pets allowed, wheelchair access, a/c, TV, room service, laundry facilities, meeting facilities, senior citizen rates, major credit cards. SGL/DBL$59-$72.

Totowa
Area Code 201

Holiday Inn (One Rte 46 West, 07512; 785-9000, 800-HOLIDAY) 155 rooms, restaurant, lounge, entertainment, outdoor pool, exercise facilities, children under 19 stay free with parents, wheelchair access, a/c, TV, no-smoking rooms, fax service, room service, no pets, laundry service, meeting facilities for 300, senior citizen rates, major credit cards. SGL/DBL$87-$100.

Vineland
Area Code 609

Days Inn (Landis Ave, 08360; 696-5000, Fax 692-6006, 800-325-2525) 106 rooms and efficiencies, restaurant, lounge, pool, children stay free with parents, room service, laundry service, a/c, game room, TV, free local calls, no pets, wheelchair access, no-smoking rooms, senior citizen rates, major credit cards. SGL/DBL$50-$56.

Ramada Inn (2216 West Landis Ave, 08360; 696-3800, Fax 696-2371, 800-2-RAMADA) 103 rooms, restaurant, lounge, entertainment, outdoor pool, wheelchair access, no-smoking rooms, airport transportation, free parking, pets allowed, wheelchair access, a/c, TV, room service, laundry facilities, meeting facilities, senior citizen rates, major credit cards. SGL/DBL$50-$70.

Wall
Area Code 908

Econo Lodge (Wall 07727; 938-3110, 800-4-CHOICE) 30 rooms and 2-room suites, children under 12 stay free with parents, no pets, senior citizen rates, wheelchair access, a/c, TV, major credit cards. SGL/DBL$45-$75.

Warren
Area Code 908

Somerste Hills (200 Liberty Corner Rd, 07060; 647-6700, Fax 647-8053, 800-688-0700) 111 rooms and suites, restaurant, lounge, entertainment, pool, exercise facilities, a/c, TV, gift shop, major credit cards. SGL/DBL$90-$150.

Wayne
Area Code 201

Holiday Inn (334 Hwy 46E, 07470; 256-7000, 890-5406, 800-HOLIDAY) 140 rooms, restaurant, lounge, entertainment, outdoor pool, exercise facilities, children under 19 stay free with parents, wheelchair access, a/c, TV, no-smoking rooms, fax, room service, no pets, laundry service, meeting facilities, senior citizen rates, major credit cards. SGL/DBL$80-$100.

Howard Johnson (1850 Hwy 23, 07470; 696-8060, Fax 696-8050 ext 555, 800-I-GO-HOJO) 151 rooms and efficiencies, restaurant, lounge, pool, children stay free with parents, wheelchair access, no-smoking rooms, TV, a/c, pets allowed, free parking, meeting facilities, senior citizen rates, meeting facilities, major credit cards. SGL/DBL$53-$70.

Weehawken
Area Code 201

Ramada Suite Hotel at Lincoln Harbor Five (500 Harbor Blvd, 07087; 617-5600, Fax 617-5627, 800-2-RAMADA) 246 rooms and 2-room suites, restaurant, complimentary breakfast, lounge, entertainment, indoor pool, wheelchair access, in-room refrigerators, microwaves and coffee makers, no-smoking rooms, airport transportation, free parking, pets allowed, wheelchair access, a/c, TV, room service, laundry facilities, meeting facilities, senior citizen rates, major credit cards. SGL/DBL$58-$108.

West Atlantic City
Area Code 609

Comfort Inn West (Black Horse Pike, 08232; 645-1818, 800-458-1138, 800-221-2222) 200 rooms, restaurant, outdoor pool, hot tubs, in-room coffee makers, wheelchair access, no-smoking rooms, no pets, children under 18 stay free with parents, senior citizen rates, a/c, TV, meeting facilities, major credit cards. SGL/DBL$49-$130.

Hampton Inn (210 Black Horse Pike, 08232; 484-1900, Fax 383-0731, 800-HAMPTON) 143 rooms, restaurant, complimentary breakfast, pool, exercise facilities, children under 18 stay free with parents, airport transportation, no-smoking rooms, wheelchair access, computer hookups, transportation to local attractions, fax service, TV, a/c, free local calls, pets allowed, meeting facilities, major credit cards. LS SGL$49, DBL$56; HS SGL$53, DBL$60-$65.

Sheraton Inn West (6821 Black Horse Pike, 08232; 272-0200, Fax 646-3703, 800-782-9237, 800-325-3535) 213 rooms and suites, restaurant, lounge, entertainment, outdoor pool, exercise facilities, no-smoking rooms, a/c, TV, children stay free with parents, wheelchair access, 9,000 square feet of meeting and exhibition space, 8 meeting rooms, meeting facilities for 300, major credit cards. SGL/DBL$65-$85.

Westfield
Area Code 908

Best Western Inn (240 North Ave, 07090, 800-528-1234) 40 rooms and efficiencies, restaurant, complimentary breakfast, lounge, pool, exercise facilities, children stay free with parents, a/c, TV, no-smoking rooms, TV, wheelchair access, pets allowed, laundry facilities, senior citizen rates, meeting facilities, major credit cards. SGL/DBL$80-$100.

West Long Branch
Area Code 908

Ramada Inn Monmouth Park (West Long Branch 07764; 229-9000, Fax 229-7565, 800-2-RAMADA) 100 rooms, restaurant, lounge, entertainment, pool, wheelchair access, no-smoking rooms, airport transportation, free parking, pets allowed, wheelchair access, a/c, TV, room service, laundry facilities, meeting facilities for 300, senior citizen rates, major credit cards. SGL/DBL$59-$95.

Wildwood, Wildwood Crest & North Wildwood
Area Code 609

Acropolis Motor Inn (3rd Ave, 08260; 522-5400) restaurant, pool, limousine service, water view, TV, a/c, room service, senior citizen discounts.

Apollo/St. Paul Motel (St. Paul Ave, 08260; 522-9300) rooms, suites and 2-bedroom apartments, a/c, TV, game room, outdoor pool, laundry facilities, free parking, open May to October. LS SGL/DBL$36-$70; HS SGL/DBL$73-$126.

Aquarius (4712 Ocean Ave, 08260; 729-0054) 27 rooms and efficiencies, restaurant, pool, in-room refrigerators, a/c, TV, laundry facilities, major credit cards. SGL/DBL$100-$165.

The Candlelight Inn (2310 Central Ave, 08260; 522-6200) 7 rooms, complimentary breakfast, whirlpools, 1905 inn, antique furnishings, no smoking, a/c, major credit cards. SGL/DBL$80-$105.

Chez Alain Apartments, Cottages and Rooms (325 East 26th Ave, 08260; 729-5813) rooms, cottages and apartments, in-room refrigerators, TV, free parking, a/c. SGL/DBL$195W-$375W.

Crusader Resort Motor Inn (6101 Ocean Ave, 08260; 522-6991, 800-462-3260) 61 rooms and suites, restaurant, pool, sauna, a/c, TV, laundry facilities, gift shop, meeting facilities. SGL/DBL$110-$165.

Days Inn (4610 Ocean Ave, 08360; 522-0331, 800-325-2525) 36 rooms, restaurant, lounge, pool, children stay free with parents, room service, laundry service, a/c, TV, free local calls, no pets, wheelchair access, no-smoking rooms, senior citizen rates, major credit cards. LS SGL$62, DBL$69; HS SGL$125-$155, DBL$130-$175.

Grand Hotel (Wildwood Crest 08260; 729-6000, 800-582-5991 in New Jersey, 800-257-855) rooms and efficiencies, restaurant, lounge, entertainment, indoor and outdoor pool, in-room refrigerators, TV, a/c, gift shop. senior citizen rates, major credit cards. SGL/DBL$55-$110.

Heart of Wildwood Motel (3915 Ocean Ave, 08260; 522-4090) rooms and 1- and 2-room efficiencies, 2 pools, TV, a/c, in-room refrigerators, free parking, open May 1 to October 1, major credit cards. LS SGL/DBL$30-$70; HS SGL/DBL$70-$150.

Jolly Roger Motel (6805 Atlantic Ave, 08260; 522-6915) 74 rooms and efficiencies, restaurant, pool, tennis, a/c, TV, in-room refrigerators, laundry facilities. SGL/DBL$85-$135.

Le Voyageur Motel (232 East Andrew Ave, 08260; 522-6407) rooms and 2-room suites, outdoor pool, free parking, in-room refrigerators, TV, a/c, open April to October. LS SGL/DBL$35; HS SGL/DBL$65.

Marlborough Apartments (215 East Roberts Ave, 08260; 522-8018) rooms and 1-, 2- and 3-bedroom apartments, a/c, free parking, TV, open May 1 to October 1, private baths. SGL/DBL$250W-$650W.

Newport Motel (4900 Ocean Ave, 08260; 522-4911) 35 rooms and efficiencies, pool, in-room refrigerators, a/c, TV. SGL/DBL$75-$125.

Oakview Hotel (315 East Oak Ave, 08260; 522-2768) 2-room apartments, TV, a/c, in-room refrigerators, open May 15 to September 30. SGL/DBL$315W-$380W.

Ocean Holiday Motor Inn (Rosemary Rd, 08260; 729-2900, 800-321-6232) 2-room suites and efficiencies, outdoor pool, laundry facilities, game room, a/c, TV, open April 1 to October 1. LS SGL/DBL$20-$40; HS SGL/DBL$44-$95.

Ocean Towers condos (5301 Ocean Ave, 08260; 301-649-3184) 1- and 2-bedroom condos, TV, a/c, pool, sauna, exercise facilities, no pets, water view. SGL/DBL$400W-$1000W.

Pan American Motor Inn (5901 Ocean Ave, 08260; 552-6939) 78 rooms, pool, a/c, TV, meeting facilities. SGL/DBL$75-$100.

Park Lane Motel (5900 Ocean Ave, 08260; 522-5900) 36 rooms and efficiencies, restaurant, pool, in-room refrigerators, a/c, TV. SGL/DBL$100-$120.

Port Royal Motor Inn (6805 Ocean Ave, 08260; 729-2000) 100 rooms, pool, beach, open May 6 to mid-October, meeting facilities. SGL/DBL$75-$100.

Quebec Motel (Atlantic Ave, 08260; 522-4664, 800-432-6774) rooms and suites, outdoor pool, a/c, TV, in-room refrigerators, meeting facilities, open year-round.

Reges Motel (Trenton Rd, 08260; 729-9300) rooms and 2-room apartments, heated outdoor pool, game room, laundry facilities, a/c, TV, water view.

Rio Motel (4850 Ocean Ave, 08260; 522-1461) rooms and efficiencies, outdoor pool, a/c, TV, gift shop, game room, open April 15 to October 1, meeting facilities. LS SGL/DBL$35-$65, EFF$650W-$750W; HS SGL/DBL$62-$95.

Rosemont Hotel (230 East Glenwood Ave, 08260; 522-6204) open June through September. SGL$20.

Royal Hawaiian (Wildwood Crest 08260; 522-3414) 88 rooms, restaurant, pool, laundry facilities, beach, a/c, TV, in-room refrigerators, major credit cards. SGL/DBL$95-$135.

Sand Castle Motel (7400 Ocean Ave, 08260; 522-6946) rooms and efficiencies, restaurant, outdoor pool, a/c, TV, in-room refrigerators, open May 1 to October 10, major credit cards. LS SGL/DBL$26; HS SGL/DBL$65.

Saratoga Inn (7505 Ocean Ave, 08260; 522-7712) rooms and 2-room efficiencies, restaurant, outdoor pool, in-room refrigerators, open May 1 to October 15, major credit cards. LS SGL/DBL$28; HS SGL/DBL$68.

Satellite Resort Motel (5909 Atlantic Ave, 08260; 522-5650) rooms and efficiencies, pool, in-room refrigerators and microwaves, children stay free with parents. SGL/DBL$35-$80.

Sea Gull Motel (5305 Atlantic Ave, 08260; 522-3333) rooms and efficiencies, pool, in-room refrigerators, a/c, TV, free parking. EFF$62-$42.

Waikiki Motor Inn (6211 Ocean Ave, 08260; 522-0115, Fax 523-8817, 800-622-5642) 55 rooms, efficiencies and suites, restaurant, pool, sauna, in-room refrigerators, a/c, TV, major credit cards. SGL/DBL$125-$15-.

Williamstown
Area Code 609

HoJo Inn (105 North Blackhorse Pike, 08094; 728-8000, Fax 875-6162, 800-I-GO-HOJO) 25 rooms, restaurant, lounge, pool, children stay free with parents, wheelchair access, no-smoking rooms, TV, a/c, no pets, free parking, meeting facilities, senior citizen rates, all major credit cards. LS SGL$40-$75, DBL$45-$85; HS SGL$45-$85, DBL$44-$95.

Windsor & East Windsor
Area Code 609

Days Inn (460 Rte 33, 08520; 448-3200, Fax 443-8535, 800-325-2525) 100 rooms and suites, restaurant, lounge, pool, children stay free with parents, room service, laundry service, a/c, TV, free local calls, no pets, wheelchair access, no-smoking rooms, senior citizen rates, major credit cards. SGL$40-$55, DBL$55-$65, STS$75-$90.

Ramada Inn (399 Monmouth St, 08520; 448-7000, 800-2-RAMADA) 200 rooms, restaurant, lounge, entertainment, pool, wheelchair access, no-smoking rooms, airport transportation, free parking, pets allowed, wheelchair access, a/c, TV, room service, laundry facilities, meeting facilities, senior citizen rates, major credit cards. SGL$55-$65, DBL$65-$75.

Woodbine
Area Code 609

Ludlam Inn (Woodbine 08270; 861-5847) bed and breakfast, no pets, private baths, 1700s home, no pets, children stay free with parents, major credit cards. SGL/DBL$20-$95.

Woodbridge
Area Code 908

Budget Motor Lodge (350 Hwy 9N, 07095; 636-4000, Fax 636-0636) 168 rooms, restaurant, a/c, TV, exercise facilities, laundry facilities, meeting rooms, wheelchair access, no-smoking rooms, major credit cards. SGL/DBL$40-$53.

Woodcliff Lake
Area Code 201

Hilton Hotel (200 Tice Blvd, 07675; 391-3600, Fax 391-3600 ext 502, 800-HILTONS) 336 rooms and suites, restaurant, lounge, entertainment, indoor and outdoor pools, jogging track, exercise facilities, tennis courts, children stay free with parents, no-smoking rooms, wheelchair access, pets allowed, a/c, free parking, TV, business services, meeting facilities, major credit cards. SGL/DBL$125-$155.

Wrightstown
Area Code 609

Days Inn (Rte 616 East, 08562; 723-6900, Fax 724-0054, 800-325-2525) 90 rooms, restaurant, lounge, pool, children stay free with parents, room service, laundry service, a/c, TV, free local calls, pets allowed, wheelchair access, no-smoking rooms, senior citizen rates, major credit cards. SGL/DBL$59-$85.

New York

Acra
Area Code 315

Acra Manor (Acra, 12405; 622-3253) 13 rooms, restaurant, lounge, entertainment, indoor pool, jacuzzi, sauna, water view, open year-round. SGL/DBL$45-$65.

Forstl's Cottages (Star Rte, 12405; 622-3556) rooms and 2-bedroom chalets, kitchenettes, pool, laundry facilities, on 135 acres. SGL/DBL$95-$135.

Lange's Grove Side (Rte 23, 12405; 622-3393) 23 rooms, restaurant, pool, jacuzzi, a/c, TV, Modified American Plan available, major credit cards. SGL/DBL$32-$72.

New Mohican House (Old Rte 23, 12405; 622-9802) bed and breakfast, pool, open year-round, major credit cards. SGL/DBL$48-$68.

Adams & Adams Center
Area Code 315

Cozy Rest Motel (Rte 11, 13605; 232-4811) 10 rooms, open April to October, a/c, TV. SGL/DBL$30-$50.

DeHart's Motel (Rte 11, 13606; 583-5612) 10 rooms, restaurant, a/c, open May 1 to November 1, TV. SGL/DBL$30-$60.

Hotel Adams (Four West Church St, 13605; 232-2623) 14 rooms, restaurant, lounge, open year-round. SGL/DBL$15-$50.

Afton
Area Code 607

Farm Jericho Inn (155 East Main St, 13730; 639-1842) 5 rooms, bed and breakfast, open year-round. SGL/DBL$35-$50.

Diamond Motel (Rte 20, Alden 14004; 937-9150) 7 rooms, no-smoking rooms, a/c, TV, wheelchair access, free parking, major credit cards. SGL/DBL$28-$38.

Albany
Area Code 518

Albany Inn (1579 Central Ave, 12205; 869-8471, 800-273-6855) 60 rooms, no-smoking rooms, wheelchair access, a/c, TV, major credit cards. SGL/DBL$40-$60.

Albany Travelers Motor Inn (1620 Central Ave, 12205; 456-0222) 102 rooms, exercise facilities, no-smoking rooms, major credit cards. SGL/DBL$40-$60.

Ambassador Motor Inn (1600 Central Ave, 12205; 456-8982, 800-950-STAY) 56 rooms, no-smoking rooms, a/c, TV, pets allowed, major credit cards. SGL/DBL$40-$60.

Blue Bell Motel (1927 Central Ave, 12205; 456-1330) 48 rooms and efficiencies, kitchenettes, pets allowed, major credit cards. SGL/DBL$25-$40.

Central Motel (1384 Central Ave, 12205; 459-3300, 800-540-6108) 31 rooms. SGL/DBL$35-$65.

Cocca's Motel (2 Wolf Rd, 12205; 459-2240) 36 rooms, no-smoking rooms, a/c, TV. SGL/DBL$25-$40.

Colonie Motel (1901 Central Ave, 12205; 456-1304) 48 rooms and efficiencies, kitchenettes, pets allowed, major credit cards. SGL/DBL$25-$40.

Comfort Inn (2800 East Trucumcari Blvd, 88401; 800-221-2222) 55 rooms, restaurant, indoor pool, wheelchair access, no-smoking rooms, no pets, children under 18 stay free with parents, kitchenettes, laundry facilities, gift shop, senior citizen rates, a/c, TV, exercise facilities, major credit cards. SGL$63-$90, DBL$68-$95.

Comfort Inn Airport (Albany-Shaker Rd, 12110; 783-1216, 99 800-221-2222) restaurant, pool, wheelchair access, no-smoking rooms, pets allowed, children under 18 stay free with parents, senior citizen rates, laundry facilities, airport transportation, a/c, TV, meeting facilities, major credit cards. SGL/DBL$54-$63.

Days Inn (16 Wolf Rd, 12205; 459-3600, Fax 459-3677, 800-325-2525) 167 rooms, restaurant, lounge, pool, children stay free with parents, room service, laundry service, airport courtesy car, a/c, TV, free local calls, no pets, wheelchair access, no-smoking rooms, senior citizen rates, major credit cards. SGL/DBL$48-$80.

Days Inn (Rte 9W, 12077; 465-8811, 800-325-2525) 100 rooms, restaurant, lounge, pool, children stay free with parents, room service, laundry service, a/c, TV, free local calls, no pets, wheelchair access, no-smoking rooms, senior citizen rates, major credit cards. SGL/DBL$54-$80.

The Desmond Hotel (660 Albany-Shaker Rd, 12211; 869-8100) 322 rooms, restaurant, lounge, indoor pool, gift shop, airport transportation, no pets, whirlpools, TV, a/c, no-smoking rooms, wheelchair access, Modified American Plan available, major credit cards. SGL/DBL$115-$130.

Econo Lodge (300 Broadway, 12207; 434-4111, 800-333-1177, 800-4-CHOICE) 135 rooms, restaurant, lounge, complimentary breakfast, pool, TV, children under 12 stay free with parents, pets allowed, senior citizen rates, wheelchair access, a/c, transportation to local attractions, major credit cards. SGL/DBL40-$60.

Econo Lodge (1632 Central Ave, 12205; 456-8811, 800-4-CHOICE) 100 rooms, complimentary breakfast, pool, children under 12 stay free with parents, pets allowed, senior citizen rates, wheelchair access, a/c, TV, major credit cards. SGL/DBL$39-$75.

Empire State Inn (1606 Central Ave, 12205; 869-5327) 50 rooms, restaurant, lounge, no-smoking rooms, a/c, TV, major credit cards. SGL/DBL$35-$55.

Hampton Inn (10 Ulenski Dr., 12205; 438-2822, Fax 438-2822 ext 610, 800-HAMPTON) 155 rooms, restaurant, complimentary breakfast, pool, exercise facilities, children under 18 stay free with parents, no-smoking rooms, wheelchair access, in-room computer hookups, fax service, TV, VCRs, a/c, free local calls, pets allowed, meeting facilities, major credit cards. SGL/DBL$66-$78.

Hilton Hotel (Ten Eyck Plaza, 12207; 462-6611, Fax 462-2901, 800-HILTONS) 387 rooms and suites, restaurant, lounge, entertainment, indoor pool, exercise facilities, children stay free with parents, no-smoking rooms, gift shop, free parking, car rental desk, airport courtesy car, limousine service, wheelchair access, pets allowed, a/c, TV, business services, meeting facilities, major credit cards. SGL/DBL$65-$135, STS$145-$250.

Holiday Inn (205 Wolf Rd, 12205; 458-7250, Fax 458-7377, 800-HOLIDAY) 309 rooms, restaurant, lounge, outdoor pool, exercise facilities, whirlpools, lighted tennis courts, airport transportation, children under 19 stay free with parents, wheelchair access, a/c, airport transportation, TV, no-smoking rooms, fax service, room service, no pets, laundry service, meeting facilities for 800, senior citizen rates, major credit cards. SGL/DBL$72-$150.

Howard Johnson Lodge (416 Southern Blvd, 12209; 462-6555, Fax 462-2547, 800-562-7253, 800-I-GO-HOJO) 177 rooms, restaurant, lounge, pool, hot tubs, tennis courts, laundry facilities, children stay free with parents, pets allowed, wheelchair access, no-smoking rooms, TV, a/c, free parking, senior citizen rates, meeting facilities for 200, major credit cards. SGL$50-$150, DBL$67-$175.

Howard Johnson Hotel (1614 Central Ave, 12205; 869-0281, Fax 869-9205, 800-I-GO-HOJO) 154 rooms, restaurant, lounge, pool, children stay free with parents, wheelchair access, no-smoking rooms, TV, a/c, pets allowed, free parking, senior citizen rates, major credit cards, meeting facilities for

200, major credit cards. LS SGL$45-$75, DBL$52-$95; HS SGL$57-$95, DBL$62-$105.

Jeremy's Inn (500 Northern Blvd, 12204; 462-5562) 69 rooms, restaurant, lounge, kitchenettes, in-room refrigerators, no-smoking rooms, a/c, TV, major credit cards. SGL/DBL$35-$55.

Journey's End Motel (100 Watervliet Ave, 12205; 800-668-4200) complimentary breakfast, TV, a/c, free local calls, senior citizen rates, major credit cards. SGL/DBL$60-$70.

Marriott Hotel (189 Wolf Rd, 12205; 458-8444, Fax 458-7365, 800-443-8952, 800-541-1881 in New York, 800-228-9290) 360 rooms and suites, restaurant, lounge, entertainment, indoor pool, exercise facilities, whirlpools, sauna, jogging track, airport courtesy car, free parking, wheelchair access, TV, a/c, no-smoking rooms, pets allowed, gift shop, children stay free with parents, business services, meeting facilities, major credit cards. SGL/DBL$99-$157.

Motel 6 (100 Watervliet Ave, 12206; 438-7447) 100 rooms, pool, free local calls, children under 17 stay free with parents, a/c, TV, major credit cards. SGL/DBL$37-$42.

Northway Inn (1517 Central Ave, 12205; 869-0277, Fax 869-0097) 84 rooms, restaurant, lounge, entertainment, pool, no pets, a/c, TV, major credit cards. SGL/DBL$45-$110.

Omni Albany Hotel (State and Lodges Streets, 12207; 462-6611, 800-THE-OMNI) 386 rooms and suites, restaurant, lounge, entertainment, indoor pool, sauna, exercise facilities, limousine service, laundry service, wheelchair access, airport transportation, no pets, no-smoking rooms available, a/c, TV, major credit cards. SGL/DBL$120-$155.

Pine Haven Bed and Breakfast (531 Western Ave, 12203; 482-1574) free breakfast, no smoking, no pets, Victorian home. SGL/DBL$50-$65.

Quality Inn (1 Watervliet Ave, 12206; 438-8431, Fax 438-8356, 800-368-5689) 217 rooms and suites, restaurant, indoor and outdoor pools, room service, exercise facilities, children stay free with parents, a/c, TV, laundry service, no-smoking rooms, pets allowed, kitchenettes, meeting facilities, major credit cards. SGL/DBL$63-$92.

Quality Inn Airport (622 Watervliet Ave, 12205; 459-1971, 800-368-5689) 56 rooms and suites, restaurant, room service, exercise facilities, children stay free with parents, a/c, TV, in-room refrigerators, lighted tennis court, pets allowed, laundry service, no-smoking rooms, meeting facilities, major credit cards. SGL/DBL$49-$90.

Ramada Inn (1228 Western Ave, 12203; 489-2981, Fax 489-8967, 800-2-RAMADA) 195 rooms, restaurant, complimentary breakfast, lounge, indoor pool, exercise facilities, sauna, barber and beauty shop, airport transportation, no-smoking rooms, airport transportation, free parking, pets allowed, wheelchair access, a/c, TV, room service, laundry facilities, meeting facilities for 400, senior citizen rates, major credit cards. SGL/DBL$59-$79.

Red Roof Inn (188 Wolf Rd, 12205; 459-1971, 800-843-7663) 116 rooms, no-smoking rooms, fax service, wheelchair access, complimentary newspaper, children stay free with parents, pets allowed, free local calls, in-room computer hookups, major credit cards. SGL/DBL$38-$72.

Residence Inn (1 Residence Inn Dr., 12110; 783-0600, 800-331-3131) rooms and suites, complimentary breakfast, pool, spa, whirlpools, airport transportation, in-room refrigerators, coffee makers and microwaves, laundry facilities, free parking, TV, a/c, VCRs, pets allowed, fireplaces, children stay free with parents, airport transportation, no-smoking rooms, wheelchair access, meeting facilities, major credit cards. SGL/DBL$130-$160.

Sheraton Inn Albany Airport (200 Wolf Rd, 12205; 458-1000, 800-325-3535) 153 rooms and suites, restaurant, lounge, pool, exercise facilities, no-smoking rooms, a/c, TV, children stay free with parents, wheelchair access, meeting facilities, major credit cards. SGL/DBL$89.

State Street Mansion (281 State St, 12210; 462-6780) 12 rooms, bed and breakfast, wheelchair access. SGL/DBL$40-$60.

Suisse Chalet (44 Wolf Rd, 12205; 459-5670, 800-5-CHALET) 97 rooms, no-smoking rooms, a/c, TV, wheelchair access, pets allowed, senior citizen rates, major credit cards. SGL/DBL$40-$60.

The Thruway Inn (1375 Washington Ave, 12206; 459-3100) 213 rooms, restaurant, lounge, outdoor pool, no-smoking rooms, wheelchair access, transportation to local attraction, major credit cards. SGL/DBL$55-$85.

Tom Sawyer Motor Inn (1444 Western Ave, 12203; 438-3594, Fax 438-1453) 85 rooms, restaurant, lounge, pool, a/c, TV, no pets. SGL/DBL$52-$76.

Tomkins Motel (1922 Central Ave, 12205; 456-12205) 13 rooms, in-room refrigerators, pets allowed, airport transportation, major credit cards. SGL/DBL$25-$40.

Travelers Motor Inn (1630 Central Ave, 12205; 456-0222, Fax 452-1376) 102 rooms, restaurant, exercise facilities, whirlpools, TV, VCRs, a/c, no pets. SGL/DBL$49-$99.

Western Motel (2019 Western Ave, 12203; 456-7241) SGL/DBL$54-$64.

Alder Creek
Area Code 315

Alder Creek Golf Club and Country Inn (Rte 13, 13301; 831-5222) 5 rooms, bed and breakfast, restaurant, open year-round. SGL/DBL$48-$60.

Alexandria Bay
Area Code 315

Alexandria Motel (122 Church St, 13607; 482-2515) 38 rooms, restaurant, TV, a/c, open May 15 to October 15. SGL/DBL$34-$44.

The Boardwalk Resort (41 Walton St, 13607; 482-9371) 20 rooms, a/c, TV, pets allowed, open April 15 to October 31. SGL/DBL$47-$165.

Bonnie Castle Resort (Holland St, 13607; 482-4511, 800-955-4511) 139 rooms and suites, restaurant, lounge, indoor and outdoor pools, wheelchair access, a/c, TV, tennis courts, no pets, open year-round, major credit cards. SGL/DBL$119-$275.

Bridgeview Motel (Rte 12, 13607; 482-9961, 800-253-9229) 117 rooms, restaurant, lounge, pool, a/c, TV, no pets, wheelchair access. SGL/DBL$40-$45.

Captain Thomson's Resort (1 James St, 13607; 482-2281) 12 rooms, water view, a/c, TV, no pets, open May to October 30. SGL/DBL$59-$165.

Channelside Motel (Point Vivian Rd, 13607; 482-2281) 12 rooms, a/c, TV, no pets, open May to November. SGL/DBL$49-$65.

Edgewood Resort (Edgewood Park, 13607; 482-9922) 160 rooms, restaurant, lounge, outdoor pool, a/c, TV, pets allowed, wheelchair access. SGL/DBL$49-$149.

El Patio Motel (38 Walton St, 13607; 482-4778) 8 rooms, a/c, TV, pets allowed, wheelchair access, open May to October. SGL/DBL$45-$60.

Fisherman's Wharf Motel (15 Sisson St, 13607) 482-2230) 24 rooms, lounge, TV, open April to October, pets allowed. SGL/DBL$25-$50.

Fitz-Inn (Rte 26, 13607; 482-2641) 10 rooms and efficiencies, lounge, TV, pets allowed, open May 1 to November 1. SGL/DBL$25-$50.

Hill's Motor Court (24 Bethune St, 13607) 482-2741, 800-447-2741) 14 rooms and efficiencies, TV, a/c, no pets, open May 15 to October 15. SGL/DBL$38-$90.

Ledges Resort (Alexandria Bay 13607) 482-9334) 24 rooms and efficiencies, a/c, TV, no pets, open May 1 to October 15. SGL/DBL$58-$108.

Ledges Resort (Alexandria Bay 13607) 482-9334) 24 rooms and efficiencies, a/c, TV, no pets, open May 1 to October 15. SGL/DBL$58-$108.

Maple Crest Motel (11 Crossmon St, 13607) 482-9518) 15 rooms, a/c, TV, no pets, open year-round. SGL/DBL$40-$55.

North Star Motel (Rte 12, 13607) 482-9332, 800-243-STAR) 30 rooms, efficiencies and cabins, a/c, TV, pool, pets allowed, wheelchair access. SGL/DBL$30-$100.

Pine Tree Resort (Alexandria Bay 13607) 482-9911, 800-ALEX-BAY) 83 rooms and 2-bedroom apartments, restaurant, lounge, entertainment, pool, sauna, whirlpools, pets allowed, airport transportation, TV, a/c, major credit cards. SGL/DBL$45-$180.

Pinehurst On The St Lawrence (Rte 12, 13607) 482-9452) 53 rooms and cabins, pool, a/c, TV, pets allowed, open May 15 to October 1. SGL/DBL$35-$65.

Remp's Motel (109 Church St, 13607) 482-5312) 6 rooms, a/c, TV, pets allowed, open May 15 to September 30. SGL/DBL$45-$55.

Riveredge Resort (Alexandria Bay 13607; 482-9917, Fax 482-5010, 800-ENJOY-US) 129 rooms, restaurant, lounge, entertainment, pool, whirlpools, sauna, a/c, TV, no pets, major credit cards. SGL/DBL$118-$188.

Rock Ledge Motel (Rte 12, 13607; 482-2191) 20 rooms, a/c, TV, no pets, open May 15 to October 15. SGL/DBL$35-$50.

The Ship Motel (12 Market St, 13607; 482-4503) 31 rooms, restaurant, lounge, a/c, TV, pets allowed. SGL/DBL$45-$70.

Village Motel (Seven Bolton Ave, 13607) 482-4778) 7 rooms, a/c, TV, pets allowed, open May to October. SGL/DBL$45-$60.

Altamont
Area Code 518

Apple Inn (Rte 146, 12009; 861-8344) 4 rooms, bed and breakfast, 1760s home, on 6 acres, fireplace, no-smoking rooms, limousine service. SGL/DBL$45-$60.

Amagansett
Area Code 516

Sea Breeze Inn (30 Atlantic Ave, 11930; 267-3692) bed and breakfast, no smoking, no children allowed, open year-round, no pets, a/c. SGL/DBL$50-$120.

Amenia
Area Code 914

Troutbeck (Leedsville Rd, 12501; 373-9681) bed and breakfast, restaurant, no pets, private baths, on 400 acres, American Plan. SGL/DBL$575-$800.

Amherst
Area Code 716

Blue Dolphin Motor Lodge (1951 Niagara Falls Blvd, 14228; 691-9392) 46 rooms and efficiencies, restaurant, TV, a/c, no pets, major credit cards. SGL/DBL$38-$75.

Hampton Inn (10 Flint Ave, 14226; 689-4414, Fax 689-4382, 800-HAMPTON) 199 rooms, restaurant, complimentary breakfast, pool, exercise facilities, children under 18 stay free with parents, airport transportation, no-smoking rooms, wheelchair access, computer hookups, fax service, TV, a/c, free local calls, pets allowed, meeting facilities, major credit cards. SGL/DBL$62-$73.

Holiday Inn (1881 Niagara Falls Blvd, 14228; 691-8181, Fax 691-4965, 800-HOLIDAY) restaurant, lounge, entertainment, outdoor pool, exercise facilities, children under 19 stay free with parents, car rental desk, wheelchair access, a/c, TV, no-smoking rooms, fax service, room service, no pets, laundry service, meeting facilities for 225, senior citizen rates, major credit cards. SGL/DBL$65-$95.

Journey's End Motel (1200 Borden Rd, 14226; 834-2231, 800-668-4200 in New York) 96 rooms, complimentary breakfast, wheelchair access, no-smoking rooms, pets allowed, meeting facilities, major credit cards. SGL/DBL$48-$68.

Lincoln Park Motel (785 Niagara Falls Blvd, 14226; 837-7400, Fax 833-2904) 13 rooms, wheelchair access, major credit cards. SGL/DBL$44-$64.

Lord Amherst Motel (5000 Main St, 14266; 839-2200, Fax 839-2200 ext 458, 800-544-2200) 101 rooms and suites, restaurant, free breakfast, lounge, pool, laundry room, children under 18 stay free with parents, airport transportation, game room, wheelchair access, no-smoking rooms, pets allowed, meeting rooms, major credit cards. SGL/DBL$55-$59, STS$127.

Marriott (1340 Millersport Hwy, 14221; 689-6900, Fax 689-6900 ext 253, 800-228-9290) 356 rooms and suites, restaurant, lounge, entertainment, complimentary breakfast, indoor and outdoor pool, sauna, whirlpool, exercise facilities, free parking, gift shop, boutiques, airport courtesy car, concierge, wheelchair access, no-smoking rooms, pets allowed, meeting facilities, major credit cards. SGL/DBL$122, STS$275.

Marriott Residence Inn (100 Maple Rd, 14221; 632-6622, Fax 632-5247, 800-331-3131) 112 suites, complimentary breakfast, indoor jacuzzi, kitchens, in- room refrigerators, airport transportation, free parking, laundry room, fireplaces, wheelchair access, no-smoking rooms, pets allowed, VCRs, meeting facilities for 20, major credit cards. SGL/DBL$95.

Motel 6 (4400 Maple Rd, 14226; 834-2231, 505-891-6161) 95 rooms, pool, free local calls, children under 17 stay free with parents, a/c, TV, major credit cards. SGL/DBL$37-$45.

Red Roof Inn (42 Flint Rd, 14226; 689-7474, Fax 689-2051) 109 rooms, children under 18 stay free with parents, wheelchair access, no-smoking rooms, a/c, TV, pets allowed, major credit cards. SGL/DBL$40-$50.

Super 8 Motel (One Flint Rd, 14226; 688-0811, Fax 688-2365, 800-800-8000) 104 rooms, complimentary breakfast, children under 18 stay free with parents, no smoking rooms, a/c, TV no pets, wheelchair access, computer hookups, fax service, free local calls, meeting facilities, major credit cards. SGL/DBL$

University Manor Motel (3612 Main St, 14226; 837-3344) 41 rooms, kitchenettes, major credit cards. SGL/DBL$54-$65.

Amsterdam
Area Code 315

Dutchman Motor Inn (116 Minaville Rd, 02010; 843-4610) 14 rooms, restaurant, open year-round. SGL/DBL$43.

Holiday Inn (10 Market St, 02010; 843-5760, Fax 842-0940, 800-HOLIDAY) 125 rooms, restaurant, lounge, indoor pool, exercise facilities, children under 19 stay free with parents, wheelchair access, a/c, TV, no-smoking rooms, fax service, room service, pets allowed, laundry service, meeting facilities for 250, senior citizen rates, major credit cards. SGL/DBL$52-$65.

Super 8 Motel (Rte 30 South, 12010; 843-5888, 800-800-8000) 67 rooms and suites, restaurant, no pets, children under 12 stay free with parents, free local calls, a/c, TV, VCRs, no pets, fax service, no-smoking rooms, senior citizen rates, wheelchair access, meeting facilities, major credit cards. SGL/DBL$45-$64.

Valley View Motor Inn (Rtes 5S and 30, 12010; 842-5637) 60 rooms, restaurant, open year-round, a/c, TV, VCRs, laundry facilities, pets allowed. SGL/DBL$25-$45.

Windsor Motel (Rte 30, 12010; 843-0243) 36 rooms, pool, wheelchair access. SGL/DBL$45.

Angelica
Area Code 716

Angelica Bed and Breakfast (64 West Main St, 14709; 466-3295) 5 rooms and 1 apartment, complimentary breakfast, Victorian inn, no pets, major credit cards. SGL/DBL$45-$65.

Arcade
Area Code 716

Kings Brook Motel (574 Main St, 14009; 492-3600) 15 rooms, restaurant, a/c, TV, open year-round, senior citizen rates, major credit cards. SGL/DBL$32-$47.

Armonk
Area Code 914

Ramada Inn (94 Business Park Dr., 10504; 273-9090, Fax 272-9090 ext 616, 800-2-RAMADA) 140 rooms and suites, restaurant, lounge, outdoor pool, exercise facilities, wheelchair access, no-smoking rooms, airport transportation, free parking, pets allowed, wheelchair access, a/c, TV, room service, laundry facilities, 7 meeting rooms, meeting facilities for 400, senior citizen rates, major credit cards. SGL/DBL$59-$119.

Ashland
Area Code 518

Ashland Farmhouse (West Settlement Rd, 12407; 734-3358) 4 rooms, bed and breakfast, private baths, hot tub, fireplace, no children allowed. SGL/DBL$55-$75.

Athens
Area Code 518

Belnest Bed and Breakfast (Rte 385, 12015; 731-2519) 3 rooms, complimentary breakfast, on 8 acres, Victorian home, open year-round, shared baths, no smoking. SGL/DBL$65-$105.

Catskill Starlight Motel (Box 151, 12015; 943-9358) restaurant, a/c, private baths, TV, open year-round. SGL/DBL$46-$56.

The Stewart House (Two North Water St, 12015; 945-1357) restaurant, complimentary breakfast, private bath, lounge, 1880s home, water view, private baths, SGL/DBL$50-$75.

Atttica
Area Code 716

Attican Motel (Rte 98, 14011; 591-0407) 28 rooms, pets allowed, a/c. SGL/DBL$36-$44.

Auburn
Area Code 315

Days Inn (37 Williams St, 13021; 252-7567, 800-325-2525) 51 rooms, restaurant, lounge, pool, whirlpools, children stay free with parents, room service, laundry service, a/c, TV, free local calls, pets allowed, wheelchair access, no-smoking rooms, senior citizen rates, meeting facilities for 300, major credit cards. SGL/DBL$46-$76.

Grant Motel (255 Grant Ave, 13201; 253-8447) 20 rooms, a/c, TV, no pets, senior citizen rates. SGL/DBL$32-$48.

Holiday Inn (75 N St, 13021; 253-4531, Fax 252-5843, 800-HOLIDAY) restaurant, lounge, indoor pool, exercise facilities, children under 19 stay free with parents, car rental desk, wheelchair access, a/c, TV, no-smoking rooms, fax, room service, pets allowed, laundry service, meeting facilities for 700, senior citizen rates, major credit cards. SGL/DBL$64-$100.

Irish Rose Bed and Breakfast (102 South St, 13021; 255-0196) 4 rooms, complimentary breakfast, pool, fireplaces, no pets, private baths, pool, 1870s home, major credit cards. SGL/DBL$55-105.

Sleepy Hollow Motel (Auburn 13021; 253-3281) 15 rooms, pool, a/c, TV, no pets, in-room refrigerators, major credit cards. SGL/DBL$35-$55.

Super 8 Motel (9 McMaster St, 13021; 253-8886, Fax 253-8329, 800-800-8000) 48 rooms and suites, no pets, VCRs, children under 12 stay free with parents, free local calls, a/c, TV, fax service, no-smoking rooms, senior citizen rates, wheelchair access, meeting facilities, major credit cards. SGL$45, DBL$55-$65.

Averill Park
Area Code 518

Ananas Hus Bed and Breakfast (Rte Three, 12018; 766-5035) complimentary breakfast, on 30 acres, no smoking, no pets, antique furnishings, a/c. SGL/DBL$45-$55.

The Gregory House Country Inn (Averill Park 12018; 674-3774) 12 rooms, restaurant, pool, 1830s inn, a/c, TV, no pets, major credit cards. SGL/DBL$60-$85.

Avoca
Area Code 607

Goodrich Center Motel (8620 Rte 415; 566-2216) 23 rooms and suites, restaurant, pool, a/c, TV, pets allowed. SGL/DBL$30-$38.

Bainbridge
Area Code 607

Berry Hill Farm (Bainbridge 13733; 967-8745) bed and breakfast, 1820s home, antique furnishings. SGL/DBL$40+.

Ballston Lake & Ballston Spa
Area Code 518

Apple Tree Bed and Breakfast (49 West High St, 12020; 885-1113) free breakfast, open year-round, Victorian home, major credit cards. SGL/DBL$65-$90.

Robin Hood Motel (Rte 50, 12020; 584-9037) 17 rooms, pool, a/c, TV. SGL/DBL$50-$75.

Rolling Meadows Farm (161 White Rd, 12019; 885-3248) 3 rooms and suite, bed and breakfast, working farm, pool. SGL$60-$75, DBL$120-$150.

Triple Crown Motel (1031 Saratoga Rd, 12019; 885-4645) pool, TV. LS SGL/DBL$40-$47; HS SGL/DBL$70-$80.

Westwood Motel (1012 Saratoga Rd, 12019; 399-3612) rooms and efficiencies, pool, TV, major credit cards. LS SGL/DBL$40-$50; HS SGL/DBL$60-$70.

Barneveld
Area Code 315

Sugarbush (Old Poland Rd, 13304; 896-6860) rooms and suites, bed and breakfast. SGL/DBL$45+.

Batavia
Area Code 716

Batavia Motel (3768 West Main St, 14020; 343-5531) 23 rooms and efficiencies, pets allowed, kitchenettes, TV, a/c. SGL/DBL$55-$65.

Colonial West Motel (3910 West Main St, 14020; 343-5816) 24 rooms and efficiencies, kitchenettes, a/c, TV, pets allowed. SGL/DBL$46-$48.

Crown Inn (8212 Park Rd, 14020; 343-2311, Fax 343-2053) 20 rooms, a/c, TV, no pets, senior citizen rates, major credit cards. SGL/DBL$42-$72.

Days Inn (200 Oak St, 14020; 343-1440, Fax 343-5322, 800-325-2525) 175 rooms and suites, restaurant, lounge, outdoor pool, children stay free with parents, room service, laundry service, a/c, TV, free local calls, no pets, wheelchair access, no-smoking rooms, senior citizen rates, meeting facilities for 300, major credit cards. SGL/DBL$49-$72, STS$78-$99.

Lock's Motel (3700 West Main St, 14020; 343-8551) 13 rooms, a/c, TV, kitchenettes, pets allowed. SGL/DBL$46-$56.

Holiday Inn (Rte 98 and I-90, 14020; 343-1440, 800-HOLIDAY) restaurant, lounge, entertainment, outdoor pool, exercise facilities, children under 19 stay free with parents, free parking, wheelchair access, a/c, TV, no-smoking rooms, fax service, room service, no pets, laundry service, meeting facilities, senior citizen rates, major credit cards. SGL/DBL$65-$85.

Sheraton Inn (8250 Park Rd, 14020; 344-2100, 800-325-3535) 196 rooms and suites, restaurant, lounge, entertainment, indoor and outdoor pool, jacuzzi, sauna, exercise facilities, no-smoking rooms, a/c, TV, children stay free with parents, wheelchair access, 15,000 square feet of meeting and exhibition space, 8 meeting rooms, meeting facilities for 600, major credit cards. SGL/DBL$55-$110.

Treadway Inn (8204 Park Rd, 14020; 343-1000, Fax 343 8608) 75 rooms, restaurant, lounge, entertainment, pool, a/c, TV, no pets. SGL/DBL$50-$80.

Bath
Area Code 607

Days Inn (330 West Morris St, 14810; 776-7644, Fax 776-7650, 800-325-2525) 104 rooms, restaurant, lounge, indoor pool, children stay free with parents, room service, laundry service, a/c, TV, free local calls, pets allowed, wheelchair access, no-smoking rooms, senior citizen rates, major credit cards. SGL/DBL$50-$75.

Holland-American Motel (Bath 14810; 776-6057) 15 rooms, a/c, TV, no pets, major credit cards. SGL/DBL$28-$40.

Old National Hotel (13 East Steuben St, 14810; 776-4104) 24 rooms, restaurant, lounge, a/c, TV, no pets. SGL/DBL$45-$50.

Super 8 Motel (333 West Morris, 14810; 776-2187, Fax 776-3206, 800-800-8000) 50 rooms and suites, no pets, children under 12 stay free with parents, free local calls, a/c, TV, VCRs, no pets, fax service, no-smoking rooms, senior citizen rates, wheelchair access, meeting facilities, major credit cards. SGL/DBL44-$55.

Bay Shore
Area Code 516

Summit Motor Inn (501 East Main St, 11706; 666-6000, Fax 588-6815) 42 rooms, restaurant, a/c, TV, no pets, major credit cards. SGL/DBL$59-$100.

Bayside
Area Code 718

Adria Hotel and Conference Center (220-33 Northern Blvd, 11360; 631-5900) 105 rooms and suites, restaurant, lounge, pool, wheelchair access, TV, a/c, major credit cards. SGL/DBL$65-$155.

Anchor Motor Inn (215-34 Northern Blvd, 11360; 428-8000) 61 rooms, wheelchair access, entertainment, TV, a/c, major credit cards. SGL/DBL$72-$87.

Bear Mountain
Area Code 914

Bear Mountain Inn (Bear Mountain 10911; 786-2731) 60 rooms, restaurant, lounge, pool, no pets, a/c, TV, major credit cards. SGL/DBL$60-$85.

Bellport
Area Code 516

Shell Cottage (21 Brown's Lane, 11713; 286-9421) 3 rooms, bed and breakfast, no smoking, no pets, antique furnishings, 1880s home. SGL/DBL$45-$70.

Berkshire
Area Code 607

Kinship Bed and Breakfast (Rte 38 North, 13736; 657-4455) 4 rooms, complimentary breakfast, 1809 home, fireplace, antique furnishings, private baths, no smoking, no pets. SGL/DBL$55-$60.

Berlin
Area Code 518

The Sedgwick Inn (Berlin 12002; 658-2334) 11 rooms and 1- and 2-bedroom apartments, restaurant, pets allowed, private baths, 1790s inn, a/c, TV, major credit cards. SGL/DBL$55-$85.

Bethany
Area Code 716

The Hillside Inn (890 East Bethany Rd, 14591; 495-6800, 800-544-2249) 12 rooms, bed and breakfast, open year-round, private baths, jacuzzis. SGL/DBL$60-$175.

Binghamton
Area Code 607

Banner Motel (1169 Front St, 13905; 607-723-8211) 42 rooms, wheelchair access, TV, a/c, open year-round. SGL/DBL$28-$42.

Binghamton

Best Western Binghamton Regency (One Harbor Square, 13901; 722-7575, 800-528-1234) 203 rooms, restaurant, complimentary breakfast, lounge, pool, exercise facilities, children stay free with parents, a/c, TV, no-smoking rooms, TV, wheelchair access, pets allowed, senior citizen rates, meeting facilities, major credit cards. SGL/DBL$50-$100.

Binghamton Regency Hotel and Conference Center (225 Water St, 13901; 722-7575) 194 rooms and suites, restaurant, lounge, pool, exercise facilities, no-smoking rooms, a/c, TV, children stay free with parents, wheelchair access, meeting facilities, major credit cards. SGL/DBL$80-$95.

Clarion (80 State St, 13901; 722-0000, 800-221-2222) 61 rooms, restaurant, lounge, complimentary breakfast, pool, pets allowed, no-smoking rooms, jacuzzi, children under 18 stay free with parents, senior citizen rates, meeting facilities, a/c, TV, major credit cards. SGL/DBL$50-$100.

Comfort Inn (1156 Front St, 13905; 722-5353, 800-221-2222) 67 rooms and efficiencies, restaurant, whirlpools, wheelchair access, no-smoking rooms, no pets, children under 18 stay free with parents, senior citizen rates, a/c, TV, meeting facilities, major credit cards. SGL$44-$64, DBL$52-$74.

Days Inn (1000 Front St, 13905; 724-3297, Fax 771-0206, 800-325-2525) 106 rooms and suites, restaurant, lounge, pool, children stay free with parents, room service, laundry service, a/c, TV, free local calls, pets allowed, wheelchair access, no-smoking rooms, senior citizen rates, major credit cards. SGL/DBL$55-$95, STS$110-$175.

Del Motel (Upper Court St, 13904; 775-2144) 23 rooms, wheelchair access, SGL/DBL$27-$38.

Econo Lodge (Upper Court St, 13904; 775-3443, 800-4-CHOICE) 105 rooms, pool, children under 12 stay free with parents, whirlpools, jacuzzi, pets allowed, senior citizen rates, wheelchair access, a/c, TV, major credit cards. SGL/DBL$30-$75.

Econo Lodge (Upper Court St, 13904; 775-3443, 800-4-CHOICE) 20 rooms, complimentary breakfast, pool, TV, children under 12 stay free with parents, pets allowed, senior citizen rates, wheelchair access, a/c, TV, major credit cards. SGL/DBL$49-$54.

Foothills Motel (Binghamton 13904; 775-1515) 20 rooms, a/c, TV, open year-round. SGL/DBL$35.

Holiday Inn Arena (Hawley St, 13901; 722-1212, 800-HOLIDAY) 250 rooms, restaurant, lounge, outdoor pool, exercise facilities, children under 19 stay free with parents, wheelchair access, a/c, TV, no-smoking rooms, fax service, room service, no pets, laundry service, meeting facilities, senior citizen rates, major credit cards. SGL/DBL$55-$79.

Holiday Inn (4105 Vestal Pkwy, 13850; 729-6371, 800-HOLIDAY) 145 rooms, restaurant, lounge, outdoor pool, exercise facilities, children under 19 stay free with parents, wheelchair access, a/c, TV, no-smoking rooms, fax service, room service, pets allowed, laundry service, meeting facilities for 200, senior citizen rates, major credit cards. SGL/DBL$35-$75.

Howard Johnson Inn at SUNY (3601 Vestal Pkwy East, 13850; 729-6181, 800-I-GO-HOJO) 60 rooms and efficiencies, restaurant, lounge, pool, children stay free with parents, wheelchair access, no-smoking rooms, TV, a/c, pets allowed, free parking, in-room refrigerators, meeting facilities, senior citizen rates, meeting facilities, major credit cards. SGL/DBL$40-$80.

Howard Johnson (700 Front St, 13905; 724-1341, Fax 773-8287, 800-I-GO-HOJO) 107 rooms, restaurant, lounge, pool, jacuzzi, children stay free with parents, wheelchair access, no-smoking rooms, TV, a/c, pets allowed, transportation to local attractions, free parking, meeting facilities, senior citizen rates, meeting facilities for 100, major credit cards. SGL/DBL$35-$65.

Motel 6 (1012 Front St, 13905; 771-0400) 118 rooms, pool, free local calls, children under 17 stay free with parents, a/c, TV, major credit cards. SGL/DBL$32-$38.

Parkway Motel (900 Vestal Pkwy East, 13850; 785-3311) 58 rooms and efficiencies, restaurant, pool, no pets, a/c, TV, no-smoking rooms, major credit cards. SGL/DBL$30-$60.

Ramada Inn (65 Front St, 13905; 724-2412, Fax 722-4000, 800-2-RAMADA) 135 rooms, restaurant, lounge, entertainment, indoor pool, wheelchair access, no-smoking rooms, airport transportation, free parking, pets allowed, wheelchair access, a/c, TV, room service, laundry facilities, meeting facilities for 350, senior citizen rates, major credit cards. SGL$54-$64, DBL$64-$74.

Red Roof Inn (560 Fairview St, 13790; 729-8940, Fax 729-8949, 800-843-7663) 107 rooms, no-smoking rooms, fax, wheelchair access, complimentary newspaper, children stay free with parents, pets allowed, free local calls, in-room computer hookups, major credit cards. SGL/DBL$40-$60.

Residence Inn (4610 Vestal Pkwy East, 13903; 770-8500, 800-331-3131) rooms and suites, complimentary breakfast, pool, spa, in-room refrigerators, coffee makers and microwaves, laundry facilities, free parking, TV, a/c, VCRs, pets allowed, fireplaces, children stay free with parents, no-smoking rooms, wheelchair access, meeting facilities for 20, major credit cards. SGL/DBL$85-$135.

Parkway Motel of Vestal (907 Vestal Pkwy East, 13903; 785-3311) 50 rooms, pool, restaurant, wheelchair access, a/c, TV, open year-round. SGL/DBL$55-$70.

Ramada Inn (65 Front St, 13905; 724-2412, 800-2-RAMADA) 135 rooms, restaurant, lounge, pool, wheelchair access, no-smoking rooms, airport transportation, free parking, pets allowed, wheelchair access, a/c, TV, room service, laundry facilities, meeting facilities, senior citizen rates, major credit cards. SGL/DBL$54-$65.

Super 8 Motel (650 Front St, 13905; 773-8111, Fax 773-8111 ext 138, 800-800-8000) 63 rooms and suites, restaurant, complimentary breakfast, VCRs, in-room microwaves, pets allowed, children under 12 stay free with parents, free local calls, a/c, TV, fax service, no-smoking rooms, senior citizen rates, wheelchair access, meeting facilities, major credit cards. SGL/DBL$40-$45.

Vestal Motel (Vestal Pkwy East, 13903; 754-8090) 23 rooms, wheelchair access, a/c, TV, open year-round. SGL/DBL$24-$44.

Blasdell
Area Code 315

Buffalo South Motor Inn (4344 Mile Strip Rd, Blasdell 14219; 825-7530, 800-488-3360) 115 rooms, restaurant, lounge, entertainment, laundry room, kitchenettes, no-smoking rooms, pets allowed. SGL/DBL$49.

McKinley Park Inn (3950 McKinley Pkwy, Blasdell 14219; 648-5700, Fax 648-5700. 75 rooms, restaurant, lounge, wheelchair access, airport transportation, major credit cards. SGL/DBL$65-$78.

Blue Mountain Lake
Area Code 518

The Hedges (Blue Mountain Lake 12812; 352-7325) 28 rooms, restaurant, wheelchair access, a/c, TV, open June through October. SGL/DBL$65-$110, EFF$80-$125.

Hemlock Hall Resort (Blue Mountain Lake 12812; 352-7706) 30 rooms and 1- and 2-bedroom efficiencies, restaurant, a/c, no pets, in-room refrigerators, TV, open May through October. SGL/DBL$97-$13.

Mountain Motel (Blue Mountain Lake 12812; 352-7781) 4 rooms, open year-round, a/c, TV. SGL/DBL$32.

Steamboat Landing (Blue Mountain Lake 12812; 352-7323) 10 rooms, a/c, TV, open May through September. SGL/DBL$40-$60.

Stephenson's Motel (Blue Mountain Lake 12812; 352-7713) 6 rooms, wheelchair access, a/c, TV, open May through October. SGL/DBL$40-$50.

Bolton Landing
Area Code 518

Bonnie View Resort and Motel (Hwy 9N, 12814; 644-5591) 50 rooms and efficiencies, pool, tennis court, a/c, TV, open May to September, no pets, major credit cards. SGL/DBL$45-$75.

Candlelight Housekeeping Cottages (Hwy 9N, 12814; 644-3321) 19 housekeeping cottages, a/c, TV, water view, no pets. SGL/DBL$65-$725.

Haye's Bed and Breakfast Guest House (7181 Lakeshore Dr., 12814; 644-5941) complimentary breakfast, no smoking, water view, no pets, private baths, major credit cards. SGL/DBL$70-$100.

Hilltop Cottage Bed and Breakfast (6883 Lakeshore Dr., 12814; 644-2492) 3 rooms, complimentary breakfast, water view, no pets, private bath. SGL/DBL$32-$60.

Melody Manor Resort (Hwy 9N, 12814; 644-9750) 40 rooms and 1- and 2-bedroom efficiencies, restaurant, lounge, pool, water view, tennis court, no pets, in-room refrigerators, major credit cards. SGL.DBL$85-$115.

The Omni Sagamore Resort (Sagamore Island, 12814; 644-9400, Fax 644-2604) 350 rooms and suites, restaurant, lounge, entertainment, indoor pool, no pets, in-room refrigerators, sauna, a/c, TV, major credit cards. SGL/DBL$99-$300.

Victorian Village Motel (Bolton Landing 12814; 644-9401) 30 rooms, TV, tennis court, no pets. SGL/DBL$48-$78.

Boonville
Area Code 315

Best Western Inn (Rte 12, 13309; 942-4493, 800-528-1234) 37 rooms, restaurant, complimentary breakfast, lounge, pool, exercise facilities, children stay free with parents, a/c, TV, no-smoking rooms, TV, wheelchair access, pets allowed, senior citizen rates, meeting facilities, major credit cards. SGL/DBL$40-$55.

Hulbert House (106 Main St, 13309; 942-4318) 7 rooms, restaurant, wheelchair access, a/c, TV, open year-round. SGL/DBL$25.

Wishing Well Motel (Rte 12, 13309; 942-2102) 4 rooms, a/c, TV, open year-round. SGL/DBL$20-$25.

Bouckville
Area Code 315

Hinman Motel (Rte 20, 13310; 893-1801) 10 rooms, a/c, TV, open year-round. SGL/DBL$28.

The Landmark Tavern (Rte 20, 13310; 893-1818) 4 rooms, bed and breakfast, restaurant, a/c, open April to December. SGL/DBL$50-$68.

Bowmansville
Area Code 607

Red Roof Inn (146 Maple Dr., 14026; 633-1100, Fax 633-1100 ext 444) 109 rooms, wheelchair access, no-smoking rooms. SGL/DBL$45-$53.

Branchport
Area Code 607

Gone With The Wind Bed and Breakfast (453 West Lake Rd, 14418; 868-4603) complimentary breakfast, no smoking, 1880s home, on 14 acres, fireplace, hot tub, no pets. SGL/DBL$85.

Bridgewater
Area Code 315

Lake Chalet Motel (Rte 8, 13313; 822-6074) 4 rooms, a/c, TV, open year-round. SGL/DBL$30.

Brockport
Area Code 716

Econo Lodge (Brockport 14420; 637-3157, Fax 637-0434, 800-4-CHOICE) 39 rooms, pool, children under 12 stay free with parents, no pets, senior citizen rates, wheelchair access, a/c, TV, major credit cards. SGL/DBL44-$53.

The Portico Bed and Breakfast (3741 Lake Rd, 14420; 637-0220) 3 rooms, complimentary breakfast, 1850s home, no pets, fireplaces, antique furnishings. SGL/DBL$45-$50.

Brookfield
Area Code 315

Bivona Hill Bed and Breakfast (Academy Rd, 13314; 899-8921) 4 rooms, complimentary breakfast, open year-round. SGL/DBL$55.

Gates Hill Homestead (Dugway Rd, 13314; 899-5837) 3 rooms, bed and breakfast, wheelchair access, restaurant, open April to March. SGL/DBL$55.

Mountain Meadow Ranch (Giles Rd, 13314; 899-8975) 3 housekeeping cabins, complimentary breakfast, restaurant, open May to October. SGL/DBL$25.

Brooklyn
Area Code 718

Bed and Breakfast On The Park (113 Prospect Park West, 11215; 499-6116) complimentary breakfast, 1890s Victorian home, no smoking, no pets, private baths, major credit cards. SGL/DBL$100-$175.

Buffalo
Area Code 716

Rental and Reservations Services

Rainbow Hospitality Bed and Breakfast (466 Amherst St, 14207; 874-8797, 800-373-8797).

Downtown Buffalo

Best Western Inn Downtown (510 Delaware Ave, 14202; 886-8333, Fax 884-3070, 800-528-1234) 61 rooms, restaurant, lounge, complimentary breakfast, exercise center, children under 18 stay free with parents, room service, kitchenettes, fax service, no-smoking rooms, a/c, TV, meeting facilities, major credit cards. SGL69-$86, DBL$75-$99, AP$6-$10.

Buffalo Hilton Hotel (120 Church St, 14202; 845-5100, Fax 845-5377, 800-445-8667, 800-HILTONS) 468 rooms, restaurant, lounge, entertainment, pool, exercise center, sauna, tennis courts, gift shop, free parking, airport courtesy car, in-room refrigerators and microwaves, wheelchair access, no-smoking rooms, a/c, TV, business services, meeting facilities for 850, major credit cards. SGL/DBL$118-$140.

Holiday Inn (620 Delaware Ave, 14202; 886-2121, 800-HOLIDAY) 168 rooms, restaurant, lounge, exercise center, children under 12 stay free with parents, wheelchair access, no-smoking rooms, a/c, TV, fax, room service, airport transportation, major credit cards. SGL$72-$85, DBL$80-$93.

Hyatt Regency (Two Fountain Plaza, 14202; 856-1234, Fax 852-6157, 800-233-1234) 400 rooms and suites, Gold Passport Floors, restaurant, 2 lounges, indoor pool, exercise center, sauna, concierge, wheelchair access, in-room refrigerators and microwaves, room service, complimentary newspaper, no-smoking rooms, a/c, TV, beauty shop, airport transportation, 12 meeting rooms, 18,000 square feet of meeting and exhibition space, major credit cards. SGL/DBL$135.

Buffalo

Journey's End Suites (601 Main St, 14203; 854-5500, Fax 854-550 ext 103, 800-668-4200) 146 2-room suites, restaurant, complimentary breakfast, free local calls, children under 16 stay free with parents, business service, free parking, airport transportation, major credit cards. SGL/DBL$100.

Lafayette Hotel (391 Washington St, 14230; 852-5470) 50 rooms, restaurant, lounge. SGL/DBL$45-$65.

Lenox Hotel (140 North St, 14201; 884-1700) 50 rooms and suites, restaurant, lounge, airport courtesy car, children under 18 stay free, in-room refrigerators and microwaves, wheelchair access, kitchenettes, room service, meeting facilities. SGL$48, DBL$55.

Towne House Hotel (999 Main St, 14203; 884-2160) 90 rooms, restaurant, lounge, complimentary breakfast, in-room refrigerators, free parking, wheelchair access, no-smoking rooms. SGL/DBL$65-$85.

Airport Area

Comfort Suites (901 Dick Rd, 14225; 633-6000, 800-221-2222) 100 rooms, complimentary breakfast, indoor pool, sauna, in-room refrigerators and microwaves, no pets, wheelchair access, no-smoking rooms, a/c, TV, meeting facilities, major credit cards. SGL/DBL$60-$80.

Days Inn Airport (4345 Genesee St, 14225; 631-0800, Fax 631-7589, 800-325-2525) 130 rooms, restaurant, outdoor pool, airport transportation, valet laundry, children under 12 stay free with parents, free local calls, wheelchair access, no-smoking rooms, a/c, TV, no pets, meeting facilities for 100, major credit cards. SGL$49-$69, DBL$57-$77, AP$8.

Quality Inn Airport (4217 Genesee St, 14225; 633-5500, 800-228-5151, 800-221-2222) 105 rooms, complimentary breakfast, indoor pool, sauna, exercise center, no pets, wheelchair access, no-smoking rooms, a/c, TV, room service, complimentary newspaper, room service, airport transportation, major credit cards. SGL/DBL$45-$65.

Radisson Hotel (4243 Genesee St, 14225; 634-2300, Fax 632-2387, 800-333-3333) 275 rooms and suites, restaurant, lounge, entertainment, indoor and outdoor pool, exercise center, sauna, children under 18 stay free with parents, wheelchair access, no-smoking rooms, a/c, TV, airport transportation, gift shop, business services, 5 meeting rooms, 20,000 square feet of meeting and exhibition space, meeting facilities for 1,000, major credit cards. SGL/DBL$115.

Ramada Inn Airport (6643 Transit Rd, 14221; 634-2700, Fax 634-1644, 800-2-RAMADA) 123 rooms, restaurant, lounge, outdoor pool, children under 18 stay free with parents, wheelchair access, no-smoking rooms, a/c, TV, airport transportation, free parking, meeting facilities for 300, major credit cards. SGL$79-$99, DBL$89-$109, AP$10.

Other Areas

Buffalo Exit 53 Motor Lodge (475 Dingens St, 14206; 896-2800, 800-437-3744, 800-237-3338 in New York) 80 rooms, restaurant, lounge, outdoor pool, room service, no-smoking rooms, major credit cards. SGL/DBL$45.

Holiday Inn Gateway (601 Dingens St, 14206; 896-2900, Fax 896-3765, 800-HOLIDAY) 118 rooms, restaurant, lounge, children under 12 stay free with parents, wheelchair access, no-smoking rooms, a/c, TV, fax, room service, airport transportation, meeting facilities, major credit cards. SGL/DBL$68.

Red Carpet Inn (1159 Main St, 14209; 882-3490, 800-251-1962) 70 rooms, restaurant, complimentary breakfast, whirlpools, children under 12 stay free with parents, no pets, major credit cards. SGL/DBL$34-$40.

Villa Niagara Hotel (1080 Sheridan Drive, 14150; 873-8197) 20 rooms, no-smoking rooms, a/c, TV, major credit cards. SGL/DBL$35-$45.

White Horse Motel (2270 Niagara Falls Blvd, 14150; 693-2732) 10 rooms, a/c, TV. SGL/DBL$28-$35.

Burdett
Area Code 607

Red House Country Inn (Picnic Area Rd, 14818; 546-8566) bed and breakfast, no smoking, antique furnishings, 1840s home, major credit cards. SGL/DBL$65-$90.

Burlington Flats
Area Code 607

Hogs Hollow Farm (Basswood Rd, 13315; 965-8555) 2 rooms, bed and breakfast, open year-round. SGL/DBL$60-$80.

Burnt Hills
Area Code 518

Oak Grove Motel (830 Saratoga Rd, 12027; 399-5284) TV, a/c. SGL/DBL$42-$58.

Cairo & South Cairo
Area Code 518

All-Seasons Motel (Rte 23B, 12482; 622-8336) 1 housekeeping cottage, kitchenette, a/c, TV, open May through September. SGL/DBL$60.

Beaver Meadow Farm Motel (Sunside Rd, 12413; 622-9287) bed and breakfast, pool, open year-round, a/c, TV, game room. SGL/DBL$45-$70.

Cedar Terrace Resort (Rte 2, 12413; 622-9313) restaurant, lounge, entertainment, outdoor pool, tennis courts, a/c, TV, meeting facilities. SGL/DBL$65-$85.

The Stage Coach Motel (Rte 23B, 12482; 622-2919) 10 rooms and efficiencies, a/c, TV, in-room refrigerators, open April 1 to December 1. SGL/DBL$38-$42.

Cambridge
Area Code 518

Blue Willow Motel (51 South Park Ave, 12816; 677-3552) 12 rooms and efficiencies, a/c, TV, pets allowed. SGL/DBL$30-$50.

Town House Motor Inn (Cambridge 12816; 677-5524) 11 rooms, a/c, pets allowed, in-room refrigerators, TV, senior citizen rates. SGL/DBL$35-$45.

Camden
Area Code 315

Katie and Karl's (Harden Blvd, 13316; 245-3958) 6 rooms, restaurant, a/c, wheelchair access, TV, open year-round. SGL/DBL$45.

The Village Inn (24 Mexico St, 13316; 245-2182) 4 rooms, a/c, TV, open year-round. SGL/DBL$35-$40.

Canaan
Area Code 518

Berkshire Spur Motel (Canaan 12029; 781-4432) 24 rooms, heated outdoor pool, no pets, a/c, TV, major credit cards. SGL/DBL$40-$75.

Canandaigua
Area Code 716

J.P. Morgan House (2920 Smith Rd, 14424; 394-9232) bed and breakfast, fireplaces, jacuzzi, on 46 acres, 1800s home, no smoking, private baths, major credit cards. SGL/DBL$60-$175.

Sheraton Inn (770 South Main St, 14424; 394-7800, Fax 394-5003, 800-325-3535) 147 rooms and suites, restaurant, lounge, entertainment, outdoor pool, exercise facilities, sauna, game room, no-smoking rooms, a/c, TV, children stay free with parents, wheelchair access, 6,400 square feet of meeting and exhibition space, 7 meeting rooms, meeting facilities for 350, major credit cards. SGL/DBL$95-$165.

Canastota
Area Code 315

Days Inn (Rte 13, 13032; 697-3309, 800-325-2525) 60 rooms, restaurant, lounge, children stay free with parents, room service, laundry service, a/c, TV, free local calls, pets allowed, wheelchair access, no-smoking rooms, senior citizen rates, major credit cards. SGL/DBL$45-$55.

Graziano's Motor Lodge (409 North Peterboro St, 13032; 697-8384) 34 rooms, restaurant, a/c, TV, open year-round. SGL/DBL$32-$42.

Midway Motel (Rte 5, 13032; 697-7928) 14 rooms, a/c, TV, open year-round. SGL/DBL$26.

Pine Valley Motel (Rte 5, 13032; 363-0490) 5 rooms, a/c, TV, open year-round. SGL/DBL$28.

Sharway Motel (Rte 5, 13032; 697-7935) 8 rooms, a/c, TV, open year-round. SGL/DBL$30-$40.

Cape Vincent
Area Code 315

Buccaneer Motel (Point St, 13618; 654-2975) 10 rooms, a/c, TV, pets allowed, open year-round. SGL/DBL$60-$75.

Cape Dairy and Motel (Cape Vincent 13618; 654-2525) 6 rooms, no pets, TV, open April 15 to October 15. SGL/DBL$40.

Martin's Marina and Motel (Valley Rd, 13618; 654-3104) 6 rooms and housekeeping cabins, no pets, open May to October 15. SGL/DBL$40-$50.

Roxy's Motel (Market and Broadway St, 13618; 654-2944) 10 rooms, restaurant, lounge, TV, wheelchair access, pets allowed, open May to October. SGL/DBL$30-$45.

Carlisle
Area Code 518

Four Acres Motel (Rte 20, 12031; 234-4266) 5 rooms, a/c, TV, open year-round. SGL/DBL$35.

Catskill
Area Code 518

Catskill Motor Court (Rte 1, 12414; 678-5559) coffee shop, complimentary breakfast, outdoor pool, a/c, open April to December, TV, major credit cards. SGL/DBL$45-$65.

Cedar Hill Motel and Efficiencies (Catskill 12414; 943-5323) rooms and efficiencies, kitchenettes. SGL/DBL$28-$32.

Friar Tuck Inn (Rte 32, 12414; 678-2271) 550 rooms, restaurant, lounge, entertainment, indoor and outdoor pool, sauna, jacuzzi, tennis courts, water view, a/c, TV, open year-round, Modified American Plan available. SGL/DBL$80-$100.

Cazenovia
Area Code 315

The Apple Farm (3073 East Pompey Hollow Rd, 13035; 655-8466) 2 rooms, bed and breakfast, pool, open year-round. SGL/DBL$50.

Brae Loch Inn (Rte 20, 13035; 655-3431) bed and breakfast, private baths, no pets, major credit cards. SGL/DBL$65-$135.

The Brewster Inn (Ledyard Ave, 13035; 655-9232) 7 rooms, bed and breakfast, open year-round. SGL/DBL$80.

Cazenovia Motel (2392 Rte 20 East, 13035; 655-9101) 45 rooms, restaurant, a/c, TV, open year-round. SGL/DBL$34-$52.

Country Bumpkin (Argos Rd, 13035; 655-8084) 2 rooms, bed and breakfast, open year-round. SGL/DBL$65.

Gail Hergert House (Cazenovia 13035; 684-9617) 2 rooms, bed and breakfast, open year-round. SGL/DBL$40.

Betty Randall House (Cazenovia 13035; 655-8084) 3 rooms, bed and breakfast, open year-round. SGL/DBL$65.

Lincklaen House (Albany St, 13035; 655-3461) 21 rooms, restaurant, a/c, TV, open year-round. SGL/DBL$65-$130.

Chaffee
Area Code 315

Josie's Brookside Motel (Routes 16 and 39, 14102; 18 rooms, restaurant, lounge, complimentary breakfast, no-smoking rooms, room service, major credit cards. SGL/DBL$38-$48.

Chappaqua
Area Code 914

Crabtree's Kittle House (11 Kittle Rd, 10514; 666-8044) bed and breakfast, restaurant, 1790s home, private baths, major credit cards. SGL/DBL$95.

Chaumont
Area Code 315

Last Resort Motel and Cottages (Point Salubrious, 13622; 649-2433) 7 rooms and housekeeping cottages, open May to October. SGL/DBL$32-$48.

Pass N'Wind Motel (New Rd, 13622; 649-2738) 6 rooms, wheelchair access, pets allowed, open April to October. SGL/DBL$19-$23.

Cheektowaga
Area Code 716

Airways Motel (4230 Genesee St, 14225; 632-8400, Fax 632-5197, 800-888-8100) 150 rooms, restaurant, lounge, entertainment, outdoor heated swimming, exercise facilities, children under 12 stay free with parents, airport transportation, gift shop, pets allowed, meeting facilities, major credit cards. SGL$35-$44, DBL$40-$50, AP$5.

Holiday Inn (4600 Genesee St, 14225; 634-6969, Fax 634-7502, 800-HOLIDAY) 210 rooms and suites, restaurant, lounge, outdoor pool, exercise facilities, children under 19 stay free with parents, wheelchair access, gift shop, car rental desk, airport transportation, a/c, TV, no-smoking rooms, fax service, room service, no pets, laundry service, meeting facilities, senior citizen rates, major credit cards. SGL/DBL$74-$90, STS$100.

Sheraton Inn Buffalo Airport (2040 Walden Ave, 14225; 681-2400, Fax 681-8067, 800-325-3535) 293 rooms and suites, restaurant, lounge, indoor pool, exercise facilities, sauna, gift shop, no-smoking rooms, a/c, TV, children stay free with parents, wheelchair access, 10,000 square feet of meeting and exhibition space, 12 meeting rooms, meeting facilities for 700, major credit cards. SGL/DBL$80-$155.

Wellesley Inn (4630 Genesee St, 14225; 631-8966, Fax 631-8977) 84 rooms, restaurant, complimentary breakfast, airport transportation, wheelchair access, no-smoking rooms, a/c, TV, pets allowed, children under 12 stay free with parents, major credit cards. SGL/DBL$36-$48.

Cherry Plain
Area Code 518

Mattison Hollow (Cherry Plain 12040; 658-2946) bed and breakfast, 1790s home, no smoking, private baths, children stay free with parents, no pets, antique furnishings. SGL/DBL$120.

Cherry Valley
Area Code 607

Marrion Cornelia Bed and Breakfast (94 Montgomery St, 13320; 264-3060) 3 rooms, complimentary breakfast, open May 15 to October 15. SGL/DBL$40-$60.

Old Story Tavern Bed and Breakfast (197 Main St, 13320; 264-3354) 4 rooms, complimentary breakfast, open May 15 to November 15, major credit cards. SGL/DBL$40-$60.

Pine Creek Farm Bed and Breakfast (Cherry Valley 13320; 264-3921) 4 rooms, complimentary breakfast, open year-round. SGL/DBL$35-$45.

Pleasant Brook Hotel (Cherry Valley 13320; 264-9394) 6 rooms, open year-round. SGL$25, DBL$50.

Pleasant View Cottages (Sharon Rd, 13320; 264-3980) 7 rooms and housekeeping cottages, restaurant, a/c, TV. Open May 26 to October 21. SGL/DBL$25-$40.

Tryon Inn (124 Main St, 13320; 264-3790) 10 rooms, restaurant, wheelchair access, open May 1 to October 1. SGL/DBL$35-$45.

Chestertown
Area Code 518

Friends Lake Inn (Friends Lake Rd, 12817; 494-4751) bed and breakfast, restaurant, no smoking, private baths, no pets, fireplace. SGL/DBL$45-$120.

Chittenango
Area Code 315

Lodge Motel (Rte 5, 13037; 687-5009) 14 rooms, wheelchair access, open year-round. SGL$22, DBL$44.

Clarence
Area Code 716

Asa Ransom House (10529 Main St, Clarence 14031; 759-2315, Fax 750-2791) 9 rooms, restaurant, lounge, no smoking, a/c, TV, antique furnishings, no pets, Modified American Plan available, major credit cards. SGL/DBL$75-$120.

Fels Crown Motel (10220 Main St, Clarence 14031; 759-8381, Fax 759-2794) 34 rooms and efficiencies, restaurant, lounge, wheelchair access, no-smoking rooms, a/c, TV free parking, major credit cards. SGL/DBL$55-$68.

Village Haven (9370 Main St, Clarence 14031; 759-6845) 30 rooms and 1- and 2-bedroom suites, complimentary breakfast, pool, in-room refrigerators, whirlpool baths, a/c, TV, VCRs, no pets, no-smoking rooms, major credit cards. SGL/DBL$35-$70.

Clayton
Area Code 315

K's Motel (1043 State St, 13624; 686-3380) 6 rooms and cabins, pets allowed, wheelchair access, TV, open May to October. SGL/DBL$28-$56.

Lanz's Motel and Cottages (Rte 12, 13624; 686-5690) 36 rooms and housekeeping cottages, TV, wheelchair access, no pets, open May to September. SGL/DBL$36-$70.

Mil's Rivershore Cottages and Apartments (Rte 12, 13624; 686-3891) 20 rooms and housekeeping cottages, TV, wheelchair access, no pets, open May 1 to October 20. SGL/DBL$36-$50.

Nash's Motel and Cottages (Clayton 13624; 686-3270) 7 rooms and housekeeping cottages, TV, pets allowed, open May 10 to October 10. SGL/DBL$32-$70.

The Pier House (Outer State St, 13624; 686-5588) 12 rooms, restaurant, lounge, a/c, TV, wheelchair access, pets allowed, open year-round. SGL/DBL$25-$65.

Riverside Acres Motel (Clayton 13624; 686-4001) 21 rooms and housekeeping cottages, pets allowed, TV, open May 15 to October 15. SGL/DBL$30-$65.

Sunset Efficiency Motel (Clayton 13624; 686-2096) 5 rooms, no pets, open March 15 to November 15. SGL/DBL$11-$59.

Thousand Island Inn (335 Riverside Dr., 13624; 686-3030) open May 14 to September 26, a/c, TV. SGL/DBL$35-$45.

West Wind Motel and Cottages (Rte 12, 13624; 686-3352) 21 rooms and cabins, TV, pets allowed, wheelchair access, May 15 to October 15. SGL/DBL$30-$65.

Cleveland
Area Code 315

The Melody Inn (East Lake Rd, 13042; 675-8616) bed and breakfast, 1820s home, antique furnishings. SGL/DBL$45+.

Clifton Park
Area Code 518

Best Western (Box 2070, 371-1811, 800-528-1234) restaurant, lounge, pool, exercise facilities, children stay free with parents, a/c, TV, no-smoking rooms, TV, wheelchair access, hot tubs, pets allowed, senior citizen rates, meeting facilities, major credit cards. LS SGL/DBL$65-$75; HS SGL/DBL$125-$150.

Cobleskill
Area Code 518

Best Western Inn (Campus Dr., 12043; 234-4321, 800-528-1234) 76 rooms, restaurant, complimentary breakfast, lounge, indoor pool, exercise facilities, children stay free with parents, a/c, TV, no-smoking rooms, TV, wheelchair access, pets allowed, senior citizen rates, meeting facilities, major credit cards. SGL/DBL$45-$55.

The Gables Bed and Breakfast Inn (62-66 West Main St, 12043; 234-4467) 7 rooms, complimentary breakfast, open year-round. SGL/DBL$45-$65.

Travel Quarters Concept (21 Mac Arthur Ave, 12043; 234-7881) 42 rooms, a/c, TV, wheelchair access, open June through August. SGL/DBL$42.

Cohoes
Area Code 518

Hampton Inn (981 New Loudon Rd, 12047; 785-0000, Fax 785-1285, 800-HAMPTON) 126 rooms, restaurant, complimentary breakfast, pool, exercise facilities, children under 18 stay free with parents, no-smoking rooms, wheelchair access, computer hookups, fax service, TV, a/c, pets allowed, free local calls, pets allowed, meeting facilities, major credit cards. SGL/DBL$58-$77.

Inn At The Century and Conference Center (997 New Loudon Rd, 12047; 785-0931, Fax 785-3274) 68 rooms and efficiencies, pool, tennis courts, airport transportation, pets allowed, a/c, TV, in-room refrigerators, major credit cards. SGL/DBL$71-$99.

Colliersville
Area Code 607

Lorenzo's Motel (Rte 7, 13747; 433-2770) 14 rooms, a/c, TV, wheelchair access, open year-round. SGL/DBL$25-$40.

Redwood Motel (Colliersville 13747; 432-1291) 8 rooms, restaurant, a/c, TV, open year-round. SGL/DBL$40-$60.

Commack
Area Code 516

Hampton Inn Long Island (680 Commack Rd, 11725; 462-5700, Fax 462-9735, 800-HAMPTON) 144 rooms, restaurant, complimentary breakfast, pool, exercise facilities, children under 18 stay free with parents, no-smoking rooms, wheelchair access, computer hookups, airport transportation, fax service, TV, a/c, free local calls, pets allowed, meeting facilities, major credit cards. SGL/DBL$75-$85.

Howard Johnson Lodge (450 Moreland Rd, 11725; 864-8820, Fax 864-8829, 800-I-GO-HOJO) 109 rooms, restaurant, lounge, complimentary breakfast, pool, exercise facilities, sauna, whirlpools, children stay free with parents, wheelchair access, airport courtesy car, no-smoking rooms, TV, a/c, pets allowed, free parking, meeting facilities, senior citizen rates, meeting facilities, major credit cards. SGL/DBL$59-$95.

Cooperstown
Area Code 607

Aalsmeer Motel and Cottages (Lake Rd, 13326; 547-8819) 18 rooms, pool, a/c, TV, wheelchair access, open May 15 to October 30, water view, pets allowed. SGL/DBL$60-$60.

Angelholm Bed and Breakfast (14 Elm St, 13326; 547-2483) 4 rooms, complimentary breakfast, open year-round. SGL/DBL$40-$80.

Baseball Town Motel (61 Main St, 13326; 547-2161) 9 rooms, a/c, TV, open year-round. SGL/DBL$40-$60.

Bay Side Motor Inn and Cottages (Lake Rd, 13326; 547-2371) 25 rooms and housekeeping cottages, restaurant, pool, a/c, TV, open year-round. SGL/DBL$60-$100.

The Blacksmith Guest House (Susquehanna Ave, 13326; 547-2317) 2 rooms, bed and breakfast, a/c, TV. SGL/DBL$60-$80.

Bourdon Guest House (60 Chestnut St, 13326; 547-9387) 1 room, complimentary breakfast, a/c, TV. SGL/DBL$30-$40.

Briar Hill Farm (Box 634, 13326; 264-8100) bed and breakfast, open year-round, on 130 acres. SGL/DBL$75.

Canyon Lodge (Cooperstown 13326; 547-2471) 2 rooms, complimentary breakfast, open year-round. SGL/DBL$30-$35.

Cobblestone Bed and Breakfast (Cooperstown 13326; 547-9502) 4 rooms, complimentary breakfast, open May through October. SGL/DBL$60.

Cooper Motor Inn (Chestnut St, 13326; 547-2567) 20 rooms, pool, a/c, TV, open year-round. SGL/DBL$80-$120.

Cooperstown Motel (Chestnut and Beaver St, 13326; 547-2301) 37 rooms, a/c, TV, wheelchair access, pets allowed, open year-round. SGL/DBL$40-$80.

Crawley Tourist Home (78 Beaver St, 13326; 547-2416) 2 rooms, open year-round. SGL$30, DBL$60.

Cooper Inn (Chestnut St, 13326; 547-2567) 15 rooms, open March to October. SGL/DBL$89-$99.

Cooperstown Motel (Chestnut and Beaver St, 13326; 547-2301) 37 rooms, a/c, TV. SGL/DBL$39-$109.

Creekside of Cooperstown (Cooperstown 13326; 547-8203) 4 rooms, bed and breakfast, open year-round. SGL/DBL$55-$95.

Deer Run Motel (Lake Rd, 13326; 547-8600) 30 rooms, restaurant, pool, TV, a/c, open April 3 to October 31. SGL/DBL$40-$80.

Edward's Bed and Breakfast (83 Chestnut St, 13326; 547-8514) 2 rooms, complimentary breakfast, open year-round. SGL$40, DBL$80.

Gray Goose Bed and Breakfast (Cooperstown 13326; 547-2763) 2 rooms, complimentary breakfast, open May through October. SGL/DBL$50.

The Guest House (49 Beaver St, 13326; 547-9276) 2 rooms, bed and breakfast, open year-round. SGL/DBL$30-$40.

Hall Tree Bed and Breakfast (11 Pine Blvd, 13326; 547-8234) 3 rooms, complimentary breakfast, open year-round. SGL/DBL$50-$60.

Hayford Tourist Home (Six Westridge Rd, 13326; 547-2787) 3 rooms, bed and breakfast, open year-round. SGL/DBL$25-$50.

Hickory Grove Motor Inn (Rte 2, 13326; 547-9874) water view, a/c, TV, open May 5 to October 22. SGL/DBL$40-$80.

Hickory Grove Inn (Lake Rd, 13326; 547-8100) 3 rooms, open year-round. SGL/DBL$45-$55.

Hill and Hollow Bed and Breakfast (Cooperstown 13326; 547-2129) 3 rooms, complimentary breakfast. SGL/DBL$50.

Hyde Park Colony (East Lake Rd, 13326; 908-725-5720) 1 rooms, pool, open June 1 to September 30. SGL/DBL$225W.

The Inn At Brook Willow (Cooperstown 13326; 547-9700) 4 rooms, bed and breakfast, no smoking, private baths, no pets, open year-round, Victorian home, antique furnishings. SGL/DBL$45-$85.

The Inn At Cooperstown (16 Chestnut St, 13326; 547-5756) 17 rooms, open year-round, wheelchair access, meeting facilities. SGL/DBL$60-$80.

J.P. Sill House (63 Chestnut St, 13326; 547-2663) 5 rooms, bed and breakfast, open April to November. SGL/DBL$80.

Lake N'Pines Motel (Lake Rd, 13326; 547-2790) 20 rooms, pool, wheelchair access, a/c, TV, open May 1 to October 15. SGL/DBL$80-$110.

Lake Front Motel (10 Fair St, 13326; 547-9511) 50 rooms, restaurant, pool, a/c, TV, wheelchair access, open year-round. SGL/DBL$40-$80.

Lake View Motel and Cottages (Lake Rd, 13326; 547-9740) 14 rooms and housekeeping cottages, kitchenettes, pool, a/c, TV, open April 1 to November 15. SGL/DBL$60-$80.

Litco Farms Bed and Breakfast (Rte 28, 13326; 547-2501) complimentary breakfast, pool, no smoking, private baths, no pets, on 70 acres. SGL/DBL$50-$60.

Mackie's Bed and Breakfast (Six Elk St, 13326; 547-2683) 4 rooms, complimentary breakfast, pool. SGL/DBL$50.

The Main Street Bed and Breakfast (202 Main St, 13326; 547-9755) 2 rooms, complimentary breakfast, open May through October. SGL/DBL$55.

Middlefield Guest House (Rte 166, 13326; 286-7056) 4 rooms, bed and breakfast, open year-round. SGL/DBL$35-$45.

Mohican Motel (90 Chestnut St, 13326; 547-5101) 13 rooms, a/c, TV, open April 1 to November 30. SGL/DBL$40-$110.

Otesaga Hotel (Lake St, 13326; 547-9931) 125 rooms and suites, restaurant, lounge, pool, a/c, TV, wheelchair access, open May 1 to October 31, 11 meeting rooms. SGL/DBL$85-$135.

Phoenix On River Road Motel (Cooperstown 13326; 547-8250) 20 rooms, complimentary breakfast, a/c, TV. SGL/DBL$45-$90.

Red Creek Guest House (Cooperstown 13326; 547-5365) 1 room, complimentary breakfast, open May through October. SGL/DBL$90.

Sleeping Lion Motel (Cooperstown 13326; 547-9015) 8 rooms, TV, water view, open July 1 to November 1. SGL/DBL$40-$60.

Tara Hills Bed and Breakfast (Cooperstown 13326; 547-9203) 2 rooms, complimentary breakfast, open year-round. SGL/DBL$40.

Terrace Motor Inn (Lake Rd, 13326; 547-9979) 15 rooms, pool, a/c, TV, wheelchair access, open May 1 to November 1. SGL/DBL$40-$100.

The Tunnicliff Inn (32-36 Pioneer St, 13326; 547-9611, 800-446-8466) 17 rooms, restaurant, TV, pets allowed, open year-round. SGL/DBL$50-$125.

Twin Pines Cabin at Hyde Bay (Otsego Lake 13326; 547-5624) 4 rooms and cabins, bed and breakfast, restaurant, open May 1 to October 15. SGL/DBL$60-$80.

Whispering Pines Bed and Breakfast (Cooperstown 13326; 547-5640) 14 rooms, complimentary breakfast, open year-round. SGL/DBL$55.

Wynterholm Bed and Breakfast (Two Chestnut St, 13326; 547-2308) 6 rooms, complimentary breakfast, open year-round. SGL/DBL$75.

Coram
Area Code 516

Be Our Guest (24 Harrison Ave, 11727; rooms, bed and breakfast, no smoking, private bath, no pets. SGL/DBL$40-$80.

Corinth
Area Code 518

Agape Farm Bed and Breakfast (4894 Rte 9, 12822; 654-7777) 6 rooms, complimentary breakfast, on 33 acres, private baths, wheelchair access, kitchenettes, no smoking, major credit cards. SGL/DBL$65-$85.

The Inn At The Edge Of The Forest (11 East Dayton Dr., 12822; 654-6656) bed and breakfast, fireplaces, no smoking, no children allows. LS SGL/DBL$60-$70; HS SGL/DBL$90-$110.

Corning
Area Code 607

Comfort Inn (66 West Pulteney St, 14830; 962-1515, 800-221-2222) 60 rooms, restaurant, indoor pool, exercise facilities, wheelchair access, no-smoking rooms, no pets, children under 18 stay free with parents, senior citizen rates, a/c, TV, meeting facilities, major credit cards. SGL$52-$85, DBL$62-$95.

Days Inn (23 Riverside, 14830; 936-9370, Fax 936-0513, 800-325-2525) restaurant, lounge, indoor pool, whirlpools, exercise facilities, children stay free with parents, room service, laundry service, a/c, TV, free local calls, no pets, wheelchair access, no-smoking rooms, senior citizen rates, major credit cards. SGL/DBL$45-$99.

The DeLevan House (188 DeLevan Ave, 14830; 962-2347) bed and breakfast, private baths, no smoking, open year-round. SGL/DBL$55-$85.

1865 White Birch (69 East First St, 14830; 962-6355) bed and breakfast, no pets, Victorian home, private baths. SGL/DBL$45-$80.

Hilton Hotel (Denison Pkwy East, 14830; 962-5000, Fax 962-4166, 800-HILTONS) 177 rooms and suites, restaurant, lounge, entertainment, indoor pool, exercise facilities, children stay free with parents, no-smoking rooms, free parking, wheelchair access, pets allowed, a/c, TV, business services, meeting facilities, major credit cards. SGL/DBL$80-$90.

Rosewood Inn (134 East First St, 14830; 962-3253) bed and breakfast, private baths, antique furnishing. SGL/DBL$65-$120.

Cornwallville
Area Code 518

Shapanack (Stone Bridge Rd, 12418; 239-4626) restaurant, entertainment, water view, tennis courts, on 300 acres, open May to September, American Plan available. SGL/DBL$45-$90.

Cortland
Area Code 607

Comfort Inn (Two Locust Ave, 13045; 753-7721, F800-221-2222) 66 rooms, restaurant, exercise facilities, wheelchair access, no-smoking rooms, no pets, children under 18 stay free with parents, senior citizen rates, a/c, TV, meeting facilities, major credit cards. LS SGL/DBL$46-$51, DBL$51-$56; HS SGL$60-$85, DBL$65-$85.

Super 8 Motel (188 Clinton Ave, 13045; 756-5622, Fax 753-6171, 800-800-8000) 58 rooms, restaurant, no pets, children under 12 stay free with parents, free local calls, a/c, TV, fax, no-smoking rooms, senior citizen rates, wheelchair access, meeting facilities, major credit cards. SGL/DBL$43-$50.

Croton-On-Hudson
Area Code 914

Alexander Hamilton House (49 Van Wyck St, 10520; 271-6737) free breakfast, pool, 1880s home, antique furnishing, a/c, water view, fireplace. SGL/DBL$45-$150.

Dansville
Area Code 716

Days Inn (Commerce Dr., 14437; 335-6023, Fax 335-2090, 800-325-2525) 20 rooms, restaurant, lounge, laundry service, a/c, TV, free local calls, pets allowed, wheelchair access, no-smoking rooms, senior citizen rates, major credit cards. SGL/DBL$28-$45.

Davenport
Area Code 607

Davenport Inn (Main St, 13750; 278-5068) 5 rooms, free breakfast, restaurant, 1800s inn, private baths. SGL/DBL$30-$60.

Delmar
Area Code 607

American Country Collection of Bed and Breakfast and Country Inns (Four Greenwood Lane, 12054; 439-7001) bed and breakfast reservation service.

Depew
Area Code 606

Pink Fountain Motor Inn (5474 Transit Rd, Depew 14043; 683-1245) 14 rooms. SGL/DBL$28-$38.

Deposit
Area Code 607

White Pillars Inn (82 Second St, 13754; 467-4191) 5 rooms, bed and breakfast, restaurant, open year-round. SGL/DBL$45-$85.

Dexter
Area Code 315

Wink's Reel'Em Inn (305 Canal St, 13634; 639-6950) 5 rooms, restaurant, open year-round. SGL/DBL$18-$36.

Dolgeville
Area Code 315

Adrianna Bed and Breakfast (44 Stewart St, 13329; 429-3249) 3 rooms, complimentary breakfast, antique furnishings, no pets, SGL/DBL$40-$45.

Downsville
Area Code 607

Adam's Farm House (Main St, 13755; 363-2757) bed and breakfast, no smoking, no pets. SGL/DBL$35-$50.

Dryden
Area Code 607

Margaret Thacher's Spruce Haven (9 James St, 13053; 844-8052) bed and breakfast, shared baths, no smoking. SGL/DBL$50-$75.

Sarah's Dream Inn (49 West Main St, 13053; 844-4321) 6 rooms and suites, bed and breakfast, fireplace, a/c, antique furnishings, private baths, TV. SGL/DBL$40-$60.

Dunkirk
Area Code 716

Quality Inn (Vineyard Dr., 14048; 366-4400, 800-368-5689) 38 rooms and suites, restaurant, room service, exercise facilities, children stay free with parents, a/c, TV, laundry service, no-smoking rooms, meeting facilities, major credit cards. SGL$44-$50, DBL$50-$60.

Sheraton Inn Harborfront (30 Lake Shore Dr. East, 14048; 366-8350, Fax 366-8899, 800-325-3535) 132 rooms and suites, restaurant, lounge, entertainment, indoor and outdoor pool, exercise facilities, sauna, whirlpools, no-smoking rooms, a/c, TV, children stay free with parents, wheelchair access, 4,200 square feet of meeting and exhibition space, 8 meeting rooms, meeting facilities for 300, major credit cards. SGL/DBL$68-$105.

Durham & East Durham
Area Code 518

Brady's Chateau Motor Lodge (Rte 145, 12422; 239-8697) pool, restaurant, a/c, open May to December, major credit cards. SGL/DBL$45-$50.

Carriage House Bed and Breakfast (Rte 145, 12423; 634-2284) complimentary breakfast, 1850s home, swimming, private baths, a/c, TV, open year-round, major credit cards. SGL/DBL$33-$64.

The Country Place (Shady Glen Rd, 12423; 239-4559, 800-888-3586) rooms and suites, restaurant, pool, tennis courts, open May to September, a/c, TV, Modified American Plan available. SGL/DBL$139-$200.

Evans New Palm Inn (Rte 145, 12423; 634-7408) 28 2-bedroom housekeeping cottages, kitchenettes, pool, open April 1 to December 15. SGL/DBL$70-$90.

Furlong's Riverside Inn (Rte 145, 12423; 634-7687) restaurant, lounge, entertainment, a/c, pool, TV, open May to November. SGL/DBL$80-$90.

Golden Harvest Bed and Breakfast (37 Golden Hill Rd, 12423; 634-2305) 2 rooms, complimentary breakfast, shared bath, open year-round. SGL/DBL$40-$45.

Stonebridge Inn (East Durham 12423; 634-7588) 4 rooms, restaurant, bed and breakfast, open May to October, private baths. SGL/DBL$85-$100.

Weldon House (Rte 145, 12423; 634-2898) restaurant, transportation to local attractions, a/c, American plan available. SGL/DBL$46-$56.

Eagle Bay
Area Code 315

Big Moose Inn (Big Moose Lake, 13331; 357-2042) bed and breakfast, restaurant, lounge, no pets, private baths, water view, wheelchair access, fireplace. SGL/DBL$35-$80.

Covewood Lodge (Big Moose, 13331; 357-3041) 18 rooms, open May to October. SG/DBL$50-$150.

Deerhead Inn at Big Moose Station (Big Moose Rd, 13331; 357-3600) 4 rooms, bed and breakfast, open year-round. SGL/DBL$27-$40.

Glenmore Hotel (Big Moose Lake, 13331; 357-4891) 11 rooms, restaurant, open year-round. SGL/DBL$17-$135.

Little Fox Hotel (Big Moose Rd, 13331; 357-6000) 7 rooms, restaurant, open year-round. SGL/DBL$30-$75.

North Star Motel (Box 91, 13331; 357-4131) 10 rooms, open year-round. SGL/DBL$32-$60.

Turner Camps (Fourth Lake, 13331; 357-4221) 10 rooms, open June through September. SGL/DBL$130-$345.

Waldheim (Big Moose Lake, 13331; 357-4331) 6 rooms, restaurant, open year-round. SGL/DBL$300-$600.

East Windham
Area Code 518

Point Lookout Mountain Inn (Rte 23, 12439; 734-3381) restaurant. SGL/DBL$40-$55.

Eaton
Area Code 315

Alice Bowie House (English Ave, 13334; 684-3760) 2 rooms, bed and breakfast, open year-round. SGL/DBL$60.

Edmeston
Area Code 607

Laurandon's Inn (West St, 965-9969) 6 rooms, restaurant, open year-round. SGL/DBL$40-$60.

Pathfinder Village Inn (Rte 80, 13335; 965-8377) 4 rooms, a/c, TV, wheelchair access, open year-round. SGL/DBL$45-$58.

Elka Park
Area Code 518

Antonio's Resort (Dale Lane, 12427; 589-5197, 800-722-2771) restaurant, entertainment, indoor and outdoor pools, jacuzzi, sauna, fireplace, game room, Modified American Plan available. SGL/DBL$65-$85.

The Cottage Bed and Breakfast (County Rd 16, 12427; 589-9496) 1 3-bedroom housekeeping cottage, complimentary breakfast, fireplace, open May to November. SGL/DBL$125.

Redcoat's Return (Elka Park 12427; 589-6379) restaurant, lounge, fireplace, a/c, open May 24 to April 1. SGL/DBL$60-$80.

Windswept Bed and Breakfast (Country Rd, 12427; 589-6275) complimentary breakfast, fireplace. SGL/DBL$45-$55.

Ellicottville
Area Code 716

Rental and Reservation Services

Alpine Rental Management (27 Washington St, 14731; 699-2000).

Century 21 Almeida Real Estate (Washington at Monroe, 14731; 699-4800).

Four Seasons Resort Realty (42 Washington St, 14731; 699-5354).

Holiday Valley Rental Managements (Rte 219, 14731; 699-2158).

Weast Realty (34 Washington St, 14731; 699-4615).

Ye Olde Town and Country Realty (38 Washington St, 14731; 699-2456).

Elmhurst & East Elmhurst
Area Code 718

Airway Motor Inn (82-20 Astoria Blvd, 11369; 565-5100) 58 rooms, a/c, TV. SGL/DBL$53-$65.

Days Inn (100-15 Ditmars Blvd, 11369; 898-1225, Fax 898-8337, 800-325-2525) 135 rooms, restaurant, lounge, outdoor pool, children stay free with parents, room service, laundry service, a/c, TV, free local calls, airport courtesy car, no pets, wheelchair access, no-smoking rooms, senior citizen rates, major credit cards. SGL/DBL$75-$105.

Holiday Inn LaGuardia Airport (104-04 Ditmars Blvd, 11369; 718-457-6300, Fax 718-899-9768, 800-HOLIDAY) 165 rooms and suites, Concierge Floor, restaurant, lounge, entertainment, indoor pool, exercise facilities, children under 12 stay free with parents, wheelchair access, no-smoking rooms, fax service, room service, gift shop, airport courtesy car, no pets, meeting facilities for 550, major credit cards. SGL/DBL$175-$185.

Kings Inn Hotel (87-02 23rd Ave, 11369; 672-7900) 76 rooms, lounge, entertainment. TV, a/c, major credit cards. SGL/DBL$38-$54.

LaGuardia Marriott Hotel (102-05 Ditmars Blvd, 11369; 565-8900, 800-228-9290) 436 rooms and suites, restaurant, lounge, entertainment, pool, exercise facilities, whirlpools, wheelchair access, TV, airport transportation, a/c, no-smoking rooms, gift shop, children stay free with parents, pets allowed, business services, meeting facilities, major credit cards. SGL/DBL$155-$175.

Quality Inn (9400 Ditmars Blvd, 11369; 335-1200, 800-368-5689) 165 rooms and suites, restaurant, room service, exercise facilities, children stay free with parents, a/c, TV, laundry service, no-smoking rooms, meeting facilities, major credit cards. SGL/DBL$90-$120, AP$10.

Ramada Hotel LaGuardia Airport (90-10 Grand Central Pkwy, East Elmhurst 11369; 718-446-4800, Fax 446-4886, 800-2-RAMADA) 288 rooms, restaurant, lounge, entertainment, outdoor pool, children under 18 stay free with parents, wheelchair access, no-smoking rooms, airport courtesy car, a/c, free parking, game room, TV, in-room refrigerators, microwaves and coffee makers, free parking, meeting facilities for 700. SGL/DBL$90-$145.

Elma
Area Code 716

Open Gate Motel (7270 Seneca St, Elma 14059; 652-9897) 12 rooms and efficiencies, no-smoking rooms, a/c, TV, free parking, major credit cards. SGL/DBL$37-$57.

Elmira
Area Code 607

Holiday Inn (One Holiday Plaza, 14901; 734-4211, Fax 734-4211 ext 295, 800-HOLIDAY) 150 rooms, restaurant, lounge, entertainment, indoor pool, exercise facilities, children under 19 stay free with parents, gift shop, wheelchair access, a/c, TV, no-smoking rooms, fax service, room service, no pets, laundry service, meeting facilities for 480, senior citizen rates, major credit cards. SGL/DBL$65-$100.

Elmsford
Area Code 914

Days Inn (Rte 119, 10523; 592-5680, Fax 592-6727, 800-325-2525) 147 rooms, restaurant, lounge, outdoor pool, children stay free with parents, room service, laundry service, a/c, TV, free local calls, pets allowed, wheelchair access, no-smoking rooms, senior citizen rates, 7 meeting rooms, meeting facilities for 150, major credit cards. SGL/DBL$59-$109.

Ramada Inn (540 Saw Mill Rd, 10523; 592-3300, Fax 592-3300 ext 199, 800-2-RAMADA) 101 rooms, restaurant, lounge, entertainment, indoor and outdoor pool, wheelchair access, no-smoking rooms, airport transportation, free parking, pets allowed, wheelchair access, a/c, TV, room service, laundry facilities, 6 meeting rooms, meeting facilities for 250, senior citizen rates, major credit cards. SGL/DBL$55-$85.

Endicott
Area Code 607

Best Western Homestead Motor Inn (740 West Main St, 13760; 754-1533, 800-528-1234) 62 rooms, restaurant, complimentary breakfast, lounge, pool, exercise facilities, children stay free with parents, a/c, TV, no-smoking rooms, wheelchair access, pets allowed, senior citizen rates, meeting facilities, major credit cards. SGL/DBL$35-$58.

Endicott Inn (214 Washington Ave, 13760; 754-6000) 57 rooms, restaurant, a/c, TV, wheelchair access. SGL/DBL$39-$48.

The Lodge (One Delaware Ave, 13760; 754-7570) 142 rooms and suites, restaurant, a/c, TV, wheelchair access. SGL/DBL$44-$50.

Endwell
Area Code 607

Endwell Motel (3211 East Main St, 13760; 748-7388) 23 rooms, restaurant, a/c, TV. SGL/DBL$27-$39.

King's Inn (2603 East Main St, 13760; 754-8020) 60 rooms, restaurant, a/c, wheelchair access, TV, open year-round. SGL/DBL$50-$75.

North Street Motor Lodge (2100 North St, 13760; 754-8020) 60 rooms, pool, a/c, TV, open year-round. SGL/DBL$45-$71.

Fair Haven
Area Code 315

Black Creek Farm (Fair Haven 13064; 947-5282) bed and breakfast, no smoking, no pets, 1880s home, no children allowed, antique furnishings, water view. SGL/DBL$38-$50.

Brown's Village Inn (Stafford St, 13064; 947-5817) bed and breakfast, no smoking, no pets, major credit cards. SGL/DBL$40-$70.

Frost Haven Retreat (West Bay Rd, 13064; 947-5331) bed and breakfast, no smoking, private baths, no pets, water view, open year-round. SGL/DBL$35-$70.

Falconer
Area Code 716

Motel 6 (1980 East Main St, 14733; 665-3670) 81 rooms, pool, free local calls, children under 17 stay free with parents, a/c, TV, major credit cards. SGL/DBL$33-$40.

Fayetteville
Area Code 315

Beard Morgan House Bed and Breakfast (126 East Genesee St, 13066; 637-4234, 800-775-4234) complimentary breakfast, 1830s home, antique furnishings, private bath. SGL/DBL$45+.

Fishkill
Area Code 914

Holiday Inn (Rte 9, 12524; 896-6281, 800-HOLIDAY) 156 rooms, restaurant, lounge, outdoor pool, exercise facilities, children under 19 stay free with parents, wheelchair access, a/c, TV, no-smoking rooms, airport transportation, fax, room service, no pets, laundry service, meeting facilities for 700, senior citizen rates, major credit cards. SGL/DBL$80-$100.

Residence Inn (Rte 9, 12524; 896-5210, 800-331-3131) rooms and suites, complimentary breakfast, pool, spa, in-room refrigerators, coffee makers and microwaves, laundry facilities, free parking, TV, a/c, VCRs, fireplaces, airport transportation, children stay free with parents, no-smoking rooms, wheelchair access, meeting facilities for 30, major credit cards. SGL/DBL$105-$135.

Fleischmanns
Area Code 914

Timberdoodle Inn (Main St, 12430; 254-4884) bed and breakfast, private bath, hiking trail. SGL/DBL$55-$85.

Floral Park
Area Code 516

Floral Park Motor Lodge (30 Jericho Turnpike, 11001; 775-7777, Fax 775-0451) 107 rooms, a/c, TV, in-room refrigerators, no pets, major credit cards. SGL/DBL$79-$109.

Flushing
Area Code 718

Sheraton Laguardia East Hotel (135-20 39th Ave, 11354; 460-6666, Fax 445-2655, 800-325-3535) 175 rooms and suites, restaurant, lounge, exercise facilities, no-smoking rooms, a/c, TV, children stay free with parents, no pets, wheelchair access, 4,000 square feet of meeting and exhibition space, meeting facilities for 400, major credit cards. SGL/DBL$140-$150.

Fly Creek
Area Code 607

Breezy Knoll (Fly Creek 13337; 547-8362) 3 rooms, bed and breakfast, open May to October. SGL/DBL$40-$45.

Lost Trolley Farm (Rte 28, 13337; 547-5729) bed and breakfast, on 96 acres, no smoking, open May to September. SGL/DBL$45+.

Major League Motor Inn (Rte 20, 13337; 547-2266) 9 rooms, a/c, TV, wheelchair access, open May 30 to October 30. SGL/DBL$40-$60.

Pine Hill Cottage (Fly Creek 13337; 547-8616) 2 rooms, bed and breakfast, open July and August only. SGL$35, DBL$70.

Toad Hall Bed and Breakfast (Fly Creek 13337; 547-5774) 3 rooms, complimentary breakfast, open year-round. SGL/DBL$70.

Fonda
Area Code 518

Camp Mohawk Motel (Fonda 12068; 853-3013) 10 rooms, open year-round, wheelchair access. SGL/DBL$30-$40.

Fort Drum
Area Code 315

The Inn At Fort Drum (4205 Point Valley Rd, 13602; 773-7777) 112 rooms, TV, a/c, wheelchair access, open year-round. SGL/DBL$65-$85.

Fort Plain
Area Code 518

Jack and Jill Motel (Rte Five, 13339; 993-3293) 8 rooms, open May to October, wheelchair access. SGL/DBL$35-$40.

Fredonia
Area Code 716

Days Inn (10455 Bennet Rd, 14063; 673-1351, Fax 672-6909, 800-325-2525) 129 rooms, restaurant, lounge, pool, children stay free with parents, room service, laundry service, a/c, TV, free local calls, pets allowed, wheelchair access, no-smoking rooms, senior citizen rates, major credit cards. SGL/DBL$40-$65.

Freehold
Area Code 518

Beverly Farm Family Resort (Box 83, 12431; 634-2550) rooms and housekeeping cottages, restaurant, entertainment, pool, a/c, kitchenettes, game room, water view. SGL/DBL$65-$85.

Pine Crest Resort (Carter Bridge Rd, 12431; 634-2858) rooms and cabins, lounge, entertainment, pool, private baths, game room, Modified American Plan available. SGL/DBL$50-$90.

Friendship
Area Code 716

Merry Maid Inn Bed and Breakfast (53 West Main St, 14739; 973-7740) complimentary breakfast. SGL/DBL$55.

Fulton
Area Code 315

Battle Island Inn (Fulton 13069; 593-3699) complimentary breakfast, no smoking, private baths, no pets, 1840s home, antique furnishings. SGL/DBL$55-$100.

Fultonville
Area Code 518

Cloverleaf Motel (Riverside Dr., 12072; 853-3456) 26 rooms, restaurant, open year-round, a/c, TV, wheelchair access. SGL/DBL$30-$60.

Poplars Inn (Riverside Dr., 12072; 853-4511) 70 rooms, restaurant, pool, wheelchair access, open year-round, a/c, TV. SGL/DBL$40.

Roadway Motor Plaza (29 Riverside Dr. 12072; 853-3411) 14 rooms, restaurant, a/c, TV, open year-round. SGL/DBL$35.

Galaway
Area Code 518

Salt Hill Farm (5209 Lake Rd, 12074; 882-9466) complimentary breakfast, outdoor pool, no pets, private baths. LS SGL/DBL$55-$75; HS SGL/DBL$95.

Gates
Area Code 716

Motel 6 (155 Buell Rd, 14624; 436-2170, 505-891-6161) 98 rooms, pool, free local calls, children under 17 stay free with parents, a/c, TV, major credit cards. SGL/DBL$33-$39.

Geneseo
Area Code 716

Days Inn (4242 Lakeville Rd, 14454; 243-0500, Fax 243-9007, 800-325-2525) 76 rooms, restaurant, lounge, pool, children stay free with parents, room service, laundry service, a/c, TV, free local calls, no pets, wheelchair access, no-smoking rooms, senior citizen rates, major credit cards. LS SGL$56-$62, DBL$62-$68; HS SGL$69-$79, DBL$75-$85.

Geneva
Area Code 315

Geneva On The Lake (1001 Lochland Rd, 14456; 789-7190, 800-3GENEVA) rooms and suites, bed and breakfast, restaurant, no smoking, private baths, no pets, major credit cards. SGL/DBL$160-$330.

Motel 6 (485 Hamilton St, 14456; 789-4050) 63 rooms, pool, free local calls, children under 17 stay free with parents, a/c, TV, major credit cards. SGL/DBL$40-$46.

Germantown
Area Code 518

Fox Run Bed and Breakfast (Germantown 12526; 537-6945) complimentary breakfast, no smoking, 1800s home, no pets, private baths, a/c, open May to October. SGL/DBL$55-$65.

Glenmont
Area Code 518

Days Inn (Rte 9W, 120771; 465-8811, 800-325-2525) 100 rooms, restaurant, lounge, pool, children stay free with parents, room service, laundry service, in-room computer hookups, laundry facilities, a/c, TV, free local calls, no pets, wheelchair access, no-smoking rooms, senior citizen rates, major credit cards. SGL/DBL$45-$80.

Stone Ends Motel (Glenmont 12077; 449-5181, 800-477-3123) 30 rooms, a/c, TV, pets allowed, major credit cards. SGL/DBL$25-$40.

Glens Falls & South Glens Falls
Area Code 518

Clearwater Motel (Rte 9, 12803; 793-9681) 88 rooms and efficiencies, kitchenettes, a/c, TV, major credit cards. SGL/DBL$45-$95.

Graylyn Motel (Rte 9, 12803; 792-1690) pool, in-room refrigerators, TV, a/c, major credit cards. LS SGL/DBL$45-$50; HS SGL/DBL$80.

Howard Johnson Lodge (54 Aviation Rd, 12804; 793-4173, Fax 793-8955, 800-I-GO-HOJO) 121 rooms, restaurant, lounge, indoor and outdoor pool, jacuzzi, laundry service, children stay free with parents, wheelchair access, no-smoking rooms, TV, a/c, pets allowed, fax service, free parking, meeting facilities, senior citizen rates, meeting facilities, major credit cards. SGL$55-$60, DBL$55-$85.

Sun Haven Motel (South Glens Falls 12803; 792-4101) a/c, TV, major credit cards. SGL/DBL$40.

Super 8 Motel (Corinth Rd, 12801; 761-9780, Fax 761-1049, 800-800-8000) 59 rooms and suites, no pets, children under 12 stay free with parents, free local calls, a/c, TV, fax service, no-smoking rooms, senior citizen rates, wheelchair access, meeting facilities, major credit cards. SGL/DBL$42-$49.

Town and Country Motel (Saratoga Rd, 12803; 793-3471) restaurant, pool, TV. LS SGL$43, DBL$50; HS SGL$57, DBL$79.

Governor's Island
Area Code 212

Super 8 Motel (Comfort Rd, 10004; 269-8878, Fax 742-0926, 800-800-8000) 52 rooms and suites, no pets, children under 12 stay free with parents, free local calls, a/c, TV, fax service, no-smoking rooms, senior citizen rates, wheelchair access, meeting facilities, major credit cards. SGL/DBL$45-$50.

Gowanda
Area Code 716

The Tepee (Gowanda 14070; 532-2168) free breakfast. SGL/DBL$30-$40.

Grafton
Area Code 518

The Grafton Inn (Rte 2, 12082; 279-9489) free breakfast. SGL/DBL$45-$60.

Grand Island
Area Code 716

Cinderella Motel (2797 Grand Island Blvd, Grand Island 14072; 773-2875) 29 rooms, free parking, wheelchair access, no-smoking rooms. SGL/DBL$48-$53.

Holiday Inn (100 Whitehaven Rd, Grand Island 14072; 773-1111, Fax 773-9386, 800-HOLIDAY) 263 rooms, restaurant, lounge, indoor and outdoor pool, exercise facilities, children under 12 stay free with parents, wheelchair access, no-smoking rooms, a/c, TV, fax service, room service, no pets, meeting facilities, major credit cards. SGL/DBL$105.

Isle Inn (3080 Grand Island Blvd, Grand Isle 14072; 773-3902) 21 rooms, no-smoking rooms, a/c, TV airport transportation, free parking, major credit cards. SGL/DBL$55-$75.

Grangerville
Area Code 518

Fish Creek Inn (120 Hughes Rd, 12871; 695-6879) 7 rooms, bed and breakfast, wheelchair access, no smoking, on 100 acres, water view. SGL/DBL$60-$100.

Great Bend
Area Code 315

Pine Grove Motel (Rte 3, 13643; 773-8331) 15 rooms, TV, a/c, pets allowed, open year-round. SGL/DBL$23-$38.

Riverrun Motel (Rte 3, 13643; 493-6056) 21 rooms, TV, a/c, wheelchair access, pets allowed, open year-round. SGL/DBL$44-$54.

Greene
Area Code 607

Sherwood Hotel (25 Genesee St, 13778; 656-4196) 34 rooms, restaurant, open year-round, a/c, TV, wheelchair access. SGL/DBL$40-$95.

The Silo (Rte 206 East, 13778; 656-4377) 3 rooms, restaurant, a/c, TV, open year-round, wheelchair access. SGL/DBL$50.

Greenfield Center
Area Code 518

The Ashley Inn (Greenfield Center 12833; 893-7232) 4 rooms, complimentary breakfast, private baths. SGL/DBL$45-$80.

Greenfield Village Inn (3234 Rte 9N, 12833; 893-2885) TV, major credit cards. SGL/DBL$60-$85.

The Wayside Inn (104 Wilton Rd, 12833; 893-7249) bed and breakfast, 1780s home, water view, private baths, on 10 acres. SGL/DBL$85-$120.

Greenville
Area Code 518

Greenville Arms (Rte 32, 12083; 966-5219) bed and breakfast, no pets, private baths, restaurant, pool, Victorian inn, open year-round. SGL/DBL$60-$120.

The Homestead Victorian Bed and Breakfast (Red Mill Rd, 12083; 966-4474) 2 rooms, complimentary breakfast, antique furnishings, private bath. SGL/DBL$65-$95.

Santa's Magic Lake Resort (Rte 26, 12083; 966-8756) restaurant, a/c, TV, water view, open year-round. SGL/DBL$40.

Sunny Hill Resort and Golf Club (Sunny Hill Rd, 12083; 634-7693) restaurant, a/c, TV, golf course, open mid-May to October. SGL/DBL$47-$67.

Groton
Area Code 607

Austin Manor Bed and Breakfast (210 Old Peroville Rd, 13073; 898-5786) 14 rooms, complimentary breakfast, Victorian home, antique furnishings, no smoking, private baths, no pets, on 180 acres. SGL/DBL$45-$70.

Gale House Bed and Breakfast (114 Williams St, 13073; 898-4904) complimentary breakfast, antique furnishings, private baths. SGL/DBL$60-$70.

Hadley
Area Code 518

Saratoga Rose Inn (Rockwell St, 12835; 696-2861) bed and breakfast, restaurant, open year-round, private baths, a/c, major credit cards. SGL/DBL$75-$135.

Haines Falls
Area Code 518

Cortina Valley (Haines Falls 12436; 589-6500) private bath, TV. SGL/DBL$45-$55.

Huckleberry Hill Inn (Rte. 23A, 12436; 589-5799) 18 rooms, bed and breakfast, private baths, fireplace, TV. SGL/DBL$60-$82.

Hunter Mountain Resort Ranch (Rte. 23A, 12436; 589-6430) restaurant, bed and breakfast, pool, open year-round, tennis court. SGL/DBL$60-$75.

Hamburg
Area Code 716

Days Inn (5220 Camp Rd, 14075; 649-8100, Fax 648-3603, 800-325-2525) 59 rooms, restaurant, lounge, children stay free with parents, room service, laundry service, a/c, TV, free local calls, no pets, wheelchair access, no-smoking rooms, senior citizen rates, major credit cards. SGL/DBL$39-$85.

Holiday Inn (5440 Camp Rd, 14075; 649-0600, Fax 648-2278, 800-HOLIDAY) 128 rooms, restaurant, lounge, outdoor pool, exercise facilities, children under 12 stay free with parents, wheelchair access, no-smoking rooms, a/c, TV, fax service, room service, meeting facilities, major credit cards. SGL/DBL$65-$75.

Hamilton
Area Code 315

Colgate Inn (On The Green, 13346; 824-2300) rooms and suites, restaurant, open year-round, a/c, TV, antique furnishings. SGL/DBL$45.

Hamlin
Area Code 716

Sandy Creek Manor House (1960 Redman Rd, 14464; 964-7528) bed and breakfast, no smoking. SGL/DBL$55-$65.

Hammondsport
Area Code 607

The Blushing Rose (11 Williams St, 14840; 569-3402) 4 rooms, bed and breakfast, no smoking, no children allowed, private baths, antique furnishing, no pets. SGL/DBL$65-$90.

The Bowman Bed and Breakfast (Hammondsport 14840; 569-2516) complimentary breakfast, no smoking, 1800s home, antique furnishing, private baths. SGL/DBL$65-$75.

Hubbs Bed and Breakfast (Hammondsport 14840; 569-2440) complimentary breakfast, 1840s home, no smoking, private baths, no pets, major credit cards. SGL/DBL$50-$65.

Hampton Bays
Area Code 516

House On The Water (Hampton Bays 11946; 728-3560) bed and breakfast, no children allowed. SGL/DBL$70-$100.

Hauppauge
Area Code 516

Marriott Wind Watch Hotel and Golf Club (1717 Vanderbilt Motor Pkwy, 11788; 232-9800, Fax 232-9853, 800-772-5897, 800-228-9290) 362 rooms and suites, restaurant, lounge, entertainment, indoor pool, exercise facilities, whirlpools, sauna, free parking, wheelchair access, TV, a/c, no-smoking rooms, gift shop, children stay free with parents, business services, meeting facilities, major credit cards. SGL/DBL$68-$108, STS$135.

Radisson Hotel (3635 Express Dr. North, 11788; 232-3000, Fax 232-3029, 800-777-1700) rooms and suites, restaurant, lounge, entertainment, pool, wheelchair access, free parking, no-smoking rooms, TV, a/c, children stay free with parents, pets allowed, major credit cards. SGL/DBL$74-$94.

Hawthorne
Area Code 914

Quality Inn (20 Saw Mill Rd, 10532; 592-8600, 800-368-5689) rooms and suites, restaurant, room service, exercise facilities, children stay free with parents, a/c, TV, laundry service, no-smoking rooms, meeting facilities, major credit cards. SGL/DBL$77-$95.

Hempstead
Area Code 516

Best Western Inn and Conference Center (Hempstead 11550; 486-4100, 800-528-1234) 182 rooms and suites, restaurant, complimentary breakfast, lounge, pool, exercise facilities, children stay free with parents, a/c, TV, no-smoking rooms, wheelchair access, pets allowed, senior citizen rates, meeting facilities, major credit cards. SGL/DBL$80-$95.

Duval Bed and Breakfast (237 Cathedral Ave, 11550; 292-9219) complimentary breakfast, antique furnishings, no smoking, TV, no pets, private baths, a/c. SGL/DBL$65-$85.

Henderson & Henderson Harbor
Area Code 315

Aspinwell House (Rte. 178, 13650; 938-5421) 24 rooms, TV, a/c, pets allowed, wheelchair access, open April 1 to October 31. SGL/DBL$54-$58.

Captain's Cove Motel (Harbor Rd, 13650; 938-5718, 800-824-FISH) 12 rooms, TV, a/c, wheelchair access, pets allowed, open April 15 to October 15. SGL/DBL$50-$60.

Dobson House Bed and Breakfast (Harbor Rd, 13650; 938-5901) 4 rooms, complimentary breakfast. SGL/DBL$55-$60.

Gill House Inn (Harbor Rd, 13650; 938-5013) 11 rooms, restaurant, lounge, pets allowed, wheelchair access, open April to October, fireplace, gift shop, a/c, TV. SGL/DBL$55.

Sunset Motel (Henderson 13650; 938-5011) 9 rooms and housekeeping cottages, no pets, open May 15 to October 15. SGL/DBL$38-$45.

West View Lodge (4001 Harbor Rd, 13650; 938-5722) 12 rooms, restaurant, lounge, TV, a/c, wheelchair access, no pets, open year-round. SGL/DBL$50-$60.

Henrietta
Area Code 716

Days Inn (4853 Henrietta Rd, 14467; 334-9300, Fax 334-8397, 800-325-2525) 192 rooms, restaurant, lounge, entertainment, pool, children stay free with parents, room service, laundry service, a/c, TV, free local calls, no pets, wheelchair access, no-smoking rooms, senior citizen rates, major credit cards. SGL/DBL$69-$89.

Super 8 Motel (1000 Lehigh Station Rd, 14467; 359-1630, Fax 359-1630, 800-800-8000) 120 rooms and suites, complimentary breakfast, no pets, children under 12 stay free with parents, car rental desk, free local calls, a/c, TV, fax service, no-smoking rooms, senior citizen rates, wheelchair access, meeting facilities, major credit cards. SGL$44, DBL$59-$51.

Hensonville
Area Code 518

Kallithea Hotel (Hensonville 12439; 734-3810) restaurant, lounge, entertainment, tennis court, open May to September, American plan available. SGL/DBL$88-$108.

Herkimer
Area Code 315

Glen Ridge (Rte. 5, 13350; 866-4149) 19 rooms, a/c, TV, wheelchair access, open year-round. SGL/DBL$35-$45.

Herkimer Motel (100 Marginal Rd, 13350; 866-0490) 60 rooms, restaurant, pool, a/c, TV, open year-round. SGL/DBL$36-$53.

Inn Towne Motel (Washington St, 13350; 866-1101) 33 rooms, restaurant, a/c, TV, wheelchair access. SGL/DBL$38-$45.

Mohawk Valley Motor Inn (715 Mohawk St, 13350; 866-6080) 15 rooms, restaurant, a/c, TV, open year-round. SGL/DBL$24.

The Prospect Inn (200 North Prospect St, 13350; 866-4400) 21 rooms, indoor pool, a/c, TV, open year-round, major credit cards. SGL/DBL$37.

Hicksville
Area Code 516

Days Inn (South Oyster Bay Rd, 11801; 433-1900, Fax 433-0218, 800-325-2525) 70 rooms and suites, restaurant, lounge, outdoor pool, children stay free with parents, room service, laundry service, a/c, TV, free local calls, no pets, wheelchair access, no-smoking rooms, senior citizen rates, major credit cards. SGL/DBL$80, STS$86.

Econo Lodge (429 Duffy Ave, 11801; 433-3900, 800-4-CHOICE) 72 rooms, complimentary breakfast, pool, TV, children under 12 stay free with parents, no pets, senior citizen rates, wheelchair access, a/c, TV, major credit cards. SGL/DBL$55-$90.

Hobart
Area Code 607

Breezy Acres Farm (Hobart 13788; 538-9338) bed and breakfast, no smoking, private baths, no pets. SGL/DBL$55-$60.

Hoosick Falls
Area Code 518

The Gypsy Lady (Hoosick Falls 12090; 686-4880) bed and breakfast, no smoking, private baths, sauna, major credit cards. SGL/DBL$50-$65.

Hornell
Area Code 607

Super 8 Motel (Rte. 36 and Webb Crossing, 14843; 324-6222, Fax 324-2990, 800-800-8000) 49 rooms and suites, restaurant, no pets, children under 12 stay free with parents, free local calls, a/c, TV, fax service, no-smoking rooms, senior citizen rates, wheelchair access, meeting facilities, major credit cards. SGL/DBL$40-$48.

Horseheads
Area Code 607

Holiday Inn (602 Corning Rd, 14852; 739-3681, Fax 739-3681 ext 160, 800-HOLIDAY) 100 rooms, restaurant, lounge, outdoor pool, exercise facilities, children under 19 stay free with parents, wheelchair access, a/c, TV, no-smoking rooms, fax, room service, no pets, laundry service, meeting facilities, senior citizen rates, major credit cards. SGL/DBL$55-$65.

Howard Johnson Lodge (Rte. 17, 14845; 739-5636, Fax 739-8630, 800-I-GO-HOJO) 76 rooms, restaurant, lounge, pool, children stay free with parents, wheelchair access, no-smoking rooms, TV, a/c, pets allowed, free parking, meeting facilities, fax service, senior citizen rates, meeting facilities, major credit cards. LS SGL/DBL$42-$56; HS SGL/DBL$48-$64.

Motel 6 (151 Rte. 17, 14845; 739-2525) 83 rooms, pool, free local calls, children under 17 stay free with parents, a/c, TV, major credit cards. SGL/DBL$36-$42.

Howes Cave
Area Code 518

Howe Caverns Motel (Howes Cave 12092; 296-8950) 22 rooms, restaurant, pool, a/c, TV, open April to October. SGL/DBL$40.

Hunter
Area Code 518

Dew Drop Inn (Cohen Rd, 12442; 263-4189) 5 rooms, bed and breakfast, open May to October. SGL/DBL$48-$56.

Fitch House Bed and Breakfast (Main St, 12442; 718-768-4138) 4 rooms, complimentary breakfast, 1890s home, private bath, fireplace, TV, open year-round. SGL/DBL$65-$75.

Hunter Inn and Motel (Hunter 12442; 263-3777) 35 rooms, restaurant, lounge, entertainment, no pets, whirlpool baths, a/c, TV, open May through October. SGL/DBL$75-$150.

Scribner Hollow Motor Lodge (Rte. 23A, 12442; 263-4211) restaurant, indoor and outdoor pools, sauna, whirlpools, a/c, TV, Modified American Plan available. SGL/DBL$72-$150.

Sunland Farm and Cottages (Rte. 23A, 12442; 263-4811, 800-333-2267) restaurant, pool, a/c, no pets, TV, open year-round, Modified American Plan available. SGL/DBL$50-$65.

Washington Irving Lodge (Rte. 23A, 12442; 589-5560) bed and breakfast, restaurant, lounge, private baths, TV, a/c, open year-round. SGL/DBL$50-$100.

Huntington Station
Area Code 516

Howard Johnson Lodge (270 West Jericho Turnpike, 11746; 421-3900, Fax 421-5287, 800-I-GO-HOJO) 63 rooms, suites and apartments, restaurant, complimentary breakfast, lounge, pool, children stay free with parents, wheelchair access, no-smoking rooms, TV, a/c, pets allowed, free newspaper, whirlpools, free parking, meeting facilities, senior citizen rates, major credit cards. LS SGL/DBL$59-$80; HS SGL/DBL$100-$125.

Hyde Park
Area Code 914

Super 8 Motel (528 Albany Post Rd, 12538; 229-0088, Fax 229-8088, 800-800-8000) 61 rooms and suites, restaurant, complimentary breakfast, no pets, children under 12 stay free with parents, free local calls, a/c, TV, fax service, no-smoking rooms, senior citizen rates, wheelchair access, meeting facilities, major credit cards. SGL/DBL$43-$50.

Ilion
Area Code 315

Wiffletree Inn (345 East Main St, 13357; 895-7777) 35 rooms, restaurant, wheelchair access, a/c, TV, open year-round. SGL/DBL$38.

Indian Lake
Area Code 518

Adirondack Trail Complex (Rte. 28, 12842; 648-5044) 10 rooms, restaurant, a/c, TV, wheelchair access, open year-round. SGL/DBL$60.

Geandreau's (Rte. 28, 12842; 648-5500) 7 rooms, open year-round. SGL/DBL$40-$280.

Lone Birch Motel (Rte. 28, 12842; 648-5225) rooms and housekeeping cabins, open year-round, kitchenettes, a/c, TV, wheelchair access, water view. SGL/DBL$40-$50.

Marty's Motel (Rte. 28, 12842; 648-5528) 3 rooms, open year-round. SGL/DBL$40.

Smith's Cottages and Cabins (Indian Lake 12842; 648-5222) 12 housekeeping cottages and cabins, kitchenettes, boating, water view, open May to October, a/c, TV. SGL/DBL$46-$53.

Squaw Brook Motel (Indian Lake 12842; 648-5262) 8 rooms, pool, open April to November, a/c, TV, wheelchair access. SGL/DBL$40.

Inlet
Area Code 315

Marina Motel (Inlet 13360; 357-3883) 16 rooms, restaurant, a/c, TV, no pets, water view, major credit cards. SGL/DBL$45-$50.

Islandia
Area Code 516

Hampton Inn (1600 Veterans Memorial Hwy, 11722; 234-0400, Fax 234-0415, 800-HAMPTON) 121 rooms, restaurant, complimentary breakfast, pool, exercise facilities, children under 18 stay free with parents, no-smoking rooms, wheelchair access, computer hookups, airport transportation, fax service, TV, a/c, free local calls, pets allowed, meeting facilities, major credit cards. SGL/DBL$74-$84.

Islip
Area Code 516

Holiday Inn (3845 Veterans Memorial Highway, 11779; 585-9500, Fax 585-9550, 800-HOLIDAY) 289 rooms, restaurant, lounge, outdoor pool, exercise facilities, children under 19 stay free with parents, wheelchair access, a/c, gift shop, car rental desk, whirlpools, TV, no-smoking rooms, fax service, room service, no pets, laundry service, meeting facilities for 425, senior citizen rates, major credit cards. SGL/DBL$65-$85.

Ithaca
Area Code 607

Buttermilk Falls Bed and Breakfast (110 East Buttermilk Falls Rd, 14850; 272-6767) 6 rooms, complimentary breakfast, jacuzzi, fireplace. SGL/DBL$36-$46.

The Danby House (1758 Danby Rd, 14850; 277-5603) 4 rooms, bed and breakfast, 1800s home, antique furnishings. SGL/DBL$55-$110.

Econo Lodge (2303 North Triphammer Rd, 14750; 257-1400, 800-4-CHOICE) 72 rooms, pool, children under 12 stay free with parents, whirlpools, no pets, senior citizen rates, wheelchair access, a/c, TV, major credit cards. SGL/DBL$39-$75.

Elmshade Guest House (402 South Albany St, 14850; 263-1707) 8 rooms, complimentary breakfast, a/c, TV. SGL/DBL$65.

Glendale Farm Bed and Breakfast (224 Bostwick Rd, 14850; 272-8756) 6 rooms, complimentary breakfast, no smoking, antique furnishings, pets allowed, private baths, major credit cards. SGL/DBL$70-$100.

Goose Lake Bed and Breakfast (400 Nelson Rd, 14850; 273-8801) 2 rooms, complimentary breakfast, on 50 acres, private bath. SGL/DBL$65-$75.

Hanshaw House (15 Sapsucker Woods Rd, 14850; 273-8034) 4 rooms, complimentary breakfast, 1830s home, water view, a/c, antique furnishings, private baths. SGL/DBL$55-$75.

Holiday Inn (2310 North Triphammer Rd, 14850; 257-3100, 800-HOLIDAY) 120 rooms, restaurant, lounge, outdoor pool, exercise facilities, children under 19 stay free with parents, wheelchair access, transportation to local attractions, airport transportation, a/c, TV, no-smoking rooms, fax service, room service, pets allowed, laundry service, meeting facilities for 350, senior citizen rates, major credit cards. SGL/DBL$48-$88.

Howard Johnson Lodge (2300 North Triphammer Rd, 14850; 257-1212, Fax 257-1212 ext 145, 800-I-GO-HOJO) 72 rooms, restaurant, lounge, pool, game rooms, fax service, VCRs, room service, children stay free with parents, wheelchair access, no-smoking rooms, TV, a/c, pets allowed, free parking, meeting facilities, senior citizen rates, major credit cards. SGL$40-$75, DBL$40-$90.

Ithaca Family Bed and Breakfast (312 Salem Dr., 14850; 257-7657) 1 2-bedroom suite, complimentary breakfast, private bath, kitchenette, TV. SGL/DBL$65-$75.

Log Country Inn (Box 581, 14851; 800-274-4771) 5 rooms, complimentary breakfast, private baths. SGL/DBL$50-$70.

MacIntire's Cottage Bed and Breakfast (217 Eastern Heights Dr., 14850; 273-8888) 2 rooms, complimentary breakfast, spa, wheelchair access. SGL/DBL$36-$46.

Meadow Court Inn (529 South Meadow St, 14850; 273-3885) 58 rooms, restaurant, a/c, TV, meeting facilities for 50, major credit cards. SGL/DBL$68+.

Ramada Inn (222 South Cayuga St, 14850; 272-1000, Fax 277-1275, 800-2-RAMADA) 177 rooms and suites, restaurant, lounge, entertainment, indoor pool, wheelchair access, no-smoking rooms, airport transportation, free parking, pets allowed, wheelchair access, a/c, TV, room service, laundry facilities, 5 meeting rooms, meeting facilities for 300, senior citizen rates, major credit cards. SGL$55-$75, DBL$60-$80.

Rita's Country Bed and Breakfast (1620 Hanshaw Rd, 14850; 257-2499, 800-231-6674) 3 rooms, complimentary breakfast, major credit cards. SGL/DBL$45-$90.

Rose Inn (Box 6576, 14850; 533-7905) 15 rooms and suites, restaurant, complimentary breakfast, fireplace, antique furnishings, meeting facilities for 75, 1840s inn, a/c, TV, major credit cards. SGL/DBL$65-$85.

Sheraton Inn and Conference Center (One Sheraton Dr., 14850; 257-2000, Fax 257-3998, 800-325-3535) 106 rooms and suites, restaurant, lounge, entertainment, indoor pool, exercise facilities, sauna, no-smoking rooms, a/c, TV, children stay free with parents, wheelchair access, 9,000 square feet of meeting and exhibition space, 13 meeting rooms, meeting facilities for 650, major credit cards. SGL/DBL$70-$135.

The Statler Hotel (Cornell University, 14850; 257-2500, 800-541-2501) 150 rooms, restaurant, a/c, TV, wheelchair access, major credit cards. SGL/DBL$115-$125.

Super 8 Motel (400 South Meadow, 14850; 273-8088, Fax 273-4832, 800-800-8000) 63 rooms and suites, no pets, children under 12 stay free with parents, free local calls, a/c, TV, fax service, no-smoking rooms, senior citizen rates, wheelchair access, meeting facilities, major credit cards. SGL/DBL$40-$50.

Whitetail Crossing Cottage (21 Belevedere Dr., 14850; 257-3946) 2 and 3-bedroom housekeeping cottages, on 52 acres, water view. SGL/DBL$85-$125.

Jackson Heights
Area Code 718

Westway Motor Inn (71-11 Astoria Blvd, 11372; 274-2800) 145 rooms, TV, a/c, major credit cards. SGL/DBL$55-$75.

Jacksonville
Area Code 607

Pleasant Grove Bed and Breakfast (1779 Trumansburg Rd, 14850; 387-5420) 3 rooms, complimentary breakfast. SGL/DBL$65-$75.

Jamaica
Area Code 718

Hilton Huntington Hotel (138-10 135th Ave, 11436; 322-8700, Fax 529-0749, 800-HILTONS) 334 rooms and suites, restaurant, lounge, entertainment, outdoor pool, exercise facilities, jacuzzi, airport courtesy car, free parking, children stay free with parents, no-smoking rooms, wheelchair access, pets allowed, a/c, TV, business services, meeting facilities, major credit cards. SGL/DBL$150-$190.

Holiday Inn JFK International Airport (144-02 135th Ave, 11436; 659-0200, Fax 322-2533, 800-HOLIDAY) 360 rooms, restaurant, lounge, indoor pool, exercise facilities, children under 12 stay free with parents, wheelchair access, no-smoking rooms, fax service, room service, a/c, TV, gift shop, airport transportation, no pets, meeting facilities for 600, major credit cards. SGL/DBL$145-$170.

Kennedy Inn (151-20 Baisley Blvd, 11434; 276-6666, Fax 276-7777, 800-826-4667) 200 rooms and suites, 2 restaurants, lounge, a/c, TV, 3,500 square feet of meeting and exhibition space, meeting facilities for 200, major credit cards. SGL/DBL$95-$165.

TraveLodge JFK Airport (Van Wyck Expressway, 11430; 995-9000, Fax 995-9075, 800-255-3050) 500 rooms and suites, restaurant, lounge, entertainment, complimentary breakfast, pool, wheelchair access, free newspaper, laundry service, gift shop, free parking, TV, a/c, free local calls, fax service, no-smoking rooms, free in-room coffee and tea service, in-room refrigerators and microwaves, no pets, meeting facilities for 800, major credit cards. SGL/DBL$99-$119, AP$10.

Jamestown
Area Code 716

The Colony Motel (620 Fairmount Ave, 14701; 488-1904) 45 rooms and efficiencies, restaurant, lounge, pool, a/c, TV, major credit cards. SGL/DBL$36-$46.

Comfort Inn (2800 North Main St, 14701; 664-5920, 800-221-2222) restaurant, whirlpools, wheelchair access, no-smoking rooms, no pets, children under 18 stay free with parents, senior citizen rates, a/c, TV, meeting facilities, major credit cards. SGL$46-$78, DBL$51-$78, AP$5.

Holiday Inn (150 West Fourth St, 14701; 664-3400, Fax 484-3304, 800-HOLIDAY) 148 rooms, restaurant, lounge, indoor pool, exercise facilities, children under 19 stay free with parents, wheelchair access, a/c, TV, no-smoking rooms, fax service, room service, no pets, laundry service, meeting facilities for 400, senior citizen rates, major credit cards. SGL/DBL$59-$69.

Jamesville
Area Code 315

High Meadows Bed and Breakfast (3740 Eager Rd, 13078; 492-3517) complimentary breakfast, no smoking. SGL/DBL$40-$55.

Jericho
Area Code 516

Comfort Inn (101 Jericho Turnpike, 11753; 334-8811, 800-221-2222) 74 rooms, restaurant, wheelchair access, transportation to local attractions, exercise facilities, no-smoking rooms, no pets, children under 18 stay free with parents, senior citizen rates, a/c, TV, meeting facilities, major credit cards. SGL$60-$100, DBL$65-$115.

Howard Johnson Lodge (120 Jericho Turnpike, 11753; 333-9700, Fax 333-9393, 800-I-GO-HOJO) 80 rooms, restaurant, lounge, pool, whirlpools, children stay free with parents, wheelchair access, no-smoking rooms, TV, a/c, pets allowed, free parking, meeting facilities, fax, senior citizen rates, major credit cards. LS SGL/DBL$59-$79; HS SGL/DBL$100-$115.

Jewett
Area Code 518

Hilltop Acres Retreat (Box 37, 12444; 734-4580) restaurant, water view, open year-round. SGL/DBL$45-$55.

Johnson City
Area Code 607

Best Western Inn (569 Harry L. Dr., 13790; 722-7575, Fax 724-7263, 800-528-1234) 102 rooms, restaurant, complimentary breakfast, lounge, indoor pool, exercise facilities, sauna, whirlpools, children stay free with parents, a/c, TV, no-smoking rooms, wheelchair access, pets allowed, senior citizen rates, meeting facilities, major credit cards. SGL/DBL$42-$60.

Johnstown
Area Code 581

Holiday Inn (308 North Comrie Ave, 12095; 762-4686, 762-4034, 800-HOLIDAY) 134 rooms, restaurant, lounge, outdoor pool, exercise facilities, children under 19 stay free with parents, wheelchair access, a/c, TV, no-smoking rooms, fax service, room service, no pets, laundry service, meeting facilities for 300, senior citizen rates, major credit cards. SGL/DBL$60-$80.

Super 8 Motel (North Comrie Ave, 12095; 736-1800, Fax 736-1838, 800-800-8000) 47 rooms and suites, no pets, children under 12 stay free with parents, free local calls, a/c, TV, fax service, no-smoking rooms, senior citizen rates, wheelchair access, meeting facilities, major credit cards. SGL/DBL$40-$50.

Keene
Area Code 518

The Bark Eater Inn (Alstead Hill Rd, 12942) rooms, complimentary breakfast, no pets. SGL/DBL$60-$130.

Kenmore
Area Code 716

Concord Inn (Sheridan Dr., 14217; 876-4020) 59 rooms, restaurant, lounge, no-smoking rooms, free parking, major credit cards. SGL/DBL$28-$48.

Kingston
Area Code 914

Days Inn (Rte. 28 West, 12401; 331-1919, Fax 338-4136, 800-325-2525) 59 rooms, restaurant, lounge, pool, children stay free with parents, room service, laundry service, a/c, TV, free local calls, in-room refrigerators, no pets, wheelchair access, no-smoking rooms, senior citizen rates, major credit cards. SGL/DBL$45-$65.

Holiday Inn (503 Washington Ave, 12401; 338-0400, Fax 338-0400 ext 389, 800-HOLIDAY) 212 rooms and suites, restaurant, lounge, entertainment, outdoor pool, exercise facilities, children under 19 stay free with parents, wheelchair access, a/c, TV, no-smoking rooms, fax service, room service, no pets, laundry service, meeting facilities for 500, senior citizen rates, major credit cards. SGL/DBL$65-$74, STS$75-$125.

HoJo Inn (129 Rte. 28, 12401; 338-4200, Fax 339-3044, 800-I-GO-HOJO) 116 rooms, restaurant, lounge, indoor pool, sauna, laundry service, children stay free with parents, wheelchair access, no-smoking rooms, TV, a/c, pets allowed, free parking, meeting facilities, senior citizen rates, major credit cards. LS SGL/DBL$49-$63; HS SGL/DBL$49-$74.

Ramada Inn (Rte. 28, 12401; 339-3900, Fax 339-3900 ext 102, 800-2-RAMADA) 147 rooms and suites, restaurant, lounge, indoor pool, exercise facilities, wheelchair access, no-smoking rooms, airport transportation, free parking, pets allowed, wheelchair access, a/c, TV, room service, laundry facilities, 4 meeting rooms, meeting facilities for 225, senior citizen rates, major credit cards. SGL$59-$125, DBL$69-$140.

Super 8 Motel (487 Washington Ave, 12401; 338-3078, Fax 338-3078, 800-800-8000) 84 rooms and suites, no pets, children under 12 stay free with parents, free local calls, a/c, TV, fax service, no-smoking rooms, senior citizen rates, wheelchair access, meeting facilities, major credit cards. SGL/DBL$49-$55.

Lake George
Area Code 518

Days Inn (Rte. 9, 12845; 793-3196, Fax 793-6028, 800-325-2525) 110 rooms, restaurant, lounge, indoor pool, jacuzzi, children stay free with parents, room service, laundry service, a/c, TV, free local calls, no pets, wheelchair access, no-smoking rooms, senior citizen rates, major credit cards. LS SGL$44-$64, DBL$48-$68; HS SGL$64-$116, DBL$68-$126.

Econo Lodge (431 Canada St, 12845; 668-2689, 800-4-CHOICE) 50 rooms, indoor pool, whirlpools, children under 12 stay free with parents, no pets, senior citizen rates, wheelchair access, a/c, TV, major credit cards. SGL/DBL$35-$98.

Holiday Inn (Canada St, 12845; 668-5781, Fax 668-9213, 800-HOLIDAY) 105 rooms, restaurant, lounge, entertainment, indoor pool, exercise facilities, children under 19 stay free with parents, game room, wheelchair access, a/c, TV, no-smoking rooms, fax service, room service, gift shop, no pets, laundry service, meeting facilities, senior citizen rates, major credit cards. SGL/DBL$65-$85.

Howard Johnson Resort Lodge (Canada St, 12845; 668-5744, Fax 668-3544, 800-I-GO-HOJO) 110 rooms and suites, restaurant, lounge, pool, children stay free with parents, wheelchair access, no-smoking rooms, TV, a/c, pets allowed, free parking, senior citizen rates, meeting facilities for 300, major credit cards. SGL/DBL$39-$69.

Ramada Inn (Rte. 9 North, 12845; 668-3131, Fax 668-3131 ext 412, 800-2-RAMADA) 96 rooms, restaurant, lounge, entertainment, indoor pool, jacuzzi, sauna, game room, wheelchair access, no-smoking rooms, airport transportation, free parking, pets allowed, a/c, TV, room service, laundry facilities, meeting facilities, senior citizen rates, major credit cards. SGL/DBL$39-$135, AP$8.

Super 8 Motel (Rte. 9, 12845; 623-2811, Fax 623-2874, 800-800-8000) 32 rooms and suites, no pets, children under 12 stay free with parents, free local calls, a/c, TV, fax, no-smoking rooms, senior citizen rates, wheelchair access, meeting facilities, major credit cards. SGL/DBL$40-$55.

TraveLodge (Canada St, 12845; 668-5421, Fax 668-4926, 800-255-3050) 102 rooms, restaurant, lounge, complimentary breakfast, pool, wheelchair access, free newspaper, laundry service, TV, a/c, free local calls, fax service, no-smoking rooms, free in-room coffee and tea service, in-room refrigerators and microwaves, no pets, major credit cards. LS SGL/DBL$42-$69; HS SGL/DBL$74-$93.

Lake Luzerne
Area Code 518

The Lamplighter Inn (2129 Lake Ave, 12846; 696-5294) 10 rooms, bed and breakfast, fireplaces, private baths, open year-round. LS SGL/DBL$70-$105; HS SGL/DBL$95-$135.

Luzerne Motor Court (Rte. 9N, 12846; 696-2734) 10 rooms and efficiencies, coffee shop, pool, a/c, TV, open May through October. SGL/DBL$50-$80.

Lake Placid
Area Code 518

The Blackberry Inn (59 Sentinel Rd, 12946; 523-3419) bed and breakfast, no pets. SGL/DBL$30-$46.

Econo Lodge (Cascade Rd, 12946; 523-2817, 800-4-CHOICE) 61 rooms, complimentary breakfast, indoor pool, TV, children under 12 stay free with parents, pets allowed, senior citizen rates, wheelchair access, laundry facilities, a/c, TV, major credit cards. SGL/DBL$45-$98.

Highland House Inn (Three Highland Place, 12946; 523-2377) bed and breakfast, private baths, no pets, major credit cards. SGL/DBL$50-$95.

Hilton Hotel (One Mirror Lake Dr., 12946; 523-4411, 523-1120, 800-HIL-TONS) 178 rooms and suites, restaurant, lounge, entertainment, indoor and outdoor pool, exercise facilities, children stay free with parents, no-smoking rooms, water view, free parking, wheelchair access, pets allowed, a/c, TV, business services, meeting facilities, major credit cards. SGL/DBL$56-$156.

Holiday Inn (One Olympic Dr., 12946; 523-2556, Fax 523-9410, 800-HOLIDAY) 202 rooms, restaurant, lounge, entertainment, indoor pool, whirlpools, exercise facilities, children under 19 stay free with parents, wheelchair access, a/c, TV, no-smoking rooms, fax service, room service, no pets, laundry service, meeting facilities for 600, senior citizen rates, major credit cards. SGL/DBL$47-$186.

Howard Johnson Resort Lodge (90 Saranac Ave, 12946; 523-9555, 800-858-4656, 800-I-GO-HOJO) 92 rooms, restaurant, lounge, pool, whirlpools, fax, laundry service, children stay free with parents, wheelchair access, no-smoking rooms, TV, a/c, pets allowed, free parking, meeting facilities, senior citizen rates, major credit cards. SGL$48-$120, DBL$58-$120.

Interlaken Inn (15 Interlaken Rd, 12946; 523-3180) bed and breakfast, restaurant, fireplace. SGL/DBL$100-$190.

Ramada Inn (8 Saranac Ave, 12946; 523-2587, Fax 523-2328, 800-2-RAMADA) 90 rooms, restaurant, lounge, indoor pool, wheelchair access, no-smoking rooms, airport transportation, free parking, pets allowed, a/c, TV, room service, laundry facilities, meeting facilities, senior citizen rates, major credit cards. LS SGL$63-$93, DBL$73-$103; HS SGL$73-$93, DBL$83-$103.

The Spruce Lodge (31 Sentinel Rd, 12946; 523-9350) bed and breakfast, no smoking rooms, private baths, major credit cards. SGL/DBL$45.

Lansing
Area Code 607

The Cuddle Duck (Lansing 14882; 257-2821) 3 rooms, bed and breakfast, water view. SGL/DBL$55-$65.

Latham
Area Code 518

Cocca's Esquire Motel and Lodge (979 Troy-Schenectady Rd, 12110; 785-5571) 37 rooms, restaurant, lounge, in-room refrigerators, no-smoking rooms, pets allowed, a/c, TV, major credit cards. SGL/DBL$25-$60.

Cocca's Thunderbird Motel (Rtes 9 and 27, 12110; 785-6626) 66 rooms, restaurant, kitchenettes, outdoor pool, a/c, TV, pets allowed, no-smoking rooms, major credit cards. SGL/DBL$25-$60.

Cocca's Travel-Rite Inn (706 New Loudon Rd, 12110; 785-0776) 49 rooms, no-smoking rooms, a/c, TV. SGL/DBL$30-$60.

Comfort Inn Airport (866 Albany-Shaker Rd, 12110; 783-1216, 800-274-9429, 800-221-2222) 99 rooms, restaurant, pool, wheelchair access, no-smoking rooms, no pets, children under 18 stay free with parents, senior citizen rates, a/c, TV, meeting facilities, major credit cards. SGL$54-$65, DBL$60-$71, AP$6.

Hampton Inn (Rte. 9, 12110; 785-0000, 800-HAMPTON) 126 rooms, restaurant, complimentary breakfast, outdoor pool, exercise facilities, children under 18 stay free with parents, no-smoking rooms, wheelchair access, in-room computer hookups, airport transportation, fax service, TV, a/c, free local calls, pets allowed, meeting facilities, major credit cards. SGL/DBL$45-$65.

Holiday Inn Airport (Rte. 9, 12110; 783-6161, Fax 783-0154, 800-HOLIDAY) 120 rooms, restaurant, complimentary breakfast, lounge, outdoor pool, exercise facilities, children under 19 stay free with parents, wheelchair access, a/c, TV, no-smoking rooms, fax service, room service, airport transportation, pets allowed, laundry service, meeting facilities for 200, senior citizen rates, major credit cards. SGL/DBL$68-$110.

Howard Johnson Hotel (611 Troy-Schenectady Rd, 12110; 785-5891, Fax 785-5805, 800-I-GO-HOJO) 146 rooms, restaurant, lounge, pool, exercise facilities, airport courtesy car, children stay free with parents, wheelchair access, no-smoking rooms, TV, a/c, pets allowed, free parking, senior citizen rates, meeting facilities for 50, major credit cards. SGL/DBL$75-$105.

The Lookout Inn (622 Watervliet-Shaker Rd, 12110; 785-1414, 800-4-LATHAM) 56 rooms, restaurant, lounge, pool, kitchenettes, in-room refrigerators, TV, a/c, wheelchair access, no-smoking rooms, major credit cards. SGL/DBL$40-$60.

Super 8 Motel (681 Troy Schenectady Rd, 12110; 783-8808, Fax 783-1002, 800-800-8000) 44 rooms and suites, restaurant, no pets, children under 12 stay free with parents, free local calls, a/c, TV, fax service, no-smoking rooms, senior citizen rates, wheelchair access, meeting facilities, major credit cards. SGL/DBL$49-$74.

Sycamore Motel (956 New Loudon Rd, 12211; 753-5095) SGL/DBL$45-$53.

Laurens
Area Code 607

Fina's Cottages (Gilbert Lake Rd, 13796; 432-5818) 5 housekeeping cottages, open year-round. SGL/DBL$80-$100.

Leeds
Area Code 518

Jolly House Motel Resort (Rte. 32B, 12451; 943-2990, 800-752-0232 in New York) restaurant, lounge, entertainment, TV, a/c, no-smoking rooms, wheelchair access, open May to October. SGL/DBL$55-$75.

The Place Motor Court (Old Rte. 23B, 12451; 943-9734) efficiencies, restaurant, coffee shop, pool, a/c, kitchenettes, TV, open year-round. SGL/DBL$60.

Pleasant Acres (Leeds 12451; 943-4011) restaurant, lounge, entertainment, indoor and outdoor pool, sauna, tennis courts, a/c, TV, open June to mid-September, major credit cards. SGL/DBL$80-$140.

LeRoy
Area Code 716

Bentley House (123 East Main St, 14482; 768-4512) 3 rooms, bed and breakfast, open year-round, private bath. SGL/DBL$45-$50.

Edson House (LeRoy 14482; 768-2340) complimentary breakfast, private baths, no pets. SGL/DBL$40-$60.

Liberty
Area Code 914

Days Inn (Sullivan Ave, 12754; 292-7600, Fax 292-3303, 800-325-2525) 120 rooms, restaurant, lounge, indoor and outdoor pool, children stay free with parents, room service, laundry service, a/c, TV, free local calls, no pets, wheelchair access, no-smoking rooms, senior citizen rates, major credit cards. SGL/DBL$50-$80.

Holiday Inn (Rte. 17, 12754; 292-7171, Fax 292-0203, 800-HOLIDAY) 70 rooms, restaurant, lounge, outdoor pool, exercise facilities, children under 19 stay free with parents, wheelchair access, a/c, TV, no-smoking rooms, fax service, room service, pets allowed, laundry service, meeting facilities for 30, senior citizen rates, major credit cards. SGL/DBL$50-$75.

Little Falls
Area Code 315

Best Western Motor Inn (20 Albany St, 13365; 823-4954, 800-528-1234) 56 rooms, restaurant, complimentary breakfast, lounge, pool, exercise facilities, children stay free with parents, a/c, TV, game room, no-smoking rooms, wheelchair access, pets allowed, senior citizen rates, major credit cards. SGL/DBL$54-$60.

The Gansevoort House Bed and Breakfast (42 West Gansevoort St, 13365; 823-3969) complimentary breakfast, 1880s home, fireplace. SGL/DBL$40+.

Liverpool
Area Code 315

Days Inn (400 7th North St, 13088; 451-1511, 800-325-2525) 126 rooms, restaurant, lounge, pool, children stay free with parents, room service, laundry service, a/c, TV, free local calls, no pets, wheelchair access, no-smoking rooms, senior citizen rates, major credit cards. SGL/DBL$62-$93.

Econo Lodge (401 7 North St, 13088; 4651-6000, 800-4-CHOICE) 84 rooms, pool, children under 12 stay free with parents, no pets, senior citizen rates, wheelchair access, a/c, TV, major credit cards. SGL/DBL$42-$68.

Friendship Inn (629 Old Liverpool Rd, 13088; 457-1240, 800-424-4777) 64 rooms, restaurant, lounge, entertainment, exercise facilities, a/c, TV, no pets, no-smoking rooms, children stay free with parents, wheelchair access, no-smoking rooms, major credit cards. SGL/DBL$39-$83.

Homewood Suites (275 Elwood Davis Rd, 13088; 451-3800, 800-CALL-HOME) 1- and 2-bedroom suites, free breakfast, pool, whirlpool, exercise facilities, in-room refrigerators, coffee makers and microwaves, fireplace, fax, airport transportation, pets allowed, TV, a/c, complimentary newspaper, no-smoking rooms, wheelchair access, senior citizen rates, business services, meeting facilities. 1BR$79-$89, 2BR$89-$109.

Knights Inn (430 Electronics Pkwy, 13088; 453-6330, 800-843-5644) pool, wheelchair access, no-smoking rooms, TV, a/c, in-room refrigerators and microwaves, fax service, free parking, VCRs, senior citizen rates, major credit cards. SGL/DBL$45-$65.

Sheraton Inn (7 North St, 13088; 457-1122, 800-325-3535) 280 rooms and suites, restaurant, lounge, entertainment, indoor pool, exercise facilities, whirlpools, airport courtesy car, no-smoking rooms, a/c, TV, children stay free with parents, wheelchair access, gift shop, 25,000 square feet of meeting and exhibition space, 13 meeting rooms, meeting facilities for 2,500, major credit cards. SGL/DBL$85-$105.

Super 8 Motel (421 7th North St, 13088; 451-8888, Fax 451-0043, 800-800-8000) 99 rooms and suites, complimentary breakfast, no pets, children under 12 stay free with parents, free local calls, a/c, TV, fax service, no-smoking rooms, senior citizen rates, wheelchair access, meeting facilities, major credit cards. SGL/DBL$45, DBL$50.

Lockport
Area Code 716

Comfort Inn (551 South Transit Rd, 14094; 434-4411, 800-221-2222) 50 rooms, restaurant, exercise facilities, wheelchair access, no-smoking rooms, no pets, children under 18 stay free with parents, senior citizen rates, a/c, TV, meeting facilities, major credit cards. SGL$50-$125, DBL$60-$150, AP$10.

Long Island City
Area Code 718

Best Western Airport (33-17 Greenpoint Ave, 11101; 392-8400, Fax 392-2110, 800-528-1234) 165 rooms, restaurant, exercise facilities, airport transportation, no pets, no-smoking rooms, wheelchair access, TV, a/c, children stay free with parents. SGL/DBL$89-$115.

Turf Club Motor Inn (31-62 14th St, 11101; 932-2100) 32 rooms, TV, a/c, major credit cards. SGL/DBL$45-$56.

Long Lake
Area Code 518

Sandy Point Motel (Long Lake 12847; 624-3817) 10 rooms and efficiencies, a/c, TV, beach, water view, no pets, major credit cards. SGL/DBL$40-$58.

Shamrock Motel (Long Lake 12847; 624-3861) 17 rooms and 2-bedroom housekeeping cottages, laundry facilities, no pets, TV, beach, water view, major credit cards. SGL/DBL$40-$55, 2BR$400W-$500W.

Whispering Woods Campground and Cottages (Walker Rd, 12847; 624-5121) housekeeping cottages, water view. SGL/DBL$38-$46.

Malone
Area Code 518

Econo Lodge (227 West Main St, 12953; 483-0500, 800-4-CHOICE) 45 rooms, restaurant, complimentary breakfast, pool, TV, children under 12 stay free with parents, pets allowed, senior citizen rates, wheelchair access, a/c, major credit cards. SGL/DBL$40-$50.

Malta
Area Code 518

Cocca's Motel (2624 Rte. 9, 12020; 581-1033) 14 rooms, complimentary breakfast, a/c, in-room refrigerators. SGL/DBL$36-$46.

The Post Road Lodge (2865 Rte. 9, 12020; 584-4169, 800-TENANTS) rooms and efficiencies, a/c, TV. SGL/DBL$44.

Manchester
Area Code 716

Friendship Inn (Highway 96, 14504; 289-3811; 800-424-4777) 36 rooms, exercise facilities, a/c, TV, no pets, no-smoking rooms, major credit cards. SGL/DBL$42-$52.

Maplecrest
Area Code 518

Salisbury Inn (Maplecrest 12454; 734-9834) 6 rooms, restaurant, private baths, game room, TV, open year-round, Modified American Plan available. SGL/DBL$65-$105.

Sugar Maples (Main St, 12454; 734-4000) 150 rooms, restaurant, lounge, entertainment, pool, fireplaces, a/c, TV. SGL/DBL$53-$75.

Massena
Area Code 315

Econo Lodge (Massena 13662; 764-0246, 800-4-CHOICE) 44 rooms, complimentary breakfast, pool, TV, children under 12 stay free with parents, no pets, senior citizen rates, wheelchair access, a/c, major credit cards. SGL/DBL$50-$90.

Super 8 Motel (Grove St Extension, 13662; 764-1065, Fax 764-9710, 800-800-8000) 41 rooms and suites, no pets, children under 12 stay free with parents, free local calls, a/c, TV, fax service, no-smoking rooms, senior citizen rates, wheelchair access, meeting facilities, major credit cards. SGL/DBL$42-$50.

Maybrook
Area Code 914

Days Inn (125 Neelytown Rd, 12549; 457-3163, Fax 457-3492, 800-325-2525) 36 rooms, restaurant, lounge, pool, children stay free with parents, room service, laundry service, a/c, TV, free local calls, no pets, wheelchair access, no-smoking rooms, senior citizen rates, major credit cards. SGL/DBL$37-$45.

Melville
Area Code 516

Hilton Huntington Hotel (598 Broad Hollow Rd, 11747; 845-1000, Fax 845-1223, 800-HILTONS) 305 rooms and suites, restaurant, lounge, entertainment, indoor and outdoor pool, exercise facilities, whirlpools, sauna, gift shop, children stay free with parents, no-smoking rooms, 24-hour room service, wheelchair access, pets allowed, a/c, TV, business services, meeting facilities, major credit cards. SGL/DBL$110.

Radisson Hotel (1350 Old Walt Whitman Rd, 11747; 423-1600, Fax 423-1790, 800-777-1700) rooms and suites, restaurant, lounge, entertainment, pool, wheelchair access, free parking, no-smoking rooms, TV, a/c, children stay free with parents, pets allowed, major credit cards. SGL/DBL$110-$200.

Menands
Area Code 518

Ramada Inn Capital District (575 Broadway, 12204; 463-1121, Fax 449-5984, 800-2-RAMADA) 120 rooms, restaurant, lounge, entertainment, pool, wheelchair access, no-smoking rooms, airport transportation, free parking, pets allowed, wheelchair access, a/c, TV, room service, laundry facilities, meeting facilities for 200, senior citizen rates, major credit cards. LS SGL$44-$70, DBL$50-$92; HS SGL$60-$82, DBL$70-$92, AP$10.

Middle Grove
Area Code 518

Daybreak Motel (2909 Rte. 29, 12850; 882-6538) restaurant, open year-round, pets allowed, major credit cards. LS SGL/DBL$35-$45; HS SGL/DBL$60-$85.

Middletown
Area Code 914

Holiday Inn (Middletown Rd, 10940; 343-1474, 800-HOLIDAY) 164 rooms, restaurant, lounge, indoor pool, exercise facilities, children under 19 stay free with parents, wheelchair access, a/c, TV, no-smoking rooms, fax service, room service, no pets, laundry service, meeting facilities for 400, senior citizen rates, major credit cards. SGL/DBL$65-$75.

Howard Johnson Lodge (551 Rte. 211 East, 10940; 342-5822, Fax 695-2140, 800-I-GO-HOJO) 117 rooms, restaurant, lounge, pool, sauna, laundry facilities, children stay free with parents, wheelchair access, no-smoking rooms, TV, a/c, pets allowed, free parking, meeting facilities, senior citizen rates, major credit cards. LS SGL$53-$68, DBL$73-$78; HS SGL$73-$88, DBL$83-$98.

Super 8 Motel (563 Rte. 211 East, 10940; 692-5828, Fax 692-5828, 800-800-8000) 82 rooms and suites, pets allowed, children under 12 stay free with parents, free local calls, a/c, TV, fax service, no-smoking rooms, senior citizen rates, wheelchair access, meeting facilities, major credit cards. SGL/DBL$54-$57.

Milford
Area Code 607

Barb's Inn (East Main St, 13807; 286-7621) 7 rooms and suites, restaurant, TV, open year-round. SGL/DBL$50-$100.

Brookside Motel (North Main St, 13807; 286-9821) 9 rooms, TV, open May 15 to November 15. SGL/DBL$40-$60.

Montauk
Area Code 516

The Beachcomber Resort (Montauk 11954; 668-2894) 88 rooms and 1- and 2-bedroom suites, pool, tennis court, sauna, laundry facilities, a/c, TV, no pets, no-smoking rooms, major credit cards. SGL/DBL$75-$250.

Gurney's Inn (Old Montauk Hwy 11964; 668-2345, Fax 668-3576) 109 rooms, cottages and efficiencies, restaurant, indoor pool, exercise facilities, whirlpools, a/c, TV, kitchenettes, no pets, major credit cards. SGL/DBL$250-$350.

Montgomery
Area Code 914

Super 8 Motel (207 Montgomery Rd, 12549; 457-3143, Fax 457-3143, 800-800-8000) 96 rooms and suites, in-room microwaves, pets OK, children under 12 stay free with parents, free local calls, a/c, TV, fax service, no-smoking rooms, senior citizen rates, wheelchair access, meeting facilities, major credit cards. SGL/DBL$47-$52.

Monticello
Area Code 914

Econo Lodge (190 Broadway, 12701; 794-8800, 800-4-CHOICE) 47 rooms, complimentary breakfast, pool, TV, children under 12 stay free with parents, no pets, senior citizen rates, wheelchair access, a/c, free local calls, whirlpools, major credit cards. SGL/DBL$46-$80.

Friendship Inn (104 East Broadway, 12701; 794-4700, 800-424-4777) 41 rooms, exercise facilities, a/c, TV, no pets, no-smoking rooms, major credit cards. SGL/DBL$36-$40.

Morris
Area Code 607

Morris Inn (Rte. 51, 13808; 263-5903) 10 rooms, restaurant, a/c, TV, open May 15 to November 15. SGL/DBL$30-$40.

Mt. Kisco
Area Code 914

Holiday Inn (One Holiday Dr., 10549; 241-2600, Fax 241-4742, 800-HOLIDAY) 111 rooms and suites, restaurant, lounge, entertainment, outdoor pool, exercise facilities, car rental desk, children under 19 stay free with parents, wheelchair access, a/c, TV, no-smoking rooms, fax service, room service, no pets, laundry service, meeting facilities, senior citizen rates, major credit cards. SGL/DBL$65-$90.

Mt. Tremper
Area Code 914

Mt. Tremper Inn (Wittenberg Rd, 12457; 688-5329) bed and breakfast, Victorian home, no smoking, private baths, antique furnishings, no children allowed. SGL/DBL$65-$100.

Mount Vision
Area Code 607

Aspen Acres Bed and Breakfast (166 Otto Stahl Rd, 13810; 293-8009) complimentary breakfast, 1880s home, on 118 acres. SGL/DBL$45-$60.

Nanuet
Area Code 914

Days Inn (260 Rte. 59, 10954; 623-0600, Fax 623-1859, 800-325-2525) 115 rooms, restaurant, lounge, outdoor pool, children stay free with parents, room service, laundry service, a/c, TV, free local calls, no pets, wheelchair access, no-smoking rooms, senior citizen rates, major credit cards. SGL/DBL$59-$80.

Sheraton Inn (415 East Rte. 59, 10954; 623-6000, Fax 623-9338, 800-325-3535) 100 rooms and suites, restaurant, lounge, outdoor pool, exercise facilities, no-smoking rooms, a/c, TV, children stay free with parents, wheelchair access, 6 meeting rooms, meeting facilities for 500, major credit cards. SGL/DBL$90-$110.

Nelliston
Area Code 518

Historian Bed and Breakfast (Rte. 5, 13410; 993-2233) complimentary breakfast, 1840s home, water view, fireplace. SGL/DBL$45+.

New York
(area code 212 unless otherwise noted)

Midtown

Aberdeen Hotel (17 West 32nd St, 10001; 736-1600, Fax 695-1813, 800-826-4667, 800-826-INNS) 200 rooms and suites, restaurant, lounge, a/c, TV, major credit cards. Near Madison Square Garden and Penn Station. SGL$65, DBL$75, STS$95.

Algonquin Hotel (59 West 44th St, 10036; 840-6800, Fax 944-1419, 800-228-3000, 800-548-0345) 165 rooms and suites, 2 restaurants, lounge, in-room refrigerators, wheelchair access, 24-hour room service, no-smoking rooms, TV, a/c, complimentary newspaper, meeting facilities for 150, major credit cards. Near 5th Ave, Rockefeller Center and the Avenue of The Americas, 30 minutes from the JFK International Airport. SGL$160-$170, DBL$170-$180, STS$300.

Ameritania Hotel (1701 Broadway at 54th St, 10019; 247-5000, 800-922-0330, Fax 247-3316) 250 rooms and suites, a/c, TV, SGL$119-$129, DBL$129-$148, STS$135-$185.

Ashley Hotel (157 West 47th St, 10036; 768-3700, Fax 768-3403, 800-826-INNS) 114 rooms and suites, restaurant, complimentary breakfast, valet parking, a/c, TV, major credit cards. SGL$85-$105, DBL$125.

Beekman Tower Suite (3 Mitchell Place, 10017; 355-7300, Fax 753-9366, 800-ME-SUITE) 171 studio, 1- and 2-bedroom suites, lounge, entertainment, exercise center, airline ticket desk, a/c, TV, children under 12 stay free, in-room refrigerators, business services, fax service, audio visual equipment, 3 meeting rooms, meeting facilities for 160, major credit cards. Near the United Nations. 1BR$220-$239, DBL$375-$395.

The Bedford (118 East 40th St, 10016; 697-4800, Fax 697-1093, 800-221-6881) 30 rooms and suites, restaurant, lounge, children under 13 stay free, laundry room, airport transportation, a/c, TV, major credit cards. SGL$139, DBL$149, STS$179.

Best Western Milford Plaza (270 West 45th St, 10036; 869-3600, Fax 944-8357, 800-528-1234) 1,300 rooms and suites, restaurant, lounge, entertainment, in-room refrigerators, exercise center, children under 12 stay free with parents, fax service, meeting facilities, a/c, TV, major credit cards. SGL$95-$135, DBL$110-$150, STS$190-$480.

Best Western Residence Hotel (234 West 48th St, 10036; 246-8800, Fax 974-3922, 800-528-1234) 341 rooms and suites, restaurant, lounge, exercise center, cable TV, children under 12 stay free with parents, no-smoking rooms, TV, a/c, fax, major credit cards. SGL$99-$165, DBL$109-$180, AP$20.

New York 197

Best Western Woodward (210 West 55th St, 10019; 247-2000, Fax 581-2248, 800-336-4110, 800-826-4667, 800-528-1234) 232 rooms and suites, restaurant, children under 12 stay free with parents, laundry room, a/c, TV, no pets, fax service, major credit cards. SGL$85-$99, DBL$99-$135, STS$150-$270.

Best Western Skyline (725 10th Ave, 10019; 586-3400, 800-528-1234) 240 rooms, a/c, TV, meeting facilities, major credit cards. SGL/DBL$135.

Beverly (125 East 50th St, 10022; 753-2700, Fax 753-2700 ext 48, 800-223-0945) 200 rooms and suites, restaurant, lounge, barber and beauty shop, in-room refrigerators, airport transportation, children under 12 stay free, a/c, TV, meeting facilities for 100, wheelchair access, major credit cards. SGL$129-$159, DBL$139-$169, STS$170-$200

The Carter Hotel (250 West 43rd St, 10036; 944-6000, Fax 398-8541) 700 rooms and suites, a/c, TV, major credit cards. SGL/DBL$55-$75, STS$119.

Chatwall Inn (132 West 45th St, 10036; 921-7600, Fax 719-0171, 800-845-559, 800-826-4667) 80 rooms and suites, laundry service, a/c, TV, major credit cards. Near Grand Central Station and the Empire State Building. SGL$75, DBL$85, STS$115.

Comfort Inn Murray Hill (42 West 35th St, 10001; 947-0200, Fax 594-3047, 800-221-2222) 120 rooms, complimentary breakfast, wheelchair access, no-smoking rooms, TV, a/c, no pets, children under 18 stay free with parents, major credit cards. Near Grand Central Station and the Rockefeller Center, SGL$145-$175, DBL$165-$195, STS$175-$375.

Days Inn (440 West 57th St, 10019; 581-8100, Fax 581-8719, 800-325-2525) 595 rooms, restaurant, outdoor pool, fax, boutiques, lounge, gift shop, car rental desk, valet laundry, children under 12 stay free with parents, cable TV, free local calls, wheelchair access, pets allowed, room service, no-smoking rooms, a/c, meeting facilities for 900, major credit cards. Near the Lincoln Center and Rockefeller Center, 8 miles from the JFK and LaGuardia airports. SGL$88-$159, DBL$104-$174, STS$175-$375, AP$10.

Doral Court (130 East 39th St, 10016; 685-1100, Fax 889-0287, 800-624-0607) 248 rooms and suites, restaurant, lounge, exercise center, in-room refrigerators, no-smoking rooms, TV, a/c, children under 12 stay free with parents, airport transportation, major credit cards. SGL/DBL$135.

Doral Inn (541 Lexington Ave, 10022; 755-1200, Fax 319-8344, 800-223-5824 in New York) 700 rooms and suites, restaurant, lounge, exercise center, in-room refrigerators, a/c, TV, transportation to local attractions, concierge, laundry service, major credit cards. SGL/DBL$155.

Doral Park Avenue (70 Park Ave, 10016; 687-7050, Fax 949-5924, 800-847-4135) 320 rooms and suites, restaurant, lounge, wheelchair access, children under 12 stay free with parents, a/c, TV, in-room refrigerators, meeting facilities, major credit cards. SGL$175-$235, DBL$195-$255, STS$275-$475.

Dorset Hotel (30 West 54th St, 10019; 247-7300, Fax 581-0153, 800-227-2348) 320 rooms and suites, restaurant, lounge, a/c, TV, meeting facilities, major credit cards. SGL$175-$235, DBL$195-$255, STS$265-$475.

The Drake Swissotel (440 Park Ave, 10022; 421-0900, Fax 371-4190, 800-372-5369, 800-63-SWISS) 552 1- and 2-bedroom suites, restaurant, lounge, entertainment, transportation to local attractions, concierge, a/c, TV, children under 16 stay free with parents, 24-hour room service, in-room computer hookups, limousine service, meeting facilities for 150, major credit cards. SGL$145, DBL$155-$300.

Dumont Plaza Hotel (150 East 34th St, 10016; 481-7600, Fax 889-8856, 800-637-8483, 800-ME-SUITE) 250 studios and 1- and 2-bedroom suites, exercise center, sauna, airline ticket office, children under 12 stay free with parents, wheelchair access, a/c, TV, laundry room, concierge, business services, fax service, meeting facilities. Near Lexington Ave, the Javits Convention Center, Dupont Plaza and the 34th St Heliport. 1BR$215-$235, 2BR$395-$415, AP$20.

Eastgate Towers (222 East 39th St, 10016; 687-8000, Fax 490-2634, 800-637-8484, 800-ME-SUITE) 192 studios, 1- and 2-bedroom suites, restaurant, lounge, in-room refrigerators, a/c, TV, airline ticket office, major credit cards. Near Grand Central Station. SGL$180-$230, DBL$195-$250, STS$350-$390.

The Edison Hotel (228 West 47th St, 10036; 840-5000, Fax 719-9541, 800-637-7070) 1,000 rooms and suites, restaurant, lounge, gift shop, airport transportation, a/c, TV, beauty shop, meeting facilities, major credit cards. SGL/DBL$84-$90.

Elysee (60 East 54th St, 10022; 753-1066, Fax 980-9270, 800-5EL-YSEE, 100 rooms and suites, restaurant, lounge, entertainment, children under 12 stay free with parents, a/c, TV, pets allowed, major credit cards. SGL$150-$210, DBL$170-$230, STS$275-$600.

The Essex House Hotel Nikko (160 Central Park South, 10019; 247-0300, Fax 315-1839, 800-NIK-KOUS) 591 rooms and suites, restaurant, lounge, entertainment, exercise center, airport transportation, in-room refrigerators, 24-hour room service, no-smoking rooms, TV, a/c, wheelchair access, pets allowed, business services, meeting facilities, major credit cards. Near Central Park, Lincoln Center, Broadway and 5th Ave, 45 minutes from JFK International Airport. SGL$240-$420, DBL$265-$345, STS$450-$1200.

Flatotel International (135 West 52nd St, 10019; 887-9400, Fax 247-7327, 800-FLATOTEL) 201 suites, restaurant, jacuzzis, kitchenettes, a/c, TV, babysitting services, business services. STS$165-$900.

Gorham Hotel (136 West 55th St, 10019; 245-1800, Fax 245-1800 ext 2234, 800-245-1800) 120 rooms and suites, restaurant, lounge, concierge, a/c, TV, kitchenettes, major credit cards. SGL/DBL$150-$195, STS$180$250.

Grand Bay Hotel (152 West 51st St, 10019; 765-1900, Fax 541-6604, 800-237-0990) 200 rooms and suites, restaurant, lounge, entertainment, exercise center, no-smoking rooms, TV, a/c, wheelchair access, transportation to local attractions, gift shop, concierge, airport transportation, in-room refrigerators, free newspaper, meeting rooms, major credit cards. SGL$95, DBL$115.

Grand Hyatt New York (Park Ave at Grand Central, 10017; 883-1234, Fax 697-3772, 800-228-9000, 800-233-1234) 1,047 rooms and suites, Regency Club, restaurant, lounge, entertainment, 24-hour room service, indoor tennis courts, exercise center, no-smoking rooms, TV, a/c, complimentary newspaper, concierge, wheelchair access, children under 18 stay free with parents, airport transportation, in-room refrigerators, meeting facilities for 2,000, major credit cards. Near Park Ave and Grand Central Station. SGL$220, DBL$245, STS$350-$1200.

Grand Union Hotel (34 East 32nd St, 10016; 683-5890, Fax 689-7397) 93 rooms and suites, a/c, TV, major credit cards. SGL$65-$75, DBL$65-$85, STS$85-$100.

Helmsley Carlton House (680 Madison Ave, 10021; 838-3000, Fax 753-8575, 800-221-4982) 464 rooms and suites, restaurant, lounge, a/c, TV, major credit cards. SGL$175-$195, DBL$200-$220, STS$215-450.

Helmsley Middletowne (148 East 48th St, 10017; 755-3000, Fax 832-0261, 800-221-4982) 193 rooms and suites, kitchenettes, children under 12 stay free with parents, a/c, TV, major credit cards. Near the United Nations Building and Grand Central Station. SGL$135-$175, DBL$145-$175, STS$195-$380.

Helmsley Palace (455 Madison Ave, 10022; 888-7000, Fax 306-6000, 800-321-2323, 800-221-4982) 1,050 rooms and suites, 2 restaurants, 2 lounge, entertainment, a/c, TV, boutiques, airport transportation, in-room refrigerators, barber and beauty shop, concierge, meeting facilities for 300, major credit cards. Near Rockefeller Center. SGL$230, DBL$255, STS$695.

Helmsley Park Lane (36 Central Park, 10019; 371-4000, Fax 319-9065, 800-221-4982) 640 rooms and suites, restaurant, children under 12 stay free with parents, 24-hour room service, in-room refrigerators, no-smoking rooms, TV, a/c, barber and beauty shop, 4 meeting rooms, meeting facilities for 275, major credit cards. Near 5th Ave and Central Park. SGL/DBL$215-$285, STS$350-$1200.

Helmsley Windsor Hotel (100 West 58th St, 10019; 265-2100, Fax 315-0371) 300 rooms and suites, kitchenettes, restaurant. Near Central Park and

Lincoln Center, major credit cards. SGL$135-$145, DBL$145-$155, STS$215-$325.

Helmsley Hotel (212 East 42nd St, 10017; 490-8900, Fax 986-7756, 800-221-4982) 800 rooms and suites, restaurant, 7 meeting rooms, a/c, TV, meeting facilities for 300, major credit cards. In the theater district, near 5th Ave and the United Nations Building. SGL$180-$230, DBL$205-$255, STS$390.

Hilton & Towers (1335 Avenue of the Americas, 10019; 587-7000, Fax 757-7423) 2,042 rooms and suites, Executive Tower, 2 restaurants, lounge, entertainment, exercise center, in-room refrigerators, 24-hour room service, barber and beauty shop, pets allowed, no-smoking rooms, TV, a/c, wheelchair access, business services, meeting facilities for 3,500, major credit cards. Near 5th Ave and Rockefeller Center, 15 miles from LaGuardia Airport and JFK International Airport. SGL/DBL$209-$269, STS$375-$450.

Holiday Inn Crowne Plaza (1605 Broadway, 10019; 977-4000, Fax 333-7393, 800-243-6969) 770 rooms and suites, 3 restaurants, lounge, entertainment, indoor pool, exercise center, children under 12 stay free with parents, wheelchair access, no-smoking rooms, TV, a/c, fax service, in-room computer hookups, room service, pets allowed, meeting facilities for 1,700, major credit cards. Near the Convention Center and Rockefeller Center, 17 miles from the JFK International Airport. SGL$149-$220, DBL$159-$240, STS$250.

Howard Johnson Plaza Hotel (851 8th Ave, 10019; 581-4100, Fax 974-7502) 300 rooms, restaurant, lounge, entertainment, children under 18 stay free, room service, babysitting services, gift shop, airport transportation, gift shop, valet laundry, a/c, TV, no-smoking rooms, major credit cards. In the theatre district near Radio City Music Hall and Madison Square Garden, 20 miles from JFK International Airport, 15 miles from LaGuardia Airport. SGL$99-$142, DBL$105-$154.

Hyatt Grand New York (Park Ave and Grand Central, 10017; 883-1234, 800-228-9000) 1,407 rooms, restaurant, lounge, beauty shop, a/c, TV, meeting facilities, major credit cards. SGL/DBL$125.

InterContinental Hotel (111 East 48th St, 10017; 755-5900, Fax 644-0079, 800-332-4246, 800-327-0200) 692 rooms and 1-bedroom suites, restaurant, lounge, exercise center, 24-hour room service, concierge, wheelchair access, beauty shop, a/c, TV, airport transportation, children under 12 stay free with parents, 16 meeting rooms, meeting facilities for 320, major credit cards. SGL/DBL$159, STS$275.

Iroquois Hotel (49 West 44th St, 10036; 840-3080, Fax 398-1754, 800-332-7220) 100 rooms and suites, major credit cards. SGL$75-$85, DBL$85-$100, STS$100-$175.

Journey's End (Three East 40th St, 10016; 447-1500, Fax 683-7839, 800-668-4200) 189 rooms, a/c, TV, major credit cards. SGL$126, DBL$136.

Kimberly Hotel (145 East 50th St, 10022; 755-0400, Fax 486-6915, 800-683-0400) 192 suites, restaurant, lounge, entertainment, concierge, a/c, TV, major credit cards. SGL$170-$205, DBL$190-$205, STS$265-$370.

Lexington Hotel (511 Lexington Ave, 10017; 755-4400, Fax 751-4091, 800-448-4471) 400 rooms and suites, restaurant, lounge, in-room refrigerators, a/c, airport transportation, cable TV, barber shop, major credit cards. SGL$120, DBL$130, STS$200-$500.

Loews New York (569 Lexington Ave, 10022; 752-7000, Fax 758-6311, 800-23-LOEWS) 728 rooms and suites, restaurant, lounge, in-room refrigerators, a/c, TV, concierge, business services, 12 meeting rooms, meeting facilities for 400, major credit cards. SGL$185, DBL$199, STS$225-$475.

Lyden House Suites (320 East 53rd St, 10022; 888-6070, Fax 935-7690, 800-ME-SUITES) 81 studio, 1-bedroom suites, in-room computer and fax hookups, limousine service. 1BR$210-$240, 2BR$235-$325, AP$20.

Macklowe Conference Center (145 West 44th St, 10036; 768-4400, Fax 768-0847, 800-934-9953) 638 rooms and suites, restaurant, lounge, a/c, TV, in-room refrigerators, exercise center, meeting facilities for 300, major credit cards. SGL$210, DBL$230, STS$425.

Madison Towers (22 East 38th St, 10016; 685-3700) 270 rooms, exercise center, a/c, TV, major credit cards. SGL/DBL$85.

Marriott East Side (525 Lexington Ave, 10017; 755-4000, Fax 980-6175, 800-242-8684, 800-228-9290) 665 rooms and suites, Concierge Level, restaurant, lounge, no-smoking rooms, TV, a/c, wheelchair access, major credit cards. Near Grand Central Station. SGL$99, DBL$109, STS$300.

Mayfair Regent Hotel (610 Park Ave, 10021; 288-0542, Fax 737-0538, 800-223-0542) 201 rooms and suites, restaurant, lounge, exercise center, room service, a/c, TV, in-room refrigerators, major credit cards. SGL$275-$410, DBL$295-$410, STS$440-$1700.

Mayflower On The Park (15 Central Park West, 10023; 265-0060, Fax 265-5098, 800-223-4164) 577 rooms and suites, exercise center, in-room refrigerators, room service, a/c, TV, 5 meeting rooms, meeting facilities for 100, major credit cards. SGL$145-$164, DBL$160-$180, STS$200-$500.

Morgans (237 Madison Ave, 10016; 686-0300, Fax 779-8352, 800-334-3408) 154 rooms and suites, free breakfast, 24-hour room service, in-room refrigerators and microwaves, laundry service, no-smoking, a/c, TV, wheelchair access, pets allowed, airport transportation, business services, meeting facilities for 100, major credit cards. 1 mile from Central Park, 1 hour from JFK International Airport, SGL$180-$210, DBL$205-$235, STS$275-$400.

Novatel Hotel (226 West 52nd St, 10019; 315-0100, Fax 765-5369, 800-221-3185) 474 rooms and suites, restaurant, lounge, entertainment, children under 16 stay free with parents, airport transportation, wheelchair access, no-smoking rooms, TV, a/c, pets allowed, meeting facilities, major credit cards. SGL$169, DBL$179, STS$380.

Omni Berkshire (21 East 52nd St, 10022; 753-5800, Fax 355-7646, 800-THE-OMNI) 415 rooms and suites, restaurant, lounge, children under 18 stay free with parents, a/c, TV, transportation to local attractions, major credit cards. 8 miles from LaGuardia Airport, 15 miles from JFK International Airport. SGL$85-$115, DBL$125.

Omni Park Central (870 5th Ave, 10019; 247-8000, Fax 484-3374, 800-THE-OMNI) 1,450 rooms and suites, restaurant, lounge, entertainment, 12 meeting rooms, a/c, TV, meeting facilities for 1,000, major credit cards. Near Central Park, Carnegie Hall and Lincoln Center, 9 miles from LaGuardia Airport, 13 miles from JFK International Airport. SGL/DBL$175-$195.

Paramount Hotel (235 West 46th St, 10036; 764-5500, Fax 354-5237, 800-225-7474) 600 rooms and suites, exercise center, children under 16 stay free with parents, concierge, airport transportation, gift shop, a/c, TV, major credit cards. SGL$95-$180, DBL$145-$200, STS$300-$430.

Park Center Hotel (870 7th Ave; 247-8000) 1,269 rooms and suites, restaurant, lounge, concierge, room service, 12 meeting rooms, meeting facilities for 1,000, a/c, TV, major credit cards. SGL/DBL$150.

Parker Meridien Hotel (118 West 57th St, 10019; 245-5000, Fax 307-1776, 800-543-4300) 700 rooms and suites, restaurant, lounge, pool, whirlpool, a/c, TV, sauna, 24-hour room service, concierge, children under 14 stay free with parents, 6 meeting rooms, meeting facilities for 160, major credit cards. SGL$200-$250, DBL$225-$275, STS$250-$1500.

Peninsula Hotel (700 5th Ave, 10019; 247-2200, Fax 903-3949, 800-262-9467) 250 rooms and suites, restaurant, lounge, entertainment, pool, spa, concierge, 24-hour room service, wheelchair access, no-smoking rooms, TV, a/c, 6 meeting rooms, meeting facilities for 120, major credit cards. SGL/DBL$275-$395, STS$460-$2,750.

The Penn Plaza (215 West 34th St, 10001; 947-5050, Fax 268-4829, 800-633-1911) 74 rooms, a/c, TV, major credit cards. SGL$61, DBL$71.

Penta Hotel (7th and 33rd St, 10001; 736-5000, Fax 502-8798, 800-223-8585) 1,705 rooms and suites, restaurant, lounge, exercise center, sauna, concierge, wheelchair access, no-smoking rooms, TV, a/c, barber and beauty shop, meeting facilities, major credit cards. SGL/DBL$175.

The Penthouse Hostel (250 West 43rd St; 391-4202; Fax 354-8156) 26 rooms, a/c, TV, major credit cards. SGL/DBL$17-$45.

Pickwick Arms (230 East 51st St, 10022; 355-0300, Fax 755-5029, 800-PICKWIK) 400 rooms and suites, a/c, TV, major credit cards. SGL$40-$60, DBL$80-$100.

The Pierre (5th Ave and 61st St, 10021; 838-8000, Fax 940-8109) 206 rooms and suites, restaurant, lounge, 24-hour room service, no-smoking rooms, TV, a/c, limousine service, in-room refrigerators, concierge, barber and beauty shop, boutiques, 5 meeting rooms, meeting facilities for 750, major credit cards. Near Central Park. SGL$280-$400, DBL$310-$430, STS$575-$1300.

The Plaza Hotel (5th Ave at Central Park; 10019; 759-3000, Fax 759-3167, 800-759-3000, 800-228-3000) 815 rooms and suites, 5 restaurants, lounge, boutiques, gift shop, barber and beauty shop, pets allowed, concierge, business services, no-smoking rooms, TV, a/c, 24-hour room service, wheelchair access, limousine service, 12 meeting rooms. Near Central Park, Lincoln Center. 30 minutes for LaGuardia, 45 minutes from JFK Airport, major credit cards. SGL$235-$500, DBL$260-$585, STS$500-$1500.

Plaza Fifty Suite (155 East 50th St, 10022; 757-5710, Fax 753-1468, 800-ME-SUITE) 206 rooms and suites, complimentary breakfast, in-room refrigerators, children under 12 stay free with parents, a/c, TV, SGL$165-$210, DBL$230-$280, STS$385-$410.

Portland Square Hotel (132 West 47th St, 10036; 382-0600, Fax 382-0684, 800-388-8988) 105 rooms, a/c, TV, major credit cards. SGL$40-$60, DBL$75-$95.

The President (234 West 48th St, 10036; 826-4667, Fax 964-3922, 800-826-4667) 400 rooms and suites, restaurant, lounge. In the theater district near Rockefeller Center and Radio City Music Hall, major credit cards. SGL$75-$95, DBL$85-$105, STS$139-$175.

Quality Inn Midtown (157 West 47th St, 10036; 768-3700, Fax 768-3403, 800-826-4667, 800-334-4667) 200 rooms and suites, restaurant, lounge, wheelchair access, no-smoking rooms, TV, a/c, meeting facilities. In the theater district near the Convention Center and Empire State Building, major credit cards. SGL$95-$125, DBL$115-$145, STS$150-$175.

Quality Inn (511 Lexington Ave, 10017; 755-4400, Fax 751-4091, 800-221-2222) 720 rooms, 3 restaurants, lounge, entertainment, no pets, wheelchair access, no-smoking rooms, TV, a/c, meeting facilities. In the theater district, 15 minutes from the Convention Center, major credit cards. SGL/DBL$95-$125.

Ramada Hotel Midtown (790 8th Ave, 10019; 581-7000, Fax 974-0291, 800-228-0888) 366 rooms, restaurant, lounge, pool, children under 18 stay free with parents, wheelchair access, no-smoking rooms, TV, a/c, meeting room, meeting facilities for 40, major credit cards. In the theater district. SGL$98-$138, DBL$110-$150, AP$20.

Ramada Renaissance (2 Times Square, 10036; 228-9898, Fax 765-1962, 800-628-5222, 800-228-9898) 305 rooms and suites, restaurant, lounge, entertainment, 24-hour room service, exercise center, children under 18 stay free with parents, wheelchair access, no-smoking rooms, TV, a/c, airport transportation, concierge, major credit cards. SGL$235, DBL$165, STS$475.

Ramada Hotel Pennsylvania (401 7th Ave, 10001; 736-5000, 800-2-RAMADA) 1,705 rooms, 5 restaurants, 2 lounges, 18-hour room service, indoor pool, whirlpool, children under 18 stay free with parents, wheelchair access, no-smoking rooms, TV, a/c, airport transportation, meeting facilities, major credit cards. Near the Empire State Building, garment district and Javits Convention Center. SGL$89-$150, DBL$109-$170, STS$200, AP$20.

Regency (540 Park Ave, 10021; 759-4100, Fax 826-5674, 800-233-2356) 384 rooms and suites, restaurant, lounge, entertainment, exercise center, whirlpool, sauna, room service, in-room refrigerators, wheelchair access, no-smoking rooms, TV, a/c, barber and beauty shop, concierge, business services, meeting facilities, major credit cards. SGL$245, DBL$270, STS$350-$550.

Remington (129 West 46th St, 10036; 221-2600, Fax 764-7481) 80 rooms, major credit cards. SGL/DBL$75.

Righa Royal (151 West 54th St, 10019; 307-5000, Fax 765-6530, 800-937-5454) 500 suites. STS$260-$390.

Ritz Carlton (112 Central Park South, 10019; 757-1900, Fax 757-9620, 800-241-3333) 220 rooms and suites, restaurant, lounge, 24-hour room service, a/c, TV, limousine service. Near the business district, major credit cards. SGL$200-$350, DBL$230-$380, STS$550-$1300.

Roger Smith (501 Lexington Ave, 10017; 755-1400, Fax 319-9130, 800-445-0277) 136 rooms and suites, complimentary breakfast, restaurant, lounge, in-room refrigerators, a/c, TV, meeting facilities, major credit cards. SGL$160-$185, DBL$175-$200, STS$225-$390.

Roosevelt Hotel (45th and Madison Ave, 10017; 661-9600, Fax 661-4475, 800-223-1870) 1,100 rooms and suites, restaurant, lounge, entertainment, in-room refrigerators, laundry service, concierge, boutiques, transportation to local attractions, barber and beauty shop, meeting facilities, major credit cards. SGL$109-$149, DBL$124-$169, STS$250-$500.

Royalton Hotel (44 West 44th St, 10036; 869-4400, Fax 869-8965, 800-635-9013) 157 rooms and suites, restaurant, lounge, children under 16 stay free with parents, in-room refrigerators, a/c, TV, major credit cards. SGL/DBL$95-$165.

Salisbury (123 West 57th St, 10019; 246-1300, Fax 977-7752, 800-223-0680) 320 rooms and suites, children under 12 stay free with parents, a/c, TV, in-room refrigerators, meeting facilities, major credit cards. SGL$124-$134, DBL$134-$144, STS$144-$174.

San Carlos Hotel (150 East 50th St, 10022; 755-2800, Fax 688-9778, 800-722-2012) 200 rooms and suites, children under 14 stay free with parents, a/c, TV, laundry service, airport transportation, major credit cards. SGL$139, DBL$149, STS$179.

Shelburne Suite Hotel (303 Lexington Ave, 10016; 689-5200, Fax 779-7068, 800-637-8483) 258 studios, 1- and 2-bedroom suites, restaurant, lounge, entertainment, exercise center, laundry service, barber and beauty shop, no-smoking rooms, TV, a/c, in-room computer and fax hookups, children under 12 stay free with parents, business services, audio-visual equipment, 1,850 square feet of meeting space, meeting facilities for 235. Near the Empire State Building, Grand Central Station and Madison Ave. 1BR$215-$245, 2BR$395-$435.

Sheraton Hotel & Towers (811 7th Ave, 10019; 581-1000, Fax 262-4410, 800-325-3535) 1,756 rooms and suites, 2 restaurants, lounge, entertainment, 18-hour room service, indoor pool, exercise center, wheelchair access, no-smoking rooms, TV, a/c, 32 meeting rooms, 80,000 square feet of meeting and exhibition space, meeting facilities for 3,000, major credit cards. Near Rockefeller Center, Radio City and the theater district, 10 miles from LaGuardia Airport. SGL/DBL$159-$229, STS$300.

Sheraton Manhattan Hotel (790 7th Ave, 10019; 581-3300, Fax 582-5489, 800-325-3535) 650 rooms and suites, restaurant, lounge, indoor pool, sauna, exercise center, wheelchair access, no-smoking rooms, TV, a/c, pets allowed, 11 meeting rooms, 5,400 square feet of meeting and exhibition space, meeting facilities for 450. Near the theater district, Central Park and Rockefeller Center, 10 miles from LaGuardia Airport, major credit cards. SGL/DBL$159-$229, STS$300.

Sheraton Park Avenue (45 Park Ave, 10016; 685-7676, Fax 889-3293, 800-537-0075) 150 rooms and suites, restaurant, lounge, 24-hour room service, exercise center, wheelchair access, pets allowed, no-smoking rooms, TV, a/c, 3 meeting rooms, meeting facilities for 150, major credit cards. Near the Empire State Building and Chrysler Building, 12 miles from LaGuardia Airport. SGL$195-$260, DBL$215-$270, STS$325-$600.

Shoreham (33 West 55th St, 10019; 247-6700, Fax 765-9741, 800-553-3347) 123 rooms and suites, a/c, TV, major credit cards. SGL$95, DBL$99, STS$130.

St. Moritz On The Park (50 Central Park South, 10019; 755-5800, Fax 751-2952, 800-221-4774) 679 rooms and suites, beauty shop, a/c, TV, meeting facilities, major credit cards. SGL/DBL$99-$165, STS$165-$350.

St. Regis Hotel (2 East 55th St, 10022; 753-4500, Fax 787-3447, 800-325-3535) 310 rooms and suites, restaurant, lounge, 24-hour room service, sauna, exercise center, wheelchair access, no-smoking rooms, TV, a/c, business services, 6 meeting rooms, major credit cards. Near Central Park and 5th Ave. SGL/DBL$200.

Stanford Hotel (43 West 32nd St, 10001; 563-1480, Fax 629-0043, 800-365-1114) 130 rooms and suites, a/c, TV, major credit cards. SGL$80, DBL$90, STS$130-$180.

Stanhope (995 5th Ave, 10028; 288-5000, Fax 517-0088, 800-828-1123) 132 rooms and suites, restaurant, lounge, exercise center, 24-hour room service, concierge, a/c, TV, limousine service, meeting facilities for 175, major credit cards. Near the Lincoln Center, 10 minutes from Carnegie Hall. SGL/DBL$250, STS$475-$2,500.

Southgate Tower Suite Hotel (371 7th Ave, 10019; 563-1800, Fax 643-8028, 800-ME-SUITE) 522 studios, 1- and 2-bedroom suites, restaurant, lounge, exercise center, gift shop, beauty shop, business services, a/c, TV, fax, meeting facilities for 300, major credit cards. Near Penn Plaza, the Javits Convention Center and Herald Square. 1BR$170-$210, 2BR$395-$495.

TraveLodge Skyline (725 10th Ave, 10019; 586-3400, Fax 582-4604, 800-433-1982) 231 rooms and suites, restaurant, lounge, entertainment, pool, sauna, a/c, TV, no pets, room service, fax service. Near the theater district, 5 minutes from the Jacob Javits Convention Center, major credit cards. SGL$105-$115, DBL$115-$125, STS$250-$300.

Travel Inn (515 West 42nd St, 10036; 695-4630, Fax 967-5025, 800-869-7171) 160 rooms, pool, meeting facilities, a/c, TV, major credit cards. SGL$90-$115, DBL$105-$120.

Tudor Hotel (304 East 42nd St, 10017; 986-8800, Fax 986-1758, 800-879-8836) 303 rooms and suites, a/c, TV, major credit cards. SGL$160-$210, DBL$180-$250, STS$280-$400.

U.N. Plaza Park Hyatt (1 United Nations Plaza, 10017; 355-3400, Fax 702-5051, 800-233-1234) 428 rooms and suites, indoor pool, indoor tennis court, exercise center, no-smoking rooms, TV, a/c, free newspaper, wheelchair access, transportation to local attractions, meeting facilities for 200, major credit cards. Twenty minutes from LaGuardia Airport. SGL$240-$260, DBL$260-$280, STS$350.

Vanderbilt YMCA (224 East 47th St, 10017; 755-2410, Fax 752-0210) 430 rooms, a/c, major credit cards. DBL$39-$88.

The Waldorf Astoria (301 Park Ave, 10022; 355-3000, Fax 421-8103, 800-HILTONS) 1,410 rooms and suites, 4 restaurants, 2 lounges, entertainment, exercise center, wheelchair access, no-smoking rooms, TV, a/c, in-room refrigerators, 24-hour room service, concierge, business services, 5 meeting rooms, meeting facilities for 1,600, major credit cards. SGL$225-$300, DBL$250-$325, STS$375-$650.

The Waldorf Towers (100 East 50th St, 10022; 872-4635, Fax 872-4799, 800-HILTONS) 191 rooms and suites, exercise center, limousine service, a/c, TV, 24-hour room service, boutiques, business services, meeting facilities, major credit cards. SGL$325-$350, DBL$350-$375, STS$850-$4000.

The Wales Hotel (1295 Madison Ave, 10128; 876-6000, Fax 860-7000, 800-428-5252) 95 rooms and suites, a/c, TV, major credit cards. DBL$125-$145, STS$175-$225.

Warwick Hotel (65 West 54th St, 10019; 247-2700, Fax 957-8915, 800-223-4099, 800-522-5634 in New York) 425 rooms and suites, restaurant, lounge, children under 15 stay free with parents, a/c, TV, barber shop, in-room refrigerators, meeting facilities, major credit cards. SGL$180-$225, DBL$205-$245, STS$350-$500

Wellington (55th St and 7th Ave, 10019; 247-3900, Fax 581-1719, 800-652-1212) 70 rooms and suites, a/c, TV, major credit cards. SGL$89-$109, DBL$99-$119, STS$140-$165.

Wentworth Hotel (59 West 46th St, 10036; 719-2300, Fax 768-3473, 800-223-1900) 194 rooms and suites, a/c, TV, major credit cards. SGL$70-80, DBL$80-$105, STS$100-$150.

Westpark Hotel (308 West 58th St, 10019; 246-6440, Fax 246-3131, 800-248-6440) 99 rooms and suites, a/c, TV, major credit cards. SGL$70-$100, DBL$80-$110, STS$150-$180.

Wolcott Hotel (4 West 31st St, 10001; 268-2900, Fax 563-0096) 280 rooms, a/c, TV, major credit cards. SGL/DBL$55-$65.

Wyndham (42 West 58th St, 10019; 753-3500) 200 rooms and suites, restaurant, lounge, in-room refrigerators, major credit cards. SGL$115-$125, DBL$130-$140, STS$175-$205.

YMCA West Side (5 West 63rd St, 10023; 787-4400, Fax 580-0441) 550 rooms, a/c, TV, major credit cards. SGL/DBL$34-$48.

Upper East Side

The Barbizon Hotel (140 East 63rd St, 10021; 838-5700, Fax 888-4271) 355 rooms and suites, complimentary breakfast, pool, sauna, a/c, exercise center. cable TV, airport transportation, meeting facilities, major credit cards. SGL /DBL$185.

The Carlyle (Madison Ave and East 76th St, 10021; 744-1600, Fax 717-4682) 190 rooms and 1- and 2-bedroom suites, restaurant, lounge, entertainment, 24-hour room service, exercise center, sauna, a/c, TV, pets allowed, in-room refrigerators, VCRs, beauty shop, fax service, concierge, 24-hour room service, major credit cards. SGL/$225-$325.

The Lowell New York (28 East 63rd St, 10021; 838-1400, Fax 319-4230, 800-221-4444) 61 rooms and suites, restaurant, lounge, children under 12 stay free with parents, a/c, TV, airport transportation, pets allowed, in-room refrigerators, concierge, major credit cards. SGL/$155.

Lyden Gardens Suites (215 East 64th St, 10021; 355-1230, Fax 758-7858, 800-ME-SUITE) 133 studios and 1- and 2-bedroom suites. business services, a/c, TV, audio-visual equipment, meeting facilities, fax service. 1BR$210-$240, 2BR$235-$325, AP$20.

The Mark Hotel (25 East 77th St, 10002; 744-4300, Fax 744-2749, 800-843-6275, 800-THEMARK) 180 rooms and suites, restaurant, lounge, 24-hour room service, a/c, TV, VCRs, children under 12 stay free with parents, kitchenettes, airport transportation, meeting facilities for 180, major credit cards. SGL/$275-$295, STS$450-$2000.

The Plaza Athenée (37 East 64th St, 10021; 734-9100, Fax 772-0958, 800-225-5843) 202 rooms and suites, restaurant, lounge, 24-hour room service, a/c, TV, pets allowed, major credit cards. SGL/$250-$500.

Surrey Suite Hotel (20 East 76th St, 10021; 288-3700, Fax 628-1549, 800-ME-SUITE) 130 studios and 1- and 2-bedroom suites, business services, computer and fax hookups in rooms, children under 14 stay free with parents, meeting facilities for 20, major credit cards. Near Madison Ave and Central Park. 1BR$315-355, 2BR$500-$580, AP$20.

Westbury Club (15 East 69th St, 10021; 535-2000, Fax 535-5056, 800-321-1569) 231 rooms and suites, restaurant, lounge, room service, children under 18 stay free with parents, meeting facilities, major credit cards. SGL/$230-$600, STS$325-$2000.

Upper West Side

American Youth Hostels (891 Amsterdam Ave, 10025; 932-2300, Fax 932-2574) 90 rooms, kitchen, a/c, TV, meeting facilities for 100, transportation to local attractions, major credit cards. SGL$19-$20, DBL$190$20.

The Beacon Hotel (2130 Broadway, 10023; 787-1100, Fax 724-0839, 800-572-4969) 45 rooms and suites, a/c, TV, major credit cards. SGL$45, DBL$89-$99, STS$140-$160.

The Broadway American (2178 Broadway, 10024; 362-1100, Fax 787-9521) 200 rooms, a/c, TV, major credit cards. SGL$45-$79, DBL$65-$89.

Embassy Suites (1568 Broadway, 10036; 719-1600, Fax 921-5212, 800-EMBASSY) 423 2-room suites, restaurant, free breakfast, exercise center, a/c, TV, room service, laundry service, wheelchair access, business service, meeting facilities. Near Carnegie Hall, Lincoln Center and Central Park, major credit cards. SGL/DBL$150.

Empire Hotel (44 West 63rd St, 10023; 265-7400, Fax 315-0349, 800-545-7400) 500 rooms and suites, restaurant, lounge, exercise center, a/c, TV, children under 12 stay free with parents, airport transportation, meeting facilities, major credit cards. SGL/$100-$200.

Esplanade Hotel and Suites (305 West End Ave, 10023; 874-5000, Fax 496-0367, 800-367-1763) 200 rooms and suites, a/c, TV, major credit cards. SGL$65-$90, DBL$75-$99, STS$85-$180.

Excelsior Hotel (41 West 81st St, 10024; 362-9200, Fax 721-2994, 800-368-4575) 150 rooms and suites, a/c, TV, major credit cards. SGL$65-$75, DBL$75-$75-$87, STS$94-$150.

Fitzpatrick Manhattan (687 Lexington Ave, 10022; 355-0100, Fax 308-5166, 800-367-7710) 92 rooms and suites, a/c, TV, SGL$160, DBL$180, STS$230.

Friendship Inn (765 8th Ave, 10036; 247-5400, Fax 586-6201, 800-777-6933) 50 rooms, major credit cards. SGL$65-$75, DBL$75-$95.

Malibu Studios (2688 Broadway, 10025; 222-2954, Fax 678-6842, 800-647-2247) 100 rooms, a/c, TV, major credit cards. SGL$10-$20, DBL$20-$85.

Marriott Marquis (1535 Broadway, 10036; 398-1900, Fax 704-8930, 800-843-4898, 800-228-9290) 1,871 rooms and suites, restaurant, lounge, entertainment, exercise center, whirlpool, sauna, 24-hour room service, children stay free with parents, concierge, no-smoking rooms, TV, a/c, wheelchair access, business services, meeting facilities. In the theatre district near the Convention Center and Wall St, major credit cards. SGL$169-$270, DBL$169-$285, STS$425-$750.

Milburn Hotel (242 West 76th St, 10023; 326-1006, Fax 721-5476, 800-833-9622) 85 rooms and suites, a/c, TV, major credit cards. SGL$79-$99, DBL$85-$100, STS$120-$180.

Radisson Empire Hotel (44 West 63rd St, 10022; 265-7400, Fax 315-0349, 800-545-7400) 375 rooms and suites, restaurant, lounge, exercise center, a/c, TV, in-room computer hookups, VCRs, 24-hour room service, SGL$120-$180, DBL$120-$200, STS$210-$550.

Riverside Tower (80 Riverside Drive, 10024; 877-5200, Fax 315-2664, 800-448-8355) 120 rooms and suites, a/c, TV, major credit cards. SGL$45-$50, DBL$55, STS$65-$85.

Lower Manhattan

Arlington Hotel (18 West 25th St, 10010; 768-3700, Fax 768-3403, 800-826-INNS) 125 rooms and suites, restaurant, lounge, a/c, TV, meeting facilities for 75, major credit cards. SGL/$55, STS$90.

Chelsea Inn (46 West 17th St, 10011; 645-8989, Fax 645-1903, 800-640-6469) 13 rooms and suites, a/c, TV, major credit cards. SGL/$78, STS$135.

Gershwin Hotel (3 East 27th St, 10001; 391-4282, Fax 345-8156) 147 rooms and suites, a/c, TV, major credit cards. SGL$40-$45, DBL$50-$60, STS$70.

Herald Square (19 West 31st St, 10001; 294-4017, Fax 643-9208, 800-727-1888) 120 rooms, a/c, TV, major credit cards. SGL$50-$65, DBL$55-$85.

Gramercy Park (2 Lexington Ave, 10010; 475-4320, 800-221-4083) 507 rooms, meeting facilities, a/c, TV, major credit cards. SGL/$185-$300.

Manhattan Seaport Suites (129 Front St, 10005; 742-0003, Fax 742-0124, 800-77-SUITE) 49 suites. STS$195-$235.

Maria Hotel (138 Lafayette St, 10013; 966-8898, Fax 966-3933, 800-282-3933) 227 rooms and suites, major credit cards. SGL$125, DBL$225, STS$225-$275.

Marriott Financial Center (85 West St, 10006; 385-4900, Fax 385-9174, 800-242-8685) 504 rooms and suites, restaurant, lounge, indoor pool, exercise center, sauna, in-room computer and fax hookups, no-smoking rooms, TV, a/c, wheelchair access, business service, 11 meeting rooms, meeting facilities for 400, major credit cards. In the financial district near the World Trade Center and Wall St SGL$209-$245, DBL$229-$265, STS$1500.

McBurney YMCA (206 West 24th St, 10011; 741-9226, Fax 741-0012) 275 rooms, a/c, TV, major credit cards. SGL$35-$37, DBL$47-$84.

Millenium Hotel (55 Church St, 10007; 693-2001, Fax 571-2316, 800-835-2220) 561 rooms and suites, restaurant, lounge, pool, exercise center, a/c, TV, in-room computer hookups, concierge, limousine service, major credit cards. SGL$225-$350, DBL$245-$360, STS$375.

Off-Soho Suites (11 Rivington St, 10002; 979-9808, Fax 979-9801, 800-OFF-SOHO) 36 rooms and suites, a/c, TV, major credit cards. SGL/$66, STS$66-$99.

Vista International (3 World Trade Center, 10048; 938-9100, Fax 321-2237, 800-258-2505) 821 rooms and suites, restaurant, lounge, entertainment, indoor pool, exercise center, sauna, wheelchair access, no-smoking rooms, TV, a/c, major credit cards. SGL$215-$280, DBL$240-$305, STS$425.

Washington Square (103 Waverly Place, 10011; 777-9515, Fax 979-8383, 800-222-0418) 180 rooms, a/c, TV, major credit cards. SGL$70-$86, DBL$86-$120.

JFK/LaGuardia Airport Areas

Best Western Midway Hotel (108-25 Horace Harding Expressway, 11368; 699-4400, Fax 760-3916, 800-528-1234) 149 rooms, restaurant, lounge, children under 12 stay free with parents, no pets, fax, car rental desk, a/c, TV, airport courtesy carmajor credit cards. 2 miles from LaGuardia , 4 miles from JFK. SGL$95-$110, DBL$105-$120, AP$10.

Newark
Area Code 315

Quality Inn (125 North Main St, 14513; 800-368-5689) 107 rooms and suites, restaurant, lounge, entertainment, indoor pool, whirlpools, sauna, room service, exercise facilities, children stay free with parents, a/c, TV, no pets, laundry service, no-smoking rooms, meeting facilities for 350, major credit cards. SGL$55-$65.

New Baltimore
Area Code 518

Fox Run Parc Motel (Rte. 9W, 12124; 731-2722) 30 rooms, restaurant, TV, game room, gift shop, major credit cards. SGL/DBL$65.

River Hill Bed and Breakfast (New Baltimore 12124; 756-3313) complimentary breakfast, antique furnishings, fireplace, water view, private baths. SGL/DBL$45-$55.

Newburgh
Area Code 914

Comfort Inn (5 Lakeside Rd, 12550; 567-0567, 800-221-2222) 128 rooms, restaurant, pool, exercise facilities, wheelchair access, no-smoking rooms, no pets, children under 18 stay free with parents, senior citizen rates, a/c, TV, meeting facilities, major credit cards. LS SGL/DBL$50-$60; HS SGL/DBL$58-$70, AP$6.

Days Inn (845 Union Ave, 12550; 564-7550, Fax 564-7551, 800-325-2525) 88 rooms, restaurant, lounge, pool, children stay free with parents, room service, laundry service, a/c, TV, free local calls, airport courtesy car, no pets, wheelchair access, no-smoking rooms, senior citizen rates, major credit cards. SGL/DBL$45-$72.

Holiday Inn (Newburgh 12550; 564-9020, Fax 564-9040, 800-HOLIDAY) 121 rooms, restaurant, lounge, entertainment, outdoor pool, exercise facilities, children under 19 stay free with parents, wheelchair access, a/c, TV, no-smoking rooms, fax service, room service, airport transportation, pets allowed, laundry service, meeting facilities, senior citizen rates, major credit cards. SGL/DBL$45-$68.

Howard Johnson Lodge (Rte 17K, 12550; 564-4000, Fax 564-0620, 800-I-GO-HOJO) 74 rooms, restaurant, lounge, pool, children stay free with parents, wheelchair access, no-smoking rooms, laundry facilities, TV, a/c, pets allowed, free parking, meeting facilities, senior citizen rates, major credit cards. SGL/DBL$45-$65.

Ramada Inn Airport (1055 Union Ave, 12550; 564-4500, Fax 564-4524, 800-2-RAMADA) 153 rooms and suites, restaurant, lounge, entertainment, pool, wheelchair access, no-smoking rooms, airport transportation, free parking, pets allowed, a/c, TV, room service, laundry facilities, meeting facilities for 300, senior citizen rates, major credit cards. SGL$59-$69, DBL$79-$89, STS$75, AP$9.

Super 8 Motel (1058 Union Ave, 12550; 564-5700, Fax 564-7338, 800-800-8000) 108 rooms and suites, restaurant, car rental desk, no pets, children under 12 stay free with parents, free local calls, a/c, TV, fax service, no-smoking rooms, senior citizen rates, wheelchair access, meeting facilities, major credit cards. SGL/DBL$47-$57.

Newfane
Area Code 716

Creekside Bed and Breakfast (2516 Lockport Olcott Rd, 14108; 778-9834) free breakfast, no smoking. SGL/DBL$30-$40.

Newfield
Area Code 607

Decker Pond Inn (1076 Elmira Rd, 14867; 273-7133) 4 rooms, bed and breakfast, no smoking, private baths, water view, no pets, 1830s home, gift shop, on 10 acres, fireplace, antique furnishings. SGL/DBL$75-$85.

Newfield Hills Bed and Breakfast (Trumbull Corners Rd, 14867; 564-7724) 2 rooms, free breakfast, private baths. SGL/DBL$45-$55.

New Hampton
Area Code 914

Days Inn (Rte 17, 10958; 374-2411, Fax 374-0011, 800-325-2525) 41 rooms, restaurant, free breakfast, lounge, outdoor pool, whirlpools, children stay free with parents, room service, laundry service, a/c, TV, free local calls, pets allowed, wheelchair access, no-smoking rooms, senior citizen rates, major credit cards. SGL/DBL$42-$80.

New Hartford
Area Code 315

Consort Inn (202 Campion Rd, 13413; 735-3392) 113 rooms, restaurant, lounge, outdoor pool, a/c, TV, open year-round, meeting facilities. SGL/DBL$55-$60.

Holiday Inn (1777 Burrstone Rd, 13413; 797-2131, 800-HOLIDAY) 100 rooms and 2-room suites, restaurant, lounge, entertainment, outdoor pool, exercise facilities, children under 19 stay free with parents, wheelchair access, a/c, TV, no-smoking rooms, fax service, room service, pets allowed, laundry service, meeting facilities for 250, senior citizen rates, major credit cards. SGL/DBL$60-$80.

New Windsor
Area Code 914

Days Inn (Rte 9W, 12553; 562-7661, 800-325-2525) 30 rooms, restaurant, lounge, pool, children stay free with parents, room service, laundry service, a/c, TV, free local calls, no pets, wheelchair access, no-smoking rooms, senior citizen rates, major credit cards. SGL/DBL$37-$55.

Econo Lodge (310 Windsor Hwy, 12550; 561-6620, 800-4-CHOICE) 40 rooms, free breakfast, pool, TV, children under 12 stay free with parents, no pets, laundry facilities, senior citizen rates, wheelchair access, a/c, major credit cards. SGL/DBL$44-$70.

New Paltz
Area Code 914

Days Inn (601 Main St, 12561; 883-7373, Fax 883-7383, 800-325-2525) 21 rooms, children stay free with parents, room service, laundry service, a/c, TV, free local calls, no pets, wheelchair access, no-smoking rooms, senior citizen rates, major credit cards. SGL/DBL$49-$69.

Econo Lodge (530 Main St, 12561; 255-6200, 800-4-CHOICE) 36 rooms, complimentary breakfast, pool, TV, children under 12 stay free with parents, no pets, senior citizen rates, wheelchair access, a/c, major credit cards. SGL/DBL$47-$60.

Super 8 Motel (Seven Terwilliger Rd, 12561; 255-8865, Fax 255-1629, 800-800-8000) 66 rooms and suites, free breakfast, no pets, children under 12 stay free with parents, free local calls, a/c, TV, fax, no-smoking rooms, senior citizen rates, wheelchair access, meeting facilities, major credit cards. SGL/DBL$48-$54.

Newport
Area Code 315

What Cheer Hall (North Main St, 13416; 845-8312) bed and breakfast, 1812 home, antique furnishings, private baths. SGL/DBL$40+.

New Rochelle
Area Code 914

Ramada Hotel Plaza (One Ramada Plaza, 10801; 576-3700, Fax 576-3711, 800-2-RAMADA) 128 rooms and suites, restaurant, lounge, entertainment, outdoor pool, exercise facilities, wheelchair access, no-smoking rooms, airport transportation, pets allowed, a/c, TV, room service, limousine service, free parking, laundry facilities, 5,700 square feet of meeting and exhibition space, meeting facilities, senior citizen rates, major credit cards. SGL$79-$122, DBL$85-$132, STS$225.

Niagara Falls
Area Code 716

Rental and Reservation Service

Rainbow Hospitality Bed and Breakfast Reservation Service (7009 Plaza Dr., 14304; 874-8797, 800-373-8797).

□ □ □

Algiers Motel (9820 Niagara Falls Blvd, 14304; 297-0395) 9 rooms, pool, wheelchair access, a/c, TV, major credit cards. SGL/DBL$38-$42.

Niagara Falls 215

Ameri-Cana Motor Inn (9401 Niagara Falls Blvd, 14303; 297-2660) 49 rooms and efficiencies, pool, wheelchair access, a/c, TV. SGL/DBL$52-$68.

American Youth Hostel (1100 Ferry Ave, 14301; 282-3700) dormitory beds. SGL/DBL$12.

Beacon Motel (9900 Niagara Falls Blvd, 14303; 297-3647) 22 rooms, pool, jacuzzis, wheelchair access, a/c, TV. SGL/DBL$38-$68.

Bit O'Paris Motel (9890 Niagara Falls Blvd, 14303; 297-1710) 27 rooms, pool, a/c, TV, wheelchair access, major credit cards. SGL/DBL$63-$73.

Budget Host (219 Fourth St, 14302; 282-1734, Fax 282-1881, 800-BUD-HOST) 23 rooms, restaurant, in-room refrigerators, no-smoking rooms, TV, VCRs, whirlpools, a/c, wheelchair access, children stay free with parents, laundry service, airport transportation, no pets, senior citizen rates, meeting facilities, major credit cards. SGL$45-$85, DBL$50-$90.

Coachman Motel (523 Third St, 14301; 285-2295) 18 rooms, wheelchair access, major credit cards. SGL/DBL$66.

Comfort Inn The Pointe (One Prospect Place, 14303; 284-6835, Fax 284-5177, 800-284-6835, 800-221-2222) 116 rooms, restaurant, wheelchair access, no-smoking rooms, no pets, children under 18 stay free with parents, senior citizen rates, a/c, TV, meeting facilities, major credit cards. LS SGL/DBL$49-$89; HS SGL/DBL$67-$127.

Days Inn (201 Rainbow Ave, 14303; 285-9321, Fax 285-2539, 800-325-2525) 200 rooms and suites, restaurant, lounge, children stay free with parents, room service, laundry service, a/c, TV, free local calls, no pets, wheelchair access, no-smoking rooms, senior citizen rates, major credit cards. SGL/DBL$59-$118, STS$118-$150.

Econo Lodge (7708 Niagara Falls Blvd, 14304; 283-0621, 800-4-CHOICE) 59 rooms, pool, children under 12 stay free with parents, no pets, senior citizen rates, wheelchair access, a/c, TV, major credit cards. SGL/DBL$39-$69.

Envoy Motor Inn (102 Niagara St, 14303; 282-5584) 28 rooms, restaurant, lounge, wheelchair access, TV, a/c. SGL/DBL$55-$75.

The Family YMCA (Portage and Main St, 14301; 285-8491) 10 rooms, pool, exercise facilities, a/c. SGL/DBL$15-$18.

Holiday Inn (114 Buffalo Ave, 14303; 285-2521, Fax 285-0963, 800-HOLIDAY) 202 rooms, restaurant, lounge, indoor pool, exercise facilities, jacuzzis, children under 19 stay free with parents, wheelchair access, a/c,

TV, no-smoking rooms, fax, room service, no pets, laundry service, meeting facilities, senior citizen rates, major credit cards. SGL/DBL$89-$134.

Holiday Inn (231 Third St, 14303; 282-2211, Fax 282-2748, 800-955-2211, 800-HOLIDAY) 161 rooms, restaurant, lounge, outdoor pool, exercise facilities, jacuzzi, children under 19 stay free with parents, wheelchair access, a/c, TV, no-smoking rooms, fax service, room service, no pets, laundry service, meeting facilities, senior citizen rates, major credit cards. SGL/DBL$39-$130.

Holly Rankine House Bed and Breakfast (525 Riverside Drive, 14303; 285-4790) 2 rooms, complimentary breakfast, major credit cards. SGL/DBL$45-$65.

Howard Johnson Lodge (454 Main St, 14301; 285-5261, Fax 285-8536, 800-I-GO-HOJO) 75 rooms, restaurant, lounge, indoor pool, sauna, game room, laundry facilities, children stay free with parents, wheelchair access, no-smoking rooms, TV, a/c, pets allowed, free parking, senior citizen rates, meeting facilities, major credit cards. LS SGL/DBL$45-$80; HS SGL/DBL$50-$90.

Howard Johnson Lodge (8505 Niagara Falls Blvd, 14304; 283-8791, Fax 283-9313, 800-I-GO-HOJO) 84 rooms, restaurant, lounge, pool, children stay free with parents, laundry facilities, game room, wheelchair access, no-smoking rooms, TV, a/c, pets allowed, free parking, senior citizen rates, meeting facilities for 100, major credit cards. LS SGL$39-$52, DBL$44-$60; HS SGL$43-$60, DBL$48-$68.

Inn At The Falls Hotel (240 Rainbow Blvd, 14303; 282-1212, 800-223-2557) restaurant, lounge, indoor pool, jacuzzi, free parking, a/c, TV, meeting facilities. SGL/DBL$65.

Olde Niagara House (610 Fourth St, 14301; 285-9408) 4 rooms, bed and breakfast, major credit cards. SGL/DBL$36-$56.

Quality Inn Rainbow Bridge (443 Main St, 14302; 284-8801, 800-777-2280, 800-368-5689) 168 rooms and suites, restaurant, indoor pool, room service, exercise facilities, children stay free with parents, a/c, TV, laundry service, no-smoking rooms, meeting facilities, major credit cards. LS SGL/DBL$45-$90; HS SGL/DBL$79-$129.

Radisson Hotel (Third and Old Falls St, 14303; 285-3361, Fax 285-3900, 800-777-1700) rooms and suites, restaurant, lounge, entertainment, pool, wheelchair access, free parking, no-smoking rooms, TV, a/c, children stay free with parents, pets allowed, major credit cards. SGL/DBL$60-$140.

Rainbow House Bed and Breakfast (423 Rainbow Blvd, 14303; 282-1135, 800-724-3536) 6 rooms, complimentary breakfast, private baths, major credit cards. SGL/DBL$65.

Rainbow Tourist Lodge (403 Rainbow Blvd, 14303; 284-8470) 11 rooms and efficiencies. SGL/DBL$36-$46.

Ramada Inn (401 Buffalo Ave, 14303; 285-2541, Fax 285-8841, 800-2-RAMADA) 194 rooms, restaurant, lounge, entertainment, pool, wheelchair access, water view, no-smoking rooms, airport transportation, free parking, pets allowed, a/c, TV, room service, laundry facilities, meeting facilities for 750, senior citizen rates, major credit cards. SGL/DBL$65-$130.

The Red Coach Inn (Two Buffalo Ave, 14303; 800-282-1459) rooms and suites, restaurant, fireplace, no pets, a/c, TV. SGL/DBL$75-$175.

TraveLodge (200 Rainbow Blvd, 14303; 285-7316, Fax 285-8541, 800-255-3050) 48 rooms and suites, restaurant, lounge, complimentary breakfast, pool, wheelchair access, free newspaper, laundry service, TV, a/c, free local calls, fax service, no-smoking rooms, free in-room coffee and tea service, in-room refrigerators and microwaves, no pets, major credit cards. SGL$45-$89, DBL$50-$93, AP$5.

Nichols
Area Code 607

Fawn's Grove (East River Rd, 13812; 699-3222) bed and breakfast, no smoking, no pets, private baths. SGL/DBL$45-$55.

North Creek
Area Code 518

The Copperfield Inn (224 Main St, 12853; 251-2500, Fax 251-4132, 800-424-9910) 25 rooms and suites, restaurant, lounge, pool, a/c, TV, VCRs, no pets, lighted tennis courts, whirlpools, Modified American Plan available, major credit cards. SGL/DBL$90-$140.

The Inn On Gore Mountain (North Creek 12853; 251-2111) 16 rooms, restaurant, a/c, TV, no pets, major credit cards. SGL/DBL$50-$75.

North Hudson
Area Code 518

Pine Tree Inn (Rte. 9, 12855; 532-9255) complimentary breakfast, no pets, open year-round. SGL/DBL$40-$60.

North Tonawanda
Area Code 716

Abbey Lane Motel (2931 Niagara Falls Blvd, 14120; 692-2277) 11 rooms, pool, a/c, TV, wheelchair access. SGL/DBL$38-$43.

Esquire Motel (3930 Niagara Falls Blvd, 14120; 692-4222) 14 rooms, pool, TV, a/c. SGL/DBL$45-$65.

Norwich
Area Code 607

Grove Park Motel (Rte. 12, 13815; 334-2251) restaurant, a/c. SGL/DBL$44-$54.

Howard Johnson Hotel (75 North Broad St, 13815; 334-2200, Fax 336-5619, 800-I-GO-HOJO) 85 rooms and suites, restaurant, lounge, pool, whirlpools, children stay free with parents, wheelchair access, no-smoking rooms, TV, a/c, pets allowed, free parking, senior citizen rates, meeting facilities, major credit cards. SGL/DBL$55-$85.

Super 8 Motel (Rte. 12, 13815; 336-8880, Fax 336-2076, 800-800-8000) 41 rooms and suites, no pets, children under 12 stay free with parents, free local calls, a/c, TV, fax, no-smoking rooms, senior citizen rates, wheelchair access, meeting facilities, major credit cards. SGL/DBL$40-$50.

Nyack
Area Code 914

Super 8 Motel (47 West Main St, 10960; 353-3880, Fax 353-0271, 800-800-8000) 43 rooms and suites, no pets, children under 12 stay free with parents, free local calls, a/c, TV, fax service, no-smoking rooms, senior citizen rates, wheelchair access, meeting facilities, major credit cards. SGL$53, DBL$56.

Oak Hill
Area Code 517

Hill House Bed and Breakfast (Rte. 81, 12460; 239-4722) 3 rooms, complimentary breakfast, shared bath, 1880s home, open year-round. SGL/DBL$60-$80.

Ogdensburg
Area Code 315

Friendship Inn (37 South Riverside Dr., 13669; 393-3730, 800-424-4777) 21 rooms, exercise facilities, a/c, TV, no pets, no-smoking rooms, children stay free with parents, wheelchair access, major credit cards. SGL/DBL$35-$65.

Holiday Inn (119 West River St, 13669; 393-2222, Fax 393-9602, 800-HOLIDAY) 78 rooms, restaurant, lounge, entertainment, indoor pool, spa, exercise facilities, children under 19 stay free with parents, wheelchair access, water view, a/c, TV, no-smoking rooms, fax service, room service, pets allowed, laundry service, meeting facilities for 400, senior citizen rates, major credit cards. SGL/DBL$56-$76.

Quality Inn Gran-View (State Rd 37, 13669; 393-4550, 800-368-5689) 48 rooms and suites, restaurant, lounge, entertainment, pool, room service, exercise facilities, children stay free with parents, a/c, TV, laundry service, no-smoking rooms, meeting facilities, major credit cards. SGL$51-$59, DBL$58-$95, AP$8.

Old Forge
Area Code 315

Sunset Motel (Rte. 28, 13420; 369-6836) indoor pool, a/c, sauna, jacuzzi, TV, tennis court, major credit cards. SGL/DBL$40-$65.

Olean
Area Code 716

Best Western Motel De Soto (3211 West State St, 14760; 373-1400, 800-528-1234) restaurant, complimentary breakfast, lounge, pool, exercise facilities, children stay free with parents, a/c, TV, no-smoking rooms, wheelchair access, pets allowed, senior citizen rates, meeting facilities, major credit cards. SGL/DBL$43-$55.

Castle Inn (3220 West State St, 14760; 372-1050, 800-422-7853) 160 rooms. SGL/DBL$52-$68.

The Old Library Bed and Breakfast (120 South Union St, 14760; 373-9804) 7 rooms, complimentary breakfast, 1890s home, a/c, TV, no pets, major credit cards. SGL/DBL$65-$125.

Park Inn Club and Breakfast Olean (2711 West State St, 373-1500, Fax 373-2920, 800-437-PARK) 143 rooms, restaurant, complimentary breakfast, lounge, outdoor pool, a/c, TV, children stay free with parents, free newspaper, senior citizen rates. SGL/DBL$49-$68.

Shady Rest Motel (1542 East State Rd, 14760; 372-3786) SGL/DBL$40-$50.

Oneida
Area Code 315

Super 8 Motel (215 Genessee St, 13421, 362-5168, Fax 363-4628, 800-800-8000) 39 rooms and suites, no pets, children under 12 stay free with parents, free local calls, a/c, TV, fax service, no-smoking rooms, senior citizen rates, wheelchair access, meeting facilities, major credit cards. SGL/DBL$42-$49.

Oneonta
Area Code 607

Cathedral Farms Inn (Rte. 23, 13820; 432-7483, 800-FARMS90) 16 rooms, restaurant, a/c, TV, open year-round, major credit cards. SGL/DBL$60-$80.

Celtic Motel (112 Oneida St, 13820; 432-0860) 20 rooms, a/c, TV, open year-round. SGL/DBL$35-$45.

Christopher's Country Lodge (Rte. 28, 13820; 432-2444) 28 rooms, restaurant, lounge, a/c, TV, meeting facilities, open year-round. SGL/DBL$60-$80.

Holiday Inn (Southside Rte. 23, 13820; 433-2250, 800-HOLIDAY) 86 rooms, restaurant, lounge, outdoor pool, exercise facilities, children under 19 stay free with parents, wheelchair access, a/c, TV, no-smoking rooms, fax service, room service, pets allowed, laundry service, meeting facilities for 400, senior citizen rates, major credit cards. SGL/DBL$40-$80.

Knott's Motel On The Lake (Rte. 28, 13820; 432-5948) 25 rooms, pool, a/c, TV, water view, open year-round, major credit cards. SGL/DBL$40-$80.

Maple Terrace (Rte. 7, 13820; 432-0790) 12 rooms, restaurant, pool, a/c, TV, open year-round, major credit cards. SGL/DBL$30-$40.

Master Host Inn (Rte. 7, 13820; 432-1280) 30 rooms, a/c, TV, open year-round, major credit cards. SGL/DBL$40-$100.

Riverview Motel (Rte. 23, 13830; 432-5301) 16 rooms, a/c, TV, pets allowed, open year-round. SGL/DBL$40-$60.

Super 8 Motel (Rte. 23 Southside, 13820; 432-9505, Fax 432-9505, 800-800-8000) 60 rooms and suites, restaurant, no pets, children under 12 stay free with parents, free local calls, a/c, open year-round, TV, fax service, no-smoking rooms, senior citizen rates, wheelchair access, meeting facilities, major credit cards. SGL/DBL$55-$64.

Town House Motor Inn (318 Main St, 13830; 432-1313) 40 rooms, a/c, TV. SGL/DBL$40-$60.

Oquaga Lake
Area Code 607

Scott's Lake House (Oquaga Lake, 13754; 467-3094) 125 rooms, restaurant, wheelchair access, open May to October. SGL/DBL$71-$82.

Orangeburg
Area Code 914

Holiday Inn (329 Hwy 303, 10962; 359-7000, Fax 359-7000 ext 396, 800-243-8287, 800-HOLIDAY) 138 rooms and suites, restaurant, lounge, outdoor pool, exercise facilities, children under 19 stay free with parents, wheelchair access, a/c, TV, no-smoking rooms, fax service, room service, no pets, laundry service, meeting facilities, senior citizen rates, major credit cards. SGL/DBL$75-$100.

Orchard
Area Code 716

Maple Court Motel (3940 Southwestern Blvd, Orchard Park 14127; 649-5809) 24 rooms, wheelchair access. SGL/DBL$55.

Ossining
Area Code 914

Hudson River Inn and Conference Center (Ossining 10562; 762-5600) 150 rooms and suites, restaurant, lounge, indoor pool, exercise facilities, sauna, tennis court, 33 meeting rooms, major credit cards. SGL/DBL$125-$165.

Oswego
Area Code 315

Days Inn (Rte. 104 East, 13126; 343-3136, Fax 343-6187, 800-325-2525) 44 rooms and suites, restaurant, lounge, pool, children stay free with parents, in-room refrigerators, room service, laundry service, a/c, TV, free local calls, no pets, wheelchair access, no-smoking rooms, senior citizen rates, major credit cards. SGL/DBL$55-$71, STS$89.

Friendship Inn (309 West Seneca St, 13126; 343-4900, 800-424-4777) 47 rooms, restaurant, exercise facilities, a/c, TV, no pets, children stay free with parents, wheelchair access, no-smoking rooms, major credit cards. SGL/DBL$42-$59.

Owego
Area Code 607

Econo Lodge (20 Hickory Park Rd, 13827; 687-9000, 800-4-CHOICE) 74 rooms and suites, pool, children under 12 stay free with parents, no pets, senior citizen rates, wheelchair access, laundry facilities, a/c, TV, major credit cards. SGL/DBL$40-$75.

Owego Treadway (Rte. 17, 13826; 687-4500) restaurant, indoor pool, sauna, water view. SGL/DBL$65-$85.

Oxford
Area Code 607

Whitegate (Oxford 13850; 843-6965) complimentary breakfast, 1820s home, on 196 acres. SGL/DBL$40+.

Painted Post
Area Code 607

Holiday Inn (304 South Hamilton St, 14870; 962-5021, Fax 962-5021 ext 299, 800-HOLIDAY) 105 rooms, restaurant, lounge, entertainment, outdoor pool, exercise facilities, children under 19 stay free with parents, beauty shop, wheelchair access, a/c, TV, no-smoking rooms, fax service, room service, no pets, laundry service, meeting facilities for 325, senior citizen rates, major credit cards. SGL/DBL$65-$95.

Super 8 Motel (255 South Hamilton, 14870; 937-5383, Fax 962-7115,800-800-8000) 61 rooms and suites, no pets, children under 12 stay free with parents, free local calls, a/c, TV, fax service, no-smoking rooms, senior citizen rates, wheelchair access, meeting facilities, major credit cards. SGL/DBL$40-$50.

Palatine Bridge
Area Code 518

Friendship Inn (East Grand St, 13428; 673-3233, 800-424-4777) 30 rooms, exercise facilities, a/c, TV, no pets, no-smoking rooms, children stay free with parents, wheelchair access, major credit cards. SGL/DBL$35-$66.

Palenville
Area Code 518

Arlington House Bed and Breakfast (Main St, 12463; 678-9081) 4 rooms, free breakfast, private bath, open year-round. SGL/DBL$48-$68.

Hans' County Line Motel (Rte. 32A, 12463; 678-3101) 42 rooms, restaurant, lounge, pool, in-room refrigerators, laundry facilities, a/c, TV, open year-round, major credit cards. SGL/DBL$40-$95.

Kaaterskill Creek Bed and Breakfast (Kaaterskill Ave, 12463; 678-9052) 3 rooms, complimentary breakfast, shared bath, fireplace, swimming, open year-round. SGL/DBL$65-$90.

The Kenmore Bed and Breakfast (Malden Ave, 12463; 678-3494) 5 rooms and 1 four-bedroom housekeeping cabin, complimentary breakfast, shared baths, kitchenettes, open year-round. SGL/DBL$90-$100.

Oak Lodge Cabins (Rte. 32A, 12463; 678-9929) 9 housekeeping cottages and cabins, kitchenettes, open May 15 to September 15. SGL/DBL$55-$68.

Palenville House Bed and Breakfast (Rte. 23A, 12463; 678-5649) complimentary breakfast, 1901 home, jacuzzi, antique furnishings, private baths. SGL/DBL$45.

Pearl's Place Bed and Breakfast (Rte. 23A, 12463; 678-5649) free breakfast, 1901 home, private baths, no smoking, no pets, major credit cards. SGL/DBL$55-$65.

Parish
Area Code 315

Springbrook Farm (Rte. 38, 13131; 625-7665) 4 rooms, bed and breakfast, kitchenettes. SGL/DBL$30-$45.

Pearl River
Area Code 914

Hilton Hotel (500 Veterans Memorial Dr., 10965; 735-9000, Fax 735-9000 ext 105, 800-HILTONS) 150 rooms and suites, restaurant, lounge, entertainment, outdoor pool, exercise facilities, jacuzzi, sauna, free parking, children stay free with parents, no-smoking rooms, wheelchair access, pets allowed, a/c, TV, business services, meeting facilities, major credit cards. SGL/DBL$85-$115, STS$125.

Pembroke
Area Code 716

Econo Lodge (Pembroke 14036; 599-4681, 800-4-CHOICE) 73 rooms, pool, children under 12 stay free with parents, no pets, senior citizen rates, wheelchair access, a/c, TV, major credit cards. SGL/DBL$45-$75.

Penfield
Area Code 716

Strawberry Castle (1883 Penfield Rd, 14526; 385-3266) bed and breakfast, pool, antique furnishings, no pets, major credit cards. SGL/DBL$85-$125.

Penn Yan
Area Code 315

The Fox Inn (158 Main St, 14527; 536-3101) 5 rooms, bed and breakfast, no smoking, private baths, no pets, 1800s home, antique furnishings, a/c, major credit cards. SGL/DBL$60-$85.

Heirlooms Bed and Breakfast (2756 Coates Rd, 14527; 536-7682) 4 rooms, complimentary breakfast, 1820s home, no pets, no smoking, major credit cards. SGL/DBL$60-$75.

Phelps
Area Code 315

Days Inn (Phelps 14532; 789-4510, Fax 789-0749, 800-325-2525) 35 rooms, restaurant, lounge, pool, children stay free with parents, room service, laundry service, a/c, TV, free local calls, pets allowed, wheelchair access, no-smoking rooms, senior citizen rates, major credit cards. SGL/DBL$40-$55.

Philadelphia
Area Code 315

Indian River Lodge (Rte. 11, 13673; 642-5666) 12 rooms, no pets, open year-round. SGL/DBL$30-$45.

Pittstown
Area Code 518

Maggie Towne's Bed and Breakfast (Pittstown 12185; 663-8369) complimentary breakfast, no smoking, private baths, Colonial home. SGL/DBL$25-$35.

Plainview
Area Code 516

Holiday Inn (215 Sunnyside Blvd, 11803; 349-7400, Fax 349-7491, 800-HOLIDAY) 155 rooms, restaurant, lounge, entertainment, outdoor pool, exercise facilities, children under 19 stay free with parents, wheelchair access, a/c, TV, no-smoking rooms, fax service, room service, no pets, laundry service, meeting facilities for 350, senior citizen rates, major credit cards. SGL/DBL$70-$85.

Howard Johnson Hotel (150 Sunnyside Blvd, 11803; 349-9100, Fax 349-9106, 800-I-GO-HOJO) 182 rooms, restaurant, lounge, pool, children stay free with parents, wheelchair access, free local calls, laundry service, room service, no-smoking rooms, TV, a/c, pets allowed, free parking, meeting facilities, senior citizen rates, major credit cards. SGL$55-$89, DBL$55-$99.

Residence Inn (9 Gerhard Rd, 11803; 433-3600, Fax 433-2569, 800-331-3131) rooms and 1- and 2-bedroom suites, indoor and outdoor pool, spa, whirlpools, in-room refrigerators, coffee makers and microwaves, laundry facilities, free parking, TV, a/c, VCRs, pets allowed, fireplaces, children stay free with parents, no-smoking rooms, wheelchair access, meeting facilities, major credit cards. SGL/DBL$130-$140.

Plattsburgh
Area Code 518

Comfort Inn (495 Cornelia St, 12901; 562-2730, 800-221-2222) 107 rooms, restaurant, lounge, entertainment, indoor pool, exercise facilities, wheelchair access, no-smoking rooms, no pets, children under 18 stay free with parents, senior citizen rates, a/c, TV, meeting facilities, major credit cards. SGL$60-$92, DBL$70-$99.

Days Inn (587 Upper Cornelia St, 12901; 561-0403, Fax 561-4192, 800-325-2525) 112 rooms, restaurant, lounge, children stay free with parents, room service, laundry service, a/c, TV, free local calls, no pets, wheelchair access, no-smoking rooms, senior citizen rates, major credit cards. SGL/DBL$37-$71.

Econo Lodge (610 Upper Cornelia, 12901; 561-1500, 800-4-CHOICE) 100 rooms and suites, indoor pool, children under 12 stay free with parents, no pets, senior citizen rates, wheelchair access, a/c, TV, major credit cards. SGL/DBL$50-$70.

Holiday Inn (I-87 and State Rd 3, 12901; 561-5000, 800-HOLIDAY) 86 rooms, restaurant, lounge, entertainment, indoor pool, exercise facilities, children under 19 stay free with parents, wheelchair access, a/c, TV, no-smoking rooms, fax, room service, no pets, laundry service, meeting facilities, senior citizen rates, major credit cards. SGL/DBL$56-$86.

Howard Johnson Lodge (Box 1278, 12901; 561-7750, Fax 561-9431, 800-243-HOJO, 800-I-GO-HOJO) 120 rooms, 3 restaurants, lounge, pool, exercise facilities, sauna, game room, laundry facilities, room service, in-room refrigerators, VCRs, children stay free with parents, wheelchair access, no-smoking rooms, TV, a/c, pets allowed, free parking, meeting facilities, senior citizen rates, major credit cards. LS SGL/DBL$45-$67; HS SGL/DBL$59-$77.

Super 8 Motel (Rte. 9 North, 12901; 562-8888, 800-800-8000) 61 rooms and suites, pets allowed, children under 12 stay free with parents, free local calls, a/c, TV, fax service, no-smoking rooms, senior citizen rates, wheelchair access, meeting facilities, major credit cards. SGL/DBL$47-$51.

Point Peninsula
Area Code 315

Golden's Cottages (North Shore Rd, 13693; 649-5206) 14 rooms and housekeeping cottages, no pets, wheelchair access, open April 15 to October 1. SGL/DBL40-$50/$150W-$225W.

Shangri-La Marina (Box 625, 13693; 649-2979) 16 rooms and cabins, restaurant, wheelchair access, pets allowed, open April 15 to October 15. SGL/DBL$40-$60.

Port Jefferson
Area Code 516

Compass Rose (415 West Broadway, 11888; 474-1111) bed and breakfast, no pets, private baths, TV, 1820s home, a/c, major credit cards. SGL/DBL$50-$125.

Danford's Inn (25 East Broadway, 11777; 928-5200) 85 rooms, restaurant, exercise facilities, no pets, fireplaces, a/c, TV, VCRs, no-smoking rooms, major credit cards. SGL/DBL$110-$210.

Port Jervis
Area Code 914

Holiday Inn (Rte. 23, 12771; 865-6611, 800-HOLIDAY) 124 rooms, restaurant, complimentary breakfast, lounge, children under 19 stay free with parents, wheelchair access, VCRs, a/c, TV, no-smoking rooms, fax service, room service, pets allowed, laundry service, meeting facilities for 150, senior citizen rates, major credit cards. SGL/DBL$80-$90.

Poughkeepsie
Area Code 914

Days Inn (62 Haight Ave, 12603; 454-1010, Fax 454-0127, 800-325-2525) 41 rooms, restaurant, free breakfast, lounge, outdoor pool, children stay free with parents, room service, laundry service, a/c, TV, free local calls, no pets, wheelchair access, no-smoking rooms, senior citizen rates, major credit cards. SGL/DBL$53-$63.

Econo Lodge (418 South Rd, 12601; 452-6600, 800-4-CHOICE) 113 rooms, restaurant, pool, children under 12 stay free with parents, no pets, senior citizen rates, wheelchair access, a/c, TV, major credit cards. SGL/DBL$43-$61.

Friendship Inn (576 South Rd, 12601; 462-4400, 800-424-4777) 99 rooms, restaurant, pool, exercise facilities, a/c, TV, no pets, no-smoking rooms, children stay free with parents, wheelchair access, major credit cards. SGL/DBL$44-$95.

Holiday Inn (Sharon Dr. and Rte. 9, 12601; 473-1151, Fax 485-8127, 800-HOLIDAY) 123 rooms, children under 19 stay free with parents, wheelchair access, free local calls, a/c, TV, no-smoking rooms, fax service, room service, no pets, laundry service, meeting facilities for 24, senior citizen rates, major credit cards. SGL/DBL$65-$77.

Radisson Hotel (40 Civic Center Plaza, 12601; 485-5300, Fax 485-4720, 800-777-1700) rooms and suites, restaurant, lounge, entertainment, pool, wheelchair access, free parking, no-smoking rooms, TV, a/c, children stay free with parents, pets allowed, major credit cards. SGL/DBL$89-$119.

Ramada Inn (679 South Rd, 12601; 462-4600, Fax 462-4638, 800-2-RAMADA) 154 rooms, restaurant, lounge, wheelchair access, no-smoking rooms, airport transportation, free parking, pets allowed, a/c, TV, room service, laundry facilities, meeting facilities for 850, senior citizen rates, major credit cards. SGL/DBL$58.

Prattsville
Area Code 518

Hideaway Hotel (Huntersfield Rd, 12468; 299-3616) 14 rooms, restaurant, open year-round, Modified American Plan available. SGL/DBL$65-$75.

Moore's Motel & Resort (Rte. 23, 12468; 299-3404). SGL/DBL$38-$40.

Pulaski
Area Code 315

Super 8 Motel (7611 Rome Rd, 13142; 298-4888, Fax 298-3293, 800-800-8000) 39 rooms and suites, no pets, children under 12 stay free with parents, free local calls, a/c, TV, fax service, no-smoking rooms, senior citizen rates, wheelchair access, meeting facilities, major credit cards. LS SGL$40, DBL$47; HS SGL/DBL$62.

Purling
Area Code 518

Bavarian Manor (Purling 12740; 622-3261, 800-999-MANOR) 53 rooms, complimentary breakfast, restaurant, entertainment, Victorian inn, water view, American plan available. SGL/DBL$75-$130.

Dellwood Resort (Mountain Ave, 12470; 622-3292) restaurant, pool, TV, a/c, game room, open May to September, major credit cards. SGL/DBL$65-$75.

Tumblin' Falls Bed and Breakfast (Purling 12740; 622-3981) 3 rooms, complimentary breakfast, shared baths. SGL/DBL$40-$60.

Queensbury
Area Code 518

Crislip's Bed and Breakfast (Ridge Rd, 12804; 793-6869) complimentary breakfast, no smoking, antique furnishings, private baths, major credit cards. SGL/DBL$50.

Ramada Inn (Aviation Rd, 12804; 793-7701, Fax 792-5463, 800-2-RAMADA) 110 rooms, restaurant, lounge, indoor pool, wheelchair access, no-smoking rooms, in-room coffee makers, airport transportation, free parking, pets allowed, a/c, TV, room service, laundry facilities, meeting facilities, senior citizen rates, major credit cards. SGL$53-$88, DBL$68-$103.

Randolph
Area Code 716

The Colonial House (252 Main St, 14772; 358-9067) bed and breakfast, no smoking, antique furnishings. SGL/DBL$35-$40.

Remsen
Area Code 315

Stor Felen Bed and Breakfast (Starr Hill and Fuller Rd, 13428; 831-5442) complimentary breakfast, 1800s home, on 23 acres. SGL/DBL$40+.

Rexford
Area Code 518

Rexford Crossing Bed and Breakfast (1643 Rte. 146, 12148; 399-1777) complimentary breakfast, Victorian home, a/c, TV, antique furnishings. LS SGL/DBL$85-$105; HS SGL/DBL$104-$125.

Rhinebeck
Area Code 914

Village Victorian Inn (31 Center St, 12572; 876-8345) bed and breakfast, no smoking, private baths, no pets, antique furnishings, no children allowed, a/c. SGL/DBL$150-$225.

Richfield Springs
Area Code 315

Aunt Martha's Bed and Breakfast (McKoons Rd, 13439; 858-1648) complimentary breakfast, no pets. SGL/DBL$45+.

Country Spread Bed and Breakfast (23 Prospect St, 13439; 858-1870) complimentary breakfast, no smoking, no pets, private baths, a/c. SGL/DBL$50-$65.

Fieldstone Farm and Cabins (Richfield Springs 13439; 858-0295, 800-336-4629) 15 rooms and housekeeping cabins, pool, pets allowed, kitchenettes, open year-round. SGL/DBL$40-$80.

Pine Grove Motel (Rte. 28, 13439; 858-9914) 5 rooms, restaurant, open May 29 to October 9. SGL/DBL$40-$60.

Red Maple Leaf Guest House (27 East Main St, 13439; 858-0482) 2 rooms, a/c, TV, open year-round. SGL/DBL$40-$50.

Spring Park Motel (East Main St, 13439; 858-1220) 5 rooms, TV, open year-round. SGL/DL$30-$40.

Stony Brook Motel (62 East Main St, 13439; 858-9929) 7 rooms, a/c, TV, open year-round. SGL/DBL$35-$50.

Summerwood (72 East Main St, 13439; 858-2024) bed and breakfast, Victorian home, antique furnishings, TV, no pets, private baths. SGL/DBL$40-$75.

Village Motel (East Main St, 13439; 858-1540) 10 rooms, a/c, TV, open year-round. SGL/DBL$35-$50.

Wolfe Hall (32 Church St, 13439; 858-1510) bed and breakfast, 1850s home, antique furnishings. SGL/DBL$40+.

Riverhead
Area Code 516

Holiday Inn (Rte. 25, 00901; 369-2200, 800-HOLIDAY) restaurant, lounge, indoor pool, exercise facilities, children under 19 stay free with parents, wheelchair access, a/c, TV, no-smoking rooms, fax service, room service, no pets, laundry service, meeting facilities, senior citizen rates, major credit cards. SGL/DBL$65-$95.

Rochester
Area Code 716

Best Western Diplomat Hotel (1956 Lyell Ave, 14606; 254-1000, Fax 254-1510, 800-528-1234) 91 rooms and efficiencies, restaurant, complimentary breakfast, lounge, pool, exercise facilities, children stay free with parents, a/c, TV, no-smoking rooms, airport transportation, wheelchair access, no pets, senior citizen rates, meeting facilities, major credit cards. SGL/DBL$50-$70.

Comfort Inn Airport (395 Buell Rd, 14624; 436-4400, 800-221-2222) restaurant, airport transportation, wheelchair access, no-smoking rooms, no pets, children under 18 stay free with parents, senior citizen rates, a/c, TV, meeting facilities, major credit cards. SGL/DBL$48-$59.

Comfort Inn (1501 West Ridge Rd, 14615; 621-5700, 800-221-2222) 83 rooms, restaurant, exercise facilities, wheelchair access, no-smoking rooms, no pets, children under 18 stay free with parents, senior citizen rates, a/c, TV, meeting facilities, major credit cards. SGL/DBL$47-$74.

Dartmouth House (215 Dartmouth St, 14607; 271-7872) bed and breakfast, antique furnishings, no pets, no smoking, private baths, no children allowed, fireplace. SGL/DBL$65-$75.

Days Inn (384 East Ave, 14607; 325-5010, Fax 454-3158, 800-325-2525) 133 rooms, restaurant, lounge, pool, children stay free with parents, room service, laundry service, a/c, TV, free local calls, pets allowed, wheelchair access, no-smoking rooms, senior citizen rates, major credit cards. SGL/DBL$63-$76.

Econo Lodge (940 Jefferson Rd, 14623; 427-2700, 800-4-CHOICE) 102 rooms, children under 12 stay free with parents, no pets, laundry facilities, whirlpools, senior citizen rates, wheelchair access, a/c, TV, major credit cards. SGL/DBL$40-$91.

Hampton Inn (717 East Henrietta Rd, 14623; 272-7800, Fax 272-1211, 800-HAMPTON) 113 rooms, restaurant, complimentary breakfast, pool, exercise facilities, children under 18 stay free with parents, no-smoking rooms, wheelchair access, computer hookups, fax service, TV, a/c, free local calls, pets allowed, meeting facilities, major credit cards. SGL/DBL$58-$68.

Highland Bed and Breakfast (1969 Highland Ave, 14618; 442-4813) bed and breakfast, no pets. SGL/DBL$55-$70.

Holiday Inn South (1111 Jefferson Rd, 14623; 475-1510, Fax 427-8673, 800-HOLIDAY) 250 rooms, restaurant, lounge, entertainment, outdoor pool, exercise facilities, children under 19 stay free with parents, wheelchair access, a/c, TV, no-smoking rooms, airport transportation, fax service, room service, no pets, laundry service, meeting facilities, senior citizen rates, major credit cards. SGL/DBL$85-$105.

Holiday Inn (120 Main St East, 14604; 546-6400, Fax 546-3908, 800-HOLIDAY) 466 rooms, restaurant, lounge, outdoor pool, exercise facilities, children under 19 stay free with parents, wheelchair access, a/c, gift shop, TV, no-smoking rooms, fax service, room service, airport transportation, pets allowed, laundry service, meeting facilities for 1,500, senior citizen rates, major credit cards. SGL/DBL$95-$110.

Holiday Inn Airport (911 Brooks Ave, 14624; 328-6000, Fax 328-1012, 800-HOLIDAY) restaurant, lounge, entertainment, indoor pool, exercise facilities, gift shop, children under 19 stay free with parents, wheelchair access, a/c, TV, no-smoking rooms, fax service, room service, no pets, laundry service, meeting facilities, senior citizen rates, major credit cards. SGL/DBL$90-$110.

Howard Johnson Lodge (3350 West Henrietta Rd, 14623; 475-1661, Fax 475-1667, 800-I-GO-HOJO) 96 rooms, restaurant, complimentary breakfast, lounge, pool, children stay free with parents, wheelchair access, no-smoking rooms, TV, a/c, fax service, laundry facilities, no pets, free parking, meeting facilities, senior citizen rates, major credit cards. SGL/DBL$45-$65.

Hyatt Regency Rochester (125 East Main St, 14604; 546-1234, Fax 546-6160, 800-233-1234) 350 rooms and suites, restaurant, lounge, entertainment, outdoor pool, whirlpool, exercise facilities, room service, TV, a/c, no-smoking rooms, wheelchair access, 13,600 square feet of meeting and exhibition space, meeting facilities, major credit cards. SGL/DBL$120-$160.

Marketplace Inn (800 Jefferson Rd, 14623; 475-9190) 145 rooms, restaurant, lounge, pool, pets allowed, a/c, TV, airport transportation, major credit cards. SGL/DBL$60-$65.

Marriott Airport Hotel (1890 West Ridge Rd, 14615; 225-6880, Fax 225-8188, 800-228-9290) 210 rooms and suites, restaurant, lounge, entertainment, indoor pool, exercise facilities, whirlpools, jogging track, sauna, airport courtesy car, free parking, wheelchair access, TV, a/c, no-smoking rooms, gift shop, children stay free with parents, business services, meeting facilities, major credit cards. SGL/DBL$140-$150.

Marriott Thruway Hotel (5257 West Henrietta Rd, 14623; 359-1800, Fax 359-1349, 800-228-9290) 307 rooms and suites, restaurant, lounge, indoor and outdoor pool, exercise facilities, whirlpools, wheelchair access, game room, jogging track, sauna, airport courtesy car, free parking, TV, a/c, no-smoking rooms, gift shop, children stay free with parents, business services, meeting facilities, major credit cards. SGL/DBL$95-$125.

Ramada Inn Airport (1273 Chili Ave, 14624; 464-8800, 800-2-RAMADA) 155 rooms and suites, restaurant, lounge, pool, wheelchair access, no-smoking rooms, airport transportation, free parking, pets allowed, a/c, TV, room service, laundry facilities, 5 meeting rooms, meeting facilities for 200, senior citizen rates, major credit cards. SGL/DBL$49-$75, STS$125, AP$10.

Residence Inn (1300 Jefferson Rd, 14623; 272-8850, Fax 272-7822, 800-331-3131) rooms and suites, complimentary breakfast, pool, spa, in-room refrigerators, coffee makers and microwaves, laundry facilities, free parking, TV, a/c, VCRs, pets allowed, fireplaces, children stay free with parents, no-smoking rooms, wheelchair access, meeting facilities for 25, major credit cards. SGL/DBL$89-$140.

Strathallan Hotel (550 East Ave, 14607; 461-5010) 150 rooms and 1- and 2-bedroom suites, restaurant, a/c, TV, exercise facilities, in-room refrigerators, airport transportation, no pets, no-smoking rooms. SGL/DBL$85-$145.

Wellesley Inn (1635 Ridge Rd, 14615; 621-2060) 99 rooms and suites, restaurant, a/c, TV, VCRs, pets allowed, no-smoking rooms, senior citizen rates, major credit cards. SGL/DBL$40-$85.

Rock City Falls
Area Code 518

The Mansion Inn (Rte. 29, 12863; 885-1607) bed and breakfast, private baths, 1860s home, open year-round. SGL/DBL$65-$100.

Rock Hill
Area Code 914

Howard Johnson Lodge (Rock Hill Drive, 12775; 796-3000, 800-I-GO-HOJO) 70 rooms, restaurant, lounge, outdoor pool, children stay free with parents, wheelchair access, no-smoking rooms, TV, a/c, in-room refrigerators and coffee makers, pets allowed, free parking, senior citizen rates, meeting facilities, major credit cards. SGL/DBL$49-$79.

Rockville Centre
Area Code 516

Holiday Inn (173 Sunrise Hwy, 11570; 678-1300, Fax 678-5657, 800-HOLIDAY) restaurant, lounge, outdoor pool, exercise facilities, children under 19 stay free with parents, wheelchair access, a/c, TV, no-smoking rooms, fax service, room service, pets allowed, laundry service, meeting facilities for 250, senior citizen rates, major credit cards. SGL/DBL$90-$130.

Rome
Area Code 315

American Heritage Motor Inn (799 Lower Lawrence St, 13440; 339-3610, 800-836-1203) 27 rooms, restaurant, a/c, TV, major credit cards. SGL/DBL$35-$45

Esquire Motor Lodge (1801 Black River Blvd, 13440; 336-5320, 800-336-1808) TV, in-room coffee makers, a/c, no-smoking rooms. SGL/DBL$48-$68.

Family Inns of Rome (145 East Whitesboro St, 13440; 337-9400) 56 rooms, restaurant, lounge, TV, kitchenettes, a/c, major credit cards. SGL/DBL$60.

Green Lantern Motor Court (8189 Turin Rd, 13440; 336-5200) 11 rooms, restaurant, a/c, TV, kitchenettes, in-room refrigerators and microwaves, no pets, major credit cards. SGL/DBL$38-$53.

The Little Schoolhouse (690 Dix Rd, 13440; 336-4474) bed and breakfast, 1840s home. SGL/DBL$45+.

Maplecrest Bed and Breakfast (6480 Williams Rd, 13440; 337-0070) complimentary breakfast, private bath, fireplace, a/c. SGL/DBL$45+.

Park Inn International (Rome 13440; 336-4300, 800-437-PARK) 104 rooms and suites, restaurant, lounge, outdoor pool, a/c, TV, laundry facilities, children stay free with parents, complimentary newspaper, senior citizen rates, major credit cards. SGL/DBL$65-$105.

Paul Revere Motor Lodge (Rte. 26N, 13440; 336-1776) pool, coffee shop, TV, on 52 acres, putting green. SGL/DBL$42-$46.

Quality Inn (200 James St, 13440; 336-4300, 800-368-5689) 104 rooms and suites, restaurant, lounge, outdoor pool, room service, exercise facilities, children stay free with parents, a/c, TV, free parking, laundry service, no-smoking rooms, meeting facilities, major credit cards. SGL$46-$65, DBL$55-$75, AP$10.

Rome Motel (8257 Turin Rd, 13440; 336-4200) rooms and efficiencies, TV, a/c, major credit cards. SGL/DBL$36-$38.

Wright Settlement Bed and Breakfast (Wright Settlement Rd, 13440; 337-2417) 3 rooms, complimentary breakfast, pool, 1800s Victorian farmhouse, antique furnishings, on 50 acres, cross-country skiing, open year-round. SGL/DBL$50-$60.

Ronkonkoma
Area Code 516

Econo Lodge (3055 Veterans Memorial Hwy, 11779; 588-6800, 800-4-CHOICE) 60 rooms, complimentary breakfast, pool, TV, children under 12 stay free with parents, no pets, senior citizen rates, wheelchair access, a/c, major credit cards. SGL/DBL$54-$80.

Round Lake
Area Code 518

Chamber Lane Motel (2142 Rte. 9, 12151; 899-2520) efficiencies and cabins, TV, in-room refrigerators, a/c, no pets, major credit cards. LS SGL/DBL$39-$65; HS SGL/DBL$55-$105.

Grand Prix Motor Inn (Box 5, 12151; 899-6633) restaurant, a/c, TV. SGL/DBL$40-$85.

Rogers Motor Court (Round Lake 12151; 899-6386) efficiencies and cabins, pool, TV, major credit cards. LS SGL/DBL$20-$60; HS SGL/DBL$45-$98.

Round Top
Area Code 518

Blackhead Mountain Lodge and Country Club (Round Top 12473; 622-3157) restaurant, entertainment, pool, tennis courts, on 100 acres, a/c, TV, 9-hole golf course, open May to October. SGL/DBL$65-$85.

Riedlbauer's Resort (Round Top 12473; 622-9584) 24 rooms, restaurant, outdoor pool, tennis courts, hiking trail, open May to October, American plan available. SGL/DBL$48-$68.

Winter Clove Inn (Round Top 12473; 622-3267) restaurant, indoor and outdoor pool, tennis courts, fireplace, on 400 acres, private baths, open May to October. SGL/DBL$75.

Rushville
Area Code 716

Lakeview Farm (4761 Rte. 364, 14544; 554-6973) 2 rooms, bed and breakfast, on 170 acres, antique furnishings, no smoking, shared baths, no pets, major credit cards. SGL/DBL$40-$60.

Rye
Area Code 914

Courtyard by Marriott (631 Midland Ave, 10580; 921-1110, 800-321-2211) 145 rooms and suites, restaurant, lounge, indoor pool, exercise facilities, whirlpools, children stay free with parents, laundry service, 2 meeting rooms, meeting facilities for 80, senior citizen rates, major credit cards. SGL/DBL$82-$115.

Inn At Old Harbor (130 Apawamis Ave, 10580; 967-4670) bed and breakfast, antique furnishings, no pets, private bath, Victorian home. SGL/DBL$85-$140.

Rye Brook
Area Code 914

Arrowhead Resort and Conference Center (Anderson Hill Rd, 10573; 939-5500, Fax 939-1877) 276 rooms and suites, restaurant, lounge, indoor and outdoor pool, exercise facilities, hiking trails, whirlpools, lighted tennis courts, sauna, transportation to local attractions, a/c, TV, no-smoking rooms, wheelchair access, 36 meeting rooms, meeting facilities. SGL/DBL$145-$400.

Hilton Ryetown Hotel (699 Westchester Ave, 01573; 939-6300, Fax 939-5328, 800-HILTONS) 438 rooms and suites, restaurant, lounge, entertainment, indoor and outdoor pool, exercise facilities, sauna, whirlpools, children stay free with parents, car rental desk, free parking, no-smoking rooms, wheelchair access, pets allowed, a/c, TV, business services, meeting facilities, major credit cards. SGL/DBL$115-$165.

Sabael
Area Code 518

Timberlock (Sabael 12864; 648-5494) cabins, kitchenettes, boating, water view, tennis courts, open June 23 to September 31, American plan available. SGL/DBL$38-$48.

Sardinia
Area Code 716

Ben's Nichlos Brook Motel (Rtes 16 and 39, Sardinia 14134; 496-7226) 24 rooms and efficiencies, complimentary breakfast, no-smoking rooms, room service. SGL/DBL$55.

Springville
Area Code 716

Leland House (26 East Main St, Springville 14141; 592-7631) 6 rooms, no-smoking rooms, wheelchair access. SGL/DBL$38.

Syracuse, East Syracuse & North Syracuse
Area Code 315

Benedict House (1402 James St, 13202; 476-6541) bed and breakfast, no smoking, no pets, private bath, TV, a/c, no children allowed. SGL/DBL$50-$60.

Comfort Inn Fairgrounds (7010 Interstate Island Rd, 13209; 453-0045, 800-221-2222) 110 rooms, restaurant, exercise facilities, wheelchair access, no-smoking rooms, no pets, children under 18 stay free with parents, senior citizen rates, a/c, TV, meeting facilities, major credit cards. LS SGL$40-$51, DBL$45-$56; HS SGL$54-$90, DBL$59-$90, AP$5.

Comfort Inn Downtown (454 James St, 13202; 425-0015, 800-221-2222) 50 rooms, restaurant, wheelchair access, no-smoking rooms, no pets, children under 18 stay free with parents, senior citizen rates, a/c, TV, meeting facilities, major credit cards. LS SGL$38-$46, DBL$43-$51; HS $45-$60, DBL$50-$70, AP$6.

Days Inn (6609 Thompson Rd, 13206; 437-5998, Fax 437-5965, 800-325-2525) 100 rooms, restaurant, lounge, pool, children stay free with parents, room service, laundry service, a/c, TV, free local calls, pets allowed, wheelchair access, no-smoking rooms, senior citizen rates, major credit cards. SGL/DBL$43-$58.

Days Inn University (1100 James St, 13203; 472-6961, Fax 472-5514, 800-325-2525) 127 rooms and suites, restaurant, lounge, indoor pool, children stay free with parents, room service, laundry service, a/c, TV, free local calls, pets allowed, wheelchair access, no-smoking rooms, senior citizen rates, major credit cards. SGL$50-$70, DBL$60-$85, STS$90-$125.

Embassy Suites (6646 Old Collamer Rd, 13057; 446-3200, Fax 437-3302, 800-EMBASSY) 2-room suites, restaurant, lounge, free breakfast, lounge, pool, whirlpool, exercise facilities, sauna, room service, laundry service, wheelchair access, free newspaper, free local calls, no-smoking rooms, gift shop, transportation to local attractions, business services, meeting facilities, major credit cards. SGL/DBL$100.

Fairfield Inn (6611 Old Collamer Rd, 13057; 432-9333, Fax 432-9333, 800-228-2800) complimentary morning coffee, outdoor pool, children under 18 stay free with parents, no-smoking rooms, remote control TV, free cable TV, free local calls, laundry service, a/c, wheelchair access, fax, meeting facilities, senior citizen rates, major credit cards. SGL/DBL$37-$60.

Hampton Inn (6605 Old Collamer Rd, 13057; 463-6443, Fax 432-1080, 800-HAMPTON) 117 rooms, restaurant, complimentary breakfast, pool, exercise facilities, children under 18 stay free with parents, no-smoking rooms, wheelchair access, computer hookups, fax service, TV, a/c, free local calls, pets allowed, meeting facilities, major credit cards. SGL/DBL$47-$57.

Hilton Syracuse Square Hotel (500 South Warren St, 13202; 471-7300, Fax 422-3440, 800-HILTONS) 201 rooms and suites, restaurant, lounge, entertainment, outdoor pool, exercise facilities, children stay free with parents, room service, no-smoking rooms, wheelchair access, pets allowed, a/c, TV, free parking, beauty shop, airline ticket desk, gift shop, business services, meeting facilities, major credit cards. SGL/DBL$85-$115.

Holiday Inn (North Syracuse 13212; 457-4000, 800-HOLIDAY) 187 rooms, restaurant, lounge, indoor pool, exercise facilities, children under 19 stay free with parents, wheelchair access, a/c, TV, no-smoking rooms, fax service, room service, no pets, laundry service, meeting facilities, senior citizen rates, major credit cards. SGL/DBL$80-$85.

Holiday Inn (Carrier Circle, 13057; 437-2761, 800-HOLIDAY) 203 rooms, restaurant, lounge, indoor pool, exercise facilities, children under 19 stay free with parents, wheelchair access, a/c, TV, no-smoking rooms, fax service, room service, no pets, laundry service, meeting facilities for 300, senior citizen rates, major credit cards. SGL/DBL$80-$85.

Holiday Inn (Farrell Rd, 13209; 457-8700, 800-HOLIDAY) restaurant, lounge, outdoor pool, exercise facilities, children under 19 stay free with parents, wheelchair access, a/c, TV, no-smoking rooms, fax service, room service, pets allowed, laundry service, meeting facilities for 325, senior citizen rates, major credit cards. SGL/DBL$52-$73.

Holiday Inn (701 Genessee St, 13210; 474-7251, 800-HOLIDAY) 290 rooms, restaurant, lounge, indoor pool, jacuzzi, exercise facilities, children under 19 stay free with parents, wheelchair access, a/c, TV, no-smoking rooms, fax service, room service, no pets, laundry service, meeting facilities for 300, senior citizen rates, major credit cards. SGL/DBL$75-$85.

Howard Johnson Lodge (Thompson Rd, 13206; 437-2711, Fax 437-1734, 800-I-GO-HOJO) 90 rooms, restaurant, lounge, complimentary breakfast, pool, children stay free with parents, wheelchair access, VCRs, no-smoking rooms, TV, a/c, pets allowed, free parking, meeting facilities, senior citizen rates, major credit cards. SGL/DBL$50-$90.

Marriott Hotel (6302 Carrier Pkwy, 13057; 432-0200, Fax 433-1210, 800-782-9847, 800-228-9290) 248 rooms and suites, restaurant, lounge, entertainment, indoor and outdoor pool, exercise facilities, whirlpools, sauna, jogging track, free parking, wheelchair access, TV, a/c, no-smoking rooms, gift shop, children stay free with parents, business services, meeting facilities, major credit cards. SGL/DBL$65-$95, STS$95-$150.

Motel 6 (6577 Court St Rd, 13057; 433-1300, 505-891-6161) 89 rooms, pool, free local calls, children under 17 stay free with parents, a/c, TV, major credit cards. SGL/DBL$27-$43.

Quality Inn North (1308 Buckley Rd, 13212; 451-1212, 800-368-5689) 143 rooms and suites, restaurant, room service, exercise facilities, children stay free with parents, a/c, TV, laundry service, no-smoking rooms, meeting facilities, major credit cards. SGL$68-$83, DBL$78-$93.

Ramada Inn (1305 Buckley Rd, 13212; 457-8670, Fax 457-8633, 800-2-RAMADA) 150 rooms and suites, restaurant, lounge, pool, wheelchair access, no-smoking rooms, airport transportation, free parking, pets allowed, a/c, TV, room service, laundry facilities, meeting facilities for 300, senior citizen rates, major credit cards. SGL$60-$89, DBL$70-$99, STS$150, AP$10.

Residence Inn (Yorktown Circle, 13057; 432-4488, 800-331-3131) 102 rooms and suites, complimentary breakfast, pool, spa, in-room refrigerators, coffee makers and microwaves, laundry facilities, free parking, TV, a/c, VCRs, pets allowed, fireplaces, children stay free with parents, no-smoking rooms, wheelchair access, major credit cards. SGL/DBL$75-$140.

Sheraton University Inn and Conference Center (801 University Ave, 13210; 475-3000, Fax 475-3311, 800-325-3535) 232 rooms and suites, restaurant, lounge, indoor pool, exercise facilities, sauna, jacuzzi, no-smoking rooms, a/c, TV, children stay free with parents, wheelchair access, 13,000 square feet of meeting and exhibition space, 17 meeting rooms, meeting facilities for 1,100, major credit cards. SGL/DBL$130-$157.

Tannersville
Area Code 518

Deer Mountain (Rte. 25, 12485; 589-6269). SGL/DBL$45-$70.

The Eggery Inn (County Rd 16, 12485; 589-5363) bed and breakfast, private bath, fireplace, TV. SGL/DBL$75-$95.

Greene Mountain View Inn (South Main St, 12485; 589-5511) complimentary breakfast, private baths, a/c, open year-round. SGL/DBL$65-$75.

The Kennedy House (Spring St, 12485; 589-6082) bed and breakfast, private baths, on 12 acres, fireplace, antique furnishing, open year-round. SGL/DBL$50-$100.

Washington Irving Lodge (Rte. 23A, 12485; 589-5560) bed and breakfast, restaurant, lounge, outdoor pool, game room, tennis court, private baths, antique furnishings, on 8 acres, open year-round. SGL/DBL$45-$85.

Tarrytown
Area Code 914

Courtyard by Marriott (475 White Plains Rd, 10591; 631-1122, Fax 631-1357, 800-321-2211) 139 rooms and suites, restaurant, lounge, indoor pool, exercise facilities, whirlpools, children stay free with parents, laundry service, 2 meeting rooms, meeting facilities for 80, senior citizen rates, major credit cards. SGL/DBL$80-$120.

Hilton Hotel (455 South Broadway, 01591; 631-5700, Fax 631-0075, 800-HILTONS) 242 rooms and suites, restaurant, lounge, entertainment, indoor and outdoor pool, exercise facilities, tennis courts, sauna, jacuzzi, free parking, limousine service, airport transportation, children stay free with parents, no-smoking rooms, wheelchair access, pets allowed, a/c, TV, business services, 16 meeting rooms, major credit cards. SGL/DBL$103-$175.

Marriott Hotel (670 White Plains Rd, 10591; 631-2200, Fax 631-7819, 800-882-1042, 800-228-9290) 444 rooms and suites, restaurant, lounge, entertainment, indoor and outdoor pool, exercise facilities, whirlpools, beauty shop, sauna, free parking, free newspaper, wheelchair access, TV, a/c, no-smoking rooms, gift shop, children stay free with parents, business services, meeting facilities, major credit cards. SGL/DBL$110-$150.

Tarrytown House Executive Conference Center (East Sunnyside Lane, 10591; 591-8200) 150 rooms, restaurant, indoor an outdoor pool, exercise facilities, sauna, whirlpools, a/c, TV, senior citizen rates, on 26 acres, major credit cards. SGL/DBL$95-$110.

Ticonderoga
Area Code 518

Circle Court Motel (440 Montcalm St, 12883; 585-7660) 14 rooms, a/c, TV, no-smoking rooms, pets allowed, major credit cards. SGL/DBL$36-$60.

Super 8 Motel (Rte. 9 North, 12883; 585-2617, Fax 585-3521, 800-800-8000) 39 rooms and suites, no pets, children under 12 stay free with parents, free local calls, a/c, TV, fax service, no-smoking rooms, senior citizen rates, wheelchair access, meeting facilities, major credit cards. LS SGL$40, DBL$49; HS SGL$44, DBL$52.

Tonawanda
Area Code 716

Beckers Motel (2468 Niagara Falls Blvd, 14150; 693-4407) 9 rooms. SGL/DBL$28-$36.

Boulevard Office Suites and Motel (1620 Niagara Falls Blvd, 14150; 832-1695) 46 rooms, no-smoking rooms, free parking. SGL/DBL$48-$58.

Cavalier Motor Lodge (1120 Niagara Falls Blvd, 14150; 835-5916, 800-445-1390) 51 rooms, wheelchair access. SGL/DBL$37.

Ellicott Park Court (2740 Niagara Falls Blvd, 14150; 693-6412) 14 rooms, whirlpool, in-room refrigerators. SGL$37, DBL$42.

Grand Motor Inn (2000 Niagara Falls Blvd, 14150; 694-6696) 31 rooms, no-smoking rooms, kitchenettes, major credit cards. SGL/DBL$44.

Horseless Carriage Motor Inn (1378 Niagara Falls Blvd, 14150; 836-2940, Fax 836-2982) 27 rooms, restaurant, lounge, entertainment, major credit cards. SGL/DBL$68-$108.

Olympic Family Motel (1601 Military Rd, 14217; 874-0771) 8 rooms, restaurant, lounge, major credit cards. SGL/DBL$44-$48.

Troy
Area Code 518

Super 8 Motel (One Fourth St, 12180; 274-8800, Fax 274-0427, 800-800-8000) 77 rooms and suites, no pets, children under 12 stay free with parents, free local calls, a/c, TV, fax service, no-smoking rooms, senior citizen rates, wheelchair access, meeting facilities, major credit cards. SGL/DBL$42-$49.

Trumansburg
Area Code 607

The Archway Bed and Breakfast (7020 Searsburg Rd, 14886; 387-6175) complimentary breakfast, fireplace, 1860s home. SGL/DBL$55-$65.

Kingtown Beach Cottages (9305 Kingtown Beach Rd, 14886; 387-6606) 2-bedroom cottages, water view, open May to October. SGL/DBL$65-$80.

Podunk House Hostel International (6383 Podunk Rd, 14886; 387-9277) 9 dormitory beds, open April 1 to October 30. SGL/DBL$55-$70.

Unadilla
Area Code 607

Country Motel (Rte. 7, 13849; 563-1035) 15 rooms, a/c, TV, wheelchair access, pets allowed, open year-round. SGL/DBL$40-$50.

Uniondale
Area Code 516

Marriott Long Island Hotel and Conference Center (101 James Doolittle Blvd, 11533; 794-3800, Fax 794-5936, 800-832-6255, 800-228-9290) 622 rooms and suites, restaurant, lounge, entertainment, indoor pool, exercise facilities, whirlpools, wheelchair access, TV, a/c, no-smoking rooms, gift shop, barber shop, free parking, children stay free with parents, business services, meeting facilities, major credit cards. SGL/DBL$135.

Utica
Area Code 315

Adam Bowman Manor Bed and Breakfast (197 Riverside Dr., 13502; 738-0276) complimentary breakfast, antique furnishings, 1820s Victorian home, fireplace, major credit cards. SGL/DBL$45+.

Best Western Adirondack Gateway Motor Inn (175 North Genesee St, 13502; 732-4121) 90 rooms, complimentary breakfast, TV, a/c, free parking, no-smoking rooms, wheelchair access, pets allowed, major credit cards. SGL/DBL$56-$88.

The Country Motel (1477 Herkimer Rd, 13502; 732-4628) 25 rooms, TV, a/c, in-room coffee makers, wheelchair access, major credit cards. SGL/DBL$48-$58.

Happy Journey Motel (300 Genesee St, 13502; 738-1959) 18 rooms, a/c, TV, pets allowed, major credit cards. SGL/DBL$27-$41.

Herbs and Hospitality (2806 Ogden Place, 13501; 797-0079) bed and breakfast. SGL/DBL$45.

Howard Johnson Lodge (302 North Genesee St, 13502; 724-4141, Fax 724-4141 ext 195, 800-I-GO-HOJO) 144 rooms, restaurant, complimentary breakfast, lounge, outdoor pool, children under 18 stay free with parents, wheelchair access, no-smoking rooms, TV, a/c, pets allowed, free parking, meeting facilities, senior citizen rates, major credit cards. SGL$35-$70, DBL$35-$80.

The Iris Stonehouse Bed and Breakfast (16 Derbyshire Place, 13501; 732-6720, 800-446-1456) 3 rooms, complimentary breakfast, private bath, a/c, no smoking, no pets, major credit cards. SGL/DBL$40+.

Motel 6 (150 North Genesee St, 13502; 797-8743, 505-891-6161) 61 rooms, pool, free local calls, children under 17 stay free with parents, a/c, TV, major credit cards. SGL/DBL$34-$40.

Quality Inn (One Champion Rd, 13412; 753-3392, 800-368-5689) 89 rooms and suites, restaurant, lounge, entertainment, pool, room service, exercise facilities, children stay free with parents, a/c, TV, laundry service, no-smoking rooms, meeting facilities, major credit cards. SGL$45-$60, DBL$60-$72.

Radisson Hotel Utica Centre (200 Genesee St, 13502; 797-8010, Fax 797-1490, 800-777-1700) 158 rooms and suites, restaurant, lounge, entertainment, indoor pool, wheelchair access, free parking, no-smoking rooms,

TV, a/c, children stay free with parents, pets allowed, major credit cards. SGL/DBL$86-$109.

Red Carpet Inn (309 North Genesee St, 13502; 797-0964, 800-251-1962) TV, a/c, children under 12 stay free with parents, senior citizen rates, major credit cards. SGL/DBL$43-$48.

Red Roof Inn (20 Weaver St, 13502; 724-7128, 800-THE-ROOF) 112 rooms, no-smoking rooms, wheelchair access, children under 18 stay free with parents, free newspaper. SGL/DBL$48-$53.

TraveLodge (1700 Genesee St, 13502; 724-2101, Fax 792-5211, 800-255-3050) 46 rooms, restaurant, lounge, free breakfast, pool, wheelchair access, complimentary newspaper, laundry service, TV, a/c, free local calls, fax, no-smoking rooms, free in-room coffee and tea service, in-room refrigerators and microwaves, no pets, major credit cards. SGL/DBL$45-$57.

Vernon
Area Code 315

Lavender Inn (Rte. 5, 13476; 829-2440) complimentary breakfast, 1790s home, private baths, antique furnishings, a/c, major credit cards. SGL/DBL$45+.

Verona Beach
Area Code 315

Dwarf Line Motel and Cottages (Lake Shore Rd, 13162; 762-4645) rooms and 1-bedroom housekeeping cottages, kitchenettes, TV, open May to September, major credit cards. SGL/DBL$55-$65.

Wales
Area Code 716

Aurora Motel (6421 Olean Rd, South Wales 14139; 652-3638) 16 rooms, complimentary breakfast, free parking, no-smoking rooms. SGL/DBL$55.

Walton
Area Code 607

Sunrise Inn Bed and Breakfast (Walton 13856; 865-7254) complimentary breakfast, no smoking, private bath, 1800s home, antique furnishings, TV, no pets, a/c. SGL/DBL$37-$60.

Warrensburg
Area Code 518

The Merrill Magee House (Two Hudson St, 12885; 623-2449) 26 rooms, bed and breakfast, outdoor pool, no pets, private baths, no children allowed. SGL/DBL$75-$95.

Waterloo
Area Code 315

Front Porch Bed and Breakfast (Waterloo 13165; 539-8325) 3 rooms, complimentary breakfast, no smoking, private baths, no pets, Victorian home. SGL/DBL$50-$550.

Watertown
Area Code 315

Allen's Budget Motel (Rte. 342, 13601; 782-5319) 19 rooms, a/c, TV, open year-round. SGL/DBL$32-$60.

Arsenal Street Motel (1165 Arsenal St, 13601; 788-3760) 15 rooms, a/c, TV, no pets, open year-round. SGL/DBL$40-$55.

Days Inn (1142 Arsenal St, 13601; 782-2700, Fax 782-7691, 800-325-2525) 135 rooms and suites, restaurant, lounge, indoor pool, children stay free with parents, room service, laundry service, a/c, TV, free local calls, no pets, wheelchair access, no-smoking rooms, senior citizen rates, major credit cards. LS SGL/DBL$60-$75, DBL$60-$80; HS SGL$70-$85, DBL$70-$90, STS$80-$99.

Econo Lodge (1030 Arsenal St, 13601; 782-5500, 800-4-CHOICE) 60 rooms, restaurant, lounge, pool, children under 12 stay free with parents, no pets, senior citizen rates, wheelchair access, a/c, TV, major credit cards. SGL/DBL$46-$75.

Holiday Inn (300 Washington St, 13601; 782-8000, Fax 782-8000 ext 399, 800-HOLIDAY) restaurant, lounge, entertainment, indoor pool, exercise facilities, children under 19 stay free with parents, barber and beauty shop, wheelchair access, a/c, TV, no-smoking rooms, fax service, room service, no pets, laundry service, meeting facilities for 400, senior citizen rates, major credit cards. SGL/DBL$55-$75.

Quality Inn (1190 Arsenal St, 13601; 788-6800, 800-368-5689) 96 rooms and suites, restaurant, room service, exercise facilities, children stay free with parents, a/c, TV, laundry service, no-smoking rooms, meeting facilities, major credit cards. SGL$50-$60, DBL$60-$72.

Ramada Inn (6300 Arsenal Rd, 13601; 788-0700, Fax 785-9875, 800-2-RAMADA) 145 rooms, restaurant, lounge, entertainment, pool, wheelchair access, no-smoking rooms, airport transportation, free parking, pets allowed, a/c, TV, room service, laundry facilities, 4 meeting rooms, meeting facilities for 350, senior citizen rates, major credit cards. SGL/DBL$62-$90, AP$6.

Starbuck House (253 Clinton St, 13601; 788-7324) 17 rooms, bed and breakfast, no smoking, 1860s home, no pets, private baths, no children allowed, major credit cards. SGL/DBL$60-$85.

Waterville
Area Code 315

Bed and Breakfast of Waterville (211 White St, 13480; 841-8295) complimentary breakfast, private bath, Victorian home. SGL/DBL$40+.

Hubbard House Bed and Breakfast (339 White St, 13480; 841-8385) 2 rooms, complimentary breakfast, private bath, no children allowed, no pets, fireplaces, no smoking. SGL/DBL$40-$80.

Watkins Glen
Area Code 607

Chieftain Motel (Rte. 14, 14891; 535-4759) 14 rooms and efficiencies, pool, a/c, TV, VCRs, in-room refrigerators and microwaves, no pets. SGL/DBL$34-$52.

Longhouse Lodge Motel (Watkins Glen 14891; 535-2565) 21 rooms and 1- and 2-bedroom efficiencies, pool, a/c, TV, VCRs, no pets, in-room refrigerators, no-smoking rooms, wheelchair access, major credit cards. SGL/DBL$30-$80.

Vintage View Bed and Breakfast (Watkins Glen 14891; 535-7909) complimentary breakfast, pool, 1860s home, no smoking, no pets, private baths. SGL/DBL$45-$55.

Wells Bridge
Area Code 607

The Deer Head Inn (Wells Bridge 13859; 369-9567) 7 rooms, open year-round. SGL/DBL$55.

Wellsville
Area Code 716

Long Vue Motel (Rte. 17 West, 14895; 593-2450) 17 rooms, a/c, TV, VCRs, in-room refrigerators, no pets. SGL/DBL$49-$59.

Palmiter's Tourist Home (467 North Main St, 14895; 593-4561) SGL/DBL$48-$58.

Wellsville Motel (Rte. 417, 14895; 593-2494) SGL/DBL$36-$42.

Westhampton Beach
Area Code 516

1880 Seafield House (Two Seafield, 11978; 288-1559, 800-346-3290) suites, bed and breakfast, 1890s home, no smoking, no pets, private bath. SGL/DBL$195.

Westkill
Area Code 518

Albino's Guest Lodge (State Rd 149, 12492; 989-6075) 7 rooms and 1 housekeeping cottage, complimentary breakfast, TV, private baths, open year-round. SGL/DBL$65-$75.

Marie's Dream House Country Inn (Rte. 42, 12492; 989-6565) restaurant, fireplace, game room, open year-round. SGL/DBL$40-$68.

Westmoreland
Area Code 315

Carriage Motor Inn (Rte. 233, 13490; 853-3561) 22 rooms, restaurant, lounge, TV, a/c, laundry facilities, pets allowed, no-smoking rooms, open year-round, free parking, major credit cards. SGL/DBL$30-$42.

Westport
Area Code 518

Inn On The Library Lawn (Westport 12993; 962-8666) 20 rooms, restaurant, complimentary breakfast, pool, transportation to local attractions, antique furnishings, a/c, TV, no-smoking rooms, major credit cards. SGL/DBL$55-$75.

Wevertown
Area Code 914

Mountainaire Adventures (Rte. 28, 12886; 251-2194, 800-950-2194) sauna, no pets, children under 3 stay free with parents, major credit cards. SGL$43, DBL$75.

White Plains
Area Code 914

Holiday Inn Crowne Plaza (66 Hale Ave, 10601; 682-0050, Fax 682-0405, 800-556-6680, 800-HOLIDAY) 400 rooms and suites, restaurant, lounge, indoor pool, exercise facilities, whirlpool tub, sauna, car rental desk, children under 19 stay free with parents, wheelchair access, a/c, gift shop, airport transportation, TV, no-smoking rooms, fax service, room service, no pets, laundry service, 11 meeting rooms, meeting facilities for 800, senior citizen rates, major credit cards. SGL/DBL$115-$165.

La Reserve (Five Bakers Ave, 10601; 761-7700, 800-431-2906) 139 suites, restaurant, lounge, complimentary breakfast, exercise facilities, free parking, airport transportation, in-room refrigerators, children stay free with parents, a/c, TV, wheelchair access, no-smoking rooms, meeting facilities, major credit cards. SGL/DBL$150-$180.

Stouffer Westchester Hotel (80 West Red Oak Lane, 10604; 694-5400, Fax 694-5616, 800-HOTELS-1) 364 rooms and 1-and 2-bedroom suites, restaurant, lounge, entertainment, indoor pool, exercise facilities, lighted tennis courts, airport courtesy car, wheelchair access, no-smoking rooms, gift shop, free parking, transportation to local attractions, free newspaper, TV, a/c, children under 18 stay free with parents, fax service, in-room refrigerators, 5,400 square feet of meeting and exhibition space, 17 meeting rooms, major credit cards. SGL/DBL$150-$200, STS$190-$250.

White Plains Plaza Hotel (White Plains 10601; 761-8100, Fax 761-9015, 800-247-5322) 304 rooms and suites, restaurant, lounge, entertainment, complimentary breakfast, exercise facilities, whirlpools, barber and beauty shop, free parking, no-smoking rooms, wheelchair access, a/c, TV, major credit cards. SGL/DBL$100-$115.

Whitney Point
Area Code 607

Point Motel (Rte. 1, 13862; 692-4451) TV, a/c. SGL/DBL$38-$56.

Willet
Area Code 607

Woven Waters Bed and Breakfast (Cincinnatus Lake, 13863; 656-8672) complimentary breakfast, water view. SGL/DBL$35-$70.

Williamsville
Area Code 716

Clarence Motel (8411 Main St, 14221; 633-9486) 50 rooms and efficiencies, a/c, TV, major credit cards. SGL/DBL$48-$53.

Econo Lodge (7200 Transit Rd, 14221; 634-1500, 800-4-CHOICE) 65 rooms, pool, children under 12 stay free with parents, no pets, senior citizen rates, wheelchair access, free parking, a/c, TV, major credit cards. SGL/DBL$25-$45.

Fairfield Inn Airport (52 Freeman Dr., 14221; 626-1500, Fax 626-1500, 800-228-2800) 165 rooms, outdoor pool, children stay free with parents, free local calls, no-smoking rooms, a/c, TV, wheelchair access, laundry service, fax, meeting facilities, major credit cards. SGL/DBL$45-$95.

Heritage House Country Inn (8261 Main St, 14221; 633-4900, Fax 633-4900) 57 rooms, free breakfast, kitchenettes, wheelchair access, no-smoking rooms, major credit cards. SGL$30-$33, DBL$41.

Holiday Inn (6700 Transit Rd, 14221; 634-7500, Fax 634-7502, 800-HOLIDAY) 80 rooms, restaurant, lounge, outdoor pool, exercise facilities, children under 19 stay free with parents, wheelchair access, a/c, TV, no-smoking rooms, fax service, room service, no pets, laundry service, meeting facilities for 400, senior citizen rates, major credit cards. SGL/DBL$55-$75.

Holiday Hotel (5801 Mains St, 14221; 632-2140) 20 rooms, kitchenettes, gift shop. SGL/DBL$65-$75.

Microtel Lancaster (50 Freeman Rd, 14221; 633-6200, Fax 633-1329) 100 rooms, wheelchair access, no-smoking rooms, major credit cards. SGL/DBL$64.

Residence Inn (100 Maple Rd, 14221; 632-6622, Fax 632-5247, 800-331-3131) 112 rooms and suites, free breakfast, pool, jacuzzi, spa, in-room refrigerators, coffee makers and microwaves, laundry facilities, free parking, TV, a/c, VCRs, pets allowed, fireplaces, children stay free with parents, no-smoking rooms, wheelchair access, meeting facilities for 20, major credit cards. SGL/DBL$80-$120.

Sheraton Court Motel (8005 Sheridan Dr., 14221; 634-2200) 32 rooms. SGL/DBL$28-$58.

Thunderbird Motel (8255 Main St, 14221; 634-6622) 10 rooms, in-room refrigerators and microwaves, major credit cards. SGL/DBL$44.

Williamsville Inn (5447 Main St, 14221; 634-1111, Fax 631-3367) 99 rooms, restaurant, lounge, entertainments, airport courtesy car, exercise facilities, wheelchair access, no-smoking rooms, a/c, TV, pets allowed, room service, laundry room, meeting facilities, major credit cards. SGL$38-$48, DBL$40-$50.

Wilmington
Area Code 518

High Valley Motel (Wilmington 12997; 946-2355) 20 rooms, pool, major credit cards. SGL/DBL$35-$55.

Hungry Trout Motel (Wilmington 12997; 947-2217) 20 rooms, restaurant, lounge, pool, pets allowed, water view. SGL/DBL$60-$100, STS$105-$120.

Wilton
Area Code 518

The Birches Motel (7442 Rte. 9, 12866; 584-1484) no pets, in-room refrigerators, TV, a/c, major credit cards. LS SGL/DBL$47-$60; HS SGL/DBL$50-$70.

Mountain View Acres Motel (327 Rte. 9, 12866; 793-2909) a/c, TV, major credit cards. SGL/DBL$43-$48.

Windham
Area Code 518

Albergo Allegria Bed and Breakfast (Rte. 296, 12496; 734-5560) 20 rooms and suite, complimentary breakfast, fireplaces, Victorian home, antique furnishings, jacuzzi, private baths, open year-round. SGL/DBL$45-$90.

Alpine Lodge (Box 225, 12496; 734-3541) 1-, 2- and 3-bedroom efficiencies, TV, open year-round. SGL/DBL$80.

Christman's Windham House (Windham 12496; 734-4230) 50 rooms, complimentary breakfast, pool, on 250 acres, private baths, Modified American Plan available. SGL/DBL$36-$72.

Country Suite Bed and Breakfast (Rte. 23, 12496; 734-4079) complimentary breakfast, no pets, 1890s home, fireplace, private baths, major credit cards. SGL/DBL$75-$85.

Danske Has Bed and Breakfast (South St, 12496; 734-6335) 4 rooms, complimentary breakfast, shared baths, sauna, fireplace, TV, VCR, open year-round. SGL/DBL$65-$125.

Point Lookout Mountain Inn (Rte. 23, 12496; 734-3381) bed and breakfast, restaurant, fireplace, private baths. SGL/DBL$55-$65.

The Windham Ridge Club (Rte. 23, 12496; 734-5800) 24 1-bedroom apartments, pool, sauna, whirlpools, tennis courts, transportation to local attractions, fireplaces, a/c, TV. SGL/DBL$125.

West Winfield
Area Code 315

Five Gables Bed and Breakfast (489 East Main St, 13491; 822-5764) complimentary breakfast, antique furnishings, jacuzzi, 1890s home. SGL/DBL$40+.

Woodbury
Area Code 516

Quality Inn Heritage (7758 Jericho Turnpike, 11797; 921-6900, 800-368-5689) 85 rooms and suites, restaurant, room service, exercise facilities, children stay free with parents, transportation to local attractions, a/c, TV, laundry service, no-smoking rooms, meeting facilities, major credit cards. SGL$65-$120, DBL$70-$130.

Ramada Inn (8030 Jericho Turnpike, 11797; 921-8500, 800-2-RAMADA) 103 rooms and suites, restaurant, free breakfast, lounge, pool, wheelchair access, no-smoking rooms, airport transportation, free parking, pets allowed, a/c, TV, room service, laundry facilities, meeting facilities for 100, senior citizen rates, major credit cards. SGL/DBL$70-$95, STS$100, AP$5.

Woodgate
Area Code 315

The Red House Bed and Breakfast (Rte. 28, 13494; 392-5479) complimentary breakfast, 1860s home, antique furnishings, no smoking. SGL/DBL$45.

Pennsylvania

Abbottstown
Area Code 717

The Atland House (Town Square, 17301; 259-9535) 5 rooms, restaurant, no pets, a/c, TV, major credit cards. SGL/DBL$58-$64.

Adamstown
Area Code 215

Adamstown Inn (62 West Main St, 19501; 484-0800, 800-594-4808) 13 rooms, bed and breakfast, no smoking, no children allowed, Victorian inn, antique furnishings, jacuzzi, no pets, private baths, major credit cards. SGL/DBL$55-$100.

Airville
Area Code 717

Spring House Bed and Breakfast (Airville 17302; 927-6906) 12 rooms, complimentary breakfast, no smoking, no pets, major credit cards. SGL/DBL$55-$90.

Akron
Area Code 717

Motel Akron (116 South 7th St, 17501; 859-1654) 14 rooms and 1- and 2-bedroom efficiencies, no pets, a/c, TV, no smoking, major credit cards. SGL/DBL$29-$38.

Allentown
Area Code 215

Comfort Inn Lehigh Valley West (7625 Imperial Way, 18106; 391-0344, 800-221-2222) 128 rooms, restaurant, complimentary breakfast, whirlpools, exercise facilities, airport transportation, wheelchair access, no-smoking rooms, no pets, children under 18 stay free with parents, senior citizen rates, a/c, TV, meeting facilities, major credit cards. SGL$48-$61, DBL$57-$82, AP$5.

Comfort Inn (3712 Hamilton Blvd, 18103; 437-9100, 800-221-2222) 122 rooms, restaurant, complimentary breakfast, exercise facilities, wheelchair access, no-smoking rooms, no pets, children under 18 stay free with parents, whirlpools, senior citizen rates, a/c, TV, meeting facilities, major credit cards. LS SGL$69-$75, DBL$79-$85; HS SGL/DBL$79-$99, AP$10.

Comfort Suites (3612 Hamilton Blvd, 18103; 437-9100) 122 rooms and suites, restaurant, lounge, pool, exercise facilities, whirlpools, in-room refrigerators and microwaves, airport transportation, no pets, a/c, TV, VCRs, major credit cards. SGL/DBL$69-$95.

Days Inn (1715 Plaza Lane, 18104; 435-7880, Fax 432-2555, 800-325-2525) 84 rooms, restaurant, lounge, pool, children stay free with parents, room service, laundry service, a/c, TV, free local calls, pets allowed, wheelchair access, no-smoking rooms, senior citizen rates, major credit cards. SGL$36-$48, DBL$40-$58.

Days Inn Conference Center (Rte 11 and Rte 309, 18104; 395-3731, Fax 395-9899, 800-325-2525) 277 rooms and suites, restaurant, lounge, pool, children stay free with parents, room service, laundry service, a/c, TV, free local calls, pets allowed, wheelchair access, no-smoking rooms, senior citizen rates, major credit cards. LS SGL/DBL$44-$64, STS$65-$110; HS SGL/DBL$54-$74, STS$79-$129.

Days Inn (2622 Lehigh St, 18103; 797-1234, 800-325-2525) 36 rooms, restaurant, lounge, whirlpools, in-room refrigerators and microwaves, children stay free with parents, room service, laundry service, a/c, TV, free local calls, no pets, wheelchair access, no-smoking rooms, senior citizen rates, major credit cards. SGL/DBL$44-$85.

Econo Lodge (2115 Downyflake Lane, 18103; 797-2200, 800-4-CHOICE) 50 rooms, pool, children under 12 stay free with parents, no pets, senior citizen rates, wheelchair access, whirlpools, a/c, TV, major credit cards. SGL/DBL$43-$79.

Hampton Inn (7471 Keebler Way, 18106; 391-1500, Fax 391-0386, 800-HAMPTON) 126 rooms, restaurant, free breakfast, pool, exercise facilities, children under 18 stay free with parents, no-smoking rooms, wheelchair access, computer hookups, airport transportation, fax, TV, a/c, free local calls, no pets, meeting facilities, major credit cards. SGL/DBL$54-$69.

Hilton Hotel (904 Hamilton Mall, 18101; 433-2221, Fax 433-6455, 800-HILTONS) 224 rooms and suites, restaurant, lounge, entertainment, indoor pool, exercise facilities, sauna, gift shop, children stay free with parents, no-smoking rooms, wheelchair access, airport transportation, no pets, a/c, TV, business services, meeting facilities, major credit cards. SGL/DBL$65-$112.

Howard Johnson Lodge (3220 Hamilton Blvd, 18103; 439-4000, Fax 439-4000 ext 200, 800-I-GO-HOJO) 43 rooms, restaurant, free breakfast, lounge, pool, jacuzzi, children stay free with parents, wheelchair access, no-smoking rooms, TV, a/c, no pets, free parking, meeting facilities, senior citizen rates, major credit cards. LS SGL$36-$40, DBL$44-$48; HS SGL$40-$48, DBL$48-$51.

McIntosh Inn (Airport Rd, 18103; 264-7531, Fax 264-5474) 107 rooms, restaurant, no pets, in-room refrigerators and microwaves, a/c, TV, major credit cards. SGL/DBL$37-$49.

Motel Allenwood (1058 Hausman Rd, 18104; 395-3707) 22 rooms, a/c, TV, major credit cards. SGL/DBL$40.

Radisson Hotel (Sixth and Hamilton Sts., 18101; 434-6101, Fax 434-0159, 800-777-1700) 134 rooms and suites, restaurant, lounge, entertainment, pool, wheelchair access, free parking, no-smoking rooms, TV, a/c, children stay free with parents, pets allowed, major credit cards. SGL/DBL$80-$105.

Ramada Inn (McArthur Rd, 18052; 439-1037, Fax 770-1425, 800-2-RAMADA) 123 rooms, restaurant, lounge, pool, wheelchair access, no-smoking rooms, airport transportation, free parking, no pets, a/c, TV, VCRs, room service, laundry facilities, meeting facilities, senior citizen rates, major credit cards. SGL/DBL$49-$65.

Red Roof Inn (1846 Catasauqua Rd, 18103; 264-5404, 800-843-7663) 116 rooms, restaurant, no-smoking rooms, fax service, wheelchair access, complimentary newspaper, children stay free with parents, pets allowed, free local calls, in-room computer hookups, major credit cards. SGL/DBL$37-$55.

Sheraton Inn Jetport (3400 Airport Rd, 18103; 266-1000, Fax 266-1888, 800-325-3535) 143 rooms and suites, restaurant, lounge, indoor pool, jacuzzi, sauna, airport courtesy car, no-smoking rooms, a/c, TV, children stay free with parents, wheelchair access, 5,500 square feet of meeting and exhibition space, 7 meeting rooms, meeting facilities for 400, major credit cards. SGL/DBL$65-$105.

Altoona
Area Code 814

Days Inn (3306 Pleasant Valley Blvd, 16602; 944-9661, 800-325-2525) 111 rooms, restaurant, lounge, pool, children stay free with parents, room service, laundry service, a/c, TV, free local calls, no pets, wheelchair access, no-smoking rooms, senior citizen rates, major credit cards. SGL/DBL$52-$67.

Econo Lodge (2906 Pleasant Valley Blvd, 16601; 944-3555, 800-4-CHOICE) 90 rooms, pool, children under 12 stay free with parents, no pets, senior citizen rates, wheelchair access, a/c, TV, meeting facilities, major credit cards. SGL/DBL$36-$50.

HoJo Inn (1500 Sterling St, 16602; 946-7601, Fax 946-5162, 800-I-GO-HOJO) 112 rooms, restaurant, complimentary breakfast, lounge, outdoor pool, children stay free with parents, wheelchair access, no-smoking rooms, TV, a/c, pets allowed, free parking, meeting facilities, senior citizen rates, major credit cards. SGL/DBL$35-$50.

Holiday Inn (2915 Pleasant Valley Blvd, 16602; 944-4581, Fax 943-4996, 800-HOLIDAY) 142 rooms, restaurant, lounge, children under 19 stay free with parents, wheelchair access, a/c, TV, no-smoking rooms, fax service, room service, no pets, laundry service, meeting facilities, senior citizen rates, major credit cards. SGL/DBL$58-$64.

Ramada Hotel (Plank Rd Exit, 16601; 946-1631, Fax 946-0785, 800-2-RAMADA) 220 rooms and suites, restaurant, lounge, indoor pool, wheelchair access, no-smoking rooms, airport transportation, free parking, pets allowed, a/c, TV, room service, laundry facilities, meeting facilities, senior citizen rates, major credit cards. SGL$61-$70, DBL$66-$75, STS$75-$130, AP$5.

Super 8 Motel (3535 Fairway Dr., 16602; 942-5350, 800-800-8000) 63 rooms and suites, pets allowed, children under 12 stay free with parents, free local calls, a/c, TV, fax, no-smoking rooms, senior citizen rates, wheelchair access, meeting facilities, major credit cards. SGL/DBL$38-$44.

Annville
Area Code 717

Swatara Creek Inn (Annville 17003; 865-3259) 10 rooms, no smoking, a/c, no pets, major credit cards. SGL/DBL$48-$70.

Barkeyville
Area Code 814

Days Inn (Gibb Rd, 16038; 786-7901, Fax 786-9693, 800-325-2525) 83 rooms, restaurant, lounge, pool, children stay free with parents, room service, laundry service, a/c, TV, free local calls, pets allowed, wheelchair access, no-smoking rooms, senior citizen rates, major credit cards. SGL/DBL$44-$60.

Bartonsville
Area Code 717

Comfort Inn (Box 184, 18321; 476-1500, 800-221-2222) 120 rooms, restaurant, pool, wheelchair access, no-smoking rooms, no pets, children under 18 stay free with parents, whirlpools, hot tubs, senior citizen rates, a/c, TV, meeting facilities, major credit cards. SGL/DBL$50-$110, AP$7.

Holiday Inn (Rte 611, 18321; 424-6100, Fax 421-4293, 800-HOLIDAY) 350 rooms, restaurant, lounge, entertainment, indoor pool, exercise facilities, game room, fireplaces, children under 19 stay free with parents, wheelchair access, a/c, TV, no-smoking rooms, fax service, room service, no pets, laundry service, meeting facilities for 350, senior citizen rates, major credit cards. SGL/DBL$65-$75.

Beaver Falls
Area Code 412

Beaver Valley Motel (Beaver Falls 15010; 843-0603) 27 rooms and efficiencies, wheelchair access, a/c, TV, major credit cards. SGL/DBL$37-$52.

Conley's Inn (Rte 18, 15010; 843-9300) 58 rooms and efficiencies, restaurant, lounge, a/c, TV, no pets, major credit cards. SGL/DBL$49-$59.

Holiday Inn (Rte 18N, 15010; 846-3700, 800-HOLIDAY) 158 rooms, restaurant, lounge, outdoor pool, sauna, whirlpools, exercise facilities, children under 19 stay free with parents, wheelchair access, a/c, TV, no-smoking rooms, fax service, room service, no pets, laundry service, meeting facilities for 450, senior citizen rates, major credit cards. SGL/DBL$68-$86.

The Inn On College Hill (3233 Sixth Ave, 15010; 843-6048) 6 rooms, bed and breakfast, antique furnishings, private bath, no smoking, no pets. SGL$40-$60, DBL$45-$65.

The Lark Motel (Rte 18N, 15010; 846-6507) 12 rooms, no pets, a/c, TV, in-room refrigerators, wheelchair access, major credit cards. SGL/DBL$33-$49.

Bedford
Area Code 814

Best Western Inn (Bedford 15522; 623-9006, Fax 623-7120, 800-528-1234) 107 rooms, restaurant, lounge, free breakfast, lounge, pool, exercise facilities, whirlpools, sauna, children stay free with parents, a/c, TV, no-smoking rooms, wheelchair access, pets allowed, senior citizen rates, meeting facilities, major credit cards. SGL/DBL$38-$62.

Friendship Inn (Transport St, 15522; 623-5174, 800-424-4777) 32 rooms, restaurant, lounge, entertainment, exercise facilities, a/c, TV, no pets, no-smoking rooms, children stay free with parents, wheelchair access, major credit cards. SGL/DBL$35-$45.

Janey Lynn Motel (Bedford 15522; 623-9515) 21 rooms and 1- and 2-bedroom efficiencies, a/c, in-room refrigerators, pets allowed, TV, major credit cards. SGL/DBL$24-$39.

Judy's Motel (Bedford 15522; 623-9118) 12 rooms, a/c, TV, no pets, major credit cards. SGL/DBL$22-$30.

Motel Town House (200 South Richard St, 15522; 623-5138) 19 rooms, a/c, TV, in-room refrigerators and microwaves, major credit cards. SGL/DBL$25-$50.

Quality Inn (Hwy 220, 15522; 623-5188, 800-368-5689) 66 rooms and suites, restaurant, pool, room service, exercise facilities, children stay free with parents, a/c, TV, laundry service, pets allowed, no-smoking rooms, meeting facilities, major credit cards. LS SG/DBL$46-$58; HS SGL/DBL$54-$66, AP$6.

Super 8 Motel (Rte 220, 15522; 623-5880, 800-800-8000) 57 rooms and suites, restaurant, children under 12 stay free with parents, free local calls, a/c, whirlpools, TV, VCRs, pets allowed, fax service, no-smoking rooms, senior citizen rates, wheelchair access, meeting facilities, major credit cards. SGL/DBL$38-$44.

Bensalem
Area Code 215

Comfort Inn (3660 St Rd, 19020; 245-0100, 800-221-2222) 141 rooms, restaurant, lounge, entertainment, exercise facilities, wheelchair access, no-smoking rooms, no pets, children under 18 stay free with parents, senior citizen rates, a/c, TV, meeting facilities, major credit cards. SGL/DBL$49-$89.

Courtyard by Marriott (3327 St Rd, 19020; 800-321-2121) 167 rooms, pool, exercise facilities, whirlpool, sauna, 4 meeting rooms, meeting facilities for 300, major credit cards. SGL/DBL$85-$115.

Days Inn Northeast (1329 Bristol Pike, 19020; 245-5222, Fax 245-1314, 800-325-2525) 140 rooms, restaurant, lounge, pool, exercise facilities, jacuzzi, wheelchair access, no-smoking rooms, no pets, a/c, TV, fax service, children stay free with parents. SGL$49-$95, DBL$59-$95, AP$10.

Holiday Inn Northeast (3499 St Rd, 19020; 638-1500, Fax 638-2163, 800-HOLIDAY) 120 rooms and suites, restaurant, lounge, entertainment, outdoor pool, children stay free with parents, transportation to local attractions, no-smoking rooms, wheelchair access, meeting facilities for 400, major credit cards. SGL/DBL$70-$90.

Berwick
Area Code 717

Budget Host Patriot Inn (6305 New Berwick Hwy, 17815; 387-1776, Fax 387-9611, 800-BUD-HOST) restaurant, lounge, in-room refrigerators, no-smoking rooms, TV, VCRs, a/c, wheelchair access, children stay free with parents, laundry facilities, senior citizen rates, meeting facilities, major credit cards. SGL$37-$46, DBL$41-$49.

Berwyn
Area Code 215

Residence Inn (600 West Swedesford Rd, 19312; 640-9494, Fax 993-0330, 800-331-3131) rooms and suites, free breakfast, pool, spa, in-room refrigerators, coffee makers and microwaves, laundry facilities, free parking, TV, a/c, VCRs, pets allowed, fireplaces, children stay free with parents, no-smoking rooms, wheelchair access, meeting facilities for 20, major credit cards. SGL/DBL$50-$90.

Bethlehem
Area Code 215

Comfort Inn (3191 Highfield Dr., 18017; 865-6300, 800-221-2222) 116 rooms, restaurant, wheelchair access, no-smoking rooms, no pets, children under 18 stay free with parents, senior citizen rates, a/c, TV, meeting facilities, major credit cards. SGL/DBL$49-$64.

Comfort Suites (120 West Third St, 18015; 882-9700) 124 suites, lounge, kitchenettes, a/c, TV, pets allowed, major credit cards. SGL/DBL$55-$100.

Econo Lodge Airport (Airport Rd South, 18018; 867-8681, 800-4-CHOICE) 119 rooms, pool, children under 12 stay free with parents, no pets, senior citizen rates, wheelchair access, a/c, TV, major credit cards. SGL/DBL$37-$50.

Holiday Inn (Hwy 22, 18017; 866-5800, Fax 867-9120, 800-HOLIDAY) 192 rooms, restaurant, lounge, entertainment, exercise facilities, children under 19 stay free with parents, gift shop, airport transportation, wheelchair access, a/c, TV, no-smoking rooms, fax service, room service, no pets, laundry service, meeting facilities for 900, senior citizen rates, major credit cards. SGL/DBL$78-$88.

Hotel Bethlehem (437 Main St, 18018; 867-3711) 128 rooms and efficiencies, restaurant, lounge, a/c, TV, whirlpools, airport transportation, in-room refrigerators, major credit cards. SGL/DBL$47-$150.

Bird In Hand
Area Code 717

Amish Country Motel (3013 Old Philadelphia Pike, 17505; 768-8396, 800-538-2535) 25 rooms, pool, transportation to local attractions, open March to November, no pets, a/c, TV, major credit cards. SGL/DBL$49-$69.

Bird In Hand Family Inn (Bird In Hand 17505; 768-8271, 800-537-2535) 100 rooms, restaurant, indoor and outdoor pool, lighted tennis courts, transportation to local attractions, a/c, TV, VCRs, whirlpools, no pets, major credit cards. SGL/DBL$57-$80.

Greystone Manor (2658 Old Philadelphia Pike, 17505; 393-4233) 12 rooms, complimentary breakfast, no pets, private baths, antique furnishings, major credit cards. SGL/DBL$65-$70.

Village Inn (2695 Old Philadelphia Pike, 17505; 293-8369) 11 rooms, a/c, TV, whirlpools, no pets, major credit cards. SGL/DBL$60-$140.

Bloomsburg
Area Code 717

Econo Lodge (189 Columbia Mall Dr., 17815; 387-0460, Fax 387-0893, 800-4-CHOICE) 80 rooms and suites, pool, children under 12 stay free with parents, no pets, senior citizen rates, wheelchair access, a/c, TV, major credit cards. SGL/DBL$41-$90.

Quality Inn (One Buckhorn Rd, 17815; 784-5300, 800-368-5689) 120 rooms and suites, restaurant, lounge, entertainment, room service, exercise facilities, children stay free with parents, a/c, TV, laundry service, no-smoking rooms, meeting facilities, major credit cards. SGL/DBL$44-$70, AP$5.

Boalsburg
Area Code 814

Springfield House (126 East Main St, 16827; 466-6290) 6 rooms, bed and breakfast, no smoking, private baths, Victorian home, major credit cards. SGL/DBL$70.

Brackney
Area Code 717

Indian Mountain Inn (Tripp Lake Rd, 18812; 663-2645) 8 rooms, bed and breakfast, no smoking, whirlpool tub, no pets, private baths, major credit cards. SGL/DBL$50-$65.

Bradford
Area Code 814

Howard Johnson Lodge (100 South Davis St, 16701; 362-4501, Fax 362-2709, 800-I-GO-HOJO) 120 rooms, restaurant, lounge, pool, children stay free with parents, wheelchair access, no-smoking rooms, TV, a/c, pets allowed, laundry facilities, gift shop, free parking, senior citizen rates, meeting facilities for 250, major credit cards. SGL/DBL$61-$81.

Breezewood
Area Code 814

Econo Lodge (Rte One, 15533; 735-4341, 800-4-CHOICE) 64 rooms, pool, children under 12 stay free with parents, no pets, senior citizen rates, wheelchair access, free local calls, a/c, TV, major credit cards. SGL/DBL$30-$65.

Knights Inn (Box 309, 15533; 735-4314, 800-843-5644) restaurant, pool, wheelchair access, no-smoking rooms, TV, a/c, in-room refrigerators and microwaves, fax service, free parking, VCRs, senior citizen rates, major credit cards. SGL/DBL$38-$54.

Quality Inn Breeze Manor (Hwy. 30 and I-70, 15533; 735-4311, 800-368-5689) rooms and suites, restaurant, room service, exercise facilities, children stay free with parents, a/c, TV, laundry service, no-smoking rooms, meeting facilities, major credit cards. LS SGL/DBL$38-$48; HS SGL/DBL$43-$54.

Ramada Inn (Rte 30, 15533, 735-4005, Fax 735-3228, 800-2-RAMADA) 125 rooms, restaurant, lounge, entertainment, indoor pool, exercise facilities, wheelchair access, no-smoking rooms, airport transportation, free parking, pets allowed, a/c, TV, room service, laundry facilities, meeting facilities, senior citizen rates, major credit cards. SGL$44-$52, DBL$49-$60, AP$8.

Bridgeville
Area Code 412

Knights Inn (111 Hickory Grade Rd, 15017; 221-8110, 800-843-5644) pool, wheelchair access, no-smoking rooms, TV, a/c, in-room refrigerators and microwaves, fax service, free parking, VCRs, senior citizen rates, major credit cards. SGL/DBL$48-$58.

Bristol
Area Code 215

Days Inn (Rte 13, 19007; 788-8400, 800-325-2525) 70 rooms and suites, restaurant, lounge, pool, jacuzzi, children stay free with parents, room service, laundry service, a/c, TV, free local calls, no pets, wheelchair access, no-smoking rooms, senior citizen rates, major credit cards. SGL/DBL$42-$70, STS$60-$150.

Brookville
Area Code 814

Bluebird Hollow (Brookville 15825; 856-2858) 13 rooms, bed and breakfast, private baths, 1890s home, major credit cards. SGL/DBL$35-$60.

Budget Host Gold Eagle Inn (250 West Main St, 15825; 849-7344, Fax 849-7345, 800-BUD-HOST) 29 rooms, restaurant, lounge, in-room refrigerators, no-smoking rooms, TV, VCRs, kitchenettes, a/c, wheelchair access, children stay free with parents, senior citizen rates, meeting facilities, major credit cards. SGL$25-$34, DBL$27-$39.

Days Inn (Brookville 15825; 849-8001, Fax 849-8943, 800-325-2525) 134 rooms, restaurant, lounge, entertainment, outdoor pool, children stay free with parents, room service, laundry service, a/c, TV, free local calls, pets allowed, wheelchair access, no-smoking rooms, senior citizen rates, major credit cards. SGL/DBL$30-$55.

Econo Lodge (295 Allegheny Blvd, 15825; 849-8381, 800-4-CHOICE) 69 rooms, restaurant, pool, children under 12 stay free with parents, no pets, senior citizen rates, wheelchair access, a/c, TV, meeting facilities, major credit cards. SGL/DBL$29-$50.

HoJo Inn (245 Allegheny Blvd, 15825; 849-3051, Fax 849-5259, 800-I-GO-HOJO) 40 rooms, restaurant, lounge, pool, children stay free with parents, wheelchair access, no-smoking rooms, gift shop, laundry facilities, TV, a/c, pets allowed, free parking, senior citizen rates, meeting facilities, major credit cards. SGL$25-$33, DBL$30-$39.

Super 8 Motel (Box 149, 15825; 849-8840, 800-800-8000) 57 rooms and suites, no pets, children under 12 stay free with parents, free local calls, a/c, TV, fax service, no-smoking rooms, senior citizen rates, wheelchair access, meeting facilities, major credit cards. SGL/DBL$35-$41.

Burnham
Area Code 717

Super 8 Motel (19 Windmill Hill, 17044; 242-8888, 800-800-8000) 57 rooms and suites, no pets, children under 12 stay free with parents, free local calls, a/c, TV, fax service, no-smoking rooms, senior citizen rates, wheelchair access, meeting facilities, major credit cards. SGL/DBL$43-$48.

Butler
Area Code 412

Days Inn (139 Pittsburgh Rd, 16001; 287-6761, Fax 287-4307, 800-325-2525) 139 rooms, restaurant, lounge, entertainment, indoor pool, children stay free with parents, room service, laundry service, a/c, TV, free local calls, pets allowed, wheelchair access, no-smoking rooms, senior citizen rates, major credit cards. SGL/DBL$39-$60.

Super 8 Motel (128 Pittsburgh Rd, 16001; 287-8888, 800-800-8000) 66 rooms and suites, no pets, children under 12 stay free with parents, free local calls, a/c, TV, fax, no-smoking rooms, senior citizen rates, wheelchair access, meeting facilities, major credit cards. SGL/DBL$35-$41.

Canadensis
Area Code 717

Dreamy Acres (Rte 447, 18325; 595-7115) 4 rooms, bed and breakfast, water view, no pets, no children allowed, open from May to late October, private baths, on 3 acres. SGL/DBL$40-$55.

Laurel Grove Inn (Rte 447, 18325; 595-7262, 800-842-0497) cottages, bed and breakfast, restaurant, private baths, 1890s inn, major credit cards. SGL/DBL$48-$85.

Nearbrook (Canadensis 18325; 595-3152) 3 rooms, bed and breakfast, no smoking, private baths, 1930s home, major credit cards. SGL/DBL$30-$45.

Carlisle
Area Code 717

Alwayspring Farm (McClures Gap Rd, 17013; 249-1455) 6 rooms, bed and breakfast, no smoking, no children allowed, on 45 acres, working farm, private baths, no pets. SGL/DBL$40-$45.

Budget Host Coast-To-Coast Motel (1252 Harrisburg Pike, 17013; 243-8585, 800-BUD-HOST) 71 rooms, restaurant, in-room refrigerators, no-smoking rooms, TV, VCRs, a/c, wheelchair access, children stay free with parents, pets allowed, laundry facilities, senior citizen rates, meeting facilities, major credit cards. SGL$28-$36, DBL$35-$41.

Days Inn (Alexander Springs Rd, 17013; 258-4147, 800-325-2525) 95 rooms, restaurant, lounge, pool, children stay free with parents, room service, laundry service, a/c, TV, free local calls, no pets, wheelchair access, no-smoking rooms, senior citizen rates, major credit cards. SGL/DBL$47-$56.

Econo Lodge (1460 Harrisburg Pike, 17013; 249-7775, 800-882-2975, 800-4-CHOICE) 72 rooms, restaurant, lounge, pool, children under 12 stay free with parents, no pets, senior citizen rates, wheelchair access, a/c, TV, major credit cards. SGL/DBL$37-$65.

Knights Inn (1153 Harrisburg Pike, 17013; 249-7622, 800-843-5644) pool, wheelchair access, no-smoking rooms, TV, a/c, in-room refrigerators and microwaves, fax service, free parking, VCRs, senior citizen rates, major credit cards. SGL/DBL$37-$44.

Howard Johnson Lodge (1255 Harrisburg Pike, 17013; 243-6000, Fax 258-4123, 800-I-GO-HOJO) 96 rooms, restaurant, lounge, pool, children stay free with parents, wheelchair access, no-smoking rooms, TV, a/c, pets allowed, laundry service, free parking, senior citizen rates, meeting facilities, major credit cards. LS SGL$38-$46, DBL$46-$54; HS SGL$40-$50, DBL$48-$60.

Line Limousine Farmhouse (Ritner Hwy, 17013; 243-1281) 2 rooms, complimentary breakfast, no smoking, on 100 acres, 1860s home, no pets, private baths, major credit cards. SGL/DBL$40-$160.

Rodeway Inn (1239 Harrisburg Pike, 17013; 249-2800, 800-102 424-4777) pool, wheelchair access, no-smoking rooms, a/c, TV, major credit cards. SGL/DBL$32-$70.

Super 8 Motel (100 Alexander Spring Rd, 17013; 245-9898, 800-800-8000) 61 rooms and suites, no pets, children under 12 stay free with parents, free local calls, a/c, TV, fax, no-smoking rooms, senior citizen rates, wheelchair access, meeting facilities, major credit cards. SGL/DBL$37-$43.

Center Valley
Area Code 215

Center Valley Motor Lodge (Center Valley 18034; 797-0128) 29 rooms, a/c, TV, pets OK, major credit cards. SGL/DBL$35-$50.

Chadds Ford
Area Code 215

Brandywine River Hotel (Rtes 1 and 100, 19317; 388-1200) 40 rooms and suites, complimentary breakfast, fireplace, antique furnishings, a/c, TV, major credit cards. SGL/DBL$119, STS$125.

Hedgerow Bed and Breakfast (268 Kennett Pike, 19317; 388-6080) 2 rooms and a 2-room apartment, complimentary breakfast, private bath, TV, a/c, no smoking, major credit cards. SGL/DBL$55-$100.

Chambersburg
Area Code 717

Days Inn (30 Falling Spring Rd, 17201; 263-1288, Fax 263-6514, 800-325-2525) 107 rooms and suites, restaurant, lounge, children stay free with parents, room service, laundry service, a/c, TV, free local calls, no pets, wheelchair access, no-smoking rooms, senior citizen rates, major credit cards. SGL/DBL$47-$70, STS$65-$75.

Hampton Inn (955 Lesher Rd, 17201; 261-9185, 800-HAMPTON) 84 rooms, restaurant, complimentary breakfast, pool, exercise facilities, children under 18 stay free with parents, no-smoking rooms, wheelchair access, computer hookups, fax service, TV, a/c, free local calls, pets allowed, meeting facilities, major credit cards. SGL/DBL$47-$62.

Holiday Inn (Rte 316, 17201; 263-3400, Fax 263-3400 ext 101, 800-HOLIDAY) restaurant, lounge, outdoor pool, exercise facilities, children under 19 stay free with parents, wheelchair access, a/c, TV, no-smoking rooms, fax service, room service, pets allowed, laundry service, meeting facilities, senior citizen rates, major credit cards. SGL/DBL$55-$75.

Howard Johnson Lodge (1123 Lincoln Way East, 17201; 263-9191, Fax 263-4752, 800-I-GO-HOJO) 132 rooms, restaurant, lounge, pool, sauna, children stay free with parents, wheelchair access, no-smoking rooms, in-room refrigerators and coffee makers, TV, a/c, pets allowed, free parking, senior citizen rates, meeting facilities for 130, major credit cards. SGL/DBL$53-$67.

TraveLodge (565 Lincoln Way East, 17201; 264-4187, Fax 267-2887, 800-255-3050) 51 rooms, restaurant, lounge, complimentary breakfast, pool, wheelchair access, free newspaper, laundry service, TV, a/c, free local calls, fax service, no-smoking rooms, free in-room coffee and tea service, in-room refrigerators and microwaves, no pets, meeting facilities for 50, major credit cards. SGL$44-$60, DBL$49-$64, AP$7.

Cherry Hill
Area Code 215

Hyatt Cherry Hill (2349 West Marlton Pike, 08022; 923-4075, Fax 662-3676, 800-233-1234) 409 rooms and suites, restaurant, lounge, entertainment, outdoor pool, whirlpool, exercise facilities, lighted tennis courts, room service, TV, a/c, no-smoking rooms, wheelchair access, 11,000 square feet of meeting and exhibition space, meeting facilities for 1,500, major credit cards. SGL/DBL$69-$159+.

Chester
Area Code 215

Howard Johnson Hotel (1300 Providence Rd, Chester 19013; 876-7211, Fax 874-5210, 800-654-9122) 116 rooms, restaurant, free breakfast, indoor pool, exercise facilities, children stay free with parents, no-smoking rooms, meeting facilities for 200, major credit cards. SGL$51-$56, DBL$56-$61.

Chestnut Hill
Area Code 717

Chestnut Hill Hotel (8229 Germantown Ave, 19118; 242-5905) 19 rooms and suites, restaurant, lounge, pets allowed, airport transportation, laundry service, children stay free with parents, 1 meeting room, meeting facilities for 50. SGL/DBL$75-$98, STS$108+.

Christiana
Area Code 215

Winding Glen Farm Guest House (107 Noble Rd, 17509; 593-5535) 12 rooms, free breakfast, no pets, no smoking, farm. SGL/DBL$30-$40.

Churchtown
Area Code 215

The Churchtown Inn (Rte 23, 17555; 445-7794) complimentary breakfast, no pets, private baths, 1730s inn, major credit cards. SGL/DBL$50-$95.

The Foreman House (2129 Main St, 17555; 445-6713) bed and breakfast, no children allowed, no smoking, private baths, antique furnishings, no pets, major credit cards. SGL/DBL$48-$58.

Clarion
Area Code 814

Days Inn (Rte 68, 16214; 226-8682, Fax 226-8372, 800-325-2525) 150 rooms and suites, restaurant, lounge, outdoor pool, children stay free with parents, room service, laundry service, a/c, TV, free local calls, no pets, wheelchair access, no-smoking rooms, senior citizen rates, meeting facilities for 300, major credit cards. SGL/DBL$45-$70, STS$75-$90.

Knights Inn (Rte 3, 16214; 226-4550, 800-843-5644) pool, wheelchair access, no-smoking rooms, TV, a/c, in-room refrigerators and microwaves, fax service, free parking, VCRs, senior citizen rates, major credit cards. SGL/DBL$38-$41.

Holiday Inn (Rte 68, 16215; 226-8850, 800-HOLIDAY) 122 rooms, restaurant, lounge, indoor pool, exercise facilities, children under 19 stay free with parents, wheelchair access, game room, a/c, TV, no-smoking rooms, fax service, room service, pets allowed, laundry service, meeting facilities for 250, senior citizen rates, major credit cards. SGL/DBL$58-$75.

Clarks Summit
Area Code 717

Days Inn (Clarks Summit 18411; 586-9100, Fax 586-9111, 800-325-2525) 67 rooms, restaurant, lounge, children stay free with parents, room service, laundry service, a/c, TV, free local calls, pets allowed, wheelchair access, no-smoking rooms, senior citizen rates, major credit cards. SGL/DBL$45-$63.

Ramada Inn Clarks Summit (Rte 6 and 11, 18411; 586-2730, Fax 587-0740, 800-2-RAMADA) 108 rooms, restaurant, lounge, outdoor pool, wheelchair access, no-smoking rooms, airport transportation, game room, free parking, pets allowed, wheelchair access, a/c, TV, room service, laundry facilities, meeting facilities, senior citizen rates, major credit cards. SGL/DBL$65-$87.

Clearfield
Area Code 814

Days Inn (Rte 879, 16830; 765-5381, Fax 765-7885, 800-325-2525) 120 rooms, restaurant, lounge, outdoor pool, children stay free with parents, room service, laundry service, a/c, TV, free local calls, pets allowed, wheelchair access, no-smoking rooms, senior citizen rates, meeting facilities for 225, major credit cards. SGL/DBL$39-$60.

Columbia
Area Code 717

The Columbian (360 Chestnut St, 17512; 684-5869, 800-422-5869) free breakfast, a/c, private baths, antique furnishings. SGL/DBL$45-$65.

Concordville
Area Code 215

Best Western Concordville Hotel (Rte 322, 19331; 358-9400, 800-528-1234) 118 rooms and suites, restaurant, complimentary breakfast, lounge, indoor pool, exercise facilities, children stay free with parents, a/c, TV, no-smoking rooms, wheelchair access, pets allowed, senior citizen rates, meeting facilities for 500, major credit cards. SGL/DBL$83-$105.

Conshohocken & West Conshohocken
Area Code 215

Marriott Hotel West (111 Crawford Ave, 19428; 941-5600, Fax 940-1060, 800-228-9290) 288 rooms and suites, restaurant, lounge, entertainment, indoor pool, sauna, exercise facilities, whirlpools, wheelchair access, free parking, TV, a/c, no-smoking rooms, gift shop, children stay free with parents, business services, meeting facilities, major credit cards. SGL/DBL$89-$154.

Cooksburg
Area Code 814

Clarion River Lodge (River Rd, 16217; 800-648-6743) 20 rooms, bed and breakfast, no pets, private baths, no children allowed, open year-round, TV, a/c, major credit cards. SGL/DBL$60-$110.

Coraopolis
Area Code 412

Consort Inn Airport (1500 Beers School Rd, 15108; 264-7900, 800-325-2525) 198 rooms and suites, restaurant, outdoor pool, sauna, exercise facilities, airport courtesy car, no-smoking rooms, limousine service, meeting facilities for 50. SGL$48-$56, DBL$54-$64.

Days Inn (1170 Thorn Run Rd, 15108; 269-0990, Fax 269-0462, 800-325-2525) 98 rooms, complimentary breakfast, transportation to local attractions, wheelchair access, no-smoking rooms, fax service, children stay free with parents, pets allowed. SGL$42-$52, DBL$46-$56, AP$6.

Embassy Suites Hotel (550 Cherrington Pkwy, 15108; 269-9070, Fax 262-4119, 800-EMBASSY) 223 2-room suites, restaurant, lounge, complimentary breakfast, pool, whirlpool, exercise facilities, sauna, room service, laundry service, wheelchair access, free newspaper, free local calls, no-smoking rooms, gift shop, transportation to local attractions, business services, meeting facilities, major credit cards. SGL/DBL$70-$105.

Hampton Inn Airport (1420 Beers School Rd, 15108; 264-0022, Fax 264-0020 ext 185, 800-HAMPTON) 128 rooms, free breakfast, children stay free with parents, airport transportation, pets allowed, no-smoking rooms, wheelchair access, in-room computer hookups, fax, free local calls, meeting facilities, major credit cards. SGL$55-$60, DBL$60-$65.

Holiday Inn Pittsburgh Airport (1406 Beers School Rd, 15108; 262-3600, Fax 262-3600 ext 1190) 257 rooms, restaurant, lounge, entertainment, indoor pool, whirlpool, exercise facilities, children stay free with parents, wheelchair access, no-smoking rooms, limousine service, fax, room service, 14 meeting rooms, meeting facilities for 1,100. SGL$105, DBL$115.

Marriott Hotel and Conference Center (100 Aten Rd, 15108; 788-8800, 788-0743, 800-228-9290, 800-328-9297) 318 rooms and suites, restaurant, lounge, complimentary breakfast, entertainment, indoor and outdoor pools, hot tub, whirlpool, sauna, exercise facilities, children stay free with parents, babysitting service, room service, complimentary newspaper, concierge, gift shop, car rental desk, wheelchair access, no-smoking rooms, limousine service, free parking, fax service, business services, 11 meeting rooms, 9,000 square feet of meeting and exhibition space, meeting facilities for 400, major credit cards. SGL$129, DBL$139, STS$259-$459.

Ramada Inn Airport (1412 Beers School Rd, 15108; 264-8950, Fax 262-5598, 800-2-RAMADA) 135 rooms and suites, restaurant, lounge, entertainment, pool, wheelchair access, no-smoking rooms, airport transportation, free parking, pets allowed, a/c, TV, room service, laundry facilities, 7 meeting rooms, meeting facilities for 600, senior citizen rates, major credit cards. SGL$65-$75, DBL$75-$85, STS$125, AP$10.

Red Roof Inn (1454 Beers School Rd, 15108; 264-5678, Fax 264-8034, 800-843-7663) 118 rooms, no-smoking rooms, fax service, wheelchair access, free newspaper, airport courtesy car, free local calls, in-room computer hookups, major credit cards. SGL/DBL$40-$49.

Royce Hotel Airport (1160 Thorn Run Extension, 15108; 262-2400) 198 rooms, restaurant, lounge, outdoor pool, airport courtesy car, no-smoking rooms, wheelchair access, limousine service, 8 meeting rooms, meeting facilities for 1,000, major credit cards. SGL$65, DBL$68-$88.

Cresco
Area Code 717

LaAnna Guest House (Cresco 18326; 676-4225) bed and breakfast, on 25 acres, antique furnishings, Victorian home, no pets. SGL/DBL$25-$40.

Dallas
Area Code 717

Ponda Rowland Bed and Breakfast (Rte 1, 18612; 639-3245) complimentary breakfast, on 130 acres, working farm, fireplace, antique furnishings, no smoking, major credit cards. SGL/DBL$25-$30.

Danville
Area Code 717

Days Inn (Rte 54, 17821; 275-5510, Fax 275-7918, 800-325-2525) 146 rooms and suites, restaurant, lounge, indoor pool, whirlpools, children stay free with parents, room service, laundry service, a/c, TV, free local calls, no pets, wheelchair access, no-smoking rooms, senior citizen rates, major credit cards. SGL/DBL$48-$80, STS$75-$125.

Howard Johnson Lodge (15 Valley West Rd, 17821; 275-5100, Fax 275-1886, 800-I-GO-HOJO) 77 rooms, restaurant, lounge, pool, children stay free with parents, wheelchair access, no-smoking rooms, TV, a/c, pets allowed, laundry facilities, game room, fax service, free parking, senior citizen rates, meeting facilities, major credit cards. SGL/DBL$35-$53.

Delaware Water Gap
Area Code 717

Ramada Inn (Interstate 80, 18327; 476-0000, 800-2-RAMADA) 104 rooms, restaurant, lounge, entertainment, indoor pool, wheelchair access, no-smoking rooms, airport transportation, free parking, pets allowed, a/c, TV, room service, laundry facilities, meeting facilities, senior citizen rates, major credit cards. SGL/DBL52-$69.

Denver
Area Code 215

Black Horse Lodge and Suites (Rte 272, 17517; 267-7563) rooms and suites, restaurant, lounge, pool, on 10 acres, a/c, TV, free local calls, major credit cards. SGL/DBL$65-$75.

Holiday Inn (Hwy 272, 17517; 267-7541, Fax 267-0515, 800-437-5711, 800-HOLIDAY) 110 rooms, restaurant, lounge, entertainment, exercise facilities, children under 19 stay free with parents, wheelchair access, a/c, TV, no-smoking rooms, fax service, room service, no pets, laundry service, meeting facilities for 60, senior citizen rates, major credit cards. SGL/DBL$48-$96.

Donegal
Area Code 412

Days Inn (Rte 31, 15628; 593-7536, Fax 593-6167, 800-325-2525) 35 rooms, restaurant, lounge, pool, children stay free with parents, room service, laundry service, a/c, TV, free local calls, no pets, wheelchair access, no-smoking rooms, senior citizen rates, major credit cards. SGL/DBL$49-$69.

Downingtown
Area Code 215

Holiday Inn (Rte 100S, 19335; 363-1100, Fax 524-2329, 800-HOLIDAY) 225 rooms, restaurant, lounge, indoor pool, exercise facilities, children under 19 stay free with parents, wheelchair access, a/c, TV, no-smoking rooms, fax service, room service, pets allowed, laundry service, meeting facilities for 450, senior citizen rates, major credit cards. SGL/DBL$65-$73.

Drums
Area Code 717

Econo Lodge (Drums 18222; 788-4121, 800-4-CHOICE) 43 rooms, pool, children under 12 stay free with parents, no pets, senior citizen rates, wheelchair access, a/c, TV, major credit cards. SGL/DBL$38-$44.

Lookout Motor Lodge (Drums 18222; 788-4131) 20 rooms, restaurant, complimentary breakfast, a/c, TV, major credit cards. SGL/DBL$60-$75.

Super 8 Motel (Drums 18222; 788-5887, 800-800-8000) 64 rooms and suites, no pets, children under 12 stay free with parents, free local calls, a/c, TV, in-room refrigerators and microwaves, fax service, no-smoking rooms, senior citizen rates, wheelchair access, meeting facilities, major credit cards. SGL/DBL$48-$54.

DuBois
Area Code 814

Holiday Inn (Hwy 219, 15801; 371-5100, Fax 375-0230, 800-HOLIDAY) 161 rooms, restaurant, lounge, outdoor pool, exercise facilities, children under 19 stay free with parents, wheelchair access, a/c, TV, no-smoking rooms, fax service, room service, no pets, laundry service, meeting facilities, senior citizen rates, major credit cards. SGL/DBL$55-$72.

Ramada Inn (Rte 255, 15801; 371-7070, Fax 371-1055, 800-2-RAMADA) 96 rooms, restaurant, lounge, entertainment, indoor pool, wheelchair access, no-smoking rooms, airport transportation, free parking, pets allowed, a/c, TV, room service, laundry facilities, meeting facilities for 400, senior citizen rates, major credit cards. SGL$51-$59, DBL$61-$69, STS$72, AP$10.

Duncansville
Area Code 814

Wye Motor Lodge (Duncansville 16635; 695-4407) 38 rooms, a/c, TV, in-room microwaves, no pets, major credit cards. SGL/DBL$27-$36.

Dunmore
Area Code 717

Days Inn (1100 O'Niell Hwy, 18512; 348-6101, Fax 348-5064, 800-325-2525) 90 rooms, restaurant, lounge, pool, children stay free with parents, room service, laundry service, a/c, TV, free local calls, in-room refrigerators and microwaves, pets allowed, wheelchair access, no-smoking rooms, senior citizen rates, major credit cards. SGL/DBL$50-$60.

East Stroudsburg
Area Code 717

Sheraton Pocono Inn (1220 West Main St, 18360; 424-1930, Fax 424-5909, 800-325-3535) 134 rooms and suites, restaurant, lounge, entertainment, indoor pool, exercise facilities, sauna, game room, gift shop, no-smoking rooms, wheelchair access, a/c, TV, children stay free with parents, 4,000 square feet of meeting and exhibition space, 4 meeting rooms, meeting facilities for 225, major credit cards. SGL/DBL$80-$120, STS$125.

Super 8 Motel (340 Green Tree Dr, 18301; 424-7411, 800-800-8000) 57 rooms and suites, no pets, children under 12 stay free with parents, free local calls, a/c, TV, fax, no-smoking rooms, senior citizen rates, wheelchair access, meeting facilities, major credit cards. SGL/DBL$42-$57.

Easton
Area Code 215

Days Inn (Rte 22, 18042; 253-0546, Fax 252-8952, 800-325-2525) 84 rooms and suites, restaurant, lounge, pool, children stay free with parents, room service, laundry service, a/c, TV, free local calls, pets allowed, wheelchair access, no-smoking rooms, senior citizen rates, major credit cards. SGL/DBL$42-$66, STS$56-$76.

Ebensburg
Area Code 814

Howard Johnson Lodge (Rte 22 West, 15931; 472-7201, 800-I-GO-HOJO) 40 rooms, restaurant, lounge, entertainment, children stay free with parents, wheelchair access, no-smoking rooms, TV, a/c, pets allowed, free parking, meeting facilities, senior citizen rates, major credit cards. SGL/DBL$38-$48.

Elizabethtown
Area Code 717

Conewago Valley Motor Inn (1688 Hershey Rd, 17022; 367-4320) SGL/DBL$55-$65.

Enlenton
Area Code 412

The Barnard House (109 River Ave, 16373; 867-2261) 5 rooms, bed and breakfast, no smoking, no pets, water view, major credit cards. SGL/DBL$43.

Enola
Area Code 717

Quality Inn (501 North Enola Rd, 17025; 732-0785, 800-368-5689) 72 rooms and suites, restaurant, room service, exercise facilities, children stay free with parents, a/c, TV, laundry service, no-smoking rooms, meeting facilities, major credit cards. SGL/DBL$46-$73.

Ephrata
Area Code 717

Gerhart House (287 Duke St, 17522; 733-0263) bed and breakfast, private baths, antique furnishings, major credit cards. SGL/DBL$55-$80.

The Guesthouse and 1777 House (318 North State St, 17522; 733-8696) rooms and suites, restaurant, complimentary breakfast, no pets, private baths, fireplace, jacuzzi, a/c, major credit cards. SGL/DBL$60-$140.

Erie
Area Code 814

Comfort Inn (8051 Peach St, 16509; 866-6666, 800-221-2222) 110 rooms, restaurant, pool, exercise facilities, wheelchair access, no-smoking rooms, no pets, children under 18 stay free with parents, senior citizen rates, a/c, VCRs, TV, meeting facilities, major credit cards. LS SGL$59-$75, DBL$69-$105; HS SGL$69-$89, DBL$85-$120.

Days Inn (7400 Schultz Rd, 16509; 868-8521, 800-325-2525) 112 rooms, restaurant, lounge, pool, children stay free with parents, room service, laundry service, a/c, TV, in-room computer hooks, airport transportation, free local calls, no pets, wheelchair access, no-smoking rooms, senior citizen rates, meeting facilities for 120, major credit cards. SGL/DBL$35-$90.

Knights Inn (7455 Schultz Rd, 16509; 868-0879, 800-843-5644) pool, wheelchair access, no-smoking rooms, TV, a/c, in-room refrigerators and microwaves, fax service, free parking, VCRs, senior citizen rates, major credit cards. SGL/DBL$36-$46.

Holiday Inn Downtown (18 West 19th St, 16501; 456-2961, Fax 456-7067, 800-HOLIDAY) 134 rooms, restaurant, lounge, outdoor pool, exercise facilities, children under 19 stay free with parents, wheelchair access, a/c, TV, no-smoking rooms, fax service, room service, no pets, laundry service, meeting facilities for 125, senior citizen rates, major credit cards. SGL/DBL$65-$68.

Holiday Inn South (8040 Perry Hwy, 16509; 864-4911, Fax 864-3643, 800-HOLIDAY) 216 rooms, restaurant, lounge, entertainment, outdoor pool, exercise facilities, spa, gift shop, children under 19 stay free with parents, wheelchair access, a/c, TV, no-smoking rooms, fax service, room service, no pets, laundry service, meeting facilities for 400, senior citizen rates, major credit cards. SGL/DBL$65-$73.

Howard Johnson Lodge (7575 Peach St, 16509; 864-4811, 864-4811 ext 146, 800-I-GO-HOJO) 111 rooms, restaurant, lounge, complimentary breakfast, pool, sauna, children stay free with parents, wheelchair access, no-smoking rooms, TV, a/c, laundry facilities, fax service, pets allowed, free parking, meeting facilities, senior citizen rates, major credit cards. SGL$49-$60, DBL$55-$78.

Ramada Inn (6101 Wattsburg Rd, 16509; 825-3100, Fax 825-0857, 800-2-RAMADA) 122 rooms, outdoor pool, wheelchair access, no-smoking rooms, airport transportation, free parking, pets allowed, a/c, TV, room service, laundry facilities, meeting facilities for 200, senior citizen rates, major credit cards. SGL$46-$54, DBL$54-$67.

Erwinna
Area Code 215

Evermay On The Delaware (River Rd, 18920; 294-1900) bed and breakfast, no pets, private bath, on 25 acres, major credit cards. SGL/DBL$48-$135.

Essington
Area Code 215

Holiday Inn Airport (45 Industrial Hwy, Essington 19029; 521-2400, Fax 521-1605, 800-HOLIDAY) 307 rooms, restaurant, lounge, children stay free with parents, wheelchair access, no-smoking rooms, fax service, room service, free parking, airport transportation, meeting facilities for 400, major credit cards. SGL/DBL$84-$104.

Knights Inn (43 Industrial Hwy, 19029; 521-6650, 800-843-5644) 87 rooms, kitchenettes, wheelchair access, no-smoking rooms, in-room refrigerators and microwaves, major credit cards. SGL$37-$42.

Ramada Inn Airport (76 Industrial Hwy, 19029; 521-9600, Fax 521-9388, 800-2-RAMADA) 290 rooms, restaurant, pool, exercise facilities, wheelchair access, no-smoking rooms, airport transportation, free parking, pets allowed, wheelchair access, a/c, TV, room service, laundry facilities, meeting facilities for 1,000, senior citizen rates, major credit cards. SGL$49-$89, DBL$49-$99, AP$12.

Exton
Area Code 215

Comfort Inn (5 North Pottstown Pike, 19341; 524-8811, 800-221-2222) 104 rooms, restaurant, indoor pool, whirlpools, wheelchair access, no-smoking rooms, no pets, children under 18 stay free with parents, senior citizen rates, a/c, TV, meeting facilities, major credit cards. LS SGL/DBL$50-$67; HS SGL/DBL$56-$73.

Holiday Inn (120 North Pottstown Pike, 19341; 524-9000, Fax 524-7259, 800-HOLIDAY) 124 rooms, restaurant, complimentary breakfast, lounge, outdoor pool, exercise facilities, airport transportation, children under 19 stay free with parents, wheelchair access, a/c, TV, no-smoking rooms, fax service, room service, no pets, laundry service, meeting facilities, senior citizen rates, major credit cards. SGL/DBL$60-$70.

Fogelsville
Area Code 215

Cloverleaf Motel (Fogelsville 18051; 395-3367, 800-540-3367) 29 rooms, restaurant, a/c, no-smoking rooms, TV. SGL/DBL$40-$43.

Fort Washington
Area Code 215

Holiday Inn (432 Pennsylvania Ave, 19034; 643-3000, 800-HOLIDAY) 224 rooms, restaurant, lounge, entertainment, outdoor pool, exercise facilities, children under 19 stay free with parents, wheelchair access, a/c, car rental desk, game room, TV, no-smoking rooms, fax service, room service, pets allowed, airport transportation, laundry service, meeting facilities, senior citizen rates, major credit cards. SGL/DBL$65-$85.

Ramada Inn (285 Commerce Dr, 19034; 542-7930, Fax 641-0969, 800-2-RAMADA) 102 rooms and suites, restaurant, lounge, pool, exercise facilities, wheelchair access, no-smoking rooms, airport transportation, free parking, pets allowed, a/c, TV, room service, laundry facilities, meeting facilities, senior citizen rates, major credit cards. SGL$60-$68, DBL$66-$74, AP$8.

Frazer
Area Code 215

Sheraton Great Valley Hotel (707 Lancaster Pike, 19355; 524-5500, Fax 524-1808, 800-325-3535) 156 rooms and suites, restaurant, lounge, indoor pool, whirlpools, exercise facilities, no-smoking rooms, a/c, TV, children stay free with parents, wheelchair access, 6,000 square feet of meeting and exhibition space, meeting facilities for 220, major credit cards. SGL/DBL$83-$103, STS$103-$225.

Gap
Area Code 717

Fassitt Mansion Bed and Breakfast (6051 Old Philadelphia Pike, 17527; 442-3139) complimentary breakfast, 1845 home, fireplaces, antique furnishings, no smoking, no pets, private baths, no children allowed, major credit cards. SGL/DBL$58.

Gettysburg
Code 717

Appleford Inn (218 Carlisle St, 17325; 337-1711) 12 rooms, bed and breakfast, antique furnishings, a/c, no smoking, major credit cards. SGL/DBL$35-$65.

The Brafferton Inn (44 York St, 17325; 337-3423) free breakfast, 1780s inn, no smoking, no pets, private baths, major credit cards. SGL/DBL$65-$85.

Budget Host 3 Crowns Motor Lodge (205 Steinwehr Ave, 17325; 334-3168, 800-BUD-HOST) 30 rooms, pool, in-room refrigerators, no-smoking rooms, TV, VCRs, a/c, laundry facilities, pets allowed, wheelchair access, children stay free with parents, senior citizen rates, meeting facilities, major credit cards. SGL$28-$36, DBL$32-$48, AP$4.

Gettysburg 271

Comfort Inn (871 York Rd, 17325; 337-2400, 800-221-2222) 2 rooms, restaurant, whirlpools, wheelchair access, no-smoking rooms, no pets, children under 18 stay free with parents, senior citizen rates, a/c, TV, meeting facilities, major credit cards. LS SGL/DBL$35-$60; HS SGL/DBL$45-$84.

Days Inn (865 York Rd, 17325; 334-0030, Fax 337-1002, 800-325-2525) 113 rooms, restaurant, lounge, outdoor pool, exercise facilities, children stay free with parents, room service, laundry service, a/c, TV, free local calls, no pets, wheelchair access, no-smoking rooms, senior citizen rates, meeting facilities for 100, major credit cards. LS SGL$53-$66, DBL$63-$76; HS SGL$69-$75, DBL$79-$85.

Doubleday Inn (104 Doubleday Ave, 17325; 334-9119) 6 rooms, bed and breakfast, a/c, TV, major credit cards. SGL/DBL$65.

Friendship Inn-Penn Eagle Motel (1031 York Rd, 17325; 334-1804, 800-453-4511, 800-424-4777) 21 rooms, pool, exercise facilities, a/c, TV, no pets, no-smoking rooms, children stay free with parents, wheelchair access, major credit cards. SGL/DBL$52-$58.

Gettysburg Inn (1980 Biglerville Rd, 17325; 334-2263) a/c, TV, no pets, major credit cards. SGL/DBL$45.

Gettysburg International Youth Hostel (27 Chambersburg St, 17325; 334-1020) a/c, TV, kitchen, game room. SGL/DBL$20-$25.

Holiday Inn Battlefield (516 Baltimore St, 17325; 334-6211, Fax 334-7183, 800-HOLIDAY) 100 rooms, restaurant, lounge, outdoor pool, exercise facilities, whirlpools, children under 19 stay free with parents, wheelchair access, a/c, TV, no-smoking rooms, fax service, room service, pets allowed, laundry service, 3 meeting rooms, meeting facilities for 350, senior citizen rates, major credit cards. SGL/DBL$40-$90.

Holiday Inn Express (869 York Rd, 17325; 337-1400, 800-HOLIDAY) 49 rooms, restaurant, complimentary breakfast, lounge, indoor pool, spa, exercise facilities, children under 19 stay free with parents, wheelchair access, a/c, TV, no-smoking rooms, fax service, room service, no pets, laundry service, meeting facilities, senior citizen rates, major credit cards. SGL/DBL$40-$85.

The Homestead Motor Lodge (1650 York Rd, 17325; 334-3866) a/c, TV, no pets, no-smoking rooms, major credit cards. SGL/DBL$33-$56.

Howard Johnson Lodge (301 Steinwehr Ave, 17325; 334-1188, Fax 334-1103 ext 325, 800-446-4656, 800-I-GO-HOJO) 77 rooms, restaurant, lounge, pool, children stay free with parents, wheelchair access, no-smoking rooms, TV, a/c, pets allowed, free parking, meeting facilities, senior citizen rates, major credit cards. LS SGL$34-$75, DBL$45-$80; HS SGL$55-$68, DBL$60-$74.

Old Mill Manor (1681 Camp Betty Washington Rd, 17325) 7 rooms and suites, complimentary breakfast, whirlpool tub, antique furnishings, 1890s home. SGL/DBL$60-$80.

Quality Inn Larson's (401 Buford Ave, 17325; 334-3141, 800-368-5689) 41 rooms and suites, restaurant, room service, exercise facilities, children stay free with parents, a/c, TV, laundry service, no-smoking rooms, meeting facilities, major credit cards. LS SGL/DBL$36-$50; HS SGL/DBL$48-$68, AP$5.

Quality Inn Motor Lodge (380 Steinwehr Ave, 17325; 334-1103, 800-221-2222) 105 rooms and suites, restaurant, outdoor pool, exercise facilities, sauna, children stay free with parents, a/c, TV, room service, laundry service, no-smoking rooms, meeting facilities, major credit cards. SGL$35-$94, DBL$46-$98, AP$6.

Ramada Inn (2634 Emmitsburg Rd, 17325; 334-8121, Fax 334-6066, 800-776-8349, 800-2-RAMADA) 195 rooms and suites, restaurant, lounge, indoor pool, exercise facilities, jacuzzi, jogging track, sauna, game room, wheelchair access, no-smoking rooms, airport transportation, free parking, pets allowed, wheelchair access, a/c, TV, room service, laundry facilities, meeting facilities for 1,200, senior citizen rates, major credit cards. SGL/DBL$79-$130, STS$175-$235, AP$7.

Sunstar (3641 Trout Run Rd, 17325; 755-7511) 4 suites, complimentary breakfast, on 12 acres, private bath, fireplace, a/c. SGL/DBL$40-$48.

Smyser-Bair House (30 South Beaver St, 17325; 854-3411) 4 rooms and suites, complimentary breakfast, 1880s home, antique furnishings. SGL/DBL$100.

Western Inn (2520 Emmitsburg Rd, 17325; 334-1339) 15 rooms, pool, a/c, TV, no pets, major credit cards. SGL/DBL$40-$50.

Glenn Mills
Area Code 215

Crier In The Country (Baltimore Pike, 19342; 358-2411) rooms and suites, restaurant, complimentary breakfast, kitchenettes, antique furnishings. SGL/DBL$45-$55.

Ramada Inn Chadds Ford (Rte 202, 19342; 358-1700, Fax 558-0842, 800-2-RAMADA) 148 rooms, restaurant, lounge, entertainment, pool, exercise facilities, wheelchair access, no-smoking rooms, airport transportation, free parking, pets allowed, gift shop, a/c, TV, room service, laundry facilities, meeting facilities, senior citizen rates, major credit cards. SGL$55-$80, DBL$60-$85, AP$5.

Grantville
Area Code 717

Holiday Inn (Hwy 81, 17028; 469-0661, 800-HOLIDAY) restaurant, lounge, entertainment, indoor pool, exercise facilities, game room, children under 19 stay free with parents, wheelchair access, a/c, TV, no-smoking rooms, fax, room service, no pets, laundry service, meeting facilities for 600, senior citizen rates, major credit cards. SGL/DBL$86-$170.

Greencastle
Area Code 717

Phaeton Farm (9762 Browns Mill Rd, 17225; 597-8656) bed and breakfast, major credit cards. SGL/DBL$35.

Quality Inn (50 Pine Dr, 17225; 597-8164, 800-368-5689) 71 rooms and suites, restaurant, room service, exercise facilities, children stay free with parents, a/c, TV, laundry service, no-smoking rooms, meeting facilities, major credit cards. SGL/DBL$55-$65, AP$6.

Welsh Run Inn Bed and Breakfast (11299 Welsh Run Rd, 17225; 328-9506) complimentary breakfast, major credit cards. SGL/DBL$45-$65.

Greensburg
Area Code 412

Knights Inn (1215 South Main St, 15601; 836-7100, 800-843-5644) pool, wheelchair access, no-smoking rooms, TV, a/c, in-room refrigerators and microwaves, fax service, free parking, VCRs, senior citizen rates, major credit cards. SGL/DBL$37-$45.

Greenville
Area Code 412

Phillips House (32 Eagle St, 16125; 588-4169) bed and breakfast, 1890s home, no pets, antique furnishings, private baths, major credit cards. SGL/DBL$38-$54.

Hamlin
Area Code 717

Comfort Inn (State Rd 191 and I-84; 689-4148, 800-523-4426, 800-221-2222) 124 rooms, restaurant, exercise facilities, whirlpools, wheelchair access, no-smoking rooms, no pets, children under 18 stay free with parents, senior citizen rates, a/c, TV, meeting facilities, major credit cards. SGL$48-$128, DBL$52-$140.

Hanover
Area Code 717

Beechmont Inn (315 Broadway, 17331; 632-3013, 800-553-7009) 7 rooms and suites, complimentary breakfast, 1830s inn, antique furnishings, private baths, no pets, whirlpool tub, fireplace, no children allowed, water view, a/c, major credit cards. SGL/DBL$68-$100.

Harmarville
Area Code 412

Holiday Inn (2802 Freeport Rd, 15238; 828-9300, Fax 828-7916, 800-HOLIDAY) restaurant, lounge, outdoor pool, exercise facilities, children under 19 stay free with parents, wheelchair access, a/c, TV, no-smoking rooms, fax service, room service, pets allowed, laundry service, meeting facilities for 300, airport transportation, senior citizen rates, major credit cards. SGL/DBL$38-$56.

Harrisburg
Area Code 717

Budget Host American Inn (495 Eisenhower Blvd, 17110; 561-1885, 800-BUD-HOST) 30 rooms, restaurant, in-room refrigerators, laundry facilities, no pets, no-smoking rooms, TV, VCRs, a/c, wheelchair access, children stay free with parents, senior citizen rates, meeting facilities, major credit cards. SGL$28-$40, DBL$35-$45, AP$5.

Budgetel Inn (990 Eisenhower Blvd, 17111; 939-8000, Fax 939-0500, 800-428-3438) rooms and suites, complimentary breakfast, children under 18 stay free with parents, a/c, wheelchair access, no-smoking rooms, free local calls, in-room computer hookups, fax service, VCRs, TV, meeting facilities, major credit cards. SGL$38-$40, DBL$45-$48, STS$45-$54.

Comfort Inn East (4021 Union Deposit Rd, 17109; 561-8100, 800-221-2222) 117 rooms, restaurant, pool, wheelchair access, no-smoking rooms, no pets, children under 18 stay free with parents, senior citizen rates, a/c, TV, meeting facilities, major credit cards. SGL/DBL$49-$69, AP$7.

Compri-Doubletree Club Hotel (765 Eisenhower Blvd, 17111; 558-9500, Fax 558-8956, 800-528-0444) 171 rooms and suites, restaurant, lounge, pool, sauna, hot tub, exercise facilities, fax service, free parking, airport courtesy car, meeting facilities for 100, major credit cards. SGL/DBL$80-$100.

Days Inn (State Rd 39, 17112; 652-9578, Fax 657-5012, 800-325-2525) 30 rooms, restaurant, lounge, gift shop, children stay free with parents, room service, laundry service, a/c, TV, free local calls, no pets, wheelchair access, no-smoking rooms, senior citizen rates, major credit cards. SGL/DBL$29-$58.

Days Inn (3919 North Front St, 17110; 233-3100, Fax 233-6415, 800-325-2525) 116 rooms, restaurant, complimentary breakfast, lounge, outdoor pool, children stay free with parents, room service, in-room refrigerators and microwaves, laundry service, a/c, TV, in-room computer hookups, free local calls, no pets, wheelchair access, no-smoking rooms, senior citizen rates, major credit cards. SGL/DBL$45-$72.

Hilton Hotel (1 North Second St, 17101; 233-6000, Fax 233-6271, 800-HILTONS) 341 rooms and suites, restaurant, lounge, entertainment, outdoor pool, exercise facilities, children stay free with parents, no-smoking rooms, wheelchair access, pets allowed, a/c, TV, free parking, business services, meeting facilities, major credit cards. SGL/DBL$85-$135.

HoJo Inn (1450 North 7th St, 17102; 234-5931, Fax 255-0638, 800-I-GO-HOJO) 48 rooms, restaurant, complimentary breakfast, lounge, pool, children stay free with parents, fax service, wheelchair access, no-smoking rooms, TV, a/c, pets allowed, free parking, senior citizen rates, meeting facilities, major credit cards. SGL$35-$55, DBL$40-$70.

Holiday Inn East (4751 Lindle Rd, 17111; 939-7841, 800-HOLIDAY) 300 rooms and suites, restaurant, lounge, indoor pool, exercise facilities, children under 19 stay free with parents, wheelchair access, a/c, TV, VCRs, no-smoking rooms, fax service, room service, no pets, laundry service, meeting facilities for 500, senior citizen rates, major credit cards. SGL/DBL$95-$106.

Howard Johnson Lodge (473 Eisenhower Blvd, 17111; 564-4730, Fax 564-6300, 800-343-5982, 800-I-GO-HOJO) 176 rooms, restaurant, lounge, pool, children stay free with parents, wheelchair access, no-smoking rooms, TV, a/c, no pets, free parking, senior citizen rates, meeting facilities for 75, major credit cards. SGL$53-$80, DBL$55-$85.

Marriott Hotel (4650 Lindle Rd, 17111; 564-5511, Fax 564-6173, 800-228-9290) 348 rooms and suites, restaurant, lounge, entertainment, outdoor pool, exercise facilities, whirlpools, sauna, jogging track, airport courtesy car, free parking, wheelchair access, TV, a/c, no-smoking rooms, gift shop, children stay free with parents, business services, meeting facilities, major credit cards. SGL/DBL$75-$90, STS$100-$115.

Quality Inn (525 South Front St, 17104; 233-1611, 800-368-5689) 124 rooms and suites, restaurant, room service, exercise facilities, children stay free with parents, a/c, TV, laundry service, no-smoking rooms, meeting facilities, major credit cards. SGL/DBL$40-$80.

Ramada Inn (Turnpike and I-83, 17070; 774-2721, Fax 774-2485, 800-2-RAMADA) 197 rooms, restaurant, lounge, indoor pool, jacuzzi, game room, exercise facilities, wheelchair access, no-smoking rooms, airport transportation, free parking, pets allowed, a/c, TV, room service, laundry facilities, meeting facilities, senior citizen rates, major credit cards. SGL/DBL$49-$99, DBL$59-$109, AP$10.

Residence Inn (4480 Lewis Rd, 17111; 561-1900, Fax 561-8617, 800-331-3131) rooms and suites, free breakfast, pool, spa, in-room refrigerators, coffee makers and microwaves, laundry facilities, free parking, TV, a/c, VCRs, pets allowed, fireplaces, children stay free with parents, no-smoking rooms, wheelchair access, meeting facilities for 30, major credit cards. SGL/DBL$65-$85.

Sheraton Inn (800 East Park Dr, 17111; 561-2800, Fax 561-8398, 800-325-3535) 173 rooms and suites, restaurant, lounge, indoor pool, exercise facilities, whirlpools, sauna, no-smoking rooms, a/c, TV, children stay free with parents, wheelchair access, 11,000 square feet of meeting and exhibition space, 10 meeting rooms, meeting facilities for 1,000, major credit cards. SGL/DBL$75-$135.

Super 8 Motel (4131 Executive Park Dr, 17111; 564-7790, Fax 564-7790 ext 165, 800-800-8000) 48 rooms and suites, no pets, children under 12 stay free with parents, free local calls, a/c, TV, fax service, no-smoking rooms, senior citizen rates, wheelchair access, meeting facilities, major credit cards. SGL/DBL$35-$46.

Super 8 Motel (4125 Front St, 17110; 233-5891, Fax 233-5891, 800-800-8000) 57 rooms and suites, no pets, children under 12 stay free with parents, free local calls, a/c, TV, fax, no-smoking rooms, senior citizen rates, wheelchair access, meeting facilities, major credit cards. SGL/DBL$38-$56.

Hawley
Area Code 717

Academy Street Bed and Breakfast (528 Academy St, 18424; 226-3430) 7 rooms, complimentary breakfast, a/c, private baths, water view, major credit cards. SGL/DBL$45-$75.

Hazleton & West Hazleton
Area Code 717

Best Western Genetti Motor Lodge (32nd and North Church St, 18201; 454-2494, 800-528-1234) 100 rooms and 2-room suites, restaurant, complimentary breakfast, lounge, entertainment, pool, exercise facilities, children stay free with parents, a/c, TV, no-smoking rooms, wheelchair access, pets allowed, senior citizen rates, meeting facilities, major credit cards. SGL/DBL$45-$75.

Comfort Inn (Kiwanis Blvd, 18201; 455-9300, 800-221-2222) 119 rooms, restaurant, pool, wheelchair access, no-smoking rooms, jacuzzi, no pets, children under 18 stay free with parents, senior citizen rates, a/c, TV, 2 meeting rooms, major credit cards. SGL/DBL$51-$80.

Forest Hill Inn (Hazleton 18201; 459-2730) a/c, TV, children under 12 stay free with parents, major credit cards. SGL/DBL$35-$50.

Hampton Inn (Rte 93, 18201; 454-3449, 800-HAMPTON) 123 rooms, restaurant, complimentary breakfast, pool, exercise facilities, children under 18 stay free with parents, no-smoking rooms, wheelchair access, computer hookups, fax service, TV, a/c, free local calls, pets allowed, meeting facilities, major credit cards. SGL/DBL$56-$67.

Holiday Inn (Rte 309 North, 18201; 455-2061, 800-HOLIDAY) 107 rooms, restaurant, lounge, outdoor pool, exercise facilities, children under 19 stay free with parents, wheelchair access, a/c, TV, no-smoking rooms, fax service, room service, no pets, laundry service, meeting facilities, senior citizen rates, major credit cards. SGL/DBL$66-$75.

Mount Laurel Motel (Rte 309 South, 18201; 455-6391) 38 rooms and efficiencies, a/c, TV. SGL/DBL$28-$43.

Hershey
Area Code 717

Budgetel Inn (200 North Mountain Rd, 17112; 540-9339, Fax 540-9486, 800-428-3438) rooms and suites, complimentary breakfast, children under 18 stay free with parents, a/c, wheelchair access, no-smoking rooms, free local calls, in-room computer hookups, fax service, VCRs, TV, meeting facilities, major credit cards. SGL/DBL$43-$51, STS$50-$57.

Days Inn (350 West Chocolate Ave, 17033; 534-2162, Fax 533-6409, 800-325-2525) 75 rooms, restaurant, free breakfast, lounge, pool, children stay free with parents, room service, laundry service, in-room refrigerators, a/c, TV, free local calls, no pets, wheelchair access, no-smoking rooms, senior citizen rates, major credit cards. LS SGL/DBL$55-$89; HS SGL/DBL$75-$113.

Pinehurst Inn (50 Northeast Dr, 17033; 533-2603) 12 rooms, bed and breakfast, restaurant, no smoking, private baths, fireplace, no children allowed, major credit cards. SGL/DBL$48.

Holicong
Area Code 215

Ash Mill Farm (5358 Rte 202, 18928; 794-5373) 5 rooms, free breakfast, on 11 acres, working farm, 1790s home, no smoking, no pets, private baths, no children allowed, antique furnishings, fireplace, major credit cards. SGL/DBL$80-$135.

Horsham
Area Code 215

Residence Inn (Three Walnut Grove Dr, 19044; 443-7330, 800-331-3131) rooms and suites, complimentary breakfast, pool, spa, in-room refrigerators, coffee makers and microwaves, laundry facilities, free parking, TV, a/c, VCRs, pets allowed, fireplaces, children stay free with parents, no-smoking rooms, wheelchair access, major credit cards. SGL/DBL$64-$84.

Hummelstown
Area Code 717

Comfort Inn (Hwy 422, 17033; 566-2050, 800-221-2222) 125 rooms, restaurant, indoor pool, wheelchair access, no-smoking rooms, no pets, children under 18 stay free with parents, senior citizen rates, a/c, TV, meeting facilities, major credit cards. LS SGL$45-$58, DBL$55-$68; HS SGL$93-$103, DBL$103-$113, AP$10.

Huntingdon
Area Code 814

Days Inn (Rte 11 and Fourth St, 16652; 643-3934, Fax 643-3005, 800-325-2525) 76 rooms, restaurant, lounge, children stay free with parents, room service, laundry service, a/c, TV, free local calls, pets OK, wheelchair access, no-smoking rooms, senior citizen rates, meeting facilities for 300, major credit cards. SGL/DBL$38-$54.

Indiana
Area Code 412

Holiday Inn (1395 Wayne Ave, 15701; 463-3561, 800-HOLIDAY) 156 rooms, restaurant, lounge, indoor pool, exercise facilities, children under 19 stay free with parents, wheelchair access, a/c, TV, no-smoking rooms, fax service, room service, no pets, laundry service, meeting facilities for 450, senior citizen rates, major credit cards. SGL/DBL$67-$80.

Industry
Area Code 643

Willows Motel (Rte 68, 15052; 643-4500) major credit cards. SGL/DBL$38-$42.

Irwin
Area Code 412

Knights Inn (7990 Rte 30, 15601; 863-2600, 800-843-5644) restaurant, lounge, airport transportation, pool, wheelchair access, no-smoking rooms, TV, a/c, in-room refrigerators and microwaves, fax service, free parking, VCRs, senior citizen rates, major credit cards. SGL/DBL$38-$54.

Johnstown
Area Code 814

Comfort Inn (455 Theatre Dr, 15904; 266-3678, 800-221-2222) 117 rooms, restaurant, indoor pool, exercise facilities, whirlpools, wheelchair access, no-smoking rooms, no pets, children under 18 stay free with parents, senior citizen rates, a/c, TV, meeting facilities, major credit cards. SGL/DBL$48-$65.

Days Inn (1540 Scalp Ave, 15904; 269-3366, 800-325-2525) 147 rooms, restaurant, lounge, indoor pool, exercise facilities, children stay free with parents, room service, laundry service, a/c, TV, free local calls, no pets, wheelchair access, no-smoking rooms, senior citizen rates, major credit cards. SGL/DBL$40-$50, STS$80.

Holiday Inn (250 Market St, 15907; 535-7777, 800-HOLIDAY) 164 rooms, restaurant, lounge, indoor pool, whirlpools, exercise facilities, children under 19 stay free with parents, wheelchair access, a/c, TV, no-smoking rooms, fax service, room service, no pets, laundry service, meeting facilities for 300, senior citizen rates, major credit cards. SGL/DBL$59-$79.

Super 8 Motel (1440 Scalp Ave, 15904; 266-8789, Fax 266-5285, 800-822-9194, 800-800-8000) 105 rooms and suites, no pets, children under 12 stay free with parents, free local calls, a/c, TV, fax service, no-smoking rooms, senior citizen rates, wheelchair access, in-room refrigerators and microwaves, laundry service, meeting facilities, major credit cards. SGL/DBL$40-$45.

Kennett Square
Area Code 215

Meadow Spring Farm (201 East St Rd, 19348; 444-3903) bed and breakfast, no pets, private bath, 1830s home, antique furnishings, major credit cards. SGL/DBL$48-$80.

Mrs. K's Bed and Breakfast (404 Ridge Ave, 19348; 444-5559) complimentary breakfast, a/c, no smoking, open year-round, major credit cards. SGL/DBL$55.

King of Prussia
Area Code 215

Comfort Inn Valley Forge National Park (550 West Dekalb Pike, 19406; 962-0700, 800-221-2222) 121 rooms, restaurant, exercise facilities, wheelchair access, no-smoking rooms, no pets, children under 18 stay free with parents, senior citizen rates, a/c, TV, meeting facilities, major credit cards. SGL$49-$85, DBL$59-$95.

Pennsylvania

Hampton Inn (530 West Dekalb Pike, 19406; 962-8111, Fax 962-5494, 800-HAMPTON) 148 rooms, restaurant, complimentary breakfast, pool, exercise facilities, children under 18 stay free with parents, no-smoking rooms, wheelchair access, computer hookups, fax service, TV, a/c, free local calls, pets allowed, meeting facilities, major credit cards. SGL/DBL$56-$78.

Hilton Valley Forge Hotel (251 West Dekalb Pike, 19406; 337-1200, Fax 337-2224, 800-HILTONS) 340 rooms and suites, restaurant, lounge, entertainment, indoor and outdoor pool, exercise facilities, sauna, children stay free with parents, no-smoking rooms, free parking, gift shop, wheelchair access, pets allowed, a/c, TV, business services, meeting facilities, major credit cards. SGL/DBL$75-$105.

Hilton and Towers (Broad St and Locust, 19107; 893-1600, Fax 893-1663, 800-HILTONS) 428 rooms and suites, restaurant, lounge, entertainment, indoor pool, exercise facilities, sauna, room service, children stay free with parents, no-smoking rooms, wheelchair access, pets allowed, a/c, TV, business services, meeting facilities, major credit cards. SGL/DBL$75-$135.

Holiday Inn (260 Goddard Ave, 19406; 265-7500, 800-HOLIDAY) 305 rooms, restaurant, lounge, entertainment, indoor pool, exercise facilities, children under 19 stay free with parents, wheelchair access, boutiques, gift shop, barber shop, car rental desk, a/c, TV, no-smoking rooms, fax service, room service, pets allowed, laundry service, meeting facilities for 1,000, senior citizen rates, major credit cards. SGL/DBL$89-$105.

Howard Johnson Lodge (South Gulph Rd, 19406; 265-4500, Fax 337-0672, 800-I-GO-HOJO) 168 rooms, restaurant, complimentary breakfast, lounge, pool, children stay free with parents, wheelchair access, no-smoking rooms, TV, a/c, in-room computer hookups, laundry service, fax service, pets allowed, free parking, senior citizen rates, meeting facilities for 20, major credit cards. SGL/DBL$59-$90.

Sheraton Plaza Hotel (North Gulph Rd, 19406; 265-1500, Fax 768-3290, 800-325-3535) 160 rooms and suites, restaurant, lounge, entertainment, pool, tennis courts, sauna, whirlpools, exercise facilities, no-smoking rooms, a/c, TV, children stay free with parents, wheelchair access, meeting facilities for 5,000, major credit cards. SGL/DBL$115-$135.

Sheraton Valley Forge Hotel (King of Prussia 19406; 337-2000, Fax 768-3222, 800-325-3535) 326 rooms and suites, restaurant, lounge, entertainment, outdoor pool, exercise facilities, tennis courts, no-smoking rooms, a/c, TV, children stay free with parents, wheelchair access, meeting facilities. SGL/DBL$95-$120.

Kittanning
Area Code 415

Quality Inn (405 Butler Rd, 16201; 543-1159, 800-368-5689) 61 rooms and suites, restaurant, pool, tennis court, room service, exercise facilities, children stay free with parents, a/c, TV, laundry service, no-smoking rooms, meeting facilities, major credit cards. SGL/DBL$43-$52, AP$4.

Kulpsville
Area Code 215

Days Inn (Sunneytown Pike, 19443; 368-5391, Fax 368-7671, 800-325-2525) 53 rooms, restaurant, lounge, children stay free with parents, room service, laundry service, a/c, TV, free local calls, no pets, wheelchair access, no-smoking rooms, senior citizen rates, major credit cards. SGL/DBL$49-$69.

Holiday Inn (1750 Sunneytown Pike, 19443; 368-3800, Fax 368-7824, 800-HOLIDAY) 184 rooms, restaurant, lounge, children under 19 stay free with parents, wheelchair access, a/c, TV, no-smoking rooms, fax service, room service, pets allowed, airport transportation, laundry service, meeting facilities, senior citizen rates, major credit cards. SGL/DBL$60-$70.

Kutztown
Area Code 215

Super 8 Motel (Golden Key Rd, 19530; 285-4880, 800-800-8000) 38 rooms and suites, no pets, children under 12 stay free with parents, free local calls, a/c, TV, fax service, no-smoking rooms, senior citizen rates, wheelchair access, meeting facilities, major credit cards. SGL$35, DBL$38.

Lahaska
Area Code 215

Lahaska Hotel (Rte 202, 18931; 794-0440) complimentary breakfast, restaurant, no smoking, no children allowed, private baths, Victorian home, antique furnishings, no pets, a/c, major credit cards. SGL/DBL$85-$100.

Lake Harmony
Area Code 717

Days Inn Poconos (Lake Harmony 18624; 443-0391, Fax 443-7542, 800-325-2525) 40 rooms, restaurant, lounge, children stay free with parents, room service, laundry service, a/c, TV, free local calls, pets allowed, wheelchair access, no-smoking rooms, senior citizen rates, major credit cards. SGL$55-$120, DBL$65-$130.

Ramada Inn Pocono (Rte 940, 18624; 443-8471, Fax 443-0326, 800-2-RAMADA) 135 rooms and suites, restaurant, lounge, entertainment, indoor pool, wheelchair access, no-smoking rooms, airport transportation, free parking, pets allowed, game room, gift shop, a/c, TV, room service, laundry facilities, meeting facilities, senior citizen rates, major credit cards. SGL$60-$80, DBL$70-$130, STS$95-$130, AP$5.

Lamar
Area Code 717

Comfort Inn (State Rd 64 and I-80, 16848; 726-4901, 800-221-2222) 155 rooms, restaurant, complimentary breakfast, pool, wheelchair access, no-smoking rooms, no pets, children under 18 stay free with parents, senior citizen rates, a/c, TV, meeting facilities, major credit cards. LS SGL/DBL$39-$57; HS SGL/DBL$75-$95.

Lampeter
Area Code 717

The Walkabout Inn (837 Village Rd, 17537; 464-0707) bed and breakfast, no smoking, no pets, private baths, antique furnishings, major credit cards. SGL/DBL$43.

Lancaster
Area Code 717

Best Western Eden Resort Inn (222 Eden Rd, 17601; 569-6444, 800-223-8963, 800-528-1234) 166 rooms, restaurant, complimentary breakfast, lounge, indoor and outdoor pool, exercise facilities, tennis courts, game rooms, children stay free with parents, a/c, TV, no-smoking rooms, wheelchair access, pets allowed, senior citizen rates, meeting facilities, major credit cards. SGL/DBL$85-$115.

Comfort Inn (500 Centerville Rd, 17601; 898-2431, 800-221-2222) restaurant, pool, wheelchair access, no-smoking rooms, no pets, children under 18 stay free with parents, senior citizen rates, a/c, TV, meeting facilities, major credit cards. SGL/DBL$39-$82.

Country Living Motor Inn (2406 Old Philadelphia Pike, 17602; 295-7295) 34 rooms and suites, restaurant, whirlpools, no pets, a/c, TV, major credit cards. SGL/DBL$40-$70.

Days Inn East (Rte 896N, 17572; 299-6900, 800-325-2525) 52 rooms, restaurant, complimentary breakfast, lounge, pool, children stay free with parents, room service, laundry service, a/c, TV, free local calls, no pets, wheelchair access, no-smoking rooms, senior citizen rates, major credit cards. LS SGL/DBL$37-$57; HS SGL/DBL$55-$69.

Dutch Family Inn (2250 Lincoln Hwy East, 17602; 393-5499) SGL/DBL$38-$43.

Econo Lodge South (2140 Hwy 30 East, 17602; 397-1900, 800-4-CHOICE) complimentary breakfast, pool, children under 12 stay free with parents, pets allowed, senior citizen rates, wheelchair access, a/c, TV, major credit cards. SGL/DBL$30-$70.

Garden Spot Motel (2291 Hwy 30 East, 17602; 394-4736) restaurant, a/c, TV, no-smoking rooms, major credit cards. SGL/DBL$45-$55.

Hampton Inn (Rte 30 and Greenfield Rd, 17602; 299-1200, 800-HAMPTON) restaurant, complimentary breakfast, outdoor pool, exercise facilities, children under 18 stay free with parents, no-smoking rooms, wheelchair access, whirlpools, in-room computer hookups, fax service, TV, a/c, free local calls, pets allowed, meeting facilities, major credit cards. SGL/DBL$65-$67.

Hilton Garden Inn (101 Granite Run Dr, 17601; Hotel 800-HILTONS) 155 rooms and suites, restaurant, lounge, entertainment, indoor pool, exercise facilities, free local calls, in-room coffee makers, children stay free with parents, no-smoking rooms, wheelchair access, pets OK, a/c, TV, business services, meeting facilities, major credit cards. SGL/DBL$85-$100.

Historic Smithton Country Inn (900 West Main St, 17522; 733-6094) complimentary breakfast, fireplace, antique furnishings, no smoking, major credit cards. SGL/DBL$55-$115.

Holiday Inn (521 Greenfield Rd, 17601; 299-2551, Fax 397-0220, 800-HOLIDAY) 189 rooms, restaurant, lounge, entertainment, indoor pool, exercise facilities, children under 19 stay free with parents, wheelchair access, a/c, TV, no-smoking rooms, fax, room service, no pets, laundry service, meeting facilities for 350, senior citizen rates, major credit cards. SGL/DBL$55-$68.

Holiday Inn (1492 Lititz Pike, 17601; 393-0771, Fax 299-6238, 800-HOLIDAY) 160 rooms, restaurant, lounge, outdoor pool, exercise facilities, children under 19 stay free with parents, wheelchair access, a/c, TV, no-smoking rooms, fax service, room service, no pets, laundry service, meeting facilities for 300, senior citizen rates, major credit cards. SGL/DBL$55-$89.

Hollinger House (2336 Hollinger Rd, 17602; 464-3050) bed and breakfast, no smoking, private baths, no pets, 1870s home, children under 6 stay free with parents. SGL/DBL$38-$60.

Hotel Brunswick (Lancaster, 17602; 397-4801, 800-233-0182) 225 rooms and suites, restaurant, lounge, indoor pool, exercise facilities, a/c, TV, major credit cards. SGL/DBL$48-$68.

Howard Johnson Lodge (2100 Lincoln Hwy East, 17602; 397-7781, Fax 397-6340, 800-I-GO-HOJO) 112 rooms, restaurant, lounge, pool, children stay free with parents, wheelchair access, game room, VCRs, gift shop, no-smoking rooms, TV, a/c, no pets, free parking, meeting facilities, senior citizen rates, major credit cards. LS SGL$44-$48, DBL$50-$60; HS SGL$58-$62, DBL$75-$92.

Kings Cottage (1949 King St, 17603; 397-1017) complimentary breakfast, no smoking, no pets, private baths, a/c, fireplace, no children allowed, major credit cards. SGL/DBL$80-$115.

Lancaster Host Resort (2300 Lincoln Hwy, 17602; 299-5500, 800-233-0121) restaurant, lounge, pool, tennis courts, game room, golf, a/c, TV, major credit cards. SGL/DBL$65-$85.

Lincoln Haus Inn (1687 Lincoln Hwy, 17602; 392-9412) free breakfast, 1680s inn, private baths, a/c, major credit cards. SGL/DBL$35-$65.

Super 8 Motel (2129 Lincoln Hwy, 17602; 393-8888, Fax 393-8888 ext 343, 800-800-8000) 101 rooms and suites, no pets, children under 12 stay free with parents, free local calls, a/c, TV, fax service, no-smoking rooms, senior citizen rates, wheelchair access, meeting facilities, major credit cards. LS SGL$31, DBL$37; HS SGL$35, DBL$41.

New Life Homestead Bed and Breakfast (1400 East King St, 17602; 398-8928) complimentary breakfast, no smoking, no pets, major credit cards. SGL/DBL$37-$60.

O'Flaherty's Dingeldein House (1105 East King St, 17602; 293-1723) bed and breakfast, no smoking, private baths, no pets, major credit cards. SGL/DBL$59-$69.

TraveLodge (2101 Columbia Ave, 17603; 397-4201, Fax 397-7842, 800-255-3050) 58 rooms, restaurant, lounge, entertainment, complimentary breakfast, pool, wheelchair access, free newspaper, laundry service, TV, a/c, free local calls, fax service, no-smoking rooms, free in-room coffee and tea service, in-room refrigerators and microwaves, no pets, meeting facilities for 100, major credit cards. LS SGL/DBL$44-$62; HS SGL/DBL$75-$85.

Witmer's Tavern (2014 Old Philadelphia Pike, 17602; 299-5305) free breakfast, 1725 inn, no pets, antique furnishings, fireplace. SGL/DBL$60-$80.

Landenberg
Area Code 215

Cornerstone Bed and Breakfast (Newark and Buttonwoods Rds., 19350; 274-2143) rooms and apartments, complimentary breakfast, pool, antique furnishings, kitchenettes, major credit cards. SGL/DBL$55-$70.

Langhorn
Area Code 215

Red Roof Inn (3100 Cabot Blvd West, 19047; 750-600, Fax 750-6205, 800-843-7663) 92 rooms, wheelchair access, no-smoking rooms, children stay free with parents, major credit cards. SGL/DBL$50.

Royce Hotel Bucks County (400 Oxford Valley Rd, 19047; 547-4100, Fax 547-4100 ext 297) 167 rooms and suites, restaurant, lounge, indoor pool, sauna, exercise facilities, major credit cards. SGL/DBL$79-$135.

Sheraton Bucks County Hotel (400 Oxford Valley Rd, 19047; 547-4100, Fax 547-4100 ext 297, 800-325-3535) 167 rooms and suites, restaurant, lounge, indoor pool, exercise facilities, whirlpools, sauna, no-smoking rooms, a/c, TV, children stay free with parents, wheelchair access, 10,500 square feet of meeting and exhibition space, meeting facilities for 1,200, major credit cards. SGL/DBL$110-$150.

Lebanon
Area Code 717

Quality Inn Lebanon Valley (625 Quentin Rd, 17042; 273-6771, 800-368-5689) 130 rooms and suites, restaurant, room service, exercise facilities, children stay free with parents, a/c, TV, laundry service, no-smoking rooms, meeting facilities, major credit cards. SGL/DBL$63-$94.

Lehigh Valley
Area Code 215

Holiday Inn (Lehigh Valley, 18002; 391-1000, Fax 391-1664, 800-HOLIDAY) 182 rooms, restaurant, lounge, entertainment, exercise facilities, children under 19 stay free with parents, wheelchair access, a/c, TV, no-smoking rooms, fax service, room service, no pets, laundry service, meeting facilities for 1,200, senior citizen rates, major credit cards. SGL/DBL$55-$78.

Leola
Area Code 717

Turtle Hill Bed and Breakfast (Turtle Hill Rd, 17540; 656-6163) complimentary breakfast, no smoking, no pets, water view, major credit cards. SGL/DBL$30-$45.

Levittown
Area Code 215

Comfort Inn (6401 Bristol Pkwy, 19057; 547-5000, 800-221-2222) 75 rooms, restaurant, exercise facilities, wheelchair access, no-smoking rooms, no pets, children under 18 stay free with parents, senior citizen rates, a/c, TV, meeting facilities, major credit cards. SGL/DBL$48-$85.

Lewisburg
Area Code 717

Days Inn (Rte 15, 17837; 523-1171, Fax 524-4667, 800-325-2525) 108 rooms and suites, restaurant, lounge, outdoor pool, exercise facilities, in-room computer hookups, free parking, children stay free with parents, room service, laundry service, a/c, TV, free local calls, no pets, wheelchair access, no-smoking rooms, senior citizen rates, major credit cards. SGL/DBL$50-$64, STS$95-$120.

The Inn on Fiddler's Tract (Rte 192W, 17837; 523-7197) 5 suites, bed and breakfast, 1800s inn, on 33 acres, no smoking, no pets, private baths, jacuzzi, sauna, major credit cards. SGL/DBL$65-$96.

Lewistown
Area Code 717

Holiday Inn (State Rd 322, 17009, 800-HOLIDAY) 124 rooms, restaurant, lounge, outdoor pool, exercise facilities, children under 19 stay free with parents, wheelchair access, a/c, TV, no-smoking rooms, fax service, room service, no pets, laundry service, meeting facilities for 225, senior citizen rates, major credit cards. SGL/DBL$39-$65.

Lionville
Area Code 215

Hampton Inn (4 North Pottstown Pike, 19341; 363-5555, Fax 363-4969, 800-HAMPTON) 122 rooms, restaurant, complimentary breakfast, pool, exercise facilities, children under 18 stay free with parents, no-smoking rooms, wheelchair access, computer hookups, fax service, TV, a/c, free local calls, pets allowed, meeting facilities, major credit cards. SGL$52, DBL$57-$69.

Lock Haven
Area Code 717

Days Inn (101 East Walnut St, 17745; 748-3297, Fax 748-5390, 800-325-2525) 53 rooms, restaurant, lounge, pool, children stay free with parents, room service, laundry service, a/c, TV, free local calls, no pets, airport courtesy car, wheelchair access, no-smoking rooms, senior citizen rates, meeting facilities for 150, major credit cards. SGL/DBL$47-$52.

Lumberville
Area Code 215

1740 House (River Rd, 18933; 297-5661) 24 rooms, complimentary breakfast, no smoking, no pets, water view, private baths, major credit cards. SGL/DBL$65.

Malvern
Area Code 215

Hilton Great Valley Hotel and Conference Center (One Liberty Blvd, 19355; 296-9800, Fax 889-9869, 800-HILTONS) 201 rooms and suites, restaurant, free breakfast, lounge, entertainment, indoor pool, exercise facilities, whirlpools, tennis courts, free parking, children stay free with parents, no-smoking rooms, wheelchair access, pets allowed, free newspaper, a/c, TV, business services, meeting facilities, major credit cards. SGL/DBL$75-$135.

Summerfield Suites Hotel (20 Morehall Rd, 19355; 296-4343, Fax 296-3942, 800-833-4353) 1- and 2-bedroom suites, complimentary breakfast, pool, whirlpools, exercise facilities, VCRs, TV, a/c, no-smoking rooms, major credit cards. SGL/DBL$119-$159.

Mansfield
Area Code 717

Comfort Inn (300 Gateway Dr, 16933; 662-3000, 800-221-2222) 100 rooms, restaurant, whirlpools, exercise facilities, wheelchair access, no-smoking rooms, no pets, children under 18 stay free with parents, senior citizen rates, a/c, TV, meeting facilities, major credit cards. SGL/DBL$49-$79.

Crossroads Bed and Breakfast (131 South Main St, 16933; 662-7008) 4 rooms, complimentary breakfast, no smoking, private baths, whirlpool tub, no children allowed, a/c, no pets, TV. SGL/DBL$40-$65.

Marietta
Area Code 717

The Vogt Farm (1225 Colebook Rd, 17547; 653-4810) bed and breakfast, TV, a/c, no smoking, no pets, fireplace, 1860s home. SGL/DBL$32-$50.

Mars
Area Code 412

Days Inn (909 Sheraton Dr, 16046; 772-2700, Fax 772-2710, 800-325-2525) 104 rooms, restaurant, lounge, children stay free with parents, room service, laundry service, a/c, TV, free local calls, pets allowed, wheelchair access, no-smoking rooms, senior citizen rates, major credit cards. SGL/DBL$48-$64.

Sheraton Inn North (910 Sheraton Drive, 16046; 776-6900, Fax 776-1115, 800-325-3535) 194 rooms and suites, restaurant, lounge, indoor and outdoor pool, exercise facilities, jacuzzi, sauna, no-smoking rooms, a/c, TV, children stay free with parents, wheelchair access, beauty shop, limousine service, boutiques, 17,800 square feet of meeting and exhibition space, 13 meeting rooms, meeting facilities for 1,400, major credit cards. SGL/DBL$65-$125.

Meadville
Area Code 814

Days Inn (240 Conneaut Lake Rd, 16335; 337-4264, Fax 337-7304, 800-325-2525) 163 rooms, restaurant, lounge, indoor pool, hot tubs, children stay free with parents, room service, laundry service, a/c, TV, free local calls, no pets, wheelchair access, no-smoking rooms, senior citizen rates, major credit cards. SGL/DBL$39-$75.

Super 8 Motel (845 Conneaut Lake Rd, 16335; 333-8883, Fax 333-8883, 800-800-8000) 62 rooms and suites, no pets, children under 12 stay free with parents, free local calls, a/c, TV, fax service, no-smoking rooms, senior citizen rates, wheelchair access, meeting facilities, major credit cards. SGL/DBL$38-$44.

Mechanicsburg
Area Code 717

Comfort Inn (6325 Carlisle Pike, 17055; 790-0924, 800-221-2222) 125 rooms, restaurant, exercise facilities, wheelchair access, no-smoking rooms, no pets, children under 18 stay free with parents, senior citizen rates, a/c, TV, meeting facilities, major credit cards. SGL/DBL$49-$99.

Hampton Inn (4950 Ritter Rd, 17055; 691-1300, Fax 691-9692, 800-HAMPTON) 129 rooms, restaurant, free breakfast, pool, exercise facilities, children under 18 stay free with parents, no-smoking rooms, wheelchair access, computer hookups, fax service, TV, a/c, free local calls, pets allowed, meeting facilities, major credit cards. SGL$62-$65, DBL$69-$72.

Holiday Inn (5401 Carlisle Pike, 17055; 697-0321, Fax 697-7594, 800-HOLIDAY) 100 rooms, restaurant, lounge, outdoor pool, exercise facilities, children under 19 stay free with parents, wheelchair access, a/c, TV, no-smoking rooms, fax, room service, no pets, laundry service, meeting facilities for 150, senior citizen rates, major credit cards. SGL/DBL$68-$74.

Mendenhall
Area Code 215

Fairville Inn (Kennett Pike, 19357; 388-5900) 15 rooms and suites, complimentary breakfast, fireplaces, major credit cards. SGL/DBL$45-$65.

Mercer
Area Code 412

Howard Johnson Lodge (Rte 19, 16137; 748-3030, Fax 748-3484, 800-I-GO-HOJO) 102 rooms, restaurant, lounge, pool, sauna, children stay free with parents, wheelchair access, no-smoking rooms, free local calls, room service, gift shop, laundry facilities, game room, TV, a/c, pets allowed, free parking, meeting facilities, senior citizen rates, major credit cards. SGL/DBL$58-$64.

Stranahan House Bed and Breakfast (117 East Market St, 16127; 662-4516) complimentary breakfast, no smoking, private baths, no pets, antique furnishings, major credit cards. SGL/DBL$55-$65.

Mercersburg
Area Code 717

Mercersburg Inn (405 South Main St, 17236; 328-5231, Fax 328-3403) 15 rooms, bed and breakfast, restaurant, private baths, major credit cards. SGL/DBL$75-$125.

Mertztown
Area Code 215

Longswamp Bed and Breakfast (Mertztown 19539; 682-6197) complimentary breakfast, on 40 acres, no smoking, no pets, private baths, major credit cards. SGL/DBL$55-$70.

Middlesex & West Middlesex
Area Code 412

Comfort Inn (State Rd 18 and Wilson Rd, 16159; 342-7200, 800-221-2222) 61 rooms, restaurant, indoor pool, whirlpools, wheelchair access, no-smoking rooms, no pets, children under 18 stay free with parents, senior citizen rates, a/c, TV, meeting facilities, major credit cards. SGL/DBL$40-$70.

Holiday Inn (3200 South Hermitage Rd, 16159; 981-1530, 981-1518, 800-HOLIDAY) 180 rooms, restaurant, lounge, outdoor pool, exercise facilities, children under 19 stay free with parents, wheelchair access, a/c, game room, TV, no-smoking rooms, fax service, room service, no pets, laundry service, meeting facilities for 150, senior citizen rates, major credit cards. SGL/DBL$62-$75.

Ramada Inn (Rte 19, 16159; 528-2501, Fax 528-2306, 800-2-RAMADA) 154 rooms, restaurant, lounge, entertainment, indoor pool, sauna, whirlpools, wheelchair access, no-smoking rooms, airport transportation, free parking, pets allowed, a/c, TV, room service, laundry facilities, meeting facilities for 600, senior citizen rates, major credit cards. SGL$57-$80, DBL$65-$90, STS$100, AP$8.

Middletown
Area Code 717

Days Inn Airport (815 Eisenhower Blvd, 17057; 939-1600, Fax 939-8763, 800-325-2525) 183 rooms, restaurant, complimentary breakfast, lounge, indoor pool, children stay free with parents, room service, laundry service, a/c, TV, airport transportation, free local calls, no pets, wheelchair access, no-smoking rooms, senior citizen rates, major credit cards. LS SGL/DBL$49-$64, STS$64-$75; HS SGL/DBL$73-$79, STS$89-$99.

Mifflinville
Area Code 717

Super 8 Motel (Mifflinville, 18631; 759-6778, 800-800-8000) 30 rooms and suites, no pets, children under 12 stay free with parents, free local calls, a/c, TV, fax service, no-smoking rooms, senior citizen rates, wheelchair access, meeting facilities, major credit cards. SGL/DBL$38-$46.

Milesburg
Area Code 814

Days Inn State College (Milesburg, 16853; 355-7521, 800-325-2525) 115 rooms, restaurant, lounge, outdoor pool, children stay free with parents, room service, laundry service, a/c, TV, free local calls, pets allowed, wheelchair access, no-smoking rooms, senior citizen rates, meeting facilities for 225, major credit cards. SGL/DBL$35-$50.

Milford
Area Code 717

Black Walnut Bed and Breakfast (Milford, 18337; 296-6322) complimentary breakfast, on 160 acres, no smoking, private baths, no pets, major credit cards. SGL/DBL$60-$85.

Monroeville
Area Code 412

Howard Johnson (2750 Mosside Blvd, 15146; 372-1022) 190 rooms, restaurant, lounge, entertainment, pool, airport transportation, 11 meeting rooms, meeting facilities for 300, major credit cards. SGL/DBL$48-$59.

The Palace Inn (Monroeville 15146; 372-5500, Fax 372-5500 ext 402) 261 rooms and suites, restaurant, lounge, entertainment, indoor pool, airport transportation, no-smoking rooms, wheelchair access, laundry service, meeting facilities, major credit cards. SGL/DBL$65-$95.

Radisson Hotel (101 Mall Blvd, 15146; 800-245-EXPO) 330 rooms and suites, restaurant, lounge, entertainment, indoor and outdoor pool, exercise facilities, spa, limousine service, in-room refrigerators, wheelchair access, no-smoking rooms, airport transportation, 5 meeting rooms, meeting facilities for 1,300, major credit cards. SGL/DBL$115.

Red Roof Inn (2729 Mosside Blvd, 15146; 856-4738, Fax 856-4758, 800-843-7663) 123 rooms, no-smoking rooms, fax service, wheelchair access, complimentary newspaper, free local calls, in-room computer hookups, major credit cards. SGL/DBL$35-$48.

Montgomery
Area Code 215

Comfort Inn (678 Bethlehem Pike, 18936; 361-3600, 800-221-2222) 84 rooms, restaurant, whirlpools, wheelchair access, no-smoking rooms, no pets, children under 18 stay free with parents, senior citizen rates, a/c, TV, meeting facilities, major credit cards. SGL$60-$90, DBL$65-$102.

Montoursville
Area Code 717

Super 8 Motel (2815 Old Montoursville Rd, 17754; 368-8111, Fax 368-8555, 800-800-8000) 43 rooms and suites, no pets, children under 12 stay free with parents, free local calls, a/c, TV, fax service, no-smoking rooms, senior citizen rates, wheelchair access, meeting facilities, major credit cards. SGL/DBL$40-$52.

Montrose
Area Code 717

The Montrose House (26 South Main St, 18801; 278-1124) bed and breakfast, open year-round, private baths, major credit cards. SGL/DBL$35-$60.

Moosic
Area Code 717

Days Inn (4130 Birney Ave, 18507; 457-6713, Fax 457-4479, 800-325-2525) 46 rooms and 3-room suites, restaurant, lounge, children stay free with parents, room service, laundry service, a/c, TV, free local calls, kitchenettes, no pets, wheelchair access, no-smoking rooms, senior citizen rates, meeting facilities for 1,000, major credit cards. SGL/DBL$35-$55, STS$75-$225.

Morgantown
Area Code 215

Holiday Inn (Turnpike Exit 22, 19543; 286-3000, Fax 286-0520, 800-HOLIDAY) 197 rooms, restaurant, lounge, entertainment, indoor pool, exercise facilities, children under 19 stay free with parents, wheelchair access, a/c, TV, no-smoking rooms, fax service, room service, pets allowed, laundry service, meeting facilities for 350, senior citizen rates, major credit cards. SGL/DBL$65-95.

Mount Joy
Area Code 717

Cameron Estate Inn (1895 Donegal Springs Rd, 17552; 653-1773) 18 rooms, restaurant, fireplace, a/c, TV, on 15 acres, 1885 inn, major credit cards. SGL/DBL$60-$110.

Cedar Hill Farm (305 Longenecker Rd, 17552; 653-4655) complimentary breakfast, 1817 home, no smoking, private baths, no pets, major credit cards. SGL/DBL$48-$65.

Green Acres Farm (1382 Pinkerton Rd, 17552; 653-4028) bed and breakfast, private baths, on 160 acres, working farm, antique furnishings, major credit cards. SGL/DBL$32-$53.

Mt. Pocono
Area Code 717

Country Road Bed and Breakfast (Grange Rd, 18344; 839-9234) 5 rooms, complimentary breakfast, no smoking, private baths, no pets, on 4 acres. SGL/DBL$60-$100.

Muncy
Area Code 717

The Bodine House (302 South Main St, 17756; 546-8949) bed and breakfast, no smoking, private baths, no pets, antique furnishings, 1800s home, no children allowed, major credit cards. SGL/DBL$38-$60.

New Bloomfield
Area Code 717

The Tressler House Bed and Breakfast (41 West Main St, 17068; 582-2914) complimentary breakfast, no smoking, private baths, antique furnishings, no pets, no children allowed, major credit cards. SGL/DBL$43-$53.

New Brighton
Area Code 412

New Brighton Bed and Breakfast (928 Sixth Ave, 15066; 847-2094) 2 rooms, complimentary breakfast, major credit cards. SGL$25, DBL$40.

New Castle
Area Code 412

Comfort Inn (1740 New Butler Rd, 16101; 658-7700, 800-221-2222) 79 rooms, restaurant, lounge, entertainment, sauna, exercise facilities, wheelchair access, no-smoking rooms, no pets, children under 18 stay free with parents, senior citizen rates, a/c, TV, meeting facilities, major credit cards. LS SGL/DBL$44-$85; HS SGL/DBL$50-$110.

Days Inn (30 East St, 16101; 652-9991, Fax 652-2092, 800-325-2525) 50 rooms and suites, restaurant, complimentary breakfast, lounge, pool, jacuzzis, children stay free with parents, room service, laundry service, a/c, TV, free local calls, no pets, wheelchair access, no-smoking rooms, senior citizen rates, major credit cards. SGL/DBL$42-$74, STS$90-$120.

Super 8 Motel (1699 Butler Rd, 16101; 658-8849, 800-800-8000) 57 rooms and suites, no pets, children under 12 stay free with parents, free local calls, a/c, TV, fax service, no-smoking rooms, senior citizen rates, wheelchair access, meeting facilities, major credit cards. SGL/DBL$35-$41.

New Columbia
Area Code 717

Comfort Inn (Hwy 15 and I-80, 17856; 568-8000, 800-221-2222) 120 rooms, restaurant, pool, whirlpools, wheelchair access, no-smoking rooms, no pets, children under 18 stay free with parents, senior citizen rates, a/c, TV, meeting facilities, major credit cards. SGL/DBL$44-$68.

New Cumberland
Area Code 717

Farm Fortune (204 Limekiln Rd, 17070; 774-2683) 4 rooms, complimentary breakfast, 1730s home, private baths, children over 10 welcome, antique furnishings. SGL/DBL$65-$85.

Radisson Hotel (175 Beacon Hill Blvd, 17070; 774-6200, Fax 774-6200, 800-777-1700) rooms and suites, restaurant, lounge, entertainment, pool, wheelchair access, free parking, no-smoking rooms, TV, a/c, children stay free with parents, pets allowed, senior citizen rates, major credit cards. SGL/DBL$80-$125.

New Holland
Area Code 717

Comfort Inn (624 West Main St, 17557; 355-9900, 800-296-4661, 800-221-2222) 69 rooms, restaurant, pool, exercise facilities, wheelchair access, no-smoking rooms, no pets, children under 18 stay free with parents, senior citizen rates, a/c, TV, meeting facilities, major credit cards. SGL/DBL$50-$75.

New Hope
Area Code 215

The Golden Plough Inn (New Hope, 18938; 794-4004) 45 rooms, free breakfast, no smoking, jacuzzis, in-room refrigerators, a/c, no pets, private baths, TV, major credit cards. SGL/DBL$115.

Holiday Inn (Rte 202, 18938; 862-5221, 800-222-HOPE, 800-HOLIDAY) 159 rooms, restaurant, lounge, entertainment, outdoor pool, exercise facilities, children under 19 stay free with parents, wheelchair access, a/c, TV, no-smoking rooms, fax service, room service, no pets, laundry service, meeting facilities for 300, senior citizen rates, major credit cards. SGL/DBL$79-$95.

The Wedgewood Inn Of New Hope (111 West Bridge St, 18938; 862-2570) free breakfast, no smoking, no children allowed, private baths, a/c, fireplaces, major credit cards. SGL/DBL$65-$170.

New Stanton
Area Code 412

Days Inn (127 West Byers Ave, 15672; 925-3591, Fax 925-9859, 800-325-2525) 140 rooms, restaurant, lounge, outdoor pool, children stay free with parents, room service, laundry service, a/c, TV, beauty shop, free local calls, no pets, wheelchair access, no-smoking rooms, senior citizen rates, meeting facilities for 300, major credit cards. SGL/DBL$45-$60.

Knights Inn (110 North Main St, 15672; 925-6755, 800-843-5644) restaurant, pool, wheelchair access, no-smoking rooms, TV, a/c, in-room refrigerators and microwaves, fax service, free parking, VCRs, senior citizen rates, major credit cards. SGL/DBL$60-$70.

Howard Johnson Lodge (112 West Byers Ave, 15672; 925-3511, Fax 925-3511, ext 500, 800-I-GO-HOJO) 87 rooms, restaurant, lounge, pool, children stay free with parents, wheelchair access, no-smoking rooms, in-room refrigerators, free local calls, room service, TV, a/c, pets allowed, free parking, meeting facilities, senior citizen rates, major credit cards. LS SGL$37-$45, DBL$40-$49; HS SGL$38-$48, DBL$44-$52.

Super 8 Motel (103 Blair Blvd, 15672; 925-8915, 800-800-8000) 62 rooms and suites, no pets, children under 12 stay free with parents, free local calls, a/c, TV, fax service, no-smoking rooms, senior citizen rates, wheelchair access, meeting facilities, major credit cards. SGL/DBL$35-$41.

North Wales
Area Code 215

Joseph Amber Inn (1005 Horsham Rd, 19454; 362-7500) 26 rooms, complimentary breakfast, on 13 acres, no pets, private baths, antique furnishings, major credit cards. SGL/DBL$80-$140.

Oakdale
Area Code 412

Comfort Inn Parkway West (7011 Old Steubenville Pike, 15071; 787-2600, 800-221-2222) 75 rooms, restaurant, lounge, complimentary breakfast, exercise facilities, airport courtesy car, wheelchair access, no-smoking rooms, no pets, major credit cards. SGL/DBL$40-$65.

Oil City
Area Code 814

Holiday Inn (1 Seneca St, 16301; 677-1221, Fax 677-0492, 800-HOLIDAY) 104 rooms, restaurant, lounge, outdoor pool, exercise facilities, children under 19 stay free with parents, wheelchair access, a/c, TV, no-smoking rooms, fax, room service, no pets, laundry service, meeting facilities for 150, senior citizen rates, major credit cards. SGL/DBL$59-$76.

Old Bethlehem
Area Code 215

Sign Of The Sorrel Horse (Old Bethlehem 18951; 536-4651) 5 rooms, complimentary breakfast, restaurant, 1740s home, no smoking, antique furnishings, no children allowed, private baths, major credit cards. SGL/DBL$90-$130.

Orrtanna
Area Code 717

Hickory Bridge Farm (96 Hickory Bridge Rd, 17353; 642-5261) bed and breakfast, no smoking, private baths, 1750s home, no pets, major credit cards. SGL/DBL$50-$80.

Oxford
Area Code 215

Log House Bed and Breakfast (15250 Limestone Rd, 19363; 932-9257) complimentary breakfast, no smoking, private baths, open year-round. SGL/DBL$35-$40.

Paradise
Area Code 717

Best Western Revere Inn (Rte 30, 17562; 687-7683, 800-528-1234) 29 rooms and suites, restaurant, complimentary breakfast, lounge, outdoor pool, exercise facilities, children stay free with parents, a/c, TV, no-smoking rooms, wheelchair access, pets allowed, senior citizen rates, meeting facilities, major credit cards. SGL/DBL$34-$66.

Maple Lane Guest House (505 Paradise Lane, 17562; 687-7479) 4 rooms, complimentary breakfast, on 200 acres, no smoking, no pets, private baths, antique furnishings, major credit cards. SGL/DBL$40-$60.

Philadelphia
Area Code 215

Rental and Reservation Services

All About Town Bed and Breakfast In Philadelphia (Box 562, Valley Forge 19481; 783-7838, Fax 783-7783, 800-344-0123).

Bed and Breakfast Connection (Box 21, Devon 10333; 687-3565, 800-448-3619).

Pennsylvania

Bed and Breakfast in Philadelphia (1616 Walnut St, 19103; 735-1917, 800-220-1917).

Bed and Breakfast Center City (1804 Pine St, 19103; 735-1137).

University City Guest House Rentals (2933 Morris Rd, 19151; 387-3731).

Downtown Area and Business District

Bag and Baggage Bed and Breakfast (338 South 10th St, 19103; 546-3807) 18 rooms, complimentary breakfast, private baths. SGL$44-$69, DBL$54-$79.

The Barclay Hotel (237 South 18th St, 19103; 545-0300, Fax 545-2896, 800-533-6622) 240 rooms and suites, restaurant, lounge, entertainment, exercise center, transportation to local attractions, wheelchair access, no-smoking, a/c, pets allowed, airport courtesy car, 11 meeting rooms, meeting facilities for 300, major credit cards. Near Rittenhouse Sq. SGL/DBL$68.

Center City B&B (1804 Pine St, 19103; 735-1137, 800-354-8401) 15 rooms and suites, complimentary breakfast. SGL/DBL$45-$74.

Embassy Suites Hotel Center City (1776 Ben Franklin Pkwy, 19103; 561-1776, 800-EMBASSY) 288 2-room suites, free breakfast, exercise center. in-room refrigerators and microwaves, airport transportation, wheelchair access, no-smoking, a/c, meeting facilities for 50, major credit cards. SGL/DBL$95-$135.

Four Seasons Hotel (One Logan Sq., 19103; 963-1500, Fax 963-9562, 800-332-3442) 377 rooms and suites, 2 restaurants, 2 lounges, indoor pool, sauna, exercise center, laundry service, beauty shop, wheelchair access, no-smoking, a/c, pets allowed, 24-hour room service, airport courtesy car, meeting facilities for 1,000, major credit cards. SGL/DBL$125-$155.

Holiday Inn (1800 Market St, 19103; 561-750, Fax 561-4484, 800-HOLIDAY) 447 rooms and suites, 2 restaurants, lounge, outdoor pool, exercise center, children stay free with parents, wheelchair access, laundry service, no-smoking, a/c, fax service, room service, gift shop, meeting facilities for 900, major credit cards. 6 miles from the Philadelphia International Airport, 1 mile from the Civic Center. SGL/DBL$85-$135.

Holiday Inn Midtown (1305-11 Walnut St, 19107; 735-9300, Fax 732-2682, 800-HOLIDAY) 161 rooms and suites, restaurant, lounge, children stay free with parents, wheelchair access, no-smoking rooms, a/c, fax service, room service, meeting facilities for 250, major credit cards. 6 miles from the Philadelphia International Airport, 2 miles from the Civic Center. SGL/DBL$70-$125.

Hotel Atop The Bellevue (1415 Chancellor Court, 19102; 893-1776, Fax 893-9868, 800-221-0833) 170 rooms and suites, restaurant, lounge, indoor pool, exercise center, whirlpools, barber and beauty shop, VCRs, boutiques, transportation to local attractions, free newspaper, 24-hour room service, in-room computer hookups, babysitting services, wheelchair access, no-smoking rooms, a/c, 24,000 square feet of meeting and exhibition space, meeting facilities for 1,000, major credit cards. In the theater and financial districts, 1 mile from the Liberty Bell. SGL$210-$230, DBL$230-$260, STS$260.

Korman Suites Hotel (2001 Hamilton St, 19130; 569-7000, Fax 569-0584, 800-626-2651) 304 rooms and 1- and 2-bedroom suites, restaurant, lounge, entertainment, complimentary breakfast, outdoor pool, exercise center, in-room refrigerators and microwaves, free parking, VCRs, transportation to local attractions, meeting facilities for 1,500, major credit cards. SGL/DBL$132, 1BR$152, 2BR$182.

Latham Hotel (135 South 17th St, 19103; 563-7474, Fax 563-4034, 800-528-4261) 140 rooms and suites, 2 restaurants, lounge, entertainment, indoor pool, exercise center, in-room refrigerators, free newspaper, meeting facilities for 120, major credit cards. Near Rittenhouse Sq. SGL$130-$160, DBL$150-$180, STS$325-$425.

Hilton & Towers (Broad St and Locust, 19107; 893-1600, Fax 893-1663, 800-HILTONS) 439 rooms and suites, Towers Floor, restaurant, lounge, indoor pool, whirlpools, exercise center, jogging track, wheelchair access, no-smoking rooms, a/c, room service, business services, 25,000 square feet of meeting and exhibition space, meeting facilities for 700, major credit cards. Near Independence Hall, 8 miles from the Philadelphia International Airport, 3 miles from Veterans Stadium. SGL$130, DBL$145, STS$250.

Palace Hotel (Ben Franklin Pkwy and 18th St, 19103; 963-2222) 276 rooms, pool, exercise center, airport courtesy car, meeting facilities, major credit cards. SGL/DBL$85-$135.

Radisson Suites (Benjamin Franklin Pkwy, 19103; 963-2222, Fax 963-2299, 800-333-3333) 253 suites, restaurant, lounge, in-room refrigerators, wheelchair access, no-smoking rooms, a/c, airport transportation, meeting facilities, major credit cards. SGL/DBL$90-$125.

Ramada Inn Center City (501 North 22nd St, 19130; 568-8300, Fax 557-0259, 800-2-RAMADA) 278 rooms, restaurant, lounge, entertainment, outdoor pool, children stay free with parents, wheelchair access, no-smoking rooms, a/c, airport transportation, gift shop, free parking, business services, 4 meeting rooms, meeting facilities for 190, major credit cards. 7 miles from the Philadelphia International Airport. SGL/DBL$59-$85, STS$85, AP$15.

The Rittenhouse Hotel (210 West Rittenhouse Sq., 19103; 546-9000, Fax 732-3364, 800-635-1042) 100 rooms and suites, 2 restaurants, 2 lounges, entertainment, indoor pool, exercise center, sauna, pets allowed, boutiques, airport transportation, barber and beauty shop, wheelchair access, 24-hour room service, VCRs, no-smoking rooms, a/c, 6 meeting rooms, meeting facilities for 350, major credit cards. On Rittenhouse Sq., 20 minutes from the Philadelphia International Airport. SGL$190-$235, DBL$215-$260, STS$300-$1,000.

Ritz Carlton (17th and Chestnut St, 19103; 563-1600, Fax 564-9559, 800-241-3333) 290 rooms and suites, Ritz Carlton Club, restaurant, lounge, entertainment, exercise center, sauna, 24-hour room service, no-smoking rooms, a/c, transportation to local attractions, gift shop, 2,500 square feet of meeting and exhibition space, 3 meeting rooms, meeting facilities for 600, major credit cards. SGL/DBL$125-$165, STS$250-$500.

Warwick Hotel (1701 Locust St, 19103; 735-6000, Fax 790-7766, 800-523-4210) 203 rooms and suites, 3 restaurants, lounge, entertainment, children stay free with parents, 24-hour room service, in-room refrigerators, boutiques, beauty shop, wheelchair access, no-smoking rooms, a/c, limousine service, airport transportation, fax service, business service, 11,000 square feet of meeting and exhibition space, meeting facilities for 800, major credit cards. Near Rittenhouse Sq., 8 miles from the airport. SGL$125-$140, DBL$135-$155, STS$155.

Wyndham Franklin Plaza (17th and Race St, 19103; 448-2000, Fax 448-2864, 800-822-4200) 758 rooms and suites, restaurant, lounge, entertainment, indoor pool, exercise center, jogging track, sauna, barber and beauty shop, transportation to local attractions, wheelchair access, no-smoking rooms, a/c, 55,000 square feet of meeting and exhibition space, major credit cards. meeting facilities for 2,500. Fifteen minutes from the Philadelphia International Airport. SGL$145-$165, DBL$165-$185, STS$275-$1,000.

Airport Area

Comfort Inn Airport (53 Industrial Hwy, 19029; 521-9800, 800-221-2222) 150 rooms, sauna, exercise center, wheelchair access, no-smoking rooms, a/c, meeting facilities, major credit cards. 3 miles from the Greater Philadelphia International Airport, 10 miles from the downtown area, 6 miles from the Convention Center. SGL/DBL$48-$78.

Days Inn Airport (4101 Island Ave, 19153; 492-0400, Fax 365-0635, 800-325-2525) 177 rooms, restaurant, lounge, outdoor pool, jogging track, free parking, airport courtesy car, wheelchair access, no-smoking rooms, a/c, 9 meeting rooms, meeting facilities for 350, major credit cards. 7 miles from the downtown area. SGL/DBL$59-$99.

Days Inn (2 Gateway Center, 19153; 492-0400, Fax 365-6035; 800-325-2525) 177 rooms, restaurant, lounge, outdoor pool, jogging track, exercise center, children stay free with parents, cable TV, fax service, free local calls, airport courtesy car, laundry service, wheelchair access, no-smoking rooms, a/c, meeting facilities for 120, major credit cards. 1 mile from the Philadelphia International Airport, 8 miles from the downtown area. SGL/DBL$59.

Embassy Suites Airport (9000 Bartram Ave, 19153; 365-4500, Fax 365-3195, 800-EMBASSY) 265 2-room suites, restaurant, complimentary breakfast, indoor pool, sauna, whirlpools, exercise center, gift shop, room service, laundry service, airport transportation, in-room refrigerators and microwaves, wheelchair access, meeting facilities for 600, major credit cards. 8 miles from the downtown area, 1.6 miles from the Philadelphia International Airport, 4 miles from the Civic Center and Veterans Stadium. SGL/DBL$78-$128.

Guest Quarters Suites Airport (1 Gateway Center, 19153; 365-6600, Fax 492-9858, 800-424-2900) 252 suites, complimentary breakfast, indoor and outdoor pool, exercise center, jogging track, airport courtesy car, gift shop, in-room refrigerators, meeting facilities for 200, major credit cards. SGL/DBL$89-$155.

Marriott Airport (4509 Island Ave, 19153; 365-4150, Fax 365-3875, 800-228-9290) 331 rooms and suites, 2 restaurants, lounge, entertainment, indoor pool, exercise center, whirlpools, sauna, gift shop, airport courtesy car, free parking, wheelchair access, no-smoking rooms, a/c, meeting facilities for 1,200, major credit cards. At the Philadelphia International Airport, 15 minutes from the downtown area. SGL$112, DBL$127.

Philadelphia Court Hotel (10th and Packer Ave, 19148; 755-9500, Fax 462-6947, 800-HILTONS) 238 rooms and suites, restaurant, lounge, outdoor pool, exercise center, wheelchair access, no-smoking rooms, a/c, limousine service, free parking, airport courtesy car, gift shop, business services, meeting facilities for 700, major credit cards. SGL$99-$119, DBL$114-$134.

Quality Inn Airport (2015 Penrose Ave, 19145; 755-6500, 800-228-5151) 240 rooms, pool, exercise center, airport courtesy car, meeting facilities, major credit cards. SGL/DBL$50-$53.

Radisson Hotel Airport (500 Stevens Drive, 19113; 521-5900, Fax 521-4362, 800-333-3333) 352 rooms and suites, restaurant, lounge, entertainment, indoor pool, whirlpools, exercise center, airport courtesy car, free parking, gift shop, car rental desk, 10,000 square feet of meeting and exhibition space, meeting facilities for 1,400. At the Philadelphia International Airport. SGL$109-$139, DBL$119-$149, STS$150.

Ramada Hotel and Conference Center (2015 Penrose Ave, 19145; 755-6500, Fax 465-7517, 800-2-RAMADA) 224 rooms, restaurant, lounge, children stay free with parents, wheelchair access, no-smoking rooms, a/c, airport transportation, pets allowed, meeting facilities, major credit cards. 1 mile from the

Convention Center, 3.5 miles from the Philadelphia International Airport, 7 miles from the downtown area. SGL$55-$85, DBL$65-$95, AP$6.

Historic Area

Antique Bed and Breakfast (341 South 12th St, 19107; 592-7802, Fax 592-9692) 8 rooms. SGL/DBL$45-$65

The Bank Street Hostel (32 South Bank St, 19106; 922-0222, Fax 922-4082, 800-392-HOSTEL) 23 rooms. SGL$14.

Best Western Independence Park Inn (235 Chestnut St, 19106; 922-4443, Fax 922-4487, 800-624-2988) 36 rooms, complimentary breakfast, wheelchair access, no-smoking rooms, a/c, meeting facilities, major credit cards. Near Independence Mall. SGL/DBL$90-$140.

Comfort Inn Penn's Landing (100 North Delaware Ave, 19106; 627-7900, Fax 238-0809, 800-221-2222) 188 rooms and suites, lounge, complimentary breakfast, transportation to local attraction, wheelchair access, no-smoking rooms, a/c, no pets, free parking, transportation to local attractions, meeting facilities for 200, major credit cards. Near Independence Hall and the Liberty Bell. SGL$68-$100, DBL$75-$110.

Hershey Hotel (Broad and Locust St, 19107; 893-1600, Fax 893-1663, 800-533-3131) 431 rooms and suites, restaurant, lounge, entertainment, indoor pool, exercise center, sauna, whirlpools, in-room refrigerators, gift shop, transportation to local attractions, wheelchair access, no-smoking rooms, a/c, airport courtesy car, meeting facilities, major credit cards. SGL/DBL$95-$250.

Holiday Inn (400 Arch St, 19106; 923-8660, Fax 923-4633, 800-843-2366, 800-HOLIDAY) 365 rooms and suites, 2 restaurants, 2 lounges, entertainment, outdoor pool, children stay free with parents, wheelchair access, no-smoking rooms, a/c, fax, gift shop, room service, meeting facilities for 500, major credit cards. Near Penns Landing, 4 miles from the Philadelphia International Airport and Sports Stadium. SGL/DBL$95-$105.

Independence Park Inn (235 Chestnut St, 19106; 922-4443, Fax 922-4487, 800-624-2988) 36 rooms, restaurant, complimentary breakfast, lounge, 4 meeting rooms, meeting facilities for 25, major credit cards. Near Independence National Historic Park and the Liberty Bell. SGL$115-$130, DBL$125-$140.

Omni Hotel At Independence Park (Fourth and Chestnut St, 19106; 925-0000, Fax 925-1263, 800-THE-OMNI) 150 rooms and suites, restaurant, lounge, entertainment, pool, exercise center, 24-hour room service, wheelchair access, VCRs, no a/c, business services, meeting facilities for 120, major credit cards. Near the historic area, Penn's Landing and South St, 8 miles from the Philadelphia International Airport. SGL$190, DBL$220.

Penns View Inn (Front and Market St, 19106; 922-7600, Fax 922-7642, 800-331-7634) 28 rooms, restaurant, complimentary breakfast, jacuzzi, room service, meeting facilities for 45, major credit cards. Near the Independence National Historic Park and the Liberty Bell. SGL/DBL$84-$140.

Quality Inn Chinatown Downtown Suites (1010 Race St, 19107; 922-1730, 800-221-2222) 96 rooms, complimentary breakfast, lounge, sauna, exercise center. wheelchair access, children stay free with parents, airport transportation, pets allowed, free parking, no-smoking rooms, a/c, 4 meeting rooms, meeting facilities for 350, major credit cards. Near Independence Hall and the Liberty Bell. SGL$75-$89, DBL$85-$99.

Sheraton Society Hill Hotel (1 Dock St, 19106; 238-6000, Fax 922-2709, 800-325-3535) 365 rooms and suites, restaurant, 2 lounges, entertainment, 24-hour room service, pool, sauna, exercise center, gift shop, children stay free with parents, boutiques, car rental desk, wheelchair access, no a/c, business services, 10 meeting rooms, 20,500 square feet of meeting and exhibition space, meeting facilities for 1,000, major credit cards. Near Independence Hall, Society Hill and the Liberty Bell, 10 miles from the Philadelphia International Airport. SGL$99-$175, DBL$99-$185.

Society Hill Inn (301 Chestnut St, 19106; 925-1395) 12 rooms, bed and breakfast, entertainment. SGL/DBL$80-$140.

Thomas Bond House (129 South Second St, 19106; 923-8523, 800-845-BOND) 12 rooms, complimentary breakfast, free parking, whirlpools, private baths, airport transportation, major credit cards. At the Independence National Historic Park. SGL/DBL$80-$150.

Northeast Philadelphia

Best Western of Philadelphia (11580 Roosevelt Blvd, 19116; 464-9500, Fax 464-8511, 800-528-1234) 101 rooms and suites, restaurant, complimentary breakfast, lounge, pool, jacuzzi, exercise center, free parking, transportation to local attractions, children stay free with parents, laundry service, 5 meeting rooms, meeting facilities for 900, major credit cards. Twelve miles from the downtown area. SGL/DBL$65-$105.

Chamounix Mansion Hostel (Chamounix Drive, 19131; 878-3676) 6 rooms, kitchen, laundry service. SGL$10-$12.

Sheraton Inn Northeast (9461 Roosevelt Blvd, 19114; 671-9600, Fax 464-7759, 800-354-4332, 800-325-3535) 192 rooms and suites, restaurant, lounge, entertainment, indoor pool, exercise center, no-smoking rooms, a/c, wheelchair access, free airport transportation, room service, 5 meeting rooms, 4,000 square feet of meeting and exhibition space, meeting facilities for 320, major credit cards. 20 minutes from the downtown area, 20 miles from the Philadelphia International Airport. SGL/DBL$65-$95, DBL$75-$105.

City Line

Adam's Mark (City Ave and Monument Rd, 19131; 581-5000, Fax 581-5069, 800-231-5858) 515 rooms and suites, restaurant, lounge, entertainment, indoor and outdoor pool, exercise center, jacuzzi, sauna, transportation local attractions, car rental desk, free parking, beauty shop, gift shop, wheelchair access, no-smoking rooms, a/c, in-room refrigerators, beauty shop, airport courtesy car, 50,000 square feet of meeting and exhibition space, major credit cards. SGL$120-$154, DBL$132-$164, STS$285-$810.

Holiday Inn (4100 Presidential Blvd, 19131; 477-0200, Fax 473-2709, 800-HOLIDAY) 343 rooms, restaurant, lounge, indoor and outdoor pool, whirlpools, exercise center, children stay free with parents, wheelchair access, no-smoking rooms, a/c, fax service, room service, gift shop, no pets, free parking, airport transportation, meeting facilities for 400, major credit cards. 6 miles from the downtown historic area, 12 miles from the Philadelphia International Airport, 10 miles from the Sports Complex. SGL/DBL$88-$98.

University City

Divine Tracy Hostel Hotel (20 South 36th St, 19104; 382-4310) 100 rooms, restaurant, laundry service, boutique. Near the University of Pennsylvania and Civic Center. SGL/DBL$20-$30.

International House Of Philadelphia (3701 Chestnut St, 19104; 387-5125, Fax 895-6562) 397 rooms and efficiencies, restaurant, gift shop, major credit cards. Near the University of Pennsylvania and Drexel University. SGL/DBL$49.

Penn Tower (Civic Center Blvd and 34th St, 19104; 387-8333, 800-356-7366) 182 rooms and suites, Concierge Level, restaurant, lounge, entertainment, sauna, exercise center, room service, wheelchair access, no-smoking rooms, a/c, children stay free with parents, airport transportation, business service, 9 meeting rooms, 5,000 square feet of meeting and exhibition space, meeting facilities for 500, major credit cards. Ten minutes from the downtown area, 8 miles from the airport. SGL/DBL$225-$375, STS$225-$475.

Sheraton University City Hotel (36th and Chestnut Sts, 19104; 387-8000, Fax 387-7920, 800-325-3535) 377 rooms and suites, restaurant, lounge, entertainment, outdoor pool, gift shop, wheelchair access, no-smoking rooms, a/c, 23 meeting rooms, 10,160 square feet of meeting and exhibition space, meeting facilities for 1,213, major credit cards. Near the Civic Center and University of Pennsylvania, 6 miles from the Philadelphia International Airport. SGL$124-$128, DBL$134-$138, STS$250-$350.

Other Locations

Days Inn (245 Easton Rd, 19044; 674-2500, 800-325-2525) 171 rooms, restaurant, complimentary breakfast, whirlpools, exercise center, children stay free with parents, cable TV, free local calls, wheelchair access, no-smoking rooms, a/c, meeting facilities for 70, major credit cards. SGL/DBL$58-$63.

Days Inn (530 Pennsylvania Ave, 19034; 643-1111, Fax 643-2159; 800-325-2525) 135 rooms and suites, restaurant, lounge, entertainment, children stay free with parents, cable TV, free local calls, wheelchair access, no-smoking rooms, a/c, pets allowed, fax service, meeting facilities for 300, major credit cards. 8 miles from the Philadelphia Zoo, 14 miles from Independence Hall. SGL$55-$85, DBL$65-$95, STS$116-$120, AP$10.

Days Inn (4200 Roosevelt Blvd, 19124; 289-9200, 800-325-2525) 115 rooms, free breakfast, jacuzzis, fax service, children stay free with parents, cable TV, fax service, no pets, free local calls, wheelchair access, no-smoking rooms, a/c, meeting facilities, major credit cards. 5 miles from the downtown area, 20 miles from the Philadelphia International Airport. SGL$50-$55, DBL$62-$67, AP$7.

Shippen Way Inn (416-418 Bainbridge St, 19147; 627-7266) 9 rooms, bed and breakfast, private baths. Near Penn's Landing. SGL/DBL$70-$150.

Pittsburgh
Area Code 412

Downtown Pittsburgh

Howard Johnson University Center (3401 Blvd of the Allies, 15213; 683-6100, Fax 682-6116, 800-245-4444, 800-441-3979 in Pennsylvania) 119 rooms, restaurant, lounge, outdoor pool, free parking, a/c, TV, 2 meeting rooms, meeting facilities for 100, major credit cards. Seventeen miles from Pittsburgh International Airport. SGL$64-$74, DBL$74-$84.

Hyatt Regency Chatham Center (112 Washington Place, 15219; 471-1234, Fax 355-0315, 800-228-9000) 400 rooms and suites, Regency Club, restaurant, lounge, entertainment, indoor pool, sauna, exercise center, wheelchair access, no-smoking rooms, a/c, TV, free newspaper, 14 meeting rooms, 24,000 square feet of meeting and exhibition space, audio-visual equipment, major credit cards. Near the Civic Area and Chatham Center, 20 minutes from the Greater Pittsburgh International Airport. SGL/DBL$135-$155.

Pittsburgh Hilton and Towers (Commonwealth Place, 15222; 391-4600, Fax 594-5161, 800-HILTONS) 718 rooms and suites, Towers Floor, 2 restaurants, 2 lounges, exercise center, sauna, no-smoking rooms, barber and beauty shop, airport courtesy car, in-room refrigerators, a/c, TV, wheelchair access, audio-visual equipment, airline ticket office, limousine service, 21 meeting rooms, meeting facilities for 1,900, major credit cards. Sixteen miles from the Greater Pittsburgh International Airport. SGL$75-$105, DBL$95-$135.

Ramada Suites Hotel (1 Bigelow Sq., 15219; 281-5800, Fax 281-8467, 800-228-2828, 800-225-5858) 300 suites, restaurant, lounge, entertainment, indoor pool, sauna, exercise center, jogging track, children stay free with parents, wheelchair access, no-smoking rooms, a/c, TV, airport transportation, barber and beauty shop, travel agency desk, business services, 5 meeting rooms, meeting facilities for 150, major credit cards. Within 5 miles of 3 Rivers Stadium and the University of Pittsburgh, .5 miles from the Convention Center and downtown area. STS$99-$165, AP$10.

Sheraton Hotel at Station Square (7 Station Square Drive, 15219; 261-2000, 800-325-3535) 293 rooms and suites, 2 restaurants, 2 lounges, entertainment, indoor pool, sauna, whirlpool, exercise center, free parking, no-smoking rooms, a/c, TV, wheelchair access, airport courtesy car, beauty shop, 21 meeting rooms, 22,650 square feet of meeting and exhibition space, meeting facilities for 2,260, major credit cards. Near Station Square, 16 miles from the Greater Pittsburgh International Airport. SGL/DBL$95-$105, STS$150.

Vista International Hotel (1000 Penn Ave, 15222; 281-3700, Fax 281-2652, 800-367-8478) 614 rooms and suites, 2 restaurants, lounge, entertainment, indoor pool, sauna, whirlpool, exercise center, children stay free with parents, 24-hour room service, in-room refrigerators, laundry service, concierge, no-smoking rooms, a/c, TV, wheelchair access, airport transportation, fax, audio-visual equipment, 18 meeting rooms, meeting facilities for 1,000, major credit cards. 16 miles from the Greater Pittsburgh International Airport. SGL$153-$196, DBL$175-$210, STS$240-$1,400.

Westin William Penn (530 William Penn Place, 15219; 281-7100, 800-228-3000) 595 rooms and suites, 3 restaurants, 2 lounges, entertainment, exercise center, jogging track, boutiques, pets allowed, 24-hour room service, no-smoking rooms, a/c, TV, barber shop, transportation to local attractions, wheelchair access, audio-visual equipment, 9 meeting rooms, meeting facilities for 1,000, major credit cards. In the business district near Mellon Square and 3 Rivers Stadium, 20 minutes from the Greater Pittsburgh International Airport. SGL$130-$155, DBL$150-$175, STS$275-$1450, AP$20.

East Pittsburgh

Conley Motor Inn (3550 William Penn Highway, 15235; 824-6000) 150 rooms, restaurant, lounge, indoor and outdoor pools, sauna, wheelchair access, a/c, TV, 4 meeting rooms, meeting facilities for 500, major credit cards. 8 miles from the downtown area. SGL/DBL$48-$68.

Hampton Inn (3315 Hamlet St, 15213; 681-1000, Fax 681-1000, 800-HAMPTON) 135 rooms, complimentary breakfast, children stay free with parents, no pets, no-smoking rooms, a/c, TV, wheelchair access, in-room computer hookups, fax service, free local calls, meeting facilities, major credit cards. 2 miles from the 3 Rivers Stadium, 16 miles from the Greater Pittsburgh International Airport. SGL$69-$79, DBL$77-$87.

Harley Hotel of Pittsburgh (699 Rodi Rd, 15235; 244-1600, 800-321-2323) 152 rooms and suites, restaurant, lounge, entertainment, indoor and outdoor pools, sauna, whirlpool, exercise center, tennis courts, no-smoking rooms, a/c, TV, wheelchair access, free parking, audio-visual equipment, limousine service, airport courtesy car, 11 meeting rooms, audio-visual equipment, meeting facilities for 250, major credit cards. Ten miles from the downtown area. SGL/DBL$97.

Holiday Inn Parkway East (915 Brinton Rd, 15221; 247-2700, 800-HOLIDAY) 180 rooms, restaurant, lounge, indoor pool, wheelchair access, no-smoking rooms, a/c, TV, 7 meeting rooms, meeting facilities for 300, major credit cards. 8 miles from the downtown area. SGL/DBL$65-$105.

Holiday Inn At University Center (100 Lytton Ave, 15213; 682-6200, Fax 682-5745, 800-HOLIDAY) 253 rooms, restaurant, lounge, entertainment, indoor pool, exercise center, children stay free with parents, wheelchair access, no-smoking rooms, a/c, TV, fax service, room service, transportation to local attractions, pets allowed, meeting facilities for 400, major credit cards. SGL/DBL$65-$105.

Shadyside Inn (5405 5th Ave, 15235; 441-4444) 100 rooms and apartment suites, a/c, TV, free local calls, VCRs. 3 miles from the downtown area, near the shopping district. SGL$85, DBL$95.

North Pittsburgh

Days Inn (Turnpike Exit 5, 15238; 828-5400, Fax 826-8544, 800-325-2525) 102 rooms, restaurant, free breakfast, children stay free with parents, pets allowed, cable TV, free local calls, fax service, wheelchair access, no-smoking rooms, a/c, TV, major credit cards. 9 miles from the downtown area, 24 miles from the Greater Pittsburgh International Airport. SGL$44-$54, DBL$49-$59, AP$5.

Holiday Inn Allegheny Valley (180 Gamma Drive, 15238; 412-963-0600, Fax 412-963-7852, 800-HOLIDAY) 186 rooms and suites, restaurant, lounge, outdoor pool, exercise center, sauna, children stay free with parents, wheelchair access, no-smoking rooms, a/c, TV, fax service, room service, audio-visual equipment, airport transportation, 9 meeting rooms, meeting facilities for 600, major credit cards. 7 miles from the downtown area, 24 miles from the Greater Pittsburgh International Airport. SGL/DBL$65-$75.

Holiday Inn McKnight (4859 McKnight Rd, 15237; 931-7791, 800-HOLIDAY) 146 rooms and suites, restaurant, lounge, outdoor pool, exercise center, children stay free with parents, wheelchair access, no-smoking rooms, a/c, TV, fax service, room service, audio-visual equipment, 9 meeting rooms, meeting facilities for 700, major credit cards. 6 miles from River Stadium, 22 miles from the Greater Pittsburgh International Airport. SGL/DBL$68-$88.

Holiday Inn (2801 Freeport Rd, 15238; 412-828-9300, Fax 412-828-7916, 800-HOLIDAY) 168 rooms, restaurant, lounge, entertainment, children stay free with parents, wheelchair access, no-smoking rooms, a/c, TV, fax service, room service, pets allowed, meeting facilities for 300, major credit cards. 8 miles from the Convention Center, 24 miles from the Greater Pittsburgh International Airport, 9 miles from the downtown area. SGL/DBL$70-$95.

The Priory – A City Inn (614 Pressley St, 15212; 231-3338) 27 rooms and suites, complimentary continental breakfast and newspaper, free parking, audio-visual equipment, children stay free with parents, wheelchair access, no-smoking rooms, a/c, TV, limousine service, meeting facilities for 150, major credit cards. A half-mile from the downtown area. SGL/DBL$85.

South Pittsburgh

Days Inn (1150 Banksville Rd, 15216; 531-8900, 800-325-2525) 70 rooms and suites, restaurant, lounge, entertainment, pool, children stay free with parents, cable TV, free local calls, free parking, fax service, wheelchair access, no-smoking rooms, a/c, TV, meeting facilities for 300, major credit cards. 5 minutes from the downtown area, Civic Arena and 3 Rivers Stadium. SGL/DBL$49-$65, STS$75-$90.

Howard Johnson Lodge (5300 Clairton Blvd, 15236; 884-6000, Fax 884-6009, 800-654-9122) 95 rooms, restaurant, complimentary breakfast, lounge, pool, children stay free with parents, no-smoking rooms, a/c, TV, wheelchair access, airport transportation, 5 meeting rooms, meeting facilities for 120, major credit cards. 23 miles from the Greater Pittsburgh International Airport, 7.5 miles from the downtown area. SGL$48, DBL$58-$68.

Hampton Inn (555 Trumbull Drive, 15205; 922-0100, Fax 922-0100 ext 109, 800-HAMPTON) 133 rooms, free breakfast, children stay free with parents, no-smoking rooms, a/c, TV, wheelchair access, airport courtesy car, pets allowed, in-room computer hookups, fax, free local calls, 2 meeting rooms, meeting facilities for 20, major credit cards. 3 miles from the Convention Center, the downtown area and 3 Rivers Stadium, 12 miles from the Greater Pittsburgh International Airport. SGL$58-$64, DBL$62-$68.

Marriott Residence Inn (700 Mansfield Ave, 15205; 279-6300, 800-331-3131) 1- and 2-bedroom suites, kitchens, in-room refrigerators, cable TV, free parking, laundry service, fireplaces, wheelchair access, no-smoking rooms, a/c, pets allowed, VCRs, meeting facilities for 35, major credit cards. A half-mile from the Foster Plaza Office Park, 4 miles from 3 Rivers Stadium and the downtown area, 12 miles from the Greater Pittsburgh International Airport. 1BR$114, 2BR$144.

Redwood Inn (2898 Banksville Rd, 15216; 343-5030, Fax 341-4611) 95 rooms and suites, restaurant, lounge, entertainment, outdoor pool, room service, no-smoking rooms, a/c, TV, children stay free with parents, limousine service, 4 meeting rooms, meeting facilities for 400, major credit cards. SGL/DBL$65-$75.

Sheraton Inn South Hills (164 Fort Couch Rd, 15241; 343-3535, 800-325-3535) 210 rooms and suites, restaurant, lounge, entertainment, outdoor pool, exercise center, no-smoking rooms, a/c, TV, wheelchair access, limousine service, airport courtesy car, gift shop, 12 meeting rooms, 6,800 square feet of and exhibition space, meeting facilities for 600, major credit cards. 9 miles from the downtown area, 15 miles from the Greater Pittsburgh International Airport. SGL/DBL$65-$104.

Airport Area and West Pittsburgh

Best Western Parkway Center Inn (875 Greentree Rd, 15220; 922-7070, 800-528-1234) 115 rooms and suites, 2 restaurants, free breakfast, 2 lounges, indoor pool, sauna, steam room, exercise center, airport transportation, audio-visual equipment, free parking, fax, 8 meeting rooms, meeting facilities for 300, major credit cards. SGL$79-$93, DBL$85-$99, AP$6.

Clubhouse Inn (5311 Campbells Run Rd, 15205; 788-8400, Fax 788-2577, 800-CLUB-INN) 152 rooms and suites, complimentary breakfast, outdoor pool, spa, jacuzzi, children stay free with parents, free local calls, laundry service, no-smoking rooms, a/c, TV, wheelchair access, free parking, airport courtesy car, limousine service, 3 meeting rooms, meeting facilities for 115, major credit cards. Near 1 Marquis Plaza, 9 miles from the downtown area, Carnegie Cultural Center and 3 Rivers Stadium, 7 miles from the Greater Pittsburgh International Airport. SGL$71-$86, DBL$81-$96, STS$100.

Days Inn Airport (100 Kisow Drive, 15205; 922-0120, Fax 922-0125; 800-325-2525) 118 rooms, children stay free with parents, cable TV, pets allowed, free local calls, wheelchair access, fax, no-smoking rooms, a/c, TV, major credit cards. 9 miles from the Greater Pittsburgh International Airport, 8 miles from the downtown area. SGL$42-$52, DBL$46-$56, AP$6.

Econo Lodge (4800 Steubenville Pike, 15205; 922-6900) 109 rooms and efficiencies, restaurant, pool, in-room refrigerators, no-smoking rooms, a/c, TV, wheelchair access, meeting facilities, major credit cards. SGL/DBL$45.

Fort Pitt Motel (7750 Steubenville Pike, 15071; 788-9960) 19 rooms, whirlpools, a/c, TV, major credit cards. 12 miles from the downtown area. SGL$37, DBL$42.

Hilton Airport Inn (1 Hilton Drive, 15231; 262-3800, Fax 695-1068, 800-HILTONS) 140 rooms and suites, restaurant, lounge, entertainment, outdoor pool, exercise center, wheelchair access, no-smoking rooms, a/c, TV, free parking, airport courtesy car, limousine service, audio-visual equipment, business services, 8 meeting rooms, meeting facilities for 600, major credit cards. Thirteen miles from the downtown area, 2.5 miles from the Greater Pittsburgh International Airport, 14 miles from 3 Rivers Stadium. SGL/DBL$95-$115.

Holiday Inn Greentree (401 Holiday Drive, 15220; 922-8100) 202 rooms and suites, restaurant, lounge, outdoor pool, whirlpool, children stay free with parents, wheelchair access, no-smoking rooms, a/c, TV, fax service, room service, audio-visual equipment, pets allowed, limousine service, meeting facilities for 700, major credit cards. 3 miles from 3 Rivers Stadium, 12 miles from the Greater Pittsburgh International Airport. SGL/DBL$65-$95.

Howard Johnson Lodge (2101 Montour Church Rd, 15071; 787-2244, Fax 787-3625, 800-654-9122) 155 rooms, lounge, entertainment, pool, children stay free with parents, no-smoking rooms, a/c, TV, wheelchair access, airport transportation, free parking, limousine service, laundry service, 5 meeting rooms, meeting facilities for 700, major credit cards. 5 miles from Pittsburgh International Airport, 12 miles from the downtown area, 1 mile from Town Center Mall. SGL$35-$40, DBL$40-$45.

La Quinta Motor Inn (1433 Beers School Rd, 15108; 269-0400, Fax 269-2504, 800-531-5900) 120 rooms, restaurant, lounge, pool, complimentary newspaper, free local calls, fax service, laundry service, no-smoking rooms, a/c, TV, wheelchair access, free parking, transportation to local attractions, 3 meeting rooms, meeting facilities for 30, major credit cards. 5 miles of the Morris Convention Center, 13 miles from the 3 Rivers Stadium, 20 miles from the downtown area, a half-mile from the Greater Pittsburgh International Airport. SGL/DBL$40-$60.

Marriott Greentree (101 Marriott Drive, 15205; 922-8400, Fax 922-8981, 800-228-9290) 467 rooms and suites, 2 restaurants, 2 lounges, entertainment, indoor and outdoor pool, exercise center, whirlpool, lighted tennis courts, jogging track, barber and beauty shop, free parking, gift shop, wheelchair access, no-smoking rooms, a/c, TV, limousine service, airport courtesy car, 6 meeting rooms, meeting facilities for 900, major credit cards. 3 miles from the downtown area, 15 miles from the Greater Pittsburgh International Airport. SGL/DBL$109, STS$105-$150.

Red Roof Inn (6404 Steubenville Pike, 15202; 787-7870, Fax 787-8392, 800-THE-ROOF) 120 rooms, restaurant, free newspaper, in-room computer hookups, wheelchair access, no-smoking rooms, a/c, TV, children stay free with parents, free local calls, fax service, major credit cards. Ten miles from the downtown area, 6 miles from the Pittsburgh International Airport. SGL/DBL$42-$60.

Super 8 Airport Motel (1455 Beers School Rd, 15108; 264-7888, Fax 264-3721, 800-800-8000) 62 rooms, complimentary breakfast, children stay free with parents, transportation to local attractions, pets allowed, car rental desk, in-room refrigerators and microwaves, no-smoking rooms, a/c, TV, wheelchair access, in-room computer hookups, fax service, free local calls, meeting facilities for 35, major credit cards. 6 miles from the Greater Pittsburgh International Airport, 30 minutes from 3 Rivers Stadium, 15 minutes from the downtown area. SGL$38, DBL$44.

TraveLodge West (4800 Steubenville Pike, 15205; 922-6900, Fax 922-1474, 800-255-3050) 109 rooms and suites, restaurant, lounge, pool, laundry service, no pets, fax service, meeting facilities for 25, major credit cards. Ten miles from the downtown area, 8 miles from the Greater Pittsburgh International Airport. SGL$35-$46, DBL$41-$47, AP$6.

Other Locations

Days Inn (300 Tarentum Bridge Rd, 15068; 335-9171, Fax 335-6642, 800-325-2525) 111 rooms, restaurant, lounge, entertainment, laundry service, children stay free with parents, cable TV, free local calls, pets allowed, wheelchair access, no-smoking rooms, a/c, TV, meeting facilities for 1,000, major credit cards. 35 miles from the Greater Pittsburgh International Airport, 20 miles from the downtown area. SGL/DBL$44-$65.

Pittston
Area Code 717

Knights Inn (State Rd 315, 18640; 654-6020, 800-843-5644) pool, wheelchair access, no-smoking rooms, TV, a/c, in-room refrigerators and microwaves, fax service, free parking, VCRs, senior citizen rates, major credit cards. SGL/DBL$48-$68.

Howard Johnson Lodge (307 Rte 315, 18640; 654-3301, Fax 883-0288, 800-I-GO-HOJO) 120 rooms, restaurant, lounge, pool, children stay free with parents, wheelchair access, no-smoking rooms, TV, a/c, pets allowed, free parking, senior citizen rates, meeting facilities, major credit cards. SGL/DBL$40-$60.

Plymouth Meeting
Area Code 215

Guest Quarters (640 West Germantown Pike, 19462; 800-424-2900) 252 suites, restaurant, lounge, indoor pool, exercise facilities, whirlpool, in-room refrigerators, complimentary newspaper, TV, a/c, room service, free parking, transportation to local attractions, wheelchair access, no-smoking rooms, meeting facilities, major credit cards. SGL/DBL$65-$85.

Pottstown
Area Code 215

Comfort Inn (Shoemaker Rd, 19464; 326-5000, 800-221-2222) 121 rooms, restaurant, complimentary breakfast, pool, wheelchair access, no-smoking rooms, no pets, children under 18 stay free with parents, senior citizen rates, a/c, laundry facilities, TV, meeting facilities, major credit cards. SGL$52-$67, DBL$59-$75.

Days Inn (29 High St, 19464; 970-1101, 800-325-2525) 65 rooms, restaurant, lounge, pool, children stay free with parents, room service, laundry service, a/c, TV, free local calls, no pets, wheelchair access, no-smoking rooms, senior citizen rates, major credit cards. SGL/DBL$39-$45.

Holiday Inn (1600 Industrial Hwy, 19464; 327-3300, Fax 327-9447, 800-HOLIDAY) 120 rooms, restaurant, complimentary breakfast, lounge, outdoor pool, exercise facilities, children under 19 stay free with parents, wheelchair access, a/c, TV, airport transportation, no-smoking rooms, fax service, room service, no pets, laundry service, meeting facilities for 55, senior citizen rates, major credit cards. SGL/DBL$56-$62.

Ramada Inn (Rte 100 and West King St, 19464; 326-6700, Fax 970-2665, 800-2-RAMADA) 100 rooms, restaurant, lounge, pool, wheelchair access, no-smoking rooms, airport transportation, free parking, pets allowed, wheelchair access, a/c, TV, room service, laundry facilities, meeting facilities for 100, senior citizen rates, major credit cards. SGL/DBL$49-$59, DBL$54-$64, AP$5.

Pottsville
Area Code 717

Quality Inn (100 South Centre St, 17901; 622-4600, 800-368-5689) rooms and suites, restaurant, lounge, entertainment, room service, exercise facilities, children stay free with parents, a/c, TV, laundry service, no-smoking rooms, meeting facilities, major credit cards. SGL/DBL$58-$75.

Reading
Area Code 215

Comfort Inn (2200 Stach Dr, 19605; 371-0500, 800-221-2222) 60 rooms, restaurant, lounge, entertainment, whirlpools, exercise facilities, wheelchair access, no-smoking rooms, no pets, children under 18 stay free with parents, senior citizen rates, a/c, TV, meeting facilities, major credit cards. SGL/DBL$50-$75.

Days Inn (415 South Lancaster Ave, 19607; 777-7888, Fax 777-5138, 800-325-2525) 142 rooms, restaurant, lounge, pool, children stay free with parents, room service, laundry service, a/c, TV, free local calls, no pets, wheelchair access, no-smoking rooms, senior citizen rates, major credit cards. SGL/DBL$53-$98.

Holiday Inn (Hwy 222N, 19605; 929-4741, Fax 929-5237, 800-HOLIDAY) 140 rooms, restaurant, lounge, outdoor pool, exercise facilities, children under 19 stay free with parents, wheelchair access, a/c, TV, no-smoking rooms, fax, room service, pets allowed, laundry service, meeting facilities for 300, senior citizen rates, major credit cards. SGL/DBL$65-$130.

Hunter House (118 South 5th St, 19602; 374-6608) free breakfast, 1840s home, no pets, TV, a/c, private bath, major credit cards. SGL/DBL$53-$75.

Sheraton Inn (Rte 422 West, 19610; 376-3811, Fax 375-7562, 800-325-3535) 256 rooms and suites, restaurant, lounge, entertainment, indoor pool, exercise facilities, sauna, gift shop, no-smoking rooms, a/c, TV, children stay free with parents, wheelchair access, 15,000 square feet of meeting and exhibition space, 5 meeting rooms, meeting facilities for 1,000, major credit cards. SGL/DBL$85-$95, STS$95-$165.

Reinholds
Area Code 215

Brownstone Corner Bed and Breakfast (590 Galen Hall Rd, 17560; 484-4460) 4 rooms, complimentary breakfast, major credit cards. SGL/DBL$23-$28.

Ridgway
Area Code 814

Faircroft Bed and Breakfast (Montmorenci Rd, 15853; 776-2539) complimentary breakfast, no smoking, private baths, on 75 acres, no pets, antique furnishings. SGL/DBL$40.

Ronks
Area Code 717

Black Forest Country Lodge (21 Eastbrook Rd, 17572; 393-2550) 54 rooms, a/c, TV, in-room refrigerators, no pets. SGL/DBL$40-$85.

Candlelite Inn Bed and Breakfast (2574 Lincoln Hwy East, 17572; 299-6005) 4 rooms, complimentary breakfast, no smoking, TV, a/c, no pets, antique furnishings. SGL/DBL$55-$65.

Cherry Lane Motor Inn (Ronks 17572; 687-7646) pool, game room, a/c, TV, major credit cards. SGL/DBL$38-$46.

The Olde Amish Inn (33 Eastbrook Rd, 17572; 393-3100) 25 rooms, a/c, TV, no pets. SGL/DBL$45-$65.

Quiet Haven Motel (Ronks 17572; 397-6231) 15 rooms, a/c, TV, no pets. SGL/DBL$35-$52.

Scranton
Area Code 717

Holiday Inn (One Tique St, 18512; 343-4771, Fax 343-5171, 800-HOLIDAY) restaurant, lounge, indoor pool, exercise facilities, children under 19 stay free with parents, wheelchair access, airport transportation, a/c, TV, no-smoking rooms, fax service, room service, no pets, laundry service, meeting facilities for 450, senior citizen rates, major credit cards. SGL/DBL$69-$100.

Sheraton Inn (300 Meadow Ave, 18505; 344-9811, Fax 344-7799, 800-325-3535) 125 rooms and suites, restaurant, lounge, entertainment, outdoor pool, exercise facilities, no-smoking rooms, a/c, limousine service, TV, children stay free with parents, wheelchair access, 5,000 square feet of meeting and exhibition space, 4 meeting rooms, meeting facilities for 500, major credit cards. SGL/DBL$68-$98, STS$100-$115.

Selinsgrove
Area Code 717

Comfort Inn (Highways 11 and 15, 17870; 374-8880, 800-221-2222) 62 rooms, restaurant, lounge, wheelchair access, no-smoking rooms, no pets, children under 18 stay free with parents, senior citizen rates, a/c, TV, meeting facilities, major credit cards. SGL/DBL$43-$56.

Sewickley
Area Code 412

Sewickley Country Inn (801 Ohio River Blvd, 15143; 741-4300) 149 rooms, restaurant, lounge, pool, exercise facilities, TV, room service, a/c, no-smoking rooms, 12 meeting rooms, meeting facilities for 1,000. SGL/DBL$95.

Shamokin Dam
Area Code 717

Days Inn Sunbury (Shamokin Dam, 17876; 743-1111, 800-325-2525) 151 rooms, restaurant, lounge, outdoor pool, children stay free with parents, room service, laundry service, a/c, TV, free local calls, no pets, wheelchair access, no-smoking rooms, senior citizen rates, meeting facilities for 250, major credit cards. SGL/DBL$39-$65.

Shawnee On Delaware
Area Code 717

Eagle Rock Lodge In The Poconos (River Rd, 18356; 421-2139) 7 rooms, free breakfast, no pets, water view, on 10 acres. SGL/DBL$48-$65.

Slippery Rock
Area Code 412

Applebutter Inn (152 Applewood Lane, 16057; 794-1844) 11 rooms, bed and breakfast, 1840s inn, antique furnishings, no pets, no smoking, private baths, major credit cards. SGL/DBL$55-$115.

Smoketown
Area Code 717

Mill Stream Motor Lodge (Eastbrook Rd, 17576; 299-0931) 52 rooms, restaurant, complimentary breakfast, a/c, TV, VCRs, in-room refrigerators, no pets. SGL/DBL$49-$70.

Somerset
Area Code 814

Days Inn (Somerset 15501; 445-9200, Fax 445-9222, 800-325-2525) 106 rooms, restaurant, lounge, children stay free with parents, room service, laundry service, a/c, TV, free local calls, no pets, wheelchair access, no-smoking rooms, senior citizen rates, major credit cards. SGL/DBL$42-$68.

Glades Pike Inn (Somerset 15501; 443-4978) 5 rooms, bed and breakfast, private baths, 1840s inn, fireplace, major credit cards. SGL/DBL$80-$85.

Holiday Inn (Shaffer St, 15501; 445-9611, Fax 445-5815, 800-HOLIDAY) 102 rooms, restaurant, lounge, outdoor pool, exercise facilities, children under 19 stay free with parents, wheelchair access, a/c, TV, no-smoking rooms, fax service, room service, no pets, laundry service, meeting facilities for 50, senior citizen rates, major credit cards. SGL/DBL$60-$110.

Knights Inn (Turnpike Entrance, 15501; 445-8933, 800-843-5644) pool, wheelchair access, no-smoking rooms, TV, a/c, in-room refrigerators and microwaves, fax service, free parking, VCRs, senior citizen rates, major credit cards. SGL/DBL$60-$100.

Ramada Inn (Somerset 15501; 443-4646, Fax 445-7539, 800-2-RAMADA) 152 rooms, restaurant, lounge, indoor pool, wheelchair access, no smoking rooms, airport transportation, free parking, pets allowed, wheelchair access, a/c, TV, room service, laundry facilities, meeting facilities for 500, senior citizen rates, major credit cards. SGL$52-$70, DBL$66-$80, AP$10.

Super 8 Motel (Somerset 15501; 445-8788, 800-800-8000) 55 rooms and suites, no pets, children under 12 stay free with parents, free local calls, a/c, TV, fax service, no-smoking rooms, senior citizen rates, wheelchair access, meeting facilities, major credit cards. SGL/DBL$38-$42.

St. Davids
Area Code 215

Radnor Hotel (591 East Lancaster, 19087; 688-5800, Fax 341-3299, 800-537-3000, 800-241-0001 in Pennsylvania) 170 rooms and suites, restaurant, lounge, entertainment, pool, gift shop, 24-hour rooms service, transportation to local attractions, wheelchair access, no-smoking rooms, meeting facilities for 700. SGL$65, DBL$75-$90, STS$110+.

Starlight
Area Code 717

The Inn At Starlight Lake (Starlight 18461; 798-2519) 26 rooms, bed and breakfast, no pets, water view, private baths, major credit cards. SGL/DBL$55-$110.

Starrucca
Area Code 717

Nethercott Inn (Main St, 18462; 727-2211)rooms, bed and breakfast, no pets, 1890s inn, antique furnishings, no-smoking rooms, private baths, major credit cards. SGL/DBL$45-$70.

State College
Area Code 814

Days Inn (240 South Pugh St, 16801; 238-8454, Fax 234-3377, 800-325-2525) 184 rooms and suites, restaurant, complimentary breakfast, lounge, entertainment, indoor pool, exercise facilities, car rental desk, children stay free with parents, room service, laundry service, a/c, TV, free local calls, no pets, wheelchair access, no-smoking rooms, senior citizen rates, major credit cards. SGL/DBL$45-$77, STS$150-$175.

Hampton Inn (1101 East College Ave, 16801; 231-1590, Fax 238-7320, 800-HAMPTON) 121 rooms, restaurant, complimentary breakfast, pool, exercise facilities, children under 18 stay free with parents, no-smoking rooms, wheelchair access, computer hookups, fax service, TV, a/c, free local calls, pets allowed, meeting facilities, major credit cards. SGL/DBL$49-$73.

Hilton Atherton Hotel (125 South Atherton St, 16801; 231-2100, 231-2300 ext 187, 800-HILTONS) 150 rooms and suites, restaurant, lounge, entertainment, indoor pool, exercise facilities, children stay free with parents, no-smoking rooms, in-room computer hookups, wheelchair access, pets allowed, free parking, a/c, TV, business services, meeting facilities, major credit cards. SGL/DBL$85-$165.

Holiday Inn (1450 South Atherton, 16801; 238-3001, Fax 237-1345, 800-HOLIDAY) 288 rooms, restaurant, lounge, entertainment, outdoor pool, exercise facilities, game room, children under 19 stay free with parents, wheelchair access, a/c, TV, no-smoking rooms, fax service, room service, no pets, laundry service, meeting facilities for 400, senior citizen rates, major credit cards. SGL/DBL$52-$63.

Strasburg
Area Code 717

Amish Lanterns Motel (Strasburg 17579; 687-7839) restaurant, pool, a/c, TV, major credit cards. SGL/DBL$30-$68.

Beaver Creek Farm Cabins (Two Little Beaver Rd, 17579; 687-7745) cabins. SGL/DBL$48-$68.

Carriage House Motor Inn (Rte 896, 17579; 687-7651) 114 rooms, a/c, TV, children under the age of 12 stay free with parents. SGL/DBL$59-$79.

The Decoy Bed and Breakfast (958 Eisenberger Rd, 17579; 687-8585) 4 rooms, complimentary breakfast, no smoking, a/c, open year-round, private baths. SGL/DBL$32-$53.

Fulton Steamboat Inn (Rtes 30 and 896, 17579; 299-9999) restaurant, indoor pool, exercise facilities, game room, gift shop, in-room refrigerators and microwaves, wheelchair access, no-smoking rooms, a/c, TV. SGL/DBL$65-$95.

Strasburg Inn (Rte 896, 17579; 687-7691, 800-872-0201) bed and breakfast, restaurant, outdoor pool, pets allowed, a/c, TV, major credit cards. SGL/DBL$45-$85.

Tannersville
Area Code 717

HoJo Inn (Rte 715, 18372; 629-4100, 800-442-2193, 800-I-GO-HOJO) 88 rooms, restaurant, lounge, outdoor pool, hot tubs, children stay free with parents, wheelchair access, room service, no-smoking rooms, TV, a/c, pets allowed, free parking, meeting facilities, senior citizen rates, major credit cards. LS SGL$45-$90, DBL$45-$130; HS SGL/DBL$50-$139.

Thompson
Area Code 717

Jefferson Inn (Main St, 18465; 727-2625) complimentary breakfast, restaurant, private baths, 1870s inn, major credit cards. SGL/DBL$20-$35.

Thornton
Area Code 215

Pace 1 Country Inn (Thornton and Glen Mills Rd, 19373; 459-3702, Fax 558-0825) 8 rooms, complimentary breakfast, restaurant, 1740s inn, private bath. SGL/DBL$45-$55.

Titusville
Area Code 814

McMullen House Bed and Breakfast (430 East Main St, 16354; 827-1592) complimentary breakfast, private baths. SGL/DBL$50-$60.

Trevose
Area Code 215

Holiday Inn (4700 St Rd, 19053; 364-2000, 800-HOLIDAY) 215 rooms, restaurant, lounge, indoor pool, exercise facilities, children under 19 stay free with parents, wheelchair access, a/c, TV, no-smoking rooms, fax service, gift shop, in-room refrigerators, room service, no pets, laundry service, meeting facilities for 250, senior citizen rates, major credit cards. SGL/DBL$65-$85.

Howard Johnson Hotel (2779 Hwy 1 North, 19053; 638-4554, Fax 638-7085, 800-I-GO-HOJO) 87 rooms, restaurant, lounge, pool, jacuzzis, children stay free with parents, wheelchair access, no-smoking rooms, TV, a/c, room service, no pets, free parking, senior citizen rates, meeting facilities, major credit cards. SGL/DBL$55-$60.

Ramada Hotel and Conference Center (2400 Old Lincoln Hwy, 19053; 638-8300, 800-238-3269) 286 rooms and suites, 2 restaurants, lounge, entertainment, indoor and outdoor pools, exercise facilities, jacuzzi, wheelchair access, no-smoking rooms, airport transportation, free parking, pets allowed, a/c, TV, room service, beauty shop, car rental desk, gift shop, laundry facilities, meeting facilities for 3,000, senior citizen rates, major credit cards. SGL$75-$115, DBL$85-$125, STS$125, AP$10.

Red Roof Inn (3100 Lincoln Hwy, 19053; 244-9422, 244-9469, 800-843-7663) 156 rooms, no-smoking rooms, fax service, wheelchair access, complimentary newspaper, free local calls, in-room computer hookups, major credit cards. SGL/DBL$38-$48.

Uniontown
Area Code 412

Holiday Inn (700 West Main St, 15401; 437-2816, 800-HOLIDAY) 182 rooms, restaurant, lounge, entertainment, indoor pool, exercise facilities, whirlpools, children under 19 stay free with parents, wheelchair access, a/c, TV, no-smoking rooms, fax service, room service, pets allowed, laundry service, meeting facilities for 500, senior citizen rates, major credit cards. SGL/DBL$68-$75.

Valley Forge
Area Code 215

Valley Forge Mountain Bed and Breakfast (Valley Forge 19481; 783-7838) free breakfast, on 2 acres, no smoking, private baths, senior citizen rates, major credit cards. SGL/DBL$32-$70.

Warfordsburg
Area Code 814

Days Inn Breezewood (Warfordsburg 17267; 735-3860, Fax 735-3841, 800-325-2525) 64 rooms, restaurant, lounge, children stay free with parents, room service, laundry service, a/c, TV, free local calls, no pets, wheelchair access, no-smoking rooms, senior citizen rates, major credit cards. SGL/DBL$40-$46.

Warren
Area Code 814

Holiday Inn (210 Ludlow St, 16365; 726-3000, Fax 726-3720, 800-446-6814, 800-HOLIDAY) 110 rooms, restaurant, lounge, entertainment, indoor pool, exercise facilities, game room, children under 19 stay free with parents, wheelchair access, a/c, TV, no-smoking rooms, fax service, room service, pets allowed, laundry service, meeting facilities for 300, senior citizen rates, major credit cards. SGL/DBL$51-$64.

Super 8 Motel (Warren 16365; 723-8881, 800-800-8000) 56 rooms and suites, no pets, children under 12 stay free with parents, free local calls, a/c, TV, fax service, no-smoking rooms, senior citizen rates, wheelchair access, meeting facilities, major credit cards. SGL/DBL$38-$43.

Washington
Area Code 412

Days Inn (1370 Chestnut St, 15301; 225-8500, Fax 222-7671, 800-325-2525) 104 rooms, restaurant, lounge, children stay free with parents, room service, laundry service, a/c, TV, free local calls, no pets, wheelchair access, no-smoking rooms, senior citizen rates, major credit cards. SGL$38-$64, DBL$44-$75.

Knights Inn (125 Knights Inn Dr, 15301; 223-8040, 800-843-5644) pool, wheelchair access, no-smoking rooms, TV, a/c, in-room refrigerators and microwaves, fax service, free parking, VCRs, senior citizen rates, major credit cards. SGL/DBL$41-$47.

Ramada Inn (1170 West Chestnut St, 15301; 225-9750, 800-2-RAMADA) 93 rooms and suites, restaurant, lounge, entertainment, pool, wheelchair access, no-smoking rooms, airport transportation, free parking, pets allowed, wheelchair access, a/c, TV, room service, laundry facilities, meeting facilities for 350, senior citizen rates, major credit cards. SGL$51-$55, DBL$54-$64, STS$65, AP$6.

Holiday Inn Meadowlands (340 Race Track Rd, 15301; 222-6200, 800-HOLIDAY) 138 rooms, restaurant, lounge, outdoor pool, exercise facilities, spa, children under 19 stay free with parents, wheelchair access, a/c, TV, no-smoking rooms, fax service, room service, transportation to local attractions, no pets, laundry service, meeting facilities, senior citizen rates, major credit cards. SGL/DBL$65-$86.

Wayne
Area Code 215

Courtyard by Marriott (762 West Lancaster Ave, 19087; 687-6633, Fax 687-1150, 800-321-2121) 149 rooms and suites, restaurant, lounge, entertainment, indoor pool, exercise facilities, wheelchair access, no-smoking rooms, in-room refrigerators, meeting facilities. SGL/DBL$68-$98.

Guest Quarters (888 Chesterbrook Blvd, 19087; 647-6700, 800-424-2900) 229 suites, restaurant, indoor pool, exercise facilities, jogging track, sauna, whirlpools, remote control TV, a/c, in-room refrigerators, transportation to local attractions, laundry service, fax service, no-smoking rooms, wheelchair access, meeting facilities for 200, major credit cards. SGL/DBL$47-$77.

The Wayne Hotel (139 East Lancaster, Wayne 19087; 687-5000, Fax 687-8387, 37 rooms and suites, restaurant, lounge, complimentary breakfast, in-room refrigerators, children stay free with parents, wheelchair access, no-smoking rooms, transportation to local attractions, meeting facilities. SGL/DBL$100-$150, STS$150+.

Waynesburg
Area Code 412

Super 8 Motel (80 Miller Lane, 15370; 627-8880, 800-800-8000) 56 rooms and suites, no pets, children under 12 stay free with parents, free local calls, a/c, TV, fax service, no-smoking rooms, senior citizen rates, wheelchair access, meeting facilities, major credit cards. SGL/DBL$37-$42.

Wellsboro
Area Code 717

Kaltenbach's Bed and Breakfast (Stony Fork Rd, 16901; 724-4954) 10 rooms, complimentary breakfast, no smoking, on 70 acres, private baths, fireplace, no pets, major credit cards. SGL/DBL$38-$100.

West Chester
Area Code 215

Rental and Reservation Service

Guesthouses, Inc. (West Chester 19380; 692-4575, 800-950-9130) reservation service for bed and breakfasts.

❑❑❑

The Crooked Windsor (409 South Church St, 19382; 692-4896) bed and breakfast, no smoking, no pets. SGL/DBL$65-$70.

Whitehall
Area Code 215

Ramada Inn (13455 Southwest TV Hwy, 97005; 643-9100, Fax 643-0514, 800-2-RAMADA) 143 rooms and suites, restaurant, lounge, pool, wheelchair access, free local calls, kitchenettes, airport courtesy car, no-smoking rooms, airport transportation, free parking, pets allowed, a/c, TV, room service, laundry facilities, meeting facilities, senior citizen rates, major credit cards. SGL/DBL$49-$75, DBL$57-$85, STS$75-$125, AP$10.

Wilkes Barre
Area Code 717

Days Inn (309 Hwy 315, 18702; 826-0111, Fax 824-4255, 800-325-2525) 75 rooms, restaurant, lounge, children stay free with parents, room service, laundry service, a/c, TV, free local calls, pets allowed, wheelchair access, no-smoking rooms, senior citizen rates, major credit cards. SGL/DBL$40-$61.

Hampton Inn (1063 Hwy 315, 18702; 825-3838, Fax 825-8775, 800-HAMPTON) 123 rooms, restaurant, complimentary breakfast, pool, exercise facilities, children under 18 stay free with parents, no-smoking rooms, wheelchair access, computer hookups, fax service, TV, a/c, free local calls, pets allowed, meeting facilities, major credit cards. SG/DBL$46-$67.

Holiday Inn (Rte 309, 18702; 824-8901, Fax 824-9310, 800-HOLIDAY) 180 rooms, restaurant, lounge, outdoor pool, exercise facilities, children under 19 stay free with parents, wheelchair access, game room, a/c, TV, no-smoking rooms, fax service, room service, pets allowed, laundry service, meeting facilities for 250, senior citizen rates, major credit cards. SGL/DBL$58-$68.

Howard Johnson Hotel (500 Kidder St, 18702; 824-2411, Fax 829-8593, 800-275-6579, 800-I-GO-HOJO) 160 rooms, restaurant, complimentary breakfast, lounge, pool, sauna, jacuzzi, laundry facilities, children stay free with parents, wheelchair access, no-smoking rooms, TV, a/c, pets allowed, free parking, senior citizen rates, meeting facilities for 600, major credit cards. SGL$38-$50, DBL$44-$62.

Ramada Hotel On The Square (20 Public Square, 18701; 824-7100, Fax 823-5599, 800-2-RAMADA) 192 rooms, restaurant, lounge, entertainment, wheelchair access, no-smoking rooms, airport transportation, free parking, pets allowed, a/c, TV, airport transportation, room service, laundry facilities, meeting facilities, senior citizen rates, major credit cards. SGL64-$69, DBL$69-$74, STS$125, AP$5.

Williamsport
Area Code 717

Days Inn (1840 East Third St, 17701; 326-1981, Fax 323-9590, 800-325-2525) 174 rooms, restaurant, lounge, outdoor pool, children stay free with parents, room service, laundry service, a/c, TV, free local calls, no pets, wheelchair access, no-smoking rooms, senior citizen rates, major credit cards. SGL/DBL$39-$65.

Quality Inn (234 Montgomery Pike, 17701; 323-9801, 800-368-5689) 115 rooms and suites, restaurant, lounge, entertainment, pool, room service, exercise facilities, children stay free with parents, a/c, airport courtesy car, TV, laundry service, no-smoking rooms, meeting facilities, major credit cards. LS SGL$45-$49, DBL$51-$59; HS SGL/DBL$65-$73.

Sheraton Inn (100 Pine St, 17701; 327-8231, Fax 322-2957, 800-325-3535) 148 rooms and suites, restaurant, lounge, entertainment, indoor pool, no-smoking rooms, a/c, TV, children stay free with parents, wheelchair access, 6,200 square feet of meeting and exhibition space, 6 meeting rooms, meeting facilities for 500, major credit cards. SGL/DBL$65-$85, STS$90-$115.

Willow Grove
Area Code 215

Hampton Inn (1500 Easton Rd, 19090; 659-3535, Fax 659-4040, 800-HAMPTON) 150 rooms, restaurant, complimentary breakfast, pool, exercise facilities, children under 18 stay free with parents, no-smoking rooms, wheelchair access, computer hookups, fax service, TV, a/c, free local calls, pets allowed, meeting facilities, major credit cards. SGL/DBL$68-$75.

Willow Street
Area Code 717

The Apple Bin Inn (2835 Willow St Pike, 17584; 464-5881) bed and breakfast, no smoking, 1860s inn, antique furnishings, no pets, TV, a/c. SGL/DBL$50-$70.

Wrightstown
Area Code 215

Hollileif Bed and Breakfast (677 Durham Rd, 18940; 598-3100) complimentary breakfast, antique furnishings, no pets, a/c, private baths, fireplace, major credit cards. SGL/DBL$115.

Wyomissing
Area Code 215

Hampton Inn (1800 Papermill Rd, 19610; 374-8100, Fax 374-2076, 800-HAMPTON) 125 rooms, restaurant, complimentary breakfast, pool, exercise facilities, children under 18 stay free with parents, no-smoking rooms, wheelchair access, computer hookups, fax service, TV, a/c, free local calls, pets allowed, meeting facilities, major credit cards. SGL/DBL$59-$71.

The Inn At Reading (1040 Park Rd, 19610; 372-7811, Fax 372-4545, 800-383-9713) 250 rooms and suites, restaurant, lounge, entertainment, pool, exercise facilities, whirlpools, sauna, a/c, TV, no-smoking rooms, wheelchair access, children stay free with parents, meeting facilities, senior citizen rates, major credit cards. SGL/DBL$76-$86.

Sheraton Berkshire Hotel (West Paper Mill Rd, 19610; 376-3811, Fax 375-7562, 800-325-3535) rooms and suites, restaurant, complimentary breakfast, lounge, entertainment, indoor pool, exercise facilities, sauna, in-room coffee makers, no-smoking rooms, a/c, TV, children stay free with parents, wheelchair access, meeting facilities, major credit cards. SGL/DBL$65-$105.

York
Area Code 717

Barnhart's Motel (301 East Market St, 17402; 755-2806, 800-882-7548) 23 rooms and apartments, complimentary breakfast, kitchenettes, a/c, TV, fax service, in-room coffee makers, major credit cards. SGL/DBL$32-$36.

Briarwood (Lincoln Hwy East, 17406; 252-4619) complimentary breakfast, 1830s home, fireplace, a/c. SGL/DBL$45-$75.

Cottage At Twin Brook Farm (Kreutz Creek Rd, 17406; 757-5384) bed and breakfast, no smoking, on 55 acres, no pets, private baths, no children allowed, senior citizen rates. SGL/DBL$65-$75.

Friendship House (728 East Philadelphia St, 17403; 843-8299) 3 rooms, complimentary breakfast. SGL/DBL$55-$85.

Hampton Inn (1550 Mount Zion Rd, 17402; 840-1500, Fax 840-1567, 800-HAMPTON) restaurant, complimentary breakfast, pool, exercise facilities, children under 18 stay free with parents, no-smoking rooms, wheelchair access, computer hookups, fax service, TV, a/c, free local calls, pets allowed, meeting facilities, major credit cards. SGL/DBL$59-$70.

Holiday Inn (2000 Loucks Rd, 17404; 846-9500, Fax 846-9500, 800-HOLIDAY) 181 rooms, restaurant, lounge, entertainment, outdoor pool, exercise facilities, children under 19 stay free with parents, wheelchair access, a/c, TV, no-smoking rooms, fax service, room service, pets allowed, laundry service, meeting facilities for 1,000, senior citizen rates, major credit cards. SGL/DBL$79-$99.

Holiday Inn (334 Arsenal Rd, 17402; 845-5671, 800-HOLIDAY) 100 rooms, restaurant, lounge, entertainment, outdoor pool, exercise facilities, children under 19 stay free with parents, wheelchair access, a/c, TV, no-smoking rooms, fax service, room service, pets allowed, laundry service, meeting facilities for 350, senior citizen rates, major credit cards. SGL/DBL$69-$79.

Holiday Inn (Market St, 17401; 755-1966, 800-HOLIDAY) 120 rooms, restaurant, lounge, outdoor pool, exercise facilities, children under 19 stay free with parents, wheelchair access, a/c, TV, no-smoking rooms, fax service, room service, pets allowed, laundry service, meeting facilities, senior citizen rates, major credit cards. SGL/DBL$69-$79.

Howard Johnson Lodge (Arsenal Rd, 17402; 843-9971, Fax 843-1806, 800-I-GO-HOJO) 124 rooms, restaurant, lounge, pool, children stay free with parents, wheelchair access, no-smoking rooms, TV, a/c, pets allowed, free parking, senior citizen rates, meeting facilities for 300, major credit cards. SGL$40-$69, DBL$46-$73.

Ramada Inn (Hwy I-83, 17402; 846-4940, Fax 854-0301, 800-2-RAMADA) 147 rooms, restaurant, lounge, entertainment, indoor pool, sauna, wheelchair access, no-smoking rooms, airport transportation, free parking, pets allowed, a/c, TV, room service, laundry facilities, meeting facilities for 160, senior citizen rates, major credit cards. SGL/DBL$63-$89, STS$95, AP$10.

Super 8 Motel (40 Arsenal Rd, 17404; 852-8686, 800-800-8000) 94 rooms and suites, no pets, children under 12 stay free with parents, free local calls, a/c, TV, fax service, no-smoking rooms, senior citizen rates, wheelchair access, meeting facilities, major credit cards. SGL/DBL$40-$46.

TraveLodge (132 North George St, 17401; 843-8974, Fax 852-0686, 800-255-3050) 56 rooms, restaurant, lounge, complimentary breakfast, pool, wheelchair access, complimentary newspaper, laundry service, TV, a/c, free local calls, fax service, no-smoking rooms, free in-room coffee and tea service, in-room refrigerators and microwaves, no pets. SGL$29-$39, DBL$34-$45, AP$5.

Zelienople
Area Code 412

Benvenue Manor Bed and Breakfast (Rte 68 West, 16063; 452-1710) 4 rooms, complimentary breakfast, TV. SGL/DBL$45-$55.

Virginia

Rental and Reservation Service

The Bed and Breakfast Association of Virginia (Box 791, Orange 22960).

Abingdon
Area Code 703

Alpine Motel (882 East Main St, 24210; 628-3178) 19 rooms, a/c, TV, no pets, major credit cards. SGL/DBL$40-$45.

The Cabin On The River (146 Crestview Dr, 24210; 628-8433) 2 suites, complimentary breakfast, private baths, no pets, a/c, kitchenettes, fireplace, meeting facilities for 10, major credit cards. SGL/DBL$75-$100.

Comfort Inn (State Rd, 140, 24210; 676-2222, 800-221-2222) 80 rooms, pool, wheelchair access, no-smoking rooms, no pets, children under 18 stay free with parents, senior citizen rates, a/c, TV, meeting facilities, major credit cards. SGL/DBL$36-$56.

Empire Motor Lodge (887 Empire Dr, 24210; 628-7131) 105 rooms, a/c, private baths. SGL/DBL$48-$58.

Holiday Inn (940 East Main St, 24210; 676-2829, 800-HOLIDAY) 80 rooms, restaurant, complimentary breakfast, lounge, outdoor pool, exercise facilities, children under 19 stay free with parents, wheelchair access, a/c, TV, no-smoking rooms, fax, room service, no pets, laundry service, meeting facilities, senior citizen rates, major credit cards. SGL/DBL$45-$55.

The Inn On Town Creek (445 East Valley St, 24210; 628-4560) 3 rooms and suites, complimentary breakfast, private baths, no pets, on 4 acres, a/c, antique furnishings. SGL/DBL$75-$150.

Maplewood Farm Bed and Breakfast (Abingdon 24210; 628-2640) 3 rooms, complimentary breakfast, on 66 acres, working farm, private baths, no smoking, no children allowed. SGL/DBL$70.

Martha Washington Inn (150 West Main St, 24210; 628-3161) 61 rooms, restaurant, a/c, TV, antique furnishings, airport transportation, fireplace, gift shop, whirlpool, no pets, in-room refrigerators, major credit cards. SGL/DBL$80-$250.

The Silversmith Inn (102 East Main St, 24210; 676-3924) 3 rooms, complimentary breakfast, no pets, 1870s home, private baths, children over age 12 welcome, major credit cards. SGL/DBL$75-$115.

Summerfield Inn (101 West Valley St, 24210; 628-5905) 4 rooms, bed and breakfast, 1920s home, private baths, children over age 12 welcome, no pets, major credit cards. SGL/DBL$65-$75.

Super 8 Motel (298 Town Center Rd, 24210; 676-3329, 800-800-8000) 51 rooms and suites, free breakfast, no pets, children under 12 stay free with parents, free local calls, a/c, TV, fax service, no-smoking rooms, senior citizen rates, wheelchair access, meeting facilities, major credit cards. SGL/DBL$37-$42.

Victoria Albert Inn (224 Oak St, 24210; 676-2797) 4 rooms, a/c, TV, airport transportation, laundry facilities, no pets, major credit cards. SGL/DBL$65-$85.

Afton
Area Code 703

Looking Glass House (Afton 22920; 456-6844) 4 rooms, bed and breakfast, no pets, 1848 home, private baths, antique furnishings, major credit cards. SGL/DBL$75-$90.

Amherst
Area Code 804

Bed and Breakfasts of the Blue Ridge (Box 1108, 24521; 946-7207).

Dulwich Manor (Rte Five, 24521; 946-7207) 6 rooms, bed and breakfast, fireplace, private baths, no pets, whirlpool tub, on 85 acres, antique furnishings. SGL/DBL$65-$85.

Fairview Bed and Breakfast (Rte Four, 24521; 277-8500) 3 rooms, complimentary breakfast, a/c, private baths, no pets, a/c, antique furnishings, 1860s home. SGL/DBL$50-$68.

Appomattox
Area Code 804

Budget Inn (714 West Confederate Blvd, 24552; 352-7451) 20 rooms, pool, a/c, TV, major credit cards. SGL/DBL$26-$36.

Super 8 Motel (Rte 4, 24522; 352-2339, 800-800-8000) 46 rooms and suites, no pets, children under 12 stay free with parents, free local calls, a/c, TV, fax service, in-room refrigerators and microwaves, no-smoking rooms, senior citizen rates, wheelchair access, meeting facilities, major credit cards. SGL/DBL$36-$41.

Arlington
Area Code 703

American Hotel (1400 Jefferson Davis Hwy, 22202; 979-3772, 800-548-6261) 100 rooms, free breakfast, SGL/DBL$60-$65.

Best Western Arlington Inn and Tower (2480 South Glebe Rd, 22206; 979-4400, 800-426-6886, 800-528-1234) restaurant, free breakfast, lounge, pool, exercise facilities, children stay free with parents, a/c, TV, no-smoking rooms, laundry facilities, wheelchair access, pets allowed, senior citizen rates, meeting facilities, major credit cards. SGL/DBL$36-$56.

Comfort Inn Ballston (1211 North Glebe Rd, 22201; 247-3399, 800-221-2222) 126 rooms, restaurant, pool, wheelchair access, no-smoking rooms, no pets, children under 18 stay free with parents, gift shop, senior citizen rates, a/c, TV, meeting facilities, major credit cards. SGL/DBL$49-$107.

Courtyard by Marriott (1533 Clarendon Blvd, 22209; 528-2222, 800-321-2211) 162 rooms and suites, restaurant, lounge, pool, exercise facilities, whirlpools, children stay free with parents, laundry service, meeting facilities, senior citizen rates, major credit cards. SGL/DBL$85-$105.

Crystal Gateway Marriott Hotel (1700 Jefferson Davis Hwy, 22202; 920-3230, 800-228-9290) 702 rooms and suites, restaurant, lounge, entertainment, indoor and outdoor pool, exercise facilities, whirlpools, wheelchair access, TV, a/c, no-smoking rooms, gift shop, children stay free with parents, business services, meeting facilities, major credit cards. SGL/DBL$175-$190.

Days Hotel Crystal City (2000 Jefferson Davis Hwy, 22202; 920-8600, 800-325-2525) 247 rooms, restaurant, lounge, pool, children stay free with parents, room service, laundry service, a/c, TV, free local calls, free parking, airport transportation, no pets, wheelchair access, no-smoking rooms, senior citizen rates, major credit cards. SGL/DBL$49-$96.

Days Inn (2201 Arlington Blvd, 22201; 525-0300, Fax 525-5671, 800-325-2525) 128 rooms, restaurant, lounge, pool, children stay free with parents, room service, laundry service, a/c, TV, free local calls, transportation to local attractions, no pets, wheelchair access, no-smoking rooms, senior citizen rates, major credit cards. SGL$49-$70, DBL$60-$75.

Embassy Suites Hotel Crystal City (1200 Jefferson Davis Hwy, 22202; 979-9799, 800-EMBASSY) 267 2-room suites, restaurant, lounge, complimentary breakfast, lounge, indoor pool, whirlpool, exercise facilities, sauna, room service, laundry service, wheelchair access, complimentary newspaper, free local calls, no-smoking rooms, gift shop, transportation to local attractions, business services, meeting facilities, major credit cards. SGL/DBL$89-$159.

Holiday Inn Crowne Plaza (300 Army Navy Dr, 22202; 892-4100, Fax 347-0860, 800-848-7000) 1,000 rooms and suites, 2 restaurants, lounge, indoor pool, exercise facilities, children stay free with parents, gift shop, no-smoking rooms, TV, a/c, wheelchair access, in-room refrigerators, airport courtesy car, pets allowed, major credit cards. SGL/DBL$65-$85.

Howard Johnson National Airport (2650 Jefferson Davis Hwy, 22202; 684-7200, 800-I-GO-HOJO) restaurant, lounge, pool, children stay free with parents, wheelchair access, no-smoking rooms, TV, a/c, pets allowed, free parking, meeting facilities, senior citizen rates, meeting facilities, major credit cards. SGL/DBL$44-$64.

Hyatt Arlington (1325 Wilson Blvd, 22209; 525-1234, Fax 875-3393, 800-233-1234) 302 rooms and suites, restaurant, lounge, entertainment, pool, whirlpools, exercise facilities, room service, TV, a/c, no-smoking rooms, wheelchair access, free parking, 17 meeting rooms, meeting facilities for 330, major credit cards. SGL/DBL$69-$159+.

Hyatt Regency Crystal City (2799 Jefferson Davis Hwy, 22202; 418-1234, Fax 418-1289, 800-233-1234) 685 rooms and suites, restaurant, lounge, entertainment, pool, whirlpools, exercise facilities, room service, TV, a/c, no-smoking rooms, airport courtesy car, wheelchair access, 23,000 square feet of meeting and exhibition space, meeting facilities for 1,600, major credit cards, major credit cards. SGL/DBL$69-$159+.

Marriott Crystal City (1999 Jefferson Davis Hwy, 22202; 521-5500, 800-321-9879) 348 rooms and suites, restaurant, lounge, indoor pool, exercise facilities, whirlpools, sauna, no-smoking rooms, TV, a/c, airport courtesy car, gift shop, major credit cards. SGL/DBL$55-$100.

Marriott Key Bridge (1401 Lee Hwy, 22209; 524-6400, 800-327-9789) 585 rooms and suites, restaurant, lounge, indoor and outdoor pool, exercise facilities, whirlpools, sauna, jogging track, gift shop, wheelchair access, no-smoking rooms, gift shop, complimentary newspaper, TV, a/c, free parking, major credit cards. SGL/DBL$95-$125.

Marriott Crystal Gateway (1700 Jefferson Davis Hwy, 22202; 920-3230, 800-228-9290) 764 rooms and suites, restaurant, lounge, indoor and outdoor pool, exercise facilities, sauna, whirlpool, jogging track, TV, a/c, gift shop, pets OK, airport courtesy car, major credit cards. SGL/DBL$80-$110.

Memory House Bed and Breakfast (6404 North Washington Blvd, 22205; 534-4607) 2 rooms, complimentary breakfast, no smoking, no pets, private baths, children over the age of 12 welcome, 1899 home, antique furnishings. SGL/DBL$70-$75.

Quality Hotel (1200 North Courthouse Rd, 22201; 524-4000, 800-228-5151) 398 rooms and suites, pool, exercise facilities, airport transportation, TV, a/c, complimentary newspaper, major credit cards. SGL/DBL$65-$85.

Quality Inn Iwo Jima (1501 Arlington Blvd, 22209; 524-5000, 800-228-5151) 144 rooms and suites, pool, laundry service, TV, a/c, free parking, major credit cards. SGL/DBL$65.

Ramada Renaissance Hotel Techworld 2 (950 North Stafford St, 22203; 528-6000, Fax 789-4213, 800-228-9898) 214 rooms and suites, restaurant, lounge, entertainment, indoor pool, exercise facilities, boutiques, airport transportation, barber and beauty shop, children stay free with parents, wheelchair access, no-smoking rooms, TV, a/c, free parking, pets allowed, meeting facilities, major credit cards. SGL/DBL$80-$129.

Ritz Carlton Pentagon City (1250 South Hayes St, 22202; 415-5000, 800-241-3333) 386 rooms and suites, restaurant, lounge, pool, free parking, complimentary newspaper, TV, a/c, limousine service, major credit cards. SGL/DBL$165-$325.

Rosslyn Westpark Hotel (1900 North Fort Meyer Dr, 22209; 527-4814, 800-368-3408) 338 rooms and suites, pool, exercise facilities, TV, a/c, free local calls, free parking, pets allowed, major credit cards. SGL/DBL$67-$95, STS$115.

Sheraton National (900 South Orme St, 22204; 754-2921, 800-541-5500, 800-325-3535) 444 rooms and suites, pool, exercise facilities, TV, a/c, free parking, major credit cards. SGL/DBL$95.

Stouffer Concourse Hotel (2399 Jefferson Davis Hwy, 22202; 418-6800, 800-HOTELS-1) 388 rooms and suites, restaurant, lounge, pool, exercise facilities, TV, a/c, complimentary newspaper, 24-hour room service, major credit cards. SGL/DBL$80-$110.

Ashland
Area Code 804

Best Western Hanover House (Ashland 23005; 550-2805, 800-528-1234) restaurant, complimentary breakfast, lounge, outdoor pool, exercise facilities, children stay free with parents, a/c, TV, no-smoking rooms, TV, wheelchair access, pets allowed, senior citizen rates, meeting facilities, major credit cards. SGL/DBL$38-$65.

Comfort Inn (101 Cottage Greene Dr, 23005; 752-7777, 800-221-2222) 126 rooms, restaurant, pool, exercise facilities, whirlpools, wheelchair access, no-smoking rooms, no pets, children under 18 stay free with parents, senior citizen rates, a/c, TV, meeting facilities, major credit cards. SGL/DBL$42-$61.

Econo Lodge (Hwy 54 West, 23005; 798-9221, 800-4-CHOICE) 87 rooms, free breakfast, pool, TV, children under 12 stay free with parents, no pets, senior citizen rates, wheelchair access, a/c, TV, major credit cards. SGL/DBL$30-$60.

The Henry Clay Inn (114 North Railroad Ave, 23005; 798-3100, Fax 798-0048, 800-343-4565) 15 rooms and suites, bed and breakfast, restaurant, entertainment, private baths, no pets, fireplace, antique furnishings, meeting facilities for 50, major credit cards. SGL/DBL$75-$145.

HoJo Inn (101 South Carter Rd, 23005; 798-9291, Fax 798-1281, 800-I-GO-HOJO) 98 rooms, restaurant, lounge, pool, children stay free with parents, wheelchair access, no-smoking rooms, in-room refrigerators and coffee makers, TV, a/c, pets allowed, free parking, meeting facilities, senior citizen rates, meeting facilities, major credit cards. SGL/DBL$39-$65.

Holiday Inn (Box 149, 23005; 798-4231, Fax 798-9074, 800-HOLIDAY) 165 rooms, restaurant, lounge, outdoor pool, exercise facilities, children under 19 stay free with parents, wheelchair access, a/c, TV, no-smoking rooms, fax service, free local calls, free newspaper, room service, no pets, laundry service, meeting facilities for 150, senior citizen rates, major credit cards. SGL/DBL$60-$86.

Ramada Inn (806 England St, 23005; 798-4262, Fax 798-7009, 800-2-RAMADA) 91 rooms and suites, outdoor pool, wheelchair access, no-smoking rooms, airport transportation, free parking, pets allowed, wheelchair access, a/c, TV, room service, laundry facilities, meeting facilities, senior citizen rates, major credit cards. SGL/DBL$40-$60, AP$5.

TraveLodge (I-95 and State Rd 54, 23005; 798-6011, Fax 798-7342, 800-255-3050) 24 rooms, restaurant, lounge, complimentary breakfast, pool, wheelchair access, complimentary newspaper, laundry service, TV, a/c, free local calls, fax service, no-smoking rooms, in-room refrigerators and microwaves, no pets, major credit cards. SGL/DBL$50.

Basye
Area Code 703

Sky Chalet Country Inn (Basye 22810; 856-2147) 24 rooms and suites, restaurant, a/c, TV, whirlpools, pets allowed. SGL/DBL$50-$75.

Bedford
Area Code 703

The Bedford House (422 Avenel Ave, 24523; 586-5050) 2 rooms, a/c, TV, no smoking, no pets, major credit cards. SGL/DBL$65.

Best Western Inn (921 Blue Ridge Ave, 24523; 586-8286, 800-528-1234) 78 rooms, restaurant, complimentary breakfast, lounge, pool, exercise facilities, children stay free with parents, a/c, no-smoking rooms, TV, in-room refrigerators, wheelchair access, pets allowed, senior citizen rates, meeting facilities, major credit cards. SGL/DBL$38-$47.

Beltsville
Area Code 301

Ramada Inn Calverton (4050 Powder Mill Rd, 20705; 572-7100, Fax 572-8078, 800-2-RAMADA) 168 rooms, restaurant, lounge, entertainment, pool, wheelchair access, no-smoking rooms, free parking, pets allowed, wheelchair access, a/c, TV, room service, laundry facilities, 8 meeting rooms, transportation to local attractions, senior citizen rates, major credit cards. SGL$39-$73, DBL$39-$79, AP$6.

Berkeley Springs
Area Code 304

Coolfront Resort (Rte One, 25411; 258-4500, 800-888-8768) 150 rooms and suites, complimentary breakfast, restaurant, pool, open year-round, tennis courts, laundry facilities, private baths, sauna, jacuzzi, no-smoking rooms, wheelchair access, major credit cards. SGL$75-$105, DBL$150-$210.

Berryville
Area Code 703

Battletown Inn (102 West Main St, 22611; 955-4100) 12 rooms, restaurant, a/c, TV, whirlpools, 1800s inn, no pets, Modified American Plan available. SGL/DBL$82-$96.

Bethesda
Area Code 301

Ramada Inn (8400 Wisconsin Ave, 20814; 654-1000, Fax 654-0751, 800-2-RAMADA) 160 rooms, restaurant, lounge, pool, wheelchair access, no-smoking rooms, airport transportation, free parking, pets allowed, wheelchair access, a/c, TV, room service, laundry facilities, meeting facilities, senior citizen rates, major credit cards. LS SGL/DBL$65-$82; HS SGL/DBL$72-$115.

Big Stone Gap
Area Code 703

Country Inn Motel (Big Stone Gap 24219; 523-0374) 46 rooms, a/c, TV, no pets, major credit cards. SGL/DBL$26-$31.

Blacksburg
Area Code 703

Best Western Inn (900 Plantation Rd, 24060; 552-7770, 800-528-1234) 104 rooms and suites, restaurant, complimentary breakfast, lounge, pool, exercise facilities, tennis courts, children stay free with parents, a/c, TV, no-smoking rooms, VCRs, wheelchair access, pets allowed, senior citizen rates, meeting facilities, major credit cards. SGL/DBL$42-$53.

Brush Mountain Inn (3030 Mt. Tabor Rd, 24062; 951-7530) 2 rooms, bed and breakfast, no pets, private baths, fireplace, major credit cards. SGL/DBL$80-$95.

Comfort Inn (3705 South Main St, 24060; 951-1500, 800-221-2222) 80 rooms, pool, exercise facilities, wheelchair access, no-smoking rooms, no pets, children under 18 stay free with parents, senior citizen rates, a/c, TV, meeting facilities, major credit cards. SGL/DBL$42-$62.

HoJo Inn (3333 South Main St, 24066; 951-4242, Fax 951-4913, 800-I-GO-HOJO) 47 rooms, restaurant, lounge, pool, jacuzzi, children stay free with parents, wheelchair access, no-smoking rooms, TV, a/c, pets allowed, fax service, free parking, meeting facilities, senior citizen rates, meeting facilities, major credit cards. SGL$30-$40, DBL$33-$46.

Holiday Inn (Rte 460, 24060; 951-1330, Fax 951-4847, 800-HOLIDAY) restaurant, lounge, entertainment, outdoor pool, exercise facilities, children under 19 stay free with parents, wheelchair access, a/c, TV, no-smoking rooms, fax, room service, pets allowed, laundry service, meeting facilities, senior citizen rates, major credit cards. SGL/DBL$48-$60.

L'Arche Farm Bed and Breakfast (1867 Mt. Tabor Rd, 24060; 951-1808) 3 rooms, complimentary breakfast, no pets, no smoking, children over age 12 welcome, private bath, 1790s home, on 5 acres. SGL/DBL$70.

Marriott Hotel (900 Prices Fork Rd, 24060; 552-7001, Fax 552-0827, 800-228-9290) 148 rooms and suites, restaurant, lounge, entertainment, indoor and outdoor pool, exercise facilities, game room, free parking, wheelchair access, TV, a/c, airport transportation, pets allowed, no-smoking rooms, gift shop, children stay free with parents, business services, meeting facilities, major credit cards. SGL/DBL$69-$79.

Per Diem Bed and Breakfast (401 Clay St Southwest, 24060; 953-2604, 800-272-4707) 6 rooms and suites, complimentary breakfast, pool, no pets, private baths, children over age 12 welcome, antique furnishings, meeting facilities for 25, major credit cards. SGL/DBL$65-$90.

Sycamore Tree Bed and Breakfast (Blacksburg 24062; 381-1597) 6 rooms, free breakfast, private baths, children over age 12 welcome, no pets, no smoking, meeting facilities for 12, major credit cards. SGL/DBL$75-$110.

Twin Porches Bed and Breakfast (318 Clay St Southwest, 24060; 552-0930) 3 rooms, complimentary breakfast, no pets, private baths, major credit cards. SGL/DBL$55-$75.

Bland
Area Code 703

Big Walker Motel (Bland 24315; 688-3331) 20 rooms, a/c, TV, pets allowed, major credit cards. SGL/DBL$27-$35.

Willow Bend Farm Bed and Breakfast (Bland 24315; 688-3719) 4 rooms, complimentary breakfast, no pets, no smoking, children over the age of 12 welcome, private bath, fireplace. SGL/DBL$55-$75.

Bluefield
Area Code 703

Comfort Inn (Hwy 19-460 West, 24605; 326-3688, 800-221-2222) 60 rooms, restaurant, pool, wheelchair access, no-smoking rooms, no pets, children under 18 stay free with parents, senior citizen rates, a/c, TV, meeting facilities, major credit cards. SGL/DBL$39-$58.

Boston
Area Code 703

Blue Thistle Bed and Breakfast (Boston 22713; 987-9142) 4 rooms, complimentary breakfast, restaurant, in-room refrigerators, no pets, laundry facilities, whirlpools, major credit cards. SGL/DBL$80-$145.

Bowling Green
Area Code 804

Bowling Green Motel (Hwy 207, 22427; 633-6444) 16 rooms, restaurant, a/c, TV, no pets. SGL/DBL$28-$36.

Boyce
Area Code 703

The River House (Rte 2, 22620; 837-1476, Fax 837-2399) 5 rooms, complimentary breakfast, restaurant, no-smoking rooms, wheelchair access, no pets, meeting facilities, senior citizen rates. SGL/DBL$65-$120.

Bristol
Area Code 703

Budget Host Inn (1209 West State St, 24201; 669-5187, 800-BUD-HOST) 24 rooms, in-room refrigerators, no-smoking rooms, TV, VCRs, a/c, wheelchair access, children stay free with parents, no pets, senior citizen rates, meeting facilities, major credit cards SGL$28-$40, DBL$30-$45, AP$4.

Comfort Inn (2368 Lee Hwy, 24201; 800-221-2222) 60 rooms, restaurant, pool, whirlpools, wheelchair access, no-smoking rooms, no pets, children under 18 stay free with parents, senior citizen rates, a/c, TV, meeting facilities, major credit cards. SGL/DBL$40-$50.

Days Inn (Old Airport Rd, 24203; 669-9353, Fax 669-6974, 800-325-2525) 124 rooms, restaurant, lounge, children stay free with parents, room service, laundry service, a/c, TV, free local calls, pets allowed, wheelchair access, no-smoking rooms, senior citizen rates, major credit cards. SGL/DBL$38-$55.

Econo Lodge (912 Commonwealth Ave, 24201; 466-2112, 800-4-CHOICE) 48 rooms, restaurant, complimentary breakfast, pool, TV, children under 12 stay free with parents, pets allowed, senior citizen rates, wheelchair access, a/c, TV, major credit cards. SGL/DBL$31-$45.

HoJo Inn (4766 Lee Hwy, 24201; 669-1151, Fax 669-1153, 800-I-GO-HOJO) 60 rooms, restaurant, lounge, outdoor pool, children stay free with parents, wheelchair access, no-smoking rooms, TV, a/c, room service, fax service, pets allowed, free parking, meeting facilities, senior citizen rates, meeting facilities, major credit cards. SGL/DBL$38-$46.

Holiday Inn (West State St, 24203; 669-7171, 800-HOLIDAY) 123 rooms, restaurant, lounge, outdoor pool, exercise facilities, children under 19 stay free with parents, wheelchair access, a/c, TV, no-smoking rooms, fax service, room service, no pets, laundry service, meeting facilities for 250, senior citizen rates, major credit cards. SGL/DBL$42-$54.

Scottish Inn (Bristol 24201; 669-4148) 30 rooms, restaurant, a/c, TV, no pets, open year-round. SGL/DBL$24-$30.

Siesta Motel (1970 Lee Hwy, 24201; 669-8166) 21 rooms, restaurant, no pets, a/c, TV. SGL/DBL$30-$32.

Skyland Motel (4748 Lee Hwy, 24201; 669-0166) 18 rooms, restaurant, a/c, pets allowed. SGL/DBL$20-$32.

Super 8 Motel (2139 Lee Hwy, 24201; 466-8800, 800-800-8000) 62 rooms and suites, no pets, children under 12 stay free with parents, free local calls, a/c, TV, in-room refrigerators and microwaves, fax service, no-smoking rooms, senior citizen rates, wheelchair access, meeting facilities, major credit cards. SGL/DBL$36-$41.

Brodnax
Area Code 804

Sherwood Manor Inn (Rte 2, 23920; 848-0361) 4 rooms, restaurant, 1880s inn, no smoking, a/c, no pets. SGL/DBL$75-$85.

Buchanan
Area Code 254

Wattstull Inn (Buchanan 24066; 254-1551) 26 rooms, restaurant, pool, a/c, TV, pets allowed. SGL/DBL$38-$44.

Buena Vista
Area Code 703

Buena Vista Motel (Buena Vista 24426; 261-2138) 18 rooms and 1- and 2-bedroom efficiencies, restaurant, a/c, TV, kitchenettes, pets allowed, major credit cards. SGL/DBL$34-$40.

Camp Springs
Area Code 301

Days Inn (5001 Mercedes Blvd, 20746; 423-2323, Fax 702-9420, 800-325-2525) 125 rooms, restaurant, lounge, pool, children stay free with parents, room service, laundry service, a/c, TV, free local calls, no pets, wheelchair access, no-smoking rooms, senior citizen rates, major credit cards. SGL/DBL$55-$73.

Carmel Church
Area Code 804

Comfort Inn (Hwy 207, 22546; 448-2828, Fax 448-4441, 800-221-2222) 140 rooms, restaurant, pool, wheelchair access, no-smoking rooms, no pets, children under 18 stay free with parents, senior citizen rates, a/c, TV, meeting facilities, major credit cards. SGL/DBL$42-$70.

Days Inn (Ruther Glen, 22546; 448-2011, Fax 448-1316, 800-325-2525) 122 rooms, restaurant, lounge, pool, children stay free with parents, room service, laundry service, a/c, TV, free local calls, pets allowed, wheelchair access, no-smoking rooms, senior citizen rates, major credit cards. SGL/DBL$35-$75.

Carrollton
Area Code 804

Econo Lodge Benn's Church (20080 Brewer's Neck Rd, 23314; 357-9057, 800-4-CHOICE) 48 rooms and efficiencies, complimentary breakfast, pool, TV, children under 12 stay free with parents, pets allowed, in-room refrigerators, senior citizen rates, wheelchair access, a/c, TV, major credit cards. SGL/DBL$31-$55.

Chantilly
Area Code 703

Marriott Dulles (333 Service Rd, 22021; 471-9500, Fax 661-8714, 800-462-9671) 374 rooms and suites, restaurant, lounge, indoor and outdoor pool, exercise facilities, whirlpools, sauna, room service, complimentary newspaper, free parking, airport courtesy car, pets allowed, meeting facilities, major credit cards. SGL/DBL$65-$70.

Westfields International Conference Center (14750 Conference Center Dr, 22021; 818-0300, 800-635-5666) 370 rooms and suites, restaurant, lounge, pool, tennis, exercise facilities, free parking. Located 7 miles from the Dulles International Airport, 30 minutes from the downtown area. SGL/DBL$135-$165, STS$300.

Charles City
Area Code 804

Edgewood Plantation (4800 Tyler Memorial Hwy, 23030; 829-2962) 6 rooms, pool, no pets, whirlpool tub, antique furnishings, a/c. SGL/DBL$80-$128.

Charles Town
Area Code 304

Gilbert House Bed and Breakfast (Charles Town 25414; 725-0637) 3 rooms, complimentary breakfast, fireplaces, private baths, meeting facilities. SGL/DBL$70-$150.

Hillbrook Inn (Rte Two, 25414; 725-4223) 5 rooms, free breakfast, restaurant, private baths, fireplace, open year-round. SGL/DBL$150-$240.

Charlottesville
Area Code 804

Best Western Cavalier Inn (105 Emmet St, 22905; 296-8111, 800-528-1234) 118 rooms, restaurant, pool, pets allowed, a/c, TV, VCRs, airport transportation, children stay free with parents, no smoking rooms, wheelchair access, senior citizen rates, major credit cards. SGL/DBL$50.

Best Western Inn (1613 Emmet St, 22906; 296-5501, Fax 977-6249, 800-528-1234) 110 rooms, restaurant, complimentary breakfast, lounge, pool, exercise facilities, children stay free with parents, a/c, TV, no-smoking rooms, TV, wheelchair access, pets allowed, senior citizen rates, meeting facilities, major credit cards. SGL/DBL$48-$56.

Boar's Head Inn (Charlottesville 22905; 296-2181, Fax 971-5733) 175 rooms and suites, restaurant, lounge, pool, sauna, exercise facilities, tennis courts, airport transportation, pets allowed, a/c,TV, Modified American Plan available, major credit cards. SGL/DBL$100-$155.

Budget Inn (140 Emmet St, 22903; 293-5141) 40 rooms, restaurant, a/c, TV, airport transportation, no pets, no-smoking rooms, senior citizen rates. SGL/DBL$32-$42.

Comfort Inn (1807 Emmet St, 22901; 293-6188, 800-221-2222) 64 rooms, restaurant, pool, wheelchair access, no-smoking rooms, pets allowed, children under 18 stay free with parents, senior citizen rates, a/c, TV, meeting facilities, major credit cards. SGL$45-$55, DBL$53-$63, AP$6.

Charlottesville 335

Courtyard by Marriott (638 Hillsdale Dr, 22901; 800-321-2211) rooms and suites, restaurant, lounge, pool, exercise facilities, whirlpools, children stay free with parents, laundry service, meeting facilities, senior citizen rates, major credit cards. SGL/DBL$65-$75.

Days Hotel (1901 Emmet St, 22901; 977-7700, Fax 296-2425, 800-325-2525) 174 rooms, restaurant, lounge, indoor pool, in-room refrigerators, airport transportation, pets allowed, laundry service, a/c, TV, wheelchair access, no-smoking rooms, senior citizen rates, major credit cards. SGL/DBL$44-$76.

Econo Lodge (400 Emmet St, 22903; 296-2104, 800-4-CHOICE) 60 rooms, complimentary breakfast, pool, TV, children under 12 stay free with parents, no pets, senior citizen rates, wheelchair access, a/c, TV, major credit cards. SGL/DBL$36-$50.

The 1817 Antique Inn (1211 West Main St, 22903; 979-7353) 4 rooms and suites, bed and breakfast, private baths, no pets, 1817 home, antique furnishings, major credit cards. SGL/DBL$89-$129.

The English Inn (2000 Morton Dr, 22901; 971-9900, Fax 977-8008) 88 rooms, restaurant, lounge, indoor pool, sauna, exercise facilities, pets allowed, a/c, TV, airport transportation, major credit cards. SGL/DBL$58-$90.

Hampton Inn (2035 India Rd, 22901; 978-7888, Fax 963-0436, 800-HAMPTON) 123 rooms, restaurant, complimentary breakfast, pool, exercise facilities, children under 18 stay free with parents, no-smoking rooms, wheelchair access, computer hookups, fax service, TV, a/c, free local calls, pets allowed, meeting facilities, major credit cards. SGL/DBL$47-$59.

Holiday Inn (Fifth St and I-64, 22901; 977-5100, Fax 293-5228, 800-HOLIDAY) 130 rooms, restaurant, lounge, outdoor pool, exercise facilities, children under 19 stay free with parents, wheelchair access, transportation to local attractions, a/c, TV, no-smoking rooms, fax service, room service, no pets, laundry service, meeting facilities for 150, senior citizen rates, major credit cards. SGL/DBL$58-$73.

Holiday Inn (Hwy 29N, 22901; 293-9111, Fax 977-2780, 800-HOLIDAY) 201 rooms, restaurant, complimentary breakfast, lounge, outdoor pool, exercise facilities, children under 19 stay free with parents, wheelchair access, a/c, TV, airport transportation, no-smoking rooms, fax service, room service, no pets, laundry service, meeting facilities, senior citizen rates, major credit cards. SGL/DBL$58-$68.

Howard Johnson Hotel (1309 West Main St, 22903; 296-8121, Fax 977-7848, 800-I-GO-HOJO) 126 rooms, restaurant, lounge, pool, children stay free with parents, wheelchair access, no-smoking rooms, TV, a/c, no pets, free parking, laundry service, meeting facilities, senior citizen rates, meeting facilities, major credit cards. SGL$55-$69, DBL$65-$79.

Virginia

The Inn At Monticello (Rte 19, 22902; 979-3593, Fax 296-1344) 5 rooms, bed and breakfast, a/c, antique furnishings, no smoking, children over age 12 welcome, 1850s home, no pets, meeting facilities for 12, major credit cards. SGL/DBL$95-$130.

Knights Inn (Hwy 29, 22901; 973-8133, 800-843-5644) pool, wheelchair access, no-smoking rooms, TV, a/c, in-room refrigerators and microwaves, fax service, free parking, VCRs, senior citizen rates, major credit cards. SGL/DBL$44-$64.

Omni Charlottesville Hotel (235 West Main St, 22901; 971-5500, 800-THE-OMNI) 208 rooms and suites, restaurant, lounge, entertainment, pool, sauna, exercise facilities, whirlpools, laundry service, wheelchair access, no-smoking rooms, a/c, TV, major credit cards. SGL/DBL$99-$140.

Prospect Hill (Charlottesville 23093; 967-0844, 800-277-0844) 12 rooms, restaurant, lounge, pool, whirlpools, fireplace, a/c, in-room refrigerators, TV, no pets, private baths. SGL/DBL$150-$240.

Quality Inn (Hwy 250, 22901; 977-3300, 800-368-5689) 100 rooms and suites, restaurant, room service, exercise facilities, whirlpools, children stay free with parents, a/c, TV, laundry service, no-smoking rooms, meeting facilities, major credit cards. SGL$39-$59, DBL$45-$70, AP$5.

Sheraton Inn (Rte 29N, 22901; 973-2121, Fax 978-7735, 800-325-3535) 244 rooms and suites, restaurant, lounge, pool, exercise facilities, tennis courts, airport transportation, no pets, no-smoking rooms, a/c, TV, children stay free with parents, wheelchair access, meeting facilities, major credit cards. SGL/DBL$54-$64.

Silver Thatch Inn (3001 Hollymead Dr, 22901; 978-4686, Fax 973-6156) 7 rooms, bed and breakfast, no pets, 1780s inn, fireplaces, children over age 5 welcome, private baths, no smoking, meeting facilities for 20, major credit cards. SGL/DBL$105-$125.

Slave Quarters Bed and Breakfast (611 Preston Place, 22903; 979-7264) 1 3-room suite, complimentary breakfast, private bath, no pets, 1830s home, fireplace, antique furnishings, children over age 5 welcome, major credit cards. SGL/DBL$80-$120.

Super 8 Motel (390 Greenbrier Dr, 22901; 973-0888, 800-800-8000) 65 rooms and suites, no pets, children under 12 stay free with parents, free local calls, a/c, TV, fax, no-smoking rooms, senior citizen rates, wheelchair access, meeting facilities, major credit cards. SGL/DBL$37-$44.

Two Hundred South Street Inn (200 South St, 22901; 979-0200) 20 rooms, bed and breakfast, restaurant, whirlpools, fireplace, a/c, no pets, airport transportation, major credit cards. SGL/DBL$90-$170.

Chatham
Area Code 804

House of Laird (335 South Main St, 24531; 432-2523) 4 rooms and suites, bed and breakfast, private baths, no smoking, no pets, fireplace, antique furnishings, children over age 12 welcome. SGL/DBL$38-$77.

Sims-Mitchell House Bed and Breakfast (242 Whittle St Southwest, 24531; 432-0595, 800-967-2867) 2 suites, free breakfast, private baths, no pets, 1870s home, no smoking, major credit cards. SGL/DBL$50-$70.

Chesapeake
Area Code 804

Comfort Inn (4433 South Military Hwy, 23321; 488-7900, 800-221-2222) 94 rooms, pool, whirlpools, wheelchair access, no-smoking rooms, no pets, children under 18 stay free with parents, senior citizen rates, a/c, TV, meeting facilities, major credit cards. SGL$39-$54, DBL$45-$65.

Comfort Suites (1550 Crossway Blvd, 23320; 420-1600, 800-221-2222) 123 rooms, restaurant, complimentary breakfast, pool, exercise facilities, sauna, wheelchair access, no-smoking rooms, no pets, children under 18 stay free with parents, senior citizen rates, a/c, TV, meeting facilities, major credit cards. LS SGL/DBL$50-$65; HS SGL/DBL$60-$95.

Days Inn (1439 George Washington Hwy, 23323; 487-8861, Fax 485-1549, 800-325-2525) 53 rooms, restaurant, lounge, children stay free with parents, room service, laundry service, a/c, TV, free local calls, no pets, wheelchair access, no-smoking rooms, senior citizen rates, major credit cards. SGL/DBL$35-$48.

Days Inn (1433 North Battlefield Blvd, 23320; 547-9262, Fax 547-4334, 800-325-2525) 90 rooms, restaurant, lounge, outdoor pool, children stay free with parents, room service, laundry service, a/c, TV, free local calls, no pets, wheelchair access, no-smoking rooms, senior citizen rates, major credit cards. SGL/DBL$40-$75.

Econo Lodge (Military Hwy South, 23320; 543-2200, 800-4-CHOICE) 55 rooms and efficiencies, complimentary breakfast, pool, TV, children under 12 stay free with parents, pets allowed, senior citizen rates, wheelchair access, a/c, major credit cards. SGL/DBL$33-$50.

Hampton Inn (701A Woodlake Dr, 23320; 420-1550, Fax 424-7414, 800-HAMPTON) 119 rooms, restaurant, complimentary breakfast, pool, exercise facilities, children under 18 stay free with parents, no-smoking rooms, wheelchair access, computer hookups, fax service, TV, a/c, free local calls, pets allowed, meeting facilities, major credit cards. SGL/DBL$42-$50.

Hampton Inn (3235 Western Branch Blvd, 23321; 484-5800, 800-HAMPTON) 90 rooms, restaurant, complimentary breakfast, pool, exercise facilities, children under 18 stay free with parents, no-smoking rooms, wheelchair access, computer hookups, fax service, TV, a/c, free local calls, pets allowed, meeting facilities, major credit cards. SGL/DBL45-$50.

Holiday Inn (725 Woodlake Dr, 23320; 523-1500, Fax 523-0683, 800-HOLIDAY) 190 rooms, restaurant, lounge, entertainment, indoor pool, exercise facilities, children under 19 stay free with parents, airport transportation, wheelchair access, a/c, TV, no-smoking rooms, fax service, room service, no pets, laundry service, meeting facilities for 600, senior citizen rates, major credit cards. SGL/DBL$66-$74.

Red Roof Inn (724 Woodlake Dr, 23320; 523-0123, Fax 523-4763, 800-843-7663) no-smoking rooms, fax service, wheelchair access, complimentary newspaper, children stay free with parents, pets allowed, free local calls, in-room computer hookups, major credit cards. SGL/DBL$33-$43.

Super 8 Motel (3216 Churchland Blvd, 23321; 686-8888, 800-800-8000) 59 rooms and suites, pets allowed, children under 12 stay free with parents, free local calls, a/c, TV, in-room refrigerators and microwaves, fax service, no-smoking rooms, senior citizen rates, wheelchair access, meeting facilities, major credit cards. SGL/DBL$36-$41.

Super 8 Motel (100 Red Cedar Court, 23320; 547-8880, 800-800-8000) 62 rooms and suites, pets allowed, children under 12 stay free with parents, free local calls, a/c, TV, in-room refrigerators and microwaves, fax service, no-smoking rooms, senior citizen rates, wheelchair access, meeting facilities, major credit cards. SGL/DBL$34-$39.

TraveLodge (701 Woodland Dr, 23320; 420-2976, Fax 366-9915, 800-255-3050) 119 rooms, restaurant, lounge, free breakfast, pool, wheelchair access, complimentary newspaper, laundry service, TV, a/c, free local calls, fax service, no-smoking rooms, in-room refrigerators and microwaves, no pets, meeting facilities for 25, major credit cards. SGL$32-$38, DBL$38-$46, AP$6.

Wellesley Inn (1750 Sara Dr, 23320; 366-0100) 106 rooms, pool, a/c, TV, pets allowed, laundry facilities, major credit cards. SGL/DBL$40-$70.

Chester
Area Code 804

Comfort Inn (2100 West Hundred Rd, 23831; 751-0000, 800-221-2222) 123 rooms, restaurant, outdoor pool, exercise facilities, whirlpools, wheelchair access, no-smoking rooms, no pets, children under 18 stay free with parents, senior citizen rates, a/c, TV, meeting facilities, major credit cards. SGL/DBL$51-$67.

Days Inn (Chester 23831; 748-5871, Fax 748-3249, 800-325-2525) 172 rooms and suites, restaurant, complimentary breakfast, lounge, pool, kitchenettes, children stay free with parents, room service, laundry service, a/c, TV, free local calls, pets allowed, wheelchair access, no-smoking rooms, senior citizen rates, major credit cards. SGL/DBL$33-$50, STS$55.

Holiday Inn (2401 West Hundred Rd, 23831; 748-6321, Fax 796-9706, 800-HOLIDAY) 167 rooms, restaurant, lounge, outdoor pool, exercise facilities, children under 19 stay free with parents, wheelchair access, a/c, TV, no-smoking rooms, fax service, room service, no pets, laundry service, meeting facilities for 125, senior citizen rates, major credit cards. SGL/DBL$56-$64.

Super 8 Motel (2421 Southland Dr, 23831; 748-0050, 800-800-8000) rooms and suites, pets allowed, children under 12 stay free with parents, free local calls, a/c, TV, in-room refrigerators and microwaves, fax service, no-smoking rooms, senior citizen rates, wheelchair access, meeting facilities, major credit cards. SGL/DBL$40-$45.

Chilhowie
Area Code 703

Econo Lodge (Chilhowie 24319; 646-8981, 800-4-CHOICE) 42 rooms, complimentary breakfast, pool, TV, children under 12 stay free with parents, pets allowed, senior citizen rates, wheelchair access, a/c, TV, major credit cards. SGL/DBL$25-$58.

Chincoteague
Area Code 804

Assateague Inn (4605 Chicken City Rd, 23336; 336-3738) 27 rooms and efficiencies, pool, whirlpools, exercise facilities, no pets, a/c, TV, in-room refrigerators, major credit cards. SGL/DBL$52-$79.

Beach Road Motel (6151 Maddox Blvd, 23336; 336-6562) 19 rooms and suites, pool, a/c, TV, in-room refrigerators, no pets, major credit cards. SGL/DBL$42-$79.

Birchwood Motel (3650 Main St, 23336; 336-6133) 41 rooms and suites, pool, a/c, TV, in-room refrigerators, no pets. SGL/DBL$43-$66.

Driftwood Motor Lodge (7105 Maddox Blvd, 23336; 336-6557, 800-553-6117) 52 rooms and 1- and 2-bedroom suites, a/c, TV, no pets, in-room refrigerators, major credit cards. SGL/DBL$40-$90.

Island Motor Inn (711 Main St, 23336; 336-3141) 48 rooms and 1- and 2-bedroom apartments, pool, whirlpools, exercise facilities, a/c, TV, no pets, in-room refrigerators, major credit cards. SGL/DBL$58-$125.

Lighthouse Motel (4219 Main St, 23336; 336-5091) 17 rooms and efficiencies, restaurant, pool, no pets, a/c, TV, in-room refrigerators and microwaves, major credit cards. SGL/DBL$39-$65.

Refuge Motor Inn (7058 Maddox Blvd, 23336; 336-5511, Fax 336-6134, 800-544-8469) 68 rooms and apartments, indoor and outdoor pool, exercise facilities, sauna, a/c, TV, no pets. SGL/DBL$55-$105.

Sea Hawk Inn (6250 Maddox Blvd, 23336; 336-6527) 28 rooms and efficiencies, restaurant, pool, kitchenettes, no pets, a/c, TV, major credit cards. SGL/DBL$35-$60.

Sea Shell Motel (3720 Willow St, 23336; 336-6589) 40 rooms and apartments, pool, a/c, TV, major credit cards. SGL/DBL$36-$58.

Sunrise Motor Inn (4491 Chicken City Rd, 23336; 336-6671) 24 rooms and efficiencies, pool, kitchenettes, a/c, TV, major credit cards. SGL/DBL$36-$60.

Waterside Motor Inn (544 South Main St, 23336; 336-3434, Fax 336-1878) 45 1- and 2-bedroom apartments, pool, whirlpools, exercise facilities, in-room refrigerators, a/c, TV, no pets, major credit cards. SGL/DBL$78-$115.

The Watson House (4240 Main St, 23336; 336-1564) 6 rooms, bed and breakfast, a/c, antique furnishings, no pets. SGL/DBL$65-$99.

Christiansburg
Area Code 703

Days Inn (Christiansburg 24073; 382-0261, Fax 382-0365, 800-325-2525) 122 rooms, restaurant, lounge, outdoor pool, children stay free with parents, room service, laundry service, a/c, TV, free local calls, pets allowed, wheelchair access, no-smoking rooms, senior citizen rates, major credit cards. SGL/DBL$40-$55.

Econo Lodge (2430 Roanoke St, 24073; 382-6161, 800-4-CHOICE) 72 rooms, complimentary breakfast, pool, TV, children under 12 stay free with parents, pets allowed, senior citizen rates, wheelchair access, a/c, TV, major credit cards. SGL/DBL$32-$40.

Hampton Inn (50 Hampton Blvd, 24073; 382-2055, Fax 382-4514, 800-HAMPTON) 125 rooms, restaurant, complimentary breakfast, pool, exercise facilities, children under 18 stay free with parents, no-smoking rooms, wheelchair access, computer hookups, fax service, TV, a/c, free local calls, pets allowed, meeting facilities, major credit cards. SGL/DBL$42-$50.

HoJo Inn (100 Bristol Dr, 24073; 381-0150, 800-I-GO-HOJO) 68 rooms, restaurant, lounge, pool, children stay free with parents, wheelchair access, no-smoking rooms, free local calls, TV, a/c, pets allowed, free parking, meeting facilities, senior citizen rates, meeting facilities, major credit cards. SGL$30-$47, DBL$33-$50.

The Oaks (311 East Main St, 24073; 381-1500) 6 rooms and suites, complimentary breakfast, 1890s home, no pets, private baths. SGL/DBL$75-$115.

Super 8 Motel (Christiansburg 24073; 382-7421, 800-800-8000) 44 rooms and suites, no pets, children under 12 stay free with parents, free local calls, in-room refrigerators and microwaves, a/c, TV, fax service, no-smoking rooms, senior citizen rates, wheelchair access, meeting facilities, major credit cards. SGL/DBL$36-$41.

Super 8 Motel (55 Laurel St Northeast, 24073; 382-5813, 800-800-8000) 50 rooms and suites, no pets, children under 12 stay free with parents, free local calls, a/c, TV, in-room refrigerators and microwaves, fax service, no-smoking rooms, senior citizen rates, wheelchair access, meeting facilities, major credit cards. SGL/DBL$36-$41.

Sycamore Tree Bed and Breakfast (Demm Hill Rd, 24073; 381-1597) 6 rooms, complimentary breakfast, a/c, antique furnishings, major credit cards. SGL/DBL$75-$110.

Clarksville
Area Code 804

Needmoor (801 Virginia Ave, 23927; 374-2866) 3 rooms and suites, bed and breakfast, no pets, private bath, 1899 home. SGL/DBL$45-$55.

Noreen's Nest (906 Virginia Ave, 23927; 374-0603) 6 rooms and suites, bed and breakfast, private baths, no pets, 1790s home, meeting facilities for 10, major credit cards. SGL/DBL$80-$140.

Clifton Forge
Area Code 703

Firmstone Manor (Longdale Furnace Rd, 24422; 862-0892) 8 rooms, private baths, antique furnishing, no smoking, 1870s home, no pets, major credit cards. SGL/DBL$65-$125.

Cluster Springs
Area Code 804

Oak Grove Plantation Bed and Breakfast (Cluster Springs 24535; 575-7137) 2 rooms, complimentary breakfast, shared baths, no pets, Modified American Plan available, 1820s home, on 400 acres, open May to September. SGL/DBL$50.

Colonial Beach
Area Code 804

Days Inn (30 Colonial Ave, 22443; 224-0404, 800-325-2525) 60 rooms, restaurant, complimentary breakfast, lounge, outdoor pool, children stay free with parents, room service, laundry service, a/c, TV, free local calls, no pets, wheelchair access, no-smoking rooms, senior citizen rates, major credit cards. SGL/DBL$39-$51.

Colonial Heights
Area Code 804

Days Inn (2310 Indian Hill Rd, 23834; 520-1010, 800-325-2525) 122 rooms, restaurant, lounge, pool, children stay free with parents, room service, laundry service, a/c, TV, free local calls, no pets, wheelchair access, no-smoking rooms, senior citizen rates, major credit cards. SGL/DBL$22-$40.

Indian Hills Interstate Inn (Colonial Heights, 23834; 526-4772, 800-274-4667) 102 rooms, restaurant, lounge, entertainment, outdoor pool, a/c, TV, pets allowed, wheelchair access. SGL/DBL$26-$37.

TraveLodge (2201 Ruffinmill Rd, 23824; 526-4611, Fax 526-4611 ext 180, 800-255-3050) 60 rooms, restaurant, lounge, complimentary breakfast, pool, wheelchair access, complimentary newspaper, laundry service, TV, a/c, free local calls, laundry facilities, fax service, no-smoking rooms, in-room refrigerators and microwaves, no pets, major credit cards. SGL/DBL$28-$32.

Columbia
Area Code 804

Upper Byrd Farm Bed and Breakfast (6452 River Rd, 23038; 842-2240) 2 rooms, complimentary breakfast, private baths, no pets, children over age 12 welcome, no smoking, water view, on 26 acres. SGL/DBL$60-$70.

Covington
Area Code 703

Comfort Inn (State Rd 5 and Mallow Rd, 24426; 962-2141, 800-221-2222) 100 rooms and 2-room suites, restaurant, free breakfast, pool, exercise facilities, laundry service, wheelchair access, no-smoking rooms, no pets, children under 18 stay free with parents, senior citizen rates, a/c, TV, meeting facilities, major credit cards. SGL$48-$57, DBL$55-$64, AP$7.

Holiday Inn (Hwy 60 and I-64, 24426; 962-4951, 800-HOLIDAY) 79 rooms, restaurant, lounge, outdoor pool, exercise facilities, children under 19 stay free with parents, wheelchair access, a/c, TV, no-smoking rooms, fax service, room service, no pets, laundry service, meeting facilities for 250, senior citizen rates, major credit cards. SGL/DBL$50-$68.

Knights Court (Hwy 60, 24426; 962-7600, 800-843-5644) pool, wheelchair access, no-smoking rooms, TV, a/c, in-room refrigerators and microwaves, fax service, free parking, VCRs, senior citizen rates, major credit cards. SGL/DBL$42-$50.

Pinehurst Motel (Covington 24426; 962-2154) 30 rooms, a/c, TV, no pets, major credit cards. SGL/DBL$30-$55.

Culpeper
Area Code 703

Comfort Inn (890 Willis Lane, 22701; 825-4900, 800-221-2222) 49 rooms and suites, restaurant, pool, wheelchair access, kitchenettes, no-smoking rooms, pets allowed, children under 18 stay free with parents, senior citizen rates, a/c, TV, meeting facilities, major credit cards. SGL/DBL$45-$62, AP$8.

Fountain Hall (609 South East St, 22701; 825-8200, 800-476-2944) 5 rooms, bed and breakfast, private baths, no smoking, a/c, no pets, 1850s home, major credit cards. SGL/DBL$65-$105.

Holiday Inn (Hwy 29, 22701; 825-1253, Fax 825-7134, 800-HOLIDAY) 159 rooms, restaurant, lounge, outdoor pool, exercise facilities, children under 19 stay free with parents, wheelchair access, a/c, TV, no-smoking rooms, fax service, room service, pets allowed, laundry service, meeting facilities for 300, senior citizen rates, major credit cards. SGL/DBL$49-$59.

Super 8 Motel (889 Willis Lane, 22701; 825-8088, 800-800-8000) 62 rooms and suites, no pets, children under 12 stay free with parents, free local calls, a/c, TV, fax service, no-smoking rooms, senior citizen rates, wheelchair access, in-room refrigerators and microwaves, meeting facilities, major credit cards. SGL/DBL$36-$41.

Dahlgren
Area Code 703

Comfort Inn (Hwy 301, 22448; 663-3060, Fax 663-0803, 800-221-2222) 59 rooms, restaurant, complimentary breakfast, exercise facilities, in-room refrigerators, wheelchair access, no-smoking rooms, no pets, children under 18 stay free with parents, whirlpools, senior citizen rates, a/c, TV, meeting facilities, major credit cards. SGL/DBL$42-$55.

Danville
Area Code 804

Best Western Inn (2121 Riverside Dr, 24541; 793-4000, Fax 799-5516, 800-528-1234) 99 rooms, restaurant, complimentary breakfast, lounge, pool, exercise facilities, children stay free with parents, a/c, TV, no-smoking rooms, wheelchair access, whirlpool baths, no pets, senior citizen rates, meeting facilities, major credit cards. SGL/DBL$45-$50.

Days Inn (1390 Diney Forest Rd, 24540; 836-6745, Fax 876-1529, 800-325-2525) 46 rooms, restaurant, lounge, pool, children stay free with parents, room service, laundry service, a/c, TV, free local calls, no pets, wheelchair access, no-smoking rooms, senior citizen rates, major credit cards. SGL/DBL$29-$50.

Howard Johnson Hotel (100 Tower Dr, 24540; 793-2000, Fax 792-4621, 800-I-GO-HOJO) 118 rooms, restaurant, lounge, pool, children stay free with parents, wheelchair access, no-smoking rooms, TV, a/c, in-room refrigerators, laundry facilities, no pets, free parking, meeting facilities, senior citizen rates, meeting facilities, major credit cards. SGL$42-$57, DBL$50-$65.

Stratford Inn (2500 Riverside Dr, 24540; 793-2500, Fax 793-6960, 800-DANVILLE) 157 rooms and efficiencies, restaurant, lounge, pool, sauna, whirlpools, laundry facilities, in-room refrigerators, a/c, TV, airport transportation, major credit cards. SGL/DBL$42-$52.

Super 8 Motel (2385 Riverside Dr, 24541; 799-5845, 800-800-8000) 57 rooms and suites, no pets, children under 12 stay free with parents, free local calls, a/c, TV, in-room refrigerators and microwaves, fax service, no-smoking rooms, senior citizen rates, wheelchair access, meeting facilities, major credit cards. SGL/DBL$36-$41.

Doswell
Area Code 804

Best Western Kings Quarters (Doswell 23047; 876-3321, 800-528-1234) 248 rooms and suites, restaurant, free breakfast, lounge, outdoor pool, exercise facilities, lighted tennis courts, children stay free with parents, a/c, TV, VCRs, no-smoking rooms, wheelchair access, pets allowed, senior citizen rates, meeting facilities, major credit cards. SGL/DBL$35-$86.

Dublin
Area Code 703

Bell's Bed and Breakfast (13 Giles St, 24084; 674-6331) 5 rooms, complimentary breakfast, a/c, children over age 6 welcome, no pets, Victorian home. SGL/DBL$50-$65.

Comfort Inn (State Rd 100, 24084; 674-1100, 800-221-2222) 99 rooms, restaurant, pool, whirlpools, wheelchair access, no-smoking rooms, no pets, children under 18 stay free with parents, senior citizen rates, a/c, TV, meeting facilities, major credit cards. SGL$41-$54, DBL$47-$60.

Duffield
Area Code 713

Ramada Inn (Duffield 24244; 431-4300, Fax 431-2626, 800-2-RAMADA) 102 rooms and suites, restaurant, lounge, entertainment, pool, wheelchair access, kitchenettes, no-smoking rooms, airport transportation, free parking, pets allowed, wheelchair access, a/c, TV, room service, laundry facilities, meeting facilities for 350, senior citizen rates, major credit cards. SGL$48-$58, DBL$52-$62, STS$96-$124, AP$6.

Dumfries
Area Code 703

Econo Lodge (17005 Dumfries Rd, 22026; 221-4176, 800-4-CHOICE) 134 rooms and efficiencies, pool, children under 12 stay free with parents, no pets, senior citizen rates, wheelchair access, whirlpools, a/c, TV, senior citizen rates, major credit cards. SGL/DBL$43-$54.

Quality Inn (17133 Dumfries Rd, 22026; 221-1141, 800-368-5689) 186 rooms and suites, restaurant, room service, exercise facilities, children stay free with parents, pets allowed, a/c, TV, laundry service, no-smoking rooms, meeting facilities, major credit cards. SGL/DBL$53-$62.

Super 8 Motel (17336 Jefferson Davis Hwy, 22026; 221-8838, Fax 221-0275, 800-800-8000) 81 rooms and suites, no pets, children under 12 stay free with parents, free local calls, a/c, TV, in-room refrigerators and microwaves, fax service, no-smoking rooms, senior citizen rates, wheelchair access, meeting facilities, major credit cards. SGL/DBL$39-$41.

Emporia
Area Code 804

Best Western Inn (1100 West Atlantic Ave, 23847; 634-3200, Fax 634-5459, 800-528-1234) 97 rooms, restaurant, free breakfast, lounge, indoor and outdoor pool, exercise facilities, children stay free with parents, a/c, TV, no-smoking rooms, whirlpools, wheelchair access, pets allowed, senior citizen rates, meeting facilities, major credit cards. SGL/DBL$40-$50.

Comfort Inn (1411 Skippers Rd, 23847; 348-3282, 800-221-2222) 96 rooms, restaurant, pool, wheelchair access, no-smoking rooms, no pets, children under 18 stay free with parents, senior citizen rates, a/c, TV, meeting facilities, major credit cards. SGL/DBL$35-$43.

Days Inn (921 West Atlantic St, 23847; 634-9481, 800-325-2525) 122 rooms, restaurant, complimentary breakfast, lounge, pool, children stay free with parents, gift shop, room service, laundry service, a/c, TV, free local calls, pets allowed, wheelchair access, no-smoking rooms, senior citizen rates, major credit cards. SGL/DBL$33-$49.

Hampton Inn (1207 West Atlantic St, 23847; 634-9200, Fax 6340-9200 ext 100, 800-HAMPTON) 115 rooms, restaurant, complimentary breakfast, pool, exercise facilities, children under 18 stay free with parents, no-smoking rooms, wheelchair access, computer hookups, fax service, TV, a/c, free local calls, pets allowed, meeting facilities, major credit cards. SGL/DBL$42-$54.

Holiday Inn (311 Florida Ave, 23847; 634-4191, 800-HOLIDAY) 144 rooms, restaurant, lounge, outdoor pool, exercise facilities, children under 19 stay free with parents, wheelchair access, a/c, TV, no-smoking rooms, fax service, airport transportation, gift shop, room service, no pets, laundry service, meeting facilities, senior citizen rates, major credit cards. SGL/DBL$46-$55.

Reste Motel (3190 Sussex Dr, 23847; 535-8505) 32 rooms, restaurant, pool, a/c, TV, no pets, major credit cards. SGL/DBL$22-$28.

TraveLodge (3173 Sussex Dr, 23847; 535-8535, 800-255-3050) 64 rooms, restaurant, lounge, complimentary breakfast, pool, wheelchair access, complimentary newspaper, laundry service, TV, a/c, free local calls, fax service, no-smoking rooms, in-room refrigerators and microwaves, no pets, major credit cards. SGL/DBL$28-$32.

Fairfax
Area Code 703

Hyatt Fair Lakes (12777 Fair Lakes Circle, 22033; 818-1234, Fax 818-3140, 800-233-1234) 316 rooms and suites, restaurant, lounge, entertainment, indoor pool, whirlpools, exercise facilities, free parking, room service, TV, a/c, no-smoking rooms, wheelchair access, 7,300 square feet of meeting and exhibition space, major credit cards. SGL/DBL$69-$159+.

Quality Inn (11180 Main St, 22030; 591-5900, 800-368-5689) 214 rooms and suites, restaurant, room service, kitchenettes, whirlpools, exercise facilities, children stay free with parents, a/c, TV, laundry service, no-smoking rooms, meeting facilities, major credit cards. SGL$54-$95, DBL$64-$95.

Falls Church
Area Code 703

Marriott Fairview Park (3111 Fairview Park Dr, 22042; 849-9400, Fax 849-8692, 800-228-9290) 415 rooms and suites, restaurant, lounge, entertainment, indoor and outdoor pool, exercise facilities, whirlpools, sauna, jogging track, no-smoking rooms, wheelchair access, free parking, gift shop, TV, a/c, pets allowed, free parking, major credit cards. SGL/DBL$125.

Quality Inn Executive (6650 Arlington Blvd, 22042; 532-8900, 800-368-5689) 121 rooms and suites, restaurant, room service, exercise facilities, transportation to local attractions, children stay free with parents, a/c, TV, laundry service, no-smoking rooms, meeting facilities, major credit cards. SGL$58-$71, DBL$64-$77, AP$5.

Ramada Hotel Tysons Corners (7801 Leesburg Pike, 22043; 893-1340, Fax 847-9520, 800-2-RAMADA) 404 rooms and suites, restaurant, lounge, indoor and outdoor pool, wheelchair access, no-smoking rooms, airport transportation, free parking, pets allowed, wheelchair access, a/c, gift shop, transportation to local attractions, whirlpools, sauna, TV, room service, laundry facilities, meeting facilities, senior citizen rates, major credit cards. SGL$75-$99, DBL$85-$105, STS$175, AP$10.

Falmouth
Area Code 703

HoJo Inn (386 Warrenton Rd, 22405; 371-6000, 800-I-GO-HOJO) 100 rooms, restaurant, complimentary breakfast, lounge, outdoor pool, children stay free with parents, wheelchair access, no-smoking rooms, TV, a/c, pets allowed, free parking, meeting facilities, senior citizen rates, meeting facilities, major credit cards. SGL$32-$45, DBL$35-$55.

Fancy Gap
Area Code 703

Cascade Mountain Inn (Fancy Gap, 24328; 728-2300) 19 rooms and efficiencies, restaurant, a/c, TV, pets allowed. SGL/DBL$30-$45.

Days Inn (Fancy Gap, 24328; 728-5101, 800-325-2525) 60 rooms, restaurant, lounge, pool, children stay free with parents, room service, laundry service, a/c, TV, free local calls, no pets, wheelchair access, no-smoking rooms, senior citizen rates, major credit cards. SGL/DBL$38-$47.

Farmville
Area Code 804

Comfort Inn (Hwy 15, 23901; 392-8163, 800-221-2222) 50 rooms, restaurant, pool, exercise facilities, wheelchair access, no-smoking rooms, no pets, children under 18 stay free with parents, senior citizen rates, a/c, TV, meeting facilities, major credit cards. SGL/DBL$50-$55.

Days Inn (Highways 15 and 460, 23901; 392-6611, Fax 392-9774, 800-325-2525) 60 rooms, restaurant, complimentary breakfast, lounge, pool, children stay free with parents, room service, laundry service, a/c, TV, in-room computer hookups, free local calls, no pets, wheelchair access, no-smoking rooms, senior citizen rates, meeting facilities, major credit cards. SGL/DBL$37-$59.

Super 8 Motel (Hwy 15 South, 23901; 392-8196, 800-800-8000) 42 rooms and suites, no pets, children under 12 stay free with parents, free local calls, a/c, TV, in-room refrigerators and microwaves, fax service, no-smoking rooms, senior citizen rates, wheelchair access, meeting facilities, major credit cards. SGL/DBL$37-$42.

Flint Hill
Area Code 703

Caledonia Farm (Rte 1, 22627; 675-3693) 4 rooms and suites, complimentary breakfast, children over age 12 welcome, no pets, private baths, no smoking, meeting facilities for 10. SGL/DBL$80-$140.

Franklin
Area Code 804

Best Western Inn (Franklin, 23851; 562-4100, Fax 562-4846, 800-528-1234) 90 rooms, restaurant, complimentary breakfast, lounge, indoor pool, exercise facilities, whirlpools, children stay free with parents, a/c, TV, no-smoking rooms, wheelchair access, no pets, senior citizen rates, meeting facilities, major credit cards. SGL/DBL$43-$59.

Days Inn (1660 Amory Dr, 23851; 562-2225, 800-325-2525) 85 rooms and efficiencies, restaurant, lounge, pool, children stay free with parents, room service, laundry service, a/c, kitchenettes, TV, free local calls, no pets, wheelchair access, no-smoking rooms, senior citizen rates, major credit cards. SGL/DBL$38-$50.

Super 8 Motel (1599 Armory Dr, 23851; 562-2888, 800-800-8000) 52 rooms and suites, no pets, children under 12 stay free with parents, free local calls, a/c, TV, in-room refrigerators and microwaves, fax service, no-smoking rooms, senior citizen rates, wheelchair access, meeting facilities, major credit cards. SGL/DBL$33-$38.

Fredericksburg
Area Code 703

Best Western Inn (3000 Plank Rd, 22401; 786-7404, Fax 371-1753, 800-528-1234) 76 rooms, restaurant, complimentary breakfast, lounge, pool, exercise facilities, children stay free with parents, a/c, TV, no-smoking rooms, wheelchair access, pets allowed, senior citizen rates, meeting facilities, major credit cards. SGL/DBL$36-$50.

Best Western Inn (Williams St, 22401; 371-5050, Fax 371-1753, 800-528-1234) 108 rooms, restaurant, complimentary breakfast, lounge, pool, exercise facilities, children stay free with parents, a/c, TV, no-smoking rooms, laundry facilities, wheelchair access, pets allowed, senior citizen rates, meeting facilities, major credit cards. SGL/DBL$41-$50.

Best Western Inn (543 Warrenton Rd, 22405; 373-0000, Fax 373-8048, 800-528-1234) 88 rooms, restaurant, complimentary breakfast, lounge, pool, exercise facilities, children stay free with parents, laundry facilities, a/c, TV, no-smoking rooms, wheelchair access, pets allowed, senior citizen rates, meeting facilities, major credit cards. SGL/DBL$35-$46.

Fredericksburg 349

Comfort Inn North (557 Warrenton Rd, 22406; 371-8900, 800-221-2222) 80 rooms, restaurant, indoor pool, exercise facilities, wheelchair access, no-smoking rooms, no pets, children under 18 stay free with parents, senior citizen rates, a/c, TV, meeting facilities, major credit cards. SGL$40-$69, DBL$45-$90, AP$5.

Comfort Inn Southpoint (5422 Jefferson Davis Hwy, 22401; 898-5550, 800-221-2222) 125 rooms, restaurant, indoor pool, exercise facilities, wheelchair access, no-smoking rooms, no pets, children under 18 stay free with parents, senior citizen rates, a/c, TV, meeting facilities, major credit cards. SGL$41-$51, DBL$47-$57, AP$6.

Days Inn (14 Simpson Rd, 22405; 373-5340, 800-325-2525) 120 rooms, restaurant, lounge, outdoor pool, children under 12 stay free with parents, room service, laundry service, a/c, TV, free local calls, pets allowed, wheelchair access, no-smoking rooms, senior citizen rates, major credit cards. SGL/DBL$27-$49.

Days Inn (5316 Jefferson Davis Hwy, 22401; 898-6800, 800-325-2525) 156 rooms, restaurant, lounge, outdoor pool, children stay free with parents, room service, laundry service, a/c, TV, free local calls, pets allowed, wheelchair access, no-smoking rooms, senior citizen rates, major credit cards. SGL/DBL$27-$49.

Dunning Mills Inn (2305 Jefferson Davis Hwy, 22401; 373-1256, Fax 899-9041) 44 rooms and suites, pool, pets allowed, in-room refrigerators, TV, a/c, laundry facilities, major credit cards. SGL/DBL$55-$90.

Hampton Inn (2310 William St, 22401; 371-0330, Fax 371-1753, 800-HAMPTON) 166 rooms, restaurant, complimentary breakfast, pool, exercise facilities, children under 18 stay free with parents, no-smoking rooms, wheelchair access, computer hookups, fax service, TV, a/c, free local calls, pets allowed, meeting facilities, major credit cards. SGL/DBL$42-$53.

Holiday Inn (564 Warrenton Rd, 22405; 371-5550, Fax 373-3641, 800-HOLIDAY) 150 rooms, restaurant, lounge, outdoor pool, exercise facilities, children under 19 stay free with parents, in-room refrigerators, wheelchair access, a/c, TV, no-smoking rooms, fax service, room service, no pets, laundry service, meeting facilities for 85, senior citizen rates, major credit cards. SGL/DBL$35-$55.

Holiday Inn (5324 Jefferson Davis Hwy, 22408; 898-1102, 800-HOLIDAY) restaurant, lounge, entertainment, indoor pool, sauna, sap, game room, VCRs, exercise facilities, children under 19 stay free with parents, wheelchair access, a/c, TV, no-smoking rooms, fax service, room service, no pets, laundry service, meeting facilities, senior citizen rates, major credit cards. SGL/DBL$43-$58.

Howard Johnson Lodge (5327 Jefferson Davis Hwy, 22401; 898-1800, Fax 898-7354, 800-I-GO-HOJO) 130 rooms, restaurant, lounge, pool, children stay free with parents, wheelchair access, no-smoking rooms, fax service, TV, a/c, pets allowed, free parking, meeting facilities, senior citizen rates, major credit cards. SGL$32-$52, DBL$37-$57.

The Kenmore Inn (1200 Princess Anne St, 22401; 371-7622) 12 rooms and 1- and 2-bedroom apartments, restaurant, lounge, no pets, a/c, TV. SGL/DBL$75-$105.

La Vista Plantation (4420 Guinea Station Rd, 22408; 898-8444, Fax 898-1041) 2 rooms and suites, bed and breakfast, private baths, no pets, 1838 home, antique furnishings, TV, a/c, water view, no smoking. SGL/DBL$85.

Mary Josephine Ball Bed and Breakfast (1203 Prince Edward St, 22401; 373-7674) 3 rooms and suites, complimentary breakfast, no pets, children over the age of 10 welcome, shared baths, 1879 home, antique furnishings, a/c. SGL/DBL$45-$68.

Motel 6 (401 Warrenton Rd, 22405; 371-5443, 505-891-6161) 199 rooms, pool, free local calls, children under 17 stay free with parents, a/c, TV, major credit cards. SGL/DBL$24-$30.

Ramada Inn Spotsylvania Mall (Rte 3 West, 22404; 786-8361, Fax 786-8811, 800-2-RAMADA) 129 rooms, restaurant, lounge, pool, wheelchair access, no-smoking rooms, airport transportation, free parking, pets allowed, a/c, TV, room service, laundry facilities, meeting facilities, senior citizen rates, major credit cards. SGL$38-$55, DBL$43-$59, STS$75, AP$5.

Richard Johnson Inn (711 Caroline St, 22401; 899-7606) 11 rooms and apartments, a/c, TV, fireplaces, no pets, in-room refrigerators, no smoking, major credit cards. SGL/DBL$85-$140.

Royal Inn (5309 Jefferson Davis Hwy, 22401; 891-2700) 27 rooms, restaurant, a/c, TV, pets allowed. SGL/DBL$33-$36.

Sheraton Inn and Conference Center (Fredericksburg 22404; 786-8321, Fax 786-3957, 800-325-3535) 196 rooms and suites, restaurant, lounge, entertainment, pool, exercise facilities, tennis courts, no-smoking rooms, a/c, no pets, TV, children stay free with parents, wheelchair access, meeting facilities, major credit cards. SGL/DBL$59-$90.

Sleep Inn (595 Warrenton Rd, 22405; 800-221-2222) 66 rooms, wheelchair access, no-smoking rooms, no pets, children under 18 stay free with parents, senior citizen rates, a/c, TV, meeting facilities, major credit cards. SGL/DBL$35-$55.

Super 8 Motel (3002 Mall Court, 22401; 786-8881, 800-800-8000) 62 rooms and suites, no pets, children under 12 stay free with parents, free local calls, a/c, TV, in-room refrigerators and microwaves, fax service, no-smoking rooms, senior citizen rates, wheelchair access, meeting facilities, major credit cards. SGL/DBL$37-$42.

TraveLodge (605 Warrenton Rd, 22405; 371-6300, 800-255-3050) 40 rooms and suites, restaurant, lounge, complimentary breakfast, pool, wheelchair access, free newspaper, laundry service, TV, a/c, free local calls, fax service, no-smoking rooms, in-room refrigerators and microwaves, no pets, major credit cards. SGL$35-$48, DBL$40-$53, AP$5.

Front Royal
Area Code 603

Bluemont Inn (1525 North Shenandoah Ave, 22630; 635-9447) 28 rooms and apartments, restaurant, in-room refrigerators, whirlpools, a/c, TV, no pets, major credit cards. SGL/DBL$32-$65.

Midtown Motel (1122 North Royal St, 22630; 635-2196) 22 rooms and 1- and 2-bedroom suites, restaurant, a/c, no pets, major credit cards. SGL/DBL$28-$50.

Quality Inn Skyline Dr (10 Commerce Ave, 22630; 635-3161, 800-368-5689) 107 rooms and suites, restaurant, lounge, entertainment, pool, room service, exercise facilities, children stay free with parents, a/c, TV, laundry service, no-smoking rooms, meeting facilities, major credit cards. SGL/DBL$45-$86, AP$9.

Scottish Inn (533 South Royal Ave, 22630; 636-6168) 20 rooms, a/c, TV, no pets, major credit cards. SGL/DBL$40-$52.

Super 8 Motel (111 South St, 22630; 636-4888, 800-800-8000) 63 rooms and suites, no pets, children under 12 stay free with parents, free local calls, a/c, TV, fax service, pets allowed, no-smoking rooms, senior citizen rates, wheelchair access, meeting facilities, major credit cards. SGL/DBL$37-$47.

Twi-Lite Motel (53 West 14th St, 22630; 635-4148) 19 rooms and apartments, restaurant, pool, a/c, TV, whirlpools, in-room refrigerators, no pets, major credit cards. SGL/DBL$30-$42.

Twin Rivers Motel (1801 Shenandoah Ave, 22630; 635-4101) 20 rooms and apartments, pool, a/c, TV, no pets. SGL/DBL$35-$45.

Galax
Area Code 703

Scottish Inn (312 West Stuart Dr, 24333; 236-5117) 50 rooms and efficiencies, a/c, TV, exercise facilities, in-room refrigerators, no pets, senior citizen rates. SGL/DBL$33-$40.

Glade Spring
Area Code 703

Glade Economy Lodge (Glade Spring 24340; 429-5131) 51 rooms and 1- and 2-bedroom efficiencies, restaurant, a/c, TV, private baths, pets allowed, senior citizen rates. SGL/DBL$25-$33.

Glen Allen
Area Code 804

AmeriSuites (4100 Cox Rd, 23060; 747-9644) 126 suites, complimentary breakfast, outdoor pool, wheelchair access, a/c, TV, no-smoking rooms. SGL$59-$85, DBL$69-$94.

Quality Inn North (9001 Brook Rd, 23060; 266-2444, 800-368-5689) 63 rooms and suites, restaurant, outdoor pool, room service, exercise facilities, children stay free with parents, a/c, TV, laundry service, no-smoking rooms, meeting facilities, major credit cards. SGL/DBL$35-$50.

Gordonsville
Area Code 703

Norfields Farm Bed and Breakfast (Gordonsville 22942; 832-2952) 3 rooms and suites, complimentary breakfast, no smoking, 1850s home, on 500 acres, working farm, pets allowed. SGL/DBL$65-$75.

Sleepy Hollow Farm Bed and Breakfast (16280 Blue Ridge Turnpike, 22942; 832-5555, Fax 832-2515) 6 rooms and suites, complimentary breakfast, private baths, pets allowed, whirlpool tub, water view, fireplace, major credit cards. SGL/DBL$60-$95.

Hampton
Area Code 804

The Arrow Inn (Hampton 23666; 865-0300, Fax 766-9367) 59 rooms and 1- and 2-bedroom suites, restaurant, kitchenettes, a/c, TV, laundry facilities, pets allowed, in-room refrigerators. SGL/DBL$37-$59.

Comfort Inn (1916 Coliseum Dr, 23666; 827-5052, 800-221-2222) 66 rooms, restaurant, complimentary breakfast, pool, whirlpools, wheelchair access, no-smoking rooms, no pets, children under 18 stay free with parents, senior citizen rates, a/c, TV, meeting facilities, major credit cards. SGL/DBL$35-$52, DBL$50-$58, AP$6.

Courtyard by Marriott (1917 Coliseum Dr, 23666; 838-3300, 800-321-2211) 146 rooms and suites, restaurant, lounge, pool, exercise facilities, whirlpools, children stay free with parents, in-room refrigerators, no pets, laundry service, meeting facilities, senior citizen rates, major credit cards. SGL/DBL$55-$75.

Hampton

Days Inn (1918 Coliseum Dr, 23666; 826-4810, 800-325-2525) 144 rooms, restaurant, lounge, outdoor pool, children stay free with parents, room service, laundry service, a/c, TV, free local calls, pets allowed, wheelchair access, no-smoking rooms, senior citizen rates, major credit cards. SGL/DBL$33-$50.

Econo Lodge (1781 King St, 23669; 723-0741, 800-4-CHOICE) 48 rooms and suites, pool, children under 12 stay free with parents, no pets, senior citizen rates, wheelchair access, a/c, TV, major credit cards. SGL/DBL$35-$55.

Fairfield Inn (1905 Coliseum Dr, 23666; 827-7400, Fax 827-7400, 800-228-2800) complimentary morning coffee, outdoor pool, children under 18 stay free with parents, no-smoking rooms, remote control TV, free cable TV, free local calls, laundry service, a/c, wheelchair access, fax, meeting facilities, senior citizen rates, major credit cards. SGL/DBL$34-$60.

Hampton Inn (1813 West Mercury Blvd, 23666; 838-8484, Fax 838-8484 ext 777, 800-HAMPTON) 132 rooms, restaurant, complimentary breakfast, pool, exercise facilities, children under 18 stay free with parents, no-smoking rooms, wheelchair access, computer hookups, fax service, TV, a/c, free local calls, pets allowed, meeting facilities, major credit cards. SGL/DBL$40-$55.

Holiday Inn (1815 West Mercury Blvd, 23666; 838-0200, 800-HOLIDAY) 164 rooms, restaurant, lounge, indoor and outdoor pools, exercise facilities, children under 19 stay free with parents, wheelchair access, airport transportation, a/c, TV, no-smoking rooms, fax service, room service, no pets, laundry service, meeting facilities, senior citizen rates, major credit cards. SGL/DBL$68-$88.

La Quinta Inn (2138 West Mercury Blvd, 23888; 827-8680, Fax 827-5906, 800-531-5900) restaurant, complimentary breakfast, lounge, pool, free newspaper, free local calls, fax service, laundry service, no-smoking rooms, wheelchair access, remote control TV, a/c, free parking, meeting facilities, major credit cards. SGL/DBL$38-$48.

Radisson Hotel (700 Settlers Landing Rd, 23669; 727-9700, Fax 722-4557, 800-777-1700) rooms and suites, restaurant, lounge, entertainment, pool, wheelchair access, free parking, no-smoking rooms, TV, a/c, children stay free with parents, pets allowed, major credit cards. SGL/DBL$69-$99.

Red Roof Inn (1925 Coliseum Dr, 23666; 838-1870, Fax 838-1737, 800-843-7663) no-smoking rooms, fax service, wheelchair access, complimentary newspaper, children stay free with parents, pets allowed, free local calls, in-room computer hookups, major credit cards. SGL/DBL$35-$46.

Sheraton Inn Coliseum (1215 West Mercury Blvd, 23666; 838-5100, Fax 838-7349, 800-325-3535) 187 rooms and suites, restaurant, lounge, entertainment, indoor pool, airport courtesy car, no-smoking rooms, a/c, TV, children stay free with parents, wheelchair access, 7,000 square feet of meeting and exhibition space, 9 meeting rooms, meeting facilities for 700, major credit cards. SGL/DBL$59-$99.

Strawberry Banks Motor Inn (Hampton 23663; 723-6061, Fax 728-3712) 100 rooms and suites, pool, a/c, TV, water view, pets allowed, fireplaces, major credit cards. SGL/DBL$36-$56.

Super 8 Motel (1330 Thomas St, 23669; 723-2888, 800-800-8000) 67 rooms and suites, pets allowed, children under 12 stay free with parents, free local calls, a/c, TV, in-room refrigerators and microwaves, fax service, no-smoking rooms, senior citizen rates, wheelchair access, meeting facilities, major credit cards. SGL/DBL$34-$39.

Harpers Ferry
Area Code 304

Cliffside Inn (Rte 50, 25425; 535-6302) 100 rooms, restaurant, pool, wheelchair access, no-smoking rooms, senior citizen rates, pets allowed, major credit cards. SGL/DBL$50-$58.

Comfort Inn (Rte 240, 25425; 535-6391, 800-221-2222) 50 rooms, restaurant, pool, wheelchair access, no-smoking rooms, no pets, children under 18 stay free with parents, senior citizen rates, a/c, TV, meeting facilities, major credit cards. SGL/DBL$45-$60.

Harrisonburg
Area Code 703

Comfort Inn (1440 East Market St, 22801; 433-6066, 800-221-2222) 60 rooms, pool, wheelchair access, no-smoking rooms, no pets, children under 18 stay free with parents, senior citizen rates, a/c, TV, meeting facilities, major credit cards. SGL$43-$55, DBL$53-$65, AP$5.

Days Inn (1131 Forest Hill Rd, 22801; 433-9353, 800-325-2525) 89 rooms, restaurant, lounge, indoor pool, children stay free with parents, room service, laundry service, a/c, TV, free local calls, pets allowed, wheelchair access, no-smoking rooms, senior citizen rates, major credit cards. SGL/DBL$33-$50.

Econo Lodge (1703 East Market St, 22801; 433-2576, 800-4-CHOICE) 87 rooms and efficiencies, restaurant, pool, children under 12 stay free with parents, whirlpools, no pets, senior citizen rates, wheelchair access, a/c, TV, senior citizen rates, major credit cards. SGL/DBL$36-$42.

Hampton Inn (85 University Blvd, 22801; 432-1111, Fax 432-0748, 800-HAMPTON) 126 rooms, restaurant, complimentary breakfast, pool, exercise facilities, children under 18 stay free with parents, no-smoking rooms, wheelchair access, computer hookups, fax service, TV, a/c, free local calls, pets allowed, meeting facilities, major credit cards. SGL/DBL$45-$52.

HoJo Inn (605 Port Republic Rd, 22801; 434-6771, 800-I-GO-HOJO) 134 rooms, restaurant, lounge, pool, children stay free with parents, wheelchair access, no-smoking rooms, TV, a/c, pets allowed, free parking, meeting facilities, senior citizen rates, meeting facilities, major credit cards. SGL$35-$38, DBL$40-$43.

Holiday Inn (Pleasant Valley Rd, 22801; 434-9981, Fax 434-7088, 800-HOLIDAY) 130 rooms, restaurant, lounge, outdoor pool, exercise facilities, children under 19 stay free with parents, wheelchair access, a/c, TV, no-smoking rooms, fax service, room service, no pets, laundry service, meeting facilities for 200, senior citizen rates, major credit cards. SGL/DBL$55-$75.

The Joshua Wilton House (South Main St, 22801; 434-4464) 5 rooms and suites, restaurant, lounge, a/c, TV, 1880s inn, no pets. SGL/DBL$85-$95.

Massanutten Resort Hotel (Harrisonburg, 22801; 289-9441) 60 rooms and suites, restaurant, lounge, entertainment, indoor pool, tennis court, exercise facilities, sauna, a/c, TV, laundry facilities, no pets, major credit cards. SGL/DBL$100.

Motel 6 (10 Linda Lane, 22801; 433-6939, 505-891-6161) 115 rooms, pool, free local calls, children under 17 stay free with parents, a/c, pets allowed, TV, major credit cards. SGL/DBL$27-$34.

Rebels Roost Motel (South Main St, 22801; 434-9696) 10 rooms and efficiencies, a/c, TV, in-room refrigerators, pets allowed, major credit cards. SGL/DBL$28-$36.

Rockingham Motel (4035 South Main St, 22801; 433-2538) 12 rooms and efficiencies, a/c, TV, pets allowed, major credit cards. SGL/DBL$29-$35.

Sheraton Inn (1400 East Market St, 433-2521, Fax 434-0253, 800-325-3535) 140 rooms and suites, restaurant, lounge, indoor and outdoor pools, exercise facilities, whirlpools, sauna, pets allowed, no-smoking rooms, a/c, TV, children stay free with parents, wheelchair access, meeting facilities, major credit cards. SGL/DBL$57-$80.

Shoney's Inn (45 Burgess Rd, 22801; 433-6089) 98 rooms and efficiencies, restaurant, lounge, indoor pool, whirlpools, sauna, exercise facilities, no-smoking rooms, a/c, TV, no pets. SGL/DBL$37-$43.

Super 8 Motel (3330 South Main St, 22801; 433-8888, 800-800-8000) 49 rooms and suites, no pets, children under 12 stay free with parents, free local calls, a/c, TV, in-room refrigerators and microwaves, fax service, no-smoking rooms, senior citizen rates, wheelchair access, meeting facilities, major credit cards. SGL/DBL$35-$40.

Village Inn (Harrisonburg, 22801; 434-7355, 800-736-7355) 38 rooms and efficiencies, restaurant, complimentary breakfast, pool, a/c, TV, pets allowed, in-room refrigerators, laundry facilities, whirlpool baths. SGL/DBL$35-$50.

Herndon
Area Code 703

Comfort Inn (200 Elden St, 22070; 437-7555, 800-221-2222) 104 rooms, restaurant, complimentary breakfast, exercise facilities, wheelchair access, no-smoking rooms, no pets, children under 18 stay free with parents, senior citizen rates, airport courtesy car, in-room refrigerators and coffee makers, a/c, TV, meeting facilities, major credit cards. SGL/DBL$35-$80.

Hyatt Dulles (2300 Dulles Corner Blvd, 22071; 713-1234, Fax 713-3410, 800-233-1234) 317 rooms and suites, restaurant, lounge, entertainment, pool, whirlpool, exercise facilities, room service, in-room computer hookups, TV, a/c, no-smoking rooms, wheelchair access, airport courtesy car, 7,300 square feet of meeting and exhibition space, major credit cards. SGL/DBL$69-$159.

Marriott Suites Washington Dulles (13101 Worldgate Dr, 22070; 709-0400, Fax 709-0434, 800-228-9290) 254 suites rooms and suites, restaurant, lounge, entertainment, indoor and outdoor pool, exercise facilities, whirlpools, sauna, airport courtesy car, free parking, wheelchair access, TV, a/c, no-smoking rooms, gift shop, children stay free with parents, business services, meeting facilities, major credit cards. SGL/DBL$99-$139, STS$145-$250.

Ramada Renaissance Hotel (13869 Park Center Rd, 22071; 478-2900, Fax 478-9286, 800-2-RAMADA) 301 rooms and suites, restaurant, lounge, entertainment, pool, wheelchair access, no-smoking rooms, airport transportation, free parking, pets allowed, wheelchair access, a/c, TV, room service, laundry facilities, 19,000 square feet of meeting and exhibition space, meeting facilities for 700, senior citizen rates, major credit cards. SGL/DBL$109-$145.

Residence Inn (315 Elden St, 22071; 435-0044, Fax 435-0044, 800-331-3131) rooms and suites, complimentary breakfast, pool, spa, in-room refrigerators, coffee makers and microwaves, laundry facilities, free parking, TV, a/c, VCRs, pets allowed, fireplaces, children stay free with parents, no-smoking rooms, wheelchair access, meeting facilities for 20, major credit cards. SGL/DBL$65-$105.

Hillsville
Area Code 703

Bray's Manor Bed and Breakfast (Hillsville, 24343; 728-7901, 800-753-BRAY) 4 rooms, complimentary breakfast, no pets, TV, fireplace, private baths, major credit cards. SGL/DBL$40-$50.

Comfort Inn (State Rd 58, 24343; 728-4125, 800-221-2222) 65 rooms, restaurant, exercise facilities, whirlpools, wheelchair access, no-smoking rooms, no pets, children under 18 stay free with parents, senior citizen rates, a/c, TV, meeting facilities, major credit cards. SGL/DBL$39-$49.

Doc Run Lodge (Hillsville, 24343; 398-2212, Fax 398-2833) 41 rooms and suites, restaurant, lounge, indoor and outdoor pool, pets allowed, a/c, TV, kitchenettes, tennis courts, major credit cards. SGL/DBL$80-$105.

Econo Lodge (Hillsville, 24343; 728-9118, 800-4-CHOICE) 41 rooms and efficiencies, restaurant, pool, children under 12 stay free with parents, pets allowed, senior citizen rates, wheelchair access, a/c, TV, major credit cards. SGL/DBL$33-$43.

Knob Hill Motor Lodge (305 East Stuart Dr, 24343; 728-2131) 19 rooms and efficiencies, a/c, TV, no pets, major credit cards. SGL/DBL$30-$45.

Hopewell
Area Code 804

Comfort Inn (5380 Oaklawn Blvd, 23875; 452-0022, 800-221-2222) 128 rooms, restaurant, pool, exercise facilities, whirlpools, wheelchair access, no-smoking rooms, no pets, children under 18 stay free with parents, senior citizen rates, a/c, TV, meeting facilities, major credit cards. SGL$46-$60, DBL$52-$70.

Days Inn (4911 Oaklawn Blvd, 23860; 458-1500, Fax 458-9151, 800-325-2525) 115 rooms, restaurant, lounge, pool, jacuzzi, kitchenettes, transportation to local attractions, children stay free with parents, room service, laundry service, a/c, TV, free local calls, no pets, wheelchair access, no-smoking rooms, senior citizen rates, major credit cards. SGL/DBL$40-$80.

The Inn Keeper (3952 Courthouse Rd, 23860; 458-2600, Fax 458-1915) 104 rooms and suites, restaurant, pool, whirlpools, in-room refrigerators and microwaves, a/c, transportation to local attractions, senior citizen rates, TV, major credit cards. SGL/DBL$40-$47.

Hot Springs
Area Code 703

Cascades Inn (Hot Springs, 24445; 839-5355, Fax 839-5042) 49 rooms and suites, restaurant, lounge, pool, a/c, TV, golf, pets allowed. SGL/DBL$125-$220.

Hilcrest Motel (Hot Springs, 24445; 839-5316) 12 rooms and efficiencies, restaurant, in-room refrigerators, a/c, TV, pets allowed, major credit cards. SGL/DBL$32-$42.

The Homestead (Hot Springs, 24445; 839-5500, Fax 839-3056) 600 rooms and suites, restaurant, lounge, entertainment, indoor and outdoor pool, sauna, whirlpool, golf, exercise facilities, airport transportation, a/c, no pets, TV, fireplaces, American plan and Modified American Plan available, major credit cards. SGL/DBL$110-$300.

Kings Victorian Inn (Hot Springs, 24445; 839-3134) 5 rooms and efficiencies, 1890s inn, no smoking, in-room refrigerators, no smoking, no pets. SG/DBL$65-$95.

Roseloe Motel (Hot Springs, 24445; 839-5373) 14 rooms and effiencies, a/c, TV, kitchenettes, in-room refrigerators, pets allowed, senior citizen rates. SGL/DBL$34-$44.

Independence
Area Code 703

River View Bed and Breakfast (Independence, 24348; 236-4187, 800-841-6628) 2 rooms, complimentary breakfast, no pets, water view, children over age 12 welcome. SGL/DBL$50-$60.

Irvington
Area Code 804

The Tides Inn (Irvington, 22480; 438-5000, Fax 438-5222) 110 rooms and suites, restaurant, lounge, entertainment, pool, tennis court, water view, airport transportation, a/c, TV, pets allowed, laundry facilities, no-smoking rooms, wheelchair access, meeting facilities, major credit cards. SGL/DBL$120-$275.

The Tides Lodge (1 St Andrews Lane, 22480; 438-6000, Fax 438-5950, 800-248-4337) 60 rooms and 1- and 2-bedroom suites, restaurant, lounge, entertainment, indoor and outdoor pools, sauna, laundry facilities, tennis court, a/c, TV, pets allowed, golf, in-room refrigerators, major credit cards. SGL/DBL$110-$240.

Keysville
Area Code 804

Sheldon's Motel (Keysville, 23947; 736-8434) 39 rooms and efficiencies, restaurant, lounge, a/c, TV, no pets, in-room refrigerators, major credit cards. SGL/DBL$36-$42.

Lake Anna
Area Code 703

Light House Inn (4634 Court House Rd, 23117; 895-5249) 14 rooms and 1- and 2-bedroom efficiencies, a/c, TV, in-room refrigerators, no pets. SGL/DBL$45-$70.

Landmark
Area Code 703

Comfort Inn (6254 Duke St, 22312; 642-3422, 800-221-2222) 150 rooms, restaurant, complimentary breakfast, pool, wheelchair access, no-smoking rooms, no pets, children under 18 stay free with parents, senior citizen rates, a/c, free parking, fax service, TV, meeting facilities, major credit cards. SGL$45-$79, DBL$49-$85.

Leesburg
Area Code 703

Carradoc Hall Hotel (1500 East Market St, 22075; 771-9200, Fax 771-1575) 126 rooms and effiencies, restaurant, lounge, pool, no pets, a/c, TV, no-smoking rooms, senior citizen rates, major credit cards. SGL/DBL$49-$53.

Days Inn Downtown (721 East Market St, 22075; 777-6622, 800-325-2525) 80 rooms, restaurant, lounge, children stay free with parents, room service, laundry service, a/c, TV, free local calls, pets allowed, wheelchair access, no-smoking rooms, senior citizen rates, major credit cards. SGL/DBL$39-$51.

Fleetwood Farm (Rte 1, 22075; 327-4325, Fax 777-8236) 2 rooms, bed and breakfast, no pets, private baths, children over age 12 welcome, laundry facilities, whirlpool tub, 1745 home, a/c, antique furnishings, fireplace. SGL/DBL$95-$120.

Lansdowne Conference Resort (44050 Woodridge Pkwy, 22075; 729-8400, Fax 729-4096) 305 rooms and suites, restaurant, lounge, indoor and outdoor pools, lighted tennis courts, whirlpools, sauna, a/c, TV, VCRs, in-room refrigerators, airport transportation, no pets, no-smoking rooms, wheelchair access, senior citizen rates, major credit cards. SGL/DBL$89-$175, STS$250-$650.

Norris House Inn (108 Loudoun St Southwest, 22075; 777-1806, Fax 771-8051) 6 rooms, bed and breakfast, private baths, no pets, a/c, no pets, 1806 home, antqiue furnishings, fireplaces, major credit cards. SGL/DBL$80-$140.

Lexington
Area Code 703

Rental and Reservation Service

Historic Country Inns of Lexington (11 North Main St, 24450; 463-2044, Fax 463-7262).

ロロロ

Best Western Inn (Lexington, 24450; 463-2143, 800-528-1234) 56 rooms, restaurant, complimentary breakfast, lounge, pool, exercise facilities, children stay free with parents, a/c, TV, no-smoking rooms, in-room refrigerators, wheelchair access, pets allowed, senior citizen rates, meeting facilities, major credit cards. SGL/DBL$37-$63.

Comfort Inn (Hwy 11, 24450; 463-7311, 800-221-2222) 80 rooms, restaurant, indoor pool, wheelchair access, no-smoking rooms, pets allowed, children under 18 stay free with parents, senior citizen rates, laundry facilities, a/c, TV, meeting facilities, major credit cards. SGL/DBL$40-$65, AP$5.

Days Inn (Rte 6, 24450; 463-2143, 800-325-2525) 53 rooms and suites, restaurant, lounge, children stay free with parents, room service, laundry service, a/c, TV, free local calls, no pets, wheelchair access, no-smoking rooms, senior citizen rates, major credit cards. SGL/DBL$45-$70, STS$60-$80.

Econo Lodge (Lexington, 24450; 463-7371, 800-4-CHOICE) 48 rooms, restaurant, children under 12 stay free with parents, no pets, senior citizen rates, wheelchair access, a/c, TV, major credit cards. SGL/DBL$34-$47.

Holiday Inn (Hwy 11 and I-64, 24450; 463-7351, 800-HOLIDAY) 72 rooms, restaurant, lounge, outdoor pool, exercise facilities, children under 19 stay free with parents, wheelchair access, a/c, TV, no-smoking rooms, fax service, room service, pets allowed, laundry service, meeting facilities for 250, senior citizen rates, American plan and Modified American Plan available, major credit cards. SGL/DBL$62-$67.

Howard Johnson Hotel (Hwy 11, 24450; 463-9181, Fax 464-3448, 800-I-GO-HOJO) 100 rooms, restaurant, lounge, pool, children stay free with parents, wheelchair access, no-smoking rooms, laundry facilities, gift shop, TV, a/c, pets allowed, free parking, meeting facilities, senior citizen rates, major credit cards. LS SGL/DBL$32-$59; HS SGL/DBL$38-$65.

Llewellyn Lodge (603 South Main St, 24450; 463-3235) 6 rooms and suites, a/c, laundry facilities, no pets, no smoking, major credit cards. SGL/DBL$50-$80.

Maple Hall Country Inn (11 North Main St, 24450; 463-2044, Fax 463-7262) 21 room and suites, restaurant, pool, tennis court, no pets, a/c, TV, in-room refrigerators. SGL/DBL$80-$130.

Ramada Inn (Hwy 11, 24450; 463-6666, Fax 464-3639, 800-2-RAMADA) 80 rooms and suites, restaurant, lounge, indoor pool, wheelchair access, no-smoking rooms, airport transportation, free parking, pets allowed, wheelchair access, a/c, TV, room service, laundry facilities, meeting facilities, senior citizen rates, major credit cards. SGL$52-$56, DBL$60-$64, STS$90, AP$6.

Super 8 Motel (Rte 7, 24450; 463-7858, 800-800-8000) 50 rooms and suites, no pets, children under 12 stay free with parents, free local calls, a/c, TV, in-room refrigerators and microwaves, fax service, no-smoking rooms, senior citizen rates, wheelchair access, meeting facilities, major credit cards. SGL/DBL$37-$44.

Thrifty Inn (820 South Main St, 24450; 463-2151) 44 rooms and effiencies, restaurant, a/c, TV, VCRs, pets OK, major credit cards. SGL/DBL$30-$45.

Locust Dale
Area Code 703

The Inn At Meander Plantation (Locust Dale, 22948; 672-4912) 4 rooms, bed and breakfast, private baths, no children allowed, no smoking, 1720s home, Modified American Plan available. SGL/DBL$85-$120.

Logan
Area Code 304

Super 8 Motel (316 Riverview Ave, 25601; 752-8787, 800-800-8000) 59 rooms and suites, pets allowed, children under 12 stay free with parents, free local calls, a/c, TV, in-room refrigerators and microwaves, fax service, no-smoking rooms, senior citizen rates, wheelchair access, meeting facilities, major credit cards. SGL/DBL$42-$47.

Luray
Area Code 703

Ramada Inn Shenandoah Valley (Hwy 211 Bypass East, 22835; 743-4521, Fax 743-6863, 800-2-RAMADA) 101 rooms and suites, restaurant, lounge, pool, no-smoking rooms, airport transportation, free parking, pets allowed, wheelchair access, a/c, TV, room service, laundry facilities, meeting facilities for 200, senior citizen rates, major credit cards. LS SGL$39-$49, DBL$46-$56; HS SGL$49-$70, DBL$56-$86, STS$115, AP$7.

Lynchburg
Area Code 804

Best Western Inn (2815 Candler's Mountain Rd, 24560; 237-2986, 800-528-1234) 87 rooms, restaurant, complimentary breakfast, lounge, pool, exercise facilities, children stay free with parents, a/c, TV, no-smoking rooms, wheelchair access, pets allowed, senior citizen rates, meeting facilities, major credit cards. SGL/DBL$42-$49.

Comfort Inn (Odd Fellows Rd, 24501; 847-9041, 800-221-2222) 120 rooms, complimentary breakfast, restaurant, pool, wheelchair access, no-smoking rooms, no pets, children under 18 stay free with parents, senior citizen rates, a/c, TV, meeting facilities, major credit cards. LS SGL$42-$80, DBL$52-$85; HS SGL50-$90, DBL$60-$100.

Days Inn (3320 Candlers Mountain Rd, 24502; 847-8655, Fax 846-DAYS, 800-325-2525) 131 rooms, restaurant, complimentary breakfast, lounge, pool, children stay free with parents, room service, laundry service, a/c, TV, free local calls, no pets, wheelchair access, no-smoking rooms, senior citizen rates, major credit cards. SGL/DBL$44-$64.

Econo Lodge (2400 Stadium Rd, 24502; 847-1045, 800-4-CHOICE) 47 rooms, complimentary breakfast, pool, TV, children under 18 stay free with parents, pets allowed, senior citizen rates, wheelchair access, a/c, major credit cards. SGL/DBL$48-$56.

Hilton Hotel (2600 Chandler's Mountain Rd, 24502; 237-6333, Fax 237-4277, 800-HILTONS) 168 rooms and suites, restaurant, lounge, entertainment, indoor pool, exercise facilities, sauna, jacuzzi, children stay free with parents, no-smoking rooms, free parking, wheelchair access, pets allowed, a/c, TV, business services, meeting facilities, major credit cards. SGL/DBL$80-$120.

Holiday Inn (Odd Fellows Rd, 24506; 847-4424, Fax 846-4965, 800-HOLIDAY) restaurant, lounge, outdoor pool, exercise facilities, children under 19 stay free with parents, wheelchair access, a/c, TV, no-smoking rooms, fax service, room service, no pets, laundry service, meeting facilities for 300, airport transportation, senior citizen rates, major credit cards. SGL/DBL$60-$80.

Howard Johnson Lodge (Rte 29 North, 24506; 845-7041, 800-I-GO-HOJO) 70 rooms, restaurant, lounge, pool, children stay free with parents, wheelchair access, no-smoking rooms, room service, TV, a/c, pets allowed, free parking, meeting facilities, senior citizen rates, meeting facilities, major credit cards. SGL/DBL$42-$64.

Innkeeper of Lynchburg (2901 Chandler's Mountain Rd, 24504; 237-7771) 104 rooms, complimentary breakfast, pool, whirlpools, free newspaper, TV, a/c, meeting facilities, major credit cards. SGL/DBL$55-$100.

Langhorne Manor (313 Washington St, 24504; 846-4667) 3 rooms and suites, bed and breakfast, 1850s house, antique furnishings, private baths, a/c, no pets. SGL/DBL$70-$95.

Lynchburg Mansion Inn Bed and Breakfast (405 Madison St, 25404; 528-5400, 800-352-1199) 4 rooms, complimentary breakfast, fireplace, private bath, no smoking, no pets, TV, meeting facilities, major credit cards. SGL/DBL$89-$109.

The Madison House Bed and Breakfast (413 Madison St, 24504; 528-1503, 800-828-MHBB) 4 rooms, complimentary breakfast, private baths, no smoking, no pets, no children allowed, 1880s home, antique furnishings, a/c, TV, major credit cards. SGL/DBL$70-$95.

Ramada Inn (1500 Main St, 24504; 845-5975, Fax 846-8617, 800-2-RAMADA) 60 rooms, restaurant, lounge, entertainment, pool, wheelchair access, no-smoking rooms, airport transportation, free parking, in-room refrigerators and microwaves, pets allowed, wheelchair access, a/c, TV, room service, laundry facilities, meeting facilities, senior citizen rates, major credit cards. SGL/DBL$35-$43, AP$5.

Radisson Hotel (601 Main St, 24504; 528-2500, Fax 528-0062, 800-777-1700) rooms and suites, restaurant, lounge, entertainment, pool, wheelchair access, free parking, no-smoking rooms, TV, a/c, children stay free with parents, pets allowed, major credit cards. SGL/DBL$85-$125.

Timberlake Motel (11222 Timberlake Rd, 24504; 525-2160) 41 rooms, outdoor pool, TV, a/c, jacuzzi, in-room refrigerators, children under 12 stay free with parents, major credit cards. SGL/DBL$48-$58.

Madison
Area Code 703

Shenandoah Springs (Madison, 22727; 923-4300) 4 rooms, bed and breakfast, private baths, no pets, Modified American Plan available, fireplace, antique furnishings, meeting facilities for 100. SGL/DBL$65-$120.

Madison Heights
Area Code 804

Howard Johnson Lodge (Rte 29 North, 24572; 845-7041, 800-I-GO-HOJO) restaurant, lounge, outdoor pool, children stay free with parents, wheelchair access, no-smoking rooms, TV, a/c, pets allowed, free parking, meeting facilities, room service, senior citizen rates, meeting facilities, major credit cards. SGL/DBL$38-$46.

Winridge Bed and Breakfast (Rte 1, 24572; 384-7220) 3 rooms, complimentary breakfast, private baths, no pets, meeting facilities for 12. SGL/DBL$59-$69.

Malden
Area Code 304

Rose Cottage Bed and Breakfast (107 Georges Dr, 25306; 925-6568) 3 rooms, complimentary breakfast, a/c, water view. SGL/DBL$50-$68.

Manassas
Area Code 703

Days Inn (10653 Balls Ford Rd, 22110; 368-2800, Fax 368-0083, 800-325-2525) 113 rooms, restaurant, lounge, pool, children stay free with parents, room service, laundry service, a/c, TV, free local calls, no pets, wheelchair access, no-smoking rooms, senior citizen rates, major credit cards. SGL/DBL$35-$49.

HoJo Inn (7249 New Market Court, 22110; 369-1700, Fax 369-4451, 800-I-GO-HOJO) 150 rooms, restaurant, complimentary breakfast, lounge, pool, children stay free with parents, wheelchair access, no-smoking rooms, TV, a/c, free parking, laundry facilities, pets allowed, free parking, senior citizen rates, meeting facilities, major credit cards. SGL/DBL$38-$50.

Quality Inn (7295 Williamson Blvd, 22110; 369-1100, 800-368-5689) 125 rooms and suites, restaurant, pool, sauna, room service, exercise facilities, children stay free with parents, a/c, TV, laundry service, no-smoking rooms, meeting facilities, major credit cards. SGL/DBL$49-$69.

Ramada Inn (Manassas, 22110; 361-8000, 800-2-RAMADA) 125 rooms, restaurant, lounge, entertainment, pool, wheelchair access, no-smoking rooms, airport transportation, free parking, pets allowed, a/c, TV, room service, laundry facilities, meeting facilities, senior citizen rates, major credit cards. SGL/DBL$45-$72.

Red Roof Inn (10610 Automotive Dr, 22110; 335-9333, Fax 335-9342, 800-843-7663) no-smoking rooms, fax, wheelchair access, complimentary newspaper, children stay free with parents, pets allowed, free local calls, in-room computer hookups, major credit cards. SGL/DBL$38-$44.

Sunrise Hill Bed and Breakfast (5590 Old Farm Lane, 22110; 754-8309) 2 rooms, complimentary breakfast, private baths, no pets, no smoking, children over age 10 welcome, major credit cards. SGL/DBL$72.

Marion
Area Code 703

Budget Host Marion Motel (435 South Main St, 24345; 783-8511, 800-BUD-HOST) 15 rooms, in-room refrigerators, no-smoking rooms, TV, VCRs, a/c, wheelchair access, children stay free with parents, senior citizen rates, meeting facilities, major credit cards. SGL$28-$36, DBL$32-$48, AP$4.

Holiday Inn (1424 Main St, 24345; 783-3193, 800-HOLIDAY) 120 rooms, restaurant, lounge, outdoor pool, exercise facilities, children under 19 stay free with parents, wheelchair access, a/c, TV, no-smoking rooms, fax service, room service, no pets, laundry service, meeting facilities for 250, senior citizen rates, major credit cards. SGL/DBL$46-$53.

Martinsburg
Area Code 304

Sheraton Inn (301 Foxcroft Ave, 25401; 267-5500, 800-325-3535) 120 rooms and suites, restaurant, lounge, pool, exercise facilities, no-smoking rooms, a/c, TV, children stay free with parents, wheelchair access, meeting facilities, major credit cards. SGL/DBL$49-$99.

Martinsville
Area Code 703

Super 8 Motel (960 North Memorial Blvd, 24112; 666-8888, 800-800-8000) 55 rooms and suites, pets allowed, children under 12 stay free with parents, free local calls, a/c, TV, in-room refrigerators and microwaves, fax service, no-smoking rooms, senior citizen rates, wheelchair access, meeting facilities, major credit cards. SGL/DBL$33-$38.

Max Meadows
Area Code 703

Comfort Inn (State Rd 2, 24360; 637-4141, 800-221-2222) 37 rooms, restaurant, wheelchair access, no-smoking rooms, no pets, children under 18 stay free with parents, senior citizen rates, a/c, TV, meeting facilities, major credit cards. SGL/DBL$38-$46.

Gateway Motel (Max Meadows, 24360; 637-3119) 10 rooms, a/c, TV, in-room refrigerators, pets allowed. SGL/DBL$24-$30.

McLean
Area Code 703

Hilton At Tysons Corner (7920 Jones Branch Dr, 22101; 847-5000, Fax 761-5100, 800-HILTONS) 457 rooms and suites, restaurant, lounge, entertainment, indoor pool, exercise facilities, sauna, gift shop, in-room refrigerators and coffee makers, children stay free with parents, no-smoking rooms, wheelchair access, pets allowed, a/c, TV, business services, meeting facilities, major credit cards. SGL/DBL$65-$125, STS$125-$250.

Middletown
Area Code 793

Wayside Inn (7783 Main St, 22645; 869-1797) 24 rooms, restaurant, private baths, meeting facilities, major credit cards. SGL/DBL$65-$125.

Midlothian
Area Code 804

Days Inn Turnpike (1301 Huguenot Rd, 23113; 794-4999, Fax 794-1028, 800-325-2525) 120 rooms, restaurant, complimentary breakfast, lounge, children stay free with parents, room service, laundry service, a/c, TV, free local calls, no pets, wheelchair access, no-smoking rooms, senior citizen rates, major credit cards. SGL/DBL$44-$65.

Mineral
Area Code 703

Littlepage Inn (15701 Monrovia Rd, 23117; 854-9861, 800-248-1803) 5 rooms and suites, bed and breakfast, private baths, no pets, 1811 home, antique furnishings, no smoking, meeting facilities for 12, major credit cards. SGL/DBL$65-$195.

Mineral Wells
Area Code 304

Comfort Suites (State Rd 14 South, 26150; 489-9600, 800-221-2222) 116 rooms, restaurant, lounge, entertainment, indoor pool, exercise facilities, whirlpools, sauna, wheelchair access, no-smoking rooms, no pets, children under 18 stay free with parents, senior citizen rates, a/c, TV, meeting facilities, major credit cards. SGL/DBL$59-$85.

Monroe
Area Code 804

St. Moor House (Rte 1, 24574; 929-8228) 2 rooms, bed and breakfast, fireplace, no pets, private bath, fireplace, antique furnishings. SGL/DBL$59.

Mount Vernon
Area Code 703

Comfort Inn (7212 Richmond Hwy, 22306; 765-9000, 800-221-2222) 92 rooms, restaurant, pool, wheelchair access, no-smoking rooms, no pets, children under 18 stay free with parents, fax service, senior citizen rates, a/c, TV, meeting facilities, major credit cards. SGL$44-$64, DBL$49-$69.

Mullens
Area Code 304

Twin Falls Lodge (Mullens, 25882; 294-4000, 800-225-5982) 35 rooms, suites and cottages, pool, tennis courts, golf, exercise facilities, a/c, TV, laundry facilities, meeting facilities, major credit cards. SGL/DBL$45-$75.

Natural Bridge
Area Code 703

Natural Bridge Resort and Conference Center of Virginia (Natural Bridge, 24578; 291-2121; 800-533-1410) 180 rooms, restaurant, indoor pool, exercise facilities, tennis courts, a/c, TV, children under 18 stay free with parents, room service, major credit cards. SGL/DBL$40-$82.

Nellysford
Area Code 804

Meander Inn (Nellysford, 22958; 361-1121, Fax 361-1380) 5 rooms, bed and breakfast, private baths, no pets, hot tub, major credit cards. SGL/DBL$65-$90.

The Trillium House (Nellysford, 22958; 325-9126, Fax 325-1099, 800-325-9126) 12 rooms and suites, bed and breakfast, restaurant, no pets, private baths, meeting facilities for 30, major credit cards. SGL/DBL$90-$105.

New Market
Area Code 703

Days Inn (George Collins Pkwy, 22844; 740-4100, 800-325-2525) 85 rooms, restaurant, lounge, children stay free with parents, room service, laundry service, a/c, TV, free local calls, no pets, wheelchair access, no-smoking rooms, senior citizen rates, major credit cards. SGL/DBL$39-$68.

Quality Inn (State Rd 211, 22844; 740-3141, 800-368-5689) rooms and suites, restaurant, pool, gift shop, room service, exercise facilities, children stay free with parents, a/c, TV, laundry service, no-smoking rooms, meeting facilities, major credit cards. SGL$39-$55, DBL$47-$71.

Newport News
Area Code 804

Comfort Inn (12330 Jefferson Ave, 23602; 249-0200, 800-221-2222) 125 rooms, restaurant, pool, wheelchair access, no-smoking rooms, no pets, children under 18 stay free with parents, senior citizen rates, a/c, TV, meeting facilities, major credit cards. SGL/DBL$43-$63.

Days Inn (11829 Fishing Point Dr, 23606; 873-6700, Fax 873-3755, 800-325-2525) 125 rooms, restaurant, free breakfast, lounge, pool, children stay free with parents, room service, laundry service, a/c, TV, in-room refrigerators, free local calls, pets allowed, wheelchair access, no-smoking rooms, senior citizen rates, major credit cards. SGL/DBL$39-$60.

Days Inn (Rte 60, 23602; 874-0201, 800-325-2525) 117 rooms, restaurant, lounge, outdoor pool, children stay free with parents, room service, laundry service, a/c, TV, free local calls, pets allowed, wheelchair access, no-smoking rooms, senior citizen rates, major credit cards. SGL/DBL$38-$54.

Holiday Inn (6128 Jefferson Ave, 23605; 826-4500, 800-HOLIDAY) 163 rooms, restaurant, complimentary breakfast, lounge, outdoor pool, exercise facilities, children under 19 stay free with parents, wheelchair access, a/c, TV, no-smoking rooms, fax service, room service, no pets, laundry service, meeting facilities, senior citizen rates, major credit cards. SGL/DBL$54-$68.

Knights Inn (797 J. Clyde Morris Blvd, 23601; 595-6336, 800-843-5644) pool, wheelchair access, no-smoking rooms, TV, a/c, in-room refrigerators and microwaves, fax service, free parking, VCRs, senior citizen rates, major credit cards. SGL/DBL$38-$56.

Ramada Inn (950 J. Clyde Morris Blvd, 23601; 599-4460, Fax 599-4336, 800-2-RAMADA) 215 rooms, restaurant, lounge, entertainment, indoor pool, wheelchair access, no-smoking rooms, airport transportation, free parking, pets allowed, wheelchair access, a/c, TV, room service, laundry facilities, meeting facilities, senior citizen rates, major credit cards. SGL$36-$62, DBL$46-$72, AP$10.

Super 8 Motel (945 J. Clyde Morris Blvd, 23601; 595-8888, 800-800-8000) 62 rooms and suites, pets allowed, children under 12 stay free with parents, free local calls, a/c, TV, in-room refrigerators and microwaves, fax service, no-smoking rooms, senior citizen rates, wheelchair access, meeting facilities, major credit cards. SGL/DBL$36-$41.

Super 8 Tidewater Motel (6105 Jefferson Ave, 23605; 825-1422, 800-800-8000) rooms and suites, pets allowed, children under 12 stay free with parents, free local calls, a/c, TV, in-room refrigerators and microwaves, fax service, no-smoking rooms, senior citizen rates, wheelchair access, meeting facilities, major credit cards. SGL/DBL$36-$41.

Norfolk
Area Code 804

Comfort Inn Naval Base (8051 Hampton Blvd, 23505; 451-0000, Fax 451-8394, 800-221-2222) 120 rooms, restaurant, indoor pool, whirlpools, wheelchair access, no-smoking rooms, no pets, children under 18 stay free with parents, senior citizen rates, a/c, TV, meeting facilities, major credit cards. SGL/DBL$54-$61.

Comfort Inn Town Point (930 Virginia Beach Blvd, 23504; 623-5700, 800-221-2222) 168 rooms, restaurant, pool, exercise facilities, wheelchair access, no-smoking rooms, no pets, children under 18 stay free with parents, senior citizen rates, a/c, TV, meeting facilities, major credit cards. SGL/DBL$35-$65.

Days Inn (1631 Bayville St, 23503; 583-4521, Fax 583-9544, 800-325-2525) 118 rooms and efficiencies, restaurant, free breakfast, lounge, outdoor pool, children stay free with parents, room service, laundry service, a/c, TV, free local calls, beach, no pets, wheelchair access, no-smoking rooms, senior citizen rates, major credit cards. SGL/DBL$40-$48, EFF$40-$89.

Days Inn (5701 Chambers St, 23502; 461-0100, Fax 461-5883, 800-325-2525) 160 rooms, restaurant, lounge, pool, children stay free with parents, room service, laundry service, in-room refrigerators, a/c, TV, free local calls, pets allowed, wheelchair access, no-smoking rooms, senior citizen rates, major credit cards. SGL/DBL$34-$59.

Hampton Inn (8501 Hampton Blvd, 23505; 489-1000, Fax 489-1009, 800-HAMPTON) 119 rooms, restaurant, complimentary breakfast, pool, exercise facilities, children under 18 stay free with parents, no-smoking rooms, wheelchair access, computer hookups, fax service, TV, a/c, free local calls, pets allowed, meeting facilities, major credit cards. SGL/DBL$54-$62.

Hampton Inn Airport (1450 North Military Hwy, 23502; 466-7474, Fax 466-7474, 800-HAMPTON) 130 rooms, restaurant, complimentary breakfast, pool, exercise facilities, children under 18 stay free with parents, no-smoking rooms, wheelchair access, computer hookups, fax service, TV, a/c, free local calls, pets allowed, major credit cards. SGL/DBL$43-$54.

Hilton Airport Hotel (1500 North Military Hwy, 23502; 466-8000 ext 639, 800-HILTONS) 250 rooms and suites, restaurant, lounge, entertainment, outdoor pool, exercise facilities, tennis courts, sauna, jacuzzi, in-room refrigerators, children stay free with parents, no-smoking rooms, wheelchair access, pets allowed, a/c, TV, airport courtesy car, fax, business services, meeting facilities, major credit cards. SGL/DBL$85-$135.

HoJo Inn (515 North Military Hwy, 23502; 461-1880, Fax 461-8783, 800-I-GO-HOJO) 164 rooms, restaurant, complimentary breakfast, lounge, outdoor pool, children stay free with parents, wheelchair access, no-smoking rooms, TV, a/c, pets allowed, free parking, meeting facilities, senior citizen rates, major credit cards. SGL$27-$34, DBL$30-$40.

Holiday Inn (1010 West Ocean View Ave, 23503; 587-8761, 800-HOLIDAY) restaurant, lounge, outdoor pool, exercise facilities, children under 19 stay free with parents, wheelchair access, airport transportation, a/c, TV, no-smoking rooms, fax service, room service, water view, no pets, laundry service, meeting facilities, senior citizen rates, major credit cards. SGL/DBL$64-$85.

Howard Johnson Hotel (700 Monticello Ave, 23510; 627-5555, Fax 533-9651, 800-I-GO-HOJO) 344 rooms and suites, restaurant, lounge, outdoor pool, children stay free with parents, wheelchair access, no-smoking rooms, gift shop, airport transportation, room service, TV, a/c, pets allowed, free parking, meeting facilities, senior citizen rates, meeting facilities, major credit cards. SGL$49-$65, DBL$49-$75.

Marriott Waterside Hotel (235 East Main St, 23510; 627-4200, Fax 628-6466, 800-228-9290) 405 rooms and suites, restaurant, lounge, entertainment, indoor pool, exercise facilities, whirlpools, jogging track, sauna, game room, wheelchair access, TV, a/c, no-smoking rooms, gift shop, children stay free with parents, business services, meeting facilities, major credit cards. SGL/DBL$75-$95.

Motel 6 (853 North Military Hwy, 23502; 461-2380, 891-6161) 152 rooms, pool, free local calls, children under 17 stay free with parents, a/c, TV, major credit cards. SGL/DBL$28-$34.

Quality Inn Lake Wright Resort (6280 Northampton Blvd, 23502; 461-6251, 800-228-5157, 800-368-5689) 305 rooms and suites, restaurant, lounge, entertainment, pool, jogging track, tennis courts, beauty salon, room service, exercise facilities, children stay free with parents, a/c, TV, laundry service, no-smoking rooms, meeting facilities, major credit cards. SGL$45-$65, DBL$50-$75.

Quality Inn (719 East Oceanview Ave, 23503; 583-5211, 800-368-5689) 101 rooms and suites, restaurant, room service, exercise facilities, children stay free with parents, a/c, TV, laundry service, no-smoking rooms, meeting facilities, major credit cards. LS SGL/DBL$30-$45; HS SGL/DBL$50-$75, AP$5.

Ramada Inn (345 Granby St, 23510; 622-6682, Fax 623-5949, 800-2-RAMADA) 124 rooms, restaurant, lounge, wheelchair access, no-smoking rooms, airport transportation, free parking, pets allowed, wheelchair access, a/c, TV, room service, laundry facilities, meeting facilities, senior citizen rates, major credit cards. SGL$39-$75, DBL$46-$82, AP$7.

Ramada Inn (6360 Newtown Rd, 23502; 461-1081, Fax 471-1081 ext 181, 800-2-RAMADA) 137 rooms and suites, restaurant, lounge, entertainment, pool, wheelchair access, no-smoking rooms, airport transportation, free parking, pets OK, wheelchair access, in-room coffee makers, a/c, TV, room service, laundry facilities, meeting facilities, senior citizen rates, major credit cards. LS SGL/DBL$48-$63; HS SGL/DBL$54-$69, STS$100, AP$10.

Sheraton Inn Military Circle (870 North Military Hwy, 23502; 461-9192, Fax 461-8290, 800-325-3535) 208 rooms and suites, restaurant, lounge, entertainment, outdoor pool, exercise facilities, no-smoking rooms, a/c, boutiques, TV, children stay free with parents, wheelchair access, 4,800 square feet of meeting and exhibition space, 5 meeting rooms, meeting facilities for 350, major credit cards. SGL/DBL$65-$85.

Super 8 Motel (7940 Shore Dr, 23518; 588-7888, 800-800-8000) rooms and suites, complimentary breakfast, no pets, children under 12 stay free with parents, free local calls, a/c, TV, in-room refrigerators and microwaves, fax service, no-smoking rooms, senior citizen rates, wheelchair access, meeting facilities, major credit cards. SGL/DBL$36-$40.

Norton
Area Code 703

Holiday Inn (Highways 58 and 23, 24273; 679-7000, Fax 679-1736, 800-HOLIDAY) 121 rooms, restaurant, lounge, indoor pool, whirlpools, exercise facilities, children under 19 stay free with parents, wheelchair access, a/c, TV, no-smoking rooms, fax service, room service, no pets, laundry service, meeting facilities, senior citizen rates, major credit cards. SGL/DBL$58-$74.

Super 8 Motel (425 Wharton Lane, 24263; 679-0893, 800-800-8000) 58 rooms and suites, no pets, children under 12 stay free with parents, free local calls, a/c, TV, in-room refrigerators and microwaves, fax service, no-smoking rooms, senior citizen rates, wheelchair access, meeting facilities, major credit cards. SGL/DBL$39-$44.

Onley
Area Code 804

Comfort Inn (Four Corner Plaza, 23418; 787-7787, 800-221-2222) 80 rooms, restaurant, pool, exercise facilities, wheelchair access, no-smoking rooms, no pets, children under 18 stay free with parents, senior citizen rates, a/c, TV, meeting facilities, major credit cards. SGL$50-$69, DBL$56-$83, AP$5.

Orange
Area Code 703

Days Inn (332 Caroline St, 22960; 672-4855, Fax 672-4886, 800-325-2525) 20 rooms and suites, restaurant, children stay free with parents, room service, laundry service, a/c, TV, free local calls, no pets, wheelchair access, no-smoking rooms, senior citizen rates, major credit cards. SGL/DBL$39-$45, STS$104-$116.

Holladay House (155 West Main St, 22960; 672-4893, Fax 672-3028, 800-358-4422) 5 rooms and suites, bed and breakfast, private baths, no pets, 1830s home, meeting facilities for 5, major credit cards. SGL/DBL$75-$185.

The Willow Grove Inn (14079 Plantation Way, 22960; 672-5982, 800-949-1778) 5 rooms and suites, bed and breakfast, private baths, no pets, antique furnishings, 1770s inn, Modified American Plan available. SGL/DBL$95-$155.

Paeonian Springs
Area Code 703

Cornerstone Bed and Breakfast (Paeonian Springs, 22129; 882-3722) 2 rooms, complimentary breakfast, private baths, no smoking, no pets. SGL/DBL$65-$75.

Palmyra
Area Code 804

Danscot House (Palmyra, 22963; 589-1977) 3 rooms, bed and breakfast, no pets, private baths, 1777 home, on 100 acres, working farm, meeting facilities for 10. SGL/DBL$50-$70.

Palmer Country Manor (Palmyra, 22963; 589-1300, 800-253-4306) 12 rooms and suites, bed and breakfast, private baths, no pets, on 180 acres, fireplace, meeting facilities for 69, major credit cards. SGL/DBL$95-$125.

Paris
Area Code 703

The Ashby Inn and Restaurant (Rte 1, 22130; 592-3900) 10 rooms and suites, bed and breakfast, pool, no-smoking rooms, wheelchair access, fireplace, open year-round, meeting facilities, private baths, major credit cards. SGL/DBL$80-$175.

Petersburg
Area Code 804

Comfort Inn West (12002 South Crater Rd, 23805; 732-2000, 800-221-2222) 97 rooms, restaurant, complimentary breakfast, pool, whirlpools, wheelchair access, no-smoking rooms, no pets, children under 18 stay free with parents, senior citizen rates, a/c, TV, meeting facilities for 20, major credit cards. SGL/DBL$34-$39.

Days Inn (Petersburg, 23805; 733-4400, Fax 861-9559, 800-325-2525) 154 rooms, restaurant, lounge, pool, children stay free with parents, room service, laundry service, gift shop, a/c, TV, free local calls, pets allowed, wheelchair access, no-smoking rooms, senior citizen rates, major credit cards. SGL/DBL$39-$60.

High Street Inn (405 High St, 23803; 733-0505) 5 rooms and suites, bed and breakfast, private baths, no pets, 1895 home, antique furnishings, major credit cards. SGL/DBL$50-$80.

Holiday Inn (Washington St and I-95, 23803; 733-0730, Fax 861-3807, 800-HOLIDAY) 225 rooms, restaurant, lounge, outdoor pool, exercise facilities, children under 19 stay free with parents, wheelchair access, transportation to local attractions, game room, kitchenettes, a/c, TV, no-smoking rooms, fax service, room service, no pets, laundry service, meeting facilities for 65, senior citizen rates, major credit cards. SGL/DBL$49-$67.

Howard Johnson Hotel (530 East Washington St, 23803; 732-5950, Fax 862-9292, 800-I-GO-HOJO) 117 rooms, restaurant, lounge, pool, children stay free with parents, wheelchair access, no-smoking rooms, TV, a/c, laundry facilities, in-room refrigerators, transportation to local attractions, pets allowed, free parking, meeting facilities, senior citizen rates, meeting facilities, major credit cards. SGL/DBL$35-$54.

Quality Inn (I-95 and State Rd 35, 23805; 733-1152, 800-368-5689) 54 rooms and suites, restaurant, room service, exercise facilities, children stay free with parents, a/c, TV, laundry service, no-smoking rooms, meeting facilities, major credit cards. SGL/DBL$30-$46.

Ramada Inn Convention Center (380 East Washington St, 23803; 733-0000, Fax 733-3927, 800-2-RAMADA) 200 rooms and suites, restaurant, lounge, entertainment, pool, wheelchair access, no-smoking rooms, airport transportation, free parking, pets allowed, wheelchair access, a/c, TV, transportation to local attractions, room service, laundry facilities, meeting facilities for 750, senior citizen rates, major credit cards. SGL$49-$65, DBL$55-$71.

Super 8 Motel (555 Wythe St East, 23803; 861-0793, 800-800-8000) 48 rooms and suites, complimentary breakfast, pets allowed, children under 12 stay free with parents, free local calls, a/c, TV, in-room refrigerators and microwaves, fax service, no-smoking rooms, senior citizen rates, laundry facilities, wheelchair access, meeting facilities, major credit cards. SGL/DBL$36-$41.

TraveLodge (16600 Sunnybrook Rd, 23805; 733-5522, Fax 733-5522 ext 230, 800-255-3050) 56 rooms, restaurant, lounge, complimentary breakfast, pool, wheelchair access, free newspaper, laundry service, TV, a/c, free local calls, fax service, no-smoking rooms, in-room refrigerators and microwaves, no pets, meeting facilities for 300, major credit cards. SGL/DBL$26-$45, AP$6.

Portsmouth
Area Code 804

Holiday Inn (Eight Crawford Pkwy, 23704; 393-2573, Fax 399-1248, 800-HOLIDAY) 270 rooms, restaurant, lounge, entertainment, outdoor pool, exercise facilities, children under 19 stay free with parents, wheelchair access, a/c, TV, no-smoking rooms, fax service, room service, no pets, laundry service, meeting facilities for 500, senior citizen rates, major credit cards. SGL/DBL$69-$84.

Super 8 Motel (925 London Blvd, 23704; 398-0612, 800-800-8000) rooms and suites, pets allowed, children under 12 stay free with parents, free local calls, a/c, TV, in-room refrigerators and microwaves, fax service, no-smoking rooms, senior citizen rates, wheelchair access, meeting facilities, major credit cards. SGL/DBL$35-$40.

Pratts
Area Code 703

Colvin Hall Bed and Breakfast (Pratts 22731; 948-6211) 3 rooms, complimentary breakfast, private baths, children over age 12 welcome, no smoking, no pets, on 7 acres, 1870s home, meeting facilities for 10, major credit cards. SGL/DBL$60-$85.

Radford
Area Code 703

Super 8 Motel (1600 Tyler Ave, 24141; 731-9355, 800-800-8000) 58 rooms and suites, pets allowed, children under 12 stay free with parents, free local calls, a/c, TV, in-room refrigerators and microwaves, fax service, no-smoking rooms, senior citizen rates, wheelchair access, meeting facilities, major credit cards. SGL/DBL$36-$41.

Raphine
Area Code 703

Quality Inn (Raphine, 24462; 377-2604, 800-368-5689) 86 rooms and suites, restaurant, pool, whirlpools, room service, exercise facilities, children stay free with parents, a/c, TV, laundry service, no-smoking rooms, meeting facilities, major credit cards. SGL/DBL$39-$57.

Reston
Area Code 703

Hyatt Regency Reston (1000 Presidents St, 22090; 709-1234, Fax 709-2291, 800-233-1234) 514 rooms and suites, restaurant, lounge, entertainment, pool, whirlpools, sauna, exercise facilities, room service, TV, free parking, a/c, no-smoking rooms, wheelchair access, 32,000 square feet of meeting and exhibition space, 13 meeting rooms, major credit cards. SGL/DBL$69-$159.

Hyatt Regency Reston (1800 Freedom Dr, 22090; 709-1234, 800-233-1234). 534 rooms and suites, restaurant, lounge, pool, exercise facilities, tennis, major credit cards. SGL/DBL$135-$155.

Richmond
Area Code 804

Abbie Hill Guest Lodging (Box 4503, 23220; 355-5855, Fax 353-4656) bed and breakfast, 1910 home, antique furnishings, children over age 12 welcome, no pets, fireplace, no smoking. SGL$45-$65, DBL$75-$95.

Be My Guest Bed and Breakfast (2926 Kensington Ave, 23221; 358-9901) complimentary breakfast, 1918 home, antique furnishings, no smoking. SGL/DBL$45-$75.

The Berkeley Hotel (12th and Carry St, 23219; 780-1300) 55 rooms, restaurant, exercise facilities, no-smoking rooms, wheelchair access, a/c, TV. SGL$69-$118, DBL$69-$128.

Best Western Governor's Inn (9849 Midlothian Turnpike, 23235; 323-0007, 800-528-1234) 86 rooms and suites, restaurant, complimentary breakfast, lounge, outdoor pool, exercise facilities, children stay free with parents, a/c, TV, no-smoking rooms, wheelchair access, pets allowed, senior citizen rates, meeting facilities, major credit cards. SGL/DBL$46-$57.

Comfort Inn Executive Center (7201 West Broad St, 23294; 672-1108, 800-221-2222) 122 rooms, restaurant, complimentary breakfast, pool, whirlpools, wheelchair access, no-smoking rooms, no pets, children under 18 stay free with parents, senior citizen rates, a/c, TV, meeting facilities, major credit cards. SGL/DBL$50-$65.

Comfort Inn Corporate Gateway (8710 Midlothian Turnpike, 23235; 320-8900, Fax 320-0403, 800-221-2222) 154 rooms, restaurant, complimentary breakfast, outdoor pool, exercise facilities, wheelchair access, no-smoking rooms, no pets, children under 18 stay free with parents, senior citizen rates, a/c, TV, meeting facilities, major credit cards. SGL/DBL$54-$59.

Commonwealth Park Suites Hotel (9th and Banks Sts, 21219; 343-7300, 800-343-7302) 59 suites, restaurant, no-smoking rooms, wheelchair access, a/c, TV, pets allowed. SGL$85-$150, DBL$100-$190.

Courtyard by Marriott (6400 West Broad St, 23230; 282-1881, 800-321-2211) 155 rooms and suites, restaurant, lounge, outdoor pool, exercise facilities, whirlpools, children stay free with parents, laundry service, meeting facilities, senior citizen rates, major credit cards. SGL/DBL$59-$82.

Cricket Inn (7300 West Broad St, 23294; 672-8621, 800-CRICKET) 126 rooms and apartment, outdoor pool, wheelchair access, no-smoking rooms, a/c, TV. SGL/DBL$43-$48.

Days Inn (2100 Dickens Rd, 23230; 282-3300, Fax 288-2145, 800-325-2525) 182 rooms, restaurant, lounge, pool, children stay free with parents, room service, laundry service, a/c, TV, free local calls, no pets, wheelchair access, no-smoking rooms, senior citizen rates, major credit cards. SGL/DBL$45-$60.

Days Inn (1600 Robin Hood Rd, 23220; 353-1287, Fax 355-2659, 800-325-2525) 99 rooms, restaurant, complimentary breakfast, lounge, outdoor pool, children stay free with parents, room service, laundry service, a/c, TV, free local calls, pets allowed, wheelchair access, no-smoking rooms, senior citizen rates, major credit cards. SGL/DBL$35-$60.

Virginia

Days Inn Downtown Convention Center (Marshall and 7th Streets, 23240; 649-2378, Fax 649-7123, 800-325-2525) 140 rooms, restaurant, lounge, indoor pool, children stay free with parents, room service, laundry service, a/c, TV, free local calls, no pets, wheelchair access, no-smoking rooms, senior citizen rates, major credit cards. SGL/DBL$41-$67.

Days Inn (6346 Midlothian Turnpike, 23225; 876-6450, Fax 674-4243, 800-325-2525) 167 rooms, restaurant, lounge, pool, children stay free with parents, room service, laundry service, a/c, TV, free local calls, no pets, wheelchair access, no-smoking rooms, senior citizen rates, meeting facilities for 500, major credit cards. SGL/DBL$27-$65.

Econo Lodge North (5221 Brook Rd, 23227; 266-7603, 800-637-3297, 800-4-CHOICE) 187 rooms, complimentary breakfast, outdoor pool, TV, children under 12 stay free with parents, pets allowed, senior citizen rates, wheelchair access, a/c, TV, major credit cards. SGL/DBL$36-$56.

Econo Lodge South Kingsland (2125 Willis Rd, 23237; 271-6031, 800-4-CHOICE) 48 rooms, free breakfast, pool, TV, children under 12 stay free with parents, pets allowed, senior citizen rates, wheelchair access, a/c, major credit cards. SGL/DBL$34-$99.

Econo Lodge West (6523 Midlothian Turnpike, 23225; 276-8241, 800-4-CHOICE) 72 rooms, complimentary breakfast, pool, TV, children under 12 stay free with parents, pets allowed, senior citizen rates, wheelchair access, a/c, major credit cards. SGL/DBL$31-$38.

Econo Lodge West Broad (8008 West Broad St, 23294; 346-0000, 800-4-CHOICE) 193 rooms and suites, complimentary breakfast, outdoor pool, TV, children under 12 stay free with parents, pets allowed, senior citizen rates, wheelchair access, a/c, major credit cards. SGL/DBL$36-$51.

Economy House Motel (2302 Willis Rd, 23237; 275-1412) 70 rooms, restaurant, outdoor pool, pets allowed, a/c, TV, meeting facilities. SGL/DBL$23-$36.

Emmanuel Hutzler House (2036 Monument Ave, 23220; 353-6900) 2 rooms and suites, bed and breakfast, antique furnishings, private baths, no smoking, no pets, children over age 12 welcome, 1914 home, fireplace, TV, jacuzzi. SGL/DBL$85-$125.

Embassy Suites (2925 Emerywood Pkwy, 23294; 672-8585, Fax 672-3749, 800-EMBASSY) 2-room suites, restaurant, lounge, complimentary breakfast, lounge, pool, whirlpool, exercise facilities, sauna, room service, laundry service, wheelchair access, complimentary newspaper, free local calls, no-smoking rooms, gift shop, transportation to local attractions, business services, meeting facilities, major credit cards. SGL/DBL$94-$124.

Executive Inn (5215 West Broad St, 23230; 288-4011) 141 rooms, restaurant, outdoor pool, a/c, TV. SGL/DBL$33-$37.

HoJo Inn (801 East Parham Rd, 23227; 266-8753, Fax 261-1096, 800-I-GO-HOJO) 82 rooms, restaurant, lounge, pool, children stay free with parents, wheelchair access, no-smoking rooms, TV, a/c, pets allowed, free parking, meeting facilities, senior citizen rates, meeting facilities, major credit cards. SGL$39-$55, DBL$45-$55.

Holiday Inn (6531 West Broad St, 23230; 285-9951, Fax 282-5642, 800-HOLIDAY) restaurant, lounge, entertainment, indoor pool, hot tubs, exercise facilities, children under 19 stay free with parents, wheelchair access, a/c, TV, no-smoking rooms, fax service, room service, no pets, laundry service, meeting facilities, senior citizen rates, major credit cards. SGL/DBL$69-$89.

Holiday Inn Crossroads (2000 Staples Mill Rd, 23230; 359-6061, Fax 359-3177, 800-HOLIDAY) 147 rooms, restaurant, lounge, outdoor pool, exercise facilities, children under 19 stay free with parents, wheelchair access, a/c, TV, no-smoking rooms, fax service, room service, pets allowed, laundry service, meeting facilities, senior citizen rates, major credit cards. SGL/DBL$49-$75.

Holiday Inn Executive Conference Center (1020 Koger Center Blvd, 23235; 379-3800, 800-HOLIDAY) 204 rooms and suites, restaurant, lounge, outdoor pool, exercise facilities, children under 19 stay free with parents, wheelchair access, a/c, TV, no-smoking rooms, airport courtesy car, fax service, room service, no pets, laundry service, meeting facilities, senior citizen rates, major credit cards. SGL/DBL$60-$77.

Holiday Inn Central (3207 North Blvd, 23230; 359-9441, Fax 359-3207, 800-HOLIDAY) 181 rooms, restaurant, lounge, outdoor pool, exercise facilities, children under 19 stay free with parents, wheelchair access, a/c, TV, no-smoking rooms, fax service, room service, no pets, laundry service, meeting facilities for 425, senior citizen rates, major credit cards. SGL/DBL$50-$65.

Holiday Inn Downtown (301 West Franklin St, 23220; 644-9871, Fax 344-4380, 800-HOLIDAY) 216 rooms, restaurant, lounge, outdoor pool, exercise facilities, children under 19 stay free with parents, wheelchair access, a/c, TV, no-smoking rooms, fax service, room service, pets allowed, laundry service, meeting facilities for 500, senior citizen rates, major credit cards. SGL/DBL$65-$70.

Holiday Inn Midtown (3200 West Broad St, 23230; 359-4061, 800-HOLIDAY) 196 rooms and suites, restaurant, lounge, outdoor pool, exercise facilities, children under 19 stay free with parents, wheelchair access, a/c, TV, no-smoking rooms, fax service, room service, pets allowed, laundry service, meeting facilities, senior citizen rates, major credit cards. SGL/DBL$55-$60.

Holiday Inn South (10800 Midlothian Turnpike, 23225; 379-3800, Fax 379-2763, 800-HOLIDAY) 200 rooms and suites, restaurant, lounge, outdoor pool, exercise facilities, children under 19 stay free with parents, wheelchair access, complimentary newspaper, airport transportation, a/c, TV, no-smoking rooms, fax, room service, no pets, laundry service, meeting facilities, senior citizen rates, major credit cards. SGL/DBL$75-$85.

Holiday Inn Southeast (4303 Commerce Rd, 23234; 275-7891, Fax 275-2901, 800-HOLIDAY) 171 rooms, restaurant, lounge, outdoor pool, exercise facilities, children under 19 stay free with parents, wheelchair access, a/c, TV, no-smoking rooms, fax service, room service, no pets, laundry service, meeting facilities for 300, senior citizen rates, major credit cards. SGL/DBL$59-$68.

Howard Johnson Lodge (1501 Robin Hood Rd, 23220; 353-0116, Fax 355-2754, 800-I-GO-HOJO) 115 rooms, restaurant, lounge, outdoor pool, children stay free with parents, wheelchair access, no-smoking rooms, TV, a/c, no pets, free parking, meeting facilities, senior citizen rates, meeting facilities for 400, major credit cards. LS SGL$37-$55, DBL$39-$60; HS SGL$39-$59, DBL$41-$60.

Hyatt Richmond at Brookfield (6624 North Broad St, 23230; 285-1234, Fax 288-3961, 800-233-1234) 372 rooms and 2-room suites, restaurant, lounge, entertainment, indoor and outdoor pool, whirlpools, jogging path, lighted tennis courts, exercise facilities, room service, TV, a/c, no-smoking rooms, wheelchair access, meeting facilities for 900, major credit cards. SGL/DBL$69-$135.

Jefferson Hotel (Franklin and Adams Streets, 23220; 788-8000, 800-325-3535) 280 rooms and suites, restaurant, lounge, indoor pool, a/c, TV, no-smoking rooms. SGL/DBL$105-$135.

La Quinta Inn (6910 Midlothian Pike, 23225; 745-7100, Fax 276-6660, 800-531-5900) 130 rooms, restaurant, complimentary breakfast, lounge, pool, complimentary newspaper, free local calls, fax service, laundry service, no-smoking rooms, wheelchair access, remote control TV, a/c, free parking, meeting facilities, major credit cards. SGL/DBL$45-$58.

Linden Row Inn (100 East Franklin St, 23219; 783-7000, 800-348-7424) 77 rooms and suites, complimentary breakfast, restaurant, indoor pool, wheelchair access, a/c, TV. SGL/DBL$64-$124.

Marriott Hotel (500 East Broad St, 23219; 643-3400, Fax 788-1230, 800-228-9290) 400 rooms and suites, restaurant, lounge, entertainment, indoor pool, exercise facilities, whirlpools, wheelchair access, TV, a/c, no-smoking rooms, gift shop, children stay free with parents, business services, meeting facilities, major credit cards. SGL/DBL$82-$104.

Massad House (11 North Fourth St, 23219; 648-2893) 64 rooms and suites, restaurant, a/c, TV. SGL/DBL$30-$45.

Mr. Patrick Henry's Inn (2300 East Broad St, 23223; 644-1322) 3 suites, bed and breakfast, restaurant, private baths, no smoking, no pets, 1850 inn, fireplaces, meeting facilities for 30, major credit cards. SGL/DBL$95-$135.

Omni Hotel Richmond (100 South 12th St, 23219; 344-7000, 800-THE-OMNI) 370 rooms and suites, restaurant, lounge, entertainment, indoor pool, sauna, exercise facilities, limousine service, laundry service, wheelchair access, no-smoking rooms available, a/c, TV, all major credit cards. SGL/DBL$114-$129.

Quality Inn North (9002 Brook St, 23060; 266-2444, Fax 261-5834, 800-368-5689) 63 rooms and suites, restaurant, room service, exercise facilities, children stay free with parents, a/c, TV, laundry service, no-smoking rooms, meeting facilities, major credit cards. SGL/DBL$32-$55.

Radisson Hotel (555 East Canal St, 23219; 788-0900, Fax 788-0791, 800-777-1700) rooms and suites, restaurant, lounge, entertainment, pool, wheelchair access, free parking, no-smoking rooms, TV, a/c, children stay free with parents, pets allowed, major credit cards. SGL/DBL$59-$119.

Ramada Inn North (5701 Chamberlayne Ave, 23227; 266-7616, Fax 266-8810, 800-2-RAMADA) 186 rooms, restaurant, lounge, wheelchair access, no-smoking rooms, airport transportation, free parking, pets allowed, wheelchair access, a/c, TV, room service, laundry facilities, meeting facilities for 450, senior citizen rates, major credit cards. SGL/DBL$45-$70, AP$6.

Ramada Inn South (2126 Willis Rd, 23237; 271-1281, Fax 271-3315, 800-2-RAMADA) 98 rooms and suites, restaurant, lounge, pool, wheelchair access, no-smoking rooms, airport transportation, free parking, pets allowed, free local calls, wheelchair access, a/c, TV, room service, laundry facilities, 2 meeting rooms, meeting facilities for 100, senior citizen rates, major credit cards. SGL/DBL$45-$63, STS$70, AP$5.

Red Roof Inn (4350 Commerce Rd, 23234; 271-7240, Fax 271-7245, 800-843-7663) no-smoking rooms, fax service, wheelchair access, complimentary newspaper, children stay free with parents, pets allowed, free local calls, in-room computer hookups, major credit cards. SGL/DBL$29-$49.

Red Roof Inn (100 Greshamwood Place, 23225; 745-0600, Fax 745-1017, 800-843-7663) no-smoking rooms, fax service, wheelchair access, complimentary newspaper, children stay free with parents, pets allowed, free local calls, in-room computer hookups, major credit cards. SGL/DBL$30-$49.

Regency Suites and Inn (Parham and Quioccasin Roads, 23229; 285-9061) 121 rooms and suites, restaurant, outdoor pool, no-smoking rooms, a/c, color, wheelchair access. SGL/DBL$40-$45.

Residence Inn (2121 Dickens Rd, 23230; 285-8200, 800-331-3131) rooms and suites, complimentary breakfast, outdoor pool, spa, in-room refrigerators, coffee makers and microwaves, laundry facilities, free parking, TV, a/c, VCRs, pets allowed, fireplaces, children stay free with parents, no-smoking rooms, wheelchair access, meeting facilities for 20, major credit cards. SGL/DBL$85-$105.

Sheraton Inn Airport (4700 South Laburnum Ave, 23231; 226-4300, Fax 226-6516, 800-325-3535) 151 rooms and suites, restaurant, lounge, entertainment, indoor pool, exercise facilities, whirlpools, sauna, gift shop, beauty shop, no-smoking rooms, a/c, TV, children stay free with parents, wheelchair access, 9,000 square feet of meeting and exhibition space, 7 meeting rooms, meeting facilities for 300, major credit cards. SGL/DBL$62-$95.

Sheraton Inn Park South (9901 Midlothian Turnpike, 23235; 323-1144, Fax 320-5255, 800-325-3535) 196 rooms and suites, restaurant, lounge, indoor and outdoor pool, exercise facilities, whirlpools, sauna, gift shop, no-smoking rooms, a/c, TV, children stay free with parents, wheelchair access, 9,600 square feet of meeting and exhibition space, 12 meeting rooms, meeting facilities for 500, major credit cards. SGL/DBL$55-$98.

Shoney's Inn (7007 West Broad St, 23294; 672-7007, 800-222-2222) 123 rooms and suites, restaurant, outdoor pool, no-smoking rooms, wheelchair access, a/c, TV, pets allowed. SGL/DBL$45-$60.

Super 8 Airport Motel (5110 Williamsburg Rd, 23231; 222-8008, 800-800-8000) 51 rooms and suites, pets allowed, children under 12 stay free with parents, free local calls, a/c, TV, in-room refrigerators and microwaves, fax service, no-smoking rooms, senior citizen rates, wheelchair access, meeting facilities, major credit cards. SGL/DBL$36-$42.

Super 8 Motel (5200 West Broad St, 23294; 672-8128, 800-800-8000) 49 rooms and suites, pets allowed, children under 12 stay free with parents, free local calls, a/c, TV, in-room refrigerators and microwaves, fax service, no-smoking rooms, senior citizen rates, wheelchair access, meeting facilities, major credit cards. SGL/DBL$37-$42.

Super 8 Motel (5615 Chamberlayne Rd, 23227; 262-8880, 800-800-8000) 61 rooms and suites, pets allowed, children under 12 stay free with parents, free local calls, a/c, TV, in-room refrigerators and microwaves, fax service, no-smoking rooms, senior citizen rates, wheelchair access, meeting facilities, major credit cards. SGL/DBL$37-$42.

Super 8 Motel (7200 West Broad St, 23294; 672-8128, 800-800-8000) 49 rooms, no pets, children under 12 stay free with parents, free local calls, a/c, TV, in-room refrigerators and microwaves, fax service, no-smoking rooms, senior citizen rates, wheelchair access, meeting facilities, major credit cards. SGL/DBL$43-$58.

Super 8 Motel (8260 Midlothian Turnpike, 23235; 320-2823, 800-843-1991, 800-800-8000) 80 rooms and suites, pets allowed, children under 12 stay free with parents, free local calls, a/c, TV, in-room refrigerators and microwaves, fax service, no-smoking rooms, senior citizen rates, wheelchair access, meeting facilities, major credit cards. SGL/DBL$37-$42.

West Bocock House (1107 Grove Ave, 23220; 358-6174) 2 rooms, bed and breakfast, 1871 home, private bath, antique furnishings, no pets, meeting facilities for 25. SGL/DBL$65-$75.

William Catlin House (2304 East Broad St, 23224; 780-3746) 3 rooms, complimentary breakfast, children over age 10 welcome, no pets, 1845 home, fireplaces, a/c, antique furnishings, private baths, major credit cards. SGL/DBL$70-$90.

Riverdale
Area Code 804

Super 8 Motel (Riverdale, 24592; 572-8868, 800-800-8000) 58 rooms and suites, pets allowed, children under 12 stay free with parents, free local calls, a/c, TV, in-room refrigerators and microwaves, fax service, no-smoking rooms, senior citizen rates, wheelchair access, meeting facilities, major credit cards. SGL/DBL$36-$41.

Roanoke
Area Code 703

Comfort Inn Airport (3695 Thirlane Rd Northwest, 24109; 563-0229, 800-221-2222) 138 rooms, restaurant, outdoor pool, whirlpools, wheelchair access, no-smoking rooms, airport courtesy car, no pets, children under 18 stay free with parents, senior citizen rates, a/c, TV, meeting facilities, major credit cards. SGL/DBL$40-$56.

Days Inn Civic Center Downtown (535 Orange Ave, 24016; 342-4551, Fax 343-3547, 800-325-2525) 257 rooms, restaurant, lounge, outdoor pool, children stay free with parents, room service, airport courtesy car, laundry service, a/c, TV, free local calls, no pets, wheelchair access, no-smoking rooms, senior citizen rates, major credit cards. SGL/DBL$40-$55.

Hampton Inn (3816 Franklin Rd Southwest, 24014; 989-4000, Fax 774-1621, 800-HAMPTON) 59 rooms, restaurant, complimentary breakfast, pool, exercise facilities, children under 18 stay free with parents, no-smoking rooms, wheelchair access, computer hookups, fax service, TV, a/c, free local calls, pets allowed, meeting facilities, major credit cards. SGL/DBL$43-$50.

Holiday Inn Airport (6626 Thirlane Rd, 24019; 366-8861, 800-HOLIDAY) 163 rooms, restaurant, lounge, outdoor pool, exercise facilities, children under 19 stay free with parents, wheelchair access, a/c, transportation to local attractions, TV, no-smoking rooms, fax service, room service, no pets, laundry service, meeting facilities for 650, senior citizen rates, major credit cards. SGL/DBL$56-$70.

Holiday Inn (Williamson Rd, 24012; 342-8961, 800-HOLIDAY) 153 rooms, restaurant, lounge, outdoor pool, exercise facilities, children under 19 stay free with parents, wheelchair access, a/c, TV, no-smoking rooms, fax service, room service, no pets, laundry service, meeting facilities, senior citizen rates, major credit cards. SGL/DBL$45-$68.

Holiday Inn (1927 Franklin Rd Southwest, 24014; 343-0121, 800-HOLIDAY) 125 rooms, restaurant, lounge, entertainment, outdoor pool, exercise facilities, children under 19 stay free with parents, wheelchair access, a/c, TV, no-smoking rooms, airport transportation, fax service, room service, no pets, laundry service, meeting facilities for 250, senior citizen rates, major credit cards. SGL/DBL$38-$65.

Holiday Inn (4468 Starkey Rd Southwest, 24014; 774-4400, Fax 774-1195, 800-HOLIDAY) 196 rooms, restaurant, lounge, outdoor pool, exercise facilities, children under 19 stay free with parents, wheelchair access, airport transportation, a/c, TV, no-smoking rooms, fax service, room service, pets allowed, laundry service, meeting facilities for 700, senior citizen rates, major credit cards. SGL/DBL$54-$105.

Marriott Airport Hotel (2801 Hershberger Rd Northwest, 24017; 563-9300, 800-228-9290) 320 rooms and suites, restaurant, lounge, entertainment, outdoor pool, exercise facilities, whirlpools, sauna, airport courtesy car, free parking, 24-hour room service, wheelchair access, TV, a/c, no-smoking rooms, gift shop, children stay free with parents, business services, meeting facilities, major credit cards. SGL/DBL$58-$120.

Motel 6 (6520 Thirlane Rd, 24019; 563-2871, 505-891-6161) 120 rooms, pool, free local calls, children under 17 stay free with parents, a/c, TV, major credit cards. SGL/DBL$23-$29.

Sheraton Inn Airport (2727 Ferndale Dr, 24017; 362-4500, 800-325-3535) 148 rooms and suites, restaurant, lounge, entertainment, indoor and outdoor, pool, exercise facilities, tennis courts, jacuzzi, gift shop, no-smoking rooms, a/c, TV, children stay free with parents, wheelchair access, 10,000 square feet of meeting and exhibition space, 11 meeting rooms, meeting facilities for 500, major credit cards. SGL/DBL$60-$90, STS$125.

Sleep Inn Tanglewood (4045 Electric Rd, 24014; 772-1500, 800-221-2222) wheelchair access, no-smoking rooms, no pets, children under 18 stay free with parents, senior citizen rates, a/c, TV, meeting facilities, major credit cards. SGL/DBL$47-$56.

Super 8 Motel (6616 Thirlane Rd, 24019; 563-8888, 800-800-8000) rooms and suites, pets allowed, children under 12 stay free with parents, free local calls, a/c, TV, in-room refrigerators and microwaves, fax service, no-smoking rooms, senior citizen rates, wheelchair access, meeting facilities, major credit cards. SGL/DBL$33-$38.

Rocky Mount
Area Code 703

Claiborne House (119 Clairborne Ave, 24151; 483-4616) 5 rooms and suites, bed and breakfast, private baths, no pets, 1895 home, antique furnishings, major credit cards. SGL/DBL$65-$115.

Comfort Inn (950 North Main St, 24151; 489-4000, 800-221-2222) restaurant, pool, wheelchair access, no-smoking rooms, no pets, children under 18 stay free with parents, senior citizen rates, a/c, TV, meeting facilities, major credit cards. SGL/DBL$46-$70.

Budget Host Inn (Hwy 220 North, 24151; 483-9757, 800-BUD-HOST) 18 rooms, restaurant, lounge, in-room refrigerators, no-smoking rooms, TV, VCRs, a/c, wheelchair access, children stay free with parents, pets allowed, senior citizen rates, meeting facilities, major credit cards. SGL$25, DBL$30-$35.

Round Hill
Area Code 703

Weona Villa Motel (Round Hill, 22141; 338-7000) 8 rooms, a/c, TV, no pets, major credit cards. SGL/DBL$32-$38.

Rustburg
Area Code 804

The Ivanhoe (Rte 3, 24504; 332-7103) 3 rooms, bed and breakfast, on 21 acres, working farm, pets allowed. SGL/DBL$44-$64.

Salem
Area Code 703

Budget Host Blue Jay Motel (5399 West Main St, 24153; 380-2080, 800-BUD-HOST) 14 rooms, restaurant, pets allowed, in-room refrigerators, no-smoking rooms, TV, VCRs, a/c, wheelchair access, children stay free with parents, senior citizen rates, meeting facilities, major credit cards. SGL$30-$34, DBL$30-$38.

Knights Inn (301 Wildwood Rd, 24153; 389-0280, 800-843-5644) pool, wheelchair access, no-smoking rooms, TV, a/c, in-room refrigerators and microwaves, fax service, free parking, VCRs, senior citizen rates, major credit cards. SGL/DBL$48-$54.

Holiday Inn (1671 Skyview Rd, 24153; 389-7061, 800-HOLIDAY) 102 rooms, restaurant, lounge, outdoor pool, exercise facilities, children under 19 stay free with parents, wheelchair access, a/c, TV, no-smoking rooms, fax service, room service, no pets, laundry service, meeting facilities for 250, senior citizen rates, major credit cards. SGL/DBL$52-$78.

Quality Inn (179 Sheraton Dr, 24153; 562-1912, 800-368-5689) 120 rooms and suites, restaurant, room service, exercise facilities, children stay free with parents, a/c, airport courtesy car, TV, laundry service, no-smoking rooms, meeting facilities, major credit cards. SGL/DBL$43-$62.

Super 8 Motel (300 Wildwood Rd, 24153; 389-0297, 800-800-8000) 62 rooms and suites, pets allowed, children under 12 stay free with parents, free local calls, a/c, TV, in-room refrigerators and microwaves, fax service, no-smoking rooms, senior citizen rates, wheelchair access, meeting facilities, major credit cards. SGL/DBL$33-$38.

Sandston
Area Code 804

Days Inn Airport (5500 Williamsburg Rd, 23150; 222-2041, 800-325-2525) 100 rooms, restaurant, complimentary breakfast, lounge, children stay free with parents, room service, laundry service, a/c, TV, free local calls, airport courtesy car, no pets, wheelchair access, no-smoking rooms, senior citizen rates, major credit cards. SGL/DBL$35-$60.

Econo Lodge Airport (5408 Williamsburg Rd, 23150; 222-1020, 800-4-CHOICE) 53 rooms, free breakfast, pool, TV, children under 12 stay free with parents, pets allowed, senior citizen rates, wheelchair access, a/c, major credit cards. SGL/DBL$30-$37.

Hampton Inn Airport (5300 Airport Square Lane, 23150; 222-8200, Fax 222-4915, 800-HAMPTON) 125 rooms, restaurant, complimentary breakfast, pool, exercise facilities, children under 18 stay free with parents, no-smoking rooms, wheelchair access, computer hookups, fax service, TV, a/c, free local calls, pets allowed, meeting facilities, major credit cards. SGL/DBL$49-$54.

Hilton Airport Hotel (5501 Eubank Rd, 23150; 226-6400, Fax 226-1269, 800-HILTONS) 159 rooms and suites, restaurant, lounge, entertainment, outdoor pool, exercise facilities, children stay free with parents, no-smoking rooms, airport courtesy car, free parking, wheelchair access, pets allowed, a/c, TV, business services, meeting facilities, major credit cards. SGL/DBL$65-$115.

Holiday Inn Richmond Airport (5203 Williamsburg Rd, 23150; 222-6450, Fax 226-4305, 800-HOLIDAY) 230 rooms, restaurant, lounge, entertainment, outdoor pool, exercise facilities, children under 19 stay free with parents, wheelchair access, a/c, TV, no-smoking rooms, fax service, room service, pets allowed, laundry service, meeting facilities for 350, senior citizen rates, major credit cards. SGL/DBL$49-$75.

Knights Inn Airport (5252 Airport Square Lane, 23150; 226-4519, 800-843-5644) 123 rooms and efficiencies, outdoor pool, wheelchair access, no-smoking rooms, TV, a/c, in-room refrigerators and microwaves, pets allowed, fax service, free parking, VCRs, senior citizen rates, major credit cards. SGL/DBL$31-$45.

Motel 6 (5704 Hwy 60, 23150; 222-7600, 505-891-6161) 121 rooms, outdoor pool, free local calls, children under 17 stay free with parents, a/c, pets allowed, TV, major credit cards. SGL/DBL$24-$30.

Scottsville
Area Code 804

High Meadows Vineyard Inn (Scottsville, 24590; 286-2218, 800-232-1832) 8 rooms and suites, bed and breakfast, pets allowed, on 50 acres, private baths, fireplace, meeting facilities for 30, major credit cards. SGL/DBL$95-$145.

Smith Mountain Lake
Area Code 703

Manor At Taylor's Store (Smith Mountain Lake, 24184; 721-3951, 800-248-6267) 6 rooms and suites, bed and breakfast, on 120 acres, antique furnishings, fireplace, exercise facilities, hot tub, a/c, meeting facilities for 30, major credit cards. SGL/DBL$89-$109.

South Boston
Area Code 804

Days Inn (Rte 3, 24592; 572-4941, Fax 572-9399, 800-325-2525) 76 rooms, restaurant, lounge, outdoor pool, children stay free with parents, room service, laundry service, a/c, TV, free local calls, no pets, wheelchair access, no-smoking rooms, senior citizen rates, major credit cards. SGL/DBL$30-$40.

South Hill
Area Code 804

Comfort Inn (918 East Atlantic St, 23970; 447-2600, 800-221-2222) restaurant, sauna, wheelchair access, no-smoking rooms, no pets, children under 18 stay free with parents, senior citizen rates, a/c, TV, meeting facilities, major credit cards. SGL/DBL$35-$49.

Holiday Inn (South Hill, 23970; 447-3123, 800-HOLIDAY) 152 rooms, restaurant, lounge, outdoor pool, exercise facilities, children under 19 stay free with parents, wheelchair access, a/c, TV, no-smoking rooms, fax service, room service, no pets, laundry service, meeting facilities, senior citizen rates, major credit cards. SGL/DBL$53-$62.

Super 8 Motel (922 East Atlantic Ave, 23970; 447-7655, Fax 447-7228, 800-800-8000) 49 rooms and suites, pets allowed, children under 12 stay free with parents, free local calls, a/c, TV, in-room refrigerators and microwaves, fax service, no-smoking rooms, senior citizen rates, wheelchair access, meeting facilities, major credit cards. SGL/DBL$35-$41.

Spotsylvania
Area Code 703

Roxbury Mill Bed and Breakfast (6908 Roxbury Mill Rd, 22553; 582-6611) 2 rooms and suites, complimentary breakfast, private baths, no pets, water view, meeting facilities for 25, major credit cards. SGL/DBL$85-$150.

Springfield
Area Code 703

Days Inn (6721 Commerce St, 22150; 922-6200, Fax 922-0708, 800-325-2525) 179 rooms, restaurant, lounge, pool, children stay free with parents, room service, laundry service, a/c, TV, free local calls, no pets, wheelchair access, no-smoking rooms, senior citizen rates, major credit cards. SGL/DBL$39-$66.

Hilton Hotel (6550 Loisdale Rd, 22150; 971-8900, Fax 971-8527, 800-HILTONS) 246 rooms and suites, restaurant, lounge, entertainment, indoor pool, exercise facilities, children stay free with parents, no-smoking rooms, free parking, gift shop, wheelchair access, pets allowed, a/c, TV, business services, meeting facilities, major credit cards. SGL/DBL$65-$105.

Stafford
Area Code 703

Days Inn (2868 Jefferson Davis Hwy, 22554; 659-0022, Fax 659-0212, 800-325-2525) 123 rooms, restaurant, lounge, pool, children stay free with parents, room service, laundry service, a/c, TV, free local calls, no pets, wheelchair access, no-smoking rooms, senior citizen rates, major credit cards. SGL/DBL$40-$55.

Standardsville
Area Code 804

Edgewood Farm Bed and Breakfast (Standardsville, 22973; 985-3782) 3 rooms, complimentary breakfast, private baths, no pets, 1790s home, on 130 acres, major credit cards. SGL/DBL$60-$75.

Staunton
Area Code 703

Ashton Country House (1205 Middlebrook Ave, 24401; 885-7819, 800-296-7819) 4 rooms and suites, bed and breakfast, no pets, children over the age of 16 welcome, on 24 acres, private baths. SGL/DBL$70-$85.

Comfort Inn (1302 Richmond Ave, 24401; 886-5000, 800-221-2222) 97 rooms, restaurant, pool, wheelchair access, no-smoking rooms, no pets, children under 18 stay free with parents, whirlpools, fax, senior citizen rates, a/c, TV, meeting facilities, major credit cards. SGL/DBL$43-$59.

Days Inn (Rte 2, 24401; 337-3031, Fax 337-3274, 800-325-2525) 121 rooms, restaurant, lounge, outdoor pool, children stay free with parents, room service, laundry service, a/c, TV, free local calls, pets allowed, wheelchair access, no-smoking rooms, senior citizen rates, major credit cards. SGL/DBL$40-$55.

Holiday Inn (Woodrow Wilson Pkwy and I-81, 24401; 248-5111, 800-HOLIDAY) 100 rooms, restaurant, lounge, outdoor pool, exercise facilities, children under 19 stay free with parents, wheelchair access, a/c, TV, no-smoking rooms, fax service, room service, pets allowed, laundry service, meeting facilities, senior citizen rates, major credit cards. SGL/DBL$42-$60.

Sheraton Inn (Woodrow Wilson Pkwy, 24401; 248-6020, 248-2902, 800-325-3535) 112 rooms and suites, restaurant, lounge, entertainment, tennis courts, airport courtesy car, no-smoking rooms, a/c, TV, children stay free with parents, wheelchair access, 3,600 square feet of meeting and exhibition space, 6 meeting rooms, meeting facilities for 350, major credit cards. SGL/DBL$47-$80.

Super 8 Motel (1015 Richmond Rd, 24401; 886-2888, 800-800-8000) 63 rooms and suites, complimentary breakfast, no pets, children under 12 stay free with parents, free local calls, a/c, TV, in-room refrigerators and microwaves, fax service, no-smoking rooms, senior citizen rates, wheelchair access, meeting facilities, major credit cards. SGL/DBL$40-$43.

Stephens City
Area Code 703

Comfort Inn (State Rd 227, 22655; 869-6500, 800-221-2222) 60 rooms, restaurant, pool, wheelchair access, no-smoking rooms, no pets, whirlpools, fax service, whirlpools, children under 18 stay free with parents, senior citizen rates, a/c, TV, meeting facilities, major credit cards. SGL/DBL$40-$65.

Strasburg
Area Code 703

Hotel Strasburg (201 South Holiday St, 22657; 465-9191, 800-348-8327) 27 rooms, bed and breakfast, restaurant, sauna, jacuzzi, no-smoking rooms, pets allowed, major credit cards. SGL/DBL$69-$149.

Suffolk
Area Code 804

Comfort Inn (1503 Holland Rd, 23434; 539-3600, 800-221-2222) 53 rooms, restaurant, pool, wheelchair access, no-smoking rooms, no pets, children under 18 stay free with parents, senior citizen rates, a/c, TV, meeting facilities, major credit cards. SGL/DBL$35-$60.

Holiday Inn (2864 Pruden Blvd, 23434; 934-2311, 800-HOLIDAY) 100 rooms, restaurant, lounge, outdoor pool, exercise facilities, children under 19 stay free with parents, wheelchair access, a/c, TV, no-smoking rooms, fax service, room service, no pets, laundry service, meeting facilities for 250, senior citizen rates, major credit cards. SGL/DBL$44-$58.

Super 8 Motel (633 North Main St, 23434; 925-0992, 800-800-8000) 51 rooms and suites, restaurant, pets allowed, children under 12 stay free with parents, free local calls, a/c, TV, in-room refrigerators and microwaves, fax service, no-smoking rooms, senior citizen rates, wheelchair access, meeting facilities, major credit cards. SGL/DBL$32-$37.

Tappahannock
Area Code 804

Super 8 Motel (Tappahannock, 22560; 443-3888, 800-800-8000) 43 rooms and suites, pets allowed, children under 12 stay free with parents, free local calls, a/c, TV, in-room refrigerators and microwaves, fax service, no-smoking rooms, senior citizen rates, wheelchair access, meeting facilities, major credit cards. SGL/DBL$36-$41.

Troutdale
Area Code 703

Fox Hill Inn (Troutdale, 24378; 677-3313, 800-874-3313) 6 rooms, free breakfast, pets allowed, private baths, meeting facilities for 20. SGL/DBL$55-$65.

Troutville
Area Code 703

Comfort Inn (2654 Lee Hwy South, 24175; 992-5600, 800-221-2222) 72 rooms, restaurant, pool, wheelchair access, no-smoking rooms, no pets, children under 18 stay free with parents, senior citizen rates, a/c, TV, meeting facilities, major credit cards. SGL/DBL$39-$60.

Days Inn Airport (8118 Plantation Rd, 24019; 366-0341, Fax 366-3935, 800-325-2525) 123 rooms and suites, restaurant, lounge, pool, children stay free with parents, room service, laundry service, a/c, limousine service, TV, free local calls, no pets, wheelchair access, no-smoking rooms, senior citizen rates, major credit cards. SGL/DBL$38-$58, STS$60-$80.

Days Inn (Troutville, 24175; 992-6041, Fax 992-5069, 800-325-2525) 24 rooms, restaurant, lounge, pool, children stay free with parents, room service, laundry service, a/c, TV, free local calls, no pets, wheelchair access, no-smoking rooms, senior citizen rates, major credit cards. SGL/DBL$25-$50.

Howard Johnson Lodge (Troutville, 24175; 992-3000, 800-I-GO-HOJO) 69 rooms, restaurant, lounge, pool, children stay free with parents, wheelchair access, no-smoking rooms, TV, a/c, laundry facilities, pets allowed, free parking, senior citizen rates, meeting facilities, major credit cards. SGL/DBL$38-$70.

TraveLodge (Lee Hwy South, 24175; 992-6700, Fax 992-3991, 800-255-3050) 109 rooms and suites, restaurant, lounge, free breakfast, pool, wheelchair access, free newspaper, laundry service, TV, a/c, free local calls, fax, no-smoking rooms, in-room refrigerators and microwaves, no pets, meeting facilities for 25, major credit cards. SGL$35-$42, DBL$41-$48, AP$6.

Upperville
Area Code 703

The 1763 Inn (Rte 1, 22176; 592-3484, 800-669-1763) 16 rooms, bed and breakfast, restaurant, pool, jacuzzi, sauna, wheelchair access, private baths, open year-round. SGL/DBL$95-$165.

Vienna
Area Code 703

Marriott Tysons Corner Hotel (8028 Leesburg Pike, 22181; 734-3200, Fax 734-5763, 800-228-9290) 390 rooms and suites, restaurant, lounge, entertainment, indoor pool, exercise facilities, whirlpools, wheelchair access, free parking, TV, a/c, no-smoking rooms, gift shop, children stay free with parents, business services, meeting facilities, major credit cards. SGL/DBL$65-$135.

Residence Inn (8616 Westwood Center Dr, 22182; 893-0120, 800-331-3131) rooms and suites, complimentary breakfast, pool, spa, in-room refrigerators, coffee makers and microwaves, laundry facilities, free parking, TV, a/c, VCRs, pets allowed, fireplaces, children stay free with parents, no-smoking rooms, wheelchair access, meeting facilities for 35, major credit cards. SGL/DBL$126-$165.

Sheraton Premiere at Tysons Corner (8661 Leesburg Pike, Vienna 22182; 448-1234, 800-325-3535) 475 rooms and suites, restaurant, lounge, indoor and outdoor pool, exercise facilities, no-smoking rooms, free parking, meeting facilities, major credit cards. SGL/DBL$105-$165.

Virginia Beach
Area Code 804

Rental and Reservation Services

Siebert Realty (601 Sandbridge Rd, 23456; 426-6200, 800-231-3037).

Sand Bridge Realty (3713 South Sandpiper Rd, 23456; 426-6262, 800-933-4800).

❑ ❑ ❑

Alamar Resort Motel (311 16th St, 23451; 428-7582, 800-346-5681) 22 rooms and 1- and 2-bedroom condos, pool, in-room refrigerators and microwaves, wheelchair access, no-smoking rooms, TV, a/c, laundry service, children stay free with parents, major credit cards. SGL/DBL$28-$87, 1BR$36-$96, 2BR$64-$144.

Alicia's (306 24th St, 23454; 340-8890) 5 cottages, major credit cards. SGL/DBL$300W.

The Aloha (Pacific Ave and 15th St, 23451; 428-0800, 800-458-9259) 48 efficiencies and suites, pool, a/c, TV, children stay free with parents, no pets, major credit cards. SGL/DBL$30-$65, EFF$35-$70, STS$40-$85.

Ambassador Suites (2315 Atlantic Ave, 23451; 428-1111, 800-554-5560) 54 2-room suites, outdoor pool, laundry service, free parking, children stay free with parents, a/c, TV, no pets, major credit cards. SGL/DBL$35-$115.

Angie's Guest Cottages (302 24th St, 23451; 428-4690) 6 rooms and 1-bedroom cottages, bed and breakfast, no-smoking, free parking. SGL/DBL$26-$46, 1BR$375W-$525W.

Aquarius Oceanfront Motel Apartments (1909 Atlantic Ave, 23451; 425-0650) 60 2-room suites, pool, laundry service, a/c, TV, children stay free with parents, free parking, pets allowed, meeting facilities, major credit cards. SGL/DBL$35-$115.

Arctic Apartments (Box 1712, 23451; 425-7666, 800-428-5200) 8 1- and 2-bedroom apartments, children stay free with parents, a/c, TV, no pets, free parking. 1BR$300W, 2BR$425W.

Balboa Motel and Efficiencies (Box 901, 23451; 425-0300) 17 rooms and efficiencies, pool, children stay free with parents, a/c, TV, no pets, major credit cards. SGL/DBL$24-$54, EFF$28-$78.

Virginia Beach 391

Barclay Towers All-Suite Hotel (809 Atlantic Ave, 23451; 491-2700, 800-344-4473) 138 2-room suites, indoor pool, spa, sauna, restaurant, lounge, room service, laundry service, free parking, children stay free with parents, air conditioning, TV, meeting facilities for 100, major credit cards. SGL/DBL$85-$145.

Barco's Apartments and Cottages (305 26th St, 23451; 428-1391) 23 one-, two- and three-bedroom apartments, air conditioning, TV. 1BR$375W, 3BR$450W.

Beach Carousel (1300 Pacific Avenue, 23451; 425-1700) 38 rooms, swimming pool, air conditioning, TV, laundry service, major credit cards. SGL/DBL$42-$76.

Best Western Oceanfront (11th St and Atlantic Ave, 23451; 422-5000, Fax 422-5000, 800-528-1234) 110 rooms and suites, restaurant, lounge, pool, children stay free with parents, a/c, TV, no pets, major credit cards. SGL/DBL$44-$124, STS$99-$124, AP$7.

Best Western Inn (5718 Northampton Blvd, 23455; 863-2500, Fax 464-2309, 800-528-1234) 60 rooms, restaurant, lounge, pool, children stay free with parents, no-smoking rooms, TV, a/c, wheelchair access, computer hookups in rooms, fax service, pets allowed. 2 miles from the airport, major credit cards. SGL$40-$50, DBL$50-$70, AP$6.

The Boardwalk Inn (2604 Atlantic Ave, 23451; 425-5971, 800-777-6070) 106 rooms and efficiencies, pool, a/c, TV, free parking, laundry service, major credit cards. SGL/DBL$25-$79.

Breakers Resort Inn (16th and Oceanfront, 23451; 428-1821, 800-237-7532, 800-468-1354 in Virginia) 55 rooms and efficiencies, restaurant, pool, jacuzzi, children stay free with parents, in-room refrigerators, a/c, TV, wheelchair access rooms, meeting facilities, major credit cards. SGL/DBL$40-$78, EFF$55-$140.

The Capes Ocean Resort (Box 871, 23451; 428-5421, 800-626-5224, 800-521-5421 in Virginia) 59 rooms and 2-room efficiencies, restaurant, indoor pool, free parking, wheelchair access, no-smoking rooms, TV, a/c, children stay free with parents, no pets, major credit cards. SGL/DBL$40-$115, EFF$55-$125.

Captain's Quarters Resort (304 28th St, 23451; 491-1700, 800-333-6020) 75 rooms and one- and two-bedroom suites, swimming pool, whirlpool, free parking, no pets, air conditioning, TV, children stay free with parents, laundry service, meeting facilities, major credit cards. SGL/DBL$50-$75, STS$70-$165.

Virginia

Carriage Inn Motel (15th St and Atlantic Ave, 23451; 428-8105) 10 rooms, a/c, TV, meeting facilities, major credit cards. SGL/DBL$28-$58.

Castle Motel (Virginia Beach, 23451; 425-9330) 47 rooms, pool, free parking, a/c, TV, no pets, children stay free with parents, major credit cards. SGL/DBL$35-$55, AP$6-$8.

Cavalier (42nd St and Oceanfront, 23451; 425-8555, 800-446-8199) 400 rooms, 3 restaurants, lounge, indoor and outdoor pools, exercise facilities, children stay free with parents, a/c, TV, no pets, meeting facilities, major credit cards. SGL/DBL$55-$155.

Cerca Del Mar Motel (410 21st St, 23451; 428-6511) 55 rooms and efficiencies, pool, laundry service, a/c, TV, no pets, major credit cards. SGL/DBL$25-$70.

Clarion Resort and Conference Center (501 Atlantic Ave, 23451; 422-3186, Fax 491-3379, 800-221-2222) 168 2-room suites, restaurant, lounge, pool, exercise facilities, free parking, tennis, children stay free with parents, no pets, wheelchair access, no-smoking rooms, TV, a/c, meeting facilities. 2 miles from the Convention Center, 3 miles from the Marine Science Museum, 20 miles from the airport, major credit cards. SGL/DBL$40-$160.

Colonial Inn (2809 Atlantic Ave, 23451; 428-5370, 800-344-3342) 159 rooms, restaurant, lounge, indoor pool, free parking, wheelchair access, no-smoking rooms, TV, a/c, children stay free with parents, meeting facilities, major credit cards. SGL/DBL$49-$99.

Comfort Inn (2800 Pacific Ave, 23451; 428-2203, 800-852-2203, 800-221-2222) 135 rooms, free breakfast, indoor and outdoor pool, sauna, jacuzzi, exercise facilities, laundry service, fax service, no-smoking rooms, TV, a/c, children stay free with parents, gift shop, wheelchair access, no pets. 15 miles from the airport, major credit cards. SGL/DBL$34-$109.

Comfort Inn Lynnhaven (804 Lynnhaven Pkwy, 23452; 427-5500, 800-221-2222) 83 rooms, exercise facilities, wheelchair access, children stay free with parents, no-smoking rooms, a/c, TV, meeting facilities. 8 miles from the airport, major credit cards. SGL/DBL$45-$60.

Comfort Inn Little Creek (5189 Shore Dr, 23455; 460-5566, 800-221-2222) 59 rooms and suites, pool, no pets, wheelchair access, no-smoking rooms, children stay free with parents, a/c, TV, in-room refrigerators and microwaves. 3 miles from the airport, major credit cards. SGL/DBL$32-$50.

Comfort Inn Oceanfront (2015 Atlantic Ave, 23451; 425-8200, 800-221-2222) 83 rooms and 2-room suites, complimentary breakfast, indoor pool, exercise facilities, sauna, free parking, wheelchair access, in-room refrigerators, children stay free with parents, no-smoking rooms, TV, a/c. 15 miles from the airport, major credit cards. SGL/DBL$45-$75, STS$90-$155.

Virginia Beach 393

Courtyard by Marriott (5700 Greenwich Rd, 23462; 490-2002, Fax 490-0169) 146 rooms, restaurant, lounge, pool, whirlpool, exercise facilities, a/c, TV, children stay free with parents, wheelchair access, no-smoking rooms, meeting facilities, major credit cards. SGL/DBL$68-$92.

Cutty Sark Motel Efficiencies (3614 Atlantic Ave, 23451; 428-2116) 13 efficiencies, free parking, laundry service, a/c, TV, children stay free with parents, no pets, airport transportation, major credit cards. SGL/DBL$27-$75.

Days Inn (Oceanfront and 32nd St, 23451; 428-7233, Fax 491-1936, 800-325-2525) 120 rooms and efficiencies, restaurant, lounge, pool, whirlpool, children stay free with parents, laundry service, free local calls, fax service, no pets, in-room refrigerators, wheelchair access, no-smoking rooms, TV, a/c, meeting facilities. Near the Convention Center and Marine Science Museum, 18 miles from the Norfolk International Airport, major credit cards. SGL$46-$76, DBL$56-$86, EFF$66-$96, AP$6.

Days Inn (4564 Bonney Rd, 23462; 497-4488, Fax 671-8432, 800-325-2525) 144 rooms, restaurant, complimentary breakfast, lounge, pool, children stay free with parents, laundry service, fax service, no pets, free local calls, wheelchair access, no-smoking rooms, TV, a/c, meeting facilities, major credit cards. SGL/DBL$48-$53, AP$6.

Days Inn Airport (5708 Northampton Blvd, 23455; 460-2205, Fax 363-8089) 148 rooms, restaurant, complimentary breakfast, pool, sauna, exercise facilities, children stay free with parents, wheelchair access, no-smoking rooms, TV, a/c, meeting facilities, major credit cards. SGL/DBL$42-$85.

Diplomat Motor Inn (3305 Atlantic Ave, 23451; 752-1424) 35 rooms and efficiencies, heated outdoor pool, a/c, TV, major credit cards. SGL/DBL$40-$85, EFF$50-$95.

Dolphin Inn (1705 Atlantic Ave, 23451; 491-1420, Fax 425-8390, 800-DOLFINS) 54 2-room suites, indoor pool, whirlpools, free parking, wheelchair access, a/c, TV, laundry service, children stay free with parents, major credit cards. SGL/DBL$42-$120.

Dolphin Run Condos (303 Atlantic Ave, 23451; 425-6166) 24 1- , 2- and 3-bedroom apartments, indoor pool, exercise facilities, sauna, laundry service, a/c, TV, free local calls, no pets, laundry service, children stay free with parents. 1BR$600W-$900W, 2BR$650W-$950W, 3BR$800W-$1300W.

Dunes Motor Inn (Box 467, 23458; 38 rooms and efficiencies, gift shop, a/c, TV, children stay free with parents, no pets, major credit cards. SGL/DBL$78-$96, EFF$86-$104.

Econo Lodge (13th and Atlantic Ave, 23451; 428-1183, 800-437-2497) 96 rooms and suites, a/c, TV, no pets, major credit cards. SGL/DBL$44-$99.

Econo Lodge At The Ocean (3108 Atlantic Ave, 23451; 65 efficiencies, restaurant, lounge, laundry service, free parking, children stay free with parents, wheelchair access, no-smoking rooms, TV, a/c, major credit cards. SGL/DBL$25-$100.

Edgewater Condominium (3615 Atlantic Ave, 23451; 425-6298) 35 2-bedroom suites, free parking, no pets, a/c, TV, children stay free with parents, major credit cards. SGL/DBL$900W.

Fairfield Inn by Marriott (4760 Euclid Rd, 23462; 499-1935, Fax 499-1935 ext 709, 800-228-2800) 134 rooms, pool, children stay free with parents, free local calls, laundry service, wheelchair access, no-smoking rooms, TV, a/c, meeting facilities. 9 miles from Virginia Beach. $42-$56.

Flagship Motel and Efficiencies (Atlantic Ave and Sixth St, 23451; 425-6422, 800-338-8790) 55 rooms and efficiencies, pool, children stay free with parents, a/c, TV, laundry service, major credit cards. SGL/DBL$40-$90, EFF$35-$95.

Founders Inn and Conference Center (I-64 and Indian River Rd, 23451; 424-5511, 800-926-4466) 249 rooms and 1-bedroom suites, restaurant, indoor and outdoor pools, exercise facilities, tennis, a/c, rooms service, no-smoking rooms, wheelchair access, TV, meeting facilities, major credit cards. SGL/DBL$95-$105, STS$125.

Four Sails Resort Hotel (3301 Atlantic Ave, 23451; 491-8200, 800-227-4213) 55 1- and 2-bedroom suites, restaurant, lounge, indoor pool, exercise facilities, a/c, TV, laundry service, free parking, major credit cards. SGL/DBL$145-$275.

Golden Sands Motel (14th St and Atlantic Ave, 23451; 428-1770) 56 rooms and efficiencies, pool, a/c, TV, major credit cards. SGL/DBL$30-$60, EFF$70-$80.

The Halifax Hotel (Oceanfront and 26th St, 23451; 428-3044) 35 rooms, restaurant, complimentary breakfast, a/c, TV, free parking, major credit cards. SGL/DBL$65.

Hampton Inn (5793 Greenwich Rd, 23462; 490-9800, Fax 490-3573, 800-HAMPTON) 122 rooms, complimentary breakfast, pool, exercise facilities, children stay free with parents, no-smoking rooms, TV, a/c, wheelchair access, computer hookups, fax service, free local calls, meeting facilities. Near the Koger Executive Center, 10 miles from the Pavillion Convention Center, 7 miles from the airport, major credit cards. SGL$49-$51, DBL$55-$57.

Hilton Inn (8th St at Oceanfront, 23451; 428-8935, Fax 425-2769, 800-HILTONS) 124 rooms and suites, restaurant, lounge, indoor and outdoor pools, exercise facilities, wheelchair access, no-smoking rooms, children stay free with parents, in-room refrigerators, a/c, TV, free parking, room service, business services, meeting facilities for 350. On the Boardwalk, 20 miles from the airport, major credit cards. SGL/DBL$50-$144.

HoJo Inn (Third and Atlantic Ave, 23451; 422-0553, 800-654-9122) 52 rooms and efficiencies, restaurant, pool, children stay free with parents, no-smoking rooms, a/c, TV, room service, gift shop, laundry service. Fifteen miles from the Pavillion Convention Center and airport, major credit cards. SGL$35-$70, DBL$40-$85.

Holiday Inn On The Ocean (39th and Oceanfront, 23451; 428-1711, Fax 425-5742, 800-942-3224, 800-HOLIDAY) 266 rooms and 2-room suites, restaurant, lounge, indoor pool, whirlpools, children stay free with parents, wheelchair access, no-smoking rooms, TV, a/c, fax service, room service, gift shop, no pets, meeting facilities for 500. 4 miles from Wildwater Rapids, 3 miles from the Marine & Science Museum. $66-$199.

Holiday Inn Airport (5725 Northampton Blvd, 23455; 464-9351, Fax 464-9351 ext 542, 800-HOLIDAY) 172 rooms, restaurant, lounge, children stay free with parents, wheelchair access, no-smoking rooms, TV, a/c, fax service, room service, airport transportation, meeting facilities for 100, major credit cards. SGL/DBL$42-$68.

Holiday Inn Expressway (5655 Greenwich Rd, 23465; 499-4400, Fax 473-0517, 800-HOLIDAY) 342 rooms and suites, restaurant, indoor pool, exercise facilities, children stay free with parents, wheelchair access, no-smoking rooms, TV, a/c, fax service, room service, free local calls, gift shop, airport transportation, no pets. 5 miles from the downtown Norfolk area, 7 miles from the airport, 10 miles from the Convention Center, major credit cards. SGL/DBL$65-$82.

Holiday Inn Oceanside (21st and Atlantic, 23451; 491-1500, Fax 491-1945, 800-88-BEACH, 800-HOLIDAY) 138 rooms, restaurant, lounge, indoor pool, whirlpool, children stay free with parents, wheelchair access, no-smoking rooms, TV, a/c, fax service, room service, no pets, free parking, laundry service, meeting facilities for 150. Twelve miles from the airport, a half-mile from the Convention Center, 2 miles from Ocean Breeze Fun Park, major credit cards. SGL$48-$124, DBL$57-$145.

Holiday Sands Motor Inn (11th St and Oceanfront, 23451; 428-3773, 800-548-9467) 40 rooms, pool, children stay free with parents, a/c, TV, free parking, major credit cards. SGL/DBL$25-$45.

Holly Kove Motel (395 Norfolk Ave, 23451; 428-8374) 29 rooms, pool, free parking, children stay free with parents, a/c, TV, laundry service, major credit cards. SGL/DBL$25-$69.

Howard Johnson Lodge (5173 Shore Dr, 23455; 460-1151, Fax 460-0041, 800-654-9122) 52 rooms, free breakfast, in-room refrigerators and microwaves, airport transportation, children stay free with parents, no-smoking rooms, TV, a/c, wheelchair access. 1 mile from Chesapeake Beach, 5 miles from the airport, major credit cards. SGL$35-$40, DBL$40-$45.

Howard Johnson Oceanfront Resort Hotel (3705 Atlantic Ave, 23451; 428-7220, Fax 428-0310, 800-654-2000, 800-654-9122) 177 rooms and efficiencies, restaurant, pool, children stay free with parents, no-smoking rooms, TV, a/c, no pets, free parking, meeting facilities. Sixteen miles from the airport, near the Convention Center and Arts Center, major credit cards. SGL$35-$70, DBL$39-$75.

Idlewhyle (2705 Atlantic Ave, 23451; 425-3041) 46 rooms and efficiencies, restaurant, indoor pool, a/c, TV, free parking, no pets, major credit cards. SGL/DBL$30-$80.

Jefferson Motel Apartments (3300 Pacific Ave, 23451; 428-1321) 26 1- and 2-bedroom apartments, pool, a/c, TV, children stay free with parents. 1BR$39-$69, 2BR$49-$89.

La Coquille Motel Apartments (314 16th St, 23451; 422-3889, 800-327-0746) 13 1- and 2-bedroom apartments, a/c, TV, no pets. 1BR$45-$76, 2BR$75-$116.

La Playa Resort Motel (Box 686, 23451; 428-5933) 34 rooms, no pets, free parking, children stay free with parents, a/c, TV, major credit cards. SGL/DBL$40-$99.

La Quinta Inn (192 Newtown Rd, 23462; 497-6620, Fax 456-9780, 800-531-5900) 129 rooms, restaurant, lounge, pool, complimentary newspaper, free local calls, fax service, laundry service, no-smoking rooms, TV, a/c, wheelchair access, free parking, meeting facilities. 5 miles from the Crossroads Center and Edgar Allen Poe Museum, 17 miles from the International Airport, major credit cards. SGL/DBL$40-$60.

Mai Kai Resort Apartments (208 57th St, 23451; 428-1096) 35 efficiencies and 1- and 2-bedroom apartments, a/c, TV, laundry service, no pets, children stay free with parents. EFF$225W-$425W, 1BR$325W-$585W, 2BR$450W-$785W.

Mardi Gras Motel and Apartments (2802 Atlantic Ave, 23451; 428-3434, 800-527-6100) 42 rooms and efficiencies, laundry service, wheelchair access, a/c, TV, free parking, children stay free with parents, pets allowed, major credit cards. SGL/DBL$20-$78.

Marjac Suites (2201 Atlantic Ave, 23451; 425-1000, 800-368-3080) 60 2-room suites, outdoor pool, free parking, a/c, TV, laundry service, children stay free with parents, major credit cards. SGL/DBL$35-$115.

Murphy's Emerald Isle Motel Apartments (Box 806, 23451; 428-3462, 800-237-9717) 71 2-room apartments, pool, laundry service, free parking, children stay free with parents, a/c, TV, wheelchair access, major credit cards. SGL/DBL$30-$95.

Newcastle Motel (12th St and Oceanfront, 23451; 428-3981, Fax 491-4394, 800-346-3176) 83 rooms and 2-room suites, restaurant, indoor pool, spa, laundry service, a/c, TV, children stay free with parents, meeting facilities, major credit cards. SGL/DBL$45-$105.

Ocean Cove Motel (200 24th St, 23451; 491-1830) 13 rooms and efficiencies, a/c, TV, children stay free with parents, free parking, major credit cards. SGL/DBL$30-$50, EFF$40-$60.

Oceanfront Inn (2901 Atlantic Ave, 23451; 422-0445, 800-548-3879) 146 rooms, restaurant, lounge, indoor and outdoor pools, wheelchair access, gift shop, a/c, TV, free parking, children stay free with parents, major credit cards. SGL/DBL$40-$105.

Ocean Holiday On The Ocean (25th St and Atlantic Ave, 23451; 425-6920, 800-26-BEACH, 800-345-SAND in Virginia) 105 rooms, lounge, pool, children stay free with parents, wheelchair access, no-smoking rooms, TV, a/c, pets allowed, meeting facilities, major credit cards. SGL/DBL$50-$70.

Oceans II Studios (4005 Oceanfront, 23451; 428-9021, 800-845-4786) 42 rooms and efficiencies, restaurant, lounge, a/c, TV, free parking, laundry service, major credit cards. SGL/DBL$45-$110.

Omni Virginia Beach Hotel (4453 Bonney Rd, 23462; 473-1700, Fax 552-0477, 800-THE-OMNI) 149 rooms and suites, restaurant, lounge, entertainment, indoor and outdoor pool, whirlpool, sauna, exercise facilities, a/c, TV, 3,600 square feet of meeting and exhibition space. 7 miles from the airport, 15 miles from the downtown Norfolk area and Waterside Festival Marketplace, major credit cards. SGL/DBL$100-$155.

Park Inn International (424 Atlantic Ave, 23451; 425-2200, Fax 491-7751, 800-955-9300, 800-437-PARK) 144 2-room suites, restaurant, lounge, indoor pool, jacuzzi, a/c, TV, laundry service, free parking, complimentary newspaper, meeting facilities for 150. 2 miles from the Ocean Breeze Festival Park and Marine Science Museum, major credit cards. SGL/DBL$50-$129.

The Plantation Motel (2906 Atlantic Ave, 23451; 428-9186) 56 rooms, restaurant, lounge, indoor and outdoor pools, a/c, TV, laundry service, children stay free with parents, major credit cards. SGL/DBL$25-$75.

Prince Anne Inn (25th St and Oceanfront, 23451; 428-5611, 800-468-1111) 60 rooms, restaurant, outdoor pool, jacuzzi, sauna, a/c, TV, free parking, major credit cards. SGL/DBL$65-$200.

Quality Inn Pavillion (Parks and 21st St, 23451; 422-3617, 800-221-2222) 107 rooms and suites, restaurant, pool, wheelchair access, no-smoking rooms, laundry service, a/c, TV, no pets, meeting facilities. Near the Convention Center and Oceanfront, 3 miles from the Marine Science Museum, 15 miles from the airport, major credit cards. SGL/DBL$39-$59, STS$90.

Quality Inn Oceanfront Resort (2207 Atlantic Ave, 23451; 428-5141, Fax 422-8436, 800-221-2222) 111 rooms and efficiencies, restaurant, lounge, indoor pool, sauna, laundry service, wheelchair access, no-smoking rooms, TV, a/c, no pets, meeting facilities. 1 mile from the Convention Center, 15 miles from the airport, major credit cards. SGL/DBL$40-$140.

Radisson Hotel (1900 Pavilion Dr, 23451; 422-8900, 800-333-3333) 282 rooms and suites, restaurant, lounge, indoor pool, sauna, whirlpool, tennis, jogging track, gift shop, children stay free with parents, no-smoking rooms, a/c, TV, wheelchair access, transportation to local attractions, free parking, meeting facilities for 750, major credit cards. SGL/DBL$39-$114.

Ramada Inn Oceanfront South (615 Atlantic Ave, 23451; 425-5151, Fax 428-4901, 800-2-RAMADA) 167 rooms and suites, restaurant, lounge, entertainment, indoor pool, jacuzzi, children stay free with parents, gift shop, wheelchair access, no-smoking rooms, TV, a/c, airport transportation, meeting facilities, major credit cards. SGL/DBL$65-$100.

Ramada Inn Resort Oceanside (Oceanfront at 57th St, 23451; 428-7025, Fax 428-2921, 800-2-RAMADA) 215 rooms, Concierge Floors, restaurant, lounge, entertainment, indoor and outdoor pools, spa, jacuzzi, laundry service, children stay free with parents, wheelchair access, no-smoking rooms, TV, a/c, airport transportation, meeting facilities for 450. At the north end of the beach, major credit cards. SGL/DBL$45-$150.

Red Roof Inn (196 Ballard Court, 23462; 490-0225, Fax 490-8220, 800-843-7663) 109 rooms, restaurant, no-smoking rooms, fax service, wheelchair access, complimentary newspaper, free local calls, children stay free with parents, a/c, TV, in-room computer hookups. 6 miles from the airport, 11 miles from the Convention Center, major credit cards. SGL/DBL$40-$56.

Rodeway Inn (2707 Atlantic Ave, 23451; 428-3970, 800-228-3970) 38 rooms, complimentary breakfast, pool, no-smoking rooms, a/c, TV, free parking, wheelchair access, no pets, major credit cards. SGL/DBL$34-$124.

Royal Clipper Motor Lodge (36th St and Atlantic Ave, 23451; 428-8992) 61 rooms and efficiencies, pool, free parking, a/c, TV, no pets, children stay free with parents, major credit cards. SGL/DBL$48-$70.

Sandcastle Oceanfront Motel (14th St and Atlantic Ave, 23451; 428-2828, 800-233-0131) 154 rooms, restaurant, indoor pool, wheelchair access, no pets, a/c, TV, children stay free with parents, free parking, major credit cards. SGL/DBL$30-$99.

Sandpiper Motel Apartments (112 Pacific Ave, 23451; 422-0001, 800-457-8006) rooms and 1- and 2-room efficiencies, pool, laundry service, pets allowed, a/c, TV, wheelchair access, children stay free with parents, major credit cards. SGL/DBL$20-$74.

Schooner Inn (215 Atlantic Ave, 23451; 425-5222, 800-283-SAND) 84 rooms and efficiencies, restaurant, lounge, pool, a/c, TV, laundry service, children stay free with parents, major credit cards. SGL/DBL$25-$95, EFF$39-$105.

Sea Gull Motel On The Beach (27th St and Oceanfront, 23451; 425-5711, 800-426-4855) 51 rooms, restaurant, indoor pool, jacuzzi, room service, children stay free with parents, a/c, TV, no-smoking rooms, major credit cards. SGL/DBL$30-$100.

Sea Vacationer Resort Inn (Box 1091, 23451; 428-4413, 800-446-8388) 78 rooms, pool, free parking, a/c, TV, children stay free with parents, no pets, major credit cards. SGL/DBL$36-$79.

Seahawk Resort Motel (Box 449, 23458; 428-1296, 800-333-6921) 48 rooms and efficiencies, indoor pool, jacuzzi, children stay free with parents, no-smoking rooms, TV, a/c, no pets, major credit cards. SGL/DBL$40-$105, EFF$45-$115.

Seashire Inn (1040 Laskin Rd, 23451; 428-5511) 52 rooms, restaurant, lounge, pool, in-room refrigerators, children stay free with parents, wheelchair access, no-smoking rooms, TV, a/c, meeting facilities, major credit cards. SGL/DBL$19-$65.

Sheraton Inn (Oceanfront and 36th St, 23451; 425-9000, Fax 428-5352, 800-325-3535) 203 rooms and suites, restaurant, lounge, entertainment, outdoor pool, exercise facilities, gift shop, no-smoking rooms, wheelchair access, complimentary airport transportation, a/c, TV, 10 meeting rooms, 12,000 square feet of meeting and exhibition space, meeting facilities for 720. Near Pavilion Convention Center, the VA Marine Sciences Museum and the beach, 15 miles from the airport, major credit cards. SGL$53-$162, DBL$59-$172.

South Shore Resort Inn (1000 Atlantic Ave, 23451; 428-6141, 800-843-7096) 110 rooms, indoor pool, jacuzzi, a/c, TV, free parking, gift shop, no pets, laundry service, major credit cards. SGL/DBL$30 $100.

Station 1 Hotel (2321 Atlantic Ave, 23451; 491-2400, 800-435-2424, 800-262-2425 in Virginia) 104 2-room suites, restaurant, lounge, pool, exercise facilities, sauna, jacuzzi, laundry room, free parking, a/c, TV, children stay free with parents, meeting facilities, major credit cards. SGL/DBL$65-$85.

Virginia

Sun Up Apartments (316 27th St, 23451; 428-8289) 5 1- and 2-bedroom apartments. 1BR/2BR$300W.

Sundial Motel and Efficiencies (308 21st St, 23451; 428-2922) 5 rooms and efficiencies, a/c, TV, major credit cards. SGL/DBL$22-$48, EFF$33-$53.

Thunderbird Motor Lodge (35th St and Oceanfront, 23451; 428-3024, 800-633-6669) 135 rooms, restaurant, lounge, outdoor pool, no-smoking rooms, TV, a/c, pets allowed, children stay free with parents, meeting facilities, major credit cards. SGL/DBL$30-$115.

Tradewinds Resort Hotel (1601 Atlantic Ave, 23451; 491-8334, 800-344-3342) 50 rooms, restaurant, lounge, outdoor pool, jacuzzi, a/c, TV, free parking, children stay free with parents, major credit cards. SGL/DBL$49-$89.

TraveLodge (2109 Atlantic Ave, 23451; 428-2403, Fax 422-2530, 800-255-3050) 55 rooms and suites, restaurant, lounge, indoor pool, room service, wheelchair access, children stay free with parents, no pets, no-smoking rooms, TV, a/c, meeting facilities for 30, major credit cards. SGL/DBL$45-$90, AP$10.

TraveLodge (4600 Booney Rd, 23462; 473-9745, Fax 497-1648, 800-255-3050) 106 rooms and suites, restaurant, lounge, complimentary breakfast, pool, laundry service, a/c, TV, fax service, free parking, meeting facilities for 25. 8 miles from the airport, 10 miles from the oceanfront, major credit cards. SGL$35-$53, DBL$41-$59, AP$6.

Tropicana Resort Hotel (18th St and Atlantic Ave, 23451; 425-5511, 800-451-5161) 85 rooms and suites, free breakfast, outdoor pool, children stay free with parents, a/c, TV, major credit cards. SGL/DBL$30-$135.

Viking Motel (2700 Atlantic Ave, 23451; 428-7116, 800-828-3063) 81 rooms and efficiencies, pool, free parking, a/c, TV, no pets, children stay free with parents, major credit cards. SGL/DBL$25-$110.

Virginia Beach Resort Hotel and Tennis Club (2800 Shore Dr, 23451; 481-9000, 800-468-2722, 800-422-4747 in Virginia) 295 1- and 2-bedroom suites, restaurant, lounge, pool, laundry service, no-smoking rooms, TV, a/c, children stay free with parents, wheelchair access, meeting facilities. 1BR$79-$184, 2BR$134-$209.

Virginian Motel (310 24th St, 23451; 428-5333) 41 2-room suites, outdoor pool, children stay free with parents, a/c, TV, free parking, no pets, major credit cards. SGL/DBL$40-$80,

Windjammer Motel (Box 5, 23451; 428-0060, 800-695-0035) 72 rooms and efficiencies, outdoor pool, free parking, laundry service, no pets, children stay free with parents, a/c, TV, major credit cards. SGL/DBL$36-$100.

Warm Springs
Area Code 703

Anderson Cottage Bed and Breakfast (Old Germantown Rd, 24484; 839-2975, Fax 839-3058) 5 rooms and suites, free breakfast, a/c, TV, no pets, private baths, meeting facilities for 10. SGL/DBL$60-$110.

Warrenton
Area Code 703

Comfort Inn (6633 Lee Hwy, 22186; 348-8900, 800-221-2222) 98 rooms and 2-room suites, restaurant, pool, wheelchair access, no-smoking rooms, pets allowed, fax service, whirlpools, children under 18 stay free with parents, senior citizen rates, a/c, TV, meeting facilities, major credit cards. SGL/DBL$56-$66.

Hampton Inn (501 Blackwell Rd, 22186; 349-4200, Fax 349-4200, 800-HAMPTON) 100 rooms, restaurant, complimentary breakfast, pool, exercise facilities, children under 18 stay free with parents, no-smoking rooms, wheelchair access, computer hookups, fax service, TV, a/c, free local calls, pets allowed, meeting facilities, major credit cards. SGL/DBL$55-$63.

HoJo Inn (Six Broadview Ave, 22186; 347-4141, Fax 347-5632, 800-I-GO-HOJO) 80 rooms, restaurant, lounge, pool, children stay free with parents, wheelchair access, no-smoking rooms, fax service, TV, a/c, pets allowed, free parking, meeting facilities, senior citizen rates, meeting facilities, major credit cards. SGL$30-$36, DBL$35-$41.

Waynesboro
Area Code 703

Comfort Inn (640 West Broad St, 22980; 942-1171, 800-221-2222) 75 rooms, restaurant, pool, wheelchair access, no-smoking rooms, no pets, children under 18 stay free with parents, senior citizen rates, a/c, TV, meeting facilities, major credit cards. SGL/DBL$38-$55.

Days Inn (2060 Rosser Ave, 22980; 943-1101, Fax 949-7586, 800-325-2525) 98 rooms, restaurant, lounge, children stay free with parents, room service, laundry service, a/c, TV, free local calls, pets allowed, wheelchair access, no-smoking rooms, senior citizen rates, major credit cards. SGL/DBL$45-$85.

Super 8 Motel (2045 Rosser Ave, 22980; 943-3888, 800-800-8000) rooms and suites, pets allowed, children under 12 stay free with parents, free local calls, a/c, TV, in-room refrigerators and microwaves, fax service, no-smoking rooms, senior citizen rates, wheelchair access, meeting facilities, major credit cards. SGL/DBL$36-$41.

White Post
Area Code 703

L'Auberge Provencale (White Post, 22663; 837-1375, 800-638-1702) 10 rooms, complimentary breakfast, fireplaces, restaurant, private baths, open year-round, no pets, wheelchair access, major credit cards. SGL/DBL$120-$165.

Williamsburg
Area Code 804

Budget Host Governor Spottswood Motel (1508 Richmond Rd, 23185; 229-6444, 800-BUD-HOST) 75 rooms, restaurant, pool, laundry facilities, in-room refrigerators, no-smoking rooms, TV, VCRs, a/c, wheelchair access, children stay free with parents, senior citizen rates, meeting facilities, major credit cards. SGL$26-$36, DBL$28-$48.

Comfort Inn Historic Area (120 Bypass Rd, 23185; 229-2000, 800-544-7774, 800-221-2222) 152 rooms, restaurant, pool, wheelchair access, no-smoking rooms, no pets, children under 18 stay free with parents, senior citizen rates, a/c, TV, meeting facilities, major credit cards. LS SGL/DBL$35-$49; HS SGL/DBL$60-$70.

Comfort Inn Central (2007 Richmond Rd, 23185; 220-3888, 800-221-2222) restaurant, indoor pool, wheelchair access, no-smoking rooms, no pets, children under 18 stay free with parents, senior citizen rates, a/c, TV, meeting facilities, major credit cards. SGL/DBL$30-$75.

Days Inn (331 Bypass Rd, 23185; 253-1166, Fax 221-0637, 800-325-2525) 120 rooms, restaurant, lounge, outdoor pool, spa, jacuzzi, children stay free with parents, room service, laundry service, a/c, TV, free local calls, no pets, wheelchair access, no-smoking rooms, senior citizen rates, major credit cards. SGL/DBL$43-$99.

Days Inn (902 Richmond Rd, 23185; 229-5060, Fax 220-9153, 800-325-2525) 100 rooms, restaurant, lounge, pool, children stay free with parents, room service, laundry service, a/c, TV, free local calls, pets allowed, wheelchair access, no-smoking rooms, senior citizen rates, major credit cards. SGL/DBL$45-$95.

Days Inn (90 Old York Rd, 23185; 253-6444, 800-325-2525) 210 rooms, restaurant, lounge, pool, children stay free with parents, room service, laundry service, a/c, TV, free local calls, no pets, wheelchair access, no-smoking rooms, senior citizen rates, major credit cards. SGL/DBL$47-$85.

Days Inn (6488 Richmond Rd, 23185; 565-0090, Fax 565-3545, 800-325-2525) 73 rooms, restaurant, lounge, pool, children stay free with parents, room service, laundry service, a/c, TV, free local calls, pets allowed, wheelchair access, no-smoking rooms, senior citizen rates, major credit cards. SGL/DBL$35-$63.

Days Inn (Williamsburg, 23187; 565-2700, Fax 800-325-2525) 122 rooms, restaurant, lounge, pool, children stay free with parents, room service, laundry service, a/c, TV, free local calls, no pets, wheelchair access, no-smoking rooms, senior citizen rates, major credit cards. SGL/DBL$35-$67.

Fairfield Inn (6439 Richmond Rd, 23188; 565-1111, Fax 565-1111, 800-524-1443, 800-228-2800) complimentary morning coffee, outdoor pool, children under 18 stay free with parents, no-smoking rooms, remote control TV, free cable TV, free local calls, laundry service, a/c, wheelchair access, fax service, meeting facilities, senior citizen rates, major credit cards. SGL/DBL$45-$65.

Hampton Inn (201 Bypass Rd, 23185; 220-0880, Fax 229-7175, 800-HAMPTON) 122 rooms, restaurant, complimentary breakfast, pool, exercise facilities, children under 18 stay free with parents, no-smoking rooms, wheelchair access, computer hookups, fax service, TV, a/c, free local calls, pets allowed, meeting facilities, major credit cards. SGL/DBL$49-$69.

Hampton Inn Historic Area (505 York St, 23185; 220-3100, 800-HAMPTON) 85 rooms, restaurant, complimentary breakfast, pool, exercise facilities, children under 18 stay free with parents, no-smoking rooms, wheelchair access, computer hookups, fax service, TV, a/c, free local calls, pets allowed, meeting facilities, major credit cards. SGL/DBL$49-$74.

Holiday Inn (3032 Richmond Rd, 23185; 565-2600, Fax 564-9738, 800-446-6001, 800-HOLIDAY) rooms and suites, restaurant, lounge, entertainment, indoor and outdoor pools, whirlpools, sauna, exercise facilities, transportation to local attractions, gift shop, game room, children under 19 stay free with parents, wheelchair access, a/c, TV, no-smoking rooms, fax service, room service, no pets, laundry service, meeting facilities for 700, senior citizen rates, major credit cards. SGL/DBL$58-$75.

Holiday Inn Historic Area (110 Bypass Rd, 23185; 253-1663, Fax 220-9117, 800-283-1663, 800-HOLIDAY) 132 rooms, restaurant, lounge, outdoor pool, exercise facilities, children under 19 stay free with parents, wheelchair access, gift shop, a/c, TV, no-smoking rooms, fax service, room service, no pets, laundry service, meeting facilities for 400, senior citizen rates, major credit cards. SGL/DBL$64-$74.

Holiday Inn 1776 (Williamsburg, 23185; 220-1776, Fax 220-3124, 800-HOLIDAY) 203 rooms, restaurant, lounge, outdoor pool, exercise facilities, gift shop, children under 19 stay free with parents, wheelchair access, a/c, TV, no-smoking rooms, fax service, room service, no pets, laundry service, meeting facilities for 400 senior citizen rates, major credit cards. SGL/DBL$58-$64.

404 Virginia

Holiday Inn Downtown (814 Capitol Landing Rd, 23185; 229-0200, 800-368-0200, 800-HOLIDAY) restaurant, lounge, indoor pool, exercise facilities, children under 19 stay free with parents, wheelchair access, gift shop, a/c, TV, no-smoking rooms, fax service, room service, no pets, laundry service, meeting facilities for 200, senior citizen rates, major credit cards. SGL/DBL$51-$100.

Hilton Williamsburg Hotel and Conference Center (50 Kingsmill Rd, 23185; 220-2500, Fax 220-2500 ext 7601, 800-HILTONS) 288 rooms and suites, restaurant, lounge, entertainment, indoor and outdoor pools, exercise facilities, tennis courts, sauna, hot tubs, children stay free with parents, no-smoking rooms, wheelchair access, pets allowed, a/c, TV, business services, meeting facilities, major credit cards. SGL/DBL$85-$95, STS$100-$135.

HoJo Inn (824 Capital Landing Rd, 23185; 229-4933, 800-446-1041, 800-I-GO-HOJO) 183 rooms, restaurant, lounge, pool, children stay free with parents, wheelchair access, in-room refrigerators and microwaves, game room, no-smoking rooms, TV, a/c, no pets, free parking, meeting facilities, senior citizen rates, major credit cards. SGL/DBL$35-$55.

Howard Johnson Hotel (7135 Pocahontas Trail, 23185; 229-6900, 800-841-9100, 800-I-GO-HOJO) 100 rooms and 2-room suites, restaurant, lounge, pool, jacuzzi, laundry facilities, children stay free with parents, wheelchair access, no-smoking rooms, TV, a/c, pets allowed, free parking, meeting facilities, senior citizen rates, major credit cards. SGL/DBL$39-$99.

Howard Johnson Lodge (1800 Richmond Rd, 23185; 229-2781, 800-I-GO-HOJO) 77 rooms, restaurant, lounge, pool, children stay free with parents, wheelchair access, no-smoking rooms, TV, free local calls, a/c, no pets, free parking, meeting facilities, senior citizen rates, major credit cards. LS SGL/DBL$39; HS SGL$50, DBL$55.

Motel 6 (3030 Richmond Rd, 23185; 565-3433, 891-6161) 169 rooms, pool, free local calls, children under 17 stay free with parents, a/c, TV, major credit cards. SGL/DBL$27-$34.

Piney Grove At Southall Plantation (16920 Southall Plantation Lane, 23187; 829-2480) 4 rooms, bed and breakfast, pool, no pets, a/c. SGL/DBL$125-$140.

Quality Inn (1700 Richmond Rd, 23187; 229-2401, 800-368-5689) 64 rooms and suites, restaurant, pool, room service, exercise facilities, children stay free with parents, a/c, TV, laundry service, no-smoking rooms, meeting facilities, major credit cards. LS SGL/DBL$36-$46; HS SGL/DBL$59-$70.

Quality Inn At Kingsmill (Hwy 60 East, 23187; 220-1100, 800-368-5689) 99 rooms and suites, restaurant, pool, room service, exercise facilities, children stay free with parents, a/c, TV, laundry service, car rental desk, no-smoking rooms, meeting facilities, major credit cards. LS SGL/DBL$30-$45; HS SGL/DBL$60-$85, AP$6.

Quality Inn Downtown (300 Bypass Rd, 23185; 229-6270, 800-284-4466, 800-368-5689) 115 rooms and suites, restaurant, complimentary breakfast, pool, whirlpools, room service, exercise facilities, children stay free with parents, a/c, TV, laundry service, no-smoking rooms, meeting facilities, major credit cards. LS SGL/DBL$30-$55; HS SGL/DBL$49-$70.

Quality Inn Lord Paget (901 Capitol Landing Rd, 23185; 229-4444, 800-368-5689) 88 rooms and suites, restaurant, pool, room service, exercise facilities, children stay free with parents, a/c, TV, laundry service, no-smoking rooms, meeting facilities, major credit cards. LS SGL/DBL$35-$50; HS SGL/DBL$50-$70.

Quality Inn Colony (State Rd 162, 23187; 229-1855, 800-368-5689) 59 rooms and suites, restaurant, room service, pool, exercise facilities, children stay free with parents, a/c, TV, laundry service, no-smoking rooms, meeting facilities, major credit cards. SGL/DBL$45-$70.

Quality Inn Conference Center (6583 Richmond Rd, 23060; 565-1000, 800-368-5689) 189 rooms and suites, restaurant, pool, whirlpools, game room, room service, exercise facilities, children stay free with parents, a/c, TV, laundry service, no-smoking rooms, meeting facilities, major credit cards. LS SGL/DBL$30-$54; HS SGL/DBL$60-$94.

Quality Inn Outlet Center (5611 Richmond Rd, 23188; 565-1100, 800-368-5689) 80 rooms and suites, restaurant, pool, room service, exercise facilities, children stay free with parents, a/c, TV, gift shop, laundry service, no-smoking rooms, meeting facilities, major credit cards. LS SGL/DBL$31-$43; HS SGL/DBL$62-$68.

Quality Suites (152 Kingsgate Pkwy, 23185; 229-6800, 800-368-5689) 169 rooms and suites, restaurant, complimentary breakfast, indoor pool, whirlpools, room service, exercise facilities, children stay free with parents, a/c, TV, laundry service, no-smoking rooms, meeting facilities, major credit cards. LS SGL/DBL$68-$88; HS SGL$95-$115, DBL$102-$122, AP$7.

Ramada Inn (351 York St, 23185; 229-4100, Fax 229-0176, 800-2-RAMADA) 141 rooms, restaurant, lounge, entertainment, indoor pool, wheelchair access, no-smoking rooms, airport transportation, free parking, pets allowed, a/c, TV, room service, laundry facilities, meeting facilities, senior citizen rates, major credit cards. LS SGL$36-$44, DBL$44-$52; HS SGL$61-$77, DBL$70-$85, STS$149, AP$8.

Ramada Inn (5351 Richmond Rd, 23185; 565-2000, Fax 565-4652, 800-2-RAMADA) 164 rooms, restaurant, lounge, entertainment, wheelchair access, no-smoking rooms, airport transportation, free parking, pets allowed, wheelchair access, a/c, TV, room service, laundry facilities, meeting facilities, senior citizen rates, major credit cards. LS SGL$39-$49, DBL$45-$55; HS SGL/DBL$59-$69, AP$5.

Super 8 Motel (304 Second St, 23185; 229-0500, 800-800-8000) 107 rooms and suites, complimentary breakfast, outdoor pool, pets allowed, children under 12 stay free with parents, free local calls, a/c, TV, in-room refrigerators and microwaves, fax, no-smoking rooms, senior citizen rates, wheelchair access, meeting facilities, major credit cards. SGL/DBL$37-$40.

TraveLodge (1402 Richmond Rd, 23185; 220-2367, Fax 253-1372, 800-255-3050) 164 rooms and suites, restaurant, lounge, complimentary breakfast, indoor pool, wheelchair access, complimentary newspaper, laundry service, TV, a/c, free local calls, fax service, no-smoking rooms, in-room refrigerators and microwaves, no pets, major credit cards. SGL$36-$74, DBL$41-$79, AP$5.

Winchester
Area Code 703

Apple Blossom Motor Lodge (2951 Valley Ave, 22601; 667-1200) 66 rooms, restaurant, pool, laundry facilities, wheelchair access, no-smoking rooms, a/c, TV. SGL/DBL$36-$45.

Best Western Lee-Jackson Inn (711 Millwood Ave, 22601; 662-4154, 800-528-1234) 140 rooms, restaurant, complimentary breakfast, lounge, pool, exercise facilities, children stay free with parents, a/c, TV, no-smoking rooms, laundry facilities, in-room refrigerators and microwaves, wheelchair access, pets allowed, senior citizen rates, meeting facilities, major credit cards. SGL/DBL$38-$50.

Bond's Motel (2930 Valley Ave, 22601; 667-8881) 16 rooms, wheelchair access, no-smoking rooms, no pets. SGL/DBL$28-$34.

Budgetel Inn (800 Millwood Ave, 22601; 678-0800, Fax 722-6878, 800-428-3438) rooms and suites, complimentary breakfast, children under 18 stay free with parents, a/c, wheelchair access, no-smoking rooms, free local calls, in-room computer hookups, fax service, VCRs, TV, meeting facilities, major credit cards. SGL/DBL$37-$48, STS$45-$54.

Comfort Inn (1020 Millwood Pike, 22601; 667-5000, 800-221-2222) 116 rooms, restaurant, exercise facilities, wheelchair access, no-smoking rooms, no pets, children under 18 stay free with parents, senior citizen rates, a/c, TV, meeting facilities, major credit cards. SGL/DBL$42-$56.

Days Inn (1601 Martinsburg Pike, 22603; 667-4400, Fax 667-2818, 800-325-2525) 84 rooms, restaurant, lounge, pool, children stay free with parents, room service, laundry service, a/c, TV, free local calls, no pets, wheelchair access, no-smoking rooms, senior citizen rates, major credit cards. SGL/DBL$45-$70.

Winchester 407

Echo Village Motel (Rte. 3, 22601; 869-1900) 66 rooms, no-smoking rooms, wheelchair access. SGL/DBL$17-$30.

Econo Lodge (1593 Martinsburg Pike, 22601; 662-4700, 800-4-CHOICE) 50 rooms and efficiencies, complimentary breakfast, pool, TV, children under 12 stay free with parents, pets allowed, senior citizen rates, wheelchair access, a/c, major credit cards. SGL/DBL$36-$58.

Fort View Motel (1810 Front Royal Pike, 22602; 662-6055) 6 rooms. SGL/DBL$30-$45.

Hampton Inn (1655 Apple Blossom Dr, 22601; 667-8011, Fax 667-8033, 800-HAMPTON) 103 rooms, restaurant, complimentary breakfast, pool, exercise facilities, children under 18 stay free with parents, no-smoking rooms, wheelchair access, computer hookups, fax service, TV, a/c, free local calls, pets allowed, meeting facilities, major credit cards. SGL/DBL$44-$50.

Holiday Inn (Hwy 50 East, 22601; 667-3300, Fax 722-2730, 800-HOLIDAY) 174 rooms, restaurant, lounge, outdoor pool, exercise facilities, children under 19 stay free with parents, wheelchair access, a/c, TV, no-smoking rooms, fax service, room service, no pets, laundry service, meeting facilities for 200, senior citizen rates, major credit cards. SGL/DBL$49-$65.

Mount Vernon Motor Inn (2645 Valley Ave, 22601; 662-6878) 21 rooms, pets allowed, a/c, TV, senior citizen rates. SGL/DBL$25-$40.

Quality Inn East (603 Millwood Ave, 22601; 667-2250, 800-368-5689) 100 rooms and suites, restaurant, pool, pets allowed, room service, exercise facilities, children stay free with parents, a/c, TV, laundry service, no-smoking rooms, meeting facilities, major credit cards. SGL/DBL$40-$53.

Quality Inn Boxwood South (2649 Valley Ave, 22601; 662-2521, 800-368-5689) rooms and suites, restaurant, lounge, entertainment, pool, room service, exercise facilities, children stay free with parents, a/c, TV, laundry service, no-smoking rooms, meeting facilities, major credit cards. SGL/DBL$35-$75.

Shoney's Inn (1347 Berryville Ave, 22601; 665-1700) 98 rooms, restaurant, pool, no-smoking rooms, no pets, sauna, jacuzzi, wheelchair access, senior citizen rates, major credit cards. SGL/DBL$39-$48.

Super 8 Motel (1077 Millwood Pike, 22601; 665-4450, 800-800-8000) rooms and suites, pets allowed, children under 12 stay free with parents, free local calls, a/c, TV, in-room refrigerators and microwaves, fax service, no-smoking rooms, senior citizen rates, wheelchair access, meeting facilities, major credit cards. SGL/DBL$34-$44.

Tourist City Motel (214 Millwood Ave, 22601; 662-9011) 12 rooms, pets allowed, no-smoking rooms, senior citizen rates. SGL/DBL$24-$34.

TraveLodge (1825 Dominion Ave, 22601; 665-0685, Fax 665-0689, 800-255-3050) 149 rooms, restaurant, lounge, complimentary breakfast, pool, wheelchair access, complimentary newspaper, laundry service, kitchenettes, VCR, TV, a/c, free local calls, fax service, no-smoking rooms, in-room refrigerators and microwaves, pets allowed, meeting facilities for 450, major credit cards. SGL/DBL$43-$56, DBL$48-$61, AP$5.

Woodbridge
Area Code 703

Comfort Inn (1109 Homer Rd, 22191; 494-0300, 800-221-2222) 95 rooms, complimentary breakfast, pool, wheelchair access, whirlpools, fax service, no-smoking rooms, no pets, children under 18 stay free with parents, senior citizen rates, a/c, TV, meeting facilities, major credit cards. SGL$47-$52, DBL$51-$57.

Days Inn (14619 Potomac Mills Rd, 22192; 494-4433, Fax 385-2627, 800-325-2525) 176 rooms, restaurant, complimentary breakfast, lounge, pool, children stay free with parents, room service, laundry service, a/c, TV, free local calls, pets allowed, wheelchair access, no-smoking rooms, senior citizen rates, major credit cards. SGL/DBL$52-$88.

Woodstock
Area Code 703

Azalea House Bed and Breakfast (551 South Main St, 22664; 459-3500) 3 rooms, complimentary breakfast, private baths, no smoking, no pets, Victorian home, fireplace, major credit cards. SGL/DBL$45-$70.

Budget Host Inn (Rte. 11 South, 22665; 459-4086, 800-BUD-HOST) 43 rooms, restaurant, in-room refrigerators, no-smoking rooms, TV, VCRs, laundry facilities, kitchenettes, a/c, wheelchair access, children stay free with parents, senior citizen rates, meeting facilities, major credit cards. SGL$29, DBL$32, AP$4.

Country Fare Bed and Breakfast (402 North Main St, 22664; 459-4828) 3 rooms, complimentary breakfast, private baths, no-smoking rooms, 1790s inn, major credit cards. SGL/DBL$45-$65.

Ramada Inn (1130 Motel Dr, 22664; 459-5000, Fax 459-8219, 800-2-RAMADA) 123 rooms, restaurant, lounge, entertainment, pool, wheelchair access, no-smoking rooms, airport transportation, free parking, pets allowed, wheelchair access, a/c, TV, room service, laundry facilities, meeting facilities for 350, senior citizen rates, major credit cards. SGL/DBL$45-$58, STS$90, AP$8.

Woolwine
Area Code 703

Mountain Rose Bed and Breakfast (Woolwine, 24185; 930-1057) 5 rooms, complimentary breakfast, restaurant, pool, private baths, no smoking, Victorian home, antique furnishings, fireplace, meeting facilities for 10, major credit cards. SGL/DBL$60-$85.

Wytheville
Area Code 703

Comfort Inn (315 Holston Rd, 24382; 228-4488, 800-221-2222) 80 rooms, restaurant, pool, wheelchair access, no-smoking rooms, no pets, children under 18 stay free with parents, senior citizen rates, a/c, TV, meeting facilities, major credit cards. SGL/DBL$35-$45.

Days Inn (150 Main Dr, 24382; 228-550, 800-325-2525) 118 rooms, restaurant, lounge, pool, children stay free with parents, room service, laundry service, a/c, TV, free local calls, pets allowed, wheelchair access, no-smoking rooms, senior citizen rates, major credit cards. SGL/DBL$33-$49.

HoJo Inn (Box 552, 24382; 228-3188, 800-I-GO-HOJO) 100 rooms, restaurant, lounge, pool, children stay free with parents, wheelchair access, no-smoking rooms, TV, gift shop, fax service, a/c, pets allowed, free parking, senior citizen rates, meeting facilities, major credit cards. SGL/DBL$32-$65.

Holiday Inn (Wytheville, 24382; 228-5483, 800-HOLIDAY) 196 rooms, restaurant, lounge, outdoor pool, exercise facilities, children under 19 stay free with parents, wheelchair access, a/c, TV, no-smoking rooms, fax service, room service, no pets, laundry service, meeting facilities for 300, senior citizen rates, major credit cards. SGL/DBL$45-$65.

Motel 6 (2020 East Main St, 24382; 228-7988, 891-6161) 106 rooms, pool, free local calls, children under 17 stay free with parents, a/c, TV, major credit cards. SGL/DBL$23-$29.

Ramada Inn (955 Peppers Ferry Rd, 24382; 228-6000, Fax 228-6000 ext 151, 800-2-RAMADA) 154 rooms, restaurant, lounge, entertainment, pool, wheelchair access, no-smoking rooms, airport transportation, free parking, pets allowed, wheelchair access, a/c, TV, room service, laundry facilities, meeting facilities for 250, senior citizen rates, major credit cards. SGL/DBL$35-$55.

Super 8 Motel (130 Nye Circle, 24382; 228-6620, 800-800-8000) 95 rooms and suites, complimentary breakfast, no pets, children under 12 stay free with parents, free local calls, a/c, TV, in-room refrigerators and microwaves, fax service, no-smoking rooms, senior citizen rates, wheelchair access, meeting facilities, major credit cards. SGL/DBL$34-$46.

Washington D.C.

Area Code 202

Rental and Reservation Services

Bed and Breakfast League – Sweet Dreams and Toast (Box 9490, 20016; 363-7767).

Bed and Breakfast Ltd. (Box 12011, 20005; 328-3510).

□ □ □

Adams Inn (1744 Lanier Pl. Northwest, 20009; 745-3600) 26 rooms, bed and breakfast, major credit cards. SGL/DBL$45-$65.

Allen Lee Hotel (2224 F St Northwest, 20037; 331-1224, 800-462-0186) 85 rooms, major credit cards. SGL/DBL$40-$51.

ANA Hotel (2401 M St Northwest, 20037; 429-2400, Fax 457-5010, 800-228-3000) 421 rooms and suites, restaurant, lounge, entertainment, indoor pool, exercise facilities, sauna, whirlpool, TV, in-room refrigerators, pets allowed, 24-hour room service, major credit cards. SGL/DBL$105-$305.

Hotel Anthony (1823 L St Northwest, 20036; 223-4320, 800-424-2970) 99 suites, free newspaper, a/c, major credit cards. SGL/DBL$150.

Bellevue Hotel (15 E St Northwest, 20001; 638-0900, 800-327-6667) 140 rooms and suites, restaurant, complimentary breakfast, free parking, a/c, major credit cards. SGL$100, DBL$114, STS$295-$395.

Best Western Downtown Capitol Hill (724 Third St Northwest, 20001; 842-4466, 800-242-4831) 58 rooms, complimentary breakfast, free parking, complimentary newspaper, pets allowed, major credit cards. SGL/DBL$54-$60.

Best Western Center City Hotel (1201 13th St Northwest, 20005; 682-5300, 800-458-2817) 100 rooms, exercise facilities, sauna, jacuzzi, no-smoking rooms, TV, a/c, major credit cards. SGL/DBL$75-$130.

Best Western Regency Congress Inn (600 New York Ave Northeast, 20002; 546-9200, 800-528-1234) 49 rooms, pool, a/c, free parking, pets allowed, major credit cards. SGL/DBL$68-$80.

Best Western Skyliner Hotel (10 I St Southwest, 20024; 488-7500, 800-458-7500) 205 rooms and suites, lounge, entertainment, outdoor pool, a/c, free parking, major credit cards. SGL/DBL$75-$80.

Canterbury Hotel (1733 N St Northwest, 20036; 393-3000, Fax 785-9581, 800-424-2950) 99 rooms and suites, restaurant, lounge, complimentary breakfast, exercise facilities, in-room refrigerators, no-smoking rooms, TV, a/c, meeting facilities, major credit cards. SGL/DBL$140-$160.

Capitol Hill Hotel (200 C St, Southeast, 20003; 543-6000, Fax 547-2608, 800-424-9165) 152 1-bedroom suites, restaurant, laundry service, children stay free with parents, no-smoking rooms, TV, a/c, meeting facilities, major credit cards. SGL/DBL$115-$215.

Carlyle Suites (1731 New Hampshire Ave Northwest, 20009; 234-3200) 170 suites, kitchenettes, free parking, pets allowed, a/c, major credit cards. SGL/DBL$75.

Channel Inn Hotel (650 Water St Southwest, 20024; 554-2400, 800-368-5668) 104 rooms and suites, restaurant, lounge, entertainment, pool, room service, free parking, a/c, major credit cards. SGL/DBL$110.

Comfort Inn Downtown (500 H St Northwest, 20001; 289-5959, Fax 289-5959, 800-234-6423) 197 rooms, restaurant, lounge, jacuzzi, exercise facilities, children stay free with parents, a/c, TV, laundry service, free parking, meeting facilities, major credit cards. SGL$59-$137, DBL$67-$152.

Days Inn (1201 K St Northwest, 20005; 842-1020, Fax 289-0336, 800-325-2525) 220 rooms, restaurant, lounge, pool, children stay free with parents, room service, laundry service, a/c, TV, free local calls, no pets, wheelchair access, no-smoking rooms, senior citizen rates, major credit cards. SGL/DBL$78-$125.

Days Inn (4400 Connecticut Ave, 20008; 244-5600, Fax 244-6794, 800-325-2525) 155 rooms and suites, restaurant, complimentary breakfast, lounge, pool, children stay free with parents, room service, laundry service, a/c, TV, free local calls, no pets, wheelchair access, no-smoking rooms, senior citizen rates, major credit cards. SGL/DBL$59-$109, STS$85-$129.

Days Inn (2700 New York Ave Northeast, 20002; 832-5800, Fax 269-4317, 800-325-2525) 195 rooms, restaurant, lounge, pool, children stay free with parents, room service, laundry service, a/c, TV, free local calls, transportation to local attractions, gift shop, pets allowed, wheelchair access, no-smoking rooms, senior citizen rates, major credit cards. SGL$48-$52, DBL$50-$62.

Dupont Plaza Hotel (1500 New Hampshire Ave, 20036; 483-6000, 800-421-6662) 317 rooms and suites, restaurant, lounge, entertainment, gift shop, a/c, TV, in-room refrigerators, children stay free with parents, no pets, major credit cards. SGL/DBL$125-$200.

Econo Lodge (1600 New York Ave Northeast, 20002; 832-3200, 800-344-7687) 158 rooms, lounge, indoor pool, transportation to local attractions, pets allowed, a/c, free parking, laundry service, major credit cards. SGL/DBL$45.

Embassy Suites Hotel (4300 Military Rd, 20015; 362-9300, Fax 686-3405, 800-EMBASSY) 198 suites, restaurant, lounge, complimentary breakfast, pool, exercise facilities, whirlpool, sauna, children stay free with parents, boutiques, in-room refrigerators, no-smoking rooms, TV, a/c, wheelchair access, meeting facilities, major credit cards. SGL/DBL$70-$125.

Embassy Inn (1627 16th St Northwest, 20009; 234-7800, Fax 234-3309, 800-423-9111) 38 rooms, complimentary breakfast, a/c, major credit cards. SGL/DBL$70-$135.

Embassy Row Hotel (2015 Massachusetts Ave Northwest, 20036; 265-1600, Fax 327-7526, 800-424-2400) 224 rooms and suites, restaurant, lounge, entertainment, exercise facilities, no pets, outdoor pool, a/c, TV, room service, gift shop, children stay free with parents, meeting facilities, major credit cards. SGL/DBL$150-$200.

Embassy Square Suites (2000 N St Northwest, 20036; 659-9000, Fax 429-9546, 800-424-2999) 252 1- and 2-bedroom suites, restaurant, lounge, free breakfast, pool, exercise facilities, a/c, TV, no pets, laundry service, children stay free with parents, free newspaper, major credit cards. SGL/DBL$120-$140.

Embassy Suites Hotel (1250 22nd St Northwest, 20037; 857-3388, Fax 293-3173, 800-EMBASSY) 318 2-room suites, restaurant, lounge, pool, whirlpool, exercise facilities, sauna, room service, laundry service, wheelchair access, complimentary newspaper, free local calls, no-smoking rooms, TV, a/c, gift shop, transportation to local attractions, business services, meeting facilities, major credit cards. SGL/DBL$110-$190.

Four Seasons Hotel (2800 Pennsylvania Ave Northwest, 20007; 342-0444, 800-332-3442) 227 rooms and suites, restaurant, lounge, indoor pool, exercise facilities, a/c, TV, whirlpools, limousine service, children stay free with parents, pets allowed, major credit cards. SGL/DBL$195-$310.

Georgetown Dutch Inn (1075 Thomas Jefferson St Northwest, 20007; 337-0900, Fax 333-6526) 47 efficiencies, complimentary breakfast, free parking, children stay free with parents, a/c, major credit cards. SGL/DBL$100-$150.

Georgetown Harbour Mews (1000 29th St Northwest, 20007; 298-1600) 76 rooms and efficiencies, a/c, TV, major credit cards. SGL/DBL$95

The Georgetown Inn (1310 Wisconsin Ave Northwest, 20007; 333-8900, 800-424-2979) 95 rooms and suites, free breakfast and newspaper, a/c, major credit cards. SGL/DBL$145-$210.

Georgetown University Conference Center (Hoya Station, 20057; 687-3200, 800-446-9476) 151 rooms and suites, restaurant, lounge, pool, a/c, TV, room service, no-smoking rooms, children stay free with parents, major credit cards. SGL/DBL$45-$100.

The Grand Hotel (2350 M St Northwest, 20037; 429-0100, Fax 429-9759, 800-848-0016) 284 rooms and suites, restaurant, lounge, entertainment, outdoor pool, a/c, TV, whirlpools, exercise facilities, children stay free with parents, fireplaces, laundry service, pets allowed, major credit cards. SGL/DBL$155-$300.

Guest Quarters Suite Hotel (2500 Pennsylvania Ave, 20037; 333-8060, Fax 338-3818, 800-424-2900) 123 suites, restaurant, pool, exercise facilities, whirlpools, room service, children stay free with parents, pets allowed, remote control TV, a/c, in-room refrigerators, transportation to local attractions, laundry service, fax service, no-smoking rooms, wheelchair access, meeting facilities for 200, major credit cards. SGL/DBL$180-$200.

Guest Quarters Suite Hotel (801 New Hampshire Ave Northwest, 20037; 785-2000, 800-424-2900) 101 suites, outdoor pool, exercise facilities, whirlpools, pets allowed, remote control TV, a/c, in-room refrigerators, transportation to local attractions, laundry service, fax service, no-smoking rooms, wheelchair access, meeting facilities for 200, major credit cards. SGL/DBL$180-$200.

Hampshire Hotel (1310 New Hampshire Ave Northwest, 20036; 296-7600, 800-368-5691) 82 rooms and 1- and 2-bedroom suites, restaurant, lounge, kitchenettes, children stay free with parents, no-smoking rooms, TV, a/c, meeting facilities, major credit cards. SGL/DBL$70-$110.

Harrington Hotel (11th and E St Northwest, 20004; 628-8140, Fax 347-3924, 800-424-8532) 300 rooms and suites, restaurant, laundry service, children stay free with parents, airport transportation, in-room refrigerators, wheelchair access, free parking, pets allowed, a/c, TV, major credit cards. SGL/DBL$59-$62, STS$79-$84.

The Hay-Adams Hotel (1 Lafayette Square Northwest, 20006; 638-6600, Fax 638-2716, 800-424-5054) 160 rooms and suites, restaurant, lounge, entertainment, children stay free with parents, a/c, TV, no-smoking rooms, no pets, airport transportation, major credit cards. SGL/DBL$180-$400.

The Henley Park Hotel (926 Massachusetts Ave Northwest, 20001; 638-5200, Fax 638-6740, 800-222-8474) 96 rooms and suites, restaurant, lounge, entertainment, in-room refrigerators, limousine service, children stay free with parents, no-smoking rooms, TV, a/c, wheelchair access, meeting facilities, major credit cards. SGL$155, DBL$175, STS$295-$675.

Washington D.C.

Hilton Capitol Hotel (16th and K St Northwest, 20036; 393-1000, Fax 265-8221, 800-HILTONS) 569 rooms and suites, restaurant, lounge, entertainment, exercise facilities, sauna, TV, a/c, airline ticket office, 24-hour room service, boutiques, barber and beauty shop, pets allowed, in-room refrigerators and computer hookups, meeting facilities, major credit cards. SGL/DBL$115.

Hilton and Towers (1919 Connecticut St Northwest, 20009; 483-3000, Fax 265-8221, 800-HILTONS) 1,300 rooms and suites, restaurant, lounge, entertainment, pool, exercise facilities, sauna, lighted tennis courts, TV, a/c, no-smoking rooms, wheelchair access, pets allowed, business services, 45,000 square feet of meeting and exhibition space, 32 meeting rooms, major credit cards. SGL/DBL$90-$255.

Holiday Inn Capitol (550 C St Southwest, 20024; 479-4000, Fax 479-4353, 800-HOLIDAY) 548 rooms and suites, restaurant, lounge, pool, laundry service, children stay free with parents, no-smoking rooms, TV, a/c, wheelchair access, pets allowed, major credit cards. SGL/DBL$75-$85.

Holiday Inn Central (1501 Rhode Island Ave Northwest, 20005; 483-2000, 800-HOLIDAY) 222 rooms and suites, restaurant, lounge, pool, children stay free with parents, gift shop, no-smoking rooms, TV, a/c, wheelchair access, pets allowed, major credit cards. SGL/DBL$75-$105.

Holiday Inn Crowne Plaza at Metro Center (775 12th St Northwest, 20005; 737-2200, 800-HOLIDAY) 465 rooms and suites, restaurant, lounge, pool, children stay free with parents, no-smoking rooms, TV, a/c, pets allowed, wheelchair access, major credit cards. SGL/DBL$65-$95.

Holiday Inn Georgetown (2101 Wisconsin Ave Northwest, 20007; 338-4600, 800-HOLIDAY) 296 rooms and suites, restaurant, lounge, pool, children stay free with parents, no-smoking rooms, TV, a/c, wheelchair access, pets allowed, major credit cards. SGL/DBL$80-$110.

Holiday Inn Governor's House (1615 Rhode Island Ave Northwest, 20036; 296-2100, 800-821-4367, 800-HOLIDAY) 152 rooms and suites, restaurant, lounge, pool, children stay free with parents, no-smoking rooms, TV, no pets, a/c, wheelchair access, major credit cards. SGL/DBL$60-$125.

Holiday Inn Thomas Circle (1155 14th St Northwest, 20005; 737-1200, 800-HOLIDAY) 208 suites, restaurant, lounge, pool, a/c, TV, no-smoking rooms, children stay free with parents, pets allowed, American plan available, meeting facilities, major credit cards. SGL/DBL$90-$100.

Howard Inn (2225 Georgia Ave Northwest, 20001; 462-5400, 800-368-5729) 141 rooms and suites, kitchenettes, pool, a/c, TV, free parking, major credit cards. SGL/DBL$48-$58.

Howard Johnson Lodge (2601 Virginia Ave Northwest, 20037; 965-2700, Fax 965-2700 ext 7910, 800-654-2000) 192 rooms and suites, restaurant, outdoor pool, children stay free with parents, in-room refrigerators, pets allowed, a/c, TV, free parking, major credit cards. SGL/DBL$67-$100.

Hyatt Grand Washington (1000 H St Northwest, 20001; 582-1234, 800-233-1234) 967 rooms and suites, restaurant, lounge, pool, exercise facilities, whirlpools, sauna, room service, a/c, TV, no-smoking rooms, wheelchair access, no pets, major credit cards. SGL/DBL$190-$275.

Hyatt Park Hotel (24th and M St Northwest, 20037; 789-1234, Fax 457-8823, 800-228-9000, 800-922-PARK) 354 rooms and suites, restaurant, lounge, pool, exercise facilities, 24-hour room service, gift shop, barber and beauty shop, children stay free with parents, no-smoking rooms, TV, a/c, wheelchair access, pets allowed, meeting facilities, major credit cards. SGL/DBL$135-$155.

Hyatt Regency Capitol Hill (400 New Jersey Ave Northwest, 20001; 737-1234, Fax 737-5773, 800-233-1234) 865 rooms and suites, restaurant, lounge, pool, exercise facilities, room service, barber and beauty shop, gift shop, children stay free with parents, wheelchair access, no-smoking rooms, TV, a/c, meeting facilities, major credit cards. SGL/DBL$90-$160.

Intercontinental Willard Hotel (1401 Pennsylvania Ave Northwest, 20004; 628-9100, Fax 637-7326, 800-327-0200) 395 rooms and suites, restaurant, lounge, pool, boutiques, no-smoking rooms, TV, a/c, wheelchair access, laundry service, pets allowed, meeting facilities, major credit cards. SGL/DBL$180-$330.

Jefferson Hotel (1200 16th St Northwest, 20036; 347-2200, Fax 331-7982, 800-368-5966) 132 rooms and suites, restaurant, lounge, pool, exercise facilities, children stay free with parents, no-smoking rooms, wheelchair access, a/c, TV, pets allowed, major credit cards. SGL/DBL$145-$300.

Kalorama Guest House at Kalorama Park (1854 Mintwood Pl. Northwest, 20009; 667-6369) 33 rooms and suites, bed and breakfast, major credit cards. SGL/DBL$65.

The Latham Hotel (3000 M St Northwest, 20007; 726-5000, 800-368-5922) 143 rooms and suites, restaurant, lounge, outdoor pool, a/c, TV, no-smoking rooms, in-room refrigerators, major credit cards. SGL/DBL$145-$200.

Loew's L'Enfant Plaza Hotel (480 L'Enfant Plaza, 20024; 484-1000, Fax 646-4456, 800-243-1166) 394 rooms and suites, restaurant, lounge, entertainment, pool, exercise facilities, gift shop, boutiques, a/c, TV, children stay free with parents, in-room refrigerators, pets allowed, major credit cards. SGL/DBL$185-$225.

Hotel Lombardy (2019 I St Northwest, 20006; 828-2600, Fax 872-0503, 800-424-5486) 120 rooms and suites, restaurant, laundry service, children stay free with parents, in-room refrigerators, complimentary newspaper, meeting facilities, major credit cards. SGL/DBL$115.

The Madison Hotel (15th and M St Northwest, 20005; 862-1600, Fax 785-1255) 383 rooms and suites, restaurant, lounge, in-room refrigerators, a/c, TV, no-smoking rooms, in-room refrigerators, 24-hour room service, VCRs, meeting facilities, major credit cards. SGL/DBL$225-$400.

JW Marriott Hotel (1331 Pennsylvania Ave Northwest, 20004; 393-2000, Fax 626-6991, 800-MARRIOT) 815 rooms and suites, restaurant, lounge, entertainment, indoor pool, exercise facilities, whirlpools, sauna, game room, airport transportation, in-room refrigerators, wheelchair access, TV, a/c, no-smoking rooms, gift shop, children stay free with parents, business services, meeting facilities, major credit cards. SGL/DBL$135-$260.

Marriott Washington (1221 22nd St Northwest, 20037; 872-1500, 800-344-4445) 425 rooms and suites, indoor pool, exercise facilities, pets allowed, complimentary newspaper, whirlpools, wheelchair access, TV, a/c, no-smoking rooms, gift shop, children stay free with parents, business services, meeting facilities, major credit cards. SGL/DBL$120-$200.

Master Hosts Inn (1917 Bladensburg Rd, 20002; 832-8600, 800-251-1962) 150 rooms, pool, free parking, a/c, TV, pets allowed, major credit cards. SGL/DBL$55.

The Morrison Clark Inn (11th and Massachusetts Ave Northwest, 20001; 898-1200, 800-332-7898) 68 rooms and suites, restaurant, lounge, no pets, antique furnishings, no-smoking rooms, a/c, TV, major credit cards. SGL/DBL$115-$185.

New Hampshire Suites Hotel (1121 New Hampshire Ave Northwest, 20037; 457-0565, 800-762-3777) 75 rooms and 1-bedroom suites, major credit cards. SGL/DBL$124, STS$144-$160.

Normandy Inn (2118 Wyoming Ave Northwest, 20008; 483-1350, Fax 387-8241, 800-424-3729) 78 rooms and suites, free breakfast, pets allowed, children stay free with parents, no-smoking rooms, TV, a/c, meeting facilities, major credit cards. SGL$83, DBL$93.

Omni Georgetown Hotel (2121 P St Northwest, 20037; 293-3100, Fax 857-0134, 800-THE-OMNI) 350 rooms and suites, restaurant, lounge, pool, exercise facilities, boutiques, wheelchair access, no-smoking rooms, TV, a/c, children stay free with parents, business services, major credit cards. SGL/DBL$90-$200.

Omni Shoreham Hotel (2500 Calvert St Northwest, 20008; 234-0700, 800-THE-OMNI) 760 rooms and suites, restaurant, lounge, pool, exercise facilities, lighted tennis courts, sauna, a/c, TV, room service, wheelchair access, no-smoking rooms, no pets, major credit cards. SGL/DBL$125-$215.

One Washington Circle (One Washington Circle Northwest, 20037; 872-1680, Fax 887-4989, 800-424-9671) 151 efficiencies, restaurant, lounge, entertainment, pool, no-smoking rooms, TV, a/c, children stay free with parents, pets allowed, VCRs, meeting facilities, major credit cards. SGL/DBL$75-$225.

Phoenix Park Hotel (520 North Capitol St Northwest, 20001; 638-6900, Fax 393-3236, 800-824-5419) 90 rooms and suites, restaurant, lounge, in-room refrigerators, no-smoking rooms, TV, a/c, wheelchair access, children stay free with parents, meeting facilities, major credit cards. SGL/DBL$150-$190.

Pullman Highland Hotel (1914 Connecticut Ave Northwest, 20009; 797-2000, 800-424-2464) 143 suites, pets allowed, a/c, TV, major credit cards. SGL/DBL$125-$275.

Quality Hotel Capitol Hill (415 New Jersey Ave Northwest, 20001; 638-1616, Fax 638-0707, 800-228-5151) 349 rooms and suites, outdoor pool, gift shop, no pets, no smoking rooms, children under 18 stay free with parents, TV, a/c, senior citizen rates, meeting facilities, major credit cards. SGL/DBL$60-$165.

Quality Hotel Central (1900 Connecticut Ave Northwest, 20009; 332-9300, 800-842-4211) 149 rooms, restaurant, lounge, pool, exercise facilities, children stay free with parents, a/c, TV, laundry service, no-smoking rooms, meeting facilities, major credit cards. SGL/DBL$95-$130.

Quality Hotel Downtown (1315 16th St Northwest, 20036; 232-8000, 800-368-5689) 135 suites, restaurant, room service, exercise facilities, children stay free with parents, a/c, TV, laundry service, no-smoking rooms, meeting facilities, major credit cards. SGL$59-$110, DBL$59-$120.

Radisson Park Terrace Hotel (1515 Rhode Island Ave Northwest, 20005; 232-7000, Fax 332-7152, 800-333-3333) 260 rooms and suites, restaurant, lounge, entertainment, pool, children stay free with parents, wheelchair access, free parking, no-smoking rooms, TV, a/c, children stay free with parents, pets allowed, meeting facilities, major credit cards. SGL/DBL$119-$170.

Ramada Inn Central (1430 Rhode Island Ave Northwest, 20005; 462-7777, Fax 332-3519, 800-368-5690) 186 rooms and 2-room suites, restaurant, lounge, outdoor pool, wheelchair access, no-smoking rooms, airport transportation, free parking, pets allowed, a/c, TV, room service, laundry facilities, meeting facilities, senior citizen rates, major credit cards. SGL/DBL$70-$110.

Ramada Renaissance Hotel (9th and K St Northwest, 20001; 898-9000, Fax 789-4213, 800-2-RAMADA) 800 rooms and suites, restaurant, lounge, indoor pool, wheelchair access, no-smoking rooms, airport transportation, free parking, pets allowed, a/c, TV, room service, laundry facilities, 72,000 square feet of meeting and exhibition space, senior citizen rates, major credit cards. SGL/DBL$200-$250.

Ritz-Carlton Hotel (2100 Massachusetts Ave Northwest, 20008; 293-2100, Fax 293-0641, 800-241-3333) 221 rooms and suites, restaurant, lounge, entertainment, no-smoking rooms, TV, a/c, wheelchair access, children stay free with parents, complimentary newspaper, in-room refrigerators, pets allowed, limousine service, meeting facilities, major credit cards. SGL/DBL$150-$300.

The River Inn (924 25th St Northwest, 20037; 337-7600, Fax 337-6520, 800-424-2741) 127 efficiencies, restaurant, lounge, no-smoking rooms, TV, a/c, children stay free with parents, meeting facilities, major credit cards. SGL/DBL$155.

Savoy Suites Hotel (2505 Wisconsin Ave Northwest, 20007; 337-9700) 148 rooms, restaurant, lounge, entertainment, pool, jacuzzi, whirlpools, pets allowed, a/c, TV, free parking, major credit cards. SGL/DBL$70-$120.

Sheraton Washington (2660 Woodley Rd Northwest 20008; 328-2000, Fax 234-0015, 800-325-3535) 1,500 rooms and suites, restaurant, lounge, entertainment, pool, exercise facilities, sauna, 24-hour room service, barber and beauty shop, gift shop, airport transportation, pets allowed, meeting facilities, major credit cards. SGL/DBL$185-$270.

Sheraton City Centre Hotel and Towers (1143 New Hampshire Ave Northwest, 20037; 775-0800, Fax 331-9491, 800-526-7495) 366 rooms and suites, restaurant, lounge, entertainment, gift shop, children stay free with parents, barber and beauty shop, wheelchair access, no-smoking rooms, TV, a/c, free parking, pets allowed, major credit cards. SGL/DBL$140-$210.

The State Plaza Hotel (2117 E St Northwest, 20037; 861-8200, Fax 659-8601, 800-424-2859) 283 rooms and suites, restaurant, lounge, children stay free with parents, free newspaper, laundry service, meeting facilities, major credit cards. SGL/DBL$105-$250.

Stouffer Mayflower Hotel (1127 Connecticut Ave Northwest, 20036; 347-3000, Fax 466-9083, 800-HOTELS-1) 400 rooms and suites, restaurant, lounge, entertainment, in-room refrigerators, wheelchair access, no-smoking rooms, TV, a/c, meeting facilities, major credit cards. SGL/DBL$170-$320.

Washington Court On Capitol Hill (525 New Jersey Ave Northwest, 20001; 628-2100, Fax 879-7918, 800-321-3010) 282 rooms and suites, restaurant, lounge, exercise facilities, sauna, children stay free with parents, in-room refrigerators, free parking, meeting facilities, major credit cards. SGL/DBL$169-$229.

Washington International AYH Hostel (1009 11th St Northwest, 20001; 737-2333) 250 beds, a/c, major credit cards. SGL$20.

Washington Plaza Hotel (Massachusetts and Vermont Avenues Northwest, 20005; 842-1300, Fax 842-1300 ext 7082) 364 rooms and suites, restaurant, lounge, entertainment, pool, gift shop, wheelchair access, no-smoking rooms, TV, a/c, exercise facilities, pets allowed, meeting facilities, major credit cards. SGL/DBL$95-$255.

Washington Vista (1400 M St Northwest, 20005; 429-1700, Fax 785-0786, 800-445-8667) 401 rooms and suites, restaurant, lounge, exercise facilities, wheelchair access, no-smoking rooms, TV, a/c, gift shop, in-room refrigerators, 24-hour room service, meeting facilities, major credit cards. SGL/DBL$110-$235.

Watergate Hotel (2650 Virginia Ave, 20037; 965-2300, 800-424-2736) 365 rooms and suites, indoor pool, exercise facilities, sauna, whirlpools, VCRs, transportation to local attractions, pets allowed, a/c, TV, kitchenettes, major credit cards. SGL/DBL$235-$500.

The Windsor Inn (1842 16th St Northwest, 20009; 667-0300, Fax 234-3309, 800-423-9111) 47 rooms and suites, complimentary breakfast, a/c, TV, children stay free with parents, major credit cards. SGL/DBL$90-$110.

Windsor Park Hotel (2116 Kalorama Rd Northwest, 20008; 483-7700, 800-247-3064) 43 rooms and suites, a/c, TV, major credit cards. SGL$58, DBL$68, STS$85.

Wyndham Bristol (2430 Pennsylvania Ave Northwest, 20037; 955-6400, Fax 955-5765, 800-822-4200) 280 rooms and suites, restaurant, no-smoking rooms, TV, a/c, wheelchair access, complimentary newspaper, meeting facilities, major credit cards. $165-$185.

West Virginia

Ansted
Area Code 304

Hawk's Nest Lodge (Ansted, 25812; 658-5212, Fax 658-4549) 31 rooms and suites, restaurant, pool, tennis court, children under 12 stay free with parents, a/c, TV, no pets, senior citizen rates, major credit cards. SGL/DBL$38-$56, STS$55-$75.

Barboursville
Area Code 304

Comfort Inn (3441 Hwy 60 East, 25504; 736-9772, 800-221-2222) 131 rooms, restaurant, pool, wheelchair access, no-smoking rooms, no pets, children under 18 stay free with parents, senior citizen rates, a/c, TV, meeting facilities, major credit cards. SGL/DBL$36-$45.

Holiday Inn Gateway (6007 Rte. 60E, 25726; 736-8974, Fax 736-8974, 800-HOLIDAY) indoor pool, exercise facilities, children under 19 stay free with parents, wheelchair access, a/c, TV, no-smoking rooms, fax service, room service, no pets, laundry service, airport transportation, meeting facilities for 250, senior citizen rates, major credit cards. SGL/DBL$55-$65.

Beaver
Area Code 304

House of Grandview (Rte. 9, 25813; 763-4381) 2 rooms, bed and breakfast, TV, no-smoking rooms. SGL/DBL$45-$85.

Beckley
Area Code 304

Beckley Hotel and Conference Center (1940 Harper Rd, 25801; 252-8661, 800-274-6010) 187 rooms and suites, restaurant, lounge, entertainment, indoor pool, exercise facilities, sauna, spa, pets allowed, boutiques, room service, laundry facilities, a/c, TV, meeting facilities, major credit cards. SGL/DBL$65-$90, STS$100-$200.

Best Western Inn (1939 Harper Rd, 25801; 252-0671, 800-528-1234) 80 rooms, restaurant, free breakfast, lounge, pool, exercise facilities, children stay free with parents, a/c, TV, no-smoking rooms, whirlpools, wheelchair access, pets allowed, senior citizen rates, meeting facilities, major credit cards. SGL/DBL$36-$50.

Charles House Motel (223 South Heber St, 25801; 253-8318) 27 rooms, a/c, TV, kitchenettes, pets allowed, major credit cards. SGL/DBL$55-$75.

Comfort Inn (1909 Harper Rd, 25801; 255-2161, 800-221-2222) 130 rooms, restaurant, complimentary breakfast, pool, exercise facilities, in-room refrigerators and microwaves, fax service, wheelchair access, no-smoking rooms, laundry facilities, no pets, children under 18 stay free with parents, senior citizen rates, a/c, TV, meeting facilities, major credit cards. SGL/DBL$39-$60.

Days Inn (Harper Park Dr, 25801; 800-325-2525) 121 rooms, restaurant, complimentary breakfast, lounge, pool, children stay free with parents, room service, laundry service, a/c, TV, free local calls, no pets, wheelchair access, no-smoking rooms, senior citizen rates, major credit cards. SGL/DBL$32-$52.

Erma's Garden (245 North Kanawha St, 25801; 253-5987) 3 rooms, bed and breakfast, private baths, gift shop, no-smoking allowed. SGL/DBL$35-$65.

Green Bank Motel (505 South Eisenhower Dr, 25801; 253-3355) 18 rooms, a/c, TV, no-smoking rooms, major credit cards. SGL/DBL$43-$46.

Hampton Inn (110 Harper Park Dr, 25801; 252-2121, Fax 252-2121, 800-HAMPTON) 108 rooms, restaurant, complimentary breakfast, pool, exercise facilities, children under 18 stay free with parents, no-smoking rooms, wheelchair access, computer hookups, fax service, TV, a/c, free local calls, pets allowed, meeting facilities, major credit cards. SGL/DBL$46-$55.

Holiday Inn (1924 Harper Rd, 25801; 255-1511, 800-HOLIDAY) 105 rooms, restaurant, lounge, outdoor pool, exercise facilities, children under 19 stay free with parents, wheelchair access, a/c, TV, no-smoking rooms, fax service, room service, no pets, laundry service, meeting facilities for 20, senior citizen rates, major credit cards. SGL/DBL$57-$68.

Honey In The Rock Motel (2315 South Fayette St, 25801; 252-7391, 800-244-6884) 88 rooms, restaurant, lounge, outdoor pool, a/c, TV, pets allowed, gift shop, room service, major credit cards. SGL/DBL$65.

Super 8 Motel (2014 Harper Rd, 25801; 253-0802, 800-800-8000) rooms and suites, pets allowed, children under 12 stay free with parents, free local calls, a/c, TV, in-room refrigerators and microwaves, fax service, no-smoking rooms, senior citizen rates, wheelchair access, meeting facilities, major credit cards. SGL/DBL$36-$41.

Beckwith
Area Code 304

Woodcrest Bed and Breakfast (Rte. 2, 25840; 574-3870) 5 rooms and 1 3-bedroom cabin, complimentary breakfast, pool, a/c, no-smoking rooms, TV, gift shop, major credit cards. SGL/DBL$55-$100.

Berkeley & Berkeley Springs
Area Code 304

Cacapon Lodge (Berkeley Springs, 25411; 258-1022, 800-225-5982) 80 rooms and housekeeping cabins, restaurant, a/c, TV, gift shop, tennis courts, kitchenettes, major credit cards. SGL/DBL$48-$55.

Coolfront Resort (Cold Run Valley Rd, 25411; 258-4500, Fax 258-5499) 81 rooms and 1-, 2- and 3-bedroom suites, restaurant, lounge, indoor pool, sauna, whirlpools, a/c, TV, kitchenettes, no pets, major credit cards. SGL/DBL$79-$109.

The Country Inn (207 South Washington St, 25411; 258-2210, 800-822-6630) 72 rooms and suites, restaurant, entertainment, a/c, TV, gift shop, meeting facilities, major credit cards. SGL/DBL$35-$85, STS$70-$135.

Highlawn Inn (Berkeley Springs, 25411; 258-5700) 6 rooms, bed and breakfast, 1890s inn, no children allowed, antique furnishings, major credit cards. SGL/DBL$70-$95.

Janesway Bed and Breakfast (501 Johnson Rd, 25411; 258-4079) 4 rooms, complimentary breakfast, no smoking, private baths, no pets. SGL/DBL$60-$90.

Bluefield
Area Code 304

Brier Motel (3206 Cumberland Rd, 24701; 325-9111) 67 rooms, restaurant, lounge, no-smoking rooms, a/c, TV, major credit cards. SGL/DBL$46-$54.

Comfort Inn (Bluefield, 24701; 326-3688, 800-221-2222) 61 rooms, restaurant, complimentary breakfast, pool, wheelchair access, no-smoking rooms, no pets, children under 18 stay free with parents, senior citizen rates, a/c, TV, meeting facilities, major credit cards. SGL/DBL$45-$55.

Econo Lodge (3400 Cumberland Rd, 24701; 327-8171, 800-4-CHOICE) 48 rooms, children under 18 stay free with parents, pets allowed, senior citizen rates, wheelchair access, a/c, TV, major credit cards. SGL/DBL$30-$41.

Holiday Inn (Rte. 52, 24701; 325-6170, 800-HOLIDAY) restaurant, lounge, entertainment, outdoor pool, exercise facilities, whirlpools, gift shop, children under 19 stay free with parents, wheelchair access, a/c, TV, no-smoking rooms, gift shop, fax service, room service, pets allowed, laundry service, meeting facilities for 500, senior citizen rates, major credit cards. SGL/DBL$53-$78.

Ramada Inn (3174 East Cumberland Rd, 24701; 325-5421, Fax 325-6045, 800-2-RAMADA) 158 rooms and suites, restaurant, lounge, entertainment, indoor pool, sauna, jacuzzi, game room, exercise facilities, wheelchair access, no-smoking rooms, airport transportation, free parking, pets allowed, a/c, TV, room service, laundry facilities, meeting facilities, senior citizen rates, major credit cards. SGL/DBL$45-$52, STS$60, AP$5.

Bramwell
Area Code 304

Bluestone Inn Bed and Breakfast (One Main St, 24715; 248-7402) 2 rooms, complimentary breakfast, pets allowed, gift shop, no-smoking rooms. SGL/DBL$60-$90.

Holley House (Bramwell, 24715; 248-8145) 2 rooms, bed and breakfast, TV, private baths. SGL/DBL$45-$55.

Three Oaks and A Quilt Bed and Breakfast (Bramwell, 24715; 248-8316) 3 rooms, complimentary breakfast, TV, VCR, no-smoking rooms, room service, private baths, children over age 12 welcome, laundry service. SGL/DBL$45-$85.

Bridgeport
Area Code 304

Days Inn (112 Tolley St, 26330; 842-3710, 800-325-2525) 62 rooms, restaurant, complimentary breakfast, lounge, indoor pool, exercise facilities, children stay free with parents, room service, laundry service, a/c, TV, free local calls, no pets, wheelchair access, no-smoking rooms, senior citizen rates, major credit cards. SGL/DBL$43-$68.

Holiday Inn (100 Lodgeville Rd, 26330; 842-5411, 800-HOLIDAY) 161 rooms, restaurant, lounge, outdoor pool, exercise facilities, children under 19 stay free with parents, wheelchair access, a/c, TV, no-smoking rooms, fax service, room service, no pets, laundry service, meeting facilities for 175, senior citizen rates, major credit cards. SGL/DBL$44-$70.

Knights Inn (1235 West Main St, 26330; 842-7115, Fax 842-2707, 800-843-5644) 116 rooms, pool, wheelchair access, no-smoking rooms, TV, a/c, in-room refrigerators and microwaves, pets allowed, fax service, free parking, VCRs, senior citizen rates, major credit cards. SGL/DBL$37-$41.

Buckhannon
Area Code 304

Bicentennial Motel (90 East Main St, 26201; 472-5000) 55 rooms and efficiencies, restaurant, pool, a/c, TV, gift shop, in-room refrigerators, meeting facilities, major credit cards. SGL/DBL$35-$45.

Centennial Motel (22 North Locust St, 26201; 472-4100) 24 rooms, TV, children under 12 stay free with parents. SGL/DBL$22-$40.

Henderson House Bed and Breakfast (54 College Ave, 26201; 472-1611, 800-CALL-WVA) 6 rooms, complimentary breakfast, a/c, TV, private baths, no-smoking rooms, major credit cards. SGL/DBL$38.

Charles Town
Area Code 304

Cottonwood Inn (Mill Lane, 25414; 725-3371) 7 rooms, bed and breakfast, private baths, no pets, a/c, TV, on 6 acres. SGL/DBL$70-$100.

Gilbert House (Charles Town, 25414; 725-0637) bed and breakfast, no smoking, private baths, 1700s home, antique furnishings, fireplace. SGL/DBL$50-$135.

Hillbrook Inn (Charles Town, 25414; 725-4223) 5 rooms, complimentary breakfast, restaurant, fireplaces, antique furnishings, no smoking, no pets, major credit cards. SGL/DBL$190-$250.

Motel 6 (6311 MacCorkle Ave Southeast, 25304; 925-0471, 891-6161) 104 rooms, pool, free local calls, children under 17 stay free with parents, a/c, TV, major credit cards. SGL/DBL$30-$36.

Towne House Motel (East Washington St, 25414; 725-8441, 800-227-2339) 115 rooms, restaurant, pool, a/c, TV, major credit cards. SGL/DBL$27-$45.

The Turf Motel (608 East Washington St, 25414; 725-2081, Fax 728-7605, 800-422-8873) 46 rooms and efficiencies, restaurant, lounge, entertainment, pool, pets allowed, transportation to local attractions, a/c, TV, major credit cards. SGL/DBL$30-$70.

Charleston
Area Code 304

Days Inn (6210 MacCorkle Ave, 25117; 766-6231, 800-325-2525) 201 rooms, restaurant, lounge, pool, children stay free with parents, room service, kitchenettes, laundry service, a/c, TV, free local calls, pets allowed, wheelchair access, no-smoking rooms, senior citizen rates, major credit cards. SGL/DBL$38-$55.

Executive Inn (3300 MacCorkle Ave, 25304; 345-8820, Fax 345-8823) 58 rooms and efficiencies, a/c, TV, children under 12 stay free with parents, in-room refrigerators, meeting facilities. SGL/DBL$45-$50.

Historic Charleston Bed and Breakfast (114 Elizabeth St, 25311; 345-8156, 800-CALL-WVA) 3 rooms, complimentary breakfast, a/c, TV, children over age 12 welcome, no-smoking allowed, private baths, pets allowed. SGL/DBL$65-$105.

Holiday Inn Civic Center (100 Civic Center Dr, 25301; 345-0600, 800-HOLIDAY) 198 rooms, restaurant, lounge, outdoor pool, exercise facilities, children under 19 stay free with parents, wheelchair access, a/c, TV, no-smoking rooms, fax service, room service, no pets, laundry service, meeting facilities for 30, senior citizen rates, major credit cards. SGL/DBL$66-$76.

Holiday Inn Charleston House (600 Kanawha Blvd, 25301; 344-4092, 800-HOLIDAY) 256 rooms and suites, restaurant, lounge, outdoor pool, exercise facilities, children under 19 stay free with parents, gift shop, car rental desk, water view, wheelchair access, a/c, TV, no-smoking rooms, fax service, barber and beauty shop, airport transportation, water view, room service, no pets, laundry service, meeting facilities for 1,100, senior citizen rates, major credit cards. SGL/DBL$78-$92, STS$80-$300.

Holiday Inn (1000 Washington St East, 25302; 343-4661, 800-HOLIDAY) restaurant, lounge, outdoor pool, exercise facilities, children under 19 stay free with parents, wheelchair access, a/c, TV, no-smoking rooms, fax service, room service, no pets, laundry service, meeting facilities for 250, senior citizen rates, major credit cards. SGL/DBL$50-$63.

Kanawha City Motor Lodge (3103 MacCorkle Ave Southeast, 25304; 344-2461) 50 rooms and efficiencies, children under the age of 18 stay free with parents, TV, meeting facilities, major credit cards. SGL/DBL$39-$43.

Knights Inn (6401 MacCorkle Ave Southeast, 25304; 925-0451, 800-843-5644) pool, wheelchair access, no-smoking rooms, TV, a/c, in-room refrigerators and microwaves, fax service, free parking, VCRs, senior citizen rates, major credit cards. SGL/DBL$35-$42.

Marriott Town Center Hotel (200 Lee St East, 25301; 345-6500, Fax 353-3722, 800-228-9290) 352 rooms and suites, restaurant, lounge, entertainment, indoor pool, exercise facilities, whirlpools, wheelchair access, TV, a/c, no-smoking rooms, laundry facilities, gift shop, children under 18 stay free with parents, no pets, business services, meeting facilities, senior citizen rates, major credit cards. SGL/DBL$89-$140, STS$250-$275.

Ramada Inn (Second Ave and B St, 25303; 744-4641, Fax 744-4525, 800-2-RAMADA) 245 rooms, restaurant, lounge, entertainment, exercise facilities, wheelchair access, no-smoking rooms, airport transportation, free parking, pets allowed, a/c, TV, room service, laundry facilities, 21 meeting rooms, meeting facilities for 450, senior citizen rates, major credit cards. SGL/DBL$49-$85, AP$5.

Red Roof Inn (4006 MacCorkle Ave Southwest, 25309; 744-1500, Fax 744-8268, 800-843-7663) 109 rooms, restaurant, no-smoking rooms, fax service, wheelchair access, complimentary newspaper, children stay free with parents, pets allowed, free local calls, major credit cards. SGL/DBL$34-$47.

Red Roof Inn South Charleston (6305 MacCorkle Ave Southwest, 25304; 925-6953, 925-8111, 800-843-7663) 109 rooms, restaurant, no-smoking rooms, fax service, wheelchair access, complimentary newspaper, children under 18 stay free with parents, pets allowed, free local calls, major credit cards. SGL/DBL$34-$50.

Chloe
Area Code 304

Pennbrooke Farm Bed and Breakfast (Chloe, 25235; 655-7367) 2 rooms, complimentary breakfast, TV, water view, no-smoking rooms. SGL/DBL$35-$55.

Clarksburg
Area Code 304

Comfort Inn (250 Emily Dr, 26301; 623-2600, 800-221-2222) 113 rooms and efficiencies, restaurant, complimentary breakfast, wheelchair access, no-smoking rooms, no pets, children under 18 stay free with parents, senior citizen rates, gift shop, a/c, TV, meeting facilities, major credit cards. SGL/DBL$35-$43.

Crawley
Area Code 304

Oak Knoll Bed and Breakfast (Crawley, 24931; 392-6903) 3 rooms, complimentary breakfast, TV, no-smoking rooms. SGL/DBL$50-$70.

Cross Lanes
Area Code 304

Comfort Inn (Goff Mountain Rd, 25313; 776-8070, Fax 776-6460, 800-221-2222) 114 rooms, restaurant, complimentary breakfast, lounge, pool, whirlpools, in-room refrigerators, wheelchair access, no-smoking rooms, no pets, children under the age of 18 stay free with parents, senior citizen rates, a/c, TV, meeting facilities, major credit cards. SGL/DBL$43-$48.

Motel 6 (330 Goff Mountain Rd, 25313; 776-5911, 891-6161) 112 rooms, pool, free local calls, children under 17 stay free with parents, a/c, TV, major credit cards. SGL/DBL$28-$34.

Daniels
Area Code 304

Glade Springs Resort (3000 Lake Dr, 25832; 763-2000, 800-634-5233) 60 rooms and suites, restaurant, lounge, outdoor pool, tennis courts, gift shop, a/c, TV, no-smoking rooms, major credit cards. SGL/DBL$88.

Davis
Area Code 304

Best Western Alpine Lodge (Davis, 26260; 259-5245, 800-528-1234) 46 rooms, restaurant, complimentary breakfast, lounge, pool, exercise facilities, children stay free with parents, a/c, TV, no-smoking rooms, laundry facilities, whirlpools, wheelchair access, pets allowed, senior citizen rates, meeting facilities, major credit cards. SGL/DBL$40-$50.

Blackwater Lodge (Blackwater State Park, 26260; 259-5216) 55 rooms and 25 housekeeping cabins, restaurant, pool, TV, laundry facilities, meeting facilities, major credit cards. SGL/DBL$48-$56.

Canaan Valley Resort and Conference Center (Davis, 26260; 866-4121, Fax 866-2172) 250 rooms, suites and cabins, restaurant, lounge, indoor pool, sauna, whirlpools, lighted tennis courts, exercise facilities, a/c, TV, no pets, senior citizen rates, major credit cards. SGL/DBL$45-$75. STS$100.

Deerfield Village Resort (Davis, 26260; 866-4698, Fax 866-4015, 800-342-3217) 100 rooms and suites, restaurant, lounge, pool, tennis court, pets allowed, a/c, TV, VCRs, whirlpools, major credit cards. SGL/DBL$90-$175.

Mountain Aire Lodge (Davis 26260; 259-5211) 11 rooms and 1- and 2-bedroom suites, a/c, TV, no pets, major credit cards. SGL/DBL$33-$50.

Dunbar
Area Code 304

Super 8 Motel (911 Dunbar Ave, 25064; 768-6888, 800-800-8000) 63 rooms and suites, no pets, children under 12 stay free with parents, free local calls, a/c, TV, in-room refrigerators and microwaves, fax service, no-smoking rooms, senior citizen rates, wheelchair access, meeting facilities, major credit cards. SGL/DBL$36-$41.

TraveLodge (1007 Dunbar Ave, 25065; 768-1000, Fax 768-2705, 800-255-3050) 89 rooms and suites, restaurant, lounge, complimentary breakfast, pool, wheelchair access, free newspaper, laundry service, TV, a/c, free local calls, no pets, fax, no-smoking rooms, in-room refrigerators and microwaves, senior citizen rates, major credit cards. SGL/DBL$40-$44.

Elkins
Area Code 304

Best Western Inn (Elkins, 26241; 636-7711, 800-528-1234) 63 rooms, restaurant, indoor pool, exercise facilities, children stay free with parents, a/c, TV, no-smoking rooms, wheelchair access, pets allowed, senior citizen rates, meeting facilities, major credit cards. SGL/DBL$36-$56.

Days Inn (1200 Harrison Ave, 26241; 637-4667, 800-325-2525) 41 rooms and suites, restaurant, lounge, jacuzzi, children stay free with parents, room service, laundry service, a/c, TV, free local calls, no pets, wheelchair access, no-smoking rooms, senior citizen rates, major credit cards. SGL/DBL$32-$56, STS$48-$69.

Econo Lodge (Hwy 33E, 26241; 636-5311, 800-4-CHOICE) 72 rooms and suites, complimentary breakfast, indoor pool, whirlpools, laundry facilities, airport courtesy car, children under 12 stay free with parents, kitchenettes, no pets, senior citizen rates, wheelchair access, a/c, TV, meeting facilities, major credit cards. SGL/DBL$39-$51.

Elkins Motor Lodge (Harrison Ave, 26241; 636-1400, 800-245-5074) 54 rooms and suites, restaurant, room service, a/c, TV, pets allowed, airport transportation, wheelchair access, meeting facilities, major credit cards. SGL/DBL$33-$43.

Four Season Motel (1091 Harrison Ave, 26241; 636-1900, 800-367-7130) 13 rooms, TV. SGL/DBL$26-$30.

Super 8 Motel (Elkins, 26241; 636-6500, 800-800-8000) rooms and suites, pets allowed, children under 12 stay free with parents, free local calls, a/c, TV, in-room refrigerators and microwaves, fax service, no-smoking rooms, senior citizen rates, wheelchair access, meeting facilities, major credit cards. SGL/DBL$33-$38.

Tunnel Mountain Bed and Breakfast (Rte. 1, 16241; 636-1684) complimentary breakfast, no pets, private baths, on 5 acres. SGL/DBL$65.

Fairlea
Area Code 304

Fairlea Town House Motel (West Fair St, 24902; 645-7070) 36 rooms, a/c, TV, kitchenettes, no-smoking rooms, wheelchair access, major credit cards. SGL/DBL$46-$58.

Fairmont
Area Code 304

Acadia House Bed and Breakfast (158 Locust Ave, 26554; 367-1000) free breakfast, a/c, children over age 10 welcome, antique furnishings, pets allowed, private baths. SGL/DBL$45-$55.

Avenue Motel (816 Fairmont Ave, 26554; 366-4960) rooms and efficiencies, TV, a/c, senior citizen rates, major credit cards. SGL/DBL$38-$46.

Country Club Motor Lodge (1499 Locust Ave, 26554; 366-4141) 32 rooms and 1- and 2-bedroom suites, TV, a/c, pets allowed, no-smoking rooms, major credit cards. SGL/DBL$21-$27.

Days Inn (1185 Airport Rd, 26554; 367-1370, Fax 367-1806, 800-325-2525) 98 rooms, restaurant, complimentary breakfast, lounge, pool, children stay free with parents, room service, laundry service, a/c, TV, free local calls, no pets, in-room computer hookups, wheelchair access, no-smoking rooms, senior citizen rates, major credit cards. SGL/DBL$41-$55.

Fairmont Motor Lodge (1117 Fairmont Ave, 26554; 363-0100) 50 rooms, pool, TV, a/c, no pets, children under 18 stay free with parents, no-smoking rooms, wheelchair access, meeting facilities, major credit cards. SGL/DBL$28-$34.

Holiday Inn (Old Grafton Rd, 26554; 366-5500, 800-HOLIDAY) 106 rooms, restaurant, lounge, outdoor pool, exercise facilities, children under 19 stay free with parents, wheelchair access, a/c, TV, no-smoking rooms, fax service, room service, no pets, laundry service, meeting facilities for 150, senior citizen rates, major credit cards. SGL/DBL$42-$65.

Marino's Motor Inn (Fairmont, 26554; 366-6664) 40 rooms, restaurant, TV, a/c, in-room refrigerators and microwaves, no pets, no-smoking rooms, senior citizen rates, major credit cards. SGL/DBL$25-$35.

Red Roof Inn (Rte. 1, 26554; 366-6800, Fax 366-6812, 800-843-7663) 109 rooms, no-smoking rooms, fax service, wheelchair access, complimentary newspaper, children under 18 stay free with parents, pets allowed, free local calls, in-room computer hookups, major credit cards. SGL$28, DBL$41.

YWCA (2019 Pleasant Valley Rd, 26554; 366-4480) SGL/DBL$13-$22.

Fayetteville
Area Code 304

Comfort Inn New River (Laurel Creek Rd, 25840; 574-3443, 800-221-2222) 107 rooms, restaurant, pool, whirlpools, exercise facilities, wheelchair access, no-smoking rooms, no pets, children under 18 stay free with parents, senior citizen rates, a/c, TV, meeting facilities, major credit cards. SGL/DBL$30-$65.

Glen Ferris
Area Code 304

Glen Ferris Inn (Glen Ferris, 25090; 632-1111) 16 rooms and suites, 1840s inn, antique furnishings, no-smoking rooms, meeting facilities, major credit cards. SGL/DBL$40-$160.

Grafton
Area Code 304

Crislip Motor Lodge (300 Moritz Ave, 26354; 265-2100) 56 rooms and suites, pool, TV, major credit cards. SGL/DBL$31-$40.

Tygart Lake State Park Lodge (Grafton, 26354; 265-3383) 20 rooms, restaurant, pool, wheelchair access, children under the age of 13 stay free with parents, wheelchair access, meeting facilities. SGL/DBL$55.

Harpers Ferry
Area Code 304

Cliffside Inn (Harpers Ferry, 25425; 535-6302, Fax 535-6313, 800-782-9436) 100 rooms, restaurant, lounge, entertainment, pool, rooms service, gift shop, transportation to local attractions, wheelchair access, major credit cards. SGL/DBL$44-$62.

Comfort Inn (Harpers Ferry, 25425; 535-6391, 800-221-2222) 51 rooms, restaurant, pool, wheelchair access, no-smoking rooms, no pets, children under 18 stay free with parents, senior citizen rates, a/c, TV, meeting facilities, major credit cards. SGL/DBL$47-$62.

Harrisville
Area Code 304

Apple Alley Bed and Breakfast (500 East Main St, 26362; 643-2272) 3 rooms, free breakfast, TV, no-smoking rooms. SGL/DBL$39-$65.

Hedgesville
Area Code 304

The Woods Resort and Conference Center (Hedgesville, 25427; 754-7977, Fax 754-8344, 800-248-2222) 60 rooms and housekeeping cabins, restaurant, lounge, entertainment, indoor and outdoor pools, lighted tennis courts, exercise facilities, sauna, whirlpools, a/c, TV, laundry facilities, Modified American Plan available, major credit cards. SGL/DBL$80-$100.

Huntington
Area Code 304

Holiday Inn Downtown (1415 Fourth Ave, 25701; 525-7741, 800-HOLIDAY) restaurant, lounge, outdoor pool, exercise facilities, children under 19 stay free with parents, wheelchair access, a/c, TV, no-smoking rooms, fax service, room service, airport transportation, no pets, laundry service, meeting facilities for 250, senior citizen rates, major credit cards. SGL/DBL$53-$76.

Holiday Inn Gateway (Huntington, 25726; 736-8974, 800-HOLIDAY) restaurant, lounge, outdoor pool, lighted tennis courts, exercise facilities, children under 19 stay free with parents, wheelchair access, a/c, TV, no-smoking rooms, fax, room service, no pets, laundry service, meeting facilities, senior citizen rates, major credit cards. SGL/DBL$55-$80.

Nicotera Bed and Breakfast (431 5th Ave, 25701; 523-5118) 2 rooms, complimentary breakfast, a/c, TV, gift shop, no-smoking rooms. SGL/DBL$65-$125.

Radisson Hotel (1001 Third Ave, 25701; 525-1001, 800-777-1700) 208 rooms and suites, restaurant, lounge, entertainment, pool, exercise facilities, airport transportation, wheelchair access, free parking, whirlpools, no-smoking rooms, TV, a/c, children stay free with parents, pets allowed, major credit cards. SGL/DBL$96-$106.

Ramada Inn (5600 Rte. 60 East, 25705; 736-3451, Fax 736-3451 ext 706, 800-2-RAMADA) 159 rooms, restaurant, lounge, entertainment, pool, wheelchair access, no-smoking rooms, airport transportation, free parking, pets allowed, wheelchair access, a/c, TV, room service, laundry facilities, 3 meeting rooms, meeting facilities for 150, senior citizen rates, major credit cards. SGL/DBL$40-$62, AP$10.

Red Roof Inn (5190 Rte. 60 East, 25705; 733-3737, Fax 733-3786, 800-843-7663) 109 rooms, restaurant, no-smoking rooms, fax service, wheelchair access, complimentary newspaper, children under 18 stay free with parents, no pets, free local calls, in-room computer hookups, major credit cards. SGL/DBL$39-$50.

Hurricane
Area Code 304

Red Roof Inn (Putnam Village Shopping Center, 25526; 757-6392, 757-6734, 800-843-7663) 79 rooms, restaurant, no-smoking rooms, fax service, wheelchair access, complimentary newspaper, children stay free with parents, pets allowed, free local calls, in-room computer hookups, major credit cards. SGL/DBL$27-$35.

Smiley's Motel (419 Hurricane Creek Rd, 25526; 562-3346, 800-726-7016) 145 rooms and efficiencies, restaurant, pool, a/c, TV, pets allowed, senior citizen rates, major credit cards. SGL/DBL$35-$40.

Huttonsville
Area Code 304

The Hutton House (Huttonsville, 26273; 335-6701) bed and breakfast, no smoking, private baths, Victorian home, no pets, major credit cards. SGL/DBL$45-$50.

Jane Lew
Area Code 304

Wilderness Plantation Inn (Jane Lew, 26378; 884-7806) 39 rooms and suites, restaurant, pool, whirlpools, sauna, a/c, TV, pets allowed, in-room refrigerators, major credit cards. SGL/DBL$36-$46.

Kingwood
Area Code 304

The Preston County Inn (112 West Main St, 26537; 329-2220) 7 rooms, bed and breakfast, children over age 12 welcome, antique furnishings, gift shop, private baths, a/c, TV, major credit cards. SGL/DBL$84-$124.

Lewisburg
Area Code 304

Brier Inn (540 North Jefferson St, 24901; 645-7722, Fax 645-7865) 162 rooms and suites, restaurant, lounge, entertainment, pool, exercise facilities, pets allowed, airport transportation, a/c, wheelchair access, no-smoking rooms, children under 12 stay free with parents, TV, senior citizen rates, VCRs, meeting facilities, major credit cards. SGL/DBL$42-$47.

Budget Host Fort Savannah (204 North Jefferson St, 24901; 645-3055, Fax 645-3033, 800-BUD-HOST) 68 rooms, restaurant, pool, whirlpools, kitchenettes, in-room refrigerators, no-smoking rooms, TV, VCRs, a/c, wheelchair access, children stay free with parents, senior citizen rates, meeting facilities, major credit cards. SGL/DBL$32-$85.

Days Inn (635 North Jefferson St, 24901; 645-2345, 800-325-2525) 26 rooms, restaurant, complimentary breakfast, lounge, children stay free with parents, room service, laundry service, a/c, TV, free local calls, pets allowed, wheelchair access, no-smoking rooms, senior citizen rates, major credit cards. SGL/DBL$35-$55.

General Lewis Inn (301 East Washington St, 24901; 645-2600) 25 rooms, restaurant, a/c, TV, pets allowed, antique furnishings, 1830s inn, major credit cards. SGL/DBL$50-$100.

Super 8 Motel (550 North Jefferson St, 24901; 647-3188, 800-800-8000) 54 rooms and suites, pets allowed, children under 12 stay free with parents, free local calls, a/c, TV, in-room refrigerators and microwaves, fax service, no-smoking rooms, senior citizen rates, wheelchair access, meeting facilities, major credit cards. SGL/DBL$36-$41.

Martinsburg
Area Code 304

Arborgate Inn (1599 Edwin Miller Blvd, 25401; 267-2211, 800-843-5644) 59 rooms and efficiencies, restaurant, pool, wheelchair access, no-smoking rooms, TV, a/c, in-room refrigerators and microwaves, fax service, free parking, VCRs, senior citizen rates, major credit cards. SGL/DBL$34-$48.

Best Western Inn (Martinsburg, 25401; 263-8811, 800-528-1234) 121 rooms and efficiencies, complimentary breakfast, indoor pool, exercise facilities, whirlpools, children stay free with parents, a/c, TV, no-smoking rooms, wheelchair access, no pets, senior citizen rates, meeting facilities, major credit cards. SGL/DBL$40-$55.

Bodyville (601 South Queen St, 25401; 263-1448) bed and breakfast, no smoking, 1800s home, on 14 acres, no pets, no children allowed. SGL/DBL$110-$130.

Morgantown 433

Comfort Inn (2800 Aikens Center, 25410; 263-6200, 800-221-2222) 100 rooms, restaurant, pool, exercise facilities, wheelchair access, no-smoking rooms, no pets, children under 18 stay free with parents, whirlpools, senior citizen rates, a/c, TV, meeting facilities, major credit cards. SGL/DBL$48-$84.

Days Inn (209 Viking Way, 25401; 263-1800, 800-325-2525) 63 rooms, restaurant, lounge, children stay free with parents, room service, laundry service, a/c, TV, free local calls, no pets, wheelchair access, no-smoking rooms, senior citizen rates, major credit cards. SGL/DBL$46-$70.

Dunn Country Inn (Rte. 3, 25401; 263-8646) bed and breakfast, no smoking, on 5 acres, no children allowed, 1800s home, no pets. SGL/DBL$80-$110.

Econo Lodge (Martinsburg, 25401; 274-2181, 800-4-CHOICE) 48 rooms, restaurant, pool, children under 12 stay free with parents, pets allowed, senior citizen rates, wheelchair access, a/c, TV, major credit cards. SGL/DBL$39-$49.

Sheraton Inn (301 Foxcroft Ave, 25401; 267-5500, Fax 264-9157, 800-325-3535) 120 rooms and suites, restaurant, lounge, indoor and outdoor pools, exercise facilities, whirlpools, sauna, tennis courts, gift shop, no-smoking rooms, a/c, TV, no pets, children stay free with parents, wheelchair access, 5,000 square feet of meeting and exhibition space, 10 meeting rooms, meeting facilities for 500, major credit cards. SGL/DBL$55-$80.

Super 8 Motel (1600 Edwin Miller Blvd, 25401; 263-0801, 800-800-8000) rooms and suites, no pets, children under 12 stay free with parents, free local calls, a/c, TV, in-room refrigerators and microwaves, fax service, no-smoking rooms, senior citizen rates, wheelchair access, meeting facilities, major credit cards. SGL/DBL$37-$42.

Wheatland Motel (1193 Winchester Ave, 25401; 267-2994) 22 rooms, restaurant, pool, major credit cards. SGL/DBL$28-$32.

Windewald Motel (1022 Winchester Ave, 25401; 263-0831) 16 rooms and efficiencies, pool, no pets, gift shop, a/c, TV, major credit cards. SGL/DBL$26-$34.

Morgantown
Area Code 304

Almost Heaven Bed and Breakfast (391 Scott Ave, 26505; 296-4007) 4 rooms, complimentary breakfast, a/c, private baths, TV, no-smoking rooms, major credit cards. SGL/DBL$55-$100.

The Cabin (59 Wilson Ave, 26505; 296-1540) 1 2-bedroom cabin, bed and breakfast, a/c, TV, private bath. SGL/DBL$65.

West Virginia

Chestnut Ridge School Bed and Breakfast (1000 Stewartstown Rd, 26505; 598-2262, 800-CALL-WVA) 4 rooms, complimentary breakfast, a/c, TV, room service, no-smoking rooms. SGL/DBL$45-$80.

Comfort Inn (Hwy 119, 26505; 296-9364, 800-221-2222) 80 rooms and suites, restaurant, complimentary breakfast, pool, whirlpools, exercise facilities, wheelchair access, no-smoking rooms, no pets, children under 18 stay free with parents, gift shop, senior citizen rates, a/c, TV, meeting facilities, major credit cards. SGL/DBL$39-$57.

Days Inn (366 Boyers Ave, 26505; 598-2120, Fax 598-3272, 800-325-2525) 102 rooms, restaurant, lounge, indoor pool, jacuzzi, exercise equipment, children stay free with parents, room service, laundry service, a/c, TV, free local calls, no pets, wheelchair access, no-smoking rooms, senior citizen rates, major credit cards. SGL/DBL$37-$90.

Econo Lodge (15 Commerce Dr, 26505; 296-8774, 800-4-CHOICE) 81 rooms and efficiencies, children under 12 stay free with parents, no pets, senior citizen rates, wheelchair access, a/c, TV, major credit cards. SGL/DBL$35-$40.

Econo Lodge (3506 Monongahela Blvd, 26505; 599-8181, Fax 599-8181 ext 438, 800-4-CHOICE) 71 rooms, restaurant, children under 12 stay free with parents, no pets, senior citizen rates, wheelchair access, a/c, TV, meeting facilities, major credit cards. SGL/DBL$40-$50.

Euro-Suites Hotel (501 Chestnut Ridge Rd, 26505; 598-1000, Fax 599-2736) 79 rooms and suites, restaurant, pool, whirlpools, exercise facilities, a/c, TV, senior citizen rates, major credit cards. SGL/DBL$80-$100.

Friendship Inn (452 Country Club Rd, 26505; 599-4850, 800-424-4777) 54 rooms, a/c, TV, in-room refrigerators, no pets, no-smoking rooms, children stay free with parents, wheelchair access, major credit cards. SGL/DBL$29-$40.

Hampton Inn (1053 Van Voorhis Rd, 26505; 599-1200, Fax 599-1200 ext 133, 800-HAMPTON) 108 rooms, restaurant, complimentary breakfast, pool, exercise facilities, children under 18 stay free with parents, no-smoking rooms, wheelchair access, computer hookups, fax, TV, a/c, free local calls, no pets, meeting facilities, major credit cards. SGL/DBL$45-$53.

Holiday Inn (1400 Saratoga Ave, 26505; 599-1680, 800-HOLIDAY) 147 rooms, restaurant, lounge, entertainment, outdoor pool, exercise facilities, children under 19 stay free with parents, wheelchair access, a/c, TV, no-smoking rooms, fax, room service, no pets, laundry service, meeting facilities, senior citizen rates, major credit cards. SGL/DBL$42-$72.

Lakeview Resort and Conference Center (Morgantown, 26505; 594-1111, Fax 594-9472) 191 rooms and suites, restaurant, indoor and outdoor pools, exercise facilities, whirlpools, lighted tennis courts, a/c, TV, golf, no pets, Modified American Plan available, senior citizen rates, major credit cards. SGL/DBL$75-$135.

The Maples Bed and Breakfast (Morgantown, 26505; 594-1122) 3 rooms, complimentary breakfast, private bath, room service, a/c, TV, major credit cards. SGL/DBL$48-$58.

The Morgan Hotel (127 High St, 26505; 292-8401) 27 efficiencies and suites, restaurant, a/c, TV, children under the age of 12 stay free with parents, in-room refrigerators, meeting facilities, major credit cards. SGL/DBL$35-$45.

Ramada Inn (Morgantown, 26505; 296-3431, 800-2-RAMADA) 159 rooms and suites, restaurant, lounge, entertainment, pool, exercise facilities, game room, wheelchair access, no-smoking rooms, airport transportation, free parking, pets allowed, a/c, TV, room service, laundry facilities, meeting facilities, senior citizen rates, major credit cards. SGL/DBL$50-$70, STS$100-$125, AP$5.

Sheraton Lakeview Resort and Conference Center (Morgantown, 26505; 594-1111, Fax 594-9472, 800-325-3535) 187 rooms and suites, restaurant, lounge, indoor and outdoor pool, exercise facilities, tennis courts, airport transportation, golf, no-smoking rooms, a/c, TV, children stay free with parents, wheelchair access, meeting facilities, major credit cards. SGL/DBL$125-$135, STS$175-$300.

New Martinsville
Area Code 304

Plaza Inn (New Martinsville, 26155; 455-4490) 46 rooms and efficiencies, restaurant, a/c, TV, no pets, in-room refrigerators, senior citizen rates, major credit cards. SGL/DBL$33-$43.

Nitro
Area Code 304

Best Western Inn (4115 First Ave, 25143; 755-8341, Fax 755-2933, 800-528-1234) 26 rooms, restaurant, complimentary breakfast, lounge, pool, exercise facilities, children under 12 stay free with parents, kitchenettes, a/c, TV, no-smoking rooms, wheelchair access, pets allowed, senior citizen rates, meeting facilities, major credit cards. SGL/DBL$36-$41.

Oak Hill
Area Code 304

Holiday Inn (Oyler Ave, 25901; 465-0571, 800-HOLIDAY) 120 rooms, restaurant, lounge, indoor pool, exercise facilities, children under 19 stay free with parents, wheelchair access, a/c, TV, no-smoking rooms, fax service, room service, no pets, laundry service, meeting facilities for 300, senior citizen rates, major credit cards. SGL/DBL$42-$62.

Orlando
Area Code 304

Friend Sheep Farm (Rte 1, 26412; 462-7075) 2 rooms, bed and breakfast, TV, on 200 acres, working farm, antique furnishings, no-smoking rooms. SGL/DBL$50-$100.

Kilmarnock Rarm (Rte 1, 26412; 462-8319) 2 rooms, bed and breakfast, room service, gift shop, hiking trails. SGL/DBL$35-$65.

Parkersburg
Area Code 304

Best Western Inn (Parkersburg, 26101; 485-6551, 800-528-1234) 77 rooms, restaurant, complimentary breakfast, lounge, pool, exercise facilities, children stay free with parents, a/c, TV, no-smoking rooms, wheelchair access, pets allowed, senior citizen rates, meeting facilities, major credit cards. SGL/DBL$32-$46.

Clarion Carriage House Inn (Fourth and Market Sts, 26101; 422-3131, 800-221-2222) 104 rooms, restaurant, lounge, no pets, no smoking rooms, children under 18 stay free with parents, gift shop senior citizen rates, meeting facilities, airport courtesy car, a/c, TV, major credit cards. SGL/DBL$59-$175.

Econo Lodge (Parkersburg, 26101; 422-5401, 800-4-CHOICE) 102 rooms, restaurant, lounge, complimentary breakfast, pool, children under 12 stay free with parents, no pets, senior citizen rates, wheelchair access, a/c, in-room refrigerators, TV, meeting facilities, major credit cards. SGL/DBL$35-$45.

Harmony House Bed and Breakfast (710 Ann St, 26101; 485-1458) 3 rooms, complimentary breakfast, no-smoking rooms, a/c, private baths, TV, major credit cards. SGL/DBL$65-$85.

Holiday Inn (Rte. 50, 26101; 485-6200, 800-HOLIDAY) 148 rooms, restaurant, lounge, entertainment, indoor pool, exercise facilities, whirlpools, game room, children under age 19 stay free with parents, room service, boutiques, wheelchair access, a/c, TV, no-smoking rooms, fax service, room service, hot tubs, no pets, laundry service, meeting facilities, senior citizen rates, major credit cards. SGL/DBL$55-$75.

Red Roof Inn (3714 East 7th St, 26101; 485-1741, Fax 485-1746, 800-843-7663) 107 rooms, no-smoking rooms, fax service, wheelchair access, complimentary newspaper, children stay free with parents, pets allowed, free local calls, in-room computer hookups, major credit cards. SGL/DBL$38-$45.

Stables Motel (3604 East 7th St, 26101; 425-5100, Fax 424-5143, 800-782-2536) 208 rooms and suites, restaurant, pool, a/c, TV, in-room refrigerators, children under 18 stay free with parents, meeting facilities, major credit cards. SGL/DBL$28-$30.

Pence Springs
Area Code 304

Pence Springs Hotel (Pence Springs, 24962; 445-2606) 15 rooms and housekeeping cottages, restaurant, complimentary breakfast, lounge, TV, pets allowed, children under 12 stay free with parents, meeting facilities, wheelchair access. SGL/DBL$45-$300.

Petersburg
Area Code 304

Hermitage Motor Inn (Petersburg, 26847; 257-1711) 36 rooms and efficiencies, restaurant, pool, whirlpools, airport transoprtation, 1880s inn, children under 12 stay free with parents, a/c, TV, no pets, senior citizen rates, major credit cards. SGL/DBL$30-$42.

Homestead Inn and Motel (Petersburg, 26847; 257-1029) 12 rooms, a/c, TV, no pets, senior citizen rates, major credit cards. SGL/DBL$35-$45.

Pipestem
Area Code 304

Pipestem State Park (Pipestem, 25979; 466-1800, Fax 466-4617) 168 housekeeping cottages, restaurant, indoor and outdoor pools, sauna, lighted tennis courts, golf, water view, laundry facilities, a/c, TV, no pets, senior citizen rates, major credit cards. SGL/DBL$45-$60.

Point Pleasant
Area Code 304

Stone Manor (12 Main St, 25550; 675-3442) 3 rooms, bed and breakfast, a/c, TV, no-smoking rooms. SGL/DBL$35-$70.

Princeton
Area Code 304

Comfort Inn (Ambrose Lane, 24740; 487-6101, 800-221-2222) 51 rooms, restaurant, complimentary breakfast, whirlpools, wheelchair access, no-smoking rooms, no pets, children under age 18 stay free with parents, senior citizen rates, a/c, TV, meeting facilities, major credit cards. SGL/DBL$51-$59.

Days Inn (Princeton, 24740; 425-8100, 800-325-2525) 124 rooms, restaurant, complimentary breakfast, lounge, indoor pool, children stay free with parents, room service, laundry service, a/c, TV, free local calls, in-room refrigerators and microwaves, pets allowed, wheelchair access, no-smoking rooms, senior citizen rates, meeting facilities, major credit cards. SGL/DBL$49-$59.

Town 'N Country Motel (805 Oakvale Rd, 24740; 425-8156) 37 rooms and efficiencies, restaurant, pool, a/c, TV, pets allowed, senior citizen rates. SGL/DBL$25-$35.

Ravenswood
Area Code 304

Hemlock Farms Bed and Breakfast (Rte 1, 26164; 273-5572) 1 room, complimentary breakfast, pets allowed, a/c, TV, room service, private baths, children over age 10 welcome. SGL/DBL$65-$100.

Ripley
Area Code 304

Best Western Inn (701 West Main St, 25271; 372-9122, Fax 372-4400, 800-528-1234) 129 rooms, restaurant, complimentary breakfast, lounge, pool, exercise facilities, children under 12 stay free with parents, a/c, TV, no-smoking rooms, laundry facilities, wheelchair access, pets allowed, senior citizen rates, meeting facilities, major credit cards. SGL/DBL$40-$51.

Econo Lodge (1 Hospitality Dr, 25271; 372-5000, 800-4-CHOICE) 43 rooms, restaurant, complimentary breakfast, children under 12 stay free with parents, no pets, senior citizen rates, wheelchair access, a/c, TV, major credit cards. SGL/DBL$36-$44.

Super 8 Motel (102 Duke Dr, 25271; 372-8880, 800-800-8000) 44 rooms and suites, pets allowed, children under 12 stay free with parents, free local calls, a/c, TV, in-room refrigerators and microwaves, fax service, no-smoking rooms, senior citizen rates, wheelchair access, meeting facilities, major credit cards. SGL/DBL$34-$39.

Shepherdstown
Area Code 304

The Bavarian Inn and Lodge (Shepherdstown, 25443; 876-2551, Fax 876-9355) 42 rooms, restaurant, lounge, pool, whirlpools, a/c, TV, tennis courts, no-smoking rooms, wheelchair access, major credit cards. SGL/DBL$75-$150.

Thomas Shepherd Inn (Shepherdstown, 25443; 876-3715) 6 rooms, complimentary breakfast, 1860s inn, no-smoking allowed, major credit cards. SGL/DBL$85-$95.

Summersville
Area Code 304

Best Western Summersville Lake (1203 Broad St, 26651; 872-6900, 800-528-1234) 59 rooms, restaurant, complimentary breakfast, lounge, pool, exercise facilities, children stay free with parents, a/c, TV, no-smoking rooms, wheelchair access, pets allowed, senior citizen rates, meeting facilities, major credit cards. SGL/DBL$40-$45.

Comfort Inn (903 Industrial Dr North, 26651; 872-6500, 800-221-2222) 99 rooms, restaurant, complimentary breakfast, pool, exercise facilities, wheelchair access, no-smoking rooms, no pets, children under 18 stay free with parents, senior citizen rates, a/c, TV, meeting facilities, major credit cards. SGL/DBL$40-$57.

Super 8 Motel (306 Merchants Walk, 26651; 872-4888, 800-800-8000) rooms and suites, pets allowed, children under 12 stay free with parents, free local calls, a/c, TV, in-room refrigerators and microwaves, fax service, no-smoking rooms, senior citizen rates, wheelchair access, meeting facilities, major credit cards. SGL/DBL$36-$41.

Sutton
Area Code 304

Days Inn (2000 Sutton Lane, 26601; 765-5055, Fax 765-1067, 800-325-2525) 100 rooms and suites, restaurant, free breakfast, lounge, pool, children under 13 stay free with parents, room service, laundry service, a/c, TV, free local calls, no pets, wheelchair access, no-smoking rooms, senior citizen rates, major credit cards. SGL/DBL$49-$99, STS$100-$115.

Sutton Lane Motel (Sutton, 26601; 765-7351) 31 rooms, restaurant, a/c, TV, meeting facilities, major credit cards. SGL/DBL$29-$35.

Teays Valley
Area Code 304

Days Inn (Putnam Village Rd, 25569; 757-8721, Fax 757-0630, 800-325-2525) 90 rooms, restaurant, lounge, pool, children stay free with parents, room service, laundry service, in-room coffee makers, kitchenettes, a/c, TV, free local calls, no pets, wheelchair access, no-smoking rooms, senior citizen rates, major credit cards. SGL/DBL$27-$48.

Triadelphia
Area Code 304

Days Inn (Triadelphia, 26059; 547-0610, Fax 547-4235, 800-325-2525) 106 rooms, restaurant, lounge, outdoor pool, children stay free with parents, room service, laundry service, a/c, TV, free local calls, pets allowed, wheelchair access, gift shop, no-smoking rooms, senior citizen rates, meeting facilities for 100, major credit cards. SGL/DBL$45-$49.

Wellsburg
Area Code 304

Elmhurst Manor (1606 Pleasant Ave, 26070; 737-3675) 2 rooms, bed and breakfast, private baths, fireplaces, on 3.5 acres. SGL/DBL$44-$88.

Times Past Bed and Breakfast (555 Washington Pike, 26070; 737-0592) 2 rooms, complimentary breakfast, a/c, private baths, no-smoking rooms. SGL/DBL$50-$100.

Weston
Area Code 304

Comfort Inn (Hwy 33 East, 26452; 269-7000, 800-221-2222) restaurant, pool, wheelchair access, no-smoking rooms, no pets, children under 16 stay free with parents, senior citizen rates, a/c, TV, meeting facilities, major credit cards. SGL/DBL$34-$48.

Super 8 Motel (12 Market Pl., 26452; 269-1086, 800-800-8000) rooms and suites, pets allowed, children under 12 stay free with parents, free local calls, a/c, TV, in-room refrigerators and microwaves, fax, no-smoking rooms, senior citizen rates, wheelchair access, meeting facilities, major credit cards. SGL/DBL$36-$41.

Wheeling
Area Code 614

Best Western Wheeling Inn (10th and Main St, 26003; 233-8500, 800-528-1234) 80 rooms, restaurant, free breakfast, lounge, entertainment, pool, exercise facilities, children stay free with parents, a/c, TV, no-smoking rooms, wheelchair access, airport transportation, pets allowed, senior citizen rates, meeting facilities, major credit cards. SGL/DBL$45-$55.

Fort Henry Motor Inn (2501 National Rd, 26003; 242-3131) 64 rooms, free breakfast, pool, a/c, TV, major credit cards. SGL/DBL$30-$40.

Hampton Inn (795 National Rd, 26003; 233-0440, Fax 233-2198, 800-HAMPTON) 104 rooms, restaurant, complimentary breakfast, pool, exercise facilities, children under 18 stay free with parents, no-smoking rooms, wheelchair access, computer hookups, fax service, TV, a/c, free local calls, pets allowed, meeting facilities, major credit cards. SGL/DBL$42-$54.

McClure House (12th and Market, 26003; 232-0300, 800-862-5873) 173 rooms and suites, restaurant, lounge, meeting facilities, a/c, TV. SGL/DBL$50-$60.

Oglebay's Wilson Lodge and Conference Center (Oglebay Park, 26003; 243-4000, Fax 243-4070, 800-624-6988) 212 rooms, suites and housekeeping cabins, restaurant, lounge, indoor pool, lighted tennis courts, a/c, TV, airport transportation, wheelchair access, room service, gift shop, meeting facilities for 600. SGL/DBL$55-$135.

Yesterdays, Ltd. (827 Main St, 26003; 233-2003, 800-540-6039) 10 rooms, bed and breakfast, a/c, private baths, TV, no-smoking rooms, major credit cards. SGL/DBL$63-$83.

White Sulphur Springs
Area Code 304

The Greenbrier (White Sulphur Springs, 24986; 536-1110, Fax 536-7834, 800-624-6070) 699 rooms and suites, restaurant, lounge, entertainment, indoor and outdoor pools, golf, exercise facilities, lighted tennis courts, transportation to local attractions, wheelchair access, no-smoking rooms, a/c, TV, meeting facilities, major credit cards. SGL/DBL150-$200.

The James Wylie House (East Main St, 24986; 536-9444) rooms and suites, bed and breakfast, no smoking, no pets, private baths, major credit cards. SGL/DBL$50-$60.

Williamstown
Area Code 304

Days Inn (Williamstown, 26187; 375-3730, Fax 375-4761, 800-325-2525) 119 rooms, restaurant, complimentary breakfast, lounge, children stay free with parents, room service, laundry service, a/c, TV, free local calls, no pets, wheelchair access, no-smoking rooms, senior citizen rates, major credit cards. SGL/DBL$30-$45.

Additional Reading

Other Travel Books from Hunter Publishing

THE FLORIDA WHERE-TO-STAY BOOK
More than 4,000 places to stay in the state that is the #1 destination in the country – condos for rent, B&Bs, country inns, motels, hotels, even beach houses for rent by the week or by the month. Organized alphabetically by town, each with a listing of facilities, address, phone, fax, prices. **$12.95, 450 pp, ISBN 1-55650-539-6**

Other guides in the Where to Stay series:
NEW ENGLAND $11.95, 500 pp, 1-55650-602-3
THE MID-ATLANTIC STATES $11.95, 448 pp, 1-55650-631-7
NORTHERN CALIFORNIA $12.95, 400 pp, 1-55650-572-8
SOUTHERN CALIFORNIA $12.95, 450 pp, 1-55650-573-6
AMERICA'S EASTERN CITIES $11.95, 420 pp, 1-55650-600-7
AMERICA'S WESTERN CITIES $11.95, 420 pp, 1-55650-601-5

THE GREAT AMERICAN WILDERNESS:
TOURING AMERICA'S NATIONAL PARKS
The 41 most scenic parks and how to see them: the main access routes, where to stay, where to eat, which roads are most crowded or most beautiful, how much time to allow, what you can safely skip and what you must not miss. Special sections tell you how to tour each park if you have only limited time – or if time is not a factor. Maps of each park, showing all surrounding access routes. **$11.95, 320 pp, 1-55650-567-1**

INSIDER'S GUIDE TO NEW ENGLAND
Filled with history, tour information, local museums and galleries, where to shop, where to eat, this is the most complete guide to every state in the region. Superb color photos & maps. Complete hotel information, from the most luxurious accommodations to places for the traveller on a shoestring budget. Free fold-out map in color. **$17.95, 256 pp, 1-55650-495-0**

Other guides in the series include:
INSIDER'S GUIDE TO FLORIDA $15.95, 256 pp, 1-55650-452-7
INSIDER'S GUIDE TO CALIFORNIA $14.95, 192 pp, 1-55650-163-3
INSIDER'S GUIDE TO HAWAII $15.95, 230 pp, 1-55650-495-0
INSIDER'S GUIDE TO CANADA EAST $15.95, 224 pp, 1-55650-581-7
INSIDER'S GUIDE TO CANADA WEST $15.95, 224 pp, 1-55650-580-9
INSIDER'S GUIDE TO MEXICO $17.95, 320 pp, 1-55650-454-3

We publish hundreds of travel guides & maps to all parts of the world, from Cuba to Zaire, from Malaysia to Trinidad and Belize. Many can be found at the best bookstores, or you can order direct by sending a check for the list price (add $2.50 for postage and handling) to: **Hunter Publishing, Inc., 300 Raritan Center Parkway, Edison NJ 08818.** Write or call **(908) 225 1900** for our free color catalog.